Dimensions of Communication
An Introduction

Michael D. Scott
Steven R. Brydon
California State University, Chico

Mayfield Publishing Company
Mountain View, California
London • Toronto

To our brothers,
Kelly L. Scott and John R. Brydon

Library of Congress Cataloging-in-Publication Date

Scott, Michael D.
    Dimensions of communication : an introduction / Michael D. Scott, Steven R. Brydon.
        p.   cm.
    Includes bibliographical references and index.
    ISBN 1-55934-442-3
    1. Communication.   I. Brydon, Steven Robert.   II. Title
P90.S3886   1996
302.2—dc20   96-33498
                                                                                                       CIP

Manufactured in the United States of America
10   9   8   7   6   5   4   3   2

Mayfield Publishing Company
1280 Villa Street
Mountain View, California 94041

Sponsoring editor, Holly J. Allen; development editor, Barbara Armentrout; production editor,
Melissa Kreischer; manuscript editor, Margaret Moore; art director, Jeanne M. Schreiber; text
and cover designer, Gary Head; art manager, Jean Mailander; photo researcher, Brian Pecko;
illustrator, Joan Carol; manufacturing manager, Amy Folden. Cover art © Clem Bedwell. The
text was set in 10.5/12 Berkeley Book by American Composition & Graphics, Inc. and
printed on acid-free 45# Chromatone Matte by Banta Book Group.

Preface

Dimensions of Communication is organized around a simple but important idea: Although the context in which people communicate may change, the basic skills that define communication competence are much the same in every context. Thus, the skills that define communication competence in interactions with friends and family are largely the same skills that define communication competence in a problem-solving group or in speaking to an audience.

Organization of the Text

We organized the text to reflect our belief that communication is best mastered as a series of interdependent steps. *Dimensions of Communication*, begins with the foundations of communication and then addresses the various contexts of communication in turn: relational communication, small group communication, public speaking, and mass communication.

Part One, Foundations of Communication Competence, contains seven chapters. Chapter 1 is an overview of the communication transaction and previews the following chapters. Chapter 2 tackles the topic of perception and introduces the reader to the role attribution plays in how we perceive ourselves and others. Chapter 3 takes a comprehensive look at the relationship between language and communication competence and offers guidelines for inclusionary language. Chapter 4 explains the nature of nonverbal communication and its impact on communication competence. This chapter emphasizes the complementary relationship between verbal and nonverbal behavior while cautioning the reader not to rely too much on nonverbal communication for the meaning of a message. Chapter 5 argues that one cannot communicate competently without communicating ethically, and thoroughly explores the ethics of our everyday communication transactions. Chapter 6 introduces listening and critical thinking, two processes that we believe are inextricably linked. In addition to explaining these processes in detail, we present several exercises to help readers improve their listening skills. Chapter 7 discusses communication competence in a diverse society. Rather than focusing only on cultural diversity, however, we also consider group and individual diversity. Our approach to cultural diversity is to look at the way cultures vary on common dimensions rather than to emphasize only differences between cultures.

Part Two, Dimensions of Interpersonal Communication, assists students in applying the principles of communication present in Chapters 1 through 7 to their relationships. Chapter 8 explores the topic of relational communication and introduces the process by which communication defines and redefines our interpersonal relationships. Specific topics covered include social penetration, relationship escalation and de-escalation, self-disclosure, and the communication skills necessary to manage relational tension (dialectics). Chapter 9 then applies much of this information to family communication. We define the family as a communication system, describe some of its possible configurations, and discuss some of the roles family members play. We also look at how narrative devices, such as storytelling, shape families and examine communication skills that facilitate family health. Chapter 10 discusses the nature of conflict in relationships and presents specific communication skills to use in managing it. Our perspective is that conflict is not necessarily bad, but is often mismanaged because people do not possess the communication skills to make conflict productive. Chapter 11 looks at another type of interpersonal communication: the interview. It discusses informational, employment-selection, and performance-appraisal interviews and explains the specific skills each type involves.

Part Three, Dimensions of Small Group Communication, continues the professional emphasis of the interviewing chapter and provides knowledge and skills relevant to success both inside and outside the classroom. Chapter 12 is an overview of small group communication. In addition to covering various types of groups in today's society, it talks about the assets and liabilities of groups, giving special emphasis to groupthink. Chapter 13 introduces group process, including the topics of group development, member roles and functions, and leadership.

Part Four, Dimensions of Public Communication, contains five chapters—four that prepare students for public speaking, and the fifth examines mass communication. Much of the content of Chapters 14 through 17 is derived from the second edition of our public speaking book, *Between One and Many: The Art and Science of Public Speaking* (Mayfield, 1997). Chapter 14 leads the reader through the steps of building a speech, beginning with audience analysis and ending with patterns for arranging a speech. Chapter 15 covers the management of speech anxiety, methods of delivery, and the creation and use of effective visual aids. Chapters 16 and 17 focus on two types of public speaking: informative and persuasive. Both chapters reflect not only the rhetorical roots of public speaking but also the significance of contemporary research to public speaking as well. Finally, Chapter 18 focuses on mass communication, including a brief history, an explanation of how it differs from face-to-face communication, and a presentation of contemporary thinking about its nature and its effects. We believe that exposing students to a variety of viewpoints concerning the effects of mass media helps them to become more critical consumers.

Integrated Text and Video

Because the written word cannot fully convey the complex and dynamic process of communication, *Dimensions of Communication* is accompanied by a student video with 19 individual segments grouped into six parts. Using live action, animation, and still photographs to illustrate important concepts and skills discussed in the text, this video is designed to stimulate students to think critically and talk about how the various dimensions of communication influence their lives.

- *Part I: The Story of Communication,* designed to complement Chapters 1 through 4, introduces the rhetorical roots of communication and illustrates the significant trends that have shaped contemporary thinking about the communication transaction. Individual segments also cover perception, language, and nonverbal communication.

- *Part II: Communication and Personal Responsibility* expands on the topics covered in Chapters 5 through 7, focusing on the need for students to take personal responsibility for their communication behavior, including how they interpret and respond to cultural, group, and individual diversity. In the three segments in this part, experts and students talk about what it means to communicate ethically, listen and think critically, and appreciate human diversity.

- *Part III: Communicating Interpersonally* takes a skills-based approach to relational communication, the subject matter of Chapters 8 through 10. The three segments in this part show examples of the communication skills needed in various relationships, including those with friends and lovers, co-workers and classmates, and family members. In addition, experts talk about relational problems and conflicts and present communication skills that are useful in managing them.

- *Part IV: Interviewing and Leadership* models an effective interview in its first segment, designed to complement Chapter 11. It shows students how to conduct themselves during an interview and how to manage communication when interviewing others. Students also learn from employers what they look for when interviewing job candidates. The second segment, designed to accompany Chapters 12 and 13, shows how leaders use communication behavior to manage the behavior of participants in a small, task-oriented group.

- *Part V: Speaking in Public* includes five segments, keyed to Chapters 14 through 17. Students are shown speaking informatively and persuasively, and the elements that make for effective introductions and conclusions, sound organization, credible arguments, and effective delivery are analyzed. One segment also shows examples of the various kinds of visual aids that can enhance or detract from speech delivery.

- *Part VI: Managing Communication Anxiety* explains the sources of communication apprehension and public speaking anxiety and illustrates skills that can be used to manage both. It contains two segments, one dealing with the sources of communication anxiety, the other explaining skills for the management of communication anxiety. Finally, the video ends with three additional student speeches that you can watch and evaluate on your own. Students are reassured that some degree of anxiety is not only natural when communicating but also beneficial.

Not only does the text note when a section is illustrated by the video, but the video package also includes a guide to help students get maximum benefit from the combination of text and video. The Video Guide alerts students about what they should look for in each segment and asks questions that will help them integrate what they see on videotape with what they read in the text.

Although the textbook can be used without the companion videotape, most students own or have access to a VCR and can benefit from the new dimensions the video adds to the text. Furthermore, the video enables students to cover in depth material that cannot be covered completely in class, especially the preparation and delivery of informative and persuasive speeches.

Features of the Text

Within each chapter are instructional boxes that focus on specific topics, and at the end of each chapter are lists of suggested readings and videos as well as exercises to help students apply theory and research about communication to their own lives. We think these various instructional activities will inform students, stimulate them to talk about what they read, and serve as springboards for out-of-class assignments, such as reaction papers.

Boxes for Critical Thinking, Considering Diversity, Self-Assessment, and Skill Building   These four types of boxes appear throughout the book to help students apply key concepts presented in the text to their own experiences. Critical Thinking boxes raise questions about communication topics ranging from shock radio to the credibility of Internet information. Considering Diversity boxes also take a critical-thinking approach as they examine a variety of issues, including gender differences in communication, cultural variations in self-presentation, organizational patterns, and audience response. Self-Assessment boxes contain instruments that readers can use to measure their communication attributes and abilities, such as level of self-monitoring, leadership style, and level of public speaking anxiety. Skill Building boxes offer tips about all aspects of communication—from listening to using "I" messages to dealing with dysfunctional group members.

End-of-Chapter Suggestions for Related Books, Articles, and Videos   Each chapter is followed by "Another Look," a directory of relevant and accessible articles and books to which students can turn for more information. We also recommend videos of feature films and documentaries that illustrate and reinforce the topics covered in the chapter. We have either previewed these videos for relevance or tested them in our own classes. Our experience shows that students not only enjoy these video supplements but also draw on them in discussing such topics as family communication and relating to people from cultures other than their own.

End-of-Chapter Applications and Activities   The feature "Theory and Research in Practice" offers several exercises that enable students to apply theory and research about communication to their own lives. Emphasis is given to theories and research that have been widely reported in books, journal articles, and convention papers and thus reflect the scholarship characteristic of the communication discipline.

Teacher-Support Package

In addition to the textbook and the companion videotape, Mayfield makes available to adopters a number of other items to help solve teaching problems in introductory communication courses.

Instructor's Manual   Written by Michele Hunkele, California Polytechnic State University, the Instructor's Manual contains general information about the course and specific information for each chapter of the textbook. Part I includes sample semester and quarter syllabi and ideas for journal-keeping and other teaching strategies. We have also addressed many of the practical questions often raised by first-time teachers—everything from what to do the first day of class to how to handle office-hour meetings with students. Part II includes guidelines for evaluation and feedback and sample evaluation forms. Part III covers each chapter of the book in detail, offering lecture outlines, ideas for presenting concepts that students often have trouble with or find controversial, suggested in-class and group exercises, and a resource bank of additional examples and research to supplement each chapter.

Printed and Computerized Test Items   Approximately 750 test questions, including multiple choice, true-false, and essay questions, are printed in the Instructor's Manual. Computerized versions of these test questions for both IBM and Macintosh platforms are available at no charge from the publisher, subject to minimum adoption requirements. As with other items in the teaching-support package, many of these test questions have been class tested.

Transparencies   A wide variety of four-color overhead transparencies illustrating major concepts from the text are available free of charge to adopting instructors.

Teaching-Assistant Materials   Programs utilizing graduate teaching assistants or other first-time instructors will receive free upon request, subject to minimum adoption requirements, a guidebook, *Between Teachers and Students: A Primer for Teaching Assistants and First-Time Instructors,* and a videotape, *Agents of Change: Graduate Teaching Assistants in the Basic Course.*

Acknowledgments

The material in this book, on the Videotape, and in the Instructor's Manual represent the result of years of testing and refinement with thousands of students at California State University, Chico, as well as from adopters of our public-speaking textbook. We believe in the theories and pedagogy presented in *Dimensions of Communication* not only because they are backed by sound theory and research but also because we have used them—and they work.

We gratefully acknowledge the support and assistance of the Mayfield staff in the development and realization of this book. We want to extend a personal thanks to Holly Allen, our sponsoring editor; Barbara Armentrout, our developmental editor; Melissa Kreischer, our production editor; Margaret Moore, who copyedited the manuscript; Brian Pecko, photo researcher; and Julianna Gustafson, editorial assistant.

We are especially grateful to George Rogers of California State University, Chico, who directed and edited the videotape that accompanies this text. We also thank the numerous students who consented to be videotaped for this project. Special thanks go to the speakers who shared their talents in providing sample speeches for the text and the tape, including Sally Garber, Kelli Wells, Ryland G. Hill, Jr., Jonathan Studebaker, Jenny Rees, and David A. Sanders.

Finally, a grateful thank you for the reviews and counsel of our peers in the classroom who graciously prepared careful critiques of our manuscript in various stages of development: Jess K. Alberts, Arizona State University; Martha Ann Atkins, Iowa State University; Stanley Baran, San Jose State University; Gil Cooper, Pittsburg State University; Robbin D. Crabtree, New Mexico State University; Susan Drucker, Hofstra University; Lisa J. Goodnight, Purdue University, Calumet; Pamela J. Joraanstad, Glendale Community College; Elaine S. Klein, SUNY—Westchester Community College; Bobbie Rickner Klopp, Kirkwood Community College; Therese McGinnis, College of DuPage; Jon F. Nussbaum, University of Oklahoma; Diane T. Prusank, University of Hartford; Richard Rea, University of Arkansas—Fayetteville; Helen M. Sterk, Marquette University; Duane Varan, University of Hawaii at Manoa; Catherine Egley Waggoner, University of New Mexico; Ruth A. Wallinger, Frostburg State University; and Gale Auletta Young, California State University, Hayward.

We appreciate the help of all these individuals in preparing this book, however, we are, of course, ultimately responsible for its content.

Brief Contents

Detailed Contents

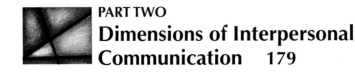

PART TWO
Dimensions of Interpersonal Communication   179

CHAPTER 8
Relational Communication   181

PART THREE
Dimensions of Small Group Communication   295

CHAPTER 13
Small Group Communication in Practice 323

CHAPTER 16
Informative Speaking   417

Foundations of Communication Competence

CHAPTER 1

Principles and Contexts

OBJECTIVES

After reading this chapter you should be able to:

- Define and describe communication.

- Critically compare models of communication.

- List and discuss the factors that make communication a transactional phenomenon.

- Describe the elements of communication competence.

- Describe mindfulness.

- Describe the similarities and dissimilarities among dyadic, small group, public, and mass dimensions of communication.

- Describe interpersonal needs such as inclusion, affection, and control.

Communication is the goal we have in mind when we choose to communicate. It also is a process in which people verbally and nonverbally attempt to create specific meanings and images in the minds of others. To be effective, communication should stimulate the meanings and images that either approximate those the communicator intended or prompt further communication to stimulate the meanings and images intended. Communicating is easier said than done. Consider the following comments from letters to the editor of *National Geographic Magazine*.[1] Each was written in response to a previous article about the West Bank region of Israel.

> I found the pro-Israel bias—or was it anti-Palestinian prejudice?—surprising. I am not used to such transparent side-taking in the usually evenhanded *Geographic*.
>
> —Donald Neff, Washington, D.C.
>
> I must take issue with your pro-Arab, anti-Israel bias.
>
> —Aharon Subar, Monsey, N.Y.

communication
Ideally, shared meaning resulting from the intentional attempt to stimulate meaning verbally and nonverbally.

My thanks to writer Don Belt for his evenhanded article.

—Mohamed Ragheb, Ottawa, Ontario

As this example illustrates, it's one thing to say something, quite another to have people interpret what is said as intended. What is difficult to achieve in a highly controlled medium such as writing, moreover, can be even more difficult when we attempt to communicate interpersonally, in small groups, before the public, or through mass systems. Not only does communication take skill and practice, it also takes a sound understanding of the principles and dimensions of communication. This initial chapter is so directed. Its aim is to show how you can better appreciate and practice effective communication. Three general topics are covered:

- models of communication,
- communication competence, and
- the major dimensions of communication in which we routinely participate.

The chapter concludes with a brief discussion of how these topics are developed in the remaining chapters of the book.

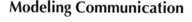

VIDEO FILE

If you have access to the videotape that accompanies this book, view Part 1, "The Story of Communication," which complements the discussion here and in Chapters 2–4.

Modeling Communication

One way to understand the principles and processes that define the nature of communication is through modeling. Models are descriptive tools meant to approximate things we otherwise would have trouble seeing, imagining, or describing. Over the years, numerous models have been offered as representations of what is involved when humans communicate. The earliest of these models (shown in Figure 1-1) depicted human communication as linear and mechanistic, usually showing a sender transmitting an encoded **message** to a receiver, who then decoded the message.[2] Later models (such as the one in Fig-

Figure 1-1
Action Model

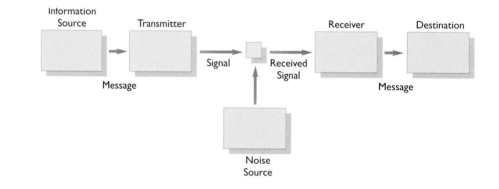

ure 1-2) depicted human communication in more interactive terms, adding concepts such as feedback.[3]

Contemporary, transactional models more accurately show that communication is far more complex than shown by these early ones. For example, the transactional model in Figure 1-3 depicts communication as a **system**.[4] The components in this system are arrayed in such a way that a change in one of its components will effect changes in all. The system includes but is not limited to

- the environment in which people communicate,
- the number of people communicating,
- their backgrounds, and
- the content and relational sides of the messages people communicate.

The transactional model also suggests communication between people is simultaneous and continuous rather than characterized by turn-taking, is characterized by interdependence rather than independence, and is heavily influenced by the process of perception.

messages Verbal and nonverbal behaviors.

system A collection of interdependent parts arrayed in such a way that a change in one will effect changes in all others.

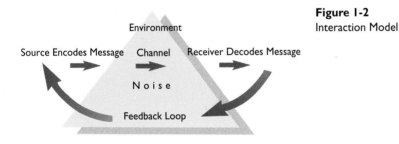

Figure 1-2
Interaction Model

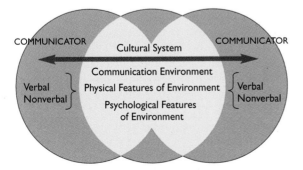

Figure 1-3
Transactional Model of Communication. Although far from perfect, transactional models of communication such as this one do a much better job of suggesting that communication is a system composed of interdependent rather than independent parts.

Environment

Consider first the environment in which people communicate. Communication exchanges between people are affected by the surroundings in which they communicate. The surroundings affect both the content of messages and the manner in which the content is exchanged. It's one thing to whisper just before a film begins. But it's annoying when two people carry on a clearly audible conversation as the film begins to unfold. Most of us, therefore, try to communicate in a manner appropriate to the environment.

Number of People

The content of our messages and the manner in which they are exchanged are influenced by the number of people communicating. The saying "Two is company and three's a crowd" is generally true. Two friends are likely to self-disclose more intimate information than will a group of three or four friends.

Consider the film *Stand by Me,* starring River Phoenix, Wil Wheaton, Corey Feldman, and Jerry O'Connell. The film shows how the lives of four adolescents change as they search for the body of a missing boy about their own age. When all four boys are shown talking, the topic of conversation ranges from TV shows to pop music. But when Phoenix and Wheaton, the most mature of the boys, are shown talking privately, topics are deeper-seated. For example, in one scene, Wheaton tells Phoenix he doesn't think his father loves him. In another, Phoenix tells Wheaton that he and the other boys only drag Wheaton down.

Backgrounds

The transactional picture of communication is further complicated by the backgrounds of the people communicating. Think about the changing face of the college campus. It is far more diverse than ever before.[5] People from different cultures frequently must interact. To do so effectively, they must learn to appreciate their differences, as well as how these differences influence their communication transactions.

Messages

The environment in which people communicate, as well as their number and background, affects both their words and the manner in which the words are said, because every message has two sides: content and relational.[6] The content side is composed of the words in a message. The relational side includes both words and such characteristics as vocal pitch, gesturing, eye contact, and touch.

Consider how the relational side affects the message conveyed by the phrase "I love you" in three different scenarios. In the first, one person shouts, "I love you," as another disappears down the gateway leading to a commercial airplane. In the second, a student softly says, "I love you," to another as they sit holding

hands, across a small table in a crowded coffee house. In the third, a man mumbles and chokes out, "I love you," his face full of anguish and his eyes moist with tears as another person stares back at him coldly.

In the film, *Stand By Me,* Wil Wheaton and River Phoenix (left) exchanged information that they withheld from the other boys.

Although the words in each scenario do not change, their meaning does. The reason is the difference in the relational dynamics of the scenarios. This doesn't mean that the content side of the message is subordinate to its relational side. Not only are they equally important, they also affect each other and serve to make a message complete. What you say always affects how you say it and vice versa.

Simultaneity

The transactional model of communication is further distinguished from the earlier models by a fifth factor, the communicators themselves. Early in the study of communication, a distinction was made between the source of a message and its receiver. This distinction implied that people take discrete turns when communicating, either playing the role of source or playing the role of receiver.

In truth, we are sources and receivers simultaneously and continuously. Even when we are listening intently to someone, we are simultaneously a source. Our face and eyes, gestures and body orientation communicate information back to the person to whom we are listening. This simultaneous feedback may cause the person to modify the content and relational dynamic of her message, even as she is speaking.

Interdependence

The transactional perspective treats communication as a system of interdependent parts. Things that are **interdependent** have a reciprocal influence on one another.[7] The context, number of communicators, and messages that characterize a system of communication are interdependent. A change in one will produce changes of varying degrees in the others. For example, topics appropriate over dinner with a lover may not generalize to conversation over pizza and beer with a group of casual friends. And spirited debate about the place of religion in politics may be acceptable in the classroom but out of line at a Thanksgiving dinner table.

Perception

Finally, the transactional model also requires an understanding and appreciation of the role of perception in communication. **Perception** is the process by which we give meaning to what we sense and experience.[8] It also is a highly selective process. For example, look at the accompanying drawing by M. C. Escher. Both what you see and how you interpret what you see depend on your life experience and on what appears most familiar and consistent with your life experience. On first glance, this drawing appears to depict the familiar and obvious, water running downhill. If you look closer, however, you will see this conclusion is impossible because the flow of water actually is continuous.

Our tendency to pick out the familiar and obvious when confronted with a new or ambiguous stimulus is both good and bad from the standpoint of communication. It is good because it enables us to quickly establish a reference point from which we can plan our own communication behavior and interpret that of others. It is bad because it can perceptually blind us to other data that may be even more important to how we behave and interpret the behavior of others.

Consider a cross-cultural example. Direct eye contact is perceived as a sign of attention and respect in most of North America. When we communicate, we use this knowledge to gauge how people are reacting to our message. This North American norm is not universal, however. Direct eye contact in some cultures, for example, Japan, may be perceived as aggressive, intrusive, and disrespectful. It is common, then, for untrained North American business people who give a speech in such cultures to walk away from the experience with their confidence

interdependence
A reciprocal effect among factors.

perception The process of giving meaning to sensations and experiences.

Waterfall. 1961.
Lithograph by M. C.
Escher. We need to
look at rather than react
to stimuli that appear
familiar.

severely shaken. They mistakenly perceive their audience's lack of eye contact as
a sign of disapproval. This mistaken perception can further undermine their
future communication transactions.

In a sense, "what we get" is what we perceive. As long as our perceptions are
based on accurate data, seeing what we choose to see may not be a problem. But
as the Escher drawing illustrates, our perceptions are not always based on accurate data. Thus, as communicators we should never assume that our initial perceptions of people, places, and things are foolproof. Box 1-1 discusses an

Box 1-1 Considering Diversity

To What Extent Does the Media Influence Our Perceptions of Other Cultures?

One of our international students recently mentioned during a class discussion that North American's perceptions of Middle Eastern people and culture were based on images received from mass media rather than direct experience. Our student also said that television and Hollywood films typically portrayed Middle Eastern men as either terrorists or religious fanatics, and Middle Eastern culture as backward and unenlightened. He then presented the class with numerous examples that countered media stereotypes of Middle Eastern men and examples of the many scientific and intellectual contributions of Middle Eastern culture that have benefited humankind.

Do you agree with our student's contention? Can you think of other groups of people whose culture has been misrepresented by mass media? What about Latino, Native American, and Southeast Asian peoples and cultures? Write a one-page position paper on how you think perceptions based on indirect experience through the mass media influences communication transactions between diverse people and cultures.

inaccurate perception of Middle Eastern men common in Hollywood films. Just because someone, some place, or some circumstance strikes us as familiar or consistent with past experience, that doesn't necessarily make it so.

Communication Competence

We have seen that communication is the intentional transmittal of a specific message in a particular context and that it is a simultaneous, reciprocal transaction between communicators. Communication is not something that automatically happens whenever we open our mouth; it is a skill that has to be learned. Although communication researchers argue over its exact meaning, most agree that **communication competence** requires two components: knowledge of the principles and practices of effective communication and a conscious decision about how to most appropriately convey a particular message.[9] In other words, effective communication is conscious communication.

Elements of Communication Competence

communication competence The ability to consciously decide how to most appropriately convey a particular message.

As the story in Box 1-2 suggests, communication competence, the ability to consciously decide how to most appropriately convey a particular message, involves more than a single element. In fact, it has at least six:[10]

1. self-competence,
2. interpretive competence,

Box 1-2   Critical Thinking

Competent Communication in the Cockpit

In 1978 a three-person cockpit crew in command of a DC-8 commercial jetliner noticed a problem with the landing gear while on approach to the International Airport in Portland, Oregon. The pilot and captain of the flight put the plane into a holding pattern, turning his attention exclusively to the problem with the landing gear.

So consumed did he become with the problem, he failed to notice the fuel was running out. Reluctant to interfere with the pilot and captain of the plane, the other two crew members did nothing, even though they could see they were almost out of fuel. The DC-8 crashed, killing 10 people.

Evidently, the reticence of the two crew members was not unusual. Upon investigating this accident and in-flight recordings of cockpit crews from other flights, safety experts were horrified to find out just how little communication occurred in the cockpit at crucial points in a flight, for example, during take-offs and landings. What's more, their findings prompted major carriers to retool their pilot training programs. All major carriers now stress cockpit communication, including speaking, listening, and challenging authority if necessary, in their training programs.

1. If you were in charge of such programs, what are some of the specific skills you would want crews to learn about communication?
2. Cockpit crews are not the only groups in which there is a chain of command. In the military, for example, there is always a formal chain personnel must follow. Is it possible to both maintain discipline and encourage honest communication? How might that balance be achieved?

SOURCE: Carl A. Lavin, "When Candor Flies as Co-Pilot," *Sacramento Bee*, 26 June 1994, C4.

3. goal competence,
4. role competence,
5. message competence, and
6. performative competence.

As Figure 1-4 shows, these elements are highly interdependent. The level of one influences the level of the others.

Self-competence is the confidence a person has in his or her communication skills. People who perceive themselves as skilled communicators approach their transactions confidently, and their self-competence shows itself in the other dimensions of communication competence.

Interpretive competence is the ability to decode communication accurately. Not everyone is equally adept at interpreting communication cues. Research suggests that women generally are better at decoding nonverbal communication than men are.[11] For example, they seem to be better at recognizing when attentiveness is a sign of romantic interest and at recognizing courtship behaviors in general.

self-competence
Confidence in communicating.

interpretive competence The ability to accurately decode communication cues.

Figure 1-4
Model of
Communication
Competence

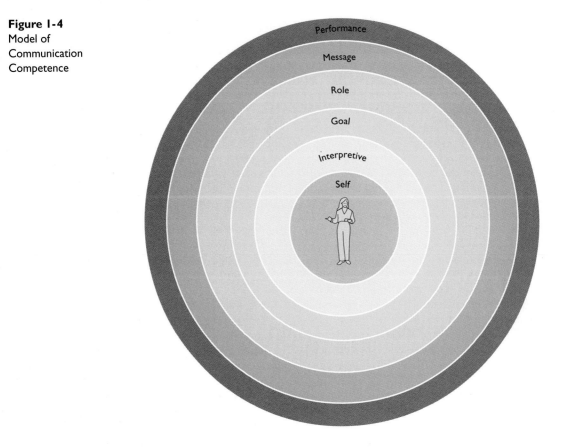

Goal competence, or the ability to establish appropriate and achievable communication goals, depends greatly on interpretive competence. To continue the example in the preceding paragraph, a man's inaccurate interpretation of a woman's attentiveness sometimes leads him to attempt to pursue a romantic relationship with her. Not only is this goal inappropriate, it also affects the final three dimensions of communication competence: role competence, message competence, and performative competence.

Role competence is the ability to choose an appropriate part to play in a specific communication situation. **Message competence** is the ability to choose appropriate verbal and nonverbal behaviors to complement the role. These two types of competence have an obvious impact on **performative competence.** No doubt you think of yourself as an adult—but your parents probably occasionally talk to you as if you were still in grade school. They probably will always think of you as their child and will feel that their appropriate role is as your parent. This assumed role will likely shape what they say to you and how they say it for most of your life.

Active Mindfulness

In addition to the six elements of competence just described, communication competence requires active mindfulness.[12] **Active mindfulness** is conscious awareness of a communication transaction as it unfolds. Active mindfulness, in other words, means focusing on the moment.

Much of people's daily communication behavior is mindless. It is a matter of habit rather than conscious thought. Students walking across campus are likely to greet one another with a set phrase like "Hey, what's up?" and to respond in kind, "What's up?" The ritualistic exchange is one of acknowledgment—nothing more and nothing less. Unless the second person were to stop the first to tell him what really was up, active mindfulness wouldn't come into play.

Active mindfulness has three requirements. The first is **cognitive flexibility**, or the ability to create new mental categories for new experiences rather than trying to force them into old ones. Have you ever noticed how some people talk louder to someone who doesn't speak much English? They seem to assume that a lack of understanding can be due to only one thing: deafness. Cognitive flexibility would enable them to imagine other reasons, such as a lack of fluency, and to use more effective communication strategies, such as simpler words, repetition, and pantomime.

The second requirement is *openness to new information* as we communicate. This receptiveness can be difficult because our first impression typically weights all our subsequent judgments about a person or a situation. We may even unconsciously distort new information so that it is consistent with our initial impression.

The third requirement is *the ability to look at someone or something from multiple perspectives*. How we see the world is biased by our experience (a point that will be discussed at length in Chapter 2). To compensate for this egocentric tendency, we have to try to see the world from other viewpoints. When we succeed in doing so, we usually learn just how limited our initial perspective was. The self-assessment in Box 1-3 will help you discover how mindful you are.

The Dimensions of Communication

A competent communicator is not only mindful but also knowledgeable about how the various dimensions of communication influence the content and relational components of a message. The four most common dimensions of communication are

- dyadic communication,
- small group communication,
- public communication, and
- mass communication.

goal competence
The ability to establish communication outcomes that are both achievable and appropriate.

role competence
The ability to achieve an appropriate pattern of communication behavior based on the interpretation of communication cues and establishment of communication goals.

message competence
The ability to communicate appropriately verbally and nonverbally.

performative competence   The overall and observable consequence of conscious communication competence.

active mindfulness
Conscious awareness of a communication transaction as it unfolds.

cognitive flexibility
The ability to create new mental categories for new experiences.

Box 1-3   Self-Assessment

How Mindful Are You?

Since so much of our communication behavior is habitual and ritualistic, it's a good idea to learn about the degree to which you are mindful when encountering others. Respond to each statement by indicating the degree to which it is representative of the way you normally communicate: always false (answer 1), usually false (answer 2), sometimes false and sometimes true (answer 3), usually true (answer 4), or always true (answer 5).

_____ 1. I pay attention to the situation and context when I communicate.

_____ 2. I think about how I will look to others when I communicate with them.

_____ 3. I seek out new information about the people with whom I communicate.

_____ 4. I ignore inconsistent signals I receive from others when we communicate.

_____ 5. I recognize that the person with whom I am communicating has a different point of view than I do.

_____ 6. I use the categories in which I place others to predict their behavior.

_____ 7. I can describe others with whom I communicate in great detail.

_____ 8. I am concerned about the outcomes of my encounters with others.

_____ 9. I try to find rational reasons why others may behave in a way I perceive negatively.

_____ 10. I have a hard time telling when others do not understand me.

To find your score, first reverse the responses for the even-numbered items (if you wrote 1, make it 5; if you wrote 2, make it 4; if you wrote 3, leave it as 3; if you wrote 4, make it 2; and if you wrote 5, make it 1). Next, add the numbers next to each statement. Scores range from 10 to 50. The higher your score, the more mindful you are when you communicate.

1. What does your score say about the degree to which you are mindful?

2. Does it suggest anything about yourself you would like to change with regard to mindfulness?

3. What would you change? How would you go about creating this change?

4. Describe the change in writing or in a communication journal if your instructor requires one.

Source: William Gudykunst, *Bridging Differences*, 2nd ed. (Newbury Park, Calif.: Sage, 1994), 121. Copyright © 1994 by Sage Publications. Reprinted by permission of Sage Publications.

Although these four dimensions are connected by a number of common threads, such as verbal and nonverbal behaviors, they also are different in significant ways. Talking with a parent, friend, or co-worker is not exactly the same as talking to both parents, several friends, or a group of co-workers. Talking with both parents or a small group of friends or co-workers is not exactly the same as speaking to an audience in which they are members. And talking to an invisible audience via a TV camera or a computer is yet another kind of communication experience.

Shown here are three of the four dimensions of communication. Our first communication experiences are dyadic (top left). Public speaking involves many of the same skills we acquire while speaking dyadically and in groups (top right). Communication becomes more complicated when a group of people talk (bottom).

Dyadic Communication

Our first communication experiences are with **dyadic communication**, or two-person communication. It is not only the most common communication dimension but also the one with which people are most comfortable. Although dyadic communication is the basic building block for other forms of communication, it is also a unique form of communication because of the following properties of dyads:[13]

1. They are characterized by a single line of communication (a line of communication which contains the channels that communicators use to send messages to each other).

dyadic communication
Communication between two people.

2. They afford communicators maximum opportunity to monitor their verbal and nonverbal behaviors.

3. They are potentially more intimate than other communication contexts.

4. They invite greater accuracy in the interpretation of messages.

The second property is especially dependent on communication competence. Although dyadic communication allows communicators maximum opportunity to monitor their respective verbal and nonverbal messages, there is no guarantee that they will do so. If they lack interpretive competence, they may not be fully aware of such messages. Monitoring verbal and nonverbal behaviors is a skill that must be developed.

Dyadic communication can satisfy a number of interpersonal needs. The three most important are the needs for inclusion, affection, and control. Communication with a best friend can fill our need for inclusion, or to be perceived by other people as significant and worthwhile. Communication with a friend or a romantic partner can fill our need for affection, or to like others and to feel likable. And communication with a co-worker can often fill our need for control, or to be perceived as competent and responsible.

Small Group Communication

Dyadic communication is comfortable because it has only one line of communication between the communicators. Not only does the number of lines of communication increase in **small group communication,** but as Figure 1-5 shows, the number of lines increases geometrically with each member added to the group. Whereas there is only one line between two people communicating, the number of lines increases to six when three people communicate.[14]

The types of small groups in which people commonly communicate are as varied as the functions they perform. In this book (especially in Chapter 12), we will consider four common types:

- informal groups,
- formal groups,
- therapeutic groups, and
- task-oriented groups.

small group communication
Communication between three or more people who have a mutually interdependent purpose, who engage in communication transactions with one another, and who identify with the norms of the group.

Informal groups range from a circle of close friends to a collection of classmates who decide to go for coffee after class. Generally, these informal, socially oriented groups satisfy some of the same needs satisfied by dyadic communication, such as inclusion and affection.

Formal groups serve similar functions but have more defined structures than informal groups do. Usually they are hierarchical, and their members have defined roles. Formal groups include fraternities, sororities, and service groups, such as Rotary International and Lions. As these examples suggest, formal groups commonly are organized around activities and interests.

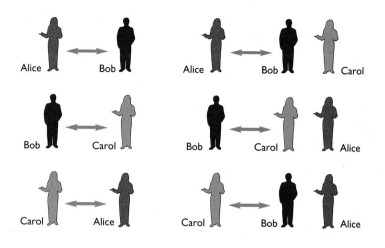

FIGURE 1-5
Lines of Communication

The number of therapeutic self-help groups, such as Alcoholics Anonymous and Al-Anon has increased dramatically in recent years. Their chief function is to assist people in overcoming physical problems, such as addiction, and psychological difficulties, such as the inability to routinely satisfy interpersonal needs.

Task-oriented problem-solving groups exist for the express purpose of completing a task or solving a problem perceived to be beyond the talents and abilities of a single person working alone. One of the best examples of such a group is the World War II–era Manhattan Project. A group of brilliant physicists, under the direction of Dr. Robert Oppenheimer, was charged by President Franklin Delano Roosevelt to develop an atomic weapon. This small group succeeded not only in meeting Roosevelt's challenge but in radically changing the course of history as well.

Public Speaking

Public speaking, or a formal presentation to an audience, is the third dimension of communication that receives major treatment in this book. Whereas dyadic and small group communication are common to the experience of most people, 40 percent of all adults report that public speaking is their number one fear.[15] This fear is understandable, if not entirely logical. Public speaking is the dimension in which most people have little or no real experience. In a class of up to 800 students, for example, probably no more than 40 people will have had substantive training and practice in the art and science of public speaking.

Anxiety about public speaking can also be due to the mistaken belief that it is about performance rather than communication. Although anxiety can be uncomfortable, a certain level can also be desirable for public speaking, as Chapter 15 explains.

The rewards from learning to speak effectively in public far outweigh the anxiety that public speaking can cause. People admire someone who can take charge of an audience as a result of speaking well. Moreover, in any type of

public speaking A formal presentation before an audience.

career, the ability to comfortably and effectively deliver a speech increases the chances of being hired and promoted.

The functions of public speaking depend on the intent of the communicator. A speech may be meant to entertain, inform, motivate, or persuade an audience. Professional and business people as well as those in politics and related arenas of public life need to be able to shape speeches to achieve these various goals.

On the surface, public speaking may seem to share little with dyadic and small group communication. Certainly, giving a speech is not the same as talking with a best friend or participating in a small group discussion. Nevertheless, public speaking has much in common with these dimensions. It is a refined and controlled extension of the communication skills people use every day.

Mass Communication

Mass communication includes print media, such as newspapers and magazines, and electronic media, such as film, radio, and television. Systems of mass communication—for example, broadcast networks like ABC, CBS, CNN, FOX, and NBC—are directed at attracting as large an audience as possible. Although they are attempting to become more interactive with their audience, they remain one-to-many systems of communication, inherently slow in responding to audience feedback.

The nature, functions, and effects of traditional mass media have been researched and written about extensively. TV, as a case in point, can be informative, entertaining, and socializing.[16] Mass media researchers also have linked TV to distorted perceptions of reality and to aggressive behavior in children.[17]

In contrast, so-called new media such as the Internet and electronic mail were designed from their inception to compensate for the inherent weaknesses of traditional mass communication systems. The Internet allows communicators to choose their audience and communicate with each other in close to real time.

Important as we think new media are to your overall communication competence, a thorough discussion of their nature and impact is both premature and beyond the scope of this book. This should not stop you from speculating, however, about the effect of new media on your life and the degree to which the skills we discuss in the following chapters are applicable to their competent use.

mass communication
Communication
directed at a large
audience through
such media as
newspapers,
magazines, radio, film,
and television.

Although these new media may modify how we think about the bounds of communication, the challenge to communicate competently remains. Being computer literate doesn't automatically make one a competent communicator in cyberspace. To the contrary: People who communicate inappropriately in real space and time probably will do likewise in their virtual realities.

Looking Forward

Up to this point, we have learned much about the nature of the communication transaction and its role in our lives. We have seen that it's one thing to want to communicate, another to achieve communication dyadically, in small groups, in

Box 1-4   Skill Building

Which Communication Skills Do You Want to Improve?

Most of us recognize that there is a high degree of correspondence between skill and training. Most of us also will admit that any skill suffers from lack of training and practice, whether it is shooting free throws or solving math problems.

1. On a scale of 1 to 10, with 1 being little and 10 being considerable, what is your training and practice with dyadic communication? Small group communication? Public speaking? Mass communication?

2. Given your score for each dimension in #1, how would you rate your effectiveness in each on a scale of 1 to 10, with 1 representing ineffective and 10 representing highly effective?

3. How well do you think the two sets of scores you gave yourself for each dimension correspond? We raise this question because students frequently think they are better communicators than their training and practice would predict.

4. Using your responses to these 3 questions as a guide, list 10 communication skills you could improve on as these skills relate to dyadic, small group, public, and mass communication—for example, listening more attentively, expressing feelings more appropriately, feeling more comfortable speaking, and thinking more critically about what you see and hear on TV. Write these skills down or record them in your journal.

SOURCE: National Organization of Women.

public, or through mass communication channels. We also have seen that in the effort to become consciously competent communicators, we must be mindful of the fact that such things as perception, our surroundings, and the number of people with whom we're in contact all affect the content of our messages and the manner in which the content is communicated.

Although we have covered much in this chapter, we have barely scratched the surface of the subject of communication. Thus, the chapters to follow extend and refine most of the ideas introduced here. For example, Chapter 2 examines perception in detail, and Chapters 3 and 4 discuss the content and relational sides of messages in the much larger context of verbal and nonverbal communication.

In Chapters 5 through 7, communication competence is examined at length as well as linked to behaviors that further define the consciously competent communicator. Chapter 5 shows how communication competence begins with ethical behavior. Chapter 6 explores how communication competence grows with increased skill in listening and thinking critically. Chapter 7 looks at the skills necessary for consciously competent communicators to respond to the increasing diversity of the human condition.

The remaining chapters of the book, 8 through 18, then lay out the specific principles and skills that enable us to better appreciate and practice communication in the four dimensions of communication introduced in this chapter. Box 1-4 will help you evaluate your skills in these four dimensions and define what skills you'd like to gain. These chapters include a thorough investigation of the role communication plays in our relational lives, in the different types of groups with which we routinely communicate, in the preparation and sharing of public speeches, and in our dealings with traditional mass media.

Summary

To close, then, this chapter previewed what lies ahead. The models, attributes, and dimensions of communication we've shared should be viewed as a small part of the complex puzzle we will join you in completing over the course of this book and over the course of your class. Remember, the goal of communication is shared meaning and images. Keep in mind, too, that communication is a transactional system in which perceptions, contexts, people, and messages are interdependently related. And finally, don't forget the fact that to consistently achieve our goal as communicators, we must remain mindful of what it means to competently communicate in dyads, in small groups, in public, and through mass communication systems.

Another Look

Articles

We have defined communication as a mindful behavior in which you try to purposefully stimulate specific images and meanings in other people's minds. Some scholars, however, have argued that communication occurs any time images and meanings are stimulated, whether intended or not. The following two articles, which should be available in your library, debate this issue and make for stimulating discussion.

Peter A. Andersen. "When One Cannot Not Communicate: A Challenge to Motley's Traditional Postulates." *Communication Studies* 42 (1991): 309–25.

Michael T. Motley. "How One May Not Communicate: A Reply to Andersen." *Communication Studies* 42 (1991): 326–39.

Books

Paul Watzlawick, Janet H. Beavin, and Donald D. Jackson. *Pragmatics of Communication: A Study of Interaction Pat-*

terns, Pathologies, and Paradoxes. New York: Norton, 1967.

This is the book that started the debate mentioned above. Although nearly 30 years old, it may be the most frequently cited text in the communication literature. The strength of this book is that it prompts people to look beyond the content of a message for meaning—for example, to look at the way something is said as well as what is said. This book should form the starting point for any term paper on the content and relational sides of communicating.

Dominic A. Infante, Andrew S. Rancer, and Deanna F. Womack. *Building Communication Theory.* 2nd ed. Prospect Heights, Ill.: Waveland Press, 1993.

This is an excellent resource if you are interested in an in-depth look at the theory and research on which the discipline of communication is founded. It also is highly recommended as an initial resource if you plan on writing about some specific facet or context in the study of communication.

Video Rentals

You could almost pick any video off the shelf and glean some lesson about communication from viewing it. Still, some films are better illustrations of the various aspects of communication than are others. As a supplement to this chapter, we recommend viewing any of the following:

Malcolm X   Spike Lee's biography shows us just how important communication was to the African American leader's life—and just how *mindful* Malcolm X was of this fact. This film also shows how communication functions in each of the contexts introduced in this first chapter. Denzel Washington was nominated for an Academy Award for his superior performance as Malcolm.

One Flew Over the Cuckoo's Nest   Michael Douglas pro-duced this adaptation of the Ken Kesey novel, and Jack Nicholson won an Oscar for best actor for his portrayal of Randall McMurphy, the book's and the film's protagonist. The film does a remarkable job of showing how one person's communication behavior disrupts and changes a rigidly defined system of communication. It also does an excellent job of showing the evolution of a small group and the ethical consequences of the communication choices people make.

Up Close and Personal   Starring Michelle Pfeiffer and Robert Redford, this film focuses on modern-day broadcast news and the romance that develops between a veteran TV correspondent, played by Redford, and his protégée, played by Pfeiffer. The film focuses on several of the dimensions of communication introduced in this chapter.

Theory and Research in Practice

1. Read either Motley's or Andersen's article cited in "Another Look." Write a one-page response in which you clearly state whether you agree or disagree with the author. In the process, also give three specific examples from your own experience you believe support your position. Come to class prepared to present and defend what you have written.

2. Research on the effects of TV is equivocal. Some research indicates that TV commercials have a direct influence on consumer behavior; other research suggests otherwise. Take a position on the effects of TV advertising and find at least three pieces of evidence you believe support your position. Share your position and evidence with the class.

3. Given their prevalence, 12-step self-help groups have become a preferred place for people to cope with their difficulties. Contact your local Alcoholics Anonymous and ask the representative about attending an "open meeting." These meetings routinely are visited by students and people in the helping professions. Attend and observe an open meeting. Afterward, write about the experience, paying particular attention to these questions:

   a. Did the person leading the meeting exhibit behaviors consistent with the dimensions of communication competence discussed in this chapter? What is the basis for your conclusion?

   b. Did the meeting and the communication characterizing it appear to be linked to any specific needs the participants appeared to feel and express? Which ones: inclusion? affection? control? What specifically leads you to these conclusions?

   c. Was this a task-oriented, social, therapeutic, or multifunctional group? What evidence leads you to this conclusion?

CHAPTER 2

The Role of Perception

OBJECTIVES

After reading this chapter you should be able to:

- Define perception.

- Describe the effects of perception on communication.

- Define and distinguish among selective perception, exposure, attention, and recall.

- Describe and use six factors that enhance selective perception.

- Describe the relationship between identity and perception.

- Define and distinguish among ideal, personal, and social selves.

- Define and critically discuss the process of attribution.

- Identify and describe common sources of attributional bias.

- List and explain skills that facilitate accurate perceptions and attributions.

The National Conference of Christians and Jews, founded in 1927 and widely recognized for its progressive values, sponsored a 1994 poll concerning perceptions among people of differing races.[1] Of the perceptions uncovered, only one was not surprising: African, Asian, and Latino Americans perceived that they have significantly less opportunity than Whites in the United States. The latter group perceived no such difference. The poll also uncovered perceptions generally not discussed. Forty percent of the African American and Latino respondents and 27 percent of the Whites, for example, agreed with the statement "Asian Americans are unscrupulous, crafty, and devious in business." And nearly 50 percent of the Whites, Latinos, and African Americans surveyed agreed with the assertion "Muslims belong to a religion that condones or supports terrorism."

Pola Lopez's graphic powerfully demonstrates how words can alter perceptions.

Needless to say, these last two perceptions are without empirical foundation. Even so, that is not likely to countermand their effect on the communication behavior of the people who subscribe to them. Because "perceiving is believing," the people who hold negative stereotypes of Asian Americans or Muslims will communicate toward them as if the perception were true.

This chapter focuses on the relationship between communication and **perception,** the process by which people give meaning to what they sense and experience. Our goal is to demonstrate the pivotal role perception plays in facilitating communication competence across the dimensions introduced in Chapter 1. Our hope is that the information covered will also shed light on the kind of bias discovered in the preceding poll. Topics discussed will include

- the nature of perception,
- selectivity in perception,
- perceiving self,
- perceiving others, and
- skills for increasing perceptual accuracy.

perception The process of giving meaning to sensations and experiences.

Box 2-1   Critical Thinking

What Does the Nose Know?

Americans, as a rule of thumb, don't like strong smells. So intense is their aversion to powerful odors, they will go to extremes in the attempt to eliminate them. The famed anthropologist Claude Lévi-Strauss, for example, relates the account of a group of American soldiers who came across a malodorous cave on the Normandy shores shortly after D-Day during WWII. To wipe out the stench of what they assumed were decaying bodies, they turned their flame throwers on the mouth of the cave. To their amazement, they later learned that they had destroyed a cache of aging Roquefort cheese stored by Frenchmen from a nearby village. Needless to say, perceptions are often culture bound.

1. Why do you think the scent of moldy cheese is heavenly to the olfactory glands of one culture and just the opposite for another?

2. Do you think the American culture is overly sensitive to smell?

3. An increasing number of people in this country are demanding scent-free environments, claiming they are allergic to perfumes and deodorizers. Is this a peculiarly American phenomenon, or do you know of similar movements in other countries? See what you can learn in this regard from foreign periodicals available in your library.

SOURCE: Claude Lévi-Strauss, *The Raw and the Cooked* (Chicago: University of Chicago Press, 1983).

The Anatomy of Perception

Once again, perception is the process by which people give meaning to the things they sense and experience. People, places, and things are sensed through sight, sound, smell, taste, and touch. The meaning people give to what they sense depends on their experience, both direct and vicarious. Racists, for example, infrequently have direct experience with the people they hate.

There is a discrepancy between the capacity of the senses and the capacity of the brain. The eye is capable of sensing much more data than the brain is capable of processing.[2] Thus, perception is a selective activity in which people give meaning to only a portion of what they sense and experience.[3] Box 2-1 takes a look at the different meanings a smell has to two different cultures.

Selective Perception

People are predisposed to give meaning to sensory data that are familiar and especially intense. This predisposition is known as **selective perception.** Three consequences of this tendency are

- selective exposure,
- selective attention, and
- selective recall.

selective perception
Predisposition to give meaning to a limited number of sensations and experiences.

Selective exposure is the choice to experience or to avoid particular stimuli. You may intensely dislike violence in movies. As a result, you purposely avoid Quentin Tarantino films such as *Pulp Fiction* and *Reservoir Dogs* because you have read or been told that these films are exceedingly bloody. Selective exposure doesn't just influence the films people choose to watch. It also influences their choices about the people with whom they communicate.

Occasionally people have no choice but to subject themselves to stimuli they otherwise would not choose. The fact that people cannot avoid being physically present in a situation, however, doesn't mean that they have to be mentally engaged. As every student knows, the gulf between going to class and being actively mindful in the class can be large.

Selective attention is the decision whether to be mindful in an encounter. It is a voluntary decision to focus on another's communication behavior. To illustrate the point, consider the degree to which students attend to the lecture of a teacher in an elective course in their major, compared to one in a required general education class. Given equal skill, which teacher do you think has an easier time getting students to actively focus on what was being said?

Selective recall, the third consequence of selective perception, centers on people's ability to remember. Selective recall is subject to a host of influences, not the least of which is the intensity of an experience. People 40 years and older, for example, typically can tell you exactly where they were and what they were doing on November 22, 1963, the day President John Kennedy was assassinated. The experience was so shocking, and so all-consuming of the nation's attention, the event was embedded deep inside people's memories.

Selectivity is a fact of life. In the mind there is no objective reality—only the reality you select to perceive. This doesn't mean selectivity cannot be manipulated. There are specific things communicators can do to increase the chances of people availing themselves, paying attention, and accurately recalling the details of a transaction.

Factors That Influence Perception

Research demonstrates that six specific factors frequently influence people's selective perception: (1) background, (2) intensity, (3) extensity, (4) concreteness, (5) contrast and velocity, and (6) impressivity.[4]

Background What does Figure 2-1 say? It was purposefully manipulated so that the background of the figure would cause confusion. Instead of the letters being made dark with clear borders on a light background, they were made light with undefined borders on a dark background. The background in which a stimulus is embedded can either facilitate or impede perception and communication.

Consider two examples. In the first, lovers converse over a secluded table in an exclusive restaurant. In the second, they attempt the same while standing at the noisiest and most crowded bar in town. Obviously, the background setting in the first example will be much more conducive to them perceiving the relevant details of their messages than the second will be.

Figure 2-1
Perceptual Task. What we perceive often depends on the degree to which a stimulus strikes us as familiar. Difficulty in perceiving the word *sly* in this example owes to the fact that the contrast has been reversed from that with which we are most familiar.

Intensity   Have you ever noticed how such things as the color of a person's hair or style of dress can attract people's attention? Intensity involves how loud, or bright, or vivid a stimulus appears. Generally speaking, the louder, brighter, or more vivid a stimulus, the greater the chances people will perceive it. This fact doesn't mean that there is always a direct and positive correlation between intensity and the meaning people give to a specific stimulus. This fact also doesn't mean that it's always to people's advantage to talk so loud or wear clothes so colorful that they draw attention to themselves.

Communicatively, messages need to be intense enough that people will *selectively perceive them*. Yet, messages shouldn't be so intense that they violate people's expectancies. Research on language intensity, which is discussed in detail in Chapter 3, is a case in point.[5] Language that is moderately intense, only slightly at odds with people's expectations, is attention-getting and involving. Language that is too intense, as is the case when it is perceived as obscene, will so violate people's expectations that it becomes a turnoff.

Extensity   When a large object is surrounded by smaller ones, people notice the large object first. Extensity involves the attention-drawing effect of size. Advertisers try to make a product big enough that it attracts attention. Along a highway numerous stimuli compete for the driver's attention. That's why signs, billboards, and oddities such as concrete figures advertising roadside attractions are made so large. They have to be made large to draw people's attention from the other stimuli competing for it.

Concreteness   Messages that are unambiguous are much more concrete. They also are more likely to gain our perceptual favor than those that are highly abstract. Concreteness explains why a scale model of an object such as an internal combustion engine is usually more successful in getting through to people than a highly detailed written or spoken description. A scale model of an internal combustion engine makes it appear less abstract and therefore more easily sensed. It also reduces the chances of the complexity of the object unnecessarily interfering with perception. Reducing complexity in this kind of situation can be next to impossible using language alone. The idea, then, is not to avoid

Extreme skier, Glenn Plake has no problem with being noticed.

complexity altogether when talking about an abstract or potentially ambiguous topic. Rather, it is to make complexity more concrete. Put another way, the idea is to give body and definition to complexity so that it is more readily sensed and grasped.

Contrast and Velocity   Contrast and velocity affect the degree to which messages and people appear striking, novel, changing, or moving. When coaching students on the delivery of speeches, most teachers urge them to vary the rate and pitch of their voice, use gestures, and make eye contact with individual audience members. Each of these techniques involves contrast and velocity. And each technique is designed to provoke and sustain the selective attention of the audience.

Contrast and velocity also are important to dyadic, small group, and mass communication. Research suggests that people who are nonverbally expressive and who use nonverbal communication to reduce perceptions of distance are

Box 2-2   Skill Building

Increase the Odds of Selective Attention

How would you prepare if you were asked to give a guest presentation to an elementary school class about your major? The teacher has told you in advance that the children, who are between 8 and 10 years old, are easily distracted. The teacher encourages you to be inventive and entertaining, if possible, to attract and maintain their attention.

How might you use your knowledge about background, intensity, extensity, concreteness, contrast and velocity, and impressivity to construct a message and set of visual aids you believe would garner the sustained attention and interest of these students? Be specific! Also, write down the ways in which you would use these perception-enhancing factors in the presentation.

perceived more positively than those who do neither. Further, although contrast and velocity have always been central to electronic media, they have become increasingly important to the new media. For example, the operating software that enables people to use computers has become increasingly animated and quick paced.

Impressivity   Finally, there is the combined long-term effect of background, intensity, extensity, concreteness, complexity, contrast and velocity, called impressivity. Advertisers don't rely on only one of these factors in order to enhance their product's chances of getting our attention. Rather, they use these factors in varying combinations so that they can sufficiently "impress" the senses to take note. Television commercials make elaborate use of impressivity to get our selective attention. Their creators use music, volume, exotic backgrounds, variation in pitch, and color in the effort to keep us from switching channels, picking up the newspaper, or turning off the TV.

To increase the chances that people will pay attention to your messages, you need to develop your skills in using the six factors we've been discussing here. The task in Box 2-2 is designed to give you practice in consciously using these techniques.

Perceiving Self

To this point, we've been concentrating on what the process of perception involves. We've also talked about some of the factors that can influence the process in its most basic sense. These factors, however, pale in comparison to the next topic: **self-perception.** Not only does self-perception define who we are, it also shapes our communication behavior toward others.

self-perception
How you see yourself.

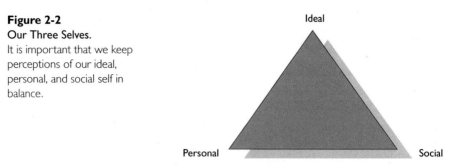

Figure 2-2
Our Three Selves.
It is important that we keep perceptions of our ideal, personal, and social self in balance.

Jonathan Studebaker was born with osteogenesis imperfecta, or brittle bones as it is commonly called. He is the founder of Project Speak Out, an organization dedicated to informing people about the disabled. One hurdle Jonathan recurrently confronts when sharing his message is getting people to ask who he is rather than what he has. Thus, it's not surprising that he enjoys sharing a speech titled "Who Am I?" which lets people know how Jonathan perceives himself.

The question "Who am I?" is one with which all people struggle. It is frequently the focus of novelists and filmmakers. J. D. Salinger's timeless novel, *The Catcher in the Rye*, is essentially about its main character, Holden Caulfield, trying to figure out who he is. The same is true of a host of recent films with female leads including *Thelma and Louise, Little Women, Boys on the Side,* and *How to Make an American Quilt.*

Philosophers and social scientists have identified at least three parts to self-perception, as shown in Figure 2-2. All parts are important to answering the question "Who am I?" The first part is the person people would like to become. The second part is how people really perceive themselves. And the third part is how people think others perceive them.

Ideal Self

Most people have some idealized version of the person they would like to become. This **ideal self** varies from one person to the next. It also changes from one stage of life to the next. Most people's idealized self evolves as they move from adolescence to puberty to adulthood. As people grow in age and experience, they not only become more realistic about who they are capable of becoming but also modify their visions of the ideal accordingly.

ideal self   The person you would like to become.

personal self   The way you really see yourself.

Personal Self

This second facet of identity, **personal self**, involves how people truly see themselves. In an interesting twist on this tendency, a British psychiatrist created a minor controversy in 1995 by suggesting that people who are happy have a

Comedians and actors like Brett Butler of the TV sitcom, "Grace Under Fire" use their audience's reactions as a kind of social mirror.

biased view of themselves. Specifically, Dr. Richard P. Bental argued that people who perceive themselves as happy "overestimate their control over environmental events," "give unrealistically positive evaluations of themselves," and "believe that others share their unrealistically positive evaluations."[6] These perceptions don't mean that happy people are communicatively incompetent. Everyone's self-perception is necessarily subjective. What's more, other researchers have reported that although happy people's self-perception may be biased, it is not completely inaccurate. These studies suggest that a major reason happy people are so joyful is that they believe others perceive them as socially attractive, based on how other people behave toward them.

Social Self

Social self, the third facet of individual identity, is obviously linked to people's ideal self and the way they really see themselves. How people see themselves reflects their beliefs about what others think of them. It is a safe bet that comedians such as Jim Carrey, Brett Butler, Damon Wayans, and George Gomez think they are funny. It's also a safe bet that they came to that conclusion as a result of people laughing at their humor.

social self   The way you perceive others see you.

reflected appraisals
Assessments of your
self based on other
people's responses to
you.

Social scientist Charles Cooley pointed out a century ago that people use each other as a kind of mirror.[7] In the process, they view other people's responses to them as a reflection of themselves. These **reflected appraisals,** as Cooley called them, lead people to judge themselves in terms of such criteria as the degree to which they are communicatively skilled, how sociable they are, and the extent to which others perceive them as attractive.

Self-Perception in Action

To sum up, these three facets of self-perception are interdependent. They operate as a system, which means a change in one will effect changes in the remaining two. Many people are what we call "late bloomers." Their interpersonal attractiveness, self-confidence, and communication skills may not "blossom" until these people are well into adulthood. To conclude that this process modifies their ideal, personal, and social selves is only reasonable.

These three facets of self-perception also affect how people see their communication competence. A negative view of self affects not only one's personal self but also one's self-confidence as a communicator. Likewise, a person who lacks self-confidence may experience difficulty in interpreting communication cues, establishing communication goals, deciding on appropriate roles, and formulating as well as sharing effective messages.

Finally, how people see themselves ideally, personally, and socially influences how they are likely to be perceived by others. As an illustration, consider how gender influences self-perception. Professor Julia T. Wood writes in her book *Gendered Lives* that young girls are often conditioned to defer to young boys.[8] Not only is this deference reflected in young girls' identity systems, but also in their language. Linguist Deborah Tannen writes that this kind of conditioning can lead women to communicate equivocally.[9] According to Tannen, instead of saying, "I think the balanced budget amendment makes sense," women often are more likely to say, "I think it makes sense, do you?"

Perceiving Others

Thus far we have defined perception, discussed the fact that it is selective, talked about factors that can affect the degree to which perception is selective, and focused on how the process of self-perception shapes our answers to the question "Who am I?" Everything we've said so far is important to our next topic, how we see others. People continuously make attributions about each other on the basis of communication behavior. Further, these attributions frequently are based on biased perceptions, such as that women are indecisive.

attribution Giving
reasons to behaviors.

The Process of Attribution

According to social psychologist Fritz Heider, the process of **attribution** involves three stages: (1) perceiving an action, (2) assigning a reason to the

Table 2-1   Types of Attributions

STABLE	UNSTABLE
Internal: I passed the test because I'm smart.	Internal: He passed the test because he studied much harder than usual.
External: I passed because the test was easy.	External: He passed because he made a lot of lucky guesses.

action, and (3) connecting the reason to the person who engaged in the action. The attribution can be directed either at oneself or at another person. As shown in Table 2-1, an attribution can be stable or unstable and internal or external.[10]

The attributions people make about themselves tend to be either generous or forgiving. When people succeed, they are quick to personally take credit for their success. When people fail, however, they are just as quick to blame someone or some other agent for the fact. This is not the case with the attributions they make about the people with whom they daily come into contact. Interpersonal communication scholar Alan Sillars studied the attributions roommates make following a conflict.[11] Sillars interviewed them individually and told them one of two things. In one condition, he told them that upon investigating the conflict, it was their fault. In the second, he said the conflict was clearly the fault of the roommate.

What did Sillars find? In the first condition, roommates attributed their behavior to an external agent, saying such things as "That's really not like me, I was ridiculed by a professor and having a terrible day." In the second condition, though, the person attributed the roommate's behavior to a personality trait, saying such things as "Well, I probably shouldn't say this, but you need to understand my roommate has the personality of a pitbull."

Attributional bias, as the chapter opening example so graphically demonstrated, is far from unusual. People routinely make negative attributions about people and their behavior based on inaccurate perceptions of race, appearance, disability, religion, ethnicity, nationality, and gender.

Although they are less likely to do so, people also use the same kind of superficial data in making positive attributions about others. For example, people commonly make attributions about others on the basis of their anatomy. If they have a mesomorphic, or athletic, physique, the attributions can be highly flattering. Research shows that mesomorphs are perceived as attractive, strong, and social. The same cannot be said for ectomorphs or endomorphs. Ectomorphs, or slender people, are perceived as nervous and edgy, while endomorphs, or people with a heavy physique, are often seen as lazy and suffering from low self-esteem.[12]

Overcoming Attributional Bias

Attributional bias, whether favorable or unfavorable, is impossible to avoid altogether. That doesn't excuse us from working to make the process of attribution more fair and accurate. Toward that end, researchers have uncovered a number of sources of attributional bias about which we should be mindful. The list includes but is not limited to centrism, xenophobia, emotional intensity, overconfidence, and power.

Centrism   In *Animal Farm,* George Orwell uses the inhabitants of a barnyard to show just how bigoted people can be.[13] He also demonstrates in the process that there is no living thing more dangerous than a person or group that sees the world from a single perspective. Centrism, as used here, refers to people who believe they are superior to others. Centrism not only is a source of attributional bias but also can lead to destructive conflict.

It is understandable that individuals and groups commonly use their own experience as a frame of reference for perception and attribution. This doesn't release people, however, from recognizing that there are other frames of reference that not only apply but also may be better suited to a specific situation. When people forget this valuable lesson, they often find themselves in a heated argument or worse.

Individuals should never generalize from a population of one. This means they should never lapse into thinking that their experience is representative of everyone else's. The same is true for groups of people who identify with each other. Gangs are a case in point. One gang presumes that it is superior to another for no reason other than that the latter is composed of different people.

Xenophobia   The fear of anything strange or foreign, including people, is called xenophobia. The most common consequence of fear is the feeling of anxiety. Research in several disciplines demonstrates that anxiety interferes with people's ability to accurately process information.[14] The implications of xenophobia for attributional bias are obvious. People fearful and anxious about others are prone to misperceive and make inaccurate attributions about them. These inaccurate attributions most likely will result in the same people communicating inappropriately with those they fear.

Xenophobia is both real and dramatic in its effect. In Northern Ireland, for instance, Catholic and Protestant children have been segregated from each other for generations in cities such as Belfast. Not only fear but hate of each other has been the unfortunate result. In a novel exchange program, Irish Catholic and Protestant children were brought together in the United States to live with American families. Although these children initially were mistrustful of each other, their perceptions and corresponding attributions changed as they played together. By the time they were scheduled to return to their homes, many had come to a new understanding, an understanding based on knowledge rather than ignorance. Xenophobia can be overcome.

Emotional Intensity   A third and even more common source of attributional bias is emotional intensity. The more intense people's beliefs and feelings, the more likely their attributions are to be biased. Examples of the relationship between emotional intensity and attributional bias are plentiful. The consequences sometimes can be extreme. Recent events in the anti-abortion movement are telling in this regard. Physicians and clinic workers have been killed, based on the attribution that they were murderers.

As these children illustrate, xenophobia can be overcome.

Conversely, emotional intensity can lead to favorable attributions about people whose behavior may actually be harmful. Studies of spousal abuse show that the abused frequently attributes the behavior of the abuser to positive motives. Corporal punishment is confused with caring; jealous rages are confused with demonstrations of love; and restrictions on personal freedoms are confused with concern for personal safety.

Overconfidence   A fourth source of attributional bias is overconfidence, or people's conviction that their interpretation of communication behavior is seldom wrong. People who put complete trust in their first impressions are representative of this group. So too are people who say they know someone as well as they know themselves.

No one's interpretive competence, to use the term introduced in Chapter 1, is infallible. Even people who are close can misinterpret each other's intentions.[15] Closeness and intimacy can breed overconfidence in people's ability to interpret their partner's communication behavior. The offices of marriage counselors are full of people who didn't know their spouse of 25 years was unhappy or felt that he or she was being taken for granted. The offices of family counselors are full of parents who saw no sign of their teenage child's thoughts of suicide and of children who failed to make the connection between personal sacrifice and parental love. The point is simple. The process of attribution is so susceptible to bias that people must be vigilant even when attributing meaning to the communication behavior of the people they think they know best.

Power   The fifth and final source of attributional bias we will discuss is power. The sources of one person's power over another are varied. A person may be powerful because of special expertise or skills, because of the ability to reward others, or because others want to be identified with the person. Power also can be legitimate or illegitimate. Legitimate power exists when we comply with a request because we believe the person making the request has the right to do so. Illegitimate power, which is coercive, exists when we have no choice but to honor another's request for compliance. Those with power often fail to see the degree to which it influences others. Those with power also sometimes confuse illegitimate requests with legitimate ones.

People who are not aware of the degree of power others perceive they possess are especially prone to attributional bias. They assume others comply with their requests because they choose to. This may or may not be the case. In the workplace, people sometimes comply with a request because they consider their job to be at stake. Every holiday season it seems that at least one letter in Dear Abby is from a secretary who was asked by the boss to do his or her holiday shopping. The secretary feels forced to comply because of the perception that the boss has the power to punish an employee who refuses. The illegitimate use of power is common. It would be less so if people in positions of power asked themselves a simple question before attempting to gain another's compliance: Does the other person perceive that he or she has any choice in the matter?

Perceiving Yourself and Others Accurately

At first glance, doesn't line A in Figure 2-3 look shorter than line B? Yet they're identical in length. This optical illusion is just another illustration of how easily we can be tricked perceptually. This final section is intended to thwart this kind of trickery by introducing skills that minimize perceptual errors. These skills involve

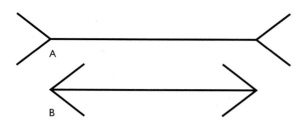

Figure 2-3
Mueller–Lyer Illusion

- behaviors necessary to increase the accuracy of attributions,
- perspective taking and a technique called reframing, and
- the coordination of meaning.

These skills are interdependent. Mastering one will increase the chances of mastering the others.

Making Accurate Attributions

Accurate attributions need to be based on evidence relevant to the attribution. Factual evidence is just as important for assessing the attributions people make about themselves as it is for assessing the attributions people make about others. People can be led to believe almost anything about themselves if they hear it said often enough by others. These beliefs also can become self-fulfilling prophecies.

When the Mattel Toy Company's talking Barbie Doll said, "Math is hard," for example, the American Association of University Women (AAUW) immediately called on Mattel to take the doll off the market.[16] The doll's statement only served to reinforce an idea, AAUW leaders said, that young girls and women have been conditioned to believe about themselves: females can't do math. Like so many of the attributions people make about themselves, this one isn't true. There is considerable evidence suggesting that women's reluctance to pursue math-dependent careers has little to do with their innate abilities.

Just as we need to have sufficient evidence to support the attributions we make about ourselves, we need to look carefully for documentation that supports the attributions we make about others. In light of what researchers call the **fundamental attribution error,** this evidence is especially important. The fundamental attribution error, or people's perception that others cause what happens to them, is found consistently by those doing research on attribution. The fundamental attribution error was exemplified earlier in Alan Sillars's research with college roommates. Fundamental attribution error expresses formally what Sillars found. People attribute another person's behavior to internal and stable rather than external and unstable factors. Those whose communication behavior offends us, for example, don't display such behavior because they are having a bad day but because they have an offensive personality. Other examples of fundamental attribution error range from the charge that welfare recipients don't

fundamental attribution error
The tendency to believe that other people's behavior is the result of internal characteristics rather than external circumstances.

want to work to the charge that women who are raped invite the act of violence as a result of the way they dress and behave.

To overcome the fundamental attribution error, people can employ at least three skills: (1) looking for signs of covariation, (2) discounting, and (3) reality checking with another source. Have you ever heard the expression "If it walks like a duck, quacks like a duck, and swims like a duck, it must be a duck"? The expression is illustrative of covariation, which involves looking for multiple cues prior to arriving at a conclusion. All too often we perceive others as unfriendly, negative, or stuck-up on the basis of very limited exposure to them. *Covariation* demands the suspension of such definitive attributions until multiple exposures in different communication environments have occurred.

Discounting is straightforward. When we are making an attribution, the tendency is to explain a person's behavior on the basis of what strikes us as most obvious. *Discounting* asks people to look beyond the obvious for alternative explanations. In the hit movie *Forrest Gump*, Tom Hanks talks to several people who share a bench at a bus stop with him. Because the character Hanks plays is mildly retarded, some of those with whom he talks immediately doubt the truth of what he says. When he talks about meeting President Kennedy or accepting the Medal of Honor from President Johnson, one man simply laughs it off. It never occurs to him that Forrest is relating a true story.

Discounting is just the opposite of the preceding example. What seems the obvious reason for a person's behavior is not necessarily the only or best reason. Going beyond the obvious can reveal alternative and equally plausible reasons. Often this translates to considerably more accurate and communication-enhancing attributions about others.

Finally, it is always a good idea to compare attributions with other sources. Because people's behavior is influenced by such things as environments, **reality checking** can be helpful. The person you perceive to be unapproachable in a specific transaction may be perceived differently by others. On the other hand, if their attribution is consistent with yours, you still are better off because it validates your initial perception.

Perspective Taking and Reframing

reality checking
Assessing the accuracy of perceptions with another source.

empathy The ability to perceive things from another person's perspective.

One of the earliest signs of moving past adolescence is the ability to take other people's perspective into consideration. As William Rawlins points out in his book *Friendship Matters*, perspective taking also is a skill that appears sooner in young women than in young men.[17] They simply are ready to understand the other person's point of view sooner than men are.

Skill in perceiving people and events from perspectives beyond our own is facilitated by the ability to empathize. This ability involves trying to sense the world as another person senses it. As Lauren Wispe, a leading authority on the subject, asserts, **empathy** also is a nonjudgmental process.[18] People are not born empathic. By the same token, it is not an automatic consequence of life. Not everyone shares the same capacity for empathy—some may even be incapable of

Box 2-3   Self-Assessment

What Is Your Empathy Level?

Respond to each statement by indicating the degree to which the statement is true regarding the way you typically communicate with others. When you think of your communication, is the statement always false (answer 1), usually false (answer 2), sometimes false and sometimes true (answer 3), usually true (answer 4), or always true (answer 5).

_____ 1. I try to understand others' experiences from their perspectives.

_____ 2. I follow the Golden Rule ("Do unto others as you would have them do unto you") when communicating with others.

_____ 3. I can "tune in" to the emotions others are experiencing when we communicate.

_____ 4. When trying to understand how others feel, I imagine how I would feel in their situation.

_____ 5. I am able to tell what others are feeling without being told.

_____ 6. Others experience the same feelings I do in any given situation.

_____ 7. When others are having problems, I can imagine how they feel.

_____ 8. I find it hard to understand the emotions others experience.

_____ 9. I try to see others as they want me to.

_____ 10. I never seem to know what others are thinking when we communicate.

To find your score, first reverse the responses for the even-numbered items (if you wrote 1, make it 5; if you wrote 2, make it 4; if you wrote 3, leave it as 3; if you wrote 4, make it 2; if you wrote 5, make it 1). Next, add the numbers next to each statement. Scores range from 10 to 50. The higher your score, the more you are able to empathize.

SOURCE: William Gudykunst, *Bridging Differences*, 2nd ed. (Newbury Park, Calif.: Sage, 1994), 90. Copyright ©1994 by Sage Publications. Reprinted by permission of Sage Publications.

it. (Box 2-3 will help you measure your capacity for empathy.) What is clear, though, is that empathy requires open-mindedness. Being open-minded means being receptive to new experience. It also means postponing the evaluation of an experience until it has been assessed from more than a single view.

Using more than a single view in assessing an experience is called **reframing**, which facilitates skill in perspective taking and the ability to empathize. Reframing is simple in theory. It involves little more than shifting one's point of view or recasting the language that is used in reference to an experience. The saying "I cried because I had no shoes until I saw a person who had no feet" is exemplary of reframing. It shifts the person's view from one that is exclusively self-centered to one in which the self is embedded in a much larger context.

reframing Shifting perspective to change one's point of view.

One of the best ways to learn how to reframe involves changing the language used to describe an experience. Language, as you'll learn in the next chapter, shapes behavior. How an experience is described, therefore, will influence the

Box 2-4   Considering Diversity

When Yes Means No

You've just concluded a meeting with a group of Japanese business people. You spent the entire day with them and feel you got to know them well. You concluded the meeting with a question: "So, do we have a deal?" They nodded and smiled in response to your question.

So, do you have a deal? Maybe not. Because saving face is so important to the Japanese, their response may have been intended to simply not offend you by saying, "No." Japanese take time in business and like to develop a personal relationship with their business associates. Thus, while you may perceive a day as sufficient to build a relationship, your Japanese counterparts probably wouldn't.

1. What steps should you take before attempting to do business with someone from a very different culture?

2. Where would you go to find information about the culture of the person with whom you planned on doing business?

3. What does this exercise in thinking say about our discussion of high and low context cultures and the coordination of the rules that govern the meaning of communication transactions?

SOURCE: Brigham Young University, *CultureGram*, Language and Intercultural Research Center (Provo, Utah: BYU 1994).

behavior that follows. Telling yourself an experience was "the pits," for instance, will lead to different behaviors than will telling yourself the experience wasn't as bad as you had envisioned. It also will serve to make similar experiences less negative than otherwise.

Coordinating Meaning

Finally, the accuracy with which people perceive each other can be enhanced dramatically if they attempt to coordinate and manage the meaning of their transaction.[19] The rules that govern communication vary across cultures. When people from different cultures with different rules meet to communicate, misperception of the meaning of the transaction easily can occur. The United States, for example, is a low context culture. The rule in low context cultures is that the content of messages carries the most meaning. In high context cultures such as Japan, however, meaning seldom is derived from only the content of what is said. Meaning depends more on the context in which something is said. Thus, as Box 2-4 illustrates, it is crucial for U.S. and Japanese communicators to coordinate and manage the rules that will govern their intercultural transaction.

Coordinating meaning is no less important to communication when talking with people from one's own culture. Parents and children, spouses, bosses and subordinates need to coordinate the rules that govern the meaning of their communication transactions. Parents have to make sure children understand when no means no, spouses have to negotiate what sharing means, and bosses and subordinates have to make sure they agree about what constitutes a legitimate use of power.

Summary

Perception is complex. Perception is the process of giving meaning to the persons, places, and things we sense and experience. Perception is a selective process because of the discrepancy between the capacity of the senses and the capacity of the brain to process what is sensed and experienced. There are three types of selective perception. These include: selective exposure—the choice to experience or avoid particular stimuli, selective attention—the decision whether to be mindful in an encounter, and selective recall—a person's ability to remember. Six factors which enhance selectivity are background, intensity, extensity, concreteness, contrast and velocity, and impressivity.

Self-perception concerns our ideal, personal, and social selves. Self-perception effects not only how we see ourselves but also the attributions we make about ourselves and others. Attribution is the process of assigning a cause to a behavior, such as a person's character or a particular situation. Attribution commonly is biased by assumptions about a person based on factors such as appearance, race, age, and gender. The accuracy of attributions about both the self and others can be increased by learning to look for signs of covariation, to discount the obvious, to do reality checks, to take the other person's perspective, and to reframe one's perspective about a particular experience. Finally, attributions also are more likely to be accurate when communicators take the time to discuss and coordinate the rules that will govern their transactions.

Another Look

Articles

S. Chaiken and P. Pilner. "Women, But Not Men, Are What They Eat: The Effect of Meal Size and Gender on Perceived Femininity and Masculinity." *Personality and Social Psychology Bulletin* 13 (1987): 166–76.

If a man eats a small meal, does that make him less masculine than one who eats a Texas-size steak? Is a woman with a healthy appetite less feminine than one who eats bird-size portions at a meal? Read this article and see how men and women are perceived differently on the basis of meal size.

E. B. Palmore. "Attitudes Toward the Aged: What We Know and Need to Know." *Research on Aging* 4 (1982): 333–48.

How do you and your peers perceive the aged? This review of research reports that older adults are often perceived in a less than favorable light by younger generations. The relationship between communication and perceptions of the aged is an excellent topic for a paper or speech. This article would be an excellent place to start your research.

Books

Negative perceptions such as those at the beginning of this chapter often are a result of ignorance, plain and simple.

The following books will help you better understand why this is so. Reading them can be a perception-changing process.

Thomas L. Friedman. *From Beirut to Jerusalem*. New York: Anchor Books, 1989.

If you've ever felt puzzled about the Arab-Israeli conflict, this winner of the National Book Award will give you new and needed insight to the centuries-old tensions in that part of the world. This fair and impartial book enables you to perceive the conflict from both Arab and Israeli perspectives. Aside from being a good read, it graphically demonstrates the relationship between perception and communication behavior.

Deborah Tannen. *You Just Don't Understand: Women and Men in Conversation*. New York: William Morrow, 1990.

In the preceding pages, we connected language with perception. This best-selling book does a terrific job of showing how gender can influence what we say and how we perceive it. In the process, Deborah Tannen also demonstrates how perceptions of power are linked to language.

Video Rentals

Fried Green Tomatoes   Based on the Fanny Flagg novel, this is a wonderful movie on many levels. In terms of perception, it does a superior job of showing why people interpret events as they do, the effect of age on perception, and the effect of gender stereotyping on perception.

Widow's Peak   Starring Mia Farrow, this is a film that purposefully manipulates the viewer's perception of the events shown. We would like to say more about the film, but to do so would ruin the experience should you choose to view it.

Rising Sun   The novel of the same name by Michael Crichton was criticized for Japan-bashing because it depicted the cutthroat competitive tactics of a large Japanese conglomerate. The film, starring Sean Connery and Wesley Snipes, takes place in Los Angeles and attempts to be more politically correct by avoiding such portrayals (the villains are all Americans). However, the film is still an interesting example of attributions that are made about the Japanese. There are several scenes where Connery analyzes "how the Japanese think" in order to generate leads to solve the sex-related murder that occurred in the board room of the Japanese corporation.

2001: A Space Odyssey   This classic Stanley Kubrick film may be the definitive "what does it mean?" film. Based on Arthur C. Clarke's novel, it depicts the evolution of humankind from Olduvai Gorge in Africa to Jupiter and beyond. In the process, it comments on everything from the meaning of God to life after death. Few people perceive the film's commentary the same way.

When Harry Met Sally   This film is about a friendship between Harry (Billy Crystal) and Sally (Meg Ryan) that after thirteen years turns into love, and the different perceptions that men and women have about their relationships. Notice how many of the perceptions are from the female perspective, such as Ryan's declaration that true friendship between a man and a woman is impossible because the issue of sex always gets in the way, and her orgasm-faking scene in a crowded café. This could be partly due to the fact that the movie was written by a woman (Nora Ephron).

Theory and Research in Practice

1. Research clearly shows that attributions about self are kinder than those made about others. One explanation for this phenomenon is the principle of psychological consistency. It suggests we rationalize our own failures to protect our self-concept. Do you agree? Record in your journal an experience in which you went out of your way to protect your self-concept. If you are not keeping a journal, describe the experience on a sheet of paper. In either case be sure to label your attribution as internal or external, stable or unstable.

2. Research also shows that we hold others accountable for their own behavior and the situation in which they find themselves. What are the implications of this research finding for public attitudes toward (1) the homeless, (2) drug addicts, (3) the disadvantaged, and (4) under-represented groups of people in the professions such as women and persons of color.

3. Research demonstrates that attributions between intimates are subject to the same kind of bias that affects less-close relationships. Married couples, for example, frequently believe they know their spouse better than they actually do, misperceive the degree to which power is shared in their relationship, and assign disproportionate blame for conflict on their spouse. Working with a partner, generate a list of 10 skills that intimates should practice to help prevent attributional bias from unnecessarily affecting their relationship with each other.

CHAPTER 3

Communication and Language

OBJECTIVES

After reading this chapter you should be able to:

- Describe the relationship between words and perception.

- Discuss the relationship between language and thought.

- Distinguish denotative from connotative meaning.

- Explain the significance of grammar and syntax to language.

- Demonstrate how language reflects cultural, group, and individual diversity.

- Create examples showing the relationship between language and power.

- Recognize examples of marginalizing language.

- Explain the effects of marginalizing and abusive language.

- Create and use examples of language that is inclusive, appropriate, uncertainty reducing, immediate, and responsive to individual learning styles.

The controversy over the effects of music lyrics on young people didn't begin with '80s punk rock or '90s gansta' rap. Decades before anyone had heard about Sid Vicious and Johnny Rotten, or Ice T and Ice Cube, parents and politicians were arguing that the day's music was corrupting the nation's youth. In the 1920s, parents and politicians worried about the lyrics of jazz. During the 1940s, they worked themselves into a frenzy over the lyrics of rhythm and blues, commonly referred to as "race music" by the white establishment. As your own parents will tell you, '60s and '70s popular music also caused the older generation to worry because many of its members thought the lyrics of rock and psychedelic music encouraged casual sex or experimentation with drugs.

The ongoing debate about the effects of music lyrics and violent language (see Box 3-1) support an incontrovertible fact: Language is not neutral. The

Box 3-1   Critical Thinking

Violent Language and Popular Culture

What's your opinion? Does the language of popular culture influence behavior? For example, does "shock radio" incite paramilitary leaders to violence? When leaders of the right-to-life movement call physicians baby murderers over radio and television, does this incite their followers to harass people who seek an abortion or to shoot a physician who practices it? Do you think the violent language in films such as *Natural Born Killers, Pulp Fiction,* and *Reservoir* *Dogs* desensitize us to violence? What about the lyrics of rappers like 2-Live Crew or alternative rockers like Trent Reznor of Nine Inch Nails? Do their lyrics promote the degradation of women and/or rape? Take a position on the subject of violent language and behavior. Find three examples from popular culture that you believe support your position. Share your position and supporting examples with your class.

words we use to express ourselves can elicit the full range of human emotion. This chapter is about **language** and its role in giving meaning to the communication transaction. It also is about the power of words in affecting the way we think about ourselves, the people with whom we come into contact, and the surroundings in which we find ourselves. On one level, the goal of this chapter is to assist you in appreciating the larger role language plays in our lives. On another, it is to show you how you can use your appreciation of language to increase your overall communication competence. We focus on

- the relationship between words and what people actually perceive,
- the relationship between language and what people think,
- the basic structure of language,
- language and diversity,
- language and power,
- inappropriate language, and
- effective language.

Language: Words and Things

language Arbitrary system of symbols for communicating.

Just as a map is not the territory it represents, a word is not the object it describes. Words are arbitrary abstractions people use in reference to the persons, places, and things with which they come into contact.[1] Meaning depends on the set of experiences people associate with the words they use. Thus, seman-

Rap is only the latest musical form to be criticized for its lyrics.

ticists, who study words and their impact on society, say, "Words don't mean—people mean."

Words and Perception

Words influence what we perceive. Further, the words we use to describe people, places, and things have a powerful effect on the mental images that result from the description. A person described as tall, dark, and handsome, for example, is likely to be perceived differently than a person described as tall, black, and handsome. Although both descriptions could be used to describe the same person, the latter has racial implications.

Contrary to what people commonly think, race and ethnicity are a perceptual consequence of the words used to describe specific groups of people, rather than biological absolutes. What's more, the language of race usually is inadequate if not inaccurate. For example, when someone is described as Asian, many people develop a mental image of the person in terms of physical features, such as hair, eyes, skin color, skeletal structure, and height. Yet, Asian could mean Chinese, Indian, or Filipino. People from China, India, and the Philippines look quite different even though they are all Asians. Moreover, there are regional variations among people from each of those countries in terms of such characteristics as height and skin color.

The point, then, is twofold. First, words influence what we perceive or, to put it another way, what we see. Second, what we perceive on hearing a word shapes both our attitudes and our communication behavior toward the person, place, or thing the word describes. Such shaping wouldn't be a problem if words and the perceptions they evoke were always accurate. As our example illustrates, though, our perceptions often are not accurate.

Language and Thinking

What is true of individual words is even more true of language. The language in which we think and speak affects how we perceive our world and the people in it. According to the **linguistic relativity hypothesis,** which can be traced to the pioneering research of cultural anthropologist Benjamin Whorf, different languages can lead to different patterns of thought.[2] Linguistic relativity is due, in part, to the fact that the words and grammatical structures of different languages can be unique.

Whorf laid the foundation for this idea while studying and writing about the Native American language of the Hopi. He discovered there are no words in their language for the concept of incremental time: no seconds, no minutes, and no hours. Thus, it would never occur to the Hopi that one could be half an hour early or late for a visit, because they have no way to express the concept.

To some extent, all languages are unique. They contain concepts so specific to the language and the culture in which the language is spoken that there are no true equivalents in other languages. For example, two concepts central to Chinese culture, *yuan* and *kuan-hsi,* vaguely concern what English speakers call fate or luck and their role in people connecting with each other. When the Chinese fail to hit it off with someone personally or professionally, they often attribute the failure to the lack of *yuan* or *kuan-hsi* in the relationship. As the Chinese will explain when asked, fate or luck are the two concepts closest to *yuan* and *kuan-shi* in the English language but are not anywhere near being their equivalent. Thus, native English speakers cannot easily understand and appreciate these two important concepts in Chinese culture.

linguistic relativity hypothesis The hypothesis that the language one speaks influences thinking.

Just as it is important to recognize how words influence perception and shape our attitudes and behavior toward people, it is important to recognize the role of language in this regard. Simply put, the language we speak and in which we

think does more than influence perception. Because language varies from culture to culture, our native tongue also can restrict our ability to see the reality perceived by people from different cultures.

In the Hopi culture, the concept of incremental time is nonexistent.

Language Structure

When we stop to think about the structure of language, the degree to which it can influence what we see and think and how we behave becomes more apparent. At its most basic level, the structure of language involves words, grammar, and syntax. On average, for example, college graduates have a vocabulary of between 10,000 and 30,000 words. These words can be used in varying combinations for the purpose of communicating. They also have different uses: standard, informal, obsolete, and slang. Standard use of the word *loser* means someone who fails to succeed at something, usually a game. Informally, *loser* frequently is used to describe a worthless person. Finally, we can also use *loser* as

denotative meaning
The dictionary definition of a word.

connotative meaning
The ideas associated with a word, often containing an emotional element.

grammar System of rules of a language governing the way words are formed and combined.

syntax System of rules of a language governing the order of words to form phrases, clauses, and sentences.

slang, meaning almost anything depending on the context and the relationship we have with a person.

Important to this discussion are the related concepts of denotation and connotation. **Denotation** involves the objective, conventional meanings for a word, or the dictionary definitions. **Connotation** involves meanings for a word you won't always find in the dictionary, or the ideas, images, and emotions people associate with a word. Although denotative meanings can be learned by reading a dictionary, connotations, which are largely determined by cultural usage, are learned over time from seeing and hearing examples. As an illustration of different kinds of connotations, consider some of the various words used to describe a person who weighs more than average. The word *chubby* is appropriate to describe a baby or toddler, but to be called chubby could hurt a teenager's feelings. A man may be described as *stocky*, but the same term applied to a woman connotes not just extra pounds but a muscular frame and even a somewhat masculine appearance. A doctor's report might note that a patient is *overweight;* the word *tubby* would seem highly unprofessional in that context. And stores don't market clothes for "fat people"; because *fat* has a negative connotation, they have departments for the "plus woman" and for "big and tall men." In summary, competent communication requires using words not only with the correct denotative meaning but also with the connotation that is appropriate for the context.

Because words vary in their meaning and function, they cannot be served up to people in just any combination. Rules are required to make sense of words that are strung together. Grammar involves such rules.[3] And so does syntax.[4] **Grammar** is a formal system of rules that tells people how words should go together. A plural noun demands a plural pronoun: "*Students* need to know *their* rights." Subjects and verbs also should agree: "How many *students were* trying to add the class?"

Syntax works in combination with grammar. Syntactical rules tell people the order in which words should appear if they are to be meaningful. As is the case with grammar, syntactical rules also vary from language to language. The French usually put their adjectives after the noun they modify, whereas in English adjectives typically are placed just before the noun they modify. Thus, English speakers say "the white house," whereas the French say "la maison blanche."

Language and Diversity

Having established that words and language color people's reality and are governed by rules, we now can examine the relationship between language and three dimensions of diversity: cultural, group, and individual. Although we will explore these dimensions of diversity in detail in Chapter 7, at this point you need a basic understanding of the connections between language and diversity in order to build your communication competence. To begin with, then, diversity is about variety. In the case of language, diversity involves the various ways language both shapes and reflects our culture, the groups with which we most identify, and our individual psychologies.

Table 3-1 Whose English Are You Speaking?

The following examples of words and terms used to describe the same thing illustrate the fact that culture involves more than what appears to be a common language.

United States	Great Britain	United States	Great Britain
What's up?	Hello.	skilled carpenter	joiner
car trunk	boot	worn out	knackered
pharmacist	chemist	license plate	number plate
buddy/partner	mate	policeman	Old Bill
brewski/a beer	pint	run away	scarper
rude	cheeky	to hurry along	to chivvy
later/good-bye	cheerio	pedestrian underpass	subway
gas	petrol	furniture removal truck	pantechnicon
baby's crib	cot	vehicle overpass	flyover
thread	cotton (for sewing)	newspaper editorial	leading article
zucchini	courgette	slot machine	fruit machine
to loaf	to skive	ladies' underwear	smalls
cotton candy	candy floss	long-distance bus	coach
period (punctuation)	full stop	petty thief	spiv
quotation marks	inverted commas	to whine	to grizzle
idiot, boor	berk	to carry a heavy load	to hump

SOURCE: Bill Bryson, *The Mother Tongue: English and How It Got That Way* (New York: William Morrow, 1990), 178. Copyright © 1990 by Bill Bryson. Used by permission of William Morrow & Co., Inc.

Language and Cultural Diversity

Culture involves the collective manner in which people in a specific society think, feel, and behave. How people collectively use language is one of the major characteristics that defines and distinguishes their culture from others.[5] Each language shapes the perceptions and patterns of thought of the people who speak it. In the effort to understand a people's culture, therefore, it is necessary to understand their language.

However, not everyone who shares a language has the same culture. The Americans and the English are a good example. The versions of the English language they speak and write are markedly different, as Table 3-1 shows. And their cultures have as many differences as similarities.

Perhaps an even better example involves Spanish-speaking people. Not only is Spanish spoken on three major continents, it also is spoken on hundreds of islands across the Atlantic and Pacific Oceans. These various Spanish-speaking people do not share one homogeneous culture. Compare Madrid, Spain, East Los Angeles, California, and South Miami, Florida. Although Spanish is the predominant language spoken by the residents of these cities, their cultures vary in significant ways.

The degree to which spoken language influences how people think, feel, and behave also depends on whether they live in what anthropologist Edward T. Hall calls a high- or low-context culture.[6] In high-context cultures, people infer much about the meaning of their communication transaction from the environment in which it occurs. Japanese businessmen may discuss certain facets of business while socializing, for example, but they don't "do" business while socializing. Whatever is said about business, therefore, is interpreted on the basis of the surroundings in which it is said.

The opposite is often true for people living in low-context cultures, where people invest considerable meaning in what they say to each other. In the North American motion picture industry, as a case in point, more deals are consummated over lunch than in the office. And U.S. business people often make no distinction between business conducted while socializing and business conducted in the workplace. What is said between U.S. business people is usually more important than where it is said.

Language and Group Diversity

Group diversity involves the various reference groups with which people most strongly identify. As Chapter 7 discusses at length, there is tremendous diversity in these reference groups. They range from our professional peers at work to the organizations we join because they reflect a hobby or an interest we share with others. Although language affects all reference groups, our discussion here focuses on three that not only are important but are affected to an extraordinary degree by language: gender, social class, and race.

Gender Gender is not the same as one's biological sex, which is genetically determined. Gender, which includes the roles people are expected to perform, is learned from the culture in which people are raised.[7] What's more, these roles and expectancies are partly shaped by the language members of a specific culture use when talking about gender. If you grew up in a household where sex determined the roles performed, you probably refer to some activities as women's work and others as men's work.

In the North American culture, gender roles traditionally have reflected people's biological sex. Historically, this fact has meant different sets of roles and expectancies for women and men. Historically, this fact also has meant that the language used in reference to women has reflected the roles and expectancies women were assigned, while the language referring to men reflected the roles and expectancies that have inhered to their cultural assignment.

These historical trends are important for a number of reasons. Chief among them are the degree to which the trends have influenced how women and men see themselves, what women talk about as opposed to what men talk about, and how men and women talk to each other. The language with which people are described, for example, clearly affects their self-concept. Thus, if women grow up hearing themselves described as weak, nurturing, emotional, timid, soft, and caring, these descriptions may very well help to shape their self-concept.

Researchers also argue that because of the different way language is applied to the sexes, women and men talk about different topics.[8] Women are predisposed to talk about relationships, whereas men are predisposed to talk about activities. This difference can complicate matters when women and men converse.

From an early age, women in the North American culture are encouraged to be cooperative and passive, even when they have good reason to be assertive or distinguish themselves in a group. In contrast, men are encouraged to compete and stand out from the crowd at an equally early age. The upshot is that the different behaviors for which young women and young men are reinforced become a feature of their conversational style. Women approach conversation as a chance to show how good they are at cooperating. Men approach conversation as an opportunity to compete or as an opportunity to individually shine.

Research illustrates how these two conversational styles often clash in women's and men's relational lives.[9] During conflict, which is the subject of Chapter 10, the competitive predisposition of men can make matters worse. In a sense, men want to win the argument, even at the risk of irreparable harm to the relationship. Women, on the other hand, are willing to cooperate to resolve the conflict, because they perceive the relationship as more important than winning the argument.

Social Class   Like gender, class is shaped by the way a culture uses language. The social class of which you consider yourself a member is in many ways a consequence of semantic training. People from different social classes not only use language differently but also tend to define class differently. To some class is defined by income, whereas for others it is defined by manners and education. Despite its ambiguity, people continue to use the language of class in describing themselves and others. Looking over several issues of various news magazines, for example, we found groups of people being referred to as the

hard-core criminal class,

permanent welfare class,

illegal immigrant class,

working-class poor,

forgotten class, and

computer-literate class.

The semantic baggage such descriptions carry is nothing to scoff at. You need only write down the images the preceding descriptions evoke, moreover, to realize the degree to which language perpetuates the idea that there are distinct classes of people, some of whom are superior to others.

Race   Race is still another reference group that owes its existence partly to language. As we said earlier in this chapter, race is an inadequate and misleading concept. It is too often used to stereotype people and assumes unique biological, and often psychological, characteristics where there are none.

Communication scholar Cheris Kramarae takes this idea a step further, arguing that language not only constructs our image of race but also is used to justify racism.[10] The Ku Klux Klan, for example, is organized in part to protect the purity of the white race. Yet, there is no purely white race just as there is no purely black or brown or red or yellow race of people. These are semantic creations, figments of language.

These examples are not meant to suggest that groups do not have any particular characteristics or that the concept of race is never used by people to identify an important reference group in which they see themselves belonging. To the contrary, these examples are meant to simply illustrate that diversity is, in part, a product of the language that people both within and outside a reference group use to describe the reference group.

People within a reference group use language to create **convergence**, the feeling that they are highly similar. People inside a reference group also use language to create **divergence**, the feeling that they have little in common with those who are outside their group. Those who are outside a reference group use language to create the feeling that they have little in common with the people within that group. Reference groups often develop their own language, which distinguishes them from each other. Scholars Mario Garcia and Rodolfo Alvarez, for example, suggest that Spanish-speaking people of Mexican descent in the United States constitute several reference groups rather than a single one.[11] Two such reference groups are Mexican Americans and Chicanos/Chicanas. The Mexican American group is composed of people who immigrated from Mexico to border states such as California and Texas following World War II. According to Garcia and Alavarez, people who consider themselves Mexican Americans are generally older and more conservative than those who identify themselves as Chicanos or Chicanas.

Chicanos and Chicanas came of age in the 1960s and gained attention in the 1970s. They perceived Mexican immigrants who wanted to assimilate with the predominant Anglo culture as abandoning their native culture. To distinguish themselves from the Mexican American reference group (divergence), Chicanos and Chicanas adopted specific patterns of behaving, including their own code words (convergence). The list of code words included *vendido* (sell out) and *socio* (the old-boy network) and nonverbal symbols such as specific styles of dress. Today, members of this reference group sometimes refer to each other as *veteranos* (veterans). The code word *veteranos* also serves to tell people that the reference group with which the *veteranos* most identify is Chicano/Chicana.

convergence The use of language to create a reference group and to define its members as highly similar.

divergence The use of language to exclude people from a reference group.

To distinguish itself from previous ones, each generation creates a language that is uniquely its own.

Language and Individual Diversity

The relationship between language and diversity is most complex at the individual level. How people perceive themselves and others is tied to the way they use language. Language also tells people a great deal about what they need to take into consideration when communicating with each other.

Individual diversity is reflected in people's personal viewpoints about such human characteristics as gender, sexual orientation, and personality. Recognizing individual diversity doesn't mean that we must agree with every viewpoint a person expresses. Rather, it means we should take such viewpoints into account when communicating with others.

All too often, we find ourselves guessing about language that is respectful of individual diversity. As a result, either we say what we think is politically correct and run the risk of patronizing the person or we say whatever pops into our mind, hoping that it doesn't prove offensive. There is a better way, one the other person is likely to appreciate: Instead of guessing or hoping you say the right thing, you ask the person, "How do you prefer to be addressed?" You'll learn that not all Blacks prefer *African American,* that some gays and lesbians don't refer to themselves as such, and that *disabled* is not a dirty word.

To learn about people's viewpoints, you also should pay attention to the words they use and how they use them. If a person uses the term "new age" in a pejorative sense, you can probably assume she won't be interested in meditation or crystals. Similarly, a person who rolls his eyes at the mention of boxing may not recognize the names George Foreman and Riddick Bowe.

Language and Power

Up to this point, we have said that language influences cultural identity, helps groups to identify themselves and distinguish themselves from each other, and shapes our viewpoints. Here we want to show that language is an instrument of tremendous power as well. The simple act of giving something a name or someone a title are cases in point. Putting a title such as Dr. in front of a name is enough to alter a person's perceptions of the individual titled Dr. when they first meet.[12] In terms of power, language shapes how people respond to each other in at least two ways. The first involves the relationship between power and talk. The second concerns the relationship between power and the manner in which people are talked about.

Power Talk

Communication research suggests there is an undeniable relationship between power and the manner in which people address and respond to each other.[13] Powerful people use competence-enhancing language. This kind of language is appropriately direct and may contain words and phrases that document with evidence the importance of what is being said. People who use powerful language are perceived as more credible, attractive, and competent than people who use powerless language.

verbal qualifiers
Tentative words and phrases that diminish the power of language.

verbal intensifiers
Words that undermine perceptions of power as a result of over-emphasis.

tag questions
Declarative sentences turned into questions to solicit approval.

Powerless language contains what powerful language doesn't: qualifiers, intensifiers, and tag questions. Examples of **verbal qualifiers** include "It's just my opinion" and "You'll probably disagree but I believe. . . ." Examples of **verbal intensifiers** include "I can't thank you enough for the simply wonderful evening" and "I need to really, really impress on you how important this is to me." Verbal intensifiers are meant to stress the significance of what a person says. In reality, however, they imply that a person lacks confidence in what he or she says and must bolster the message with unnecessarily intense language.

Tag questions frequently accompany verbal qualifiers and intensifiers.[14] They turn a declarative statement into a solicitation for approval. Tag questions are italicized in these examples:

"I think that's wrong, *but then, what do I know?*"

Box 3-2 Skill Building

Increase Your Assertiveness

Rewrite each of the following statements so that it connotes greater power:

I'm pretty sure.

It was okay, I guess.

Would it be all right to open a window?

I'm allergic to smoke; would you terribly mind not smoking?

Will you be in during your scheduled office hour? I'd like to stop by, okay?

I'm so very sorry, but I'm really, really busy. I apologize, but is there a time you could call back?

I think that's right, but what do you think?

"This looks right, *but what do you think?*"

"It's a trapezoid, *isn't it?*"

Finally, powerless people may use indirection in their speech. They say, "Wouldn't you like to go to the movies tonight?" or "Wouldn't you like to try the new Indonesian restaurant?" What they mean, of course, is "*I* would like to go to the movies," or "*I* would like to try the new restaurant." (Box 3-2 provides additional examples of the language of subordination.)

A word of caution about powerless language is needed, though. In many cultures—for example, China and Japan—powerless talk would be called appropriate talk in certain situations. Further, it would not signal weakness to others. Rather, it would reflect cultural convention acknowledging differences in age, gender, or status. Also, it was once widely reported that women use less-powerful language than men. Current research suggests that this is not necessarily the case in general nor is it the case at work specifically.

Language That Marginalizes

The way people talk isn't the only clue about the degree to which they are perceived as powerful. How people are talked about also is significant in this regard. Box 3-3 illustrates this fact. It tells the reader a Silicon Valley executive was killed and his female companion was critically injured. Later, it also tells the reader the companion was the director of an office of the California Trade and Commerce Agency. So, why was the male described as an executive and the female described with the **marginalizing** term companion, even though her job would warrant a professional title?

marginalizing language Words and phrases that disenfranchise individuals and specific groups of people.

Box 3-3   Considering Diversity

How Does Language Marginalize People?

A 53-year-old cabdriver is facing vehicular manslaughter charges in the hit-and-run accident that killed a Silicon Valley executive and critically injured his companion, a state trade official, police say.

Arthur Alan Smith of San Francisco, a driver for DeSoto Cab Co., was arrested at the Hall of Justice Thursday after a police inspector investigating the Friday night accident asked him to come in for additional questioning.

"We talked to him at the scene the night of the accident," Inspector Jeff Levin said. "He told us that another car hit the couple and threw them onto the hood of his cab. We have since been able to determine that was not what happened."

Calvin Threadgill II was killed instantly, and his companion, Tina Frank, was seriously injured when they were struck at about 9:30 p.m. last Friday as they crossed the Embarcadero near Mission Street.

Threadgill, 45, of Castro Valley, was recently appointed vice president of marketing for Zapit, a Silicon Valley environmental technology company.

Frank is the director of the Bay Area regional office of the California Trade and Commerce Agency. . . .

Investigators say the pair were walking in a marked crosswalk when they were struck.

Levin said a reconstruction of the accident by Sgt. James Hughes, evidence gathered by the police crime lab and new information from two eyewitnesses had led them to Smith.

---

1. Based on what you have read about marginalizing language, rewrite this article so that it does not unfairly marginalize anyone depicted.

2. Can you see how your changes modify the effect of the story? How so? Explain in writing.

SOURCE: John D. O'Connor, "Cops Hold Cabbie in Hit-Run Death," *San Francisco Examiner,* 12 August 1994, A4. Reprinted by permission.

Table 3-2   Describing People with Disabilities

MARGINALIZING LANGUAGE	APPROPRIATE LANGUAGE
He is a victim of cerebral palsy.	He has cerebral palsy.
She's wheelchair bound.	She's in a wheelchair.
John's physically challenged.	John's disabled.
You'll find handicapped parking in front of the office.	There's accessible parking in front of the office.
We have plenty of seating for wheelchair-bound viewers.	There's plenty of disabled seating space.

SOURCE: *Faculty Handbook: Students with Disabilities* (Disabled Student Services, California State University Chico, 1996).

Biased Language Although this example may strike you as a minor oversight, it is not. Such sexist distortions of fact are made hundreds of thousands of times each year in the mass media. What's more, they further marginalize a group of people who are routinely described as less important than men: women. To reiterate, the words people routinely use to describe their reality have a profound effect on the way they think and behave. As a result, when a group of people, such as women, are described consistently in marginal terms, it affects both how the group is viewed by others and how the group views itself. Of course, women are not the only example of an identifiable group of people who have been marginalized in the language. So too have children, the disabled, the elderly, and specific minority groups.

For years the disabled have been fighting for the adoption of language that accurately portrays them. According to people in the disability movement, the words and phrases in the left column of Table 3-2 unfavorably stereotype people with (not "suffering from") a disability. As a result, the alternatives in the right column are recommended.

The disabled are a powerful voice against marginalizing language.

Hate Speech   Finally, people on the margins of power also tend to be the preferred targets of those who use hate speech. Hate speech includes but is not limited to words and phrases that are abusive, misogynist, and racist. The intent of such language is to strip its targets of their humanity and self-worth. Examples of hate speech abound. They even have become commonplace over on-line computer services such as the Internet. Box 3-4 describes one such case. According to the Simon Wiesenthal Center in Los Angeles, at least 50 hate groups currently are disseminating abusive speech over computer networks. One is telling subscribers that all Jews should leave the United States and that the *Diary of Anne Frank* is a Jewish propaganda ploy.[15]

Anti-Semitism isn't the only example of hate speech on-line. To avoid hateful and sexist messages over the Internet such as "R U horny?" there are now women-only bulletin boards operating across the nation. And users have to speak to an operator to prove their sex before they are given access to these bulletin boards.[16]

College and university campuses haven't avoided the plague of hate speech, either. Publications such as the *Chronicle of Higher Education* are full of reports of examples of students victimized by language that could have been written in Nazi Germany. Further, on many campuses one of the most contentious debates being waged concerns whether this kind of language should be subject to disciplinary action or protected as free speech.

The Language of Communication Breakdowns

The familiar term "communication breakdown" doesn't mean that the process of communication has literally broken down between people. Instead, it means that an exchange between people wasn't understood as intended. Breakdowns can be minor, such as when two people agree to meet and then show up at two different places, or major, as when airline pilots and air traffic controllers misunderstand each other.

Ambiguous language sometimes is the root cause of a communication breakdown between people. Three common sources of ambiguity are relative terms, abstract words, and euphemisms. Relative terms include familiar forms, such as *big* and *small, a lot* and *a little,* and *smart* and *dumb.* Such words beg for a point of a comparison or a standard that will facilitate their accurate interpretation. For example, $100,000 seems like a lot to us. To someone like Bill Gates, the billionaire co-founder of Microsoft, $100,000 probably is a little. The point, then, is that relative terms need to be accompanied by a point of comparison that enables the listener to answer the question "In relation to what?" In the absence of such a point of comparison, a breakdown in the intended meaning of a communication becomes more likely.

Just as relative words need a point of comparison, so do words that are highly abstract. A favorite of conservative talk show hosts and politicians is the word

Box 3-4   Self-Assessment

Do You Think There Should Be Limits on Internet Communication?

In February of 1995, a University of Michigan sophomore was arrested by the FBI for three sexual fantasies he wrote and posted over a bulletin board on the Internet. In addition to writing such things as "torture is foreplay," he used the name of a female classmate on the campus. The FBI considered the student a threat to the community, and many professors on the Michigan campus, including antipornography attorney and author Catherine MacKinnon, charged that he clearly was guilty of sexual harassment.

1. Was he guilty of abusive language or was he simply exercising his First Amendment rights, as some have argued?

2. Read the First Amendment and take a position in writing with respect to this case. Give a synopsis of your written statement orally to your class.

SOURCE: Phillip Elmer-Dewitt, *Time Magazine*, 20 February 1995, 69.

liberal. According to *Webster's New Collegiate Dictionary,* a liberal is "one who is open-minded or not strict in the observance of orthodox, traditional or established ways." You'll also find in the same dictionary that liberals are keen on the protection of individual rights. Yet, this is hardly the meaning implied when conservative talk show hosts and politicians apply the term to "tree-hugging, anti-capitalist, gun-abolishing, welfare-supporting, criminal rights–advocating, anti–death penalty bleeding hearts." *Liberal* is an abstract word, one that people sometimes define to suit their own cause and purpose. The same is true of the word *conservative,* which the dictionary doesn't define, we should add, as a "pro-pollution, pro-business, gun-toting, Bible-thumping, woman-hating, white male."

Finally, euphemisms have contributed to more than their fair share of communication breakdowns. Euphemisms are terms that are created specifically to let people avoid talking directly about a subject. The funeral industry is legendary in its use of euphemisms, as Jessica Mitford first pointed out in her book *The American Way of Death.* The dead are put on view in "slumber rooms" and "interred" but never buried.

Society as a whole, of course, is every bit as guilty as the funeral industry in the creation of euphemisms that not only are unnecessary but also provoke communication breakdowns. In the United States, we ask for directions to the men's room, as if we were about to visit a posh club. We have catalogs and stores for big guys and full-figured women. At the same time, diet and health foods in our grocery stores are sectioned off from the rest of the food items, as if they were unhealthy and undernourishing.

Effective Language

In contrast to the language of marginalization and communication break-downs, effective language is meant to increase understanding between people. Effective language has at least five characteristics. It is (1) inclusive rather than marginalizing, (2) appropriate rather than simply correct, (3) uncertainty-reducing rather than anxiety-arousing, (4) immediate, and (5) responsive to individual learning styles.

Inclusive Language

In Chapter 1 the need for inclusion was introduced in the context of dyadic communication. This need was defined as *the need for people to believe that others perceive them as significant and worthwhile*. **Inclusive language** does exactly that. It assists people in believing that they not only have a stake in matters of societal importance but also have power in this regard. Inclusive language doesn't exclude people because of their gender, race, ethnicity, age, religion, sexual orientation or ability. But inclusive language does not draw attention to such characteristics either.[17] For example, look at the following sentences.

> "It's good to have so many aviators and aviatrixes together in the same hanger."
>
> "This is the time that we gather to recognize all the wonderful actors and actresses in the New York theater."
>
> "I think every color in the rainbow is represented here tonight."

These sentences appear to be inclusive. But in unnecessarily drawing attention to gender and race, they defeat their intended purpose. This kind of language totalizes people on the basis of their uniqueness. Totalizing language is inappropriate because it tends to define people exclusively on the basis of attributes such as color and gender. It defeats its well-intentioned purpose. Remember, then, language needs to be both inclusive and appropriate. Box 3-5 will help you practice transforming language from exclusive to inclusive.

Appropriate Language

inclusive language
Words and phrases that assist people in believing they have a stake in and power regarding matters of societal importance.

Communication competence is measured in part by a person's ability to construct appropriate messages in a specific situation. Appropriate messages demand appropriate language. What's more, long before the term "politically correct" became a part of almost everyone's vocabulary and the subject of ridicule for some, people involved in the study and practice of communication were busy trying to convince students of both facts.

Appropriate language is not censored language. It also isn't the kind of hyper politically correct language so frequently satirized by comedians such as talk show host Bill Maher. Very simply, appropriate language reflects the competent

Box 3-5   Skill Building

Use Inclusive Language

Exclusionary language is marginalizing and biased. Provide inclusive alternatives for each of the following:

actress	doorman	meter maid	Mrs. John Doe
airline stewardess	executrix	mother	old wives' tale
businessman	goddess	majorette	waitress
craftsmanship			

SOURCE: Adapted from Rosalie Maggio, *The Bias-Free Word Finder: A Dictionary of Nondiscriminatory Language* (Boston: Beacon Press, 1991).

communicator's respect for the diverse perspectives of people and the environment in which communication occurs.

Practically speaking, using appropriate language first means addressing and describing people in terms they themselves would choose—for example, African American and Latina, gay and lesbian. It also means using language that is inclusive but bias free—for instance, aviators and actors, newscasters and mail carriers. But it also means accounting for the environment in which diverse groups of people find themselves communicating.

Every environment is different. What constitutes appropriate language in one environment may not constitute appropriate language in another, even if the environments appear similar. Jargon, which is a language unique to a group bound by interests or tasks, is appropriate among experts assembled to talk about the subject that gave birth to the jargon. It is inappropriate, however, in environments where people lack the necessary background to participate, such as the first class of a college course intended to introduce students to the subject. Likewise, combative and competitive language may be appropriate in an argumentation and debate class, but inappropriate at a fraternity/sorority mixer.

Uncertainty-Reducing Language

The third characteristic of effective language is that it reduces the anxiety-causing uncertainty that can interfere with communication. At the least, **uncertainty-reducing language** specifies, invites comparison, and is unequivocal.

Uncertainty-reducing language makes a message more specific, less susceptible to multiple interpretations. Specifying language employs words that not only

uncertainty-reducing language Words and phrases that make messages more specific and less ambiguous.

are readily grasped by a listener but also enhance meaning for the listener. The word *bear,* for example, is made more specific and meaningful by modifying it with the word *polar* or *grizzly.*

Specifying language also avoids using terms such as a little or a lot. Not only are they abstract and relative, but as we have already noted, they could mean almost anything depending on the perspective of the listener. Besides specifying, then, uncertainty-reducing language also features points of comparison to assist the listener in arriving at appropriate meaning. To suggest that the music of a group is good or its sound is pure is meaningless unless some point of comparison is provided. To suggest that a group is as good as Pearl Jam or the Boston Pops, however, gives the listener something to use in evaluating the statement.

A third characteristic of uncertainty-reducing language is that it is unequivocal. Recall from our earlier discussion of powerful language that it is best to avoid verbal qualifiers, intensifiers, and tag questions. They can undermine perceptions of power, attractiveness, and credibility because they have the potential to increase rather than decrease uncertainty. Uncertainty reduction has been linked to perception of these three attributes in research focusing on the acquaintance process. When uncertainty goes up, perception of these attributes goes down, whereas the reverse is true when uncertainty is reduced by communicators.

Thus, it is to your advantage to avoid equivocal words and phrases in situations where you want to reduce uncertainty. This means avoiding relative terms, abstract words, and euphemisms as well as verbal qualifiers, intensifiers, and tag questions.

Immediate Language

Effective language is also immediate. It reduces the psychological distance separating communicators.[18] **Immediate language** is inclusive, suggesting to listeners that they are co-participants in the communication transaction. Consider the personal pronouns people choose when conversing dyadically, working in groups, speaking before an audience, or communicating through a mass medium. The personal pronouns "I" and "me" are self-centered. They also are far less immediate than the personal pronouns "we" and "us." A newscaster who routinely says, "I would like to welcome you to my broadcast" probably won't last as long as one who greets viewers with "Welcome to news about our world."

immediate language
Words and phrases that increase the perception of psychological closeness between communicators.

There is some evidence to suggest that women customarily use immediate language more than men do. Psychologist Carol Gilligan has persuasively written that women's personal pronoun of choice is "we."[19] Gilligan believes this is because women think about their reality in terms of their relationships. Men, who think of their reality in terms of individual achievement, choose "I" as their personal pronoun of choice.

According to the research, men would be well advised to follow women's lead when it comes to immediate language. Table 3-3 gives some examples. Immedi-

Table 3-3 Saying It More Immediately

LESS IMMEDIATE	MORE IMMEDIATE
I	
me	we
you	us
them	
I think	
It's my opinion	Wouldn't you agree?
I know	
tell	
show	share
explain	

acy positively affects perceptions of interpersonal attraction. Research also suggests that immediate language may enhance perceptions of one's overall communication style.

Language That Is Responsive to Learning Styles

As you know from personal experience, not all people learn in the same manner. Whereas some people do just fine on a diet of large lectures and multiple-choice exams, others learn best individually or in small groups. What is true of learning in general is also true of language and of information processing specifically. People process language differently and have different needs in this regard.[20] Some people need to "see" words to accurately process them; some need to "hear" words; and some need to "touch" them.

Although communicators cannot always meet these different information-processing needs explicitly, the use of effective language makes it possible to meet these needs implicitly. Table 3-4 gives a number of specific visual, auditory, and kinesthetic words that may help people with different learning styles better process messages. Used appropriately these words can help people see a solution, hear the point you want to make, and feel the pain of the oppressed. The point is simple: To maximize listeners' receptivity to what is said, people must make every effort to use words that reflect different styles of information processing.

Table 3-4 Learning-Style Responsive Language

VISUAL WORDS FOR VISUAL LEARNERS

focus	graphic	watch	colorful
bright	illustrate	vision	glimpse
show	color	brilliant	look
pretty	see	evident	sight
envision	picture	sketch	shining
draw	hazy	oversight	hidden
view	peek	clearly	notice
clear	imagine	perspective	

AUDITORY WORDS FOR AUDITORY LEARNERS

listen	ringing	compliment	sound
hear	resonate	loud	request
discuss	yell	silent	whispering
declare	told	shout	quiet
implore	call	talk	ask
acclaim	assert	noisy	
clap	profess	symphonic	
petition	noise	address	

KINESTHETIC WORDS FOR TACTILE-ORIENTED LEARNERS

feel	shatter	concrete	contact
pressure	shaking	irritated	nurture
hurt	burdensome	hunger	dizzy
tense	firm	graceful	
touchy	heavy	sensual	
pushy	touch	weighty problem	

SOURCE: Adapted from Loretta Malandro, *Speak with Impact* (Scottsdale, Ariz.: Malandro Communication, 1995). Used with permission from Malandro Communication.

Summary

The words people use influence what they perceive and how others perceive them. Likewise, the language people speak also influences how they perceive their reality. Language is given structure through words and rules. Because words are not always used for the same effect, their meaning varies from person to person. In order to be meaningful, words must go together in a certain way (grammar) and in a certain order (syntax).

Language is one of the factors that distinguishes one culture from the next. Groups and individuals also create language to further distinguish themselves not only from each other but also from the larger culture in which groups and individuals are found. Understanding language in relation to cultural, group, and individual diversity, then, is essential to competent communication.

Language is associated with perceptions of power as well. Powerful people avoid words and phrases that make them sound unsure of themselves. People who perceive themselves as powerless communicate more tentatively, frequently using verbal qualifiers and tag questions.

Language can be used to exclude people from the mainstream. Such marginalizing language demeans people as well. Effective language is appropriate to the context of communication and the people communicating. Effective language is inclusive and reduces rather than increases uncertainty. Finally, effective language is immediate and responsive to people's individual learning styles.

Another Look

Articles

Jo Liska. "Dominance-Seeking Language Strategies: Please Eat the Floor, Dog Breath, or I'll Rip Your Lungs Out, OK?" In *Communication Yearbook 15,* edited by S. A. Deetz. Newbury Park, Calif.: Sage, 1992.

Don't let the title mislead you. Jo Liska is a serious language researcher with a sense of humor. This article looks at how we use language in our relationships to get the upper hand. Remember, language is powerful. As a result, it simply makes good sense to see how people try to use it for leverage in their relationships.

C. Barbato and J. Feezel. "The Language of Aging in Different Age Groups." *Gerontological Society of America* 27 (1987): 527–31.

How do you describe your age group? Generation X? Baby boomer or boom buster? Senior or senior citizen? As discussed in this chapter, the language that reference groups use to describe themselves influences how they and others see them. This article looks at the language generational groups use about themselves and the implications of this use.

R. Hopper, M. Knapp, and L. Scott. "Couple-Personal Idioms." *Journal of Communication* 31 (1981): 23–33.

Although we didn't discuss the fact in this chapter, it is well known that intimate couples develop their own code words. Such words enable couples to communicate privately in even the most public of settings. If you're interested in learning about the personal language that develops between couples, reading this article would be a good place to start.

Barbara Ehrenreich. "A Term of Honor." *Time Magazine,* 23 January 1994, 64.

As you may recall, newscaster Connie Chung got Kathleen Gingrich to say on air that her son, Speaker of the House Newt Gingrich, had referred to Hillary Rodham Clinton as a "bitch." This essay argues that the term is really a badge of honor, worn by any powerful woman who upsets the "good old boy" network. Read the article and decide on the degree to which you think it is an illustration of how men use marginalizing language to subordinate women perceived as powerful.

Books

Carol Gilligan. *In a Different Voice.* Cambridge, Mass.: Harvard University Press, 1982.

When it was first published, Gilligan's book challenged people to reexamine their beliefs about the way women think, what women value, and women's language. Even though Gilligan's thinking has been challenged, this book would be an invaluable source for a paper or presentation on language and gender. It also is basic reading for anyone interested in feminist scholars.

Anthony Burgess. *A Clockwork Orange.* New York: Norton, 1963.

Burgess was not only a critically acclaimed novelist but also a respected linguist. His combined expertise is readily apparent in this prescient and critically acclaimed novel of a future in which violent gangs of teenagers terrorize the urban landscape. Burgess created a language system that readers are required to learn as they read. The novel becomes an enjoyable lesson in language and the construction of reality as a result.

Video Rentals

Nell   Academy Award winner Jodie Foster plays a woodswoman who grows up in total isolation. Following the death of her mother, the only human with whom Nell has had contact, she is confronted by people who not only are curious about the strange dialect she has created and speaks but also wish to socialize her to the modern world. This is an excellent film for studying the relationship between one's language and reality.

Little Women   Scripted for the modern audience, this 1994 film based on the classic Louisa May Alcott novel features superior performances by Winona Ryder and Susan Sarandon. This film also gives "voice" to Carol Gilligan's thinking about the relationship between women's values and their community of language. This film would be an excellent basis for a paper about how women talk to each other.

Wall Street   Director Oliver Stone's tribute to his stockbroker father clearly demonstrates how people with power communicate. Starring Charlie Sheen and Michael Douglas, who won an Oscar for his role as mega-tycoon Gordon Gecko, the film also traces the degree to which a person changes as he or she becomes more powerful. If you choose to watch this film, pay close attention to how Douglas speaks to people, and note how Sheen's language evolves as he perceives himself becoming more successful.

Quest for Fire   This 1982 French film would make an excellent bridge between language, the subject of this chapter, and nonverbal behavior, the subject of the next chapter. Anthony Burgess wrote the script. Animal behaviorist Desmond Morris coached the actors, who play members of different and competing Ice Age clans. One clan lacks language, another has it. The comparative behavior of the two clans, consequently, is relevant to this and the next chapter.

Theory and Research in Practice

1. Although the linguistic relativity hypothesis seems to make sense, researchers have had a difficult time validating it in their experiments. Interview a faculty member who teaches a foreign language on your campus. Ask the faculty member whether he or she believes that people who speak different languages think differently. Ask about the role of language in this regard. And be sure to obtain examples reflecting the faculty member's thinking that you can share with your class.

2. Anecdotal evidence has led some to theorize that women use less-powerful language than men. Watch a popular television sitcom depicting women and men who come into frequent contact, for example, *Mad About You, Murphy Brown,* or *Seinfeld.* Analyze the characters' use of verbal intensifiers, commands, verbal qualifiers, and tag questions. Note whether gender seems to make a difference in this regard. Take a stand on whether the show you watched marginalizes women in its dialogue or promotes equality between the sexes. Finally, check the credits to see the mix of women and men staff writers for the show, and form an opinion on the effect of a writer's gender on a TV script.

3. One of the most interesting and controversial issues in the research on language is whether it is uniquely human. For years, people have been teaching advanced primates, such as chimps and gorillas, to use either American Sign Language or pictorial systems of language for the purpose of communicating with humans. Some scholars argue that they have clearly demonstrated that advanced primates can be taught to use language. Others argue just the opposite, claiming that the chimps and gorillas are simply mimicking their teachers' behaviors. Before making up your mind, investigate the issue of primate communication and write a report on your findings. A good place to start would be a seminal article written by T. Gardiner and R. A. Gardiner and appearing in volume 1, edition 65, of *Science,* 1969.

4. The connotations of words reflect their user's point of view and can influence the opinion of the people who hear them or read them. Conservative commentator Rush Limbaugh knows the power of negative connotation to stir up emotions when he uses a term like "feminazi." And writers of advertising copy are masters of positive connotation: A new soap won't just make the laundry smell clean; it will smell "springtime fresh." To demonstrate the power of connotation, do one of the following:

a. Reverse the effect of an advertisement in a magazine or newspaper by substituting words and phrases with negative connotations for positive words and phrases;

b. Rewrite an editorial or a letter to the editor by substituting emotionally neutral terms for ones with intense connotations; or

c. Compare the connotative elements (both visual and verbal) in television advertisements for a luxury car, a van, and a truck. List the connotative elements in each ad, explain the connotation, and then describe the kind of person the copywriters are trying to reach in each of the ads.

CHAPTER 4

Nonverbal Communication

OBJECTIVES ───────────────────────────────

After reading this chapter you should be able to:

- List and describe the factors that distinguish nonverbal behavior from language.

- Describe the interdependent codes that define the system of nonverbal behavior, including the functions and effects of appearance, the face and eyes, the voice, the body, touch, space, distance, territory, and time.

- Describe the major functions of nonverbal behavior.

- Discuss how diversity influences nonverbal behavior.

- Discuss methods for increasing skills linked to the major functions of nonverbal behavior.

Diana Griego Erwin is a syndicated newspaper columnist. She writes about everyday experiences, including lessons learned as a result of the people she encounters. In a recent column, Erwin related a lesson about the degree to which you can read a person based on nonverbal behavior. She recounts a teenage boy boarding the commuter train on which she and her young daughter were riding:

> He looked nervous, and that is what scared me. . . . If a director needed a jittery type for a movie such as "Speed," this is the guy they would cast. By the time he sat down, beads of sweat had popped up on his nose and brow, and he pulled at one side of the black and red woolen cap he wore. He'd look over his shoulder, then look outside. In the space of about 30 seconds, he adjusted his coat twice.[1]

Erwin continues in this vein and tells the reader that she not only was frightened by the boy's appearance and "suspicious" behavior but also was prepared to protect herself should the boy move on her and her daughter. Then Erwin reveals the rest of the story. Just before the next stop, Erwin says,

nonverbal communication A wordless system of codes that, in combination, convey messages.

The boy-man looked frantically outside. Just before [the train] stopped, he looked at me; made eye contact. "Will you save these seats?" he asked.

He hurried to the doorway where a bent, aging woman struggled to climb the stairs. . . . He took her arm and helped her up. "Grandma," he said, "I worried the whole time we split up. I never should have let you talk me into leaving you like that."[2]

All of us are at least a little like columnist Diana Griego Erwin in this account. We presume much about a person based on nonverbal messages, probably much more than we should. What is true of Erwin's encounter with a young man on a commuter train, moreover, also is true whether we are encountering a stranger, working with a new group of people, or speaking to an unfamiliar audience.

This chapter complements the previous chapter's discussion of language. Our focus is on **nonverbal communication,** which we define as a wordless system of codes that, in combination, convey messages. The chapter is intended to show why people need to be mindful of their own nonverbal communication and of the inferences they make on the basis of the nonverbal communication of others. Topics covered include

- the distinguishing characteristics of nonverbal messages,
- the system of interdependent nonverbal message codes that affect communication,
- the functions of nonverbal messages, and
- practical knowledge and related skills you can immediately begin applying to more competently use and interpret nonverbal communication.

Distinguishing Characteristics of Nonverbal Communication

Recall from Chapter 1 that interpretive communication competence concerns the degree to which people accurately assess the communication cues they perceive. Since so many of these cues are nonverbal, interpretive competence is influenced by the degree to which people understand what they can reliably infer from nonverbal behavior. Reliable inferences begin with first knowing how to distinguish nonverbal from verbal communication.

Although some scholars might quibble with our earlier definition of nonverbal communication, few would disagree that there are a number of characteristics that differentiate verbal from nonverbal messages. Chief among these distinguishing characteristics are these four:[3]

1. nonverbal messages are continuous,
2. nonverbal messages are multichanneled,

3. nonverbal messages involve the simultaneous use of these multiple channels, and

4. nonverbal communication is spontaneous.

Nonverbal Communication Is Continuous

Verbal messages, composed of words, are discrete. This means verbal messages can be divided into separate units, as was the case when you first began to learn about nouns, verbs, and adjectives. These parts of speech, as you may remember them being called, are governed by complex rules, dictating how they should be combined to form phrases, clauses, and sentences. In contrast, nonverbal messages are continuous.

Consider an expression of happiness on a person's face. What you see is a complex message that involves the mouth, eyes, and eyebrows. The muscles of the face contract, affecting the eyebrows, corners of the mouth, and corners of the eyes. Unlike a verbal message, these involuntary movements of the face cannot be broken down into nonverbal counterparts of the verbal parts of speech. The eyes, for example, do not constitute a noun, the corners of the mouth do not constitute a verb, and the eyebrows do not constitute an adjective.

Nonverbal Communication Is Multichanneled

Verbal messages, whether spoken or written, are word driven. It involves either an auditory or a visual channel but never both. We hear spoken words, see written ones. Returning to the example of an expression of happiness, nonverbal messages involve multiple channels. Emotions such as happiness almost always are expressed by two or more channels. What's more, it is difficult to discern the expression of such emotions on the basis of a single channel of communication.

Nonverbal Communication Is Simultaneous

As you might infer from its multichanneled nature, the third distinguishing characteristic of nonverbal communication is that it is expressed across two or more channels simultaneously. When happy, for example, we don't show the emotion sequentially. We don't first raise the corners of our mouth, then change the position of our eyebrows, and finally constrict the corners of our eyes. These nonverbal messages occur at the same time.

Nonverbal Communication Is Spontaneous

The fourth and final distinguishing characteristic is that nonverbal behavior is spontaneous. With the possible exception of so-called Freudian slips, verbal behavior is planned behavior. We consciously think about the words we speak and write, though we do so with such speed it may not occur to us that we planned this behavior.

Smiles, hand gestures, and body language, which are all nonverbal in nature, occur at a subconscious level. This doesn't mean that people do not sometimes plan gestures and the like. When they do, however, the nonverbal behavior is likely to look phony. Most people learn to distinguish between authentic and phony nonverbal behaviors by the time they reach their teens. Unless a nonverbal behavior is rehearsed to the point it becomes habit, therefore, planned gestures will be recognized as insincere. This ability to distinguish the sincere from insincere is a major reason people put so much stock in the meaning they infer from nonverbal behavior.

The Nonverbal Communication System

Recall that a system is a collection of interdependent components arrayed so that a change in one will produce changes in them all. The nonverbal system is composed of at least seven interdependent codes of behavior:[4]

- appearance,
- the face and eyes,
- the voice,
- the body,
- touch,
- space, distance, and territory, and
- time.

Appearance

We discuss appearance first because of its disproportionate significance to communication transactions. People never get a second chance to make a first impression. First impressions largely are based on appearance, including body type and height, skin and hair color, and clothing and accessories.

The significance of appearance to communication can be measured in at least two ways. The first, involves first impressions. The second involves how people perceive themselves as a result of their appearance and the impact this perception has on their self-confidence.

According to communication expert Dale Leathers, "Our visible self functions to communicate a constellation of meanings which define who we are and what we are apt to become, in the eyes of others."[5] In his book about nonverbal behavior, Leathers also says the standards people use in this definitional process are very specific. In North America, for example, people are most impressed by those whose physical attributes are perceived as beautiful. Although beauty may be to some extent in the eye of the beholder, there also is overwhelming agree-

As Denzel Washington and Daisy Fuentes illustrate, in Hollywood, looks *and* talent are the holy grail.

ment among North Americans about what makes a person beautiful or handsome. Men with athletic physiques are seen as more physically attractive than thin or heavy-set males. People whose forehead, nose, lips, and chin are symmetrical are perceived as more attractive than those whose profile is less than proportional. In women especially, small facial features are preferred over larger ones. Although the standards people use in evaluating the degree to which others are physically attractive are precise, it is the consequence of the label "physically attractive" that is important to this discussion. People perceived as physically attractive also are perceived as *smart, successful, sociable,* and *self-confident.*[6] As a result, those with whom they come into contact are predisposed to form favorable first impressions of them.

The criteria people use in judging others' physical attractiveness, however, also affects how they see themselves. People spend billions of dollars each year on their appearance. They also are subjected to thousands of persuasive messages designed to make them believe that their satisfaction with life is inextricably tied to the way they look.

Box 4-1   Critical Thinking

My Body, My Self

Although men are becoming increasingly body conscious, women have been most affected in this regard. Aside from the fact that men emphasize women's bodies more in ratings of physical attractiveness, women are subjected to countless messages in the media designed to influence their thinking in this regard. In her best-selling book, *The Beauty Myth*, Naomi Wolf points out that models, the mass media's notion of the feminine ideal, weigh 23 percent less today than did models a generation ago.

1. Is our society's high level of body consciousness healthy? Is it responsible for the near-epidemic of self-starvation among young women and steroid abuse among young men?

2. Do the media, especially women's magazines, have an *ethical* duty to portray bodies as 95 percent of them really are?

3. Record in your journal, or write on a sheet of paper, your personal thoughts about the degree to which you are satisfied with your body. To what extent do you think your satisfaction reflects media stereotypes about the ideal form?

4. In a group with other classmates, develop a code of ethics for the fashion industry concerning the depiction of women and men.

SOURCE: N. Wolf, *The Beauty Myth* (New York: William Morrow, 1991).

This obsession, as designer Calvin Klein might call it, can do more than shake the self-confidence of those who believe their physical appearance doesn't meet society's standard of beauty. It can make them miserable. And it can make them self-destructive, as is the case with those suffering from anorexia nervosa or bulimia.

Communicators need to consider the impact of their appearance on how they are perceived. Communicators also should consider the degree to which their appearance is appropriate to the context of communication. By the same token, though, communicators should try to rely less on physical appearances in forming impressions of each other. Appearance is but a single code in the nonverbal system. Further, the research confirms what many people know from personal experience: Looks can be deceiving. Box 4-1 asks you to consider some of the social and emotional effects of today's standards of physical attractiveness.

The Face and Eyes

In North America, people infer a great deal from the face and eyes. In the mid-1970s, nonverbal behavior expert Paul Ekman and his colleagues conducted a comprehensive survey of the research on facial expression.[7] From this survey, they concluded that the face signals eight emotions with a high degree of meaning: happiness, surprise, fear, anger, disgust, contempt, sadness, and interest.

Since then, a number of other researchers have found that the face also is rich in nonverbal cues signaling the intensity of the emotion experienced or the degree of control people have over the emotion.[8] When people say they hate something, for example, their face tends to disclose the intensity of their hate. Similarly, when people sob or appear hysterical, their face suggests they have little control over the emotion they are experiencing.

Eye behavior, technically called **oculesics**, adds to the potential meaning that can be derived from facial expression. Like the face, the eyes are very expressive. Eye behavior also is very susceptible to inaccurate stereotyping. In North America, eye contact is mistakenly treated as a denotative message. People who are respectful, trustworthy, friendly, and interested look you in the eye.[9]

Although this belief about eye contact is culturally bound, some studies call its credibility into question. Many places in the world hold that the kind of immediate eye contact North Americans prefer is disrespectful and hostile. What's more, researchers have found that immediate eye contact in this culture can be an instrument of deception.[10] Champion poker players use eye contact to disguise their hands, for instance.

As is always the case with other kinds of nonverbal behavior, it makes good sense to avoid inferring too much about people on the basis of their faces and eyes. The face and eyes are potentially rich in meaning. Deciphering this meaning accurately, however, is more probable when the face and eyes are considered in conjunction with (1) other nonverbal codes and (2) the content of a person's verbal message.

oculesics   Study of eye behavior.

The Voice

Just as every person has a unique set of fingerprints, every person has a voice that is uniquely his or her own. Although people are seldom judged by their fingerprints, they are often judged by their voiceprint. On hearing the sound of someone's vocalic behavior, as the voiceprint is technically labeled, people believe they can deduce the person's age, race, and even his or her most character-defining traits.[11] As Box 4-2 illustrates, we make assumptions about what people (as well as animated characters) are like, based on the sound of their voice.

The production of sound in the voice is fairly straightforward. People take in air and expel it, first across their vocal cords and then across their teeth and tongue. Variations in the amount of air expelled, the positioning of the vocal cords, or the placement of the teeth and tongue results in variations in the sound of the voice. Shallow breathing and the rapid expulsion of air across the vocal cords produce a much different sound than breathing deeply and then slowly expelling the air. In the first case, the voice is likely to be described as "breathless" or "feminine." In the second, it is more likely to be described as "deep" or "masculine," even though a deep voice doesn't necessarily make a person any more masculine than a higher-pitched one makes a person more feminine.

The voice is a significant medium of emotional expression. Like the face and eyes, the voice can disclose happiness, sadness, anger, and contempt. Unlike the

Box 4-2 Skill Building

Vocal Stereotypes

The box office smash of 1994, *The Lion King*, was perceived by most as a tale that could be enjoyed by young and old alike. Not everyone, however, was happy with the voices behind the characters. Academy Award winning actor Jeremy Irons, the voice behind Scar, the Lion King's evil uncle, was criticized for the effeminate quality in his voice. The hyenas, whose voices included comedian Cheech Marin's, also were criticized for sounding like ethnic stereotypes.

Given the effect of voice on how people are perceived, do you think animators need to consider the consequences of their characters' voices?

_____

1. Choose an animated film or TV show, such as *The Simpsons* or *Ren and Stimpy,* and analyze the voices behind the characters.

2. Do any of the voices suggest stereotypes? What kinds of stereotypes?

3. Do any of the vocal stereotypes negatively represent particular types of people? Describe the connotations of the voices.

face and eyes, however, the voice is comparatively easy to manipulate in the attempt to project a certain image. The voice can be made louder or softer, its pitch can be made higher or lower, and its rate can be accelerated or slowed down.

How people use their voice to embellish the content of their messages depends on their interaction goals. During a speech, it is important to be perceived as confident and self-assured. This perception demands a relatively quick rate of speaking, good articulation, and a volume that is clearly audible.

During interpersonal encounters, vocal characteristics significant to speaking may be less important than the degree to which the voice promotes the perception that communicators are similar. Author and consultant Loretta Malandro coaches her corporate clients to try to pace their own voices with those of their customers. In other words, Malandro encourages her clients to try to use rates and tones similar to their customer's voice.

The Body

Some authors imply that you can learn everything you need to know about people by observing the way they sit or stand, whether or not they fold their arms when talking, and the degree to which they gesture. Although such messages are expressive, they aren't necessarily communicative. Folded arms, for example, may be more of a statement about how cold a room is than the degree to which the person is approachable. Table 4-1 lists the common ways we use our bodies to communicate and the functions such body movements perform.

kinesics Study of movement.

Technically known as **kinesics**, the way people use their bodies to embellish verbal messages changes as they move from one dimension of communication to

Table 4-1   Common Kinesic Behaviors

The following are common gestures that people use in combination with verbal behavior:

Emblems   translate directly to a few words at the most. The two-finger peace sign is an emblem.

Illustrators   complement verbal behavior and add to its clarity. Examples of illustrators include using the hands to clarify the size of an object, pointing while giving directions, or using the hands to show the shape of an object.

Affect displays   usually add to what the face tells us about an emotion. A sad face may be accompanied by slumping posture; bewilderment may be accompanied by a shoulder shrug; and anger may be accompanied by a rigid and erect posture.

Regulators   control interactions. Looking at a watch and putting your hands on top of your thighs as if beginning to stand up are examples of regulators that tell the other person it is time to end the conversation.

Self-adapters   help people compensate for feelings of anxiety by touching themselves. Examples of self-adapters include stroking their arm, touching their face, or wrapping their arms around themselves.

SOURCE: L. Malandro, L. Barker, and D. A. Barker, *Nonverbal Communication,* 2nd ed. (New York: Random House, 1989).

the next. So, too, do the functions of these nonverbal messages. In interpersonal communication, a person's gestures and movements usually are spontaneous and informal, reflecting both the context and content of a message. Further, gestures and movement used in interpersonal communication function primarily to regulate the transaction. Leaning toward a person and nodding the head signals interest and encourages continuation of the conversation. Slapping one's thighs with the palms of the hands and leaning back, in contrast, signals readiness to bring the transaction to a close.

The movements of the body also serve to regulate behavior in groups. As people move from social to task-oriented groups, for example, their gestures and movement may become more constrained, reflecting their task-oriented environment and the problem-oriented content of their messages. Behaviors such as leaning in toward the group or leaning back may indicate how involved people are in the problem. Gestures can also complement the delivery of speeches in several ways. As explained in Table 4-1, gestures can make the speech more emblematic, more illustrative, or more emotional. Further, good body posture can serve to make speakers and messages appear more authoritative to an audience.

Touch

Touch, which researchers call **haptics,** is the most intimate of the codes in the nonverbal system. It also is one with which people may need to exercise the

haptics   The study of how people use and respond to touch.

greatest care. How people use and respond to touch varies according to culture, reference groups, and individual psychologies. In some cultures, such as Italy, touch is central to communication. People touch cheek to cheek when greeting, hold hands while engaged in conversation, and vigorously hug before departing. Further, this kind of touch goes on regardless of gender.

In other cultures, such as the North American, the norms for touch are quite different. Touch among North American males is both ritualistic and kept to a minimum. It's okay for teenage males to wrestle, bump chests, or slam each other in the mosh pit at a rock concert. It's also okay for a male coach to slap a male athlete on the butt for exceptional performance. In other environments, however, this kind of nonverbal approval between North American males is taboo. Imagine, for example, the reaction of students to a male teacher slapping a male student on the butt for acing a test. The norms of touching are less restrictive for North American females. Not only are they frequently the initiators of touch with males, they also can be demonstrative when touching each other.

Given the various norms for touching, initiating and responding to touch is tricky, to say the least. Both initiation and response depend on where people communicate, the type of relationship between communicators, and knowledge of the normative and situational rules for touching. Consider a few examples, beginning with one that occurs in the workplace.

Status differences between people affect nonverbal behavior in many ways.[12] Low-status people tolerate much nonreciprocal behavior from high-status people in the workplace. The boss can interrupt the subordinate, violate the subordinate's personal space, and express emotions such as anger or frustration without fear of retribution. The boss also may touch the subordinate without consequence, but the subordinate normally may not touch the boss. This doesn't make the behavior right. A superior's nonreciprocal behavior can be invasive or harassing even if the subordinate tolerates the behavior.

The type of relationship between people also influences touch.[13] Physicians, nurses, and elementary school teachers, for example, may consider touching a necessary part of their professional relationship with patients and students. Outside an emergency, however, that doesn't excuse them from first asking the patient or student whether it is OK to touch her or him. What's more, many professionals who touch in the course of doing their job might be surprised by people's response if they were to first ask for permission to touch.

Finally, appropriate touch depends on the situation. Intimate touch between lovers in private surroundings is one thing. Intimate touch in a public setting, however, can be embarrassing not only for those sharing the public space but also for the person being touched. Rather than acting surprised as the response is received, the touch initiator should recognize that what is appropriate in private may be inappropriate in another setting.

Space, Distance, and Territory

If you were to take a trip around the world, you would learn much about nonverbal behavior. You would find that notions of individual space, distance, and

Touch is the most intimate medium of communication.

territory vary from culture to culture, group to group, and person to person. The study of the ways that space, distance, and territory affect human interaction is called **proxemics.** A number of proxemics researchers have looked at the relationship between the spatial features of an environment and the communication behaviors of people in that environment. In the process, they have discovered information both intriguing and useful.

   The configuration of space in an environment can either facilitate or impede communication. Robert Sommer, a leading authority on how space affects

proxemics Study of space, distance, and territory.

Where we communicate often influences how we communicate.

behavior, suggests some environments are **sociopetal**, meaning they stimulate human involvement.[14] Generally, such environments are perceived as warm, allow for privacy, provide comfortable seating, and are relatively intimate.

In contrast, other environments are **sociofugal**, which means that they are configured to make people feel distant. Knowing what kind of environment discourages communication, the designers of fast-food restaurants, such as McDonald's, intentionally create interior spaces that discourage people from lingering once they've eaten. Instead of making their eateries warm and inviting, they make them cold and completely public.

Besides space, proxemics researchers have looked at the concept of personal distance. Personal-distance norms are a consequence of (1) culture and (2) relationships. But what is normative for a specific culture may not hold for all groups or individuals in that culture. In North America, the distance norm is about 18 inches for intimate relationships; 2 to 4 feet for social or consultative relationships, such as that between a salesperson and a client; and 5 to 10 feet in public relationships, such as that between a speaker and an audience. Latinos and Asian Americans, however, require less social/consultative distance than do Anglo-Americans. And North Americans convicted of violent crimes have been found to require twice as much social/consultative distance as the norm.

Finally, investigations into the relationship between territory and communication have also resulted in findings of interest. Territory is geographically fixed and marked by explicit or implicit signs that are meant to communicate "ownership" of a particular territory. They can be as obvious as signs that proclaim "Pri-

sociopetal environments
Environmental spaces that stimulate human involvement, including communication.

sociofugal environments
Environmental spaces that make people feel distant, discouraging communication.

vate Property—Trespassing Expressly Forbidden by Law." Or they can be as subtle as backpacks and books strategically arranged on a table at the library.

Violations of distance norms and territory tend to invite an immediate response. People who feel their personal-distance norms have been violated behave in one of three ways. The first is the flight response, which can be as obvious as literally running away or as tentative as backing up slightly as the violator gets closer. The second response is to stand one's ground, a sort of fight response. The third response is to treat the violator as an object rather than a person. In some situations, such as a crowded elevator, people can neither flee nor stand their ground and challenge those who are intruding into their space. To compensate, they simply objectify their surroundings and the people within them.

Violating territory that is "owned," such as one's home or a private space within the home, such as a bedroom, generally results in conflict. In mild cases a war of words takes place. In the extreme, however, violence is not uncommon. Even though their house may not be a castle, most people will defend their home as if it were the Palace of Versailles.

The need for personal space, distance, and territory appears to be innate. Denied proxemic satisfaction, people (and their relationships) are likely to suffer. Overcrowding, for example, makes people anxious. Studies also show it is a prime cause of abnormal behavior.[15] And overcrowding in prisons is seen by some experts as a leading cause of prison violence.

Time

The final nonverbal code is time, technically called **chronemics,** after the mythological figure Cronus. Popular author Michael Ventura distinguishes between two kinds of time:

> Time is the medium in which we live. There is inner time—our personal sense of the rhythms of time experienced differently by each of us; and there is imposed time—the regimented time by which society organizes itself, the time of schedules and deadlines, time structured largely by work and commerce.[16]

Time varies from one individual to the next. Research confirms what you no doubt long ago suspected. Our internal body clock regulates not only when we sleep but also times of peak performance when we are awake. Some people perform best from early to mid morning, some during the middle of the day, and others late at night. What is true of performance in general, moreover, is true of communication specifically. During our time awake, there are periods of the day and night that facilitate interpersonal, group, and public communication, depending on our individual body clock.

But as Michael Ventura noted, the culture in which we live imposes time on us. What's more, this imposed time often is at odds with our individual body

chronemics Study of time.

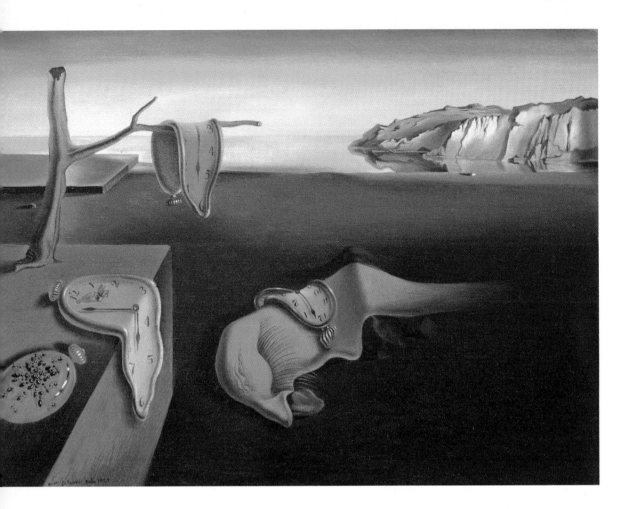

The Persistence of Memory. 1931. Salvador Dali. Oil on canvas, 9½ x 13″ (24.1 x 33cm). When considered seriously, time's control over our behavior does seem surrealistic.

clock. The North American culture is predominantly an 8-to-5 one in terms of work. We are expected to perform accordingly, regardless of our individual time needs. The upshot is that people judge us by the degree to which we adhere to the time norms of our culture. Punctuality in this culture is seen as a sign of competence and responsibility. To be habitually late suggests the opposite.

The North American culture also equates importance with urgency. Sometimes this is justified, as is the case with genuine emergencies. Yet, most of us probably can think of times when we labeled a phone message urgent, asked for a response ASAP, or sent a letter or résumé via overnight mail to give the impression of a matter being more important than it actually was.

Functions of Nonverbal Communication

Nonverbal messages serve many important functions in the communication transaction. They can assist people in more fully understanding the meaning of the verbal messages they receive. And they can help them clarify the meaning of the verbal messages they attempt to communicate to others. According to Professor Dale Leathers, who has written extensively on the subject, nonverbal messages communicated through our appearance, face and eyes, voice, touch, space, and time interact to perform six major functions:

1. to provide information,
2. to regulate interaction,
3. to express emotions,
4. to add meaning through metacommunication,
5. to control behavior, and
6. to facilitate satisfaction of needs.[17]

Information

Nonverbal behavior *provides people with information* about each other and the state of the communication transaction itself. It is possible for people to infer each other's level of comfort on the basis of their nonverbal behavior. The absence of visible signs of stress in the face and voice, for instance, can be used in conjunction with a relaxed posture to infer a person is at ease in communicating. As we said while discussing kinesics, smiling and leaning forward, moreover, may suggest that the person is interested in the conversation and wishes it to continue.

Regulation of Interaction

At the same time, behaviors such as smiling and leaning forward serve to *regulate the interaction.* They tell the other, "I'm involved with what you are saying, please go on." But if the person were to lean back and simultaneously glance toward a clock, these behaviors would regulate the interaction differently. These are classic **leave-taking behaviors.** They tell the other person it's time to wrap things up.

Expression of Emotions

The third function of nonverbal behaviors is the most obvious. Nonverbal behavior is emotionally expressive. It is the primary system that people rely on when making attributions about internal states—for instance, whether a person is happy, sad, or angry. Due to the fundamental attribution error, discussed in Chapter 2, people need to take great care in attributing behaviors to internal causes. Expressive behavior can be misleading. People cry, for example, for reasons other than sadness. They cry because they are angry, joyful, or embarrassed to name three alternatives to sadness.

leave-taking behaviors Nonverbal behaviors such as glancing at one's watch to signal a conversation should be terminated.

meta-communication
The message about the message, usually made up of nonverbal behaviors.

Meta-Communication

Fourth, nonverbal behavior is the medium through which **meta-communication** occurs. Meta-communication is defined as the message about the message. Meta-communication provides information about both the communicator and the content of the communicator's message. Meta-communication often serves to complement the meaning of verbal communication, such as when a person grins broadly and says, "It's really good to see you." Meta-communication also can be redundant with language, as is the case when a speaker holds up three fingers and says, "There are three items of business we need to discuss."

Meta-communication also may contradict and thereby appear to negate language. When our emotions have been aroused, for example, we often reveal the fact through meta-communication. What's more, people tend to believe meta-communication, even when we verbally protest otherwise. Saying "I'm not angry" carries little weight when our face is contorted and the message is emitted through clenched teeth. Although contradictory meta-communication may be a reliable indicator of the communicator's intent, it may not be. Reason sometimes takes precedence over the emotions that can cause contradictory meta-communication.

Control of Behavior

A fifth function of nonverbal communication is control of the communication transaction. Research shows that certain nonverbal behaviors are significantly linked to the perception of power. Eye contact, body orientation, and the use of space, distance, and territory are but three examples. Consider how people use their bodies to exert control over others. A teacher standing over a seated student clearly tells all students who has the power in the class. A parent gazing intently at a child as the parent says, "Look me in the eye when you talk to me," also is exercising nonverbal power. So too is the executive with the expansive office and a desk big enough for an F-14 Tomcat to use for a landing.

Thus, where you stand in relation to others, the amount of space you take when sharing a sofa, and the manner in which you dress can all connote power. Further, such symbols of power also can serve to regulate and control the behavior of those perceived as less powerful. Keep this in mind next time you invade another's space without thinking, occupy more space than you need, or decide a table in the library is exclusively yours.

Need Satisfaction

Finally, nonverbal communication can play an instrumental role in satisfying people's needs. There is no better example in this regard than touch. It is both an important need *and* the medium through which the need is satisfied. As psychology professor Stephen Thayer so well states,

Without the social vocabulary of touch, life would be cold, mechanical, distant, rational, verbal. We are created in the intimate union of two bodies and stay connected to the body of one until the cord is cut. Even after birth, we need touch for survival. Healthy human infants deprived of touch and handling for long periods develop a kind of infant depression that leads to withdrawal and apathy and, in extreme cases, wasting away to death.[18]

Of course, touch isn't the only nonverbal code that serves to assist us in the satisfaction of our needs. Infants and toddlers, for example, communicate both happiness and distress with their faces and through the sound of their voice, as do people unable to speak with words. Because space and territory also are needs, we have become good at signaling our need for space with our hands and torsos and establishing our territory with nonverbal markers such as the stacks of books we place on either side of us at the library table we are using. Finally, we can use our face and eyes to silently signal the desire to be close with a person or, conversely, to extricate ourselves from a conversation that is making us feel uncomfortable.

Nonverbal Skill Development

Up to this point, we have distinguished verbal from nonverbal behavior, characterized the codes that interact to form a system of nonverbal communication, and described some of the most important functions served by the system. This brings us to the final topic in this chapter, nonverbal skill development. Not everyone is equally skilled in using or interpreting nonverbal behavior. As mentioned earlier, women are much better at interpreting nonverbal communication than men. Adults are more skilled than children in interpreting nonverbal communication.

Even though nonverbal messages are often outside the conscious control of the communicator, there are many ways we can begin to immediately increase our skill in using and interpreting nonverbal messages. The first few involve sorting through the misconceptions about nonverbal communication that have been given unwarranted credibility in books and magazines. Others involve recognizing the role diversity plays in nonverbal communication, learning about self-monitoring, and familiarizing ourselves with the concept of nonverbal immediacy.

Misconceptions About Nonverbal Communication

Hundreds if not thousands of pieces have been written in the popular press about nonverbal communication. Books such as *Body Language* and articles in magazines such as *Glamour* not only have brought the subject of nonverbal communication to the attention of millions of people but also have given unwarranted credibility to a number of ideas about the topic.[19] Three such ideas involve (1) the degree of meaning attributable to nonverbal messages in comparison to verbal ones, (2) the ease with which people can decode nonverbal cues, and (3) which code should be believed when a nonverbal message conflicts with a verbal one.

Some people have claimed that upward of 90 percent of the meaning of a message is attributable to nonverbal behavior. This claim is confusing at best, and if it were true, it would make language redundant, as communication scholar Judee Burgoon points out.[20] First, there is a difference between a message that stimulates meaning and one that leads to shared meaning. Although nonverbal behavior is expressive and often stimulates meaning, that doesn't make it communicative. An expressive smile can mean several different things. It can mean "Hello, I think you're attractive." It can mean "This is a nice place." But it also can mean "I mustn't let them think I'm bored." To assign a specific meaning to this single nonverbal cue, therefore, is a mistake. Its meaning needs to be considered in relation to other cues, both verbal and nonverbal.

Second, communication behavior isn't additive. We cannot get to 100 percent of the meaning of a message by assigning a specific value to verbal behavior and a specific value to nonverbal behavior and then adding the two values. The best we can do is to realize that both verbal and nonverbal behavior significantly influence the meaning a person derives from a message. The degree to which one or the other behavior contributes, however, depends on such variables as culture, the immediate environment, and individual experience.

Decoding Nonverbal Cues

Is it possible to read a person's nonverbal behavior as you would read a book? The best-selling book *Body Language* said that you could. In reality, nonverbal cues are not easily decoded. Nonverbal cues are complex, vary from one culture to the next, and often are outside the conscious control of the communicator. Making an inference about what a person is thinking and feeling on the basis of a few nonverbal cues is risky at best.

As a case in point, research suggests that there is a fine line between **quasi-courtship behaviors** and real ones.[21] Quasi-courtship behaviors are predominantly nonverbal. Although they look like flirting, they are not intended as such. Quasi-courtship behaviors include smiling, sustained eye contact, primping, and occasional touching. Men frequently confuse quasi-courtship behaviors with ones that are intended to attract romantic interest. When they respond to quasi-courtship behaviors they have confused with real ones, all kinds of problems can develop. Not the least of these problems, moreover, is the perception of sexual harassment.

Research also suggests that people think they can decode nonverbal cues with greater accuracy than they actually can. Such overconfidence may lead to inappropriate conclusions about nonverbal behavior. There is an abundance of

quasi-courtship behaviors
Nonverbal behaviors frequently mistaken for flirting such as eye contact, primping, touching, and blushing.

research suggesting that jurors frequently confuse lying and truth telling on the basis of a witness's nonverbal cues.[22] Jurors assume that witnesses who look them in the eye, as a case in point, are usually telling the truth. As discussed earlier, looking someone in the eye is a cultural norm rather than a norm for truth telling. And most of us have been lied to by someone who gazed steadily and confidently into our eyes.

Does this mean nonverbal cues are impossible to accurately decode? No. But it does mean caution should be exercised in this regard. It also means people need to know much more about the subject before deciding that they can read nonverbal behavior as easily as a book.

Interpreting Conflicting Messages

When verbal and nonverbal messages appear to contradict one another, we generally believe the latter. While this can be problematic in itself, it is even more so when we act on the basis of such an interpretation. Nonverbal messages are not always superior to verbal ones. We sometimes are conflicted. Although we may want to do something, we may also know that it isn't in our best interest to do it. Such conflicted states and the physiological arousal that accompanies them commonly are the source of verbal and nonverbal messages that appear to contradict each other. Have you ever been embarrassed because you were falsely accused? Chances are your skin flushed, your pupils dilated, you stumbled on your words, and you had trouble making eye contact with your accuser. Such cues are outside your control, products of the autonomic nervous system. In the North American culture, however, each of these nonverbal cues is mistakenly assumed to be an indicator of deception. Thus, the accuser would tend to believe your nonverbal behavior, even though it was contradictory to your verbal denial.

We should be cautious when verbal and nonverbal messages conflict. First, we should be cautious in our interpretation of the conflicting messages. Second, we should be equally cautious in how we respond to these messages. Third, we should look for additional information to check the accuracy of our interpretation.

Cross-Checking Nonverbal and Verbal Cues

Simply put, it is inappropriate and misleading to assume too much about people on the basis of a few isolated nonverbal cues. When attempting to decipher the meaning of nonverbal behavior, we need to exercise good judgment. One of the best ways to verify the meaning of nonverbal cues is to check and compare all the verbal and nonverbal cues. This process is referred to as **cross-modality checking.** It means that if you notice someone with whom you're communicating seems disinterested or confused, you should check the person's overall behavior and ask whether your impression is accurate. When you are listening to someone, it means trying to determine whether what the person is saying seems consistent with the context of the transaction and with what you see in

cross-modality checking
Comparing channels of communication in the attempt to determine a message's meaning.

Box 4-3   Considering Diversity

Nonverbal Communication Outside North America

Although the ways people use their faces to communicate emotions such as anger, fear, happiness, and sadness are similar in many of the world's cultures, the nonverbal communication norms in one culture typically don't travel well to another. For example, the French and the Italians both use their hands to express themselves. Yet, how they use their hands to express themselves is quite different.

To explore these kinds of differences, make an appointment to visit an instructor on your campus who teaches about non-Western cultures. Tell the instructor that you are interested in learning about nonverbal communication norms in the culture he or she teaches about. During your meeting, ask about the norms that govern

- touch,
- personal space,
- eye contact,
- dress, and
- time.

Record what you learn and prepare a traveler's guide for nonverbal communication in the culture investigated. Share your guide with your class.

the person's face, hear in the person's voice, and feel as a consequence of the way he or she moves and gestures. Finally, it means checking out the consistency between these kinds of cues with the verbal message as well.

Recognizing Diversity

Next, we can more competently use and interpret nonverbal communication if we recognize that nonverbal behavior is influenced to an extraordinary degree by human diversity. Whereas spitting at a person's feet is a legitimate form of greeting in parts of Central Africa, the same behavior could lead to one's arrest in Singapore. Individual, group, and cultural diversity all affect nonverbal behavior.

Nonverbal communication varies from culture to culture, as Box 4-3 discusses. Cultural diversity is reflected in such things as how close people stand, whether they shake hands or kiss when greeting, and the degree to which they make eye contact. A comprehensive treatment of the variety of cultural diversity in nonverbal communication is beyond the scope of a single book, much less a single chapter. What is said here, consequently, barely scratches the surface.

The most important thing to recognize about the cultural diversity of nonverbal communication is that knowledge of the norms in one culture should not be overgeneralized to another. The competent communicator looks for more than the most obvious signs of cultural diversity in making decisions about nonverbal messages and their meaning. The competent communicator also considers the specific reference groups with which people most identify. Not everyone in Central Africa, for example, would look kindly on the fact that you had just spit at their feet. As a result, you would need to learn about the ethnic diversity of the different reference groups that populate Central Africa before using this form of greeting.

To claim real competence, though, communicators need to go beyond the nonverbal cues they learn to associate with cultures and groups. Communicators also must come to grips with individual diversity. As a case in point, research suggests that every culture has rules or norms that govern appropriate touch. But not every person in a specific culture subscribes to its touch norms. In North American culture, the degree to which people touch varies. Some people are touchers; for them, touch, is an essential part of their persona. Other North Americans are what nonverbal researcher Peter Andersen calls touch avoiders.[23] They neither touch nor like to be touched, usually for psychological reasons that are deep seated. Box 4-4 will help you assess how you feel about touching.

Most people don't recognize touch avoiders until they try to embrace them and see the latter respond. Most people also attribute another's touch avoidance to unfriendliness or worse. This kind of attributional bias, as explained in Chapter 2, often is wrong because it is based on cultural or group norms rather than the individual's unique psychological history. Touch avoiders may seem abnormal but they are not.

A person could memorize a list of every idiosyncratic nonverbal behavior that inheres to a specific culture and still inappropriately communicate in the culture. Understanding diversity relative to nonverbal communication also involves learning about the myriad reference groups to which people belong and the individual traits that make them unique. Finally, it demands that people be open to diversity and recognize diversity's value.

Self-Monitoring

Another method you can use to increase nonverbal skill is **self-monitoring**.[24] This technique involves consciously looking for cues about socially appropriate communication behavior and about how people are responding to your communication behavior. To successfully self-monitor your nonverbal communication, you need to know how to (1) recognize important cues, (2) interpret those cues once you recognize them, (3) analyze the potential consequences of your response, and (4) respond appropriately to those cues.

When people communicate in cultures other than their own, self-monitoring is particularly important. North Americans with appointments in Mexico or Argentina, for example, need to recognize that formal time is much less strict in these cultures. When North Americans think that their Central or South American counterparts are late, they need to monitor their own nonverbal behavior for signs of stress. The aggravation that the North American typically feels when someone is late will reveal itself nonverbally and will be perceived as rudeness by the member of the other culture.

self-monitoring
Behavioral skill that involves observing and responding to communication cues about appropriate behavior.

Box 4-4   Self-Assessment

How Do You Feel About Touching?

Instructions

This instrument is composed of 14 statements concerning feelings about touching other people and being touched. Please indicate the degree to which each statement applies to you by marking in the blank beside the item:

5 strongly agree   2 disagree
4 agree   1 strongly disagree
3 are undecided or neutral

Statements

While some of these statements may seem repetitious, take your time and try to be as honest as possible.

_____ 1. I don't mind if I am hugged as a sign of friendship.

_____ 2. I enjoy touching others.

_____ 3. I often put my arms around others.

_____ 4. When I see people hugging, it bothers me.

_____ 5. People shouldn't be uncomfortable about being touched.

_____ 6. I really like being touched by others.

_____ 7. I do not show my emotions by touching others.

_____ 8. I do not like touching other people.

_____ 9. I find it enjoyable to be touched by others.

_____ 10. I do not like being touched by others.

_____ 11. I dislike having to hug others.

_____ 12. Hugging and touching should be outlawed.

_____ 13. Touching others is a very important part of my personality.

_____ 14. Being touched by others makes me uncomfortable.

Calculating Your Score

1. Add together your responses to items 1, 2, 3, 5, 6, 9, and 13 = _____.

2. Add together your responses to items 4, 7, 8, 10, 11, 12, and 14 = _____.

3. Complete the following formula:

TAM (Touch Avoidance Measure) = 42 - Total from step 1 = _____.
Then, + Total from step 2. YOUR TOTAL TAM SCORE = _____.

Interpreting Your Score

Possible range of scores: 14–70. (If your own final TAM score does not fall within that range, you made a computational error.)

The midpoint on the TAM is 42. If your score falls well above that midpoint, you can be classified as a "touch approacher"; below the midpoint, a "touch avoider." Touch approachers like to touch others and, in return, to be touched. These high touchers are apparently unaware of the norms for touching and often touch even when others find it annoying. Research indicates that with the same sex, males are typically more avoidant than females; but with the opposite sex, females are more avoidant. Protestants are more touch avoidant than non-Protestants; older, married persons are more touch avoidant of opposite-sex friends.

SOURCE: P. A. Andersen and K. Leibowitz, "The Development and Nature of the Construct Touch Avoidance," *Environmental Psychology and Nonverbal Behavior* 3 (1978): 89–106.

Personal distance also is different in other cultures. Returning to Mexico and Argentina, social distance is much closer there than it is in North America. If a North American conducting business tries to establish a distance comfortable for her by increasing the distance from the Mexican or Argentine client, it can give the wrong impression. The different cultural norms for social distance can lead to inaccurate attributions about each other. The Mexican or Argentine may perceive the North American as aloof and unfriendly. In contrast, the North American may perceive the Mexican or Argentine as pushy and nonbusinesslike.

immediacy skills
Nonverbal behaviors that reduce physical distances psychologically.

Signaling Immediacy

Finally, in order to use nonverbal communication more effectively, you can work on your **immediacy skills.** Immediacy involves people's perception of how close they are to others. Immediacy skills promote the perception of closeness. They also have the power to psychologically reduce the physical distance separating people, as is the case when people make and sustain eye contact across a crowded room.

Research shows that people whose nonverbal behavior promotes immediacy are in most circumstances perceived more favorably than those whose nonverbal behavior detracts from immediacy. This research also shows that specific nonverbal behaviors promote immediacy. People who are perceived as immediate

- sustain eye contact,
- smile,
- show signs of attentiveness, such as leaning forward and nodding,
- directly face the other person,
- punctuate verbal behavior with facial expressions and illustrative gestures, and
- stand or sit in appropriately close proximity to the other person.

Those who behave just the opposite are perceived as distant, unfriendly, and uninvolved. This research finding holds true in both social and professional contexts. Thus, it pays to be perceived as immediate whether you are meeting someone for the first time, interviewing for a job, leading a problem-solving group, or delivering a speech.

Summary

Unlike language, nonverbal communication is continuous, multichanneled, simultaneous, and spontaneous. Nonverbal communication is composed of a wordless system of codes that interact in the production of messages. These codes include appearance, the face and eyes, the voice, the body, touch, space, distance, territory, and time.

Nonverbal communication is also functional. Some of the most important functions it serves include providing people with information, regulating interaction, expressing emotions, adding meaning through meta-communication, controlling the communication transaction, and satisfying certain human needs. The degree to which nonverbal communication successfully performs these functions varies with individual skill. To improve nonverbal skills, people need to recognize that nonverbal communication is much more complex than it has been portrayed in popular books and magazines and that it is influenced by cultural, group, and individual diversity. In the effort to become more skillful nonverbally, people also need to self-monitor and to exhibit appropriate immediacy behaviors.

Another Look

Articles

S. Thayer. "Close Encounters." *Psychology Today,* March 1988, 31–36.

This exceptionally well-written article on touch is an excellent introduction to the subject. Thayer reviews literature on types of touch, the functions touch performs, and some key findings in the research concerning how touch differs across cultures. Thayer also comments on the ethics of touch between professionals, such as physicians, and their patients/clients.

L. R. Cohen. "Nonverbal Miscommunication Between Managerial Men and Women." *Business Horizons,* January–February 1983, 13–17.

This article looks at an issue that may be more important today than when it was published. The workplace has more women managers than ever before, so the effect of gender on nonverbal behavior is essential to understand. Among the topics Cohen discusses are the problems created by quasi-courtship cues in the office.

Books

There are a number of excellent textbooks about the relationship between nonverbal behavior and communication. Any of the ones listed below could serve as a good initial source in researching the topic.

J. Burgoon, D. W. Buller, and W. G. Woodhall. *Nonverbal Communication: The Unspoken Dialogue.* New York: Harper and Row, 1989.

M. L. Knapp and J. A. Hall. *Nonverbal Communication in Human Interaction.* Fort Worth, Tex.: Holt, Rinehart and Winston, 1992.

D. Leathers. *Successful Nonverbal Communication: Principles and Applications.* New York: Macmillan, 1986.

L. Malandro, L. Barker, and D. A. Barker. *Nonverbal Communication.* 2nd ed. New York: Random House, 1989.

P. Ekman. *Telling Lies.* New York: Norton, 1985.

Anyone who wants to fully understand the relationship between nonverbal behavior and deception needs to read this book. Ekman is recognized as one of the world's leading authorities on the subject. In this book, he demonstrates how complicated deception is to detect and why people have such a difficult time separating lies from the truth.

Video Rentals

Triumph of the Will This propaganda film was made by Leni Riefenstahl. It depicts Nazi rallies in 1934 and is regarded by many critics as the most important example of cinematic propaganda in history. From the perspective of nonverbal behavior, it is the symbolism of the setting itself that makes this film alarmingly captivating.

Charlie Chaplin Films   Before the movies talked, actors relied on nonverbal behavior to connect with their audiences. No one was better at it than Charlie Chaplin, who to this day is perceived by many as the epitome of comedic genius. Watch any of Chaplin's films, most of which are now available on video. Analyze Chaplin's nonverbal behavior in relation to our discussion of kinesics or of the face and eyes.

House of Games   A professional gambler (Joseph Mantegna) leads a psychiatrist (Lindsay Crouse) into a world where deciphering nonverbal cues is necessary for survival. Excellent examples of the relationship between nonverbal cues and deception.

Theory and Research in Practice

1. Research clearly indicates that women display more nonverbal behaviors than men. This research also shows that women interpret nonverbal behavior more accurately than men. Scholars in communication have advanced two explanations for this fact. The first is that women are socialized to be more attentive to feelings than men so that they can nurture others. A second explanation is that because women have historically been subordinate to men, they have had to become skilled in discerning men's emotional states in order to avoid punishment. Which of these two explanations do you find most persuasive? What specifically leads you to believe this explanation is most persuasive?

2. From the following list of nonverbal behaviors, select those you believe would correlate with a successful job interview. Once you've constructed your list, compare it to the key that follows. Finally, describe in writing the reasons you selected the nonverbal behaviors on your list.

   1. intermittent eye contact
   2. eye contact of short duration
   3. steady eye contact
   4. smiling
   5. head nodding
   6. holding fist beneath chin while nodding head
   7. sitting straight in your seat
   8. leaning forward toward the interviewer
   9. considering a question before responding
   10. responding without lag time
   11. gesturing
   12. keeping hands visible but in a rested position
   13. high energy in voice
   14. relaxed and even voice
   15. shifting posture to complement interviewer's

   Answers: 3, 4, 5, 8, 10, 11, 13, 15

3. Research suggests that the degree to which people are physically attractive affects men and women differently in terms of job placement. Although the perception of physical attractiveness helps men at all levels of the organization, it does not always help women. While women perceived as physically attractive have an advantage in securing low-level positions in an organization, attractiveness is a hindrance as they move up the organizational ladder. On your own or in a group, construct a personal theory to explain this finding. Check your theory against what is said about the effects of physical attractiveness in the textbooks recommended in the "Another Look" section for this chapter.

CHAPTER 5

Ethical Communication

Objectives

After reading this chapter you should be able to:

- Demonstrate orally or in writing an understanding of the differences among ethical relativism, universalism, utilitarianism, and situational ethics.

- Apply ethical principles to a variety of different communication situations.

- Explain plagiarism and the role of attribution in avoiding plagiarism.

- Explain and apply the basic ethical obligations of both sources and receivers.

- Explain and apply dialogic ethics across varying dimensions of communication.

A reader recently wrote to a nationally syndicated advice columnist seeking guidance about a dilemma in which he found himself. The reader explained that he was seeing a woman with whom he wanted to pursue a long-term relationship. He mentioned that he and the woman had been on three dates, each more physically intimate than the one preceding it. His dilemma? The reader had genital herpes and, on the one hand, knew he was ethically obligated to inform the woman he was seeing before they became more intimate. On the other hand, he was concerned about whether the fact that he had not told her of his disease would cause her to perceive him as dishonest from the beginning of their relationship and would prompt her to break off the relationship completely.

This kind of dilemma is at the center of this chapter, which is about **ethics**, or the study of right and wrong, and the relationship of ethics to communication. Although you may never have been between a rock and a hard place quite like the one in which the advice seeker found himself, chances are you have been in a situation that caused you to ask, "When is it appropriate to disclose sensitive information about oneself to another person?"

> **ethics** The study of the principles of right and wrong that govern human conduct.

We are committed to the belief that ethical behavior is the cornerstone of communication competence. What's more, we think this belief is just as applicable to the behavior of people talking about themselves on a first date as it is to the behavior of the decision makers who determine what we see and what we read in newspapers, on TV, and over the Internet. In support of this belief, we cover the following topics in this chapter:

- some of the key ethical questions facing today's communicators,
- the ethical norms to which competent communicators subscribe,
- important ethical guidelines for communicators, and
- the significance of dialogic ethics to all dimensions which people communicate.

Key Questions About Ethical Communication

There are a number of ethical questions all of us need to consider in the process of becoming competent communicators. They include but are not limited to the following:

1. Is it ever OK to lie?
2. Does propaganda sometimes serve such a noble purpose that its methods are justified?
3. Is it better to be ambiguous about an opinion and not offend other people, or is it better to be specific regardless of outcome?
4. Should you remain silent or speak up when someone says something you think is morally outrageous?
5. Are there limits to the freedom of speech and expression?

The following perspectives, which you'll find in most books about ethics, shed some light on these questions. The first perspective is called ethical relativism.

Ethical Relativism

The most competitive market in radio and television is the daytime talk show. An increase in half a rating point can mean millions of dollars to a daytime talk show's executive producers. As a result, producers and hosts seem willing to stoop to any behavior in the attempt to attract more viewers. Shock jock Howard Stern routinely insults callers and guests on his radio and TV shows. Yet, the best example of the lengths to which talk show hosts and their producers are willing to go in the effort to attract ratings was probably in 1994 when the *Jenny Jones Show*, which invited people to go on the air and meet their secret admirers. What the producers and Jenny Jones didn't tell these people, however,

By any economic measure, Stern is a huge success, but is his communication behavior ethical?

was that these secret admirers could be heterosexual, gay, or lesbian. You may recall the tragic results of this attempt to "entertain" the viewing audience. On learning that one guest's secret admirer was gay, the guest later stalked and murdered the admirer.

The *Jenny Jones Show* staff, including Jenny Jones herself, argued that the show's tragic result was unforeseeable and outside their control. After all, Jones said, this is show business and we're simply trying to entertain people. We can't be held responsible, she continued, for the behavior of guests once they've left the studio.

VIDEO FILE

If you have access to the videotape that accompanies this book, view Part II, "Communication and Personal Responsibility," which complements this chapter and Chapters 6 and 7 as well.

The notion that one's career or profession, culture, or belief system excuses him or her from complying with any universal code of conduct is exemplary of **ethical relativism**.[1] One version of ethical relativism asserts that one person's view of ethics is as good as the next person's. Although this philosophy has the advantage of simplicity, it can lead to disastrous results. Consider groups that preach hate in print, over the radio, and on television. Aside from the fact that the messages of these groups are reminiscent of those of Nazi Germany in the 1930s and 1940s, they have been linked in courts of law to hate crimes such as murder. Basically, the courts have said that the relative belief systems of hate groups do not excuse them from the consequences of their messages over the mass media specifically.

However, many people would argue that a society or culture may establish ethical standards that vary from those of other cultures but are just as valid. In collectivist cultures, such as most Asian cultures, where "saving face" is important to the good of all society, people are often indirect and may stretch the bounds of truthfulness rather than offend someone. To do either in an individualistic culture such as the United States could very well be regarded as unethical communication. Can either culture claim superiority over the routine communication practices of the other? Not really.

The point we want to make is twofold. First, society cannot afford to let individuals and small bans of hatemongers use the concept of ethical relativism to say whatever comes to mind. Second, there is inevitable variance in what constitutes ethical communication as you move across entire cultures. Thus, you must always be mindful about the degree to which the ethical standards for communication in your own culture generalize to a culture with which you have little or no familiarity.

Universal Rules

An alternative to ethical relativism is to find universal ethical standards that transcend any group or culture. Immanuel Kant, an 18th-century philosopher, suggested just such a solution. He proposed the **categorical imperative**: "Act only on that maxim through which you can at the same time will that it should become a universal law."[2] For example, a lie is successful only if most people tell the truth. Lies cease to be effective if everyone knows that everyone else is lying. Thus, a universal law that lies are permissible would in fact make lies ineffective. You can see similar applications to other ethical rules. Imagine if cheating or stealing were universal laws. Of course, the result would be disastrous. So Kant's perspective is a way to deduce fundamental ethical rules from one basic principle that, he believes, is self-evident regardless of one's individual or cultural background.

One of the most important ethical rules that Kant proposed relates directly to communicators. Kant proposed the maxim "Act in such a way that you always treat humanity whether in your own person or in the person of any other, never simply as a means, but always at the same time as an end."[3] The practical impli-

ethical relativism
The position that there are no universal ethical principles.

categorical imperative   The proposition that behaviors should be based on universal laws.

Box 5-1 Self-Assessment

When Is It OK to Lie?

Read the following scenarios carefully. Put an * next to the scenarios in which you think it would be OK to lie. Compare your responses with those of your classmates, making sure that you thoroughly discuss any differences in your thinking.

1. You know your best friend is cheating on a lover. The lover is suspicious and asks you: "Is Jane/Joe cheating on me?"

2. The person seated next to you during an exam appears to be copying your answers. As you turn your exam in, the instructor asks you: "Was X copying from your exam?"

3. A casual friend misses several lectures in a class you both attend. He asks to borrow and make copies of your notes. While you don't want to hand over your hard work, you also don't want to appear unsympathetic. Should you make up a lie, telling the person that you failed to take notes on the days he was absent—that you too missed the same lectures?

4. A person repeatedly asks you out on a date. You've run out of excuses, but to be honest about it, you find the person completely unattractive. Do you tell the person the truth, running the risk of hurt feelings, or try to lie your way out of the situation once again?

5. Your parents have always trusted you. Over a break from school, they ask you whether you've experimented with marijuana. Even though you have used marijuana, you are of the opinion that what your parents don't know won't hurt them. Do you lie—or tell them the truth, recognizing how fragile trust can be?

cations of Kant's philosophy for communicators is that we should treat people with respect, not simply as a means of achieving our goals. Obviously, then, communication tactics that deceive or demean people are unacceptable.

While Immanuel Kant's categorical imperative is certainly preferable to ethical relativism, it is not without drawbacks. Consider truth telling. If lying is unacceptable in any circumstance, innocent people may suffer as a consequence. Nip Gies, for example, lied to authorities throughout World War II to protect the Jews she was hiding from the Nazis, including a young girl named Anne Frank. And this isn't an isolated example. History is replete with cases demonstrating that it is sometimes better to bend the truth to fit the situation. Box 5-1 will help you explore your beliefs about lying.

Utilitarian Ethics

Philosophers Jeremy Bentham and John Stuart Mill proposed another ethical standard, **utilitarianism.** They sought the greatest good for the greatest number of people. And they specifically defined "good" as that which creates happiness. But the standard of ethics they proposed was not the agent's own greatest happiness, but the greatest amount of happiness altogether."[4]

utilitarianism An ethical principle based on the greatest amount of happiness for the greatest number of people.

This ethical standard is certainly applicable to communication behavior, for example, when working to solve a problem with a task-oriented small group. Most of the problems small groups try to solve involve trade-offs between what is in the best interest of a majority of people. Before bills are voted on by Congress, for example, they first move through various committees. These congressional committees are composed of small groups of people from both parties, usually have a staff that advises the committee members about a proposed bill, and hold hearings so that people can give testimony about issues relevant to the proposed bill. Ostensibly, the complex communication transactions characteristic of this entire process are designed to create a bill that is in the majority of people's best interest.

Utilitarianism, of course, has its critics. Many would say it promotes ethical relativism. After all, the greatest good for the greatest number often discriminates against some minority. Think about the debate over prayer in schools. Many fundamentalist Christians, the minority, have argued in print, over the radio, and on TV that laws forbidding prayer in school discriminate against their constitutionally guaranteed freedom to practice the religion of their choice. The majority opposition, however, has likewise argued that to allow Christian prayer in schools would promote a state-sanctioned religion, which the Constitution also expressly forbids.

Critics of utilitarianism have a point. Seeking the greatest happiness for the greatest number does not guarantee happiness for all. There always will be some person or group of people who feel unjustifiably left out. As history bears out, moreover, a few unscrupulous communicators can influence the majority of people to accept the most inhuman of practices in the name of the public good.

Situational Ethics

Another approach to the subject of this chapter is known as **situational ethics.** Proponents of this view believe that there are overriding ethical maxims, but that sometimes it is necessary to set them aside in particular situations to fulfill a higher law. As one writer put it, "What acts are right may depend on circumstances . . . but there is an absolute obligation to will whatever may on each occasion be right."[5]

situational ethics
The view that there are overriding ethical maxims, but that sometimes it is necessary to set them aside in particular situations to fulfill a higher law.

Communicators are frequently faced with ethical choices that are situationally based. Physicians and therapists sometimes are confronted with situations in which they must debate the merits of giving or withholding information. Should a physician inform a patient about alternative treatments in which the physician personally has no faith? Along the same lines, should a therapist encourage a client to follow through on the urge to disclose past infidelities to a spouse? Or should a public speaker tell an audience that her perspective is decidedly one-sided and based on the disclosure of the facts that are most favorable to her side?

Ethical Means Versus Ethical Ends

Each of the preceding questions relates to this last one: Is ethical communication about means or ends? The answer is both. Competent communicators base their behavior first on its probable consequences not only for themselves but for others who will be affected as well.[6] By the same token, competent communicators do not buy into the idea that ethical ends justify, as a matter of course, unethical means.

Think about a not-so-uncommon dilemma in which friends may find themselves. On a Saturday night, you see your best friend's lover locked in a passionate embrace with someone else. Knowing that the bearer of bad news is sometimes greeted less than civilly, you still think that in the end, you should inform your best friend so that he or she can deal with the situation. So what do you decide to do? Do you send an anonymous note or leave an anonymous message on the friend's answering machine? Not only do these two strategies strike us as cowardly, but they seem unethical as well. Therefore, competent communicators always wrestle with this means and ends dilemma. Unless they can harmonize the two, moreover, competent communicators are likely to conclude that an end wasn't as just as initially thought.

If the ethical standards discussed on the preceding pages seem far removed from daily life, they are not. Servers in restaurants routinely flatter customers in the hope of receiving a bigger tip, which is deceptive and perhaps unethical. Students use unfortunate circumstances (death of a distant relative) to try to excuse work that would have been late in any event (teachers also do this). And we've all probably lavished insincere praise on a colleague or superior at work to curry the person's favor. It's not that any of these behaviors are so terrible, but each exemplifies how we seldom think through the ethical perspectives that should come into play in our day-to-day communication transactions.

Ethical Norms for Communication Competence

Up to this point, we have discussed the fact that ethical communication involves choice—for instance, deciding whether the ethics of communication are relative, universal, or situational. The only specific advice we've given is that ethical ends don't justify unethical means. Here we want to add to this advice, suggesting a set of ethical norms significant to your communication competence.[7] These norms are based on

- the universality of truthfulness,
- respect for the power of language,
- tolerance for differences,
- reason and the situation, and
- interaction consciousness.

Truthfulness

Recognizing that, on rare occasions, *it is best withheld,* truthfulness is a universal norm to which competent communicators subscribe. Truthfulness also defines and sustains the competent communicator's credibility with people. Credibility is composed partly of perceptions of trustworthiness. As your own experience tells you, the people we most trust are those who have consistently told us the truth.

Truthfulness is important to communication competence, regardless of the dimension of communication. Truthfulness is essential to viable interpersonal relationships, decision-making groups, public speeches, and mass media. Can you imagine, for example, a healthy family in which deceit rather than truthfulness is the norm for communicating? Would you trust the recommendations of a problem-solving group knowing that its leader was a pathological liar? Can you envision a public speaker or mass medium achieving long-term credibility without adhering to the norm of truthfulness?

To repeat, there are situations in which this norm may need to be momentarily displaced by a higher purpose, but this is the exception rather than the rule. Competent communicators recognize and accept this fact as an article of faith.

The Power of Language

In Chapter 3, we said that language isn't neutral. Language is extremely powerful and can, in the wrong hands, be put to destructive use. Competent communicators genuinely appreciate the power of language and its potentially destructive force. Competent communicators see through the ridiculous idea that "sticks and stones may break my bones, but words will never hurt me." As a result, they choose their words mindfully, a concept discussed in Chapter 1.

The relationship between communicating ethically and using language mindfully is not about the kind of "political correctness" comedians poke fun at. Rather, the ethical, and therefore competent, use of language means that communicators think through the consequences of their remarks to a friend, comments in a group, speeches in public, and in print or on TV. What's more, competent communicators also think about the relationship between their language and the ethical questions we introduced earlier. Consider two scenarios in which choosing what to say is as important as deciding to say anything at all.

In the first scenario, you receive a call from someone who is considering hiring a former co-worker of yours. You think the former co-worker is competent but unfriendly. The language you choose to describe the former co-worker and the attributes it emphasizes are of genuine consequence. If your language emphasizes competence, the recommendation would be positive. But if you shade the person's competence with language emphasizing how unpleasant it was to work with the person, your recommendation would be equivocal at best.

In the second scenario, you are at a party talking with a small group. One person tells a joke that is incredibly racist or homophobic. Do you speak up? Do

you call the person a racist or bigot? Or do you quickly let the person know you weren't amused and then shift the direction of the discussion to a neutral topic?

The language you choose in either scenario will reflect not only on your communication competence but on your ethics as well. As a result, your language needs to be based on the ethical perspectives that inhere to each scenario.

Ethics and economic profit are not always compatible, as the congressional testimony of tobacco industry executives clearly demonstrated.

Tolerance

At this point, it should be clear that what people regard as ethical or unethical depends a great deal on their culture and the set of beliefs which inhere to it. As we will discuss at length in Chapter 7, it is difficult for people to avoid imposing the ethical standards for behavior in their own culture when judging the ethical behavior of people in another culture.[8] Some cultures, groups, and individuals are more tolerant of different standards of behavior than others are. They seem to abide by the notion "different strokes for different folks." As a general rule, the North American culture, and many of the groups and individuals that live in it, historically has been intolerant of ways of behaving that are contrary to accepted norms.

As the North American culture has become more diverse, this lack of tolerance has become more apparent. Immigrants who accede to North American norms quickly are assimilated. Those who don't, however, are often singled out for disapproval. Think about this dilemma in terms of ethical relativism. Many of the cultural practices recent immigrants have brought with them are outside the bounds of what the majority of North Americans regard as ethical. Box 5-2 gives you an example.

Competent communicators recognize that the customary criteria they use in judging what is ethical may be inappropriate in judging the degree to which other people's behavior is ethical. This tolerance for differences guides competent communicators in both interpreting and responding to the communication behaviors of people who are culturally dissimilar. Tolerance for differences, however, is not synonymous with unconditional approval of ethical norms other than your own. For example, competent communicators can tolerate ethical norms with which they disagree. The fact that they are tolerant, though, can facilitate constructive talk between competent communicators and the people who subscribe to norms the communicators find disagreeable. From such dialogues, new and mutually satisfactory ethical norms can potentially emerge.

Good Reasons

good reasons
Statements, based on moral principles, offered in support of propositions concerning what we should believe or how we should act.

A fourth norm to which competent communicators subscribe is expressed in the philosophy of Karl Wallace, scholar and former president of the National Speech Communication Association. Wallace believed that communicators must offer each other "good reasons" for believing, valuing, and acting.[9] **Good reasons** are statements, based on moral principles, offered in support of propositions concerning what we should believe or how we should act. Wallace believed that ethical and moral values, as well as relevant information, are the basic materials of communication. Communicators who rely on good reasons value all people including the ethical principles to which people adhere. Not only does the use of good reasons help ensure that communicators use ethical means, it is also far more likely to be successful in accomplishing the ethical ends competent communicators seek.

interaction consciousness The practice of balancing the satisfaction of one's own needs with the satisfaction of others' needs.

Interaction Consciousness

The fifth and final norm governing ethical communication is closely linked to good reasons. Called **interaction consciousness,** this norm is a result of communication scholar Roderick Hart's thinking about the concept of rhetorical sen-

---

Box 5-2   Considering Diversity

Freedom of Religion Versus Ethical Norms

Europeans came to the North American continent, in part, so that they could freely express their religion. Many contemporary immigrants from the Caribbean and Southeast Asia think that what was good enough for the Pilgrims should apply to them equally. As a result, some Caribbean and Southeast Asian immigrants have argued that they should be able to practice their religion and express this practice through symbolic acts, which are highly communicative, such as the ritualistic sacrifice of animals.

Should people be guaranteed the freedom of religious expression in this country, even though such expression may be at odds with the ethical norms of the majority in the United States? Take a position on this question and write a one-page paper in defense of your position.

---

sitivity, a topic we discuss in detail in Chapter 7.[10] Very simply, people who exercise interaction consciousness try to balance the satisfaction of their needs with those of the people with whom they come into contact. To partners in a relationship, interaction consciousness means thinking about the relational consequences of communication behavior. In small groups, it means accepting the idea that the needs of the group outweigh the needs of any individual member of the group. In a public speaking situation, interaction consciousness means the needs of the speaker should be based on an analysis of the needs of the audience. Finally, interaction consciousness means personal profit is never more important than the consequences of one's message, an idea often ignored by people, including those in the media.

Ethical Guidelines for Sources and Receivers

Truthfulness, respect for the power of language, tolerance, good reasons, and interaction consciousness oblige communicators to behave ethically regardless of the role in which they find themselves. Next, we discuss ethical guidelines for conditions in which you are primarily a source of communication. Then we discuss conditions in which you are primarily a receiver of communication. Finally, we introduce what scholars have come to call the dialogic imperative.[11] Although these guidelines fit some contexts of communication better than others, the norms on which the guidelines are based cut across contexts.

Ethical Guidelines for Sources

Attribution is the first guideline for sources. It concerns giving credit to people whose ideas you either directly quote or borrow from liberally. Attribution is based on the ethical norm of truthfulness and is designed to protect you from

plagiarism The act of stealing the ideas of others and using them as your own.

the charge of plagiarism. **Plagiarism** involves stealing intellectual property and passing it off as one's own. Plagiarism is the epitome of intellectual dishonesty.

While always important, attribution is most significant to public speaking and the various media of mass communication. As a speaker, you have the ethical obligation to attribute the words and ideas in your message to their proper source. The same is true when writing for a mass medium such as a newspaper or magazine or when speaking over a medium such as radio or television. Box 5-3 describes the price that a public official can pay for plagiarism.

Giving good reasons is the second guideline for sources. Although it is possible to gain compliance from other people through irrational and even deceptive means, it is far from ethical. Good reasons, as scholar Karl Wallace called them, are appeals based on the best attributes rather than the worst attributes in people.

Creating conditions for informed choice is the third guideline for sources who choose to communicate ethically. Often people fail to provide others with all the information necessary for them to understand the big picture. Politicians are notorious for not mentioning information contrary to the positions they advocate. Yet many times, people need this omitted information in order to make decisions that are both sound and principled.

Withholding information from people not only is unethical but also can lead to decisions of enormous consequence for the people affected by such decisions. Journalist and former White House Press Secretary Bill Moyers, for example, argues that former President Lyndon Johnson's decisions about the Vietnam War were negatively affected by people in the military who routinely withheld information from Johnson. Moyers also argues that this unethical withholding of information led Johnson to make decisions that unnecessarily cost thousands of lives.[12] In the case of decision-making groups like the one advising Johnson on the Vietnam War, competing interests among individual group members can undermine ethical judgment. As a result, small group communication scholar Ernest Bormann's list of ethical guidelines for decision-making groups includes the following one about sources creating conditions for informed choice.

> When in the adviser role, participants should present information honestly, fairly, and accurately. They should reveal their sources, they should allow others to scrutinize their evidence and arguments. They should not lie, because lying breaks the trust necessary for participants to assess information.[13]

The fourth and final guideline for sources involves the delicate balance between *freedom of speech* and *the power of words*. Freedom of speech, guaranteed by the First Amendment to the U.S. Constitution, is a right few people in the world enjoy to the extent residents of the United States do. Yet, because of what many perceive to be an abuse of this right, there are well-intentioned people who believe freedom of speech needs to be better defined. At colleges across this nation, for example, campus speech codes are the subject of debate. Some people believe such codes are necessary to combat racist, sexist, and homophobic speech to name but three. Others have argued that speech codes violate the First Amendment and are a poor way to curtail abusive words and language. Box 5-4 suggests some guidelines for campus speech codes.

Box 5-3   Critical Thinking

Senator Joseph Biden and Plagiarism

Senator Joseph Biden was a leading contender for the Democratic nomination for president in 1988 when he spoke in Des Moines, Iowa, on August 29, 1987. Little did he know that his candidacy was about to unravel.

Biden had seen a videotape of Neil Kinnock, leader of Britain's Labor Party, asking, "Why am I the first Kinnock in a thousand generations to be able to get to university?" Kinnock then pointed to his wife and asked, "Why is Glenys the first woman in her family in a thousand generations to be able to get to university? Was it because all our predecessors were thick?" He concluded, "Does anybody really think that they didn't get what we had because they didn't have the talent or the strength or the endurance to the commitment? Of course not. It was because there was no platform on which they could stand."

Biden, at an Iowa State Fair debate, spoke almost the same words, without attribution. He said, "Why is it that Joe Biden is the first in his family to ever go to a university? Why is it that my wife who is sitting over there in the audience is the first in her family to ever go to college? Is it because our fathers and mothers were not bright?" He concluded, "No, it's not because they weren't as smart. It's not because they didn't work hard. It's because they didn't have a platform on which to stand."

Those purloined words came back to haunt Biden. When newspapers started running stories and his political opponents began circulating videotapes comparing his words with Kinnock's,

Biden's fate was sealed. Soon other instances of Biden borrowing words from politicians like Robert Kennedy and Hubert Humphrey came to light. Ultimately, Biden was forced to end his quest for the presidency.

SOURCE: Jack W. Germond and Jules Witcover, *Whose Broad Stripes and Bright Stars? The Trivial Pursuit of the Presidency, 1988* (New York: Warner Brothers, 1989), 230–31.

Competent communicators seriously consider the weight of words prior to uttering them. Competent communicators also recognize that the best way to protect freedom of speech is through ethical communication behavior. As Supreme Court Justice Oliver Wendell Holmes, Jr., once said, freedom of speech

Box 5-4   Skill Building

Campus Speech Codes

A great experiment is simultaneously being conducted on campuses across the United States. Administrators, faculty, and students are trying to come up with speech codes that strike the right balance between protecting freedom of speech as guaranteed by the First Amendment and protecting people in the campus community from hateful and demoralizing language. This task has been made all that more difficult as a result of legal decisions striking down speech codes at Stanford and the University of Michigan. Working either on your own or in an instructor-assigned group, find out if your campus has a speech code that banishes the use of certain types of words and language. If your campus has such a policy, how would you amend it to fit your thinking or your group's? Compare your code to the following one derived by scholar Richard Johannesen from existing campus codes across the United States. Johannesen's code forbids

- use of derogatory names, inappropriately directed laughter, inconsiderate jokes, and conspicuous exclusion of another person from conversation,

- language that stigmatizes or victimizes individuals or that creates an intimidating or offensive environment,

- face-to-face use of epithets, obscenities, and other forms of expression that by accepted community standards degrade, victimize, stigmatize, or pejoratively depict persons based on their personal, intellectual, or cultural diversity, and

- extreme or outrageous acts or communications intended to harass, intimidate, or humiliate a student on the basis of race, color, or national origin, thus reasonably causing him or her severe emotional distress.

SOURCE: Charles U. Larsen, *Persuasion: Reception and Responsibility,* 7th ed. (Belmont, Calif.: Wadsworth, 1975), 34.

does not give people the right to shout "fire!" in a crowded theater. Although Justice Holmes was speaking metaphorically, the principle he was expressing is as relevant to the current debate about speech codes as it was nearly a century ago. The fact that people can say almost anything that comes to mind in this country doesn't make the content of what they say either ethical or wise.

Ethical Guidelines for Receivers

People who find themselves in the primary role of receiver also need to think about their ethical obligations. Remember, even when you are primarily the recipient of a message, you are still a party to the communication transaction. Like the source of the message, you too bear some responsibility for the consequences of the message.

The first guideline for receivers is to recognize that unless coerced, they are *responsible for the choices they make* during and following a communication transaction. This means that receivers cannot blame a source for their decision to riot or to violate human rights following a speech; they cannot excuse their actions by saying that a charismatic communicator persuaded them to act. Just as the judges at the Nuremberg Trials concluded that "following orders" was not an excuse for war crimes, receivers cannot excuse their unethical behavior on the grounds that they were complying with a message.

A second guideline, which logically follows from the first, is that receivers are responsible for *keeping themselves informed* on issues of the day. People who are uninformed about important topics and vital issues are easy prey for propagandists. History is replete with examples of people who have tried to attribute unethical behavior to ignorance real or imagined. Examples range from the people who said they didn't know the Nazis were sending millions of Jews to their death during World War II to the pharmaceutical company executives who claimed they were unaware of the terrible side effects of the drug thalidomide. Simply put, ignorance is no excuse for unethical behavior.

The third guideline for receivers is related to the first two. It involves the receiver's ethical obligation to speak up when convinced that a *source of communication is misinforming or misleading people.* Most of us have been in situations where we knew a source was bending the truth, leaving out pertinent details, or passing off another's ideas as his or her own. Under some unique set of circumstances, keeping this knowledge to ourselves may be justified. In most circumstances, however, we owe it to ourselves and others to constructively speak up. Speaking up can take the form of questioning a source following a presentation, asking the appropriate agency for equal time to speak, writing a letter to the editor of a newspaper or magazine, and confronting the source one-on-one. Whatever the appropriate medium, silence generally is not an option.

The final guideline for receivers concerns their subjective view and the manner in which this view biases how they *receive and process a source's message.* As pointed out in Chapter 2, perception is colored by one's experience both real and vicarious. It is psychologically healthier and more realistic for us to admit this fact to ourselves than to deny it. Only then can we determine how much of our reaction to a communicator's message is based on its content and relational dynamic and how much is attributable to our individual biases.

The Dialogic Imperative

The final topic for discussion involves ethical communication as it applies to our relationships, the groups in which we work, the audiences we address, and the media we both create and consume. Since we will be talking about ethics in each of these dimensions of communication in Chapters 8–18, we will limit our discussion here to what we call the dialogic imperative.

Dialogic ethics relates back to our discussion of interaction consciousness. This dimension of rhetorical sensitivity involves the communicator's commitment to consider his or her needs relative to the needs of others. Dialogic ethics, which most scholars trace to the philosophy of Martin Buber, goes even further in this regard. Buber believed we are nothing by ourselves. Instead, we are the product of our relationships with others and the messages we share.[14] Buber believed we are ethically obligated to communicate in a way that nurtures the

dialogic ethics   The principle that people are ethically obligated to behave in ways that express respect in their relationships with others.

The same ethical communication obligations that apply to speaking to groups or an audience also apply when interacting over the Internet, as the man at this "cyber-cafe" is doing.

relationship between us and other people. This obligation demands viewing and treating others not as objects to be manipulated for personal gain but as richly unique entities. Buber believed this dialogic imperative requires communicators to "be" rather than to "seem." Being involves the communication of the real you. Seeming involves communicating an image of self that is false.

Richard Johannesen, a communication scholar and expert on the subject of ethics, also has addressed the subject of dialogic ethics. Johannesen has developed specific guidelines for communicating ethically with people.[15] They concern authenticity, inclusion, confirmation, presentness, mutual equality, and supportiveness. These six guidelines are designed to assist communicators in nurturing their relationships with others and, therefore, themselves.

Authenticity is similar to Buber's concept of being. Authentic communicators present genuine representations of themselves to others, rather than trying to manipulate their behavior to achieve some calculated impression. *Inclusion,* a need we introduced in Chapter 1, involves communication behaviors that assist people in feeling significant and worthwhile. *Confirmation* involves communication behaviors that let people know that what they think and what they say counts, even when we disagree. *Presentness* is a little like mindfulness, which we defined in Chapter 1 as well. Presentness means we are consciously tuned into the other person, listening to the person with our total being. *Mutual equality* and *supportiveness* are straightforward, but not always easy to achieve in relationships. Ethical communication should be egalitarian. For example, in an egalitarian relationship, the attempts of both partners to influence the relationship are equally important. Supportiveness concerns creating a relational climate based on cooperation and mutual respect rather than competition and relational "games." Supportiveness also means creating a relational environment that can withstand disagreement and conflict.

Although Johannesen suggested these guidelines to serve people who are interpersonally involved, they generalize to small group, public speaking, and mass communication transactions as well. When people are talking to groups, speaking before an audience, or interacting over the Internet, for example, wouldn't you agree that they have an ethical obligation to communicate authentically? Wouldn't you also agree that effective small group communication requires individual group members to commit to the concept of inclusion, confirmation, equality, and supportiveness? As audience members listening to a speaker, don't we have an ethical obligation to exercise presentness? Dialogic ethics, that is, ethics that govern the communication behaviors *between* people, is the cornerstone of the even more specific ethical guidelines we will discuss relative to small groups, public speaking, and systems of mass communication in later chapters.

Summary

This chapter began with a consideration of basic ethical questions: Is it ever OK to lie? Is propaganda ever justified? Is it better to be ambiguous or say exactly what is on your mind? Should you remain silent or speak up when morally outraged by another's comments? Are there limits to the freedom of speech and expression? These are not questions with simple answers. How communicators interact depends to an important extent on the ethical principles they hold in common.

Regardless of their ethical system, however, competent communicators should employ ethical means to achieve ethical ends. Although no codified system exists for communicators, ethical norms for communicators can be derived from both traditional and contemporary sources. Among these norms are truthfulness, respect for the power of language, tolerance for differences, good reasons, and interaction consciousness.

Guidelines for sources and receivers can be derived from these ethical norms. For sources, these guidelines include attribution, appealing to the best in people by giving good reasons, creating conditions for informed choice, and balancing freedom of speech with the predictable consequences of abusive words and language. Guidelines for receivers include taking responsibility for their actions during or following a communication transaction, staying informed on important topics and vital issues, speaking up when they are aware that a source is misinforming or misleading people, and taking ownership of their subjective view and its effect on receiving and processing messages.

Ethical communication cuts across the dimensions of communication that make up our daily routine. The dialogic imperative, for instance, generalizes across these dimensions and tells us that, regardless of the situation in which we find ourselves, we should practice communication that is authentic, inclusive, confirming, egalitarian, exemplary of presentness, and supportive.

Another Look

Articles

Richard L. Johannesen. "The Ethics of Plagiarism Reconsidered: The Oratory of Martin Luther King, Jr." *Southern Communication Journal* 60 (1995): 185–94.

This article addresses the issue of plagiarism and how standards may vary from oral to print-oriented cultures. The oratory of Martin Luther King, Jr., provides a key example of how standards of plagiarism are not universally held (see Box 5-5).

Books

Richard L. Johannesen. *Ethics in Human Communication.* 3rd ed. Prospect Heights, Ill.: Waveland Press, 1990.

This book is a comprehensive discussion of ethics in all communication dimensions. The author thoroughly discusses the ethical issue inherent in each dimension, ranging from interpersonal and small group communication to political campaigns.

James A. Jaska and Michael S. Pritchard. *Communication Ethics: Methods of Analysis.* 2nd ed. (Belmont, Calif.: Wadsworth, 1994).

An excellent discussion of communication ethics, this book relies on numerous real-world ethical examples, which students are encouraged to think about and discuss.

Nina Rosenstand. *The Moral of the Story: An Introduction to Ethics.* 2nd ed. (Mountain View, Calif.: Mayfield, 1997).

This author takes a narrative approach to the study of ethics. Using fiction and film storytelling, the book shows how ethical theories can be applied to real-world situations.

Video Rentals

The Conversation   In this Francis Ford Coppolla film, Gene Hackman plays a surveillance expert hired to follow and tape-record an adulterous couple. In the process, Hackman uncovers what appears to be a murder plot. The film raises important questions about the ethics of listening.

Crimes and Misdemeanors   Woody Allen directs and stars with Academy Award winner Martin Landau. The film follows the moral dilemma Landau wrestles with as a prominent physician who has his mistress murdered.

All the President's Men   This film, starring Robert Redford and Dustin Hoffman, raises interesting questions about journalistic ethics. Redford and Hoffman play *Washington Post* reporters Bob Woodward and Carl Bernstein, who help bring down a president, using unnamed sources and unorthodox reporting techniques. In some ways, this film represents an excellent case study in the relationship between ethical ends and sometimes questionable means.

Leap of Faith   This film, starring Steve Martin and Debra Winger, follows the life of an unethical evangelist who doesn't believe in what he preaches, until he is forced to make a "leap of faith." In the process, the film explores the question of whether it is ever justified to communicate unsupported messages people want to hear. The film also clearly shows the difference between a person being versus seeming.

Theory and Research in Practice

1. Self-disclosure research shows that people who reveal intimate details about themselves expect the information to remain private. Suppose a close friend discloses that she or he has successfully plagiarized a paper, receiving an A for his or her dishonesty. Given what we've discussed in this chapter, what would you do with such a disclosure? Why? Be specific in explaining your decision.

2. Communication ethics scholar Richard Johannesen suggests that plagiarism is a Eurocentric idea, not a universal ethical norm. Visit with a professor on your campus who teaches a course in non-Western civilization. Discuss Johannesen's claim with the professor. Report on your discussion in class.

3. Mediated communication using new technologies raises ethical issues that currently are being debated. If you use your e-mail account at work to interpersonally communicate, are you being unethical? Is it unethical for your employer to monitor your messages over e-mail, which many companies do? Construct a list of at least three guidelines you believe should serve users of e-mail.

4. Clearly, people who communicate over computer networks have a choice to construct either an authentic image of self or one that is contrived to suit a situational purpose. Is Martin Buber's concept of being versus seeming relevant to computer transactions? Explain your answer in writing.

CHAPTER 6

Listening and Critical Thinking

OBJECTIVES

After reading this chapter you should be able to:

- Explain what listening involves.

- Explain the significant role that listening plays in our daily transactions.

- Recognize and explain the difference between hearing and listening.

- Recognize common myths about listening.

- Practice discriminative, appreciative, comprehensive, and therapeutic listening skills.

- Recognize common obstacles to listening.

- Practice listening skills that minimize the effects of obstacles to listening.

- Practice critical listening and thinking when appropriate.

- Use Toulmin's model of reasoning to analyze the validity of an argument.

- Identify common fallacies of argument.

Most of us have been surprised to learn that the words we thought we heard while listening to a favorite song were nothing like its true lyrics. Gavin Edwards has written a book about this common experience called *'Scuse Me While I Kiss This Guy and Other Misheard Lyrics.*[1]* The book title is based on the frequently

---

*Reprinted with the permission of the publisher, Simon Schuster from *'Scuse Me While I Kiss This Guy and Other Misheard Lyrics* by Gavin Edwards. Copyright ©1995 by Gavin Edwards.

confused lyric "Excuse me while I kiss the sky," taken from Jimi Hendrix's classic psychedelic song, "Purple Haze."

According to Gavin, there is a long tradition of listeners mishearing the lyrics to rock and roll tunes specifically. Some of the best, Gavin reports, include the following ones.

Misheard lyric: "I'll never leave your pizza burnin'."

Correct lyric: "I'll never be your beast of burden."—The Rolling Stones.

Misheard lyric: "The girl with colitis goes by."

Correct lyric: "The girl with kaleidoscope eyes."—The Beatles

Misheard lyric: "Mice aroma."

Correct lyric: "My Sharona."—The Knack

Misheard lyric: "Baking carrot biscuits."

Correct lyric: "Taking care of business."—Bachman-Turner Overdrive

Misheard lyric: "And doughnuts make my brown eyes blue."

Correct lyric: "And don't it make my brown eyes blue."—Crystal Gayle

Misheard lyric: "They sent you a tie clasp."

Correct lyric: "They said you was high class."—Elvis Presley

As these examples show, hearing a message doesn't guarantee we'll understand it or interpret it correctly. Effective listening requires skill, concentration, and critical thinking.

This chapter focuses on listening. As you can see in Figure 6-1, which shows the various types of communication activities in which we engage daily, listening

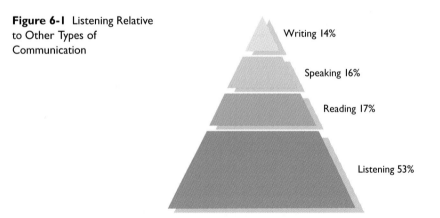

Figure 6-1 Listening Relative to Other Types of Communication

Writing 14%

Speaking 16%

Reading 17%

Listening 53%

is by far the most common. However, most of us lack the skills to be effective listeners. The average listener remembers only about half of what was said immediately after it was said. And after 48 hours the average listener remembers only about one quarter of what was said.[2]

In this chapter you'll find some thoughts, ideas, and skills that should help you become a consciously competent listener, including

- the nature of listening,
- the need to listen to others,
- obstacles to listening,
- types of listening,
- techniques to improve your listening behavior, and
- the relationship between critical listening and critical thinking.

The Nature of Listening

For starters, hearing is not the same as listening. Hearing is a physical process. **Listening** is both physical and mental. Listening also can be active or passive. **Active listening** is mindful, a concept we've repeatedly emphasized. Passive listening isn't mindless, but it is certainly less focused than active listening. Professional listeners, such as therapists, engage in active listening. People listening to radio typically engage in passive listening. Although there is no universally agreed-on definition of listening, most scholars agree that it requires consciously receiving, attending to, and assigning meaning to verbal and nonverbal messages. Most also agree that listening involves

- selective attention,
- sensorial involvement,
- comprehension/meaning, and
- retention/remembering.[3]

As noted in Chapter 2, selective attention is a conscious decision to listen. **Sensorial involvement** means listening with all applicable senses, not simply the sense of hearing. Comprehension means understanding what was said. And retention means storing what was said in either short- or long-term memory. Comprehension and retention are familiar requirements for active listening, but selective attention and sensorial involvement deserve additional discussion.

Selective Attention

Research on selective attention shows that we are most likely to attend to messages we perceive to be reinforcing.[4] In other words, we are more likely to give

listening Mentally and physically attending to, comprehending, and retaining the meaning of messages.

active listening Listening that involves participating mindfully in the communication transaction.

sensorial involvement Listening with all the applicable senses, not simply the sense of hearing.

our attention to someone whose message reflects our views than to someone whose message opposes them. For example, conservatives are more likely to watch Rush Limbaugh than Jesse Jackson, whose political beliefs are much more liberal. Thus, it's easier to consciously decide to listen to reinforcing messages than to messages we perceive otherwise.

Sensorial Involvement

Once you've made a deliberate choice to listen to the communication transaction, you then need to involve all of your applicable senses in the transaction. Not only must you try to hear what is being said, but you also must try to see and feel what is being said. As we said in Chapter 1, every message has two sides: content and relational. You must use your senses to try to comprehend both sides of the message.

Reading the text of a conversation is not the same as physically participating in it, just as reading a movie script is not the same as watching the film. You are limited to the content of the message and its compositional elements. Although content is important, how it is expressed is equally important. Gestures, movements, facial expressions, and eye contact can add meaning and emphasis to the content of a message. The reaction of people to the message and the physical setting in which the transaction occurs can also affect the meaning of the message.

The Need to Listen

The ability to listen effectively is important to succeeding in school, at work, with friends and family, and in other situations where you need to share information with others. For example, effective listening is essential to learning. As a college student you are exposed to hundreds of hours of lectures, group discussions, and mass communication. The ability to process and absorb information is the essence of learning. You need to engage in active listening if you are to obtain the maximum benefit from your college career.

Second, effective listening is essential to success in the work force. One of the key complaints of many employers is that employees do not listen effectively, costing millions each year in mistakes and inefficiencies. Among the skills employers value in listeners are "listening for content; listening to conversations; listening for long-term contexts; listening for emotional meaning; and listening to follow directions."[5]

Third, listening is also essential to family and interpersonal communication. How many times have you heard children or parents complain that no one listens to what they say? In interpersonal contexts, listening must go well beyond content—focusing on the relational components of the communication transaction, including emotion.

Finally, listening is essential to effectively communicating information to others. Your messages need to be adapted to the feedback you receive from others.

Understanding what others need because you have effectively listened is essential to successfully influencing their beliefs, attitudes, and actions.

Drawing by Ziegler; © 1982 The New Yorker Magazine, Inc.

Myths about Listening

There are a number of myths about effective listening. Three common ones are that (1) listening is easy, (2) automatically results from intelligence, and (3) does not need to be planned.

Myth 1:   *It Is Easy To Listen*

Some people think that listening is like breathing—we are born listeners. Of course, that is just as fallacious as assuming that because we can breathe, we can breathe as properly as professional singers. Successful singers train for years to master the proper breathing techniques to project and control their voices. Just because someone can carry a tune and sing in the shower does not mean that the person is ready for the New York Metropolitan Opera. Similarly, just because we've heard others talk to us all of our lives does not mean that we are effective listeners. Quite the contrary, complacency about listening is one of the things that makes people susceptible to poor listening habits.

Myth 2:   *Smart People Are Better Listeners*

Does being smart guarantee you will be a good listener? Not necessarily. Some highly intelligent people are very poor listeners. We know a widely respected scientist whose mind was so preoccupied with his scientific endeavors that he often did not listen to what members of his family said. He would often mutter, "Uh huh, sure," even though he was not paying attention to what was said. Ultimately his children learned to say, "Dad, this is important! Please listen to me." Only after they had his full attention did they then state their point. Otherwise, they knew that although their father might be hearing their words, he would not be listening. Listening is a skill. Although being intelligent may help you learn the skill, it does not guarantee you will become an effective listener.

Myth 3:   *There Is No Need to Plan Ahead*

A third common misconception is that listening just happens—there's no need to plan for it. Of course, we can't prepare for the conversations of daily life. But when we know in advance that we will be in a listening situation, we can plan ahead. For example, if you are attending a lecture, you should bring paper and pen to take notes. If your instructor has assigned reading prior to class, you will be far better prepared to listen if you have read the materials the lecturer presumes you have read. And being rested, alert, and motivated to listen are all likely to help you get the most out of the time you spend in class.

Obstacles to Listening

A number of factors can prevent listening effectively. Six of the most important obstacles to listening are the internal dialogue to which we are prone, physical conditions, cultural differences, personal problems, biases, and connotative meanings. With the exception of the first two, all of these obstacles are perceptual in nature. Box 6-1 allows you to measure your level of receiver apprehension, which can interfere with your ability to listen.

The Internal Dialogue

Listening begins within your own mind. We sometimes carry on an internal dialogue in response to another's words, though we don't verbalize it. For example, suppose you listen to someone talking about a controversial topic. If you agree with the person, you may find yourself thinking, "Yeah . . . that's right!" On the other hand, if you disagree with the person you may say to yourself, "You've got to be kidding!" Listening to the internal dialogue affects your listening to others, and not always for the best. It can interfere with your processing of the message you are receiving. This is especially true under conditions of stress, such as when meeting a large number of people at a professional meeting or social gathering. Uptight and preoccupied with the impression we are making, we frequently carry on an internal dialogue while being introduced to another person. These internal dialogues are one of the reasons we fail to process, much less remember, the names of people just introduced to us.

Listening is important to a child's self-esteem.

Physical Factors

The physical environment clearly affects the ability to listen. Among the factors that can inhibit listening are noise, an unpleasant room temperature, poor lighting, physical obstacles, and uncomfortable seating. A noisy, hot, poorly lit room, with hard, uncomfortable chairs, is hardly an ideal listening environment. On the other hand, a quiet, well-lit room, with comfortable (but not too comfortable) chairs, and a pleasant temperature allows listeners to concentrate on each other. Even though listeners cannot always do much to make the physical environment more conducive to listening, they can consciously try to ignore the physical distractions in the environment and focus on what each other is saying.

Cultural Differences

Communication patterns vary from culture to culture on a number of important dimensions.[6] For example, in the North American culture communicators look

Box 6-1   Self-Assessment

What Is Your Level of Receiver Apprehension?

Just as some people are anxious about communicating with others, some people are anxious when receiving information. Receiver apprehension can significantly interfere with effective listening. The following statements apply to how various people feel about receiving communication. Indicate if these statements apply to how you feel by noting whether you (5) strongly agree, (4) agree, (3) are undecided, (2) disagree, or (1) strongly disagree.

_____ 1. I feel comfortable when listening to others on the phone.

_____ 2. It is often difficult for me to concentrate on what others are saying.

_____ 3. When listening to members of the opposite sex I find it easy to concentrate on what is being said.

_____ 4. I have no fear of being a listener as a member of an audience.

_____ 5. I feel relaxed when listening to new ideas.

_____ 6. I would rather not have to listen to other people at all.

_____ 7. I am generally overexcited and rattled when others are speaking to me.

_____ 8. I often feel uncomfortable when listening to others.

_____ 9. My thoughts become confused and jumbled when reading important information.

_____ 10. I often have difficulty concentrating on what others are saying.

_____ 11. Receiving new information makes me feel restless.

_____ 12. Watching television makes me nervous.

_____ 13. When on a date I find myself tense and self-conscious when listening to my date.

_____ 14. I enjoy being a good listener.

_____ 15. I generally find it easy to concentrate on what is being said.

_____ 16. I seek out the opportunity to listen to new ideas.

_____ 17. I have difficulty concentrating on instructions others give to me.

_____ 18. It is hard to listen or concentrate on what other people are saying unless I know them well.

_____ 19. I feel tense when listening as a member of a social gathering.

_____ 20. Television programs that attempt to change my mind about something make me nervous.

To determine your score, first total the scores you gave yourself for statements 2, 6, 7, 8, 9, 10, 11, 12, 13, 17, 18, 19, 20. *Add* 42 to that total (maximum 107, minimum 55). From this result, *subtract* the total of the scores you gave yourself for statements 1, 3, 4, 5, 14, 15, 16. Your score should be in the range from between 20 and 100. The higher your score, the more apprehensive you are about listening. Scores above 80 indicate a relatively high level of receiver apprehension. A mid-range score would be about 60. Scores below 40 would indicate a relatively low level of receiver apprehension.

Based on your score, what sorts of listening behaviors do you think you could improve? For example, do your answers suggest a need to work harder at concentration? Should you seek greater opportunities to practice listening skills and learn new information?

Box 6-2   Considering Diversity

Listening in High- and Low-Context Cultures

As we discuss at length in the next chapter, some cultures place greater emphasis on the context in which communication occurs than on what was actually heard. In such high-context cultures, as they are called, people realize that what one hears while listening must be deciphered only after thoroughly considering the context in which it is heard. Yes may mean no and vice versa, for example, depending on where and under what circumstances they are uttered. The opposite is true in low-context cultures, where greatest emphasis is given to the spoken word. People trust what they think they hear without giving undue attention to the context in which it is heard.

What kinds of problems do you see occurring when people from high- and low-context cultures listen to each other? Which of the listening skills discussed in this chapter do you think would most help in overcoming these problems? Be specific!

SOURCE: Edward T. Hall and Mildred R. Hall, *Hidden Differences: Doing Business with the Japanese* (Garden City, N.Y.: Anchor/Doubleday, 1987).

for and appreciate communication cues that tell them active listening is taking place. In a relationship, such cues include eye contact, positive head nods, and verbal encouragements like "really?" and "uh huh." In a speaking situation, the audience tells the speaker that they're listening through additional cues such as leaning forward in their seats. This kind of feedback, telling people that active listening is occurring, is not a feature of other cultures, for instance, many African ones. Box 6-2 compares listening in high- and low-context cultures.

Although there is no simple rule of thumb for dealing with cultural differences in listening, the best advice is to be aware of the culture of the person or persons to whom you are listening and to take differences from your own culture into account. Listening to someone from a culture different from your own is more likely to occur today than at any other time. You should take advantage of every opportunity to learn about other cultures. This knowledge will improve your cross-cultural listening effectiveness.

Personal Problems

Most people have had the experience of being so preoccupied with a personal problem that they were unable to pay attention to someone else. Thinking about an argument with a significant other or financial problems can easily detract from listening to what is being said. The best advice to overcoming this obstacle is to recognize the situation and try to focus on what is being said, as difficult as that may be. For example, what would you do if you were plagued by a personal problem prior to an important job interview? Chances are you would tell yourself to "get your act together." You need to do the same thing in other dimensions of communicating—for instance, prior to listening to a troubled friend, participating in a small group, or fielding questions from an audience following a speech you think was less effective than you would have liked.

Bias

All people are biased, though not to an equal degree. Bias reflects an opinion formed without evidence, usually about a person or group of people. Racial, religious, gender, and other such biases, though forbidden by law, often exist in people's minds. Recognizing bias is an important step to overcoming it.[7]

Bias isn't always based on inaccurate stereotypes. Incomplete knowledge can also cause us to form hasty judgments. In publicized criminal cases, such as those involving the Menendez brothers, O. J. Simpson, Reginald Denny, or John and Lorena Bobbitt, it is sometimes difficult to find a jury of 12 people who can set aside their biases, listen to the evidence presented in court, and reach a fair verdict.

Regardless of its source, bias is a serious impediment to listening. To overcome bias, listeners need to recognize its existence, recognize its irrationality, and mentally set it aside.

Connotative Meanings

As discussed in Chapter 3, words have both denotative and connotative meanings. Whereas the denotative meanings of words are generally agreed on and can be found in the dictionary, connotative meanings are more subjective. A word's connotation often has a strong emotional component. In addition, connotations can be personal and subjective.

Along the same lines, connotative meaning is frequently culturally bound. Native English speakers on college campuses, for example, use words such as *buff, large,* and *style* in culturally specific ways. Yet, an international student listening to a native speaker use these words connotatively would translate them denotatively.

Understanding that people may have different connotations for the same word is essential to overcoming this obstacle to effective listening. Listeners need to recognize that their connotative meanings for words are not always shared. What's more, communicators need to avoid or define words that are connotatively rich when talking with or speaking to people from diverse cultures.

Types of Listening

Just as there is no single style of effective communication, there is no single type of listening that is appropriate in each and every situation. Table 6-1 describes five common but different types of listening: discriminative, comprehensive, appreciative, therapeutic, and critical.[8] Let's look at each in detail, as well as suggestions to improve your skills at each type of listening.

Table 6-1	Common Types of Listening
TYPE	**GOAL**
Discriminative listening	To detect such things as how consistent a verbal message is with the nonverbal message.
Comprehensive listening	To understand the overall meaning of a message; to recognize that the sum of the message is greater than the message's individual parts.
Appreciative listening	To listen for pleasure.
Therapeutic listening	To serve as a nonevaluative sounding board for someone who needs to talk.
Critical listening	To analyze the communicator's credibility and the soundness of his or her message.

Discriminative Listening

This most basic type of listening is the one on which all others are based. **Discriminative listening** involves learning to distinguish among the variety of verbal and nonverbal cues to which we are exposed. As infants we begin to listen discriminatively, learning first to recognize parental voices, then sounds, words, and eventually the complex structures of language. Visual stimuli, such as facial expression, gesture, and movement, become part of meaning for us. The careful listener is sensitive to both verbal and nonverbal nuances of messages.

One important aspect of discriminative listening is recognizing when a verbal message is intended to be contradicted by a nonverbal one. When verbal and nonverbal messages appear to conflict, people tend to believe the nonverbal one. Sometimes people intentionally contradict their verbal message with a nonverbal one, for example, when being sarcastic. Yet, not everyone is as adept at understanding a sarcastic message as they are at understanding a message that is intended to be taken literally. The sarcastic message requires a higher degree of discriminative listening than the literal message. Box 6-3 will help you improve your discriminative listening skills.

Comprehensive Listening

Once discriminative listening occurs, the next step is comprehension, listening targeted at understanding. As a student, much of your day involves **comprehensive listening**—for example, making sense of a lecture, understanding a calculus problem, or assigning meaning to a new concept. Successful comprehensive listening demands that your understanding of a message closely approximate the meaning intended by the source of the message. How well you comprehensively listen depends on several factors. Chief among them are vocabulary, concentration, and memory.

discriminative listening Listening targeted at distinguishing verbal and nonverbal cues from one another.

comprehensive listening Listening targeted at understanding.

Box 6-3   Skill Building

Improve Your Discriminative Listening Skills

Here are some helpful skills you can use to improve your discriminative listening:

• Learn to detect and isolate vocal cues such as a person raising his or her voice at the end of a sentence, which is a vocal cue seeking approval of what is being said.

• Learn to recognize environmental sounds such as distinguishing between leaves being rustled by the wind and the whispering sound wind makes as it moves through pine needles.

• Learn to detect and isolate visual cues such as a raised eyebrow suggesting surprise and a frown suggesting a person doesn't understand.

SOURCE: Adapted from Andrew D. Wolvin and Carolyn G. Coakley, *Listening*, 3rd ed. (Dubuque, Iowa: Wm. C. Brown, 1988), 144–54.

Vocabulary   Vocabulary is a two-edged sword in the context of this discussion. Obviously, you cannot comprehend something for which you don't have meaning. Thus, a limited vocabulary has the undesirable effect of limiting your ability to comprehensively listen to the messages of others.

By the same token, some communicators use their vocabulary like a sledgehammer. Rather than enlightening others, their polysyllabic messages simply pound people down into their seats. For example, consider this paragraph taken from the "Ask Marilyn" column in a *Parade Magazine*. Listed in the *Guinness Book of World Records* as having the highest I.Q. ever recorded, Marilyn Vos Savant answered a reader's mathematical question as follows:

> The resolution of this apparent paradox lies with the concept of densities of infinities and the correspondingly unique qualities of transfinite numbers; the numbers of points on any segment curve is described by the second of the transfinite numbers, known as aleph-one.[9]

Although the answer may be technically correct, it is likely that many of Vos Savant's readers quickly turned to the comics pages of their Sunday papers rather than decipher this obscure answer.

Concentration   A second important factor for comprehensive listening is concentration. As we know all too well, our minds are easily distracted from the task at hand. For example, have you ever been asked a question while your mind was wandering? Concentration can be lost in class, during a meeting, or even during a conversation. It also happens more frequently to some of us than we would like to admit.

There are two types of concentration: wide-band and pinpoint (Figure 6-2). Whereas pinpoint concentration is most relevant to critical listening, wide-band

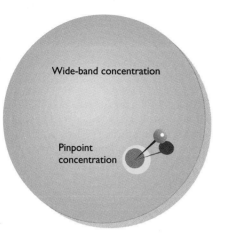

Figure 6.2 Wide-Band Concentration Compared to Pinpoint Concentration. If you were listening to a symphonic orchestra, you would use wide-band concentration to focus on the total sound of the orchestra. You would use pinpoint concentration to focus on a single section of the orchestra.

concentration is most relevant to comprehensive listening. Pinpoint concentration is a focus on specific details. Wide-band concentration is a focus on patterns rather than details. As a result, wide-band concentration assists you in listening for the gist of the conversation, the tone of the speech, or the larger meaning of the lecture.

Both types of concentration, however, demand that you try to block out stimuli that compete with the message on which you are trying to focus. These competing stimuli range from the obvious, such as heavy equipment being operated outside your office, to the subtle—for example, the growls your stomach makes when you are hungry.

Memory Closely related to concentration is the third factor that influences comprehensive listening: memory. Often the failure to remember reflects the failure to concentrate. Go back to the example of forgetting the name of someone to whom you have just been introduced. Although this common experience simply may be the result of "mental laziness," most often it is the product of the anxiety accompanying the situation. Anxiety and preoccupation have a devastating effect on our powers of concentration and memory. At a fraternity or sorority rush, or at a party, such feelings are commonplace. As you are being introduced to someone, you may be too busy thinking about how you are being perceived (remember the internal dialogue?) to concentrate on the person's name. It isn't that you forgot the name—it's that you didn't listen for and process the name in the first place.

To summarize: Much of your day is spent in situations that require comprehensive listening. And nowhere is this more likely to be true than in your classes. You must try to listen comprehensively not only to your instructors but

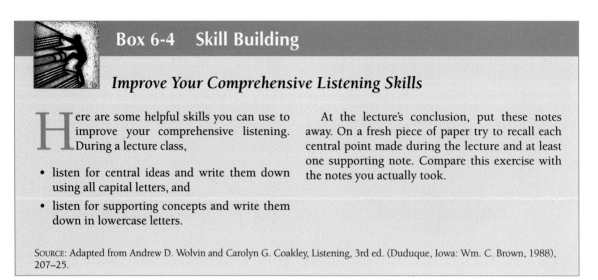

Box 6-4 Skill Building

Improve Your Comprehensive Listening Skills

Here are some helpful skills you can use to improve your comprehensive listening. During a lecture class,

- listen for central ideas and write them down using all capital letters, and

- listen for supporting concepts and write them down in lowercase letters.

At the lecture's conclusion, put these notes away. On a fresh piece of paper try to recall each central point made during the lecture and at least one supporting note. Compare this exercise with the notes you actually took.

SOURCE: Adapted from Andrew D. Wolvin and Carolyn G. Coakley, Listening, 3rd ed. (Duduque, Iowa: Wm. C. Brown, 1988), 207–25.

also to other students as they ask and answer questions, make comments, or seek out your assistance during a lab assignment. Box 6-4 will help you improve your comprehensive listening skills.

Appreciative Listening

Appreciative listening is listening that is done for enjoyment, the kind of listening you do when watching TV, attending a music concert, and seeing a play. Although it might seem that such listening just comes naturally, you can enhance your pleasure by expanding your listening experiences, increasing your understanding of what you are listening to, and developing your powers of concentration. Music appreciation classes, for example, help students learn what to listen for in different kinds of music.

Many people have a tendency to avoid a wide variety of listening experiences. For example, many of today's parents have difficulty appreciating their children's choice in music and vice versa. Yet, not appreciating each other's music may be a result of a lack of understanding and experience rather than an inherent generational difference. Understanding what you listen to is important to enhancing your listening pleasure. Listening to a symphony or opera is difficult for many people, not because they lack taste but because they simply do not understand or appreciate the art form. Just as you need to understand the rules of a sport such as hockey to genuinely appreciate the action, so it is with listening not only to music but also to poetry readings and live theater.

Therapeutic Listening

This type of listening provides a person with the opportunity to talk through a problem. **Therapeutic listening** involves helping people in a nonevaluative and

appreciative listening Listening that is done for enjoyment.

therapeutic listening Nonevaluative and nonthreatening listening to help people express feelings.

Signs of active listening are music to a speaker's ears.

nonthreatening way to express their feelings, as a therapist helps a client.[10] Therapeutic listening requires that listeners focus their attention fully and show their attentiveness verbally and nonverbally. A supportive climate is essential for therapeutic listening. Listeners should be nonjudgmental, while demonstrating empathy for the speaker. They should not interrupt, change the subject, talk about themselves, discount the speaker's feelings, blame, evaluate, or advise. Their role is to be a sounding board.

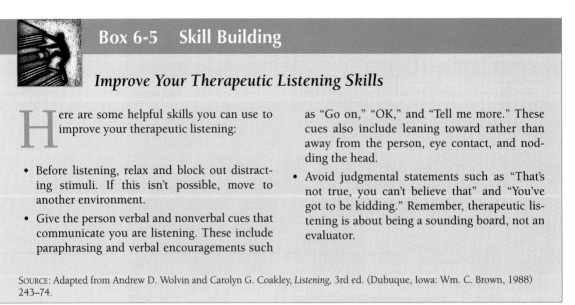

Box 6-5   Skill Building

Improve Your Therapeutic Listening Skills

Here are some helpful skills you can use to improve your therapeutic listening:

- Before listening, relax and block out distracting stimuli. If this isn't possible, move to another environment.

- Give the person verbal and nonverbal cues that communicate you are listening. These include paraphrasing and verbal encouragements such

as "Go on," "OK," and "Tell me more." These cues also include leaning toward rather than away from the person, eye contact, and nodding the head.

- Avoid judgmental statements such as "That's not true, you can't believe that" and "You've got to be kidding." Remember, therapeutic listening is about being a sounding board, not an evaluator.

SOURCE: Adapted from Andrew D. Wolvin and Carolyn G. Coakley, *Listening*, 3rd ed. (Dubuque, Iowa: Wm. C. Brown, 1988) 243–74.

Listening for what a person is feeling is a special skill. It demands that you process what a person feels while talking, and pay particular attention to emotive words that convey feelings such as anger, tension, and powerlessness. Box 6-5 will help you improve your therapeutic listening skills.

Critical Listening

Critical listening, which is the skill addressed in Box 6-6, is an extension and refinement of the other types of listening described in Table 6-1. Critical listening often requires skills similar to those required by appreciative, discriminative, comprehensive, and therapeutic listening. There is one crucial difference, however: Critical listening involves making reasoned judgments about communicators and messages. Much of the daily information we receive is targeted at influencing us, as well as making us comply with the wishes of others. Unfortunately, much of the information directed at influencing us or making us comply is not in our best interest. Cigarette advertising, for example, is notorious for encouraging people to pursue a habit that can cost them their health or even their life.

critical listening
Listening that involves making a reasoned judgment about the communicator and the message.

Thus, on the one hand, learning to listen critically is a form of self-protection. Listening critically helps us guard against being taken advantage of by unscrupulous salespeople, politicians, and plain old con artists. On the other hand, learning to listen critically will directly enhance our ability to communicate interpersonally, while dialoguing on the Internet, working in a small group, delivering a speech, or watching a TV debate between presidential candidates.

Box 6-6 Skill Building

Improve Your Critical Listening Skills

Here are some helpful skills you can use to improve your critical listening:

- Take notes if at all possible.
- Listen first for the communicator's credentials. Try to determine whether the communicator is competent and trustworthy as a result of what she or he says.
- Listen next for any claims being made.

- If one or more claims are made, then listen for grounds, backing, and qualifiers three terms discussed later in the chapter.
- If grounds and backing are offered in support of the claim, listen to determine whether the reasoning is sound or fallacious.
- If qualifiers are offered, make sure that they are substantive, not meant to simply give the impression that the communicator is being objective about the content of the message.

At a minimum, critical listening involves focusing on both the communicator and the message in the attempt to verify the validity of what is being said. Is the communicator competent and trustworthy? How do you know this to be the case? What evidence has been given to you that would make this the case? And what about the message? Is it directed at getting you to change, stay the same, or buy something? Is the message merely informative, or is it argumentative? In either case, how do you know the information is representative of the facts? Is the message logical? Is it supported with evidence; for example, are there clearly cited sources you could track down and check?

Just because someone says something is true does not make it true. Although revered by many as a paragon of truth, radio talk show host Rush Limbaugh has apparently misstated a number of "facts," according to a report by the media watchdog group FAIR (Fairness and Accuracy in Reporting). For example, Limbaugh has frequently asserted that nicotine is not addictive, despite the overwhelming medical evidence to the contrary.[11]

The critical perspective you bring to bear when listening to communicators and their messages is just as relevant to you and the message you ultimately share with others. Thus, learning to listen critically to others will assist you in becoming more objectively critical of yourself. In the case of public speaking specifically, for instance, listening critically will assist you in both the preparation and delivery of your own message because it will force you to apply a similar set of critical questions to yourself:

- What do I need to do to ensure that people will perceive me as competent and trustworthy?

- What is my goal? Do I want to inform my audience's opinions, teach them something, persuade them to stay the same, or persuade them to change in a direction I advocate?
- What are the main points I want to make in support of my overall goal?
- Do I need evidence to support my main points? If so, what kind and how much?
- Should my appeals be exclusively logical, or do I also want to appeal emotionally to people?
- What ethical bounds constrain me in communicating?

Listening Skills

To begin with, no one can make you listen. The decision to actively attend to communicators and their messages is yours and yours alone. All the techniques in the world won't help you become a better listener unless you consciously choose to attend to a specific communication transaction, learn, and practice effective listening.

Second, the techniques that follow are best viewed as a collection or system of techniques. They are interdependent—not independent. Your skill in using one of these techniques, consequently, will have a direct bearing on your skill in using them all. Nine techniques of effective listening are

- setting goals,
- blocking out distracting stimuli,
- suspending judgment,
- focusing on main points,
- recognizing highlights and signposts,
- taking effective notes,
- being sensitive to meta-communication,
- paraphrasing, and
- questioning.[12]

Setting Goals

The first technique is straightforward: Establish a goal you hope to achieve as a consequence of listening. Your goal depends on the type of listening you will be doing. The goal of therapeutic listening, for example, is not the same as the goal of critical listening. Therapeutic listening is directed toward empathic understanding of the other person, whereas critical listening is directed toward reasoned judgment.

Advertisers (such as the tobacco industry) would go broke if people listened critically to their messages.

Your goal will guide your behavior as you listen. When critically listening, for example, you will focus much of your attention on distinguishing what part of a communicator's message is fact and what part is opinion. In contrast, when therapeutically listening, you will focus much of your attention on what the communicator's message suggests the communicator is feeling.

Recall from Table 6-1 that the listening goal we establish for ourselves will tend to dictate the listening behaviors in which we engage. Thus, when we fail to establish a goal at the outset of the listening process, we run the risk of focusing on what is peripheral rather than central to our purpose.

Blocking Out Distracting Stimuli

To actively listen, you must clear your mind of distracting stimuli. Trying to shut out distracting thoughts, however, is not the answer. Relaxation may be. Research suggests that a relaxed mind is a receptive mind. Moreover, there is a mind-body relationship in this regard: When the body feels relaxed, so does the mind. As a result, anything you do to promote self-relaxation prior to listening should help you diminish the potential impact of distracting stimuli.

Suspending Judgment

We opened Chapter 2 with an example that demonstrated all people, regardless of background, are capable of racial bias. Further, people may be biased even when they have little concrete evidence on which to base their judgments. People cannot listen when they prematurely judge people and their messages. They may hear what they want to hear, but they cannot listen. Comprehensive listening and critical listening especially demand an open mind.

In the attempt to suspend judgment, you can do three things. First, recognize and accept the fact that you and everyone else bring subjective experience to the communication transaction. This subjective experience colors and filters your perceptions of the communicator and the message. Second, try not to judge a book by its cover. Stereotypes on the basis of physical appearance are notoriously unreliable. Finally, if you're having trouble listening because you don't like the communicator, try to separate the message from the communicator.

Focusing on Main Points

You may also find it helpful to prioritize what you listen for in a communication transaction. The content of all messages varies in importance. Some ideas expressed are central, whereas others are peripheral. Critically listening for the main ideas in a message is most important.

Some students make the mistake of indiscriminately writing down verbatim everything a professor says in class. They risk missing the central points of a lecture. For example, one of us had a classmate in college who tape-recorded and then transcribed every class lecture. Despite this extraordinary effort, she rarely earned better than a C. Why? Because she tried to record and memorize every word her professors said rather than learning to distinguish the important points from the insignificant ones.

Recognizing Highlights and Signposts

One way to identify the central points in a message is to pay attention to highlights and signposts. Often competent communicators go out of their way to highlight what is most important in their message. They might say, for example:

> "Of the three ideas I've shared, this one is far and away the *most important*."
>
> "In my mind, the *most precious freedom* we enjoy is the freedom of speech, followed by. . . ."
>
> "How can anyone ignore the *magnitude* of the environmental problems caused by the automobile?"

In each instance, the communicator uses a highlighting statement to emphasize the centrality of what is being said. Phrases and words such as *most important*, *central, most precious,* and *magnitude* serve to verbally italicize and set apart central ideas from subordinate ones.

To understand how the ideas in a message are related, you can look for transitional statements, or signposts, as well. Transitions indicate when one main idea is ending and another is beginning. A communicator might provide a signpost by saying, for example:

"Having established the importance of a speaker's credibility, *let's now look at. . . .*"

"This key to understanding Poe leads me to my *second point* about the interpretation of poetry."

"*Equally important to this idea is the notion* that an open society demands a free press."

Taking Effective Notes

Effective note-taking is a science. Like any other science it demands an appropriate methodology. One method we sometimes recommend to people is patterned after the flow sheet college debaters use to track the development of arguments during the course of a debate. As you can see in the flow sheet in Figure 6-3, this technique involves keeping track of central ideas and data that support these ideas. The affirmative team in a debate usually begins with the central idea that something is wrong with the status quo. Because the burden of proof falls on the affirmative's shoulders, the affirmative team must produce evidence in support of the central idea.

In college debate, the negative team usually will defend the status quo and carefully tracks not only the development of the affirmative team's main idea but also the evidence offered in support of the main idea. The negative team may write down questions that occur to it as well.

Given this framework, let's assume we are at work. Part of our job is to evaluate proposals for new product lines, for changes in policy, or for bringing in an outside consultant. Sometimes these proposals are written and sent to us for evaluation. More often, they are presented orally to us as well as in writing.

Even if we are favorably predisposed to such proposals, we should follow the lead of the negative team in college debate. We should write down the main point being made and the evidence offered in support as we listen to the presentation. We should also jot down questions that occur to us as we listen. In other words, we should use the note-taking methodology of debaters to make our listening behavior systematic and focused.

Being Sensitive to Meta-communication

Another important technique that we recommend involves listening to **meta-communication.** Meta-communication is the message about the message. It is generally conveyed nonverbally and can be rich in meaning. You can listen for the meta-message in a communicator's eyes, voice, gestures, movements,

meta-communication
The message about the message; generally conveyed nonverbally.

Figure 6-3 Note-Taking

PRESENTER AND PROPOSAL	EVALUATOR
1. Reengineering this company can save us millions of dollars each year.	1. OK, she's making a pretty strong claim. SAVINGS = Millions
2. We're bringing in a top consultant.	2. What makes her a top consultant?
3. She has a good track record and is a professor at the Wharton School.	3. That's impressive.
4. Dr. Smith has three areas she wants us to look at: R&D, manufacturing, and customer service.	4. Why those three?
5. Our own figures show inflated costs in these three areas as well.	5. Let's hear the figures.
6. In R&D it's 3%, 7.5% in manufacturing, and 4% in customer service.	6. Maybe those increases are justified. Just because they're up doesn't make them inflated.

posture, and use of time. You can also listen for the meta-message in other people's reaction to the communicator.

Chief among the reasons for listening carefully to the meta-message is cross modality checking, first introduced in Chapter 4. Cross-modality checking involves comparing what a person says verbally against the nonverbal behaviors that make up the meta-message. Cross-modality checking enables us to ferret out the subtleties in a communicator's message—for example, irony, sarcasm, and even deception.

But a word of caution about meta-communication is in order. At the outset of this discussion we stated that listening techniques are interdependent. This is especially true when listening to meta-communication. Although meta-communication can clarify meaning, you should never infer the meaning of a communicator's message on the basis of the meta-message alone. The meta-message is not a substitute for the spoken word—a point emphasized in Chapter 4 on nonverbal behavior. It also can be tremendously misleading when isolated from its spoken counterpart.

Paraphrasing

One of the key elements of active listening is for the listener to confirm that the message has been received accurately. The techniques of paraphrasing and questioning, which are used extensively in therapeutic listening, are valuable tools for ensuring accurate communication. To paraphrase a message, you repeat the essence of what has been said, but in your own words. Paraphrasing is normally done in fewer words than the original message. It should be done in a way that confirms understanding, and it should be nonevaluative. Your goal is not to convey your opinion of what was said, but merely to confirm that you understand what was said. Often you will paraphrase not only the denotative content of the message but the emotional aspects as well. For example, you might say, "You're angry," or "You feel taken advantage of," or "You feel good about this decision."

Questioning

Similar to paraphrasing, questioning is a way of determining if you correctly understand the message. But rather than simply repeating in your own words what you think you have heard, you ask the other person for information as well as confirmation. To engage in active listening, however, avoid hostile and loaded questions. Saying something like "Do you think I'm so stupid I believe the line you're feeding me?" is much different than saying "Are you saying that you're attracted to me?" Your goal is not to embarrass or trap the individual, but to give him or her an opportunity to clarify and elaborate on what you have said. You should also respect the communicator's time. Do not interrupt a communicator to ask a question unless it is appropriate. Often, paying close attention to nonverbal behaviors will help you know when it is appropriate to interrupt with a question, because nonverbal behaviors regulate the flow of conversation, especially discussion. Interpersonally, for example, a friend who is finished with a comment will usually pause and look you directly in the eyes. If the friend is pausing only momentarily, however, he or she briefly will look away and then

critical thinking
The process of making sound inferences based on accurate evidence and valid reasoning.

return to face you. This pause and glance away usually means the person is thinking about what to say next, not that he or she is finished talking.

Critical Listening and Thinking

Of the types of listening discussed thus far, critical listening is perhaps the most complex. Critical listening involves judgment of the soundness of messages. Are the message and the messenger credible? Are the inferences made by the communicator valid ones? Is the evidence offered to the listener clear and consistent in pointing to the conclusions being made? As emphasized in the previous chapter, not all communicators use their communication skills ethically. Not all communicators have thought through the credibility and consequences of the ideas they express. Thus, critical listening demands critical thinkers. **Critical thinking** involves making sound inferences based on accurate evidence and valid reasoning.

Assessing Arguments

Philosopher Stephen Toulmin suggests that much of communication involves arguments designed to elicit compliance or agreement. As a result of his belief, Toulmin developed a model of argument that is helpful in understanding the relationship between critical listening and critical thinking.[13] The model has three basic parts: (1) a claim, (2) grounds, (3) and a warrant. First, an arguer has a *claim,* or conclusion, that she or he wishes to establish. There must be *grounds,* or evidence, to support the claim. And there needs to be a link between the grounds and the claim, which is provided by a *warrant.*

Consider the process of buying a car. You consult *Consumer Reports* and narrow your choice between a Honda Civic and a Dodge Neon. You visit the Honda dealer first, whose salesperson makes the claim "This is a great car, the best in its class." A claim alone, however, does not make an argument; there must be some grounds. Thus, the salesperson might point out that Hondas get excellent gas mileage. This fact, however, is not enough for a valid argument. Maybe you are more concerned with high performance than gas mileage. Thus, there must be a warrant, or a reason to connect the grounds to the claim. In this case, the warrant would be that gas mileage is more important in choosing a car than performance.

Three additional features may be present in an argument. One feature is *backing,* which the arguer may provide to further support the warrant. Thus, the salesperson might point out that good gas mileage not only saves you money but is environmentally friendly as well. The salesperson may also present a *qualifier,* that "very likely" the Honda is the best car. Thus, he or she has admitted that some room for argument still exists.

After a while, you decide to visit the Dodge dealership. You tell the salesperson you are debating between a Honda Civic and a Dodge Neon. The Dodge salesperson immediately begins to argue against purchasing the Honda. This is called a *rebuttal*. The salesperson points out that the Neon is less expensive than the Honda, making the Neon a much better buy.

The Toulmin model can be depicted as in Figure 6-4. Figure 6-5 shows how the Toulmin model would look in our example of car shopping.

Critical listening and the companion process of critical thinking, then, frequently boil down to an analysis of grounds, warrants, and claims. In addition, critical listening and thinking may sometimes involve looking at backing, rebuttals, and qualifiers. Ultimately, however, two questions must be answered: Is the reasoning valid, that is, supported by grounds and backing, and is the evidence presented in support of the reasoning credible, that is, believable?

Recognizing Fallacies

To answer these questions, you need to listen for and recognize what constitutes sound reasoning and credible evidence. The critical thinker must be on guard against fallacies. A **fallacy** is an argument that appears sound at first glance but contains a flaw in reasoning which makes it unsound.[14] Returning to Toulmin's model, a fallacy is an argument that doesn't warrant the claim being made.

It is important to distinguish here between intentional and unintentional fallacies. Certainly not everyone who makes an error in reasoning is intending to deceive us. On the other hand, someone who is seeking to pull the wool over another person's eyes may indeed use fallacies intentionally. Either way, it is the listener and consumer of communication who must remain vigilant to avoid being misled, whether by accident or design, by fallacies.

Let's consider some of the types of fallacies that you should guard against. The discussion that follows should give you a flavor of the kinds of mistakes in reasoning that constitute fallacious argument. As a critical listener and thinker, you should watch out for these nine common fallacies.

Unsupported Assertion   There are a number of ways in which the grounds, or evidence, in support of an argument can be defective. The most serious case is the absence of any grounds to support a claim. The *unsupported assertion* is the absence of any argument at all. Fans of the syndicated sitcom *Cheers* probably recognize this tendency in Cliff Claven, who is always spouting the most absurd facts as if they were gospel. An argument without grounds is no argument at all. In the example discussed earlier about buying a car, unless the seller can prove the Honda gets good mileage (gas receipts, EPA ratings, and the like), the argument is worthless. The same is true about the rebuttal in which the seller claims that the Dodge has better performance than the Honda.

fallacy An argument based on faulty reasoning.

Distorted Evidence   Less easily discovered is the argument that relies on distorted evidence to support its claim. *Distorted evidence* occurs when significant

Figure 6-4 The Toulmin Model of Argument

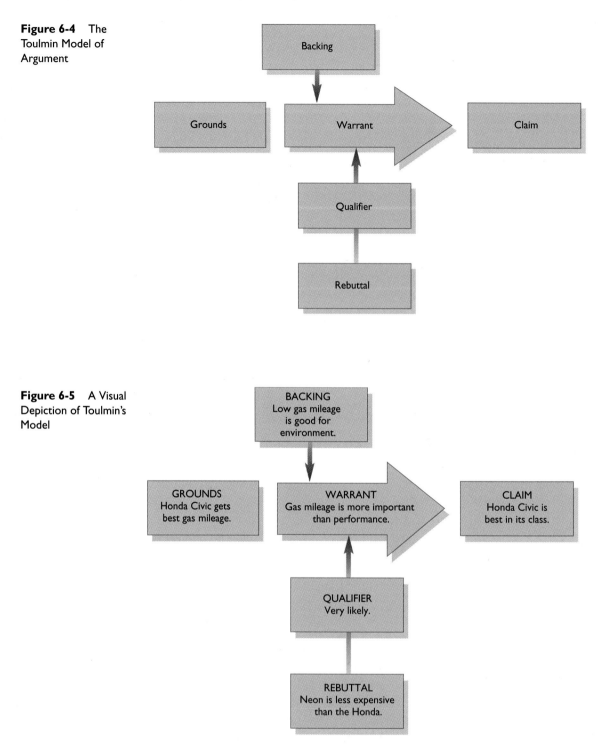

Figure 6-5 A Visual Depiction of Toulmin's Model

omissions or changes in the grounds of an argument are used to alter the argument's original intent. Political commercials are notorious for distorting evidence. For example, we recall one commercial in which one candidate, Mr. Smith, showed a brief excerpt of his opponent, Ms. Jones, stating, "I'll do anything to get reelected." The ad was highly damaging to Ms. Jones's campaign. However, the actual statement had been made in reference to what Ms. Jones predicted Mr. Smith would do if he were elected. What was actually said was something like "If Smith is elected, he's going to be one of those politicians who says, 'I'll do anything to get reelected.'"

Faulty Opinion Evidence *Faulty opinion evidence* occurs when the person expressing an opinion on a specialized topic lacks expertise in that area. Most people wouldn't trust their doctor to give stock tips, and nobody would allow their stockbroker to perform an operation. Further, even an expert may be unreliable if he or she has a biased point of view. Many of the medical experts hired by the Tobacco Institute to attempt to disprove the link between cigarette smoking and disease have impeccable credentials. However, because these medical experts usually are the recipients of grants from the tobacco industry, it is difficult to believe that their opinions are not clouded by a desire not to bite the hand that feeds their research.

Hasty Generalization Reasoning which overgeneralizes based on insufficient evidence is known as a *hasty generalization.* For example, many experiments in communication research use college students as the sample. If we are interested in how college students react to fear-arousing advertisements, we may be perfectly justified in generalizing from this group to college students as a class of people in the population. However, to generalize that the general population itself, from high school dropouts to senior citizens, would react the same way as our college sample is a hasty generalization.

False Analogy A *false analogy* occurs when two things that are not genuinely similar are compared as if they were essentially the same. Perhaps the most controversial example of an argument based on false analogy was during the trial of O. J. Simpson. Lead defense attorney Johnnie Cochran compared racist Los Angeles Police Detective Mark Fuhrman to Adolph Hitler. Despicable as Fuhrman's character was, there was no evidence that his racism had cost anyone's life. On the other hand, Hitler's racism directly led to the Holocaust, in which eight million people were put to death. To imply that Fuhrman and Hitler were exactly alike, therefore, was fallacious.

Post Hoc Reasoning and Mistaking Correlation for Cause Arguments dealing with effect-to-cause reasoning frequently commit the error of assuming that because one event preceded another, the first event must be the cause of the second. Technically, this is known as the *post hoc, ergo propter hoc* fallacy (after this, therefore because of this). Shortly after Bill Clinton was elected president in

Some people perceived that the North American Free Trade Agreement (NAFTA) was the first step down a slippery slope.

November 1992, the government reported that there had been a significant upturn in the economy. During the holiday shopping season, retailers had their best sales in years. Many Clinton supporters claimed that the optimism created by his election had bolstered consumer confidence and stimulated the economy, even before Clinton had taken office. Yet, Clinton's election in 1992 was no more responsible for the upturn in sales during the 1992 holiday shopping season than his economics alone were responsible for the downturn in sales during the 1995 holiday season. Just because one event was followed by another in no way proves that the first caused the second.

This kind of post hoc reasoning is similar to *mistaking correlation for cause,* which is the assumption that because two events occur at the same time, one event caused the other. The classic example of mistaking correlation for cause is the myth that the length of women's skirts is correlated to ups and downs in the stock market. The assumption that as one goes up, it causes the other to do likewise is truly voodoo economics.

Slippery Slope   The *slippery slope* fallacy is the assumption that a series of undesirable events will result from one action without there being any necessary relationship between the action and the projected consequences. This fallacy is expressed in the familiar saying "If you give them an inch, they'll take a mile."

How many times have you heard someone argue that a ban on assault rifles will lead to a ban on all guns? Or perhaps you've been told that if you don't get a college degree you will end up homeless and broke. As was the case with dis-

Box 6-7   Critical Thinking

Common Fallacies

When you are evaluating an argument, be sure to determine whether it contains any of the following arguments:

unsupported assertion   The absence of any argument at all.

distorted evidence   An argument in which significant omissions or changes in the grounds of a claim are used to alter the claim's original intent.

faulty opinion evidence   An opinion on a specialized topic from someone who lacks expertise in that area or has a biased point of view.

hasty generalization   An argument that over-generalizes from insufficient evidence.

false analogy   The comparison of two things that are similar in some ways as if they were essentially the same in all ways.

post hoc, ergo propter hoc (after this, therefore because of this)   The assumption that because one event preceded another, the first event must be the cause of the second.

mistaking correlation for cause   The assumption that because two events occur at the same time, one event caused the other.

slippery slope   The assumption that a series of undesirable events will result from one action without there being any necessary relationship between the action and the projected consequences.

non sequitur   A claim that does not follow from its premises.

torted evidence, politicians frequently use the slippery slope to persuade voters. Ross Perot, for example, argued while running for president in 1992 that if the North American Fair Trade Agreement was passed, the giant sucking noise we would all hear would be thousands of American jobs being swallowed by Mexico. To date, however, the number of American jobs lost to Mexico as a result of NAFTA hasn't made much of a statistical sound at all.

Non Sequitur   A *non sequitur* is a claim that does not follow from its premise, which is a proposition presumed to be true. Non sequiturs are the fallacy du jour on many talk radio programs. Some of the most frequently heard include that everyone on welfare is lazy, all liberals have bleeding hearts, there's no such thing as a conservative with a conscience, and environmentalists would rather see people starve than cut down a tree. People who say these kinds of things overstate what reasonably can be inferred from their premise. The fact that environmentalists may speak out to save trees doesn't warrant the claim that they think trees are more important than people. The same is true for those who characterize all conservatives as Ebenezer Scrooge.

Detecting these nine common fallacies, which are recapped in Box 6-7, is a major step in the process of critical listening and thinking. As a constant recipient of messages designed to influence you to spend money, vote a certain way, or comply with another person's request, you need to evaluate each message for its logical validity. These fallacies are some of the common techniques used in political propaganda, advertising, and interpersonal compliance-gaining situations. To the extent that you comply with messages based on logical fallacies, you are suspending your critical listening and thinking skills and allowing yourself to be manipulated.

Summary

Listening is but one more skill necessary to becoming a consciously competent communicator. Hearing and listening are not the same thing. Hearing involves recognition of sound whereas listening involves mental tasks such as, selective attention, sensorial involvement, comprehension/meaning, and retention/remembering.

There is more than one type of listening. We listen discriminately, comprehensively, appreciatively, therapeutically, and critically. Once we have made the conscious choice to actively listen, there are several things we can do to increase our overall listening skill. These include setting goals, blocking out distracting stimuli, suspending judgment, focusing on main points, recognizing highlights and signposts, taking effective notes, being sensitive to meta-communication, paraphrasing, and questioning.

Critical listening promotes critical thinking. To judge the validity of the messages we receive, we need to judge the validity of the arguments embedded in those messages. This involves critically thinking through an argument and examining its claim, warrant, grounds, backing, qualifiers, and relevant rebuttals. Finally, critical listening and thinking involves recognizing examples of fallacious reasoning, including unsupported assertions, distorted evidence, faulty opinion evidence, hasty generalizations, false analogies, post hoc reasoning, mistaking correlation for cause, slippery slopes, and non sequiturs.

Another Look

Articles

John Stewart. "Empathic Listening: A Symposium." *Communication Education* 32 (1983): 365-401.

This symposium includes articles by Ronald C. Arnett and Gordon Nakagawa, "The Assumptive Roots of Empathic Listening: A Critique"; John Stewart, "Interpretive Listening: An Alternative to Empathy"; and Gary T. Hunt and Louis P. Cusella, "A Field Study of Listening Needs in Organizations." The first article critiques assumptions underlying empathic listening. The second offers an alternative model of listening, termed "interpretative." The third article reports on the results of a survey of Fortune 500 companies, which found that training directors feel that listening skills of typical organizational members are inadequate.

Andrew D. Wolvin and Carolyn Gwynn Coakley. "A Survey of the Status of Listening Training in Some Fortune

500 Companies." *Communication Education* 40 (1991): 152-164.

This study reports on a survey of Fortune 500 company training directors. The majority of respondents offered listening training to their employees, focusing on active listening, paraphrasing, and nonverbal communication. Respondents reported that listening is perceived to be important in their companies.

Books

Andrew D. Wolvin and Carolyn G. Coakley. *Listening.* 3rd ed. Dubuque, Iowa: William C. Brown, 1988.

This is an excellent comprehensive book on listening. The authors deal in depth with all five types of listening—discriminative, comprehensive, therapeutic, critical, and appreciative. Specific methods for enhancing each type of listening skills are provided.

Brooke Noel Moore and Richard Parker. *Critical Thinking.* 4th ed. Mountain View, Calif.: Mayfield, 1995.

This is a very readable textbook on critical thinking, one of the most widely used in the United States. The book provides numerous examples of real-life fallacies of reasoning.

Video Rentals

In the Name of the Rose Based on semiologist Umberto Eco's critically acclaimed novel, this film stars Sean Connery and Christian Slater. It is both a murder mystery and a lesson in critical thinking as Connery employs his reasoning skills to figure out a very complicated sequence of events. Take notes as you watch, and try to discriminate between sound evidence and fallacies as they are communicated by central characters in the film's plot.

Talk Radio Oliver Stone directs Eric Bogosian, Alec Baldwin, and Ellen Green in this portrait of a person who is paid to listen and respond to callers. The film clearly demonstrates the qualitative differences among critical, discriminative, and therapeutic listening.

Theory and Research in Practice

1. Research focusing on conflict suggests we should try harder to document what we think we hear the other person saying. Documentation is needed because we often mis-hear the other person's message and react accordingly. During conflict, mis-heard messages and the reactions they provoke throw fuel on the fire, making conflict management more difficult than it needs to be. Talk to someone with whom you are close about whether this is a problem in your relationship. Explain the concept of documenting in general and paraphrasing specifically. Discuss how the two of you might use documenting and paraphrasing to better manage conflict when it occurs in your relationship.

2. This writing assignment involves becoming a fallacy detector. Pick an advertisement from any print medium—for example, magazines, newspapers, or direct mail. In a two- to three-page paper, identify at least three fallacies used in the advertisement. Define each fallacy in your own words. Cite the specific example of each fallacy from the ad, and explain why the example meets the definition. Finally, attach a copy of the ad to your paper with the fallacies highlighted on the copy.

3. Uncritical inference test:

Instructions

Read the following story. Assume that all the information presented in it is definitely accurate and true. Read it carefully because it has ambiguous parts designed to lead you astray. No need to memorize it, though. You can refer to it whenever you wish.

Next read the statements about the story and indicate whether you consider each statement true, false, or "?". "T" means that the statement is *definitely true* on the basis of the information presented in the story. "F" means that it is *definitely false*. "?" means that it may be either true or false and that you cannot be certain which on the basis of the information presented in the story. If any part of a statement is doubtful, make it "?". *Answer each statement in turn, and do not go back to change any answer later, and don't reread any statements after you have answered them. This will distort your score.*

To start with, here is a sample story with correct answers.

Sample Story

You arrive home late one evening and see that the lights are on in your living room. There is only one car parked in front of your house, and the words "Harold R. Jones, M.D." are spelled in small gold letters across one of the car's doors.

Statements About Sample Story

1. The car parked in front of your house has lettering on one of its doors.   Ⓣ F ?
   (This is a "Definitely true" statement because it is directly corroborated by the story.)

2. Someone in your family is sick.   T F ⑦
   (This could be true, and then again it might not be. Perhaps Dr. Jones is paying a social call at your home, or perhaps he has gone to the house next door or across the street, or maybe someone else is using the car.)

3. No car is parked in front of your house.   T Ⓕ ?
   (A "definitely false" statement because the story directly contradicts it.)

4. The car parked in front of your house belongs to a woman named Johnson.   T F ⑦
   (May seem very likely false, but can you be sure? Perhaps the car has just been sold.)

So much for the sample. It should warn you of some of the kinds of traps to look for. Now begin the actual test. Remember, mark each statement *in order*—don't skip around or change answers later.

The Story[1]

A businessman had just turned off the lights in the store when a man appeared and demanded money. The owner opened a cash register. The contents of the cash register were scooped up, and the man sped away. A member of the police force was notified promptly.

Statements About the Story

1. A man appeared after the owner had turned off his store lights.   T F ?

2. The robber was a *man*.   T F ?

3. The man who appeared did not demand money.
                                               T F ?

4. The man who opened the cash register was the owner.   T F ?

5. The store owner scooped up the contents of the cash register and ran away.   T F ?

6. Someone opened a cash register.   T F ?

7. After the man who demanded the money scooped up the contents of the cash register, he ran away.
                                               T F ?

8. While the cash register contained money, the story does *not* state *how much*.   T F ?

9. The robber demanded money of the owner.
                                               T F ?

10. A businessman had just turned off the lights when a man appeared in the store.   T F ?

11. It was broad daylight when the man appeared.
                                               T F ?

12. The man who appeared opened the cash register.
                                               T F ?

13. No one demanded money.   T F ?

14. The story concerns a series of events in which only three persons are referred to: the owner of the store, a man who demanded money, and a member of the police force.   T F ?

15. The following events occurred: someone demanded money; a cash register was opened; its contents were scooped up; and a man dashed out of the store.
                                               T F ?

---

[1]*The story and statements are a portion of the "Uncritical Inference Test," copyrighted 1955 and 1983 by William V. Haney. Excerpted with special permission from William V. Haney,* Communication and Interpersonal Relations, *6th ed. (Homewood, Ill.: R. D. Irwin, 1992), 231–33, 241.*

Answers to Uncritical Inference Test

1. ? Do you *know* that the "businessman" and the "owner" are one and the same?

2. ? Was there necessarily a robbery involved here? Perhaps the man was the rent collector—or the owner's son—they sometimes demand money.

3. F An easy one to keep up the test-taker's morale.

4. ? Was the owner a *man*?

5. ? May seem unlikely, but the story does not definitely preclude it.

6. T The story says that the owner opened the cash register.

7. ? We don't know who scooped up the contents of the cash register or that the man necessarily *ran* away.

8. ? The dependent clause is doubtful—the cash register may or may not have contained money.

9. ? Again, a robber?

10. ? Could the man merely have appeared *at* a door or a window without actually entering the store?

11. ? Stores generally keep lights on during the day.

12. ? Could not the man who appeared have been the owner?

13. F The story says that the man who appeared demanded money.

14. ? Are the businessman and the owner one and the same—or two different people? The same goes for the owner and the man who appeared.

15. ? "Dashed"? Could he not have "sped away" on roller skates or in a car? And do we know that he actually left the store? We don't even know that he entered it.

CHAPTER 7

Communication and Diversity

OBJECTIVES

After reading this chapter you should be able to:

- Describe and distinguish among cultural, group, and individual diversity.

- Critically discuss how the following dimensions of culture influence communication behavior: collectivism-individualism, power distance, uncertainty avoidance, and femininity-masculinity.

- Identify on your campus varying examples of cultural and group diversity.

- Distinguish among noble selves, rhetorical reflectors, and rhetorically sensitive communicators.

- Explain the role of self-monitoring and relational empathy in diversity-responsive communication.

- Construct examples of diversity-responsive speech.

Given the attention and controversy that diversity continues to stimulate, you might reasonably think that it is the exception rather than the rule. Of course, just the opposite is true. Whether or not we're always aware of it, diversity, both subtle and obvious, is all around us. It's axiomatic among biologists, moreover, that diversity is essential to the well-being of us and other living things.

The word *diversity* means "being different." Being different is a quality of which most of us are proud. Consider our ancestry or ethnic origins. Even though our ancestry or ethnic origins can be traced to one of the four hemispheres we use to geographically divide the globe, we usually do not think of our ancestry or ethnic origins in this way. We do not say, for example, "My ancestors are from the southern [or northern] hemisphere." Instead, we usually narrow our ancestry or ethnicity to a specific culture of people, proudly informing others that our roots can be traced to precolonial Africa, the penal colony of

Australia, the Anasazi forebears of the Hopi and Navajo, the Aztecs, Incans, and Mayans, the Romans and Normans, the Celts and Saxons. We celebrate, in other words, the diversity that distinguishes us from each other.

Thus, it is in this spirit of celebration that this chapter focuses on diversity-responsive communication. We believe diversity is just one more characteristic of the human condition to which competent communicators routinely adapt. We also believe and will show you that diversity-responsive communication involves many of the same competence-defining skills discussed thus far in our book. We begin by briefly revisiting the topic of perception in general and attribution specifically. We then cover

- three levels of diversity common to most dimensions of communication,
- the role of rhetorical sensitivity in diversity-responsive communication, and
- the related concepts of self-monitoring and relational empathy.

Perception and Attribution

During the 1950s, Dr. Wellington Koo, Chinese ambassador to the United States, was guest of honor and main speaker at a banquet hosted by Princeton University. As the story goes, a number of members of the student body were invited to represent their classmates, including a Princeton football player who found himself seated next to Dr. Koo. Obviously feeling out of place at the highly formal banquet, the student kept looking and smiling at Dr. Koo, completely at a loss for words. Finally, following the first course, the student turned to Dr. Koo and said, "Likee soupee?" The ambassador only smiled in return and remained silent until he was introduced to speak.

After the speech, which was delivered eloquently and in flawless English, Dr. Koo returned to his seat to face the now dumbstruck and even more embarrassed undergraduate. This time, however, Dr. Koo inquired of the undergraduate, "Likee speechee?"[1]

Recall from Chapter 2 that perception is the process by which we give meaning to experience. Remember as well that perception is easily biased by experience or the lack thereof, the latter being the case with the Princeton undergraduate in the anecdote. Although diversity is all around us, many of us have little or no experience with people whose culture, societal group, or individual background is dissimilar to our own. Not only can this lack of experience cause perceptual bias, but it can also cause inaccurate attributions about the diverse people with whom we come into contact.

Attributions are the reasons we give to explain our own behaviors and the behaviors of others as well. Typically, the more similar people are to us, the more accurate the attributions we make about them. The opposite also is typically true. The more dissimilar people are to us, the less accurate the attributions we make about them.

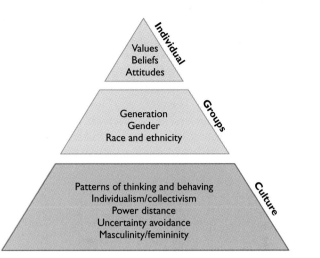

Figure 7-1 Hofstede's Levels of Diversity

Perceptual bias and inaccurate attributions are especially likely when we come into contact with people whose cultural background is dissimilar to our own. To begin with, most of us are fairly **ethnocentric** when it comes to culture. This means we are predisposed to perceive our own culture as superior to other cultures.[2] Second, many of us have little direct experience with people whose culture is dissimilar to our own. Ethnocentrism and the ignorance our inexperience can spawn can lead to very inaccurate attributions about people from other cultures. Further, this combination of ethnocentrism and ignorance can be a potent source of conflict between people from dissimilar cultures.

The best way to guard against the perceptual bias and inaccurate attributions that work against diversity-responsive communication is to learn about the levels of diversity around us. The more we know about human diversity, the more confidently we can predict what will constitute appropriate communication with the diverse people we meet.

The Levels of Diversity

Diversity is part of our culture, even though we don't always see it or treat it as such. Consider a team like the Chicago Bulls and three of its marquee players: Michael Jordan, Scottie Pippen, and Dennis Rodman. In many ways they are similar to each other. Yet both on and off the court they also are dissimilar. Jordan is the team leader and most gifted player. Pippen is the team's play maker and steadiest outside threat to consistently score from the perimeter. Rodman rarely shoots, preferring to rebound. Whereas Jordan's and Pippen's behavior is fairly straight-laced, Rodman goes out of his way to be outrageous. Off the court, Jordan and Pippen try to keep their personal lives private, whereas Rodman has posed nude for a national magazine.

ethnocentrism The belief that one's own culture is superior to other cultures.

cultural diversity
Differences in patterns of thinking, feeling, and behaving due to differences among cultures.

People sometimes mistakenly believe that diversity is exclusively a cultural issue. There is more to diversity than the culture with which people primarily identify. Diversity also is reflected in the societal groups with which people most identify and in their individual histories as well. Figure 7-1 depicts the three levels of diversity: cultural, group, and individual.

Simply put, diversity isn't always obvious. The more you know about the cultural, group, and individual diversity of the people with whom you communicate, the more likely it is that your communication behavior will be appropriate and effective.

Cultural Diversity

Cultural diversity is on the rise in the United States. Scholars generally agree that culture is better described than rigidly defined. Most would also agree that culture is the collective pattern of thinking, feeling, and acting characteristic of a specific human society. One's culture includes recorded history, literature, and music. According to communication scholar Geert Hofstede, one's culture also includes how people go about "greeting, eating, showing or not showing feelings, keeping a certain physical distance from others, making love, or maintaining body hygiene."[3]

Culture is learned. Further, people have a tendency to assume that the culture into which they were born is at the center of the universe. As we said earlier, this ethnocentrism often leads people to also believe that their culture is superior to all other cultures. Historically, this belief has been a major source of conflict between cultures. It also is a prime source of intolerance.

Overcoming this kind of intolerance and the inappropriate communication it fosters requires a commitment to learning about cultures other than our own. Since the list of specific things that distinguish one culture from the next is inexhaustible, this commitment may strike you as impossible to make. Yet, **cultural literacy,** that is, the ability to interpret and appropriately respond to the communication behaviors of people from other cultures, doesn't mean trying to memorize the millions of nuances that distinguish cultures from each other. To the contrary, discovering what is common but variable among cultures is the key to cultural literacy.

Hofstede says that all cultures are characterized by four value dimensions:[4]

cultural literacy
The ability to interpret and appropriately respond to the communication behaviors of people from cultures other than one's own.

- collectivism-individualism,
- power distance,
- uncertainty avoidance, and
- femininity-masculinity.

Hofstede contends that these dimensions vary in degree from one culture to the next. Competence in identifying and adapting to these different degrees is the first important measure of cultural literacy.

All cultures can be located somewhere on the continuum between **collectivism** and **individualism.** Some cultures, notably Asian and Native American cultures, are closer to the collectivism end and believe the good of the many far outweighs the good of the few. People in these collectivist cultures shun the individual spotlight. Singling out a member of a collectivist culture during a group discussion or while you are giving a speech is likely to embarrass the person.

In cultures where "rugged individualism" is admired and encouraged, the opposite is true. In the United States, where the predominant culture is very individualistic, we champion lone wolf entrepreneurs who strike it rich, quarterbacks who stand alone in the pocket, and politicians who march to the beat of a different drummer. There is evidence to believe, in fact, that the United States is the most individualistic nation on earth (see Table 7-1). Being singled out from the crowd here is a badge of honor.

The degree to which a culture is individualistic or collectivistic influences how the people of that culture communicate with each other. In highly individualistic countries, such as the United States, communication frequently is competitive. People use their communication skills to win arguments, make others comply with their demands, or gain the upper hand in a negotiation. People from highly collectivist countries tend to be more cooperative in their approach to communicating. Reaching consensus, mutual agreement, or harmony through communication is emphasized and valued.

Cultures and their members are not 100 percent individualistic or 100 percent collectivistic. Both dimensions are mediated by important factors such as biological sex and gender as well as by individual personality traits. Women in the United States, for instance, tend to be more collectivistic in perspective than are men. To be truly culturally literate about this or any other dimension of diversity, therefore, you need to know both the rule and the major exceptions to it. The questions in Box 7-1 will help you assess your own mix of collectivism and individualism.

The second dimension of culture is **power distance** (Table 7-2). This dimension concerns the degree to which inequality exists and how it affects people. Power distance influences communication in at least two important respects. The first is the degree to which people depend on the sources of power in their culture for directions about how to behave. In the former Soviet Union, for example, most sources of power rested with the state and the official Communist Party. Thus, people not only looked to the state and the party for behavioral guidance, but were expected to do so.

The second way power distance influences communication is in terms of deference. In some cultures, people defer to those with more power about matters ranging from where their children should go to school to the manner in which they go about a work-related task. In egalitarian cultures, however, a person with less power may openly challenge a person who obviously has more. Students in American colleges and universities are encouraged to challenge their instructors' ideas. Expectancies about their instructors being available for office hours and other consultations outside of class, moreover, are high.

collectivism
Cultural attitude that the good of the many far outweighs the good of the few.

individualism
Cultural attitude that emphasizes the individual over the group.

power distance
Cultural attitude about the degree to which inequality exists and how it affects people.

Table 7-1   Individualism-Collectivism Rankings of Countries

COUNTRY	HIGHLY INDIVIDUALISTIC COUNTRIES
United States	
Australia	
Great Britain	
Canada	
Netherlands	
New Zealand	
Italy	
Belgium	
Denmark	
France	
Sweden	
Ireland	
Norway	
Switzerland	
Germany	
South Africa	
Finland	
Austria	NOTE: A country listed near
Israel	the top of the scale indicates
Spain	an individualistic preference;
India	a listing near the bottom of
Argentina	the scale indicates a
Japan	collectivistic preference.
Iran	
Brazil	
Turkey	
Greece	
Philippines	
Mexico	
Portugal	
Chile	
Singapore	
Thailand	
Taiwan	
Peru	
Pakistan	
Colombia	
Venezuela	
Panama	
Ecuador	
Guatemala	**HIGHLY COLLECTIVISTIC COUNTRIES**

SOURCE: Adapted from Geert Hofstede, *Cultures and Organizations: Software of the Mind* (London: McGraw-Hill), 53. Reprinted with permission of the author and publisher.

Box 7-1   Self-Assessment

What Is Your Collectivism-Individualism Score?

The purpose of this questionnaire is to help you assess your individualistic and collectivistic tendencies. Respond by indicating the degree to which the values reflected in each phrase are important to you: opposed to your values (answer 1), not important to you (answer 2), somewhat important to you (answer 3), important to you (answer 4), or very important to you (answer 5).

_____ 1. Obtaining pleasure or sensuous gratification

_____ 2. Preserving the welfare of others

_____ 3. Being successful by demonstrating my individual competency

_____ 4. Restraining my behavior if it is going to harm others

_____ 5. Being independent in thought and action

_____ 6. Having safety and stability of people with whom I identify

_____ 7. Obtaining status and prestige

_____ 8. Having harmony in my relations with others

_____ 9. Having an exciting and challenging life

_____ 10. Accepting cultural and religious traditions

_____ 11. Being recognized for my individual work

_____ 12. Avoiding the violation of social norms

_____ 13. Leading a comfortable life

_____ 14. Living in a stable society

_____ 15. Being logical in my approach to work

_____ 16. Being polite to others

_____ 17. Being ambitious

_____ 18. Being self-controlled

_____ 19. Being able to choose what I do

_____ 20. Enhancing the welfare of others

To find your individualism score, add your responses to the _odd-numbered_ items. To find your collectivism score, add your responses to the _even-numbered_ items. Both scores will range from 10 to 50. The higher your scores, the more individualistic and/or collectivistic you are.

SOURCE: William B. Gudykunst, _Bridging Differences,_ 2nd ed. (Newbury Park, Calif.: Sage, 1994). © Sage Publications, Inc. Reprinted by permission.

In cultures with greater power distance, it would never even occur to students that they have the right to challenge an instructor's thinking, demand time outside of class, or mingle socially with instructors. For example, Japanese and Taiwanese students attending school in the United States are often shocked to see how informally students treat their instructors.

The manner in which people acquire power also varies from culture to culture. In some cultures, power is a consequence of entitlement, age, and education. In others, power is a consequence of how much money or fame or both a person has. Thus, when you are communicating with people from other cul-

Table 7-2 Power-Distance Rankings of Countries

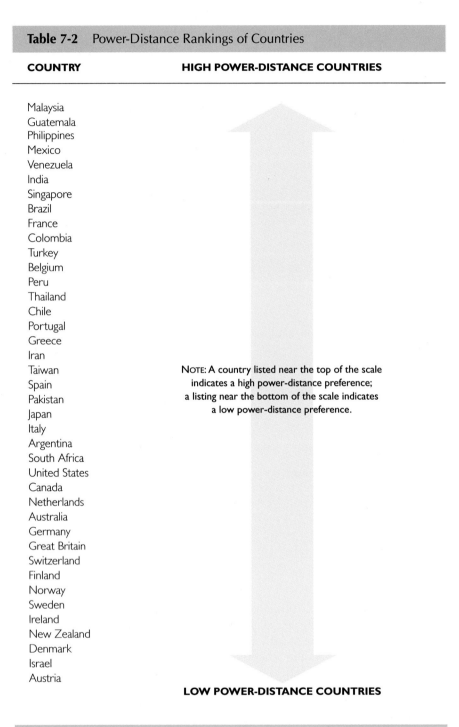

COUNTRY	HIGH POWER-DISTANCE COUNTRIES
Malaysia	
Guatemala	
Philippines	
Mexico	
Venezuela	
India	
Singapore	
Brazil	
France	
Colombia	
Turkey	
Belgium	
Peru	
Thailand	
Chile	
Portugal	
Greece	
Iran	
Taiwan	NOTE: A country listed near the top of the scale indicates a high power-distance preference; a listing near the bottom of the scale indicates a low power-distance preference.
Spain	
Pakistan	
Japan	
Italy	
Argentina	
South Africa	
United States	
Canada	
Netherlands	
Australia	
Germany	
Great Britain	
Switzerland	
Finland	
Norway	
Sweden	
Ireland	
New Zealand	
Denmark	
Israel	
Austria	**LOW POWER-DISTANCE COUNTRIES**

SOURCE: Adapted from Geert Hofstede, *Cultures and Organizations: Software of the Mind* (London: McGraw-Hill, 1991), 26. Reprinted with permission of the author and copyright holder.

tures, it is a good idea to learn about and respect both the sources of power within a culture and the manner in which power is typically acquired. It is also a good idea to then learn about the degree to which cultural norms about power distance influence communication transactions.

The third value dimension Hofstede discusses is **uncertainty avoidance.** As a student, you know all about uncertainty and the feelings of discomfort that can accompany it. Instructors who are vague about assignments, tests, due dates, and evaluation not only create uncertainty but sometimes are the ones students try to avoid. Further, just as people vary in terms of the amount of uncertainty they can tolerate, so do whole cultures vary in this regard.

Cultures with a high level of uncertainty avoidance tend to value tradition and conformity. Rules and regulations make life seem less uncertain and can reduce anxiety. Except for Japan, the top 10 countries in the ranking for uncertainty avoidance (shown in Table 7-3) are either predominantly Roman Catholic or Greek Orthodox. Both of these religions are based on the assumption that there is such a thing as absolute truth.

In contrast, cultures that have a high tolerance for uncertainty and ambiguity, such as the Netherlands and the Scandinavian countries, tend to have a more relativistic view. They tend to be more accepting of nonconformity and social deviance. Whereas single women and widows can be treated as social outcasts in many of the high-uncertainty-avoidance cultures, premarital sex and prostitution don't raise many eyebrows in cultures that have a high tolerance for uncertainty.

As befits a democracy founded on the values of civil liberties, such as the freedoms of speech, press, and religion, the United States is toward the tolerant end of the uncertainty spectrum. However, there are variations among groups and individuals within the United States. People in big cities tend to be more tolerant of a variety of lifestyles than are people in small rural towns. Conservative Christians are generally more likely to condemn a deviation from traditional "family values" than are people who are not strongly religious. Some people (such as the supporters of English-only laws, described in Box 7-2) feel strongly that everyone should speak the same language, whereas others enjoy linguistic and cultural diversity. And some individuals are anxious in the face of any kind of uncertainty, whereas others find it easy to just go with the flow.

The final value dimension of culture in Hofstede's scheme is **femininity-masculinity** (Table 7-4). As Hofstede points out, a number of biological attributes between women and men are statistically constant throughout the world. Men are taller, heavier, and physically stronger whether we're talking about Sri Lanka or Syracuse, New York. But Hofstede also points out something much more important when it comes to people communicating: The gender roles deemed suitable for men and women vary tremendously around the world. Thus, this final dimension is best viewed as one that concerns gender rather than biological sex. Biological sex is genetically determined. Gender is a cultural creation.[5]

Masculinity and femininity influence both gender roles and the manner in which people communicate. Cultures that are high in masculinity assign distinctly different gender roles to men and women. The roles assigned to men tend

uncertainty avoidance Cultural attitude about the degree to which ambiguity is tolerated.

femininity-masculinity Cultural attitude about the degree to which gender roles are assigned on the basis of biological sex.

Table 7-3   Uncertainty-Avoidance Rankings of Countries and Regions

COUNTRY	HIGH UNCERTAINTY-AVOIDANCE CULTURES
Greece	
Portugal	
Guatemala	
Belgium	
Japan	
Peru	
France	
Chile	
Spain	
Argentina	
Turkey	
South Korea	
Mexico	
Israel	
Colombia	
Venezuela	
Brazil	
Italy	NOTE: A country listed near the top of the scale
Pakistan	indicates a high uncertainty-avoidance culture;
Austria	a listing near the bottom of the scale
Taiwan	indicates a low uncertainty-avoidance culture.
Germany	
Thailand	
Iran	
Finland	
Switzerland	
Netherlands	
Australia	
Norway	
South Africa	
New Zealand	
Canada	
United States	
Philippines	
India	
Great Britain	
Ireland	
Sweden	
Denmark	
Jamaica	
Singapore	
	LOW UNCERTAINTY-AVOIDANCE CULTURES

SOURCE: Adapted from Geert Hofstede, *Cultures and Organizations: Software of the Mind* (London: McGraw-Hill, 1991), 113. Reprinted with permission of the author and copyright holder.

Box 7-2   Critical Thinking

Monolingual or Multilingual?

In cities and states where the non-English-speaking population is growing—for example, Miami, Florida, and Los Angeles, California—language is no longer a monolingual issue. Businesses, government offices, and schools find that English is no longer sufficient to accommodate the needs of the population. Whereas many residents of such cities and states have accepted and adapted to diversity in spoken and written language, others have reacted negatively. In Dade County, Florida, and the state of California, mea- sures have been passed declaring that English is the "official language."

What is your opinion of English-only laws? How do they affect the communication of people who are not fluent in English? Should schools provide bilingual classes? Should voting materials be provided in more than one language? Should hospitals and courts provide interpreters for people who do not speak English? Does society have any reasons to accommodate those who understand another language better?

to be more public, prestigious, and financially profitable than the gender roles assigned to women. The communication behaviors of men and women in cultures high in masculinity reflect men's and women's roles. Men are assertive and use powerful language like that described in Chapter 3. Conversely, women are more deferential and qualify their communication behaviors with language that undermines their credibility—for instance, tag questions.

The reverse is true of cultures high in femininity. Although men and women differ in their values in such cultures, their gender roles and communication behaviors are less distinct. In the Scandinavian countries, as a case in point, women are just as likely as men to enjoy high status and well-paying jobs. As you might predict, these powerful roles also produce styles of communicating that are not nearly as reflective of men's and women's roles as are the communication styles in the masculine cultures mentioned above.

Before moving on, we want to emphasize a couple of matters. First, these four dimensions of culture are interdependent rather than independent. Thus, the degree to which a culture is masculine or feminine will influence the degree to which the culture is individualistic or collectivistic, how strong or weak the culture is with respect to uncertainty avoidance, and the degree of power distance in the culture. Second, the fact that these dimensions are interdependent makes communication between people from different cultures more complex than would be the case if the dimensions were independent.

Social psychologist Harry Triandis illustrates the complexity of intercultural communication in an actual transaction between an American supervisor and a Greek subordinate. Their attributions and messages not only are inaccurate but also reflect the different power-distance norms that characterize the two cultures.[6]

Table 7-4 Masculinity–Femininity Rankings of Countries

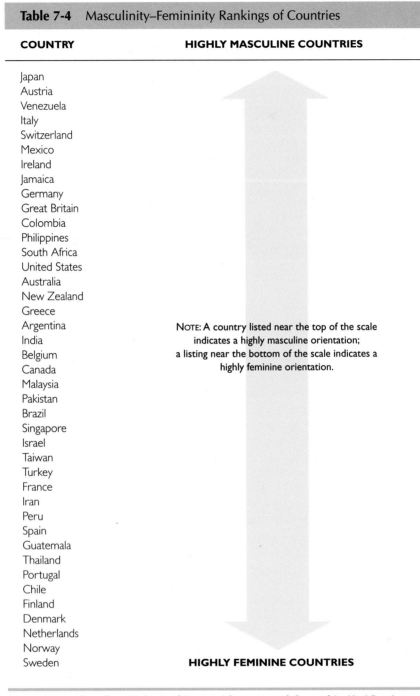

COUNTRY	HIGHLY MASCULINE COUNTRIES
Japan	
Austria	
Venezuela	
Italy	
Switzerland	
Mexico	
Ireland	
Jamaica	
Germany	
Great Britain	
Colombia	
Philippines	
South Africa	
United States	
Australia	
New Zealand	
Greece	
Argentina	NOTE: A country listed near the top of the scale indicates a highly masculine orientation; a listing near the bottom of the scale indicates a highly feminine orientation.
India	
Belgium	
Canada	
Malaysia	
Pakistan	
Brazil	
Singapore	
Israel	
Taiwan	
Turkey	
France	
Iran	
Peru	
Spain	
Guatemala	
Thailand	
Portugal	
Chile	
Finland	
Denmark	
Netherlands	
Norway	
Sweden	HIGHLY FEMININE COUNTRIES

SOURCE: Adapted from Geert Hofstede, *Cultures and Organizations: Software of the Mind* (London: McGraw-Hill, 1991), 84. Reprinted with permission of the author and copyright holder.

Message	Attribution
AMERICAN: "How long will it take you to finish this report?"	AMERICAN: I asked him to participate. GREEK: His behavior makes no sense. He is the boss. Why doesn't he tell me?
GREEK: "I do not know. How long should it take?"	AMERICAN: He refuses to take responsibility. GREEK: I asked him for an order.
AMERICAN: "You are in the best position to analyze time requirements."	AMERICAN: I press him to take responsibility for his own actions. GREEK: What nonsense! I better give him an answer.
GREEK: "Ten days."	AMERICAN: He lacks the ability to estimate time; this estimate is totally inadequate.
AMERICAN: "Take 15. It is agreed you will do it in 15 days."	AMERICAN: I offer a contract. GREEK: These are my orders. Fifteen days.

In fact the report needed 30 days of regular work. So the Greek worked day and night, but at the end of the 15th day, he still needed one more day's work.

Message	Attribution
AMERICAN: "Where is my report?"	AMERICAN: I am making sure he fulfills his contract. GREEK: He is asking for the report.
GREEK: "It will be ready tomorrow."	(Both attribute that the report is not ready.)
AMERICAN: "But we agreed that it would be ready today."	AMERICAN: I must teach him to fulfill a contract. GREEK: The stupid, incompetent boss! Not only did he give me wrong orders, but he does not appreciate that I did a 30-day job in 16 days.
The Greek hands in his resignation.	The American is surprised. GREEK: I can't work for such a man.

Important as it is to recognize how cultural dimensions influence behavior, there is still much more to the story of diversity. Collectivism-individualism, power distance, avoidance of uncertainty, and femininity-masculinity are just

group diversity
Differences in patterns of thinking, feeling, and behaving due to differences among groups in a society.

the beginning. Even if a culture is high in a particular dimension, not every member of that culture is so inclined. Our group affiliations and our personal experiences, as well as our culture, influence our personal values and behavior.

Group Diversity

Group diversity is the second characteristic you'll want to examine to better understand the people with whom you come into contact. The groups to which people belong and identify help to shape how they experience and interpret their world.[7] These groups also shape the way their members relate and communicate not only with each other but with people outside the group as well. Some of the groups in which people generally see themselves belonging reflect

- the geographic region they refer to as "home,"
- their race and ethnicity (which subsume nationality and native language),
- their gender,
- their religion,
- their socioeconomic class, and
- their generation.

Geographic Region   The student body of many colleges and universities reflects considerable geographic diversity. The place people consider "home" colors their perceptions and influences their communication behavior. Rural students, for example, often relate differently to people and environments than do students from urban backgrounds. Rural and urban students need to understand that they may see things differently. The same is true for students who consider themselves midwestern, northern, eastern, southern, and western American. These different geographic regions often lead to regional differences in such behaviors as eye contact, smiling at strangers, or simply saying "hello." Just as it is important to know about people's culture in order to communicate competently with them, you should know about their geographic region as well.

race   A socially defined category of people who share certain physical characteristics.

ethnicity   Cultural, national, and/or linguistic affiliation.

Race and Ethnicity   Similarity is a powerful agent of attraction among people. Thus, the fact that people congregate on the basis of their **race** and **ethnicity** is not surprising. A racial group is one that is socially defined on the basis of shared physical characteristics.[8] An ethnic group is one that is defined on the basis of cultural, national, or linguistic affiliation.[9] The United States is a multiracial, multiethnic nation. With the exception of Native Americans, 98 percent of the population can trace its ancestry to another country. The racial and ethnic mix varies from region to region, and as Box 7-3 shows, the mix can make a difference.

Although race and ethnicity sometimes seem obvious, they are less so than you may think. Consider the people in your class. Perhaps two of them have last names that suggest Slavic ancestry. Yet, to use their names as evidence of com-

Box 7-3   Considering Diversity

What Will a Town Without Diversity Do?

As a result of growth and the need to expand your manufacturing ability, your business is searching for a new plant site. After controlling for costs, you are wondering whether you should consider the diversity of the communities in which you are thinking about building. Sound far-fetched? Consider the case of American Type Culture Collection, a biotechnology company just outside of Baltimore. Despite being offered $25 million in incentives to open offices in Des Moines, Iowa, American Type Culture Collection decided against it. The reason? According to company officials, Des Moines simply wasn't diverse enough racially. Company officials believed that their minority employees would be adversely affected. According to 1990 U.S. Census figures, Des Moines's population was 7 percent African American, 2.4 percent each Asian and Latino, and over 87 percent white. In contrast, Baltimore was almost 60 percent black, about 1 percent each Asian and Latino, and about 38 percent white.

If you listen to Max Phillips, an executive with U.S. West and co-chairman of the Des Moines Chamber of Commerce Diversity Committee, the demographic profile of a city is increasingly important to businesses considering opening offices or relocating there. With others in your class, discuss American Type Culture Collection's racially based decision. Also, discuss the possible role that diversity plays or will play in your deliberations over such things as where to live, work, and go to school.

SOURCE: Dirk Johnson, "White Communities: A Corporate Deterrent," *New York Times*, 18 April 1994, C1.

mon ethnicity would be a serious mistake. One student could be Bosnian and the other could be Serbian. Along the same lines, two other students in your class may speak with a Spanish accent. Although they share a language, they do not necessarily share race or ethnicity. One student might be of Spanish ancestry and the other of Mayan ancestry. To confuse the two would be a mistake.

Diversity-responsive communication demands that you look beyond what you assume are obvious signs of race and ethnicity. The pigment in a person's skin, after all, can be every bit as misleading as it is informative. That's why it is so important that we talk to people about their background, including their race and ethnicity.

Gender   As we said earlier when discussing masculinity and femininity, gender is a cultural creation, not a genetic one. Gender's influence on how people perceive themselves and others is a subject receiving considerable scholarly attention. Consider the case of police officers and firefighters. Once these two occupational roles were exclusively defined as male. Of course this situation has changed and continues to change, with many women now counted in the ranks of police and fire departments. Gender roles in the United States are becoming more rather than less diverse. We cannot afford to think and communicate about gender in the narrow terms people once did. Today the gender roles of men and women may or may not have anything to do with their biological sex.

Religion   Even at well-known sectarian universities like Notre Dame, you will find diversity in the religious beliefs of groups of students. Of course, at public colleges and universities religious diversity is even greater. In some cases, people's religion may be identified on the basis of apparel and appearance. Such cases include the Amish, Hasidic Jews, some Muslims, and Sikhs. Usually, however, the religious diversity on your campus or at work will not be discernible from people's clothing and appearance.

Christian students frequently refer to their breaks from schools in sectarian terms. No matter how it is described officially, a recess in December is discussed as Christmas break, and a recess in the spring commonly is called Easter break. Asking a Jewish student about plans for Easter break or a Muslim student about Christmas plans may seem innocuous in the eyes of Christian students. Yet, when this oversight is added to the fact that there are no corresponding school-wide breaks for Jewish and Muslim holy days, its potential to unnecessarily discriminate may became apparent. We cannot emphasize enough, therefore, how important it is for you to consider religious diversity as an inherent feature of your communication environment.

Socioeconomic Class   College and university classrooms were once the exclusive domain of the socioeconomic elite. But after World War II, the G.I. Bill enabled hundreds of thousands of men and a smaller number of women from diverse socioeconomic circumstances to attend colleges and universities. This trend continues, except women (who now constitute 55 percent of all college students) are a much more prevalent part of the mix.[10] Thus, in today's classroom there may be students from impoverished backgrounds as well as students from well-to-do families. Making predictions about people on the basis of perceptions of socioeconomic status is risky at best.

Generational Diversity   Another form of group diversity that is increasingly evident on college campuses is generational. Whereas classrooms were once populated mostly by those age 25 and under, this is no longer the case. Longer life, corporate downsizing, changes in gender roles, and industrial innovation have all contributed in making today's campus multigenerational. Just as people's racial or ethnic group influences their perceptions and interactions with others, so too does the generational group with which they most identify. It remains, in many respects, people's peer group throughout their lives. Thus, one's generational group is likely to influence historical points of reference, musical preferences, beliefs, attitudes, and values.

Although the types of groups we've been discussing are representative of group diversity, they don't encompass all the types of group diversity in modern life. Other important groups include but are not limited to professional groups, political groups, and groups of activists, such as those in the disability rights movement.

Individual Diversity

Up to this point, our discussion of diversity has focused on its broader limits. People's cultural backgrounds and the groups to which they belong tell us much about how they are likely to perceive the world and communicate with the people in it. However, it is **individual diversity** that truly makes every human being unique. Recognizing people as individuals is one of the distinguishing characteristics of the competent communicator.

Individual diversity is deeply embedded in our personal beliefs, attitudes, and values. A *belief* is a conviction about whether something is true or false. Some beliefs are relatively obvious and incontrovertible. For example, we all (presumably) share a belief that the earth is round. On the other hand, some beliefs can be controversial, like those concerning issues such as the existence of God, the effects of TV violence on behavior, and the medical benefits of marijuana.

Attitudes interact with our beliefs. Attitudes are predispositions to respond in a consistently favorable or unfavorable manner to physical and psychological objects. Over the course of our lives, we develop innumerable attitudes about countless numbers of objects, ranging from our favorite food to the most heated issues of the day.

Values are more general than attitudes. They are enduring beliefs about good and evil, what is moral and immoral. Underlying opposition to capital punishment, for example, is not only the belief that capital punishment is not an effective deterrent to murder but also the value that killing is always wrong, whatever the reason.

According to psychologist Milton Rokeach, some values are terminal and others are *instrumental*.[11] *Terminal* values concern goals. A comfortable or exciting life, a sense of accomplishment, a world at peace, a world of beauty, equality, family security, freedom, and happiness are examples of terminal values. *Instrumental* values concern modes of conduct, which are guides to behavior and the means by which we achieve the goals specified in our terminal values. Examples of instrumental values include ambitiousness, broad-mindedness, capableness, cheerfulness, cleanliness, courage, forgiveness, helpfulness, and honesty.

Although one might not always agree with what constitutes a terminal value and what constitutes an instrumental value—for example, honesty can certainly be viewed as an end in itself—the basic notion is useful. Some values are desirable in and of themselves, whereas others are instruments for achieving higher, terminal values. For example, forgiveness and courage may be seen as means to achieving world peace.

Values are very difficult to change because they are learned at an early age and widely shared among people. Such values as fairness, justice, and patriotism not only are fundamental but also are taught to us in our most formative years. Depending on the degree to which they come into contact with others who are dissimilar, people can spend their entire lives without having their basic values challenged.

individual diversity
Differences in patterns of thinking, feeling, and behaving due to differences of individual characteristics and experiences.

People's beliefs, attitudes, and values are inextricably tied to both their cultural heritage and the groups to which they belong. Individual diversity isn't separate from cultural and group diversity. The point is not that cultural, group, and individual diversity are unrelated, but that we can never learn everything we need to know about people on the basis of cultural or group diversity alone. This is especially true when people are labeled on the basis of one of the groups with which they affiliate. Consider disability and sexual orientation. We commonly group people into categories of able or disabled and straight, gay, or lesbian. Yet, people with physical disabilities may have perfectly able minds, and not all gay men are feminine, nor are all lesbians masculine. People who happen to be disabled, or gay, or lesbian are individuals in their own right.

At this point, we can begin to see that diversity-responsive communication involves more than thinking multiculturally or being sensitive to legally protected groups that historically have been discriminated against. Diversity-responsive communication also involves moving beyond knowledge about people's culture and group membership to the beliefs, attitudes, and values that make every individual unique. Diversity-responsive communication is, as you are about to see, rhetorically sensitive communication.

Rhetorical Sensitivity

Knowledge and understanding of diversity are one thing. Putting this knowledge and understanding to constructive use is another. Thus, this is a good time to introduce the concept of rhetorical sensitivity and the communication skills characteristic of rhetorical sensitivity. People who are **rhetorically sensitive** do their best to appropriately adapt their communication to the environment in which they find themselves and to the diverse people who occupy the environment. To use the term introduced by scholars Roderick Hart and Don Burks, rhetorically sensitive communicators are best understood first in contrast to their two counterparts: the noble self and the rhetorical reflector.[12]

If you have read or seen Shakespeare's play *Hamlet,* then perhaps you recall the advice of one of its characters, Polonius, to his son: "This above all else, to thine own self be true." This line could be the credo of the **noble self,** the first counterpart to rhetorically sensitive communicators. Noble selves are unwavering in their belief that they must be true to their convictions. Practically speaking, this means noble selves communicate what they believe, regardless of context and people. To suggest that this inflexibility puts noble selves in the position of communicating inappropriately in today's diverse world would be an understatement. Consider the idea of cultural relativism. Introduced by the famous anthropologist Claude Lévi-Strauss, **cultural relativism** admonishes people from using the criteria for appropriate behavior in their own culture to judge appropriate behavior in another. People who subscribe to cultural relativism try to understand another culture's rules for behavior, even if they don't necessarily agree with them. Not only would noble selves reject another culture's

rhetorically sensitive communicator
Communicator who is adaptive, flexible, appreciative of human diversity, and interaction conscious.

noble self
Communicator who is unwavering in communicating his or her convictions.

cultural relativism
The idea that it is inappropriate for the members of one culture to apply the criteria for appropriate behavior in their culture to another culture.

rhetorical reflector
Communicator who tries to adapt to the situation, even if it requires communicating a false image.

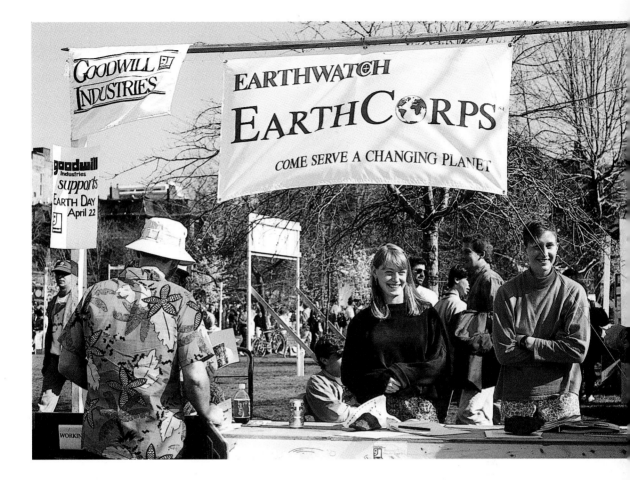

rules if they disagreed with them, their communication behavior would exemplify the fact. Noble selves' rejection of another culture's rules, moreover, would severely undermine their communication effectiveness.

In sharp contrast, **rhetorical reflectors** are chameleon-like in their communication behavior. They wouldn't dare say what they believed unless they thought it would allow them to ingratiate the people with whom they are communicating. Unlike noble selves, who are true to their convictions no matter what the consequence, rhetorical reflectors believe their messages should always be based on the ends they hope to achieve.

People who are rhetorically sensitive are adaptive communicators. While recognizing the importance of being true to oneself, rhetorically sensitive communicators also recognize the need to take into account cultural, group, and individual diversity. Unlike rhetorical reflectors, however, the rhetorically sensitive communicator isn't willing to go to any length in the effort to avoid displeasing the people with whom he or she communicates.

People belong to groups based on their individual beliefs and attitudes. For example, the people in this photo probably chose to join EarthCorps because they believe that the earth's resources are not being used wisely and think that they can make a difference by increasing the awareness of others.

Rhetorically sensitive communicators exhibit skills that are characteristic of communication competence. Their communication behavior shows that they respect people's complexity and that they are flexible enough to adapt their messages to the demands of a particular situation. Rhetorically sensitive communicators also exemplify interaction consciousness.

Respect for Human Complexity

All of us want others to treat us as individuals. We don't like being categorized and stereotyped, moreover, because it denies our individual diversity. In recognition of the fact, rhetorically sensitive communicators are skilled at constructing messages that reflect our multifaceted nature, and they try to avoid making statements like the following ones:

"Amal, what's the Arab perspective on the Israeli–Palestinian peace agreement?"

"As a woman who has been victimized by sexism, I know what it must feel like to be an African American man."

"Hey, as far as I'm concerned, the people of color in this room are just like me."

No doubt you have heard people make statements similar to these three. Perhaps you have said something to the same effect yourself.

According to communication researchers Marsha Houston and Julia T. Wood, these statements are characteristic of totalizing.[13] In Chapter 4, we said totalizing occurs when we emphasize a single attribute about a person; we are in effect defining who the person is on the basis of the single attribute. Although being African American, or Latino, or gay, or lesbian may be central to a person's identity, these terms don't tell us everything we need to know about a person.

The messages of rhetorically sensitive people acknowledge differences in race, ethnicity, gender, sexual orientation, and ability, but at the same time, they reflect other attributes important to the identity of the person or people with whom they're communicating. In other words, a rhetorically sensitive communicator's message reflects individual diversity, not simply cultural or group membership. Sometimes this means keeping one's mouth shut because there is no appropriate alternative to an offensive message. Other times, this means recasting the message. For example:

"Amal, we've heard from everyone else in terms of what they think about the Middle East conflict. Do you wish to comment?"

"I can speak only in terms of my own experience as a woman who has been victimized by sexism."

Flexibility and Adaptiveness

Research on communication competence has consistently found that competent communicators are flexible and adaptive. These attributes are also characteristic of the rhetorically sensitive. People who are rigid in their thinking behave

Like demagogues in the past, a few politicians are using linguistic diversity to bait people's natural suspicions about those who are different.

rigidly. They have a tough time being flexible enough to adapt to people whose culture is dissimilar or who belong to groups with which they are unfamiliar.

People who are open and receptive to the experience of others, as are rhetorically sensitive communicators, have little trouble being flexible and adaptive in their communication behavior. They purposely try to see things from the perspective of other cultures, groups, and individuals and actively seek information when they don't understand a behavior or an attitude.

Self-Monitoring

Flexible and adaptive communication behavior is, in part, made possible through **self-monitoring.** This skill involves focusing on the communication

self-monitoring
Surveying the communication environment for cues about appropriate communication behavior and adapting to them.

Box 7-4   Skill Building

How Much Do You Self-Monitor?

There are striking and important differences in the extent to which people can and do control their self-presentation in social situations; some people do this more often—and with greater skill—than others. Professional actors, as well as many trial lawyers, are among the best at controlling their self-presentation.

The following statements concern your personal reactions to a number of different situations. No two statements are exactly alike, so consider each statement carefully before answering. If a statement is true or mostly true as applied to you, circle it as true. If a statement is false or not usually true as applied to you, circle it as false.

T   F   1. I find it hard to imitate the behavior of other people.

T   F   2. My behavior is usually an expression of my true inner feelings, attitudes, and beliefs.

T   F   3. At parties and social gatherings, I do not attempt to do or say things others will like.

T   F   4. I can only argue for ideas that I already believe.

T   F   5. I can make impromptu speeches even on topics about which I have almost no information.

T   F   6. I guess I put on a show to impress or entertain other people.

T   F   7. When I am uncertain how to act in a social situation, I look to the behavior of others for cues.

T   F   8. I would probably make a good actor/actress.

T   F   9. I rarely seek the advice of my friends to choose movies, books, or music.

T   F   10. I sometimes appear to others to be experiencing deeper emotions than I actually am.

T   F   11. I laugh more when I watch a comedy with others than when alone.

T   F   12. In a group of people, I am rarely the center of attention.

T   F   13. In different situations and with different people, I often act like very different persons.

T   F   14. I am not particularly good at making other people like me.

T   F   15. Even if I am not enjoying myself, I often pretend to be having a good time.

T   F   16. I'm not always the person I appear to be.

Give yourself a 1 for every true response, 0 for every false response. Total your score. The higher the score you gave yourself on this measure, the greater the degree of self-monitoring in which you routinely engage. Very high scores (13+) may suggest that you are prone to be a rhetorical reflector. Very low scores (6) may suggest that you exhibit behaviors consistent with those of the noble self.

The strategies and techniques you use to control the impression you convey to others are referred to as "impression management." The self-monitoring test you just completed will provide you with insight into your skills in the area of impression management and specific skills on which you may need to work. Make a list of these skills and write down some ways in which you could improve them.

SOURCE: The Self-Monitoring Test was developed and tested by Dr. Mark Snyder, Department of Psychology, University of Minnesota. Copyright ©1974 by the American Psychological Association. Reprinted with permission from the APA and M. Snyder, "Self Monitoring of Expressive Behavior," *Journal of Personality and Social Psychology,* 30 (1974), 531.

Adapting to another culture's norms is a sign of communication competence.

environment, looking for cues about what constitutes appropriate communication behavior, and then adapting to these cues.[14]

Your score on the questions in Box 7-4 will indicate how much you self-monitor. Traveling inside a culture other than yours, for example, requires self-monitoring. Specifically, visiting another culture requires that you remain mindful of at least two things. The first is the communication behavior of those native to the culture. Their communication behavior is rich in such nonverbal cues as appropriate eye contact, the amount of distance people establish between themselves when conversing, and rituals, such as how they greet each other. Second, cross-cultural travel requires that you be mindful of how others appear to be responding to your communication behavior. Such responses can tell you a great deal about the degree to which your behavior is in line with cultural norms and expectations. Experienced travelers know that people are usually willing, if not

Communication is a bridge between diverse people.

eager, to assist them in adapting to the ways of a new culture and that when such assistance isn't forthcoming, the fault often can be found in the way the visitor is communicating.

Interaction Consciousness

The final attribute mentioned by Hart and Burks is interaction consciousness. Recall from Chapter 5's discussion of ethics that **interaction consciousness** involves balancing one's own needs with the needs of others. So it is with the rhetorically sensitive. They consciously try to avoid communicating in a manner that reflects only their own needs.

Of course, you cannot exercise interaction consciousness without knowing the diverse needs of the people with whom you communicate. Besides self-monitoring, one skill in particular that can help you recognize those needs is relational empathy.

interaction consciousness
Balancing one's own needs with the needs of others.

Relational Empathy

We discussed empathy in Chapter 2, while exploring the topic of perceptual bias. Empathy, or the ability to see things from someone else's perspective, is an important skill in overcoming perceptual bias. Empathy can be tough, even when we are communicating with people who are highly similar to us.

How, then, can we try to see the world from another's perspective when we are clueless about the experience that has given rise to the perspective? The short answer is that we can't, without first becoming familiar with the set of experiences that color another's reality. Even then, we won't be able to duplicate the other's experience or keep it uncontaminated from our own experience.

Intercultural communication scholar Benjamin J. Broome argues for what he calls relational empathy.[15] In contrast to the traditional conceptualization of empathy, which involves trying to reproduce another's reality, **relational empathy** is concerned with the reality communicators negotiate as they communicate.

What this means in practical terms is that in the attempt to be rhetorically sensitive, people should never presuppose their experience is sufficiently rich to see the world in the same way as those with whom they have little in common. Instead, people whose experiences are diverse should produce their own perspective, one that reflects the totality of their combined experience. What's more, as their relationship matures, people whose experience is diverse should periodically take stock of the perspective they've collectively produced so that it can be modified as needed.

relational empathy
A negotiated reality between communicators.

Summary

Diversity is a fact of life. Diversity-responsive communication, therefore, is important to overall communication competence. Diversity-responsive communication begins with cultural literacy. Cultural literacy requires that people reassess their perceptions of and attributions about dissimilar people. Cultural literacy also asks us to try to understand the degree to which the dimensions common to all cultures vary. There are four common value dimensions of culture: collectivism-individualism, power distance, uncertainty avoidance, and femininity-masculinity.

Diversity-responsive communication also involves the different patterns of thinking, feeling, and behaving associated with groups. Group diversity can reflect geographic region, race and ethnicity, gender, religion, socioeconomic class, and generation. These are not the only types of groups, however.

Diversity-responsive communication also respects individual differences in people's patterns of thinking, feeling, and behaving. Individual diversity is deeply embedded in people's beliefs, attitudes, and values.

Finally, diversity-responsive communication is related to rhetorical sensitivity. People who are rhetorically sensitive appreciate human complexity, are adaptive and flexible, and practice interaction consciousness. Rhetorically sensitive communicators also self-monitor and strive to achieve relational empathy with people whose experience is dissimilar to their own.

Another Look

Articles

Benjamin Schwarz. "The Diversity Myth: America's Leading Export." *The Atlantic Monthly*, May 1993, 57–67.

This article asserts that the so-called melting pot theory, in which diverse groups in America assimilate to become a common one, is a hoax. Schwarz says that minority cultures and groups of people historically have been forced by the much larger and dominant Anglo culture to conform to its pattern of thinking, feeling, and behaving.

S. Hurtado. "The Campus Racial Climate: Contexts of Conflict." *Journal of Higher Education* 63 (1992): 539–69.

Hurtado maintains that today's college campuses are rife with racial conflict and that there may be less social interaction between the races on college campuses today than 25 years ago. This article could be a starting point for a paper or a class discussion about relations between various groups on your campus.

Books

Douglas Copeland. *Generation X: Tales for Accelerated Culture*. New York: St. Martin's Press, 1991.

Having sold over 400,000 copies, Copeland's novel has gone from cult reading to best seller. Copeland writes about the attitudes, culture, and lifestyle of three friends who reject authority and mock the generations before them. If you'd like to know how 20-somethings came to be called Generation X, this book is the place to start.

H. L. Horowitz. *Campus Life: Undergraduate Cultures from the 18th Century to the Present*. New York: Alfred A. Knopf, 1987.

This historical overview traces and compares campus cultures over nearly a 200-year time span. It is fascinating in the sense that it shows that every generation of college students creates both cultures and groups unique to their times. This would be an excellent book to report on in class or in a paper.

Video Rentals

Higher Learning Although this John Singleton film doesn't pack quite the wallop of *Boyz N the Hood*, it is a film with which college students readily identify. It portrays the lives and perspectives of a multiracial group of students on a diversity-rich campus. Themes that are explored include racism, homophobia, and the white-supremacy movement.

Alamo Bay Starring Ed Harris and Amy Madigan, this film directed by Louis Malle is about contemporary intolerance. It shows how a Texas coastal town angrily reacts to an influx of Vietnamese immigrants who hope to fish the coastal waters. This film is an evenhanded treatment of a subject that continues to be volatile in this country: immigration.

El Norte This moving and critically praised film follows the lives of a brother and a sister who flee war and political intolerance in Guatemala, illegally enter the United States, and attempt to start a life in Los Angeles, California. Visually arresting, the film shows the difficulties of adapting to life in a new culture.

My Left Foot Daniel Day Lewis won the Oscar for best actor for his portrayal of Irish poet Christy Brown. The film does a wonderful job in showing the commitment and resilience of a disabled man trying to lead an ordinary life.

Brother from Another Planet John Sayles's inventive film starring Joe Morton shows what might happen if a silent, six-toed man of color from outer space paid us a visit. Because the film steps outside the normal box from which interracial relationships are viewed, Sayles's film does a marvelous job of illustrating perceptual bias and inaccurate attribution.

Theory and Research in Practice

1. Choose the one country outside North America you would most like to visit. Consulting your campus library, faculty, and perhaps international students from your country of choice, develop a travel guide predicated on the principle of diversity-responsive communication. Include in your guide cultural, group, and individual differences you may confront and how you should adapt your communication behavior to these differences. Don't forget about self-monitoring and relational empathy. Add this information to the guide you developed concerning nonverbal communication in different cultures.

2. Many campuses have official groups that represent disabled students, gay and lesbian students, and racial minorities. Make an appointment to meet with the members of one or more of these groups. Take a list of questions with you to ask group members about their diversity, including misconceptions, common instances in which they feel discriminated against, and specific diversity-responsive behaviors they would like other students to adopt. Compare what you find with the discussion of diversity shown on Segment 7 of the accompanying video.

3. With a close friend, lover, or parent, discuss the dimensions of culture introduced in this chapter. Be sure to discuss as well the North American norms for each of these dimensions. Once you both feel comfortable with your level of understanding relative to these dimensions, follow these directions:

   a. Working alone, rate the degree (with 10 being high and 1 being low) to which you think your *relationship* is (1) collectivistic or individualistic, (2) equal or unequal in terms of power, (3) traditional or nontraditional with respect to gender roles, and (4) tolerant of the differences between the two of you.

   b. Discuss your ratings with each other. In the process, discuss the degree to which your ratings conform to the North American norms discussed in the chapter. Report what you learn to your class.

PART TWO

Dimensions of Interpersonal Communication

CHAPTER 8

Relational Communication

OBJECTIVES

After reading this chapter you should be able to:

- Define and describe relational communication.

- Describe the process of social penetration.

- Explain the role of proximity, attraction, and similarity in the initiating stage of relationship development.

- Describe the communication behaviors that characterize the process of relational escalation.

- Describe the communication behaviors that characterize the process of relational de-escalation.

- Describe and distinguish among self-presentational, instrumental, and relational goals.

- Discuss the process of self-disclosure and eight guidelines important to managing the process.

- Describe the skills necessary to regulate conversation.

- Explain the role of conversational regulation in managing relational dialectics.

Over the course of our lives, we will have many kinds of interpersonal relationships—with classmates, acquaintances, best friends, co-workers, dates, lovers, and relatives. Some of these relationships will be superficial, and some intense. Some will last over many years, and others will fade away without our noticing. But the same factors, some of which we will investigate in this chapter, seem to be at work, influencing how deep a relationship goes, how long it lasts, and how it ends.

The movie *Dead Man Walking* chronicles a most unusual interpersonal relationship under the most difficult circumstances—that of a nun, Sister Helen Pre-

relational communication
Verbal and nonverbal messages that define the nature of the association between people.

jean (played by Susan Sarandon), who becomes spiritual advisor to death-row inmate Matthew Poncelet (played by Sean Penn). Nevertheless, the development of their relationship follows a pattern that has been described by communication researchers. Their first meeting is tentative as they search for things to say and try to figure out how to connect with each other. In subsequent meetings, all conducted through a window in the prison visitor's room, they search for appropriate roles. Poncelet tries flirting, probably because it is one of the ways he is most accustomed to relating with women. But Sister Helen perseveres in her role as spiritual advisor and talks to him, refusing to stereotype him or to be stereotyped. She is finally able to achieve a deeper level of relationship and enable him to take responsibility for his actions in the torture and murder of two teenagers.

Few of our relationships are as dramatic as that between Sister Helen and Poncelet, but common communication behaviors characterize all of them. Relationship development is really a consequence of **relational communication,** which involves the verbal and nonverbal messages that define the nature of the association between people. The breadth and depth of our relationships reflect the communication behaviors that characterize the relationships.

This is the first of three chapters focusing on the defining role communication plays in our relationships. This chapter provides an overview of relational communication and the process of relationship development. It discusses

- the nature of relationships,
- how relationships get started and sometimes escalate,
- how relationships sometimes come apart, and
- the constructive use of communication skills in managing our relationships.

VIDEO FILE

If you have the videotape that accompanies this book, be sure to view Part III, consisting of three segments that complement Chapters 8, 9, and 10.

How We Define Relationships: Levels of Social Penetration

Our relationships vary on a continuum from acquaintance to intimacy. What's more, we can have a perfectly satisfying relationship anywhere along this continuum. Contrary to what is sometimes implied in basic books about communication, the quality of our relationships does not automatically get better as we move in the direction of intimacy.[1] Exactly where a relationship falls on this continuum is defined by how the people communicate and what their communication behavior says about the nature of their association. Ongoing acquaintances, for example, speak more formally than intimates do; they also stand farther apart and touch each other less. Thus, the way people communicate reflects the nature of their relationship.

social penetration
The process of exchanging messages that vary in breadth and depth.

Psychologists Irwin Altman and Dalmas Taylor constructed a model that we can use to visualize the various kinds of relationships on the continuum.[2] Their model, called **social penetration,** shows the breadth and depth of the messages exchanged in a relationship. Figure 8-1 includes examples of the kinds of topics typical of messages at different levels of breadth and depth.

Communication defines our association with people, including those at work.

Breadth

When people meet and first start to become acquainted, they sometimes cover quite a bit of ground. They also talk about topics that are generally superficial, for instance, where they're from, what they're majoring in, and who they both might know. The next time these two people meet, they may add to their first conversation, this time sharing hobbies, bits of information about their respective families, and preferences in such things as food or entertainment.

Altman and Taylor refer to this process as *exploratory affective exchange.* They also suggest that although there may be considerable breadth in the topics talked about, there is likely to be little depth. People may decide to keep their relationship at this relatively superficial level of social penetration, based on the breadth of information they have shared. Then again, people may decide on the basis of what they've shared that they would like to know each other even better.

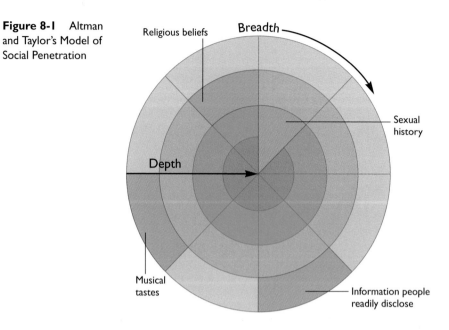

Figure 8-1 Altman and Taylor's Model of Social Penetration

Depth

Affective exchange, as Altman and Taylor call the next level of social penetration, signals that people are willing to chance sharing information about themselves that otherwise wouldn't be obtainable. This kind of purposeful self-disclosure adds depth to the relationship and signifies a potential **turning point,** which communication researchers Leslie Baxter and Carol Bullis define as "any event or occurrence that is associated with change in a relationship."[3] In their research about romantic couples, Baxter and Bullis found that when people begin disclosing their feelings about each other, their relationship is usually turning in the direction of greater commitment.

Whether self-disclosure leads to greater commitment in nonromantic relationships depends on the characteristic breadth and depth of the exchanges. It is not uncommon for co-workers, as a case in point, to exchange messages that over time add both breadth and depth to their relationship. Usually, though, the implicit rules that govern such relationships place limits on the depth of exchange. As a result, the content of self-disclosures stabilizes and doesn't get any deeper.

turning point Any event or occurrence associated with change in a relationship.

Stable Affective Exchange

Altman and Taylor suggest *stable affective exchange* exists when people seem satisfied with the characteristic breadth and depth of their messages and relationship. Stable affective exchange can occur at any level of social penetration. As Figures 8-2, 8-3, and 8-4 indicate, people who have achieved what they mutu-

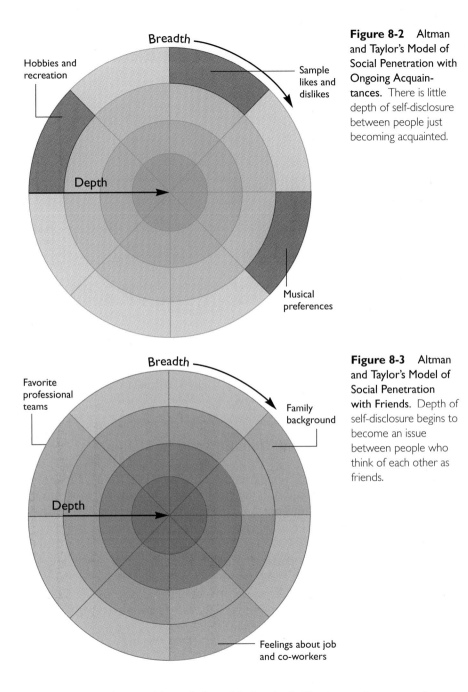

Figure 8-2 Altman and Taylor's Model of Social Penetration with Ongoing Acquaintances. There is little depth of self-disclosure between people just becoming acquainted.

Breadth

Hobbies and recreation

Sample likes and dislikes

Depth

Musical preferences

Figure 8-3 Altman and Taylor's Model of Social Penetration with Friends. Depth of self-disclosure begins to become an issue between people who think of each other as friends.

Breadth

Favorite professional teams

Family background

Depth

Feelings about job and co-workers

ally perceive to be a stable and desirable level of affective exchange can be co-workers, friends, or lovers. The strength of Altman and Taylor's model is that it can be used to describe a wide variety of mutually satisfactory interpersonal relationships, not just intimate ones. Thus, by applying their model, we can better

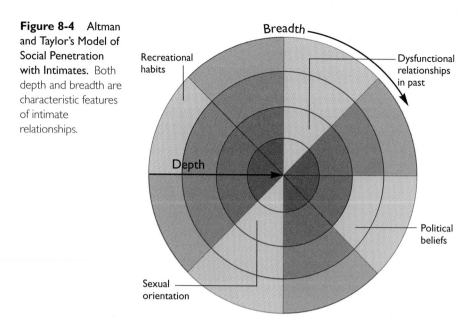

Figure 8-4 Altman and Taylor's Model of Social Penetration with Intimates. Both depth and breadth are characteristic features of intimate relationships.

understand our acquaintances, casual friends, and colleagues at work, not just the people with whom we have achieved psychological intimacy.

Relationship Development: Initiation and Escalation

Communication scholar Mark Knapp introduced a model of relationship development not long after Altman and Taylor introduced theirs. Whereas Altman and Taylor's model gives us a general idea of how relationships unfold, Knapp's model is more specific. As shown in Figure 8-5, it describes five stages through which relationships *potentially* can **escalate**: (1) initiating, (2) experimenting, (3) intensifying, (4) integrating, and (5) bonding.[4] We emphasize the word *potentially* because this model is not intended to suggest that all relationships move through each of these stages in the exact sequence described. People not only stop at specific stages, telling each other they've gone far enough in the relationship, but they also skip or revisit stages.

relational escalation
The process of initiating, experimenting, intensifying, integrating, and bonding a relationship.

Initiating

This first stage in Knapp's model is straightforward. You initiate a relationship when you start up a conversation to pass the time or to plant the seeds for a possible ongoing relationship. Although this stage can be anxiety arousing and is not unimportant, it would not be possible without the presence of one or more

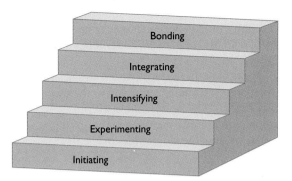

Figure 8-5   Knapp's Model of Relational Development. These are the steps that can be taken in the process of escalating a relationship.

motivating factors. There are three variables most responsible for people initiating communication: proximity, perceptions of physical attraction, and perceptions of similarity. These *pre-interaction cues,* as communication scholar Steve Duck calls them, assist us in deciding on both the appropriateness of initiating and the method of initiating.[5]

The influence of **proximity** on initiation is both obvious and subtle.[6] Unless you come into close, physical proximity with someone, the probability of initiating communication is next to impossible. This is even true of cyberspace relationships, which require a kind of electronic proximity between people. The people in the relationship have to be connected to a network to talk. Less obvious is the degree to which we use proximity to gather information about such things as the likelihood of meeting someone on a regular basis. For instance, the probability of initiating a relationship with a person who shares the bus-stop bench every day is much greater than with a person you've seen at the bus stop only once. Simply put, the more you think it is likely you will encounter someone, the better the chance you'll make the effort to initiate communication.

A second factor that motivates people to initiate communication is the perception of *physical attraction.* Fifty years of research show that the perception of physical attraction is the single best predictor of two people initiating interaction with each other, which is, of course, necessary to relationship development.[7] Perceptions of physical attraction depend on a specific culture's definition of beauty. Because mass media, especially television, have created a fairly homogeneous culture in the Western industrialized part of the world, there is a high consensus in the West about what constitutes the physical ideal in men and women.

Study after study strongly suggest that people perceived as physically attractive have a distinct relational advantage over those perceived as less so, especially with regard to first impressions. People perceived as physically attractive are seen as happier, more outgoing, smarter, and more desirable as potential partners than their less attractive counterparts.[8] These kinds of attributions make attractive people a more likely target of relationally motivated communicators.

proximity   The amount of physical distance between people.

Perceived similarity can enhance the impact of proximity and attraction on initiating a relationship. Perceived similarities between people usually promote communication. According to research, we first make judgments about how similar people are on the basis of their appearance.[9]

Appearance has an almost domino-like effect on other forms of similarity. The more similar we perceive a person's appearance to our own, the more similar we perceive the person to us in general. People who dress like us and appear to be in our age group, for example, often are perceived to have backgrounds, attitudes, beliefs, and values similar to ours. This tendency to generalize from people's appearance is not without reason.

Usually, students at four-year colleges are more alike than different. Although there are exceptions, the majority of them (1) are relatively close in age; (2) share similar backgrounds; and (3) hold similar attitudes, beliefs, and values on socially significant subjects. Chances are their sense of style also clearly identifies them as "college students." College students could spend time learning about each other's demography in the attempt to determine why they appear so similar, but most know it is quicker to do just the opposite, that is, to use appearance as an indicator of the degree to which they are demographically similar. Of course, college students are not the only ones who use appearance in this way. So, too, do people in certain professions.

Obviously, there is danger in generalizing too much about similarity from appearance. Aside from the fact that generalizing can promote unfair stereotyping, appearance is not a completely reliable indicator of similarity. Not every young male with long hair likes Metallica, nor are all males who wear oversized jackets and stocking caps pulled down over their ears "gangsta' rappers."

Three points, then, need to be clear before moving on. First, people are more attracted to people they perceive as similar than to people they perceive as dissimilar. Second, initial perceptions of similarity are based on surface cues, such as appearance. Third, surface cues can be misleading or even deceptive. Consider what happened shortly after the Tom Cruise and Val Kilmer film *Top Gun* became the most popular action film in the United States. First, crowds of young women flocked to the Miramar Club, the saloon where naval aviators attending the "Top Gun" school socialize. Second, innumerable young men showed up at the Miramar Club dressed in flight suits and looking very much like the Top Gun aviators they were impersonating.

Experimenting

The work of Steve Duck suggests that we use experimenting, the second stage in Knapp's model, as a kind of relational filter.[10] Experimenting involves information gathering, usually by asking and answering questions. In the process, we begin to learn how accurate were the pre-interaction cues that led us to initiate contact. While experimenting, we learn whether the other person is as similar as his or her appearance led us to believe.

Experimenting also lets us filter out people we don't find socially attractive. Social attraction is largely based on how skillfully people communicate.[11] The

We are predisposed to build relationships with people we perceive as similar to us.

skill with which people communicate can tell us a great deal about them, including their ability to listen, how well they self-monitor, and whether they are overly anxious.

Finally, experimenting gives people a chance to reduce the uncertainty that is characteristic of initial encounters. Uncertainty is a leading cause of anxiety when people first meet. Anxiety can undermine both our confidence and our skill when communicating. With rare exceptions, people who are successful at reducing uncertainty as they experiment have a much better chance of seeing their relationships intensify.

Intensifying

Intensifying, the third stage in Knapp's model, typically begins when people have had several opportunities to meet and communicate. During this stage we not only bring up similarities but also engage in verbal and nonverbal behaviors that reinforce them. Verbally, we remind each other about the many things we have in common. We may nonverbally complement these verbal reminders, moreover, through similar dress, time spent together, and the amount of physical distance separating us when we talk.

Intensifying behaviors signal a genuine turning point in a relationship, one marked in Baxter and Bullis's study of romantic couples by increased breadth and depth in the messages shared.[12] What people tell each other at this stage of relational development tends to be less ritualistic and more spontaneous than when experimenting. In the previous stages, messages tend to concern topics that are general and safe, such as sports, weather, school, local hangouts or even well-known professors on campus. Intensifying, however, is characterized by messages that clearly focus on the people in the relationship. Because these messages also are more emotion laden, they involve risk. The fact that we feel and express a high degree of similarity with another person doesn't guarantee the expressed feeling will be reciprocated.

Integrating

Knapp's fourth stage in the process of relational development, integrating, signals that a relationship has turned in the direction of intimacy. Again, the focus and content of communication changes. Self-disclosure, which we discuss in detail later in this chapter, tends to be more personal and potentially compromising. People typically share their pasts so that they can better understand each other's present. People are also likely to reveal their aspirations and significant life goals. Thus, integrating suggests not only an increased level of commitment between people but increased responsibility as well. Possessed with potentially volatile information about each other, people need to be increasingly mindful that what they say and do is of real consequence not just to them but also to the people with whom they've become close.

Bonding

The fifth and final stage of escalation in Knapp's model is bonding. Verbal and nonverbal communication at this stage tells people both in and outside the relationship that it is a primary and committed one. In many cultures, bonding is accompanied by ceremony. Marriage is the obvious example, where people publicly disclose the primacy of their commitment. Like each of the preceding stages, bonding adds a new dimension to a relationship. Developmental psychologist Erik Erikson argues that bonding requires willingness to give up part of your individual self in favor of one that is merged with that of the person you care about.[13] Bonding requires not only overall communication competence but also psychological maturity. People have to be emotionally capable of bonding, in other words. Box 8-1 will help you think about the reasons you would commit yourself to a relationship.

Knapp's five stages of relational development are not lock-step. People occasionally jump steps and may even revisit steps throughout their relationship.

Box 8-1   Self-Assessment

What Motivates You to Make a Commitment?

Using a scale of 1 to 5, with 1 representing low importance and 5 representing high importance, indicate how significant you believe each of the following reasons are for making a commitment to a relationship.

1. A high probability of receiving future rewards from this relationship.
   Low   1   2   3   4   5   High

2. The likelihood that this relationship is as good as any you'll ever have.
   Low   1   2   3   4   5   High

3. The other person's willingness to expend as much effort as you are on the relationship.
   Low   1   2   3   4   5   High

4. A strong desire to be identified with the other person.
   Low   1   2   3   4   5   High

5. The amount of emotional investment you already have in the relationship.
   Low   1   2   3   4   5   High

There are no right or wrong responses. Rank-order your responses on the basis of the score given. If you gave the same score to two or more items, decide which item is most important and rank the other items accordingly. Do your responses and rankings reveal anything about yourself of which you were unaware? Do you think your responses reflect your true beliefs or what you think you should believe?

SOURCE: Adapted from Mark L. Knapp and Anita L. Vangelisti, *Interpersonal Communication and Human Relationships*, 3rd ed. (Boston: Allyn and Bacon, 1996), 266.

However, only a handful of our relationships achieve some form of bonding. That's why we describe specific relationships with words such as *casual, good, best,* and *significant.* Bonding is about best friends and our most significant others.

Relationship Development: Redefinition and De-escalation

Not all relationships work out. Some end suddenly and unexpectedly, some fade as a result of physical distance, and others dissolve due to lack of attention. Whereas people generally perceive the process of relational escalation as desirable, they often have a negative view of de-escalation. We don't share this viewpoint. The process of **de-escalation** also is a process of redefining the relationship. The fact that people frequently have trouble with the process, doesn't mean that it is inherently bad. Difficulties in redefining a relationship do not necessarily owe to the process of de-escalation. Often such difficulties simply reflect the lack of skill with which people communicate during the process.

   One strength of Knapp's model is that it describes turning points in a relationship on the wane.[14] Some people may be mindful of the distance growing between them and choose not to do anything about it. Others, we suspect, are less mindful of the state of their relationship and may fail to realize what's

relational de-escalation The process of redefining a relationship through differentiating, circumscribing, stagnating, avoiding, and terminating.

happening until too late. In either case, Knapp suggests that there are five stages or turning points in the process of de-escalation: (1) differentiating, (2) circumscribing, (3) stagnating, (4) avoiding, and (5) terminating.

As was the case with the stages of escalation in Knapp's model, the stages of de-escalation are not lock-step. People may take note of what is happening to their relationship and act accordingly. Couples in counseling, for instance, usually recognize that they've reached a turning point in their relationship that one or both don't like. They seek help to identify the turning point's cause and to acquire skills which will enable them to deal constructively with it. Other people look to other sources of outside advice, like the "love doctors" described in Box 8-2.

What follows, therefore, is meant to illustrate one way the stages of de-escalation might unfold. For convenience, we'll look at the process as it might unfold between people who have bonded. However, people in a less defined relationship can also go through the stages of differentiating, circumscribing, stagnating, avoiding, and terminating.

Differentiating

Whereas intensifying is characterized by communication behaviors meant to reinforce the similarities between people, *differentiating* involves communication transactions that point out dissimilarities. Consider the following dialogue between Syd and Nancy.

SYD: "Let's go to Kamatsu's Friday. It's payday."
NANCY: "I'd rather not."
SYD: "I thought you were crazy about the sushi?"
NANCY: "Honestly? I ate it because you liked it. I'm really not that fond of it."
SYD: "You should have said something . . . so, you pick a place."
NANCY: "I vote for staying home. I'm just not the out-on-the-town person you are."
SYD: "What? Nancy? Ms. Party-time, anytime?"

During the usually protracted process of differentiating, one or both people in the relationship begin to send messages that say, "I'm not as similar to you as you think. So don't assume that you know what I'm thinking or feeling." Messages meant to create distance between people become as common as those intended to create closeness during the process of intensifying.

Circumscribing

Circumscribing, or talking around each other, is even less direct than differentiating. Circumscribing is designed to discourage meaningful dialogue, since

Box 8-2   Critical Thinking

Calling Dr. Love

Do you know who Barbara DeAngelis is? Maybe you've read one of her books or seen one of her infomercials on late-night or early-morning television. DeAngelis, who holds a Ph.D. in psychology, is an extraordinarily popular author, speaker, and seminar leader. Her books, such as *Are You the One for Me?* and videotapes, such as *Making Love Work*, sell in the hundreds of thousands. As the executive director of the Los Angeles Personal Growth Center, DeAngelis also travels all over the world dispensing relational advice to people who have paid handsomely to hear her.

DeAngelis is only one of hundreds of Doctors of Love, people who make their living prescribing principles they tell their clients will help them find the right person and avoid the wrong one.

What's your take on love doctors like DeAngelis? Do you think they serve a useful purpose? For example, do you think their advice assists people in escalating, maintaining, or de-escalating a relationship? Or do you perceive love doctors to be modern-day sellers of relational snake oil? Visit the self-help section of your local bookstore. Peruse the relational advice self-help books offer, and compare this advice with the research-based principles described in this chapter. Report back to class.

SOURCE: Fahizah Alim, "Patchwork," *Sacramento Bee*, 8 December 1994, E1–E5.

it might cause people to actually talk about the changing dynamic of their relationship.

SYD: "Did you read what Peter Smith said about Alicia Silverstone in *Spin*?"
NANCY: "I'm going back to the office. You'll have to eat alone."
SYD: "He said she was the next Winona Ryder. Do you believe that?"
NANCY: "I've got to run."

As we'll discuss at length in Chapter 10, many of us mistakenly assume that conflict is negative.[15] As a result, we've been conditioned over time to circumscribe conflict rather than use it constructively and learn from it. In this scenario, Nancy believes that if she communicates directly with Syd, it may lead to a protracted discussion, which she doesn't want. Worse yet, she assumes that a direct answer may lead to an argument and harsh words. Thus, Nancy further distances herself from Syd by physically withdrawing.

Stagnating

Stagnating is the third stage in the spiral of de-escalation Knapp describes. During this stage, a kind of relational limbo occurs. People are neither willing to invest the energy necessary to repair their relationship nor willing to hasten its end. They keep talk between them to a minimum, and when they do talk, the content of the transaction tends to reflect tasks rather than their relationship.

SYD: "You pay the utilities yet?"
NANCY: "Yeah. And I also called the mechanic and made an appointment for you to take the car in Wednesday."
SYD: "Yeah . . . sure. Whatever."

At the stage of stagnating, people will do almost anything to avoid talking about their relationship. To do so would force Nancy and Syd to deal with what is really occurring between them. Thus, they focus on "doing" rather than "relating."

Avoiding

Avoiding is the last stage before a relationship is terminated. Avoiding can be physical or psychological, if physical avoidance isn't possible. Two co-workers who are in a relationship cannot physically separate themselves all the time. Separated lovers who share many of the same friends can find it difficult to completely avoid each other, as can quarreling family members who must attend the same celebrations over the holidays. When people cannot physically avoid each other, they often treat each other as objects rather than persons. For example, they may treat each other like they treat strangers on a crowded elevator, avoiding eye contact or any other form of behavior that might signal acknowledgment. Whereas nonverbal immediacy increases during the escalating phase of relationships, it may decline to the point of disappearing as people try to disengage. In addition to less eye contact, avoiding may be signaled by less touching, by sitting or standing farther apart, and leaning away from rather than toward the person while talking.

Terminating

Terminating is the final stage of de-escalation in Knapp's model. It can be as formal as a divorce decree or as informal as people avoiding places they once frequented as a couple. Physical termination, however, doesn't mean psychological termination. People who separate may think about each other, may compare a new relationship to the just-terminated one, and may even get to the point where they are able to develop a different kind of relationship with each other. Some divorced couples with children know that it usually is in their children's interest to try to redefine their relationship. Co-workers who become romantically involved may not be able to completely terminate contact either, so they may also redefine their relationship.

Thus, terminating may signal the end of one kind of relationship and the beginning of another. Although the former relationship will always affect the new one, its influence needn't be negative. If people learn from their former relationship, in fact, it can improve the redefined one.

Managing Relational Communication

At this point, you should have a good idea about the role of communication in defining relationships, the potential turning points through which relationships can pass, and the effect of variables like proximity, attraction, and similarity in the process of relational escalation and de-escalation. You should also have a good idea about how the stages of relationship escalation and de-escalation unfold and the communication behaviors that are characteristic of these stages. Now we want to turn to the management of relational communication, which involves the verbal and nonverbal messages that define the nature of people's relationships. We'll start by looking at the three most common types of goals of relational communication. Next, we will discuss both the nature and management of self-disclosure, which is central to effective relational communication. Finally, we'll introduce a number of conversational skills that can assist you in regulating your beginning relationships, as well as in managing the dialectical tensions inherent in ongoing relationships.

Goals

Back in Chapter 1 we talked about the relationship between communication and goals. We said that competent communicators establish goals appropriate to the situation and to their relationships. Communication scholars Daniel J. Canary and Michael J. Cody have identified three kinds of goals common to relationships: self-presentational, instrumental, and relational.[16] These three goals operate in concert, though one goal may supersede another in specific instances. For example, self-presentational goals may seem less significant to a married couple than to two people on a first date.

Self-presentational goals concern the impression we want to create verbally and nonverbally. Consider the following passage from F. Scott Fitzgerald's novel *The Great Gatsby*.

> He smiled understandingly—much more than understandingly. It was one of those rare smiles with a quality of eternal reassurance in it, that you may come across four or five times in life. It faced—or seemed to face—the whole external world for an instant, and then concentrated on you with an irresistible prejudice in your favor. It understood you just as far as you wanted to be understood, believed in you as you would like to believe in yourself, and assured you that it had precisely the impression of you that, at your best, you hoped to convey.[17]

The passage is spoken by Nick, the novel's narrator, on first encountering the title character, Jay Gatsby. If you've read *The Great Gatsby* or seen the film based on it, then you know everything Jay Gatsby did in the way of impression-making was strategic. He had very specific self-presentational goals. One type of self-presentational goal concerns first impressions. First impressions are meant to convey a specific image to a person or group with whom we may want to develop an ongoing relationship. Although the relational goal for a job interview, a first date, and an initial meeting with an academic advisor may be different, the self-presentational goal generally is the same. We want the person to form a favorable impression of us.

Yet, even though our goal is the same in each scenario, our communication behavior should reflect the relevant differences in the scenarios. Interviewing for a job and meeting with an academic advisor require a more formal style of communicating than does dating someone for the first time. As a result, you refer to the interviewer as Ms. Jones, the academic advisor as Professor Smith, and your date as Kelly. At a superficial level, using the appropriate form of address is what it means to manage relational communication.

Self-presentational goals help us achieve *instrumental goals.* Our purpose in making a good impression goes beyond the desire to have a transaction go smoothly; we want to land the job, to establish a relationship with someone we can count on for regular and reliable advice, or to gain a source of steady companionship. Instrumental goals concern self-advancement.

In the Oliver Stone movie *Wall Street,* Michael Douglas plays an extraordinarily wealthy investor and corporate raider, interested in taking over companies he can monetarily exploit. Charlie Sheen plays a young stockbroker who believes that if he can get in to see Douglas and make a sales pitch, he will be able to hitch a ride on Douglas's economic shooting star. During several of the early scenes in the film, Sheen is shown rehearsing his self-presentational strategy, verbally practicing exactly what he will say to not only Douglas but to Douglas's secretary as well. Sheen knows that how he initiates contact (his self-presentational goal) with Douglas is essential to his desired success (his instrumental goal).

Finally, competent communicators are mindful of their *relational goals,* of which there are three: maintenance, escalation, and de-escalation. Frequently, our relational communication behaviors tell others that we want to maintain things just the way they are. As a result, we try to keep our communication behavior relatively constant. We try to avoid sending messages that might be taken to mean we want more or less from a relationship. This wish to maintain the status quo is evident not only in the customary way we address people but also in how close or distant we stand, how long we sustain eye contact, and the degree to which we touch.

At other times, however, we may want to manage our relational communication so that it signals our desire to escalate a relationship. Returning to Altman and Taylor's model of social penetration, we may try especially to increase the depth of our exchanges. In terms of Knapp's stages, we may begin sending messages designed to intensify perceptions of similarity.

Then there will be times when we would like to de-escalate or disengage from a relationship altogether. To review, this desire usually translates to relational communication that is indirect and distant, emphasizes dissimilarities, and is increasingly less frequent. As we implied earlier, managing the relational communication behaviors that characterize a relationship from which we're trying to disengage demands skill. How do you distance yourself from someone, for

The importance of first impressions to relationship development doesn't diminish with age and experience.

example, without hurting feelings or turning what has been a positive relationship into a negative one? Box 8-3 suggests a way to improve your ability to de-escalate a relationship.

Self-Disclosure

Regardless of the type of goal, some degree of self-disclosure is inherent in relational communication. **Self-disclosure** involves people purposefully

self-disclosure The process by which people purposefully reveal information about themselves that otherwise would be unobtainable.

Box 8-3   Skill Building

De-escalate Relationships with Care

Although people may have considerable experience in initiating and escalating a relationship, many are inexperienced when it comes to redefining a longstanding one. Further, what experience people do have with this process often is negative. With another person in class, try to develop a set of communication behaviors that would enable people to de-escalate an intimate relationship and avoid the negativity that often accompanies differentiating, circumscribing, stagnating, avoiding, and terminating. Be specific when you write down your list of communication behaviors. Then write a corresponding narrative explaining why you selected these particular behaviors.

exchanging information about themselves that otherwise would be unobtainable.[18] One person revealing to another that he or she was adopted is an example of self-disclosure. Although there is a considerable body of research concerning self-disclosing communication, there is no evidence to suggest that a specific and universal set of rules governs self-disclosive behavior. Simply put, self-disclosive communication depends on the personalities in a relationship, including their goals, the nature of their relationship, and their levels of communication competence.

Generally, three levels of self-disclosure characterize relational development. They are topical, evaluative, and intimate self-disclosure.[19] During the earliest phases of developing relationships, self-disclosure is primarily topical. It is about topics that are neutral or relatively risk-free, such as those that characterize the questions asked during the experimenting stage of a relationship. The middle level of self-disclosure is evaluative. It is about simple likes and dislikes, but seldom about things that are liked or disliked intensely (food may be the exception). Intimate self-disclosures are typically the domain of people whose relationship has grown close. Because intimate self-disclosures can make one vulnerable, they are inherently risky.

Whereas people in developing relationships tend to stick to topical and evaluative self-disclosures, people in close relationships move among all three levels of self-disclosure. One moment they may be sharing their thoughts about their greatest personal fears, the next sharing their opinions about the effects of the salary cap on professional sports.

Self-disclosure plays a key role in achieving a self-presentational goal, such as making a positive first impression. Research by communication professor Lawrence Wheeless suggests that people need to be especially careful about the depth and direction of self-disclosure during their initial encounters.[20] The norm in North America is not to reveal intimate information during an initial

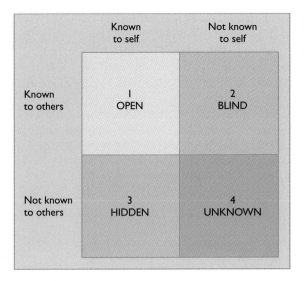

Figure 8-6 The Johari Window. These four "window panes" vary, depending on the type of relationship between people.

encounter. Revealing highly personal details about your life during a professional interview, for example, isn't appropriate. Neither is it appropriate to do so during initial social encounters.

Self-disclosure during initial encounters is most likely to result in a favorable impression when it is positive. People tend to be turned off by those who are consistently negative in their initial self-disclosures. Similarly, a sizable body of research clearly demonstrates self-disclosures should be reciprocal between people during first encounters especially.[21] This **reciprocity norm** is the closest principle social scientists have to a rule for self-disclosive behavior. Reciprocal self-disclosure, like the following dialogue, says people expect their self-disclosures to be returned in kind.

"I'm a junior in Parks and Recreation. How about you?"

"Public Relations sophomore. I'm a people person."

"Me, too. I want to work in a national park this summer."

"I just want a job."

Reciprocity also is key to making judgments about the development of a relationship. If you disclose something personal, and it's met with a response such as "That's interesting," you may have exceeded what the person considers to be appropriate at this juncture in your encounter. The person's failure to reciprocate would be the communication cue telling you this disclosure is considered inappropriate.

Finally, self-disclosure is significant to uncertainty reduction during initial encounters. Generally, the more uncertainty that appropriate self-disclosures reduces for people, the more favorable their impression of you. To better visualize the potential effects of self-disclosure, look at Figure 8-6. It depicts the

reciprocity norm
Widely documented principle that when people give something to someone they expect something similar in return.

Johari Window A matrix designed to show what is known, not known, and hidden between people, depending on the nature of their relationship.

Johari Window, named after its creators, psychologists, Joseph Luft and Harry Ingham.[22] The Johari Window suggests that when two people meet for the first time, they will know very little about each other. They also will purposefully keep certain information about themselves hidden from each other. As their conversation develops, however, this situation may change as a result of self-disclosure and corresponding uncertainty reduction. Theoretically, as a relationship develops, the windows in Luft and Ingham's model will expand and contract as shown in Figure 8-7. This theoretical conclusion assumes, of course, that the depth and breadth of self-disclosure between the two people in the relationship continues to reduce their mutual uncertainty about each other, thereby increasing their mutual attraction for each other as well.

Having overviewed the process of self-disclosure, we can introduce some useful guidelines for you to follow in making good decisions abut self-disclosure, regardless of its definitional status. All of these guidelines involve the concept of mindfulness, which you'll remember demands conscious thought about the consequences of communication behavior.

Guideline 1: Pay attention to diversity. What constitutes appropriate self-disclosure varies depending on the culture, group, and individual. While the Japanese are not especially expressive about themselves, the Koreans are just the opposite. Yet both Japan and Korea are considered collectivist cultures.[23]

What is true of cultures also is true of groups and individuals. Many 12-step groups depend on members making honest and intimate self-disclosures. What individual men and women self-disclose in such groups, however, usually reflects their gender roles. Research shows that men are more reluctant to self-disclose their feelings than are women.[24]

Guideline 2: Think through the relationship between self-disclosure and the goals that motivate it. Ask yourself what you hope to achieve as a result of self-disclosure. Also ask yourself what would constitute appropriate breadth and depth of self-disclosure, given the goal you desire to achieve.

Guideline 3: Avoid indiscriminate self-disclosure. You cannot take back what you self-disclose, though you may try to qualify what you have said. In a sense, self-disclosure is a gift because it suggests you trust someone to whom you've self-disclosed. To give this gift indiscriminately, lessens its value.

Guideline 4: Protect what is disclosed to you in your relationships. One of the quickest ways to send a relationship into a tailspin is to betray a confidence someone has given you. Relationships come with some degree of built-in responsibility. Thus, even if you don't like the fact that you have been burdened with a self-disclosure, you are still obligated to keep it in confidence. Only in the rarest of circumstances—for example, when a friend is suicidal—is this not the case.

Guideline 5: Think through the consequences of a specific self-disclosure. What's more, don't make a self-disclosure unless you are willing to take responsibility for its consequences. There can be unwelcome consequences for self-disclosing something about which you feel guilty or for self-disclosing the negative feelings you have about someone in a relationship. If you take ownership of these poten-

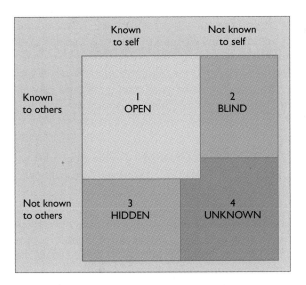

Figure 8-7 The Johari Window in a Developing Relationship. In a developing relationship, the size of Quadrant 1 will typically expand and the others decrease.

tial consequences, you'll probably find that some things truly are better left unsaid.

Guideline 6: Establish privacy boundaries in your well-defined relationships especially. Periodically, for example, an advice seeker will write Dear Abby and explain that a spouse wants to know everything about past relationships. The advice seeker feels caught in a dilemma. Withholding such information makes it appear as if there is something to hide. Self-disclosing the information may interfere with the present relationship.

Simply put, people shouldn't put each other on the defensive with such unfair demands. Instead, people should negotiate the topics about which self-disclosure is appropriate. What's more, people can renegotiate these privacy boundaries should the need arise.

Guideline 7: Practice reciprocity when appropriate. Self-disclose at a level of breadth and depth consistent with another's self-disclosure. However, don't let yourself become obligated in this regard if the breadth and depth of someone's self-disclosure is inappropriate to the situation and your relationship. Don't let someone rush you into disclosing intimate information about yourself, for example, because this person has inappropriately done so.

Guideline 8: Be positive. In relationships just beginning to be defined, it is particularly important for you to avoid being overly negative about people and issues. Aside from the fact that such self-disclosure is a turnoff, people are very quick to pick up highly negative self-disclosures.

Conversation

Knowing how to effectively manage conversation is important to all ongoing relationships. As illustrated in Box 8-4, knowing how to skillfully manage

conversational management
Managing the verbal and nonverbal rules that govern talk in the process of relational definition.

conversation also is essential to achieving your self-presentational, instrumental, and relational goals. In the last section of this chapter, therefore, we want to talk about **conversational management** in two ways. First, we want to discuss what constitutes skillful conversational management as relationships are just beginning to be defined. Second, we want to discuss what constitutes skillful conversational management once the dialectic tensions characteristic of well-defined relationships begin to emerge.

Conversational Rules   First, conversation is regulated by unwritten rules we learn over time. Your parents' admonition "Don't talk to strangers" probably was one of the first conversational rules you were taught. You later modified it to "Don't talk to certain types of strangers in certain situations."

When in the process of defining their relationships, people are expected to follow a number of ritualistic conversational rules. Verbal rules include appropriate topics for conversation, the breadth and depth of self-disclosures, and the degree to which self-disclosures are positive or negative.[25] Compare two dialogues in which people are at different but still early stages in the definition of their relationships.

Dialogue One

"Hey! . . . do you always eat lunch here?"
"I could ask the same of you. Do you want to sit down?"
"You read my mind. It's Samantha, right?"
"Samantha Davis, and . . . you're Terrence?"
"To everyone but my friends. Terry Jordan."
"Any relation to Michael?"
"Yeah, don't I wish. You from Chicago?"
"Joliet, actually. How about you?"
"Nowhere but here. Born and raised in Bloomington, Illinois."

Dialogue Two

"Can I tell you a secret?"
"Yeah, I guess so."
"It was no accident that I showed up at Friday's that time you asked me to sit down."
"That was planned?"
"Well, I don't know if I'd go so far to call it a plan. But I was definitely following a hunch."
"Do you want to know my secret? I was hoping I might see you, too."

During dialogues like the preceding two, conversational rules for appropriate verbal behavior are accompanied by rules for appropriate nonverbal behavior as well.[26] In the first case, we would expect Samantha and Terry to face each other,

Box 8-4   Considering Diversity

Conversational Management and Racism

A reader wrote Judith Martin, the nationally syndicated columnist known as Miss Manners, describing himself as an Ivy-League-educated African American on the management fast-track of the company at which he was employed. He was seeking Martin's advice about an incident at a formal party at the company president's home. The chief financial officer of the company told a racist story to a group of people. Although the story was greeted with silence, all eyes turned to the African American, as if people expected him to respond.

In such a scenario, Martin advised,

First, look unsmilingly around the room, finally allowing your eyes to rest on the person who told the joke. The room goes silent. Slowly and in a conversational tone, you ask, "Do you find that amusing?" Then you allow your eyes to travel back around the room. One person will become unfrozen, and declare, "No, I don't, as a matter of fact." Immediately, the rest of the guests will fall all over themselves to show that they didn't like it either. Before the

teller of the joke can recover enough to attempt self-defense, you say, "But I'm sure Brian didn't mean any harm by it." And then you turn to him, and engage him in innocent social conversation that has nothing to do with what just happened. Against his will, he will feel grateful to you for having rescued him. The senior executives will register that you are not to be trifled with. And the president will observe that you know how to be simultaneously smooth and firmly in charge. Miss Manners can't imagine that anyone could hope to get anything more out of an office party.

What is your opinion of Miss Manner's advice? Do you agree with the manner of conversational regulation she suggests? Certainly it allows the advice seeker to make a strong statement and impression without sacrificing an instrumental goal, namely, getting ahead in the company. Do you think the same advice would have applied equally well if the story had been sexist and the advice seeker had been female? Explain why or why not.

SOURCE: Judith Martin, "Miss Manners," *Sacramento Bee,* 19 July 1995, E3. Reprinted by permission of United Media.

look each other in the eye while talking, pause long enough to encourage the other to respond, and smile as an expression of warmth. In the second case, we would expect all of this nonverbal behavior and more. At this point, Samantha and Terry might lightly touch hands. They also might lean toward each other and spend more time gazing at each other without necessarily saying anything.

If Samantha and Terry's relationship continued to escalate, the rules governing verbal and nonverbal behavior would become less ritualistic. Samantha and Terry would continue to self-disclose but with greater depth, touch more frequently, and further reduce the physical distance separating them. With even further escalation, they also would begin to experience what communication scholar William Rawlins calls dialectic tension.[27] It's at this point that their conversational skills would begin to be tested.

relational dialectics
The contextual and interactional tensions that are inherent in relationships.

Dialectics   A dialectic is a contradiction between two conflicting forces which creates a tension. According to Rawlins, there are two contextual dialectics people need to manage communicatively. The first concerns the tension that occurs because relationships have both a public and private side.[28] Consider these two sides in terms of unmarried couples who live together compared to married couples who live together. Privately, both relationships may be similar in nature. The parties are loving and committed. Publicly, however, these two relationships are quite dissimilar. One has legal status and the other does not.

Cohabiting couples frequently are criticized by people outside the relationship because their relationship isn't publicly sanctioned. This criticism creates tension within the relationship that the couple must learn to manage. Although heterosexual couples can resort to marriage in the attempt to manage this specific dialectic tension, gay and lesbian couples cannot. Gay and lesbian couples report, moreover, that the public and private sides of their relationship are frequently a source of tension for them.[29]

A second contextual dialectic is what Rawlins refers to as the ideal and the real. Most of us have an image of what we consider the ideal relationship. This idealized image can lead us to expect more from our real relationships than they are able to deliver. TV, films, and romance novels, for example, communicate powerful but unrealistic images of what constitutes the ideal relationship. Research suggests that mass media are a potential source of tension in people's relationships in this regard. Who among us can compete with the romantic ideals portrayed on *The Young and the Restless, General Hospital,* and *Days of Our Lives?*

As if these contextual dialectics don't produce enough relational tension in our lives, Rawlins also says there are four interactional dialectics: (1) independence and dependence, (2) affection and instrumentality, (3) judgment and acceptance, and (4) expressiveness and protectiveness.[30] Friends usually have little difficulty relating to the first source of tension. On the one hand, people want friends on whom they can depend. On the other hand, people don't want friends who become overly dependent on them. There must be not only reciprocity but also balance in this regard.

Affection and instrumentality is a source of tension with which most friends and intimates can readily identify. The fact is, we pursue friendship and intimacy because they assist us in realizing our instrumental goals. The conclusion that we get something out of friendship and intimacy is inescapable. That friendship and intimacy serve an instrumental purpose isn't necessarily bad—unless the tension between affection and instrumentality becomes a defining issue in a relationship, as is the case when people perceive that they're being used.

Judgment and acceptance is the third source of dialectic tension. One benefit of friendship and intimacy is having a relationship with someone who will be honest with you. Friends don't let friends go out looking bad, jeopardize their health by gaining too much weight, or drink too much and make fools of themselves. Or do they? The line between being honest and being judgmental is thin. And friends and intimates who are unconditionally accepting are rare indeed. That this dialectic between judgment and acceptance is a common source of tension, therefore, shouldn't be surprising.

Finally, there is expressiveness and protectiveness, the fourth source of dialectic tension Rawlins links to interaction.[31] This dialectic is clearly related to our earlier discussion of the management of self-disclosure. It is important for friends and intimates to express their mutual feelings to each other. But must they always be brutally honest? Or should they be more strategic and protect themselves and others from information that might harm their relationship?

In heterosexual relationships, expressiveness and protectiveness also are influenced by one's gender. Women, in general, are more expressive than men. Women report, moreover, that they are frequently bothered by men's reluctance to express their feelings in a relationship.

These contextual and interactional dialectics are an inherent part of our most important relationships. Because the tensions owing to these dialectics don't simply disappear over time, their management is necessary throughout the life of a relationship. Thus, it is important for people to be mindful of these tensions in their day-to-day conversation, not just when these tensions cause outright conflict between them.

Left unmanaged, nonverbal communication can increase dialectical tension in a relationship.

Table 8-1 Making Conversation Coherent

Quantity Contribute as much information to a conversation as the situation demands, but never more.

Quality Avoid saying things you think are false when conversing, and try not to make claims for which you lack evidence.

Relevance Avoid saying things that strike others as completely off-the-wall. Stick to the topic of conversation.

Clarity Reduce uncertainty by avoiding ambiguity and express yourself with terms people are likely to understand. Also, try to be logical in the order of things you say, and be brief.

SOURCE: Adapted from Kathleen K. Reardon, *Interpersonal Communication: Where Minds Meet* (Belmont, Calif.: Wadsworth, 1987), 107–8.

As we said earlier, conversation is regulated by rules. Ritualistic in the beginning, conversational rules change as a relationship takes on definition. People need to be actively involved with this process of change. One way for people to handle this change is to develop consensual rules for their conversations.[32] Couples, for example, may agree to avoid saying hurtful things to each other, and co-workers may agree that it's OK to disagree.

Consensual rules for conversation can be a big help in managing the dialectic tension associated with expressiveness and protectiveness. Thinking ahead about whether an expression will be hurtful is much better than blurting it out. Agreeing in advance that it's OK to disagree can assist people in managing any dialectic tension arising from judgment and acceptance. Such a consensual rule tells people that they don't have to always accept what the other says. Consensual rules such as this also tell people that when they do disagree, it shouldn't cause unmanageable levels of tension in their relationship.

A second way people can manage dialectic tension involves conversational coherence; knowing what to say, when to say it, and how to say it.[33] Consensual rules are useless without conversational coherence. When people argue, as a case in point, they may consensually agree to stick to issues, avoid personal attacks, and take turns in elaborating their thoughts.

Rules are irrelevant, however, if people repeatedly interrupt each other, cut each other off, or dismiss the validity of a message with nonverbal behaviors that suggest the person is an idiot. Thus, people must both agree to follow the rules they establish for managing dialectic tension and display communication behaviors consistent with the principle of conversational coherence. Communication scholar Kathleen Reardon offers the advice summarized in Table 8-1 about conversational coherence, which involves the quantity of information appropriate to conversation, the quality of the information, its relevance, and its clarity.[34]

In addition to reaching consensual rules and conversing with coherence, managing dialectic tensions involves skillful nonverbal behavior. However, this is

Table 8-2	Facilitative Nonverbal Behaviors and Conversational Coherence

1. Maintain an amount of distance appropriate to the relationship.

2. Make and maintain appropriate eye contact.

3. Lean toward rather than away from the person.

4. Nod to indicate understanding, move your head from side to side when you don't understand.

5. Use vocalic encouragers such as "mm-hmm" and "ah-hah."

6. Smile, if appropriate.

SOURCE: Adapted from Mark L. Knapp and Anita L. Vangelisti, *Interpersonal Communication and Human Relationships,* 3rd ed. (Boston: Allyn and Bacon, 1996).

sometimes easier said than done. Much of our nonverbal behavior is outside our conscious control. Furthermore, when nonverbal behavior appears to contradict the content of a message, we are inclined to believe what is communicated nonverbally.

Table 8-2 lists a number of nonverbal behaviors that facilitate conversational coherence. Eye contact and facial expression, for example, can assist people in determining the degree to which they understand each other and whether or not they agree. Movements, such as nodding your head in agreement and leaning toward people, also encourage people to continue talking. Respecting people's space and pausing long enough to ensure they're finished talking also are facilitative, conversational behaviors.

Finally, conversational management of the dialectic tensions characteristic of well-defined relationships involves the concepts of complementarity and symmetry. Communication researchers Frank Millar and Edna Rogers argue that the nature of the association between people depends on whether their relational communication is complementary or symmetrical.[35] Complementary relational communication tells people they agree about the nature of their association. Consider the following conversation between Ari and Rafi. The arrows after each remark tell us whether it is controlling (↑), accepting (↓), or transitional (→).

ARI: "Let me show you how to hold the hammer. You'll drive the nails straighter and with less effort." (↑)
RAFI: "Sure, you're the boss." (↓)
ARI: "At least when it comes to carpentry." (→)
RAFI: "That's true. But I get to be boss when we start choosing colors of paint." (↑)
ARI: "Go for it." (↓)

Because the direction of the arrows is equitably distributed between Ari and Rafi, their relationship not only is complementary but egalitarian as well.

Relational communication that is symmetrical is characterized by parallel messages. Symmetrical messages also can be competitive or submissive, as illustrated in the next conversation.

JAN: "I vote for the movies." (↑)
SUSAN: "No way, we went to the movies last week." (↑)
JAN: "So, you decide." (↓)
SUSAN: "I want you to decide." (↓)

The first exchange is representative of what Millar and Rogers call competitive symmetry, and the second is representative of submissive symmetry.[36] Researchers have successfully used complementarity and symmetry to analyze couples.[37] Among other things, they have found that cooperative couples seldom engage in the kind of competitive symmetry we see in Jan and Susan's initial exchange. The implication of this finding for using conversation to manage dialectic tension is fairly obvious. Whereas competitive symmetry potentially can increase such tensions, complementarity potentially can decrease them.

Consider cohabiting couples once again. Both couples are feeling tension in their relationship as a result of having to try to balance its public and private side. The heterosexual couple is being pressured, for example, to get married and legalize their relationship by two sets of parents. The gay couple is feeling pressured because one's health insurance at work cannot be legally applied to the other, who needs a tonsillectomy.

How well the couples manage the tension resulting from these two very realistic scenarios depends on the kind of relational communication in which they engage. Competitive symmetry probably would only exacerbate the tension. Although complementarity probably would reduce it, the couples would have to first recognize which pattern of relational communication is most customary for them.

A chief role of marriage counselors is to assist couples in identifying the kind of relational communication in which they typically engage. Couples sometimes learn in the process of counseling that though they've been willing to try to work things out, the competitive and symmetrical style with which they communicate has frustrated their efforts.

As you can now see, then, the success or failure of your relationships is a matter of the communication behaviors that define them. Further, this fact is true whether a relationship is just starting out or is a long established one. Simply put, the health of your relationships is a consequence of how well you manage your relational communication. That is why it's so important that you understand the goals behind your relationship and the communication behaviors you'll need to manage in the attempt to realize those goals.

Summary

Relational communication involves the characteristic verbal and nonverbal behaviors that define the nature of the association between people. This is most evident in the process of relationship development. Satisfactory relationships can exist anywhere on a continuum from ongoing acquaintance to intimacy. Where a relationship falls on this continuum depends on the characteristic breadth and depth of the messages that the people exchanged.

Altman and Taylor's model of social penetration describes how the breadth and depth of the messages exchanged between people can evolve as they engage in exploratory affective exchange, affective exchange, and stable affective exchange. Knapp's model of the specific stages through which a relationship potentially can escalate adds information to Altman and Taylor's model of social penetration. Knapp proposes five specific stages of relationship development: (1) initiating, which is heavily influenced by proximity, perceptions of physical attraction, and perceived similarity; (2) experimenting, which serves as a relational filter for people; (3) intensifying; (4) integrating; and (5) bonding.

Knapp's model also addresses the manner in which relationships potentially can de-escalate. Knapp proposes five stages in the process of de-escalation: (1) differentiating, (2) circumscribing, (3) stagnating, (4) avoiding, and (5) terminating.

The likelihood of relationships staying as they are, escalating, or de-escalating depends on how well people manage their relational communication. Managing relational communication begins with people examining the goals they hope to achieve in their relationships. Canary and Cody suggest three goals in this regard: (1) self-presentational, (2) instrumental, and (3) relational.

Managing relational communication also involves being mindful of the process of self-disclosure. Self-disclosure concerns people purposefully revealing information that otherwise would be unobtainable. Self-disclosure varies in breadth and depth, depending on the nature of the association between people. Self-disclosure in beginning relationships is characterized by breadth. In well-defined and intimate relationships, self-disclosure is characterized by both depth and breadth.

Finally, the management of relational communication involves conversational regulation throughout the life of a relationship. During the early stages of relationships, conversational regulation involves adhering to verbal and nonverbal rules that are ritualistic. In later stages of relationship development, conversational regulation also involves the dialectic tensions that are an inherent feature of friendship and intimacy in particular. There are two broad categories of these dialectic tensions, contextual and interactional. Two contextual dialectics involve tensions between the public and the private dimensions of relations and between the ideal and the real in relationships. Interactional dialectics include independence and dependence, affection and instrumentality, judgment and acceptance, expressiveness and protectiveness. How well people use conversation in regulating these dialectic tensions, finally influences the degree to which their relationship is characterized by complementary and symmetrical relational messages.

Another Look

Articles

William W. Wilmot and Alan L. Sillars. "Developmental Issues in Personal Relationships." In *Life-Span Communication: Normative Processes,* edited by Jon F. Nussbaum, 119–35. Hillsdale, N.J.: Lawrence Erlbaum, 1989.

This authoritative article by two highly respected scholars takes an in-depth look at relationship development and how this process potentially changes over the course of a life. As Wilmot and Sillars point out, with an ever-increasing life span, it's very important for us to understand how kin, friend, and romantic relationships fluctuate as we grow older.

Elaine Hatfield. "The Dangers of Intimacy." In *Bridges Not Walls: A Book About Interpersonal Communication,* 5th ed., edited by John Stewart, 215–24. New York: McGraw-Hill, 1990.

Hatfield, who is a psychotherapist, reports that much of her practice is devoted to helping people cope with their fears of intimacy. Hatfield suggests that there are good reasons for such fears. She describes the major reasons behind them and then gives the reader some strategies for dealing with the fear of intimacy.

Books

Mark L. Knapp and Anita L. Vangelisti. *Interpersonal Communication and Human Relationships.* 3rd ed. Boston: Allyn and Bacon, 1996.

This text looks at the complex processes overviewed in this chapter. It does a good job of describing the communication behaviors that are characteristic of escalating and de-escalating relationships. This text also offers many useful communication skills for dealing with a relationship in decline.

William K. Rawlins. *Friendship Matters: Communication, Dialectics, and the Life Course.* New York: Aldine de Gruyter, 1992.

Although they make up the bulk of our relational lives, friends tend to be ignored in the research on relationships. This book explains the dialectic tensions we introduced in the context of friendship. Rawlins also looks at how these dialectics change, depending on our stage of life.

Video Rentals

The Joy Luck Club Based on Amy Tan's critically acclaimed best seller, this film shows modern Chinese daughters and their traditional mothers, struggling to accommodate each other. It does an excellent job of illustrating how secrets, self-disclosure, and goals influence communication behavior. It also shows how cultural diversity can play a significant role in families of the same ethnicity. For example, the Americanized culture of the daughters is often extremely different from the traditional Chinese culture of their mothers, which has a dramatic impact on mother–daughter communication.

Glory This probably isn't the first film that comes to mind when you think about relational definition. Yet, this remarkable telling of the 54th Massachusetts, the African American infantry unit that made history for its heroic effort during the Civil War, is an excellent illustration of how a group of diverse men meet and begin to define the nature of their association. Denzel Washington, who won an Academy Award for his performance, is especially effective in his scenes with Morgan Freeman.

Thelma and Louise Susan Sarandon and Geena Davis play two friends who spontaneously decide to take a vacation from their everyday lives. Sarandon and Davis are very effective in showing how the depth and breadth of exchange between people changes as they become more intimate. The film also does a good job of showing the differences between relationships that are complementary and those that are symmetrical.

Harold and Maude   This cult favorite, starring Ruth Gordon and Bud York, shows how a withdrawn and alienated young man is transformed by his relationship with an eccentric, hip, and wise septuagenarian. Aside from countering stereotypes about the aged, *Harold and Maude* clearly illustrates the role of communication in defining people's relationships.

Theory and Research in Practice

1. In your journal, make a list of the non-family members with whom you have been most involved. Discuss the development of these relationships, using Altman and Taylor's concepts of breadth and depth of exchange and Knapp's stages of relationship escalation. Also, compare what you perceive as the attributes that initially attracted you to these people with the attributes discussed in this chapter, specifically, proximity, physical attraction, and similarity.

2. Think back over the course of development of one of your most intimate relationships. See if you can remember the turning points that marked significant changes in the relationship, and the changes in communication behaviors that accompanied these turning points.

3. The literature on relational development suggests that women are much better at relationships than men. One explanation is the male deficit model, which argues that men lack the interest and skill to become genuinely intimate with each other. An alternative model suggests that men do become close, but they take a different path than women do. Whereas women talk with each other more and disclose more intimate information about each other, men are "doers." They become close as a result of the activities they share.

Take a stand on one of the two models. Drawing on your experience, defend in writing the stand you take, paying particular attention to the role of self-disclosure in women's and men's relationships.

4. Assess how the relationships in which you're involved have helped you to achieve your self-presentational, instrumental, and relational goals. Do these three types of goals vary with the relationship? For example, are the goals your ongoing acquaintances have helped you achieve different from those that your friends or intimates have helped you achieve? Be specific and see if you can explain any differences noted.

5. In your journal, describe how dialectic tensions affect your closest relationships. Then, for each relationship, describe how successful you and the other person have been in using conversation to manage these tensions. To what do you attribute your success or lack of it?

6. The research reported in this chapter is based on face-to-face communication. Yet, cyberspace conversations are becoming increasingly routine. How well do you think the principles of conversational regulation discussed here generalize to conversations over the Internet?

CHAPTER 9

Family Communication

OBJECTIVES

After reading this chapter you should be able to:

- Describe and distinguish among open, closed, random, enmeshed, and disengaged family systems.

- Discuss how the number of people and the roles they perform influence family systems of communication.

- Describe what can be learned about family systems boundaries and hierarchies by observing and diagramming their network of interaction.

- Construct examples showing how rules influence family communication systems.

- Discuss the role of stories, themes, and myths in the family communication system.

- Describe differences among traditional, independent, separate, and mixed-couple types.

- Create examples that demonstrate how dialectic tensions influence the transactions between couples, between couples with children, and between parents and children.

- Demonstrate communication skills associated with effective family communication.

Whenever I see the bridges that connect Los Angeles with East Los Angeles, I remember my family. I remember my father and my mother; my brothers Chucho, little Jimmy, and Memo, the lawyer; and my crazy sisters Toni and Elene. But to write the story of my family, I have to begin where millions of stories have begun—a long, long time ago.

So begins Edward James Olmos's narration of *My Family/Mi Familia,* a powerful film about the life of a Latino family.[1] The film crosses decades and generations.

As the film *Mi Familia-My Family* so vividly demonstrated, communication connects each new generation of a family with the one that preceded it.

In the process, we learn about the family's origins, its people, their successes and their tragedies. In the process, we also learn something about ourselves and the families to which we belong. Although every family is unique, every family also is a little alike.

This chapter focuses on family communication. It extends the information about relational communication presented in the previous chapter to the dimension of communication that is perhaps the most significant in which we participate. Our family first shapes how we see ourselves and how we relate to others. So that we may better understand family communication, we look at the family from a number of different vantage points, including

- family systems and their attributes,
- the communication networks that define family structure,
- the function of storytelling in family communication,
- the roles people play in families and the functions they perform,
- the kinds of dialectic tensions that occur in families, and
- what constitutes effective family communication.

The Family System

In Chapter 1, we characterized communication as a system of interdependent components. We also said that a change in one of these components will produce changes in the other components. A **family** is a system of relational communication, whose members perform interdependent roles, are bound by history or choice, and create a collective memory through storytelling, themes, and myths. Although family systems vary in type, they also share a number of common attributes, which we'll discuss shortly.

family A system of relational communication, whose members perform interdependent roles, are bound by history or choices, and create a collective memory through storytelling, themes, and myths.

Family Types

Families are increasingly diverse in nature. If you were to pick up a book on the modern family, for example, you would find discussions of families of origin, families of choice, one- and dual-wage-earning families, two-parent and single-parent families, and functional and dysfunctional families as well. And even that list doesn't exhaust the infinite variety of family types. It doesn't include blended families, for example, which are the result of couples with children divorcing and remarrying people who also have children and then perhaps also having one or more of their own children.[2]

Our discussion begins with five types of family systems.[3] Although they don't cover every possible variation, these five systems include most of the family types listed in the preceding paragraph. In addition, these five systems can be applied generally to both families of origin and families of choice, which include heterosexual couples, homosexual couples, and single parents.

Open family systems welcome family members interacting with people outside the family and encourage them to do so. Open family systems readily adapt to the inputs family members bring back from exchanges with nonmembers, and use the information to regulate or modify the primary family system. An open family in which one member is disabled, for example, is likely to encourage all family members to spend time in the disabled community. The input family members receive from the disabled community then allows the family system to adapt to the needs of the disabled family member.

Closed family systems discourage family members from interacting with people outside the family. The heads of closed family systems, which are hierarchical by nature, see little to be gained from interaction with outsiders. An extreme example of a closed family was the Branch Davidian religious sect headed by David Koresh. Not only was the group largely closed to communication from the surrounding community, but the word of Koresh was law among family members.

Random family systems are a third general type. The boundaries of the random family system are ambiguous, as are the rules governing the interaction of family members with outside subsystems. The primary difficulty members of random family systems face is the unpredictability of these systems. For instance, the heads of such systems may encourage family members to be open one moment and closed the next. Much of the time members of random systems spend communicating is targeted at deciphering the rules of the day.

Enmeshed family systems are neither completely open nor completely closed. Unlike random family systems, however, the goal of the enmeshed system is family cohesiveness. Of the five family types discussed, the enmeshed system is the most collectivistic. The family comes before the individual, no matter what.

If this means family members must sacrifice their independence for the good of the family, so be it.

Finally there is the *disengaged family system*. In stark contrast to the collectivistic orientation of enmeshed family systems, individualism in the extreme is reinforced in the disengaged family system. The danger in such systems is that members can become so distant from each other they lose sight of their interdependence. Thus, the system of mutual support we tend to associate with families may fall to the wayside in disengaged systems.

Family Attributes

Families can be thought of as systems because the members play particular roles in relation to one another. As a unit family members exchange messages with sources outside the family. Who belongs to a family is defined by its boundaries, and the place of members inside the family is defined by its hierarchy. Family life is governed by rules; and one of the primary goals of family members is to ensure the stability of the system. Let us look at each of those attributes in some detail.

Family Size and Members' Roles   The type of system characteristic of a family is influenced by the number of people in the system and the roles they perform. Because, as was noted in Chapter 1, a two-person, or dyadic, system has only a single line of communication, a two-person family is potentially more intimate and has more accurate communication than larger family systems.

In families of every size, the members each have one or more roles. A **role** is a pattern of behavior in which a family member is expected to routinely engage.[4] Some roles are expressive, such as when family members care for each other's emotional needs. Other roles are instrumental, such as one member working outside the home in the effort to contribute to the family's financial well-being. Authors Kathleen Galvin and Bernard Brommel list five essential family role functions that researchers have identified:

1. providing for adult sexual fulfillment and gender modeling for children,
2. providing nurturing and emotional support,
3. providing for individual development,
4. providing kinship maintenance and family management, and
5. providing basic resources.[5]

role   A pattern of behavior in which family members are expected to routinely engage.

Sometimes these roles are highly differentiated and fall on the shoulders of specific family members. At other times, these roles may be shared. Family communication researchers Janet Yerby, Nancy Buerkel-Rothfuss, and Authur Bochner list some familiar family roles that members may assume: family achiever, pet, clown, listener, hero, adventurer, eccentric, confronter, mediator, or scapegoat.[6] Later in the chapter, we will discuss family roles in more detail, as well as the family myths and stories that perpetuate some of these roles.

Box 9-1   Considering Diversity

Roles in Families of Choice

The traditional model of the family is based on heterosexuality. Two people meet, marry, and at some point have children. Increasingly, though, people realize that there is something called a family of choice. One kind of family of choice is the homosexual couple, gay men or lesbians who have committed to a long-term relationship.

As communication scholars Michelle Huston and Pepper Schwartz point out, the roles heterosexual couples adopt when they join to form a family tend to be based on their gender. Certainly, this is the case with traditional couples, one of four marital types uncovered by the research of Mary Anne Fitzpatrick.

But what about homosexual couples, Huston and Pepper ask? Does one adopt a male gender role and the other a female one? Or do the roles gay and lesbian couples assume mirror those of independent couples, a second marital type uncovered in Fitzpatrick's research? Independents prefer to negotiate the roles they perform, rather than divide them along gender lines.

The stereotype of gay and lesbian couples is more traditional than independent. Hollywood films and TV shows, for example, almost always cast gay and lesbian couples in masculine and feminine terms. One person performs the male role, and the other person performs the female role.

How accurate is this stereotype? Investigate this stereotype in the attempt to determine if it is more fiction than fact. If possible, discuss the stereotype with gays and lesbians. Also, visit your library and see what the research reports in journals that focus on personal and social relations, human sexuality, communication, and psychology. Report in class on what you learn.

SOURCE: Michelle Huston and Pepper Schwartz, *Gendered Dynamics in the Romantic Relationships of Lesbians and Gay Men, Gendered Relationships,* ed. Julia T. Wood (Mountain View, Calif.: Mayfield, 1996), 163–76.

For now, it is sufficient to note that the number of people in a family and the roles they play are key elements in family systems. First, the number of people in a system affects the operation of the system. The addition of new members, for example, children, dramatically alters the system. Second, the roles people are expected to perform also influence the operation of the system (see Box 9-1). Consider the stereotypical example in which a mother falls ill in a traditional family. Because the father and children may be unaccustomed to performing the mother's role, the functioning of the system suffers.

Inputs and Outputs   As Yerby, Buerkel-Rothfuss, and Bochner discuss in their highly regarded book, *Understanding Family Communication,* family systems also are influenced by inputs and outputs.[7] Inputs are messages a family receives from sources outside the system. Sometimes family members perceive these inputs as a threat to the system's health, as is the case with parents concerned with the effects of television violence or the lyrics of rock music. Thus, family members may try to filter outside inputs, letting some in and keeping some out.

By the same token, family systems produce outputs. These outputs not only influence how family members see themselves but also influence the subsystems

Our sense of appropriate gender roles is learned primarily through our interactions with parents.

surrounding them. The family that doesn't give school officials permission to include a child in a sex education class is sending a message to a specific subsystem, the school. The family actively involved with the Parent-Teacher-Student Association or a youth sports team affiliated with the school is also sending a message to the school.

Boundaries and Hierarchies   Family systems are characterized by boundaries and hierarchies. Boundaries define who belongs to the family and who doesn't.[8] Married children typically constitute a subsystem that falls within the boundaries of the overall family system. Close friends also constitute a subsystem, but close friends usually fall outside the family's true boundaries. The exception is when close friends constitute a family of choice.

Hierarchies define who has influence and who has the power to make decisions in the family.[9] In some cases, a family system's power and decision-making structure is very hierarchical, meaning influence moves from the head of the family downward. In others, the power and decision-making structure in the system may be less well defined, as is sometimes the case in dysfunctional families. Children with an alcoholic parent, for example, often make decisions that normally would be made by one or both parents. Finally, where there is no clear-cut hierarchy in the system, family members may share power and decision-making authority.

Rules   Family communication systems are governed by rules both explicit and implicit.[10] Some rules are arbitrary, as is the typical case with parents telling children what constitutes appropriate and inappropriate behavior. Other rules may be consensually developed. The family may consensually agree to rules about such matters as how they celebrate birthdays or how they decide on where to

Family members are a source of strength and comfort in times of grief.

vacation each year. Family members also may come to a consensual agreement about the rules for dividing and spending family resources.

Goals   Just as the communication behavior of family members reflects the rules of the system, their communication behavior also reflects the goals of the system.[11] A chief relational goal among families is to maintain the system . . . to keep it going. This is one of the reasons families are so resilient, capable of surviving almost any adversity. Married couples survive affairs, and the relationship between parents and children survives divorce.

Committed families in the modern world, moreover, remain intact even when visited by death. In the film *Long Time Companion,* a group of gay men clearly constitute a family system. Their family's survival is put to the test by the onslaught of the AIDS crisis. Even though they lose several members to AIDS, their commitment to the system they created keeps their family going.

Of course, the goals characteristic of family systems are not always as dramatic as survival of the system. Families also have self-presentational goals that influence the communication behaviors of individual members, such as when a parent tells a child that no one in the family has ever failed a subject in school. Finally, the communication routine of family systems is influenced by instrumental goals, such as saving money for a home or for a child's future education.

Feedback   The final shared attribute of family systems is feedback.[12] Family communication systems feature feedback mechanisms that are meant to regulate the interdependent behaviors of individual family members. When family members break rules or their behaviors get in the way of family goals, they may be punished. In rare cases, families may even go so far as to ostracize a family member who repeatedly breaks the rules of the family system.

Figure 9-1 Chain, Wheel, and Y-Type Networks. Networks often reveal where power resides in a family system.

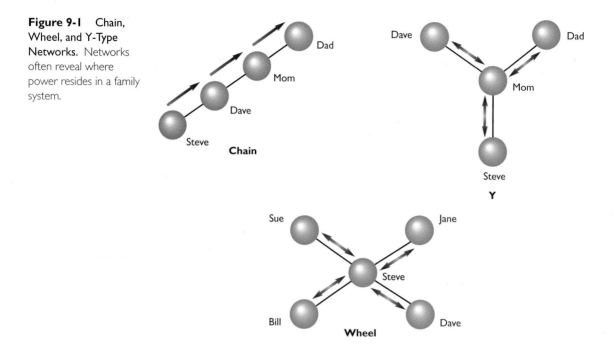

Networks and Subsystems

Family communication reflects the networks and subsystems a family develops over time. These networks and subsystems, which can cross or stay within the boundaries that define who belongs to a family, have a powerful effect on family communication. Networks tell us about not only the flow of communication inside a system but also the degree to which families are hierarchical. Figure 9-1, depicts three different networks. As you can see from the flow of communication, power in each of the three networks is concentrated in a single person.[13]

Internal Networks and Subsystems

Specifically, then, a **network** is composed of the links that connect the lines of communication in a family system. The number and configuration of these links can reveal much about the pattern of communication that is characteristic of a specific family, including who has power and authority and who is involved with decision making. In Figure 9-2, for example, there are five members in the family system. As you can see, there are ten links connecting the potential lines of communication among family members. If we were to observe the members of this family system interacting with each other, we could learn whether influence was shared or concentrated and determine whether any members had formed a clique or subsystem.

network The links that connect the lines of communication in a family system.

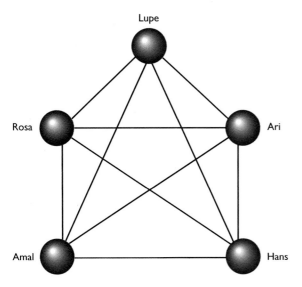

Lupe

Rosa

Ari

Amal

Hans

Figure 9-2 All Channel **Network.** In an all channel network, it is possible to directly communicate with any member of the family system.

If we discovered while observing this system that a majority of messages were directed at Lupe, for example, we might reasonably infer that she has disproportionate influence on the pattern of communication characterizing the system. Although this disproportionate influence could be a result of Lupe's role, it also could be symptomatic of dysfunctional behavior. In hierarchical family systems, as a case in point, a disproportionate number of messages is directed at the person at the top of the hierarchy. Yet, you also see the same pattern in families where one member's behavior is having a disruptive influence on the overall system.

To reiterate, we also can identify from observing a network the presence of a clique or subsystem in the family. In Figure 9-2, the amount of interaction between Amal and Hans might be abnormally high and unique to their relationship. By that, we mean Amal and Hans don't interact this much with others in the system. Subsystems are characterized by the same features that appear in the larger system. The members of subsystems have roles, establish rules and goals, and give each other feedback in the attempt to regulate the subsystem. They also may produce outputs and receive inputs. Subsystems typically develop because the larger system fails to sufficiently satisfy the needs or goals of the people who form the subsystem, as is the case among children whose needs are not being met by parents.

Subsystems also can be either complementary or symmetrical in relation to the family as a whole (Figure 9-3). Recall from Chapter 8 that complementary relationships are cooperative, whereas symmetrical ones are often competitive. Complementary subsystems, therefore, can improve the functioning of the overall family system. Symmetrical ones, on the other hand, may negatively affect the larger family system, as is the case when two family members form a coalition to compete with others in the family.

External Networks and Subsystems

It is difficult for even the most closed family system to shield itself from the influence of the external networks and subsystems surrounding it.[14] As a case in point, there are more dual-wage-earning families today than at any other time in history. The workplace and its demands constitute a powerful subsystem, one that is having a major impact on modern family life. Magazines such as *Newsweek* and *Time* have dedicated issues to the impact of the work environment on families of varying shape and size. When both parents work, the issue of who takes care of the kids is more important than ever. And working couples without children report that the amount of time they spend at their job is a major source of tension in their family life.

Work is only one example of the external subsystems and corresponding networks that influence family communication. Others include the government, which makes rules governing the behavior of family members, and schools, which may expose children to ideas and practices contrary to those taught in the family. In addition, close friends and religious organizations to which family members belong also potentially influence families.

Like subsystems in the family, external subsystems and networks may be complementary or symmetrical. Most of us can think of subsystems to which we have belonged that complemented the goals of our families. By the same token, most of us also can recall examples of subsystems that were symmetrical and competitive, as is typically the case of the network of friends we develop in adolescence.

Storytelling

Up to this point we've been talking about family systems of communication in fairly generic and inclusive terms. We described the types of systems that characterize families, the attributes common to family systems of communication, and how family systems are affected by internal and external networks and subsystems. Here we want to begin discussing the factors that give each family a unique identity and encourage family members to think of themselves as part of a collective or clan. To begin this process, we ask that you think back to Chapter 7's discussion of cultural diversity. We said that a culture is defined by a collective pattern of thinking and behaving. We also said that cultures vary in terms of collectivism-individualism, power distance, uncertainty avoidance, and femininity-masculinity.

Not only does your family constitute a culture in its own right, your sense of the larger culture and your beliefs about appropriate communication behavior relative to it are very much a product of your family experience. What's more, the degree to which your beliefs deviate from those of the culture at large also is a reflection of your family experience. If you were raised in a family that practiced collectivism, for example, the chances are good that your beliefs differ from the North American norm emphasizing the importance of being an individual.

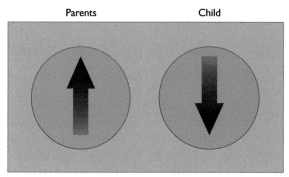

Parents   Child

Complementary Family Systems

Figure 9-3 Complementary and Symmetrical Family Systems

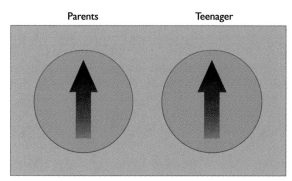

Parents   Teenager

Symmetrical and Competitive Family Systems

The cultural lessons we learn from our families are part of a larger story that families pass along from generation to generation. Like any other story that has been told and retold, the narratives that describe our family's history reflect certain themes and even myths. These stories and the themes and myths that inhere to them are what truly give us a sense of place and a sense of belonging.

Stories

Family stories clearly constitute relational communication. Not only do such stories assist us in understanding the nature of our association with our immediate family, but they also do so with family members with whom we've had little or even no direct experience—for instance, a great-great-grandmother or a great-great-grandfather. Stories are narrative descriptions of events. Believable stories are characterized by logical consistency; events as told must make sense. Believable stories also are characterized by fidelity; events as described must ring true with personal experience.[15]

Family stories are functional. Norman MacLean's book *A River Runs Through It,* for example, tells a number of canonical stories about his family living in Missoula, Montana, during the early part of the century. **Canonical stories** involve what is considered to be appropriate behavior. In *A River Runs Through It,*

canonical stories
Family stories that teach family members lessons important to the family functioning for example, appropriate behavior.

MacLean talks about his father, who is a minister, and his brother, and the lessons his father taught them about right and wrong while fly fishing on the Bigfoot River. It is only through the telling of the story, MacLean points out early in the book, that he has come to fully understand the lessons taught and learned from his father, mother, and brother.

Harper Lee does much the same thing in *To Kill a Mockingbird,* her Pulitzer Prize–winning novel about growing up in the rural South during the 1920s, as seen through the eyes of a young girl, Jean Louise Finch, who is the novel's narrator. Scout, as Jean Louise is called by her father, Atticus, and brother Jim, describes the events that shaped her childhood. Along the way, she also describes how her father helped her to understand the larger meaning of the events, including the lessons to be learned from them about prejudice and bigotry. Like MacLean's family story, Lee's also is canonical.

Besides teaching lessons and establishing the boundaries of right and wrong, family stories help to *connect* one generation to another, create a *collective memory* among family members, and shape *family identity.*[16] When Edward James Olmos begins the narration to the film *My Family/Mi Familia,* he starts out by saying, "I remember my family." He goes on to weave a complex tapestry that not only connects the present generation with past generations but serves to create a sense of shared history among family members. This shared history and the collective memory it facilitates also serve to reinforce among family members the fact that their family identity is unique and even special.

Sometimes the events described in family stories become epiphanies, detailing pivotal and seemingly miraculous events in a family's history.[17] In *My Family/ Mi Familia,* as a case in point, the mother is separated from her husband and illegally deported to Mexico. The story of her return to her family is truly heroic and gives her an almost mythic quality. This story becomes a benchmark in the history of the family's struggle to survive and prosper.

Themes and Myths

A common theme in the stories families tell involves personal sacrifice and struggle. Certainly this is true in the case of *My Family/Mi Familia.* But it is also true of the family stories of Laura Ingalls Wilder, which you may know from the still-in-syndication TV series *Little House on the Prairie.* **Myths** also are a common consequence of the stories families tell and the themes that inhere to them. According to family communication scholars, myths are not without purpose. Myths can serve to assist families in

myths Family stories that assist family members in maintaining important attitudes, beliefs, and values, managing role conflicts, reinforcing generational bonds, and coping with emotional duress.

- maintaining important attitudes, beliefs, and values;
- managing role conflicts;
- reinforcing generational bonds; and
- coping with emotional duress.[18]

Consider the Gladstones, a married couple with a 15-year-old son and a 12-year-old daughter. Mark has taken over the role of managing the family farm

Sacrifice and struggle were frequent themes on the TV series "Little House on the Prairie."

from his aging and retired father. The Gladstones have farmed for three generations, and Mark hopes his 15-year-old son, Dave, will continue the tradition. Mark's dad instilled in him a belief that he hopes to instill in his son: Farming connects a person to the cycle of life in a way that no other occupation can. It's a theme that frequently is the focus of the family stories told by Mark. It's also a myth. Although farmers may be unusually connected to the cycle of life, so too are longtime family physicians, wildlife biologists, and veterinarians.

Inside the house, Felicia works alongside her aging but active mother-in-law, who is showing her 12-year-old granddaughter, Ruth, how to can vegetables. She tells Ruth that she was about her age when she learned to can from her grandmother, which is a family tradition. She also tells Ruth that she will one day do the same for her granddaughter. Felicia chimes in, saying Gladstone women have always made good homemakers.

Yet, even at this early age, Ruth isn't buying what her grandmother is saying. Not only does she wish she were outside tending to the animals with her dad, but she knows from her Aunt Lucy, who is a professor of medicine at the nearby university, that her great-great-grandmother left the canning to the wife of a man who sharecropped on the Gladstone farm. Ruth doesn't say anything, however, because she enjoys spending time with her grandmother regardless of the activity. Further, Ruth is in the process of learning that when she objects to the traditional role her mother expects her to perform, conflict usually is the result.

Two myths in this example serve useful functions. The first myth serves to maintain an important belief among Gladstone men—a belief that is significant to the probability of the younger generation accepting the farming legacy the older generation hopes to pass on. The second myth also serves a useful purpose. Canning enables one generation to bond with another, even if the story that the grandmother is teaching the granddaughter is more fiction than fact. Ruth's going along with the idea that Gladstone women traditionally have been homemakers is also a way of managing role conflict and the emotional duress that can follow. In addition, Ruth is smart enough to know that the time will come when she not only can choose her own roles but also can do so with less hassle from other family members.

Although it may not occur to us at the time, the themes and myths we learn about our families are the result of the stories that are told to us over the course of our lives. Seldom do we hear all that a story has to tell in a single sitting. We tend to get bits and pieces of the story on a road trip, at the holiday dinner table, or while going over grades with a none-to-pleased parent. As you'll learn from the exercise in Box 9-2, these stories, their themes, and the myths the stories highlight give us a much needed sense of self and place.

Family Roles and Functions

Family stories often teach us about the various roles family members play and the functions of these roles. Earlier in the chapter, we briefly looked at roles as a family attribute. Here, we investigate family roles in more detail, looking at the roles of spouses and parents and at role conflicts.

Spousal Roles

The roles spouses perform reflect the type of relationship they have established. Communication researcher Mary Anne Fitzpatrick has identified four types of

Box 9-2   Self-Assessment

What Is Your Family Story?

If you were to write your family's story, what would you say? Where would you begin? Who would you include and exclude? What themes would you stress, and what myths would you include? Develop a written outline of the first chapter of your family's story. In the process, try to determine whether there is a unifying theme that encapsulates your family's story and the people within it.

Here is a sample outline:

I. My Family

A. Ancestry
   1. maternal side
   2. paternal side
B. Notable Ancestors
   1. great and near-great relatives
   2. saints and sinners
C. Themes and Myths
   1. lemonade from lemons
   2. dream big

---

couples based on the kinds of roles they have in the relationship: traditional couples, independent couples, separate couples, and mixed couples.[19]

Among **traditional couples,** roles are likely to be both differentiated and complementary. Men are expected to perform a largely instrumental role in the family, earning an income and paying the bills. Women are expected to perform a more expressive role, taking care of the children and the home and emotionally supporting their men. These gender-differentiated roles are complementary because traditional couples believe that men are best suited to the role of breadwinner and protector of the family and that women are best suited to be homemakers and caregivers.

The roles performed by **independent couples,** the second type described by Fitzpatrick, are more ambiguous. Because both members usually work, the clear-cut division of roles characteristic of traditional couples may be impossible for independent couples. Instead, they continuously negotiate their roles and tend to cross the gender lines that, for traditional couples, define who is responsible for doing what.

In her research, Fitzpatrick found that the relational communication behaviors of independent couples are much different than those of traditional couples. Because independent couples do not have predetermined roles and must constantly negotiate, the accuracy of communication between the members of these couples sometimes suffers. However, the accuracy of communication between members of traditional couples can suffer seriously when one of them steps outside his or her expected role; in times of crisis, traditionals, who are not accustomed to any ambiguity in their relationships, find it harder than independent couples to achieve accuracy in their communication.

traditional couples
Family system in which roles are highly differentiated and complementary.

independent couples
Family system in which autonomy is valued and encouraged and in which roles are negotiated.

Table 9-1	Fitzpatrick's Couple Types	
TYPE	**ROLE**	**DEGREE OF AUTONOMY**
traditional	gender based	low
independent	negotiated	high
separate	gender based	high
mixed	ambiguous	ambiguous

SOURCE: Adapted from Mary Anne Fitzpatrick, *Between Husbands and Wives* (Newbury, Calif.: Sage, 1988).

As Table 9-1 shows, Fitzpatrick identified two other types of couples. **Separate couples** have a fairly traditional role relationship, though they enjoy considerable independence. **Mixed couples** have different perceptions of their relationship and different role expectations. For example, one member might think the relationship is an independent one, whereas the other might see it as traditional. One member expects roles to be shared, and the other expects the roles to be complementary and differentiated along gender lines. These mismatched expectations often cause conflict over roles in the relationship, a topic we will return to shortly.

Parental Roles

Couples frequently become parents. This is true not only for married couples but also for monogamous couples of choice. Sometimes, one member of the couple ends up with all the parenting responsibilities.[20] The role of parent in a family is multifunctional. It involves nurturing children, giving them emotional support, and encouraging them to accept challenges by assuring them that they are capable. At the same time, however, society says that the role of parent involves socializing children to the larger culture to which children belong. Parents are expected not only to teach their children about the culture but also to control the behavior of their children so that it doesn't disrupt the culture's functioning.

The multifunctional role parents are expected to play is extremely challenging. A chief reason is that the functions parents are expected to perform often are at odds with each other. Parents not only are expected to nurture their children, for instance, but also are expected to discipline their children when they are antisocial.

Consider the case of parents who take their child to the symphony or a theater production. This act of nurturing is well intended, designed to instill an appreciation of the arts in the child. But suppose the child becomes restless during the performance, twisting and turning in his or her seat, gawking at the sur-

separate couple
Family system in which roles are traditional but in which there also is an unusually high level of autonomy between partners.

mixed couple
Family system in which one or both people misperceive the type of relationship between them.

rounding people. Or suppose the child begins to ask questions and make comments that are clearly audible to people seated nearby. In either case, both the child and parents are likely to receive disapproving, even hostile looks from those around them. The message conveyed by these disapproving and hostile looks is clear "Discipline your unruly child and correct his or her disruptive behavior." Taking the hint, one or both parents try to reason with the child. The parents don't want to hurry the child to the lobby, because to do so would undermine their attempted nurturing. Yet, after being repeatedly frustrated in their attempts to reason with the child, and after receiving increasingly hostile looks from the adults seated around them, that is exactly what one or both parents may end up doing.

Role Conflicts

This parent and child illustration is but a single example of the role conflicts that can occur in families. Another common one involves conflict between spousal and parental roles. As any parent will tell you, or as you may already know yourself, children are communication intensive. The amount of attention they demand can significantly subtract from the attention a spousal relationship also demands. Further, some people get jealous over the time their spouse spends parenting.

Another example of the role conflict that can occur in families with children involves the inevitable disputes between children and one of their parents. Whose side, if any, should the other parent take in the dispute? Should the parent support his or her spouse, even if he or she believes the child is right about the nature of the dispute? Certainly that's what the spouse will think. Yet, if the parent sides with his or her spouse, even though he or she thinks the spouse is wrong, what is the message communicated to the child?

Even in families without children, role conflicts are an inherent consequence of modern life. This situation seems to be especially true in mixed couples. One of the most frequently reported complaints from women in dual-career families, for instance, is that their husbands expect them also to assume the role and perform the functions of homemaker—that is, cooking and cleaning, washing and ironing. Not only do women take the defensible position that this expectancy is sexist, but they also say it is grossly unfair given the instrumental family functions they perform outside the home. Mixed couples may spend considerable energy, moreover, arguing about the nature of their relationship and the roles they expect each other to perform.

Dialectic Tensions in Families

As should be obvious in light of our examples of role conflicts, the dialectic tensions we discussed in Chapter 8 also are a feature of family life. Further, these dialectic tensions both reflect and influence the communication behaviors of family members, regardless of how conventional or nonconforming their family's structure. Here, then, we want to revisit the sources of dialectic tension introduced in the previous chapter. We also want to add a source of dialectic tension that was implied but not explicitly addressed in Chapter 8, namely, the process of change.

Remember that dialectic tensions fall into two general categories, contextual and interactional.[21] The first category reflects the subsystem and networks surrounding the family. The second reflects the relational communication that defines and redefines the nature of the association among family members.

Contextual Dialectics

The two contextual dialectics we introduced in Chapter 8 involved tensions owing to the public and private dimensions of relationships and to tensions resulting from comparing the ideal relationship with a real one. Both dialectics are a common source of tension in families.

Public and Private   The public and private sides of family life have been a staple of novelists, playwrights, and filmmakers. Families, like individuals, have presentational goals. Sometimes the impression a family hopes to convey to the public is at odds with what is going on privately in the family. In *Ordinary People,* for example, the Judith Guest novel translated by Robert Redford into an Academy Award-winning film, an affluent family is rocked by tragedy. First, Buck, the family's elder son, drowns in a boating accident that his younger brother, Conrad, survives. Second, Conrad slashes his wrists in an attempted suicide as a result of the guilt he feels because he survived the accident. Third, Conrad spends months in a psychiatric hospital and undergoes electroshock therapy.

After Conrad rejoins his parents and returns to school, it is clear that he is still a very troubled young man. Conrad's father (played by Donald Sutherland) clearly sees this and tries to be honest in responding to the well-intentioned questions of family friends who want to know about his son's progress. Conrad's mother (played by Mary Tyler Moore) wants Conrad and his family to publicly behave as if their lives were completely back to normal and to hide Conrad's difficulties even from his grandparents.

The tension that results from Conrad's mother trying to maintain a public image of the family that is contrary to what's occurring privately in the family is never fully resolved. The film closes with Conrad's mother leaving him and his father. She prefers to leave rather than change in the effort to reduce the dialectic tension that is ruining her relationship with both her husband and her son.

Ideal and Real   As we noted in the previous chapter, another common source of dialectic tension involves people comparing their real relationship with an idealized one. This situation is especially true for couples both with and without children. The ideal family is mythical. It has no historical basis in fact. Television families, such as the Brady Bunch and the Cleavers, were imagined families. So,

Much to the chagrin of Queen Elizabeth II, Charles and Diana were eventually unable to conceal from the paparazzi that their marriage was less than ideal.

too, is the family depicted in the popular TV sitcom *Mad About You*. Of course, the fact that there is no "ideal family" in real life hasn't stopped people from comparing such idealized TV families with their own.[22] Box 9-3 will help you think about the effect of media portrayals on your notions about family life.

Unrealistic comparisons of this nature can and do cause people to acquire unrealistic expectancies about family life. These expectancies may lead people to grow dissatisfied with their relationship. In turn, this dissatisfaction may cause not only dialectic tension but also conflict among family members. Left unmanaged, as we'll discuss at length in Chapter 10, this dialectic tension may instigate communication behaviors typical of the initial stages of relational de-escalation.

Interactional Dialectics

Tension from contextual dialectics can easily be compounded by the tension resulting from the interactional dialectics you read about in Chapter 8. Recall that there are four interactional dialectics that can cause relational tension: (1)

Box 9-3   Critical Thinking

Families and Real Families

Be honest: What is your image of the ideal couple and the ideal family? Do you think the images of couples and families portrayed on TV and in film contribute to unrealistic expectancies about what constitutes an effective family? Or do you think people are able to watch families on TV and in film without effect on their image of the ideal?

Take a position and write a one-page reaction paper on this topic. Before doing so, however, be sure to watch your favorite TV family in action. If the show is no longer current, maybe you can catch a rerun or rent a video. If the show is unavailable, try to recall in detail the family and a specific episode of the show that affected your thinking about families.

independence and dependence, (2) affection and instrumentality, (3) judgment and acceptance, and (4) expressiveness and protectiveness.

Independence and Dependence   The extent of independence can be a source of tension in developing relationships as well as in the developed relational systems of families. Independent married couples, for example, accept the fact that a degree of independence in the relationship is both necessary and healthy for the relationship. So central is independence to the nature of the relationship that any sign of one person infringing on the autonomy of the other could lead to tension and conflict.

Where independence and dependence most often create tension, however, is in families with maturing children. We suspect you know from your own experience that when passing from adolescence to puberty, children begin communicating their independence to their parents. Teenagers talk less with their parents, develop language and communication codes to which parents are not privy, and physically separate themselves from family activities in which they once freely participated.

The tension that results from this process can be painful for both parents and children.[23] Yet parents and children cannot afford to ignore this dialectic tension. Unmanaged, it can cause parents and children to remain alienated from each other for years to come. In worst-case scenarios, this dialectic tension also can contribute to antisocial and self-destructive behavior in children and their parents. Thus, parents need to recognize that their children's need for independence is natural and to talk openly with their children about the need.

Affection and Instrumentality   People bond and become a family partly because of their affections for each other. It would be naive to assume, however, that bonding has nothing to do with instrumental goals. At one time in history, in fact, people formed families primarily for the purpose of political or economic alliance. You still see this but to a far lesser degree among royal families, the rich and powerful, and the merely famous.

Given the phenomenal success of books such as *Men Are From Mars, Women Are From Venus,* it is clear that women and men express affection differently in their families. Women talk about their feelings of affection. Men take on instrumental roles, for instance, working longer to make more money, which men regard as a sign of their affection for their family. Women, though, want husbands and fathers to express affection verbally and nonverbally, rather than trying to show it only by performing the instrumental role of provider. It's not uncommon, moreover, for grown children of both sexes to lament the fact that though their father was a great provider, they wish he had spent more time talking with them and telling them about his feelings.[24]

Judgment and Acceptance   The third interactional dialectic, judgment and acceptance, can be a difficult source of tension for families to manage. A chief reason is the expectancies family members have about each other. These expectancies range from working hard to assist the family in achieving its goals to making an effort to maintain one's health and appearance. Advice columnists frequently receive letters from a spouse who can't accept another's unemployment, weight, or poor health. Advice columnists usually urge letter writers to seek counseling so that they can begin managing the dialectic tension they feel.

Although children have expectancies of parents, the latter's expectancies of their children can border on the extreme. Mothers and fathers push toddlers into sports, the arts, and baby genius classes. Likewise, parents may not want their children to simply succeed at soccer, the violin, or a second language, but to excel. When children do not live up to parental expectancies, parents can have a difficult time in accepting the fact. No matter how hard they try, parents also may find it impossible to avoid communicating their disappointment in nonverbal terms that even the youngest of children can recognize.

Expressiveness and Protectiveness   This fourth interactional dialectic is related to each of the preceding ones. Family members may bite their tongue to protect the ego of a specific family member. Family members also may withhold information about themselves when they perceive that the information could be injurious to the family. Striking a balance between expressiveness and protectiveness in what family members say about themselves and others in the family is not easy.

Consider close siblings. One discovers that the other shows signs of bulimia, frequently engaging in binge eating and purging. The latter pleads, "Don't tell Mom and Dad, OK? I'll quit doing it, swear to God." Does the brother or sister protect the person or tell his or her parents? Whatever the person decides, there will be consequences to pay. Protecting the sibling jeopardizes his or her health. Disclosing the discovery to parents jeopardizes the feelings of closeness that characterize the sibling relationship.

The Dialectic of Change in the Family Life Cycle

As the example between siblings implies, the course of action one sibling decides on may produce changes in the manner with which family members relate to each other. If the parents are told about the bulimic behavior, it will significantly change the way they communicate with the troubled daughter or son. If the siblings agree to a conspiracy of silence, it will affect not only how they communicate with their parents but how they communicate with each other.

Even though change is a constant in family life, it also is a source of dialectic tension in families. Research shows that people, on the whole, tend to resist change. This research also shows that this tendency to resist is true even when change is in people's best interests.

Family researchers David Olson and Hamilton McCubbin suggest there are seven stages in the development of heterosexual family life.[25] These stages are clearly characterized by changes in the family system, including changes in the relational communication behaviors of family members. Olson and McCubbin's stage one involves married couples without children. Stages two and three involve couples with preschool-age children, and couples with school-age children. Stages four and five involve families with adolescents and families with children entering adulthood. Stages six and seven are referred to as the empty-nest and retirement years. We recognize the stereotypic nature of Olson and McCubbin's models. Not all families are heterosexual, and not all families include children or two parents. Still, we think these seven stages are useful in helping us understand change as a relational dialectic in family life.

Think about a single stage, the empty-nest years that immediately follow children leaving the home and beginning lives largely independent from their parents. Aside from the obvious impact the change produces in the amount of communication that routinely occurs between parents and their children, this transition can radically alter the communication behavior between the empty nesters themselves. Children can be a common focal point of the transactions between parents. Topics of conversation include children's progress in school, relationships with others, and degree of maturity. Once adult children leave the home, the parents may find themselves increasingly outside the loop of their adult children's lives. The empty-nest couple, therefore, needs to discover topics in common other than their children.[26]

The presence of children in a family also can serve to regulate the communication between parents. Husbands and wives may develop a consensual rule that says, "Never argue in front of the children." Such a consensual rule may seriously influence the frequency of conflict between parents. With the children gone, however, the rule no longer applies, enabling dialectic tensions between the empty nesters to surface. They may find themselves arguing over the least little thing as a result.

The point we want to emphasize here is the inevitability of change. It will occur and produce tension in the lives of family members, regardless of the type of family system in which people are members. How well families manage change reflects the skill with which family members communicate.

Family Communication Skills

To begin with, almost everything we said in Chapter 8 about relational communication in general applies to family communication specifically. The principles for regulating conversation in close relationships are as applicable here as they were in Chapter 8. What follows, therefore, extends rather than replaces what we already have said about what constitutes competent verbal and nonverbal communication.

Our second point is that every system of family communication is different. These differences range from slight to great. Thus, as you read and think about the family communication skills that follow, realize that their effectiveness will depend on the specific family system in which they are applied.

Expressing Ownership

The more we own up to the potential consequences of what we do and say, the better the chances we will strike a balance between knowing what to say and what not to say to family members. Owning up to the potential consequences of what you say also requires that you identify the content and intent of your message as yours. "I" messages (such as "I feel . . .") rather than "you" messages ("You are . . .") are an important way to take responsibility for your messages. People also intuitively recognize that the plural pronoun *we* potentially carries more weight with people than the singular pronoun *I*. That's one of the reasons parents say "we think," or "we believe," or "we know from experience."

Family communication scholars Patricia Noller and Mary Anne Fitzpatrick suggest that we should use "I" messages when communicating with children especially. According to Noller and Fitzpatrick, "Effective 'I' messages include: (1) a behavior ('When you don't call and let me know that you are going to be late'), (2) a feeling ('I feel anxious,'), and (3) an interpretation ('because I think you may have been involved in an accident')."[27]

"I" messages also can be used effectively in couples without children. Consider the case of a couple experiencing dialectic tension owing to the perception that one person doesn't express feelings of affection to the extent the other person desires. As a result, this latter person says, "Why can't you tell me you love me?" The message is accusatory and implies there is something deficient about the inexpressive person. A better alternative would be, "When you don't tell me you love me, I take your silence to mean that you don't care." This "I" message clearly meets Noller and Fitzpatrick's criteria for effectiveness.

Ownership of feelings and beliefs, and the "I" messages that should be used to express them, helps families manage the dialectic tensions they are bound to

Active listening is essential to good family communication.

experience. First, ownership helps because it requires family members to be mindful of the consequences that may accrue should they express a feeling or belief. Second, "I" messages are helpful because they acknowledge that the feeling or belief belongs to you. Third, because "I" messages are not accusatory in meaning, they are much less likely to be met with a defensive response from a family member, such as "What are you talking about? I tell you how I feel all the time." The scenarios in Box 9-4 will help you practice constructing "I" messages.

Documenting

Sometimes called pinpointing, documenting requires that family members provide specific evidence to support a claim such as "You never listen to me." No matter how terrible a listener a family member happens to be, the accusation

---

Box 9-4   Skill Building

Learn to Use "I" Messages

Write an "I" message for each of the following scenarios. Be sure that your "I" message meets each of the criteria listed by Noller and Fitzpatrick.

1. A parent repeatedly invades your privacy, entering your room without your permission and opening your mail.

2. Your spouse seldom expresses her or his feelings about you.

3. A sibling borrows clothes, toiletries, and money but never once thanks you for your generosity.

4. You think your parents show favoritism toward your older or younger sibling.

5. Your spouse's behavior at a party embarrassed you, and this wasn't the first time for such an occurrence.

6. Your spouse is a selfish lover.

---

that he or she never listens would be tough to prove. What's more, the accusation is likely to produce a defensive response from the person who was accused, such as "Oh, really? How about the time I changed my mind about punishing you after hearing your side of the story? I guess you don't consider that listening?"

Whether talking with a spouse or a child, it's always a good idea to be specific about a claim, making sure you can provide concrete documentation. "The last three times I asked for your permission to go to a concert you said no" is more effective than the typical "You never let me do anything."

Protecting Self-Esteem

Because they are close, family members often share potentially destructive information about each other. Sometimes family members lose control and use this information to hurt the other person. No matter how much he or she regrets having used the information, the offending family member cannot take back the hurtful message.

As a result, family members should always consider the potential of a message to negatively and unfairly detract from another member's self-esteem.[28] After all, building self-esteem among its members is an important role played by the family. It makes little sense, then, for family members to verbally and nonverbally tear down what they've built.

Listening Actively

Since we discussed listening at length in Chapter 6, we won't go into detail here. A family member's inability to listen is a common complaint from spouses and children. Given the statistics on how poorly the average person listens, this complaint may be justified. Recall that to listen actively, you must use as many of your senses as possible, not just your sense of hearing. This means, for example, listening with your eyes, and hearing both the content and relational components of a family member's message.

In low context cultures such as in North America, listening actively also means providing family members with plenty of communication cues that signal you are listening. Recall that verbal cues in this regard include paraphrasing and encouragers such as "Go on, tell me more" and "That's interesting." Nonverbal cues of listening actively include facial expressions, eye contact, positive head nods, and leaning forward.

Being Rhetorically Sensitive

Effective family communication is rhetorically sensitive communication. It is based on recognition of the family system's complexity. It reflects the unique attributes of every member of the family system. It is adaptive to changes in the family system. Finally, it is based on the needs of the many rather than the needs of the few.

In closing, we need to repeat the fact that family communication skills are meant to be combined with the other communication skills we have talked about in earlier chapters. Although family communication may make unique demands on communicators, what constitutes competent communication in the family has much in common with what constitutes competent communication in developing relationships or while working in groups, the subject of Chapters 12 and 13. What's more, the skills just described, for instance, expressing ownership and documenting, are characteristic of competent communicators in general. So apply the skills described in this chapter outside your family system as well.

Summary

Families constitute a specific type of relational communication system. The people within the system are bound by history or choice, perform specific roles, and create a collective memory through stories, themes, and myths. Family systems minimally involve two people and can be open, closed, random, enmeshed, or disengaged. Regardless of the specific system type that best describes a family, family systems share many common attributes, including roles, inputs and outputs, boundaries and hierarchies, rules, goals, and feedback.

Family networks are composed of the links that connect the lines of communication between family members, and they vary according to number and configuration of these links. Networks reveal not only family structure but also power and decision-making authority in the family system. Networks reveal the existence of internal subsystems in the family as well.

Subsystems affect how the family functions. Subsystems can be internal, as is the case when siblings form a coalition to manage their relationship with their parents. Subsystems also can be external, as is the case when a family member works for an organization.

Storytelling is a common and important form of relational communication within family systems. Stories assist families in creating a collective memory and in teaching family members lessons significant to the family's well-being. Family stories are usually rich in themes and myths which assist families in maintaining attitudes, beliefs, values; reinforcing generational bonds; dealing with role conflicts; and managing emotional duress.

Stories also can reveal roles that family members traditionally have performed. Roles are patterns of behavior in which family members are expected to routinely engage, for example, spouse or parent. Role conflicts are common in families. Role conflicts also can reflect the dialectic tensions that inhere to all family communication systems. These dialectics can be contextual or interactional.

Managing dialectic tensions is an important function of family communication. Effective family communication reflects many of the skills previously dealt with in this book. Effective family communication includes additional skills, however, such as using "I" messages, documenting, protecting self-esteem, listening actively, and being rhetorically sensitive.

Another Look

Books

There are a number of excellent books devoted to family communication. We highly recommend the following ones.

Laurie P. Arliss. *Contemporary Family Communication: Messages and Meanings.* New York: St. Martin's Press, 1993.

Patricia Noller and Mary Anne Fitzpatrick. *Communication in Family Relationships.* Englewood Cliffs, N.J.: Prentice-Hall, 1993.

Janet Yerby, Nancy Buerkel-Rothfuss, and Arthur P. Bochner. *Understanding Family Communication.* 2nd ed. Scottsdale, Ariz.: Gorsuch Scarisbrick, 1995.

Articles

Leslie A. Baxter. "A Dialectical Perspective on Communication Strategies in Relationship Development." In *A Handbook of Personal Relationships,* edited by Steven W. Duck. New York: Wiley, 1988.

This article stimulated much of the interest about the role of dialectics in relational communication. Scholars have been receptive to the notion that communication plays a pivotal role in the management of the tensions that result from dialectics such as autonomy and interdependence, one of the central dialectics discussed in this article.

Mary Anne Fitzpatrick and Diane M. Badzinski. "All in the Family: Interpersonal Communication in Kin Relationships." In *Handbook of Interpersonal Communication*, edited by Mark L. Knapp and Gerald R. Miller, 687–736. Newbury Park, Calif.: Sage, 1985.

This article does an outstanding job of overviewing some of the most crucial issues affecting family communication. It would be a good source to initially consult if you plan on writing a paper about family communication.

Video Rentals

There is an abundance of films that do a superior job of illustrating the content of this chapter. What's more, the following films are dissimilar enough that they explore complementary issues about family communication.

I Never Sang for My Father   Starring Gene Hackman and Melvyn Douglas, this film explores the dialectic tensions that commonly exist between fathers and sons.

The Great Santini   Based on novelist Pat Conroy's book of the same title, this film explores the impact of a judgmental, headstrong, and yet admirable father of a military family. Robert Duvall does an excellent job of portraying Bo Santini, the domineering, Marine fighter pilot who heads the household. The film is worth watching for many reasons, including the one-on-one basketball game played between Duvall and Michael O'Keefe, who plays the first-born son in the family. It is also an interesting look at how family roles change when one member is away for a period of time, which is often the case in military families.

Ordinary People   Robert Redford's wrenching adaptation of the Judith Guest novel shows a family in the throes of crisis and the dialectic tensions tearing it apart. The film makes viewers feel as if they are eavesdropping on the most intimate conversations between members of a modern family.

Long Time Companion   This is a moving film about a family of choice over a 10-year span of time. This film clearly shows the commitment and resilience of the family, even when several of its members are decimated by AIDS.

Running on Empty   River Phoenix, Judd Hirsch, and Christine Lahti star in this film about a family on the run from the FBI. This film does a remarkable job of showing the pain parents and children experience as one parent fights to hold on to a teenage son at the same time the son tries to break away. This film also is a near perfect illustration of a closed family system.

Jungle Fever   Director Spike Lee's film looks at the effect of an interracial affair on the couple's families. Starring Wesley Snipes and Annabella Sciorra, the film explores the dialectic tensions the couple experience as a result of the private and public dimensions of their relationship. The film also underscores the underlying tension interracial couples stir in both the African American and White communities.

My Family/Mi Familia   Gregory Nava's multigenerational portrait of a Latino family in East Los Angeles, California, is both loving and realistic. The film does an excellent job in showing how the story of the family establishes the family's identity. It also does a good job of showing how the generations in a family can clash and the role communication plays in defining and resolving the clash.

Theory and Research in Practice

1. An epiphany is characterized by sudden and unexpected insight to a subject. Can you think of a family story you regard as an epiphany? Can you recall one that gave you new and sudden insight to your family as the whole or to a specific member of your family? Recollect in writing a family story you would label an epiphany.

2. Canonical stories teach us lessons, as is the case in Norman MacLean's *A River Runs Through It* and Harper Lee's

To Kill a Mockingbird. Recall one canonical story in particular that is recurrently told in your family. What lessons did the story specifically teach? Did the story carry a moral, for example, or did it simply teach a lesson about appropriate behavior? Describe the story and the lesson you learned from it.

3. Although Mary Anne Fitzpatrick's research focuses on married couples, try to apply her typology to both married and unmarried couples you know. Try to assess whether the relationship is traditional, independent, separate, or mixed. Also, describe in writing the communication behaviors that prompt your characterizations of the relationship type.

4. Write an essay on the dialectic tension you have experienced with one or both parents. Describe in your journal the degree to which you have been successful or unsuccessful in managing the tension. Knowing what you now know, would you have managed the tension differently? What specific communication strategies would you use in this regard?

5. Diagram the network you think best typifies power and decision making in your family. Be sure to note the pattern of interaction that characterizes the network. If possible, show your diagram to your family and ask for their reactions. Discuss these reactions in class.

CHAPTER 10

Relational Conflict

OBJECTIVES

After reading this chapter you should be able to:

- Define conflict.

- Recognize common misconceptions about conflict.

- Differentiate between destructive and constructive conflict.

- Define what is meant by an escalatory spiral.

- Describe five common sources of conflict.

- Construct examples of varying types of conflict style.

- Develop a distributive message strategy for conflict.

- Develop an integrative message strategy for conflict.

- Compare and contrast the advantages and disadvantages of distributive and integrative message strategies.

- List and explain three sets of communication skills necessary for the constructive management of relational conflict.

Family holidays, when all the grown children come back home, can be a time of joy or, often, of conflict. The film *Home for the Holidays* is in many ways a caricature of the kinds of conflicts that can arise and of the various ways they are resolved, at least partly and temporarily, letting the family remain a family in spite of their differences. The three grown children in this film have each gone their separate ways, and only two are close: Claudia (played by Holly Hunter), a divorced mother who has just lost her job as an art restorer, and Tommy (played by Robert Downey, Jr.), a gay man, who we (and his family) find out in the course of the film has recently married his lover, Jack.

Claudia dreads these family holidays, and her teenage daughter's parting advice is just to "float" rather than get drawn into any family scenes. Tommy's way of coping seems to be playing the clown, protecting himself by constantly cracking jokes, some of which he pushes too far and enrages his other sister, Joanne (played by Cynthia Stevenson), who has chosen a traditional married life with a husband, who is a banker, and two children. When her brother's playing around ends up with the half-carved turkey landing in her lap, she starts to storm out but is persuaded to stay; as a way of showing her resentment, however, she refuses Claudia's offer of some clean clothes, preferring to continue wearing her dress, spotted with turkey grease and baking soda. Claudia goes to Joanne's the next morning to try to make amends, but Joanne refuses; after Claudia leaves, Joanne starts to cry. We get the sense that she doesn't really want to be the person she has shaped for herself. We know that the family scene will be repeated, with some variations but many of the same themes, at Christmas time.

In the last two chapters, we have often noted that dialectic tension is normal in our most significant relationships and is a constant feature of the relational landscape. This chapter focuses on another constant feature: conflict and the role communication plays in its creation and management. Despite its centrality to relational life, conflict is something most of us try to avoid. As a result, we are not especially good at controlling the sources that contribute to its occurrence or at managing conflict once it occurs. Topics covered in this chapter include

- the nature of conflict, including some common misconceptions about it,
- common sources of conflict, and
- communication skills for constructively managing conflict in your ongoing relationships.

The Nature of Conflict

Certainly conflict has its darker side. You need only turn to the shocking statistics describing child and spousal abuse to affirm this fact. The question, though, is whether this darker side is inherent to conflict per se, or a consequence of ignorance and mismanagement of conflict when it occurs.

Misconceptions About Conflict

Many people think conflict is inherently bad. This belief not only is incorrect but also has given rise to a number of misleading misconceptions about the subject. Some of the most prominent ones follow.

Misconception 1: Conflict is abnormal. Nothing could be further from the truth. Conflict is normal and even necessary in some cases.[1] Intrapersonal conflict, for example, struggling with one's self-concept, accompanies nearly every developmental stage of life. And interpersonal conflict is a regular feature in even the healthiest relationships. The fact that we may not enjoy conflict or that we find it difficult to constructively manage doesn't make it abnormal.

Misconception 2: Conflict always is destructive. Perhaps the most pervasive misconception is that conflict produces nothing of value in a relationship.[2] If things are going badly between people, overt conflict only will make matters worse. But is this belief really true? Frequently, students and teachers experience conflict as a result of misperceptions about each other. The student perceives the teacher to be aloof and uncaring about student needs. The teacher perceives the student as apathetic because he or she hasn't visited during office hours to discuss his or her progress. Left unattended, these perceptions only will fester. If the student takes the initiative and confronts the teacher with the perception, it may provoke the teacher to reveal his or her perception. Once these conflicting perceptions are out in the open, the student and the teacher can try to resolve them. This will never happen, however, unless one or both of them confront the other.

Misconception 3: Conflict results from communication breakdowns. Conflict frequently and indiscriminately is said to result from what has become a catch-all

> Although conflict between people who are close is inevitable, it need not be destructive.

term—the communication breakdown.[3] Basically, a communication breakdown involves people founding their behavior on inaccurate interpretations of their respective messages. The familiar refrain "No . . . that's not what I meant" is often made in response to people not only misperceiving the intended meaning of a message but also taking offense to it.

Yet, conflict also can and often does result from a transaction in which there is complete fidelity in a communication transaction. Family members may agree on a goal but experience conflict over the best way to achieve it. While all may agree that a college degree is a good idea, they may experience conflict over the best way to go about getting it. The student in the family may want to take the shortest route possible, even if it means going into considerable debt. The parents may think little of the idea, advocating a stint in the military to finance an eventual degree. The fact that there is conflict, however, in no way means that the transaction between family members has broken down or that they have failed to communicate and accurately interpret their differences.

Misconception 4: Conflict should be resolved as quickly as possible. Once conflict does occur, we tend to believe we should do everything in our power to speedily resolve it.[4] A couple of issues need to be brought to light here. First, the dysfunctional behaviors that often accompany mismanaged conflict should not be confused with the substance of the conflict. They are a manifestation of the conflicting parties' lack of skills. Second, speedy resolution of a conflict may result in "winning the battle but losing the war." Substantial good can arise from managed conflict. Accepting a quick fix, as you probably know from your own experience, may ultimately prove to be the worse course of action.

Types of Conflict

Having now dealt with four of the many misconceptions that surround conflict, let's look at what conflict is. Therapist Joyce Hocker and communication scholar William Wilmot define **conflict** as "an expressed struggle between at least two interdependent parties who perceive incompatible goals, scarce resources and interference from others in achieving their goals."[5] Several parts of this definition deserve comment. First, conflict involves *interdependent parties.* Whether or not people are aware of it, their individual actions affect each other. Second, conflicts begin with interdependent parties *perceiving things differently.* Since perception is a product of experience, conflict is far more likely between people whose experiences are dissimilar. Third, conflict exists when people perceive that

conflict   An expressed struggle between at least two interdependent parties who perceive incompatible goals, scarce resources, and interference from others in achieving their goals.

- they can't get what they want, if others get what they want;
- whatever it is that they want, there's not enough of it to share equally; and,
- even when people do want the same thing, someone or some agency is preventing them from getting it.

Two types of conflict can emerge from such a struggle in perceptions. The first, and the one with which most people are familiar, is *destructive conflict.* The

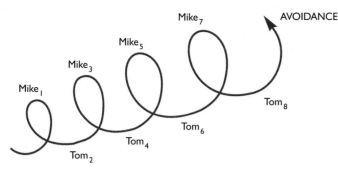

Figure 10-1
Escalatory Spiral

1. Mike tells Tom, "You've got to quit smoking."
2. Tom tells Mike, "I don't need you to tell me what to do."
3. Mike says, "You know your clothes smell like smoke."
4. Tom says, "So what are you now, the odor cop?"
5. Mike says, "Your smoking is really bothering me."
6. Tom says, "So go somewhere else."
7. Mike says, "Come on, put it out."
8. Tom says, "I'll put it out. As soon as you start minding your own business. Who made you God anyway?"

second, and the one with which we want you to become skilled, is *constructive conflict.* **Destructive conflict** most often involves people verbally and nonverbally abusing each other. Destructive conflict usually, but not always, is characterized by an **escalatory spiral,** depicted in Figure 10-1.[6] As you can see, an escalatory spiral means the conflict progressively becomes more destructive to the relationship over time.

Destructive conflict is accompanied by distinctive communication behaviors. Often motivated by the desire to make the other person suffer, messages can be very mean-spirited. Comments meant to attack the person's psyche, such as "You're just like your father," frequently are heard. So, too, are messages that communicate rigidity, such as "I'm not about to change," and messages that communicate the desire to dominate the other person, such as "You're such an emotional coward."

Constructive conflict involves change and thus can occur only between people who are willing to change. Constructive conflict is multifaceted. First, it demands that people be flexible, that they avoid rigidity in the positions they take and in the behaviors they exhibit. Second, constructive conflict is a form of communication that is intended to assist people in learning about each other and the issues at hand. It is not about hoarding information or protecting oneself at all costs. Third, constructive conflict should enhance rather than diminish the self-esteem of people. It should leave people with the impression that they accomplished a worthwhile goal. Constructive conflict, of course, doesn't just happen. It is the result of knowledge and skill, including recognition of the most common sources of relational conflict.

destructive conflict
Unmanaged struggle that jeopardizes the relationship between people (unless that is the goal of conflict).

escalatory spiral
Visual depiction of how unmanaged conflict becomes more destructive to relationships over time.

constructive conflict
Managed struggle involving change in a relationship.

Common Sources of Relational Conflict

Common sources of relational conflict are (1) perceptual bias, (2) interdependence, (3) goals, (4) scarce resources, and (5) outside interference. *Perceptual bias* is the result of such attributes as ethnocentrism, explained in Chapter 7, and emotions so intense they blind us to what other people plainly see. As Box 10-1 notes, gender can also be a source of perceptual bias. Recall that there is no objective reality, only a perceptual one. Thus, when we perceive an issue or someone in a particular way, we behave accordingly. To the extent that our perception of the issue or person is accurate, there is no conflict between perception and reality. Of course, this is not always the case. Consider teenagers and their parents. Role conflict between them not only is the rule but also may take as long as 10 years to fully dissipate. Conflict management, therefore, is a necessity. Typically, there are major differences separating teenagers from their parents. As we said in Chapter 9, they tend to think, talk, and act differently. Tastes in music, style, and leisure activities also are likely to differ. These kinds of generational differences are bound to bias the perceptual realities of teenagers and their parents. Unless recognized as the common source of dialectic tension and conflict that they are, these biases can do real harm to families.

A second source of conflict is *interdependence*. We have repeatedly emphasized the fact that individual actions have relational consequences. Your behavior affects both your partner and your relationships, even when you are not aware of the fact. In a relationship, there is no such thing as hurting only yourself. Consider the following example of a couple at a party. One person drinks too much, gets loud and obnoxious, and then passes out on a sofa in the den. The inevitable next-day conflict begins with one person saying, "I feel you humiliated me last night!" The other person retorts, "Oh . . . come on, I didn't hurt anybody but myself." This is a ridiculous statement, of course. The offending person's behavior does reflect on the other person. It may say to others, such things as "What does she see in him that's so special she'll put up with behavior like that?"

Goals are a third source of conflict in relationships. Relational partners often assume that the other person is perfectly aware of what is expected from a relationship. When the other person's behavior is perceived as inconsistent with the realization of these unstated goals, conflict is probable. Stated goals, of course, also may result in conflict. People don't always want the same thing at the same time. In rare cases, goals even may be mutually exclusive—such as spending time with the family and making enough money to become affluent. In any case, goals need to be explicit between people. They can then be prioritized on the basis of what is important to the relationship's health. Although conflict is probable in the process, it can prove to be beneficial if constructively managed.

The fourth source of conflict is the perception of *scarce resources*. Too much money is infrequently cited as an underlying cause of divorce. Too little money and the manner in which it's distributed or spent, however, is commonly cited as a major source of conflict between married couples.

Box 10-1   Critical Thinking

How Men and Women View Conflict

Back in Chapter 3 we suggested that men and women sometimes use language differently. It should come as no great surprise, then, that the attitude and manner in which men and women approach conflict is different as well. There is some reason to believe that this difference owes more to the way boys and girls are socialized than to their biological sex.

Boys, for example, are often thrust into competitive games as soon as their hands are big enough to wear a glove, grip a bat, or control a racquet. Boys learn at an early age, moreover, that competition and winning are a good way to achieve recognition and status and to achieve their instrumental goals as well.

Although the situation is changing for girls in this regard, the process of socialization for them is still largely different. Whereas boys grow up learning how to compete, girls grow up learning how to cooperate. Whereas boys enjoy competing because it calls attention to themselves, girls enjoy cooperating because it assists them in connecting with people and building relationships.

Is it any wonder, then, that when adult men and women have conflict, they respond differently? Research shows that women seem to be better conflict managers than men. The bottom line for women is loyalty to the relationship—not winning. Their verbal and nonverbal behaviors during conflict validate their commitment to the relationship. Men, on the other hand, may try to sweep conflict issues under the rug. When they do join in conflict, they also tend to revert to their competitive ways, trying to win the argument rather than collaborating in its resolution.

What do you think? Is this consistent with your experience? Interview a member of the opposite sex on the topic of conflict between men and women. Ask the person to describe his or her attitude about conflict between the sexes and how he or she behaves when engaged in such a conflict. Record the description and report back to class.

The fifth and final source of conflict is *outside interference* from a party outside a specific relationship. Do the names Capulet and Montague, or Hatfield and McCoy, ring familiar to you? Each of these families experienced the worst of conflict as a result of interfering with the individual relationships of specific family members. Of course, we need not look to Shakespeare's Verona or the hollows of Appalachia to find examples of conflict owing to outside interference.

Communication and Conflict

Once we understand the nature of conflict and its common sources, we can learn how to manage conflict. Conflict management begins with an analysis of the relationship between communication behavior and the perceptual struggles we experience over goals, resources, and outside interference. This kind of analysis involves learning about our conflict style and the customary message strategies we use under conditions of conflict.

conflict style
Customary pattern of behavior exhibited during conflict.

Conflict Styles

A style is a customary pattern of behavior. It may show itself across varying situations, or it may be situationally specific. Thus, your **conflict style** is a pattern of communication behavior you are likely to exhibit when confronted with a potential struggle over goals, resources, or people outside a relationship meddling with it. Before reading any further, therefore, fill out the self-assessment measure in Box 10-2. It will reveal your dominant conflict style.

It is important to recognize that a style is something to which you are predisposed. The fact that you typically avoid conflict, therefore, doesn't mean that you always avoid it, regardless of the circumstances. Note also that your perceptions of your own style may be at odds with others' perceptions. Research shows that most of us perceive ourselves as conflict resolvers. Research also shows that we perceive the manner in which we resolve conflict as decidedly positive. In contrast, this same research reveals just the opposite when it comes to our perceptions of other people, who we generally regard as the cause of the conflicts we experience.[7]

Table 10-1 lists five common conflict styles. The table also shows the major advantages and disadvantages of each of these styles. The first style, *avoidance,* is best represented by people who go out of their way to escape a conflict. Avoidance can range from outright denial, "I don't see the problem," to steering a transaction away from the issue at the bottom of the conflict, "Lovely weather after all, don't you think?" Avoidance may postpone conflict, but avoidance won't make the source of the conflict go away. You know this from your attempts to manage the dialectic tensions in your close relationships. Although something as simple as leaving the toilet seat up seems petty, it nonetheless irritates you terribly. Do you let your partner continue to get away with it until it becomes so frustrating you explode at the person? This is the most likely consequence for people who try to avoid conflict. Their avoidance actually escalates the conflict once it inevitably occurs.

Collaboration also is a conflict style. Not to be confused with compromise, which means adjusting positions to reach agreement, collaboration involves people working together to find a mutually discovered solution. This second style is intended to yield a long-term solution to the root cause of the conflict. Although collaboration involves real effort, researchers have shown that it works to the mutual benefit of the people involved.[8] Conflict expert Alan Sillars and his associates, for example, have found that when married couples commit to a collaborative style, they not only arrive at better solutions to their struggles but also experience greater satisfaction in their relationship.[9]

As mentioned in Chapter 9, many couples today must juggle their personal and professional lives. Conflict is an inevitable consequence of their juggling act. As we also pointed out, one of the most common sources of conflict is the perception of inequality in the roles men and women perform. Women continue to report in survey after survey that despite the fact they have a career outside the home, they still end up doing most of the household chores. Although such a conflict may seem ideally suited to compromise, this may not be the case. Con-

Box 10-2   Self-Assessment

What Is Your Conflict Style?

Respond to each of the following statements on a scale of 1 to 5, with 1 representing "strongly disagree" and 5 representing "strongly agree." These statements reflect one of three conflict styles. One is collaborative and solution oriented and includes compromise and accommodation; one is nonconfrontational and characteristic of avoidance and withdrawal; one is assertive, controlling, and competitive.

_____ 1. I blend my ideas with those of others to create new alternatives for resolving a conflict.
_____ 2. I shy away from topics that are sources of disputes.
_____ 3. I insist my position be accepted during a conflict.
_____ 4. I suggest solutions that combine a variety of viewpoints.
_____ 5. I steer clear of disagreeable situations.
_____ 6. I give in a little on my ideas when the other person also gives in.
_____ 7. I avoid a person I suspect of wanting to discuss a disagreement.
_____ 8. I integrate arguments into a new solution from issues raised in a dispute.
_____ 9. I stress my point by hitting my fist on the table.
_____ 10. I will go fifty-fifty to reach a settlement.
_____ 11. I raise my voice when trying to get another person to accept my position.
_____ 12. I offer creative solutions in discussions of disagreements.
_____ 13. I keep quiet about my views in order to avoid disagreements.
_____ 14. I frequently give in a little if the other person will meet me halfway.
_____ 15. I downplay the importance of a disagreement.
_____ 16. I reduce disagreements by saying they are insignificant.
_____ 17. I meet the opposition at a midpoint of our differences.
_____ 18. I assert my opinion forcefully.
_____ 19. I dominate arguments until the other person understands my position.
_____ 20. I suggest we work together to create solutions to disagreements.
_____ 21. I try to use everyone's ideas to generate solutions to problems.
_____ 22. I offer trade-offs to reach solutions in a disagreement.
_____ 23. I argue insistently for my stance.
_____ 24. I withdraw when someone confronts me about a controversial issue.
_____ 25. I sidestep disagreements when they arise.
_____ 26. I try to smooth over disagreements by making them appear unimportant.
_____ 27. I stand firm in my views during a conflict.
_____ 28. I make our differences seem less serious.
_____ 29. I hold my tongue rather than argue.
_____ 30. I ease conflict by claiming our differences are trivial.

Compute three sets of scores by adding your responses to items 1, 4, 6, 8, 10, 12, 14, 17, 20, 21, and 22 for Set One _____; items 2, 5, 7, 13, 15, 16, 24, 25, 26, 28, 29, 30 for Set Two _____; and items 3, 9, 11, 18, 19, 23, and 27 for Set Three _____.

Set One = Collaborative style   Set Two = Avoidance style   Set Three = Assertive/controlling style

The set on which you scored highest indicates your dominant conflict style.

SOURCE: Adapted from L. K. Putnam and C. Wilson, "Communication Strategies in Organizational Conflicts," in *Communication Yearbook 6*, ed. M. Burgoon (Newbury Park, Calif.: Sage, 1982). Reprinted by permission of Sage Publications.

Table 10-1 Conflict Styles

STYLE	ADVANTAGES	DISADVANTAGES
Avoidance	Not all goals are worth the risks that potentially inhere to all conflicts; can keep another from harming you; for short-term relationships.	Perceived as uncaring; abandons goal; supports idea that conflict should be avoided at all costs.
Collaborating	Satisfactory to both parties; promotes solutions and commitment to them; enhances relational and instrumental goals; works well in long-term associations.	Requires intense activity; can be complex if not equally balanced.
Competing	Helpful when quick decisions are needed; instrumental goal is more important than self-presentational goal.	Can lead to escalation of conflict or retreating by the other person; can hurt relational and self-presentational goals.
Compromising	Allows both parties to achieve some goals; maintains most relational goals; appears to be reasonable.	Could prove counterproductive; parties' goals may be sacrificed; does not allow creative alternatives.
Accommodating	Shows reasonableness; improves relationships (especially with superiors); can keep another from harming you.	May communicate less power; ignores relational issues; forfeits instrumental goals.

SOURCE: Adapted from Daniel J. Canary and Michael J. Cody, *Interpersonal Communication: A Goals-Based Approach* (New York: St. Martin's Press, 1993).

sider a mixed couple in which the woman perceives the relationship as independent and the man perceives it as traditional. Inequality in roles in this instance is not the result of oversight or insensitivity. It owes to a fundamental difference in the way the woman and the man perceive the nature of their marriage. The root cause of their conflict, moreover, won't be resolved through compromise. Instead, the couple will have to work together to uncover the causes of their confused perceptions about their relationship. This won't be easy. It may not even lead to a resolution with which they both can live. But consider the alternative. What are the chances of their relationship surviving if they don't work together to uncover the source of their conflict?

Competition, the third conflict style, is also ill suited to the preceding scenario. Competitive styles, which are symmetrical, are designed to produce a winner, even if winning comes at someone else's expense.[10] Although a competitive style may be ill suited to a couple trying to resolve a struggle over roles, this doesn't

mean there is no place for such a style in the world of conflict management. Competition has been shown to increase people's commitment. We know a couple, for example, who competed to see who lowered his or her cholesterol more. Even so, competition is much better suited to team sports and businesses where conflict is intended to produce a winner. With rare exception, competitive symmetry in a relationship is likely to only escalate conflict.

The fourth and perhaps most commonly used conflict style is *compromise*. Examples in which compromise is common range from labor and management disputes to parents and teenagers struggling to be civil to one another. When we compromise, we tend to barter, agreeing to give up something in order to gain something in return.[11] Sometimes compromise works fairly well. When two people perceive each other as co-equals, for example, compromise is seen as an equitable way of resolving conflict. However, if one person sees the other as more equal, he or she will see compromise as an inequitable strategy.[12] If you already own most of the pie, for instance, you will be seen as giving up a lot less than a person who owns only two or three pieces. Even if a compromise is reached, therefore, it may breed resentment. In turn, this resentment may cause the two of you to experience conflict in the near future.

Cooperation is necessary for the constructive management of conflict, even when creative differences are involved.

The point, then, is that compromise often looks better than it actually proves to be. Frequently it leads to only a temporary resolution of a conflict. The reason, of course, is that the compromise is a quick and short-term fix to a long-term problem. Although a compromising style is not necessarily bad, you need to think long and hard about the style's potential disadvantages.

The fifth and final conflict style is *accommodation*. Like the preceding four, it has both advantages and disadvantages. People in a position of power, for instance, often can afford to be accommodating. As a result, they may enjoy putting their needs on the back burner to satisfy the needs of another. The opposite is true for people with little power. They may "eat crow" because they have no choice but to accommodate the demands of the person in power. The hotel manager may accede to the wishes of the rude guest who thinks he was overcharged on his bill and is making a scene in the lobby. But the manager doesn't have to like the fact that the "customer is always right."

As a rule of thumb, all of us should be flexible enough to be willing to use accommodation as a conflict style. When we are wrong or chiefly responsible for a conflict, accommodating the other person's wishes is not only productive but warranted as well. On the other hand, we also need to be suspicious of the motives of the person who is always willing to accommodate, willing to put her or his wishes behind everyone else's. This kind of accommodation actually can be a form of control.

In practice, people rarely use the same style of conflict in all the situations they experience daily. You may be highly competitive at work but accommodating at home. The fact that you agreed to a compromise with a coworker today doesn't mean you'll do the same tomorrow. In other words, different styles are appropriate for managing conflict in different circumstances.

Message Strategies

integrative strategy
A proposal and collaborative message strategy designed to lead to a fair and equitable outcome during and following conflict.

distributive strategy
An antisocial and controlling message strategy designed to enhance one's own position during and following conflict.

The preceding five conflict styles influence the message strategies people use when in conflict with each other. A message strategy is a plan or framework that people use to guide their communication behavior during conflict. Researchers have identified two distinct message strategies which people commonly employ. **Integrative message strategies** are prosocial and collaborative, approaching conflict as a win–win situation. Table 10-2 gives examples. **Distributive message strategies** are antisocial and controlling, treating conflict as a win–lose situation.[13] Table 10-3 gives examples.

In the case of integrative messages, parties look for common ground and attempt to integrate their interests in the hope of finding a long-term solution to the conflict. Integrative messages are cooperative rather than competitive in content and tone. Integrative messages reflect the party's beliefs that the satisfaction of their needs shouldn't come at the expense of the other person's needs going unsatisfied.

In the case of distributive messages, one party tries to gain control of the situation. Distributive messages are competitive and reflect the person's desire to

Table 10-2   Integrative Message Strategies

STRATEGY	DESCRIPTION	EXAMPLE
Descriptive statement	The communicator offers a factual explanation.	"There is a big bag of trash in the kitchen."
Disclosure	The communicator discloses personal feelings about the topic.	"I get annoyed when you interrupt me."
Soliciting disclosures	The communicator asks the other person to disclose feelings.	"What are you thinking about?"
Understanding and concern	The communicator demonstrates understanding and caring.	"I'm sure you are agonizing over this decision."
Supportive remark	The communicator backs up the other person's point of view.	"Now I understand."
Concession	The communicator conveys willingness to give in a little.	"OK, I'll try not to interrupt you from now on."
Acceptance of responsibility	The communicator accepts responsibility for part of the conflict.	"You're correct. I'll try to improve my table manners."
Common ground	Both communicators try to find a mutually satisfying solution.	"Can we agree to seek counseling?"

SOURCE: Adapted from Daniel J. Canary and Michael J. Cody, *Interpersonal Communication: A Goals Based Approach* (New York: St. Martin's Press, 1993).

win at the expense of the other person losing. People who use distributive messages also engage in personal attacks and attempt to bully the other person into submitting.

Needless to say, these two message strategies have a much different impact on the probability of a relationship between people surviving their conflict. With an integrative message strategy, there is a good chance that a relationship not only will survive but also will become stronger as a result of the conflict. People usually feel good about what they have accomplished following a conflict in which an integrative message strategy prevailed.

The attacking style that inheres to a distributive message strategy is likely to leave the losing side with a bruised and battered self-concept. The win-at-all-costs philosophy that underscores the distributive strategy, moreover, is also likely to leave the losing side feeling embittered. A distributive message strategy, therefore, minimizes the chances of the relationship surviving the conflict.

Table 10-3   Distributive Message Strategies

STRATEGY	DESCRIPTION	EXAMPLE
Personal criticism	The communicator faults the other person's character.	"Hey, stupid! Think before you act!"
Rejection	The communicator dismisses the other person's ideas.	"Not a chance, no way!"
Threat	The communicator warns of punishment if argument fails.	"If your grades don't improve, you're not going to play sports."
Blame	The communicator attributes the the entire conflict to the other person.	"If only you had listened, we wouldn't have this problem."
Hostile remark	The communicator tries to intimidate.	"Who — made you God?"
Shouting	The communicator tries to overcome the other person through sheer volume.	"Don't raise your voice at me!"
Sarcasm	The communicator uses intonation to convey that a statement is to be interpreted as its opposite.	"You sure looked buffed in that Speedo."
Prescription	The communicator tells the other person what to do.	"You shouldn't be so selfish — people might invite you over more."

SOURCE: Adapted from Daniel J. Canary and Michael J. Cody, *Interpersonal Communication: A Goals Based Approach* (New York: St. Martin's Press, 1993).

Constructive Conflict Management

Alan Sillars and J. Weisberg describe conflict as a relational event.[14] This description reinforces what we've said thus far: Conflict is a normal part of the process in which people define and redefine the nature of their relationship. Viewed from this vantage, conflict is not an aberration but a natural and predictable consequence of people in ongoing relationships spending time with each other.

Still, this relational event needs to be constructively managed. The constructive management of conflict is part knowledge and part skill. The knowledge part, moreover, includes recognizing not only what you should do during conflict but also what you should not do. The skills include the following:

- considering the other,
- keeping emotions in check and arguments rational,

Box 10-3 Considering Diversity

Conflict and Saving Face

Although the concept of saving face is collectivistic and associated with cultures such as Japan and China, we think it is a relevant and useful concept, regardless of one's culture. Saving face means allowing a person to keep his or her dignity in even the most adverse of circumstances. For example, people who believe in the concept would never dream of resolving a conflict in a manner that would cause either party to lose face.

In this culture, people seem to take almost perverse joy in not only controlling the outcome of a conflict but rubbing the other person's face in the outcome. In collegiate and professional sports, for example, it is no longer sufficient to win. In addition, the winner or winning team is now compelled to taunt the opposing side in the process.

Given this framework, do you think there is a need for the concept of saving face to be taught in our schools and youth sports programs? Do you think teachers, coaches, parents, and children would be receptive to the concept? Would it detract from the satisfaction North Americans, especially males, derive from competitive conflicts? Why or why not? Take a position on this series of questions, and write a one-page paper in response.

- expressing yourself precisely,
- bringing the conflict to resolution, and
- accentuating the positive.

Consider Others

Recall that people who use distributive message strategies are interested only in winning. They have little or no consideration for the other person. The distributive message strategist's communication behavior is exemplary of the fact. Such people frequently interrupt the other person and attack his or her self-image with comments that are deprecating and insulting. People who use a distributive message strategy also may provoke a conflict with others when they either least expect it or are busy with other matters.

In contrast, people who use integrative message strategies are considerate of the other person. In the attempt to assist the other in the constructive management of the conflict, people who take an integrative approach do their best to balance their needs with those of the other person, to listen to what the other person has to say without interruption, and to avoid attacking the other person's identity. As discussed in Box 10-3, integrative strategies are practiced routinely in collectivist cultures.

Given this general framework, here are some specific techniques you can use to show the other person you are concerned with his or her well-being:[15]

1. *Listen actively to the other person.* Let the person know you are involved by leaning forward, nodding your head when you agree with a point being made. Encourage the person to continue until he or she is finished talking.

2. *Validate the person's self-worth.* Tell the person explicitly that you respect the legitimacy of his or her beliefs and feelings, even if you disagree with them.

3. *Be consistent.* Don't contradict your verbal validation of the person's self-worth nonverbally. People read between the lines when in conflict. They check out the reliability of what is said verbally by comparing it with what is being said nonverbally. Try to keep the content and relational components of your message consistent.

4. *Avoid dogmatism.* Accept the fact that there are alternate points of view to yours, and stress the fact that you are willing to learn about them.

5. *Don't patronize the other person.* No one likes to be talked down to, even if the relationship is clearly superior to subordinate, as is the case with parents and children.

6. *Don't interrupt.* Try not to interrupt the other person, even if it means biting your tongue until it bleeds. Also, try to schedule the encounter with the other person at a time during which you're not likely to be interrupted by others.

Be Calm and Stay Rational

Even though conflict over serious matters is almost always accompanied by strong emotions, the constructive management of conflict is impossible unless people make a concerted effort to keep their emotions in check. The more rational the approach people take to their conflicts, the more likely they will keep a leash on their emotions. As is the case in considering others, there are specific strategies people can use in this regard.[16]

1. *Avoid distributive messages.* Distributive messages purposely take aim at the other person's identity. The responses distributive messages elicit are likely to be defensive and hostile.

2. *Learn to distinguish among messages that are assertive, argumentative, and hostile.* Assertive messages are designed to communicate personal competence and confidence. In terms of the present discussion, assertive messages tend to take one of three forms.[17] The first involves people communicating in the effort to establish leadership and control of the situation—for example, "I'm the parent, you're the child, and I'll make the decision."

A second form of assertiveness involves people communicating in defense of their rights and interests. In families with teenage children, for instance, it is not uncommon for the teenager to assert a right to privacy, telling a parent, "This is my room and you should knock before entering!"

Finger pointing and name calling only make conflict worse.

A third and final form of assertiveness involves people communicating in the effort to protect a feeling or belief. In a group of close friends, as a case in point, two people may gang up on a third: "Come on . . . you know we're right and you're wrong." The third person may assert in response, "Ganging up on me won't work. I refuse to agree with what you're saying just because there are two of you and one of me."

Assertive messages are aggressive by nature but needn't be hostile. The same is true of argumentative messages, which are a subset of assertive messages. Assertive messages tend to be declarative, for example, "I'm the oldest and most experienced." Argumentative messages, on the other hand, involve a claim and evidence in support of the assertion. Frequently, argumentative messages also are designed to refute what another claims. Thus, a person may argue, "You may be the oldest, but you only think you have more experience. You're forgetting that I majored in marketing at the leading school in the country."[18]

Hostile messages, like assertive and argumentative ones, are aggressive by nature. Unlike assertive and argumentative messages, however, hostile ones tend to be colored with anger, irritability, negativism, and resentment.[19] Rather than helping a person keep emotions in check, hostile messages are emotional by definition. Hostile messages tend to provoke a hostile response. Whereas assertiveness and argumentativeness can be put to constructive use during conflict, hostile messages simply fan the fire.

3. *Don't catastrophize.* Catastrophic messages make things look worse than they actually are. Catastrophic messages not only exaggerate the situation but also predict improbable consequences when people don't get their way. Teenagers commonly make catastrophic statements when in conflict with parents. They say such things as "If you make me wear that, no one will ever speak to me again."

4. *Avoid trying to "one up" hostile messages.* If a person says something that is genuinely nasty, resist the temptation to reciprocate by going the person one better. The best way to handle this situation is to respond to the person's message by asking for clarification of the remark. If the person says, "You're just like your mother when you don't get your way," respond with "I'm not sure what you mean."

5. *Mind your meta-message.* Try not to intensify the emotions you feel nonverbally. Finger pointing, raising your voice, and showing anger in your face invite similar responses. Further, messages dripping with sarcasm or feigned disbelief will only make matters worse.

6. *Take control of your anger.* Take a break to cool off if emotions begin to get out of control. Otherwise, your messages and the other person's as well are likely to become increasingly hostile.

Speak Precisely

How people present issues, frame problems, and express their feelings plays a significant role in the constructive management of conflict. It is important, therefore, that we communicate precisely. There are several things you'll want to do in your effort to communicate as precisely as you can.

1. *Be specific.* Be specific about the issues underlying the conflict. Tell the other person that you perceive the conflict to be the result of incompatible goals, scarce resources, or outside interference from another party. Then state as precisely as you can which of your goals appear to be incompatible, why you think resources are so scarce that they can't be shared equitably, or why someone outside the relationship is interfering with it.

2. *Avoid generalizations.* If a person is occasionally late, don't say, "You're always late." If a person occasionally makes a mistake in balancing the checkbook, don't say, "Why do you always screw up the checkbook balance?" Such

generalizations not only overstate the issue but also make it appear that the person is always irresponsible.

3. *Use "I" messages.* As we explained in Chapter 9, "I" messages communicate ownership of the feelings or beliefs expressed. When we clearly take ownership of a message, it is less likely to be perceived as accusatory or judgmental.

4. *Be descriptive.* Try to be descriptive rather than evaluative when talking about issues. Instead of saying, "You are such a whiner," say instead, "I think you find fault in much of what I do." Note that this strategy also turns a "you" message into a less-accusatory "I" message.

5. *Stay focused and in the moment.* You have no control over the past. Besides, bringing up a person's past transgressions is likely to make the person defensive and more combative.

Keep Moving Toward Resolution

The more distributive your strategy, the more likely it is that conflict will continue. The more integrative your strategy, the more likely the conflict will be resolved to everyone's satisfaction. Remember that an integrative strategy invites collaboration and a win–win attitude among all parties involved. The following points should be helpful in your attempts to mutually satisfy conflicts.

1. *Establish a frame of reference.* If possible, establish at the very beginning of your discussion a frame of reference that will enable you and the other person to reaffirm your relationship and admit to the discomfort you feel in anticipation of trying to resolve the conflict. Also try to agree consensually to the rules of engagement, including acceptable and unacceptable behavior.

2. *Clarify the issues.* Set aside time for issue clarification. Try to identify to everyone's satisfaction mutual goals and the obstacles that stand in the way of achieving those goals.

3. *Be open.* If there is more than one potential source of resolution to the conflict, which is often the case, don't hide it. Be open about alternative solutions to problems that stand in the way of resolving the conflict.

4. *Take time to find long-term solutions.* Give yourself and the other person sufficient time to weigh and evaluate proposed courses of action. At the same time, when presented with a proposal from the other person, try to avoid making an immediate counterproposal, which will invite the same from the other person. What may sound good at the moment often loses its luster over time. Finding a long-term solution to a problem or a resolution to the conflict itself will take time.[20]

5. *Accentuate the positive.* Be sure to close each encounter by reinforcing what is good about the relationship. Counselors try to have conflicting parties

Box 10-4   Skill Building

Verbal and Nonverbal Behaviors for Managing Conflict

Revisit Chapters 3 and 4, which dealt with verbal and nonverbal communication behaviors. Review what was said there about language and its potential effects on perceptions and behavior. On the basis of your review, list five principles of effective language you believe would be useful in the constructive management of conflict.

Next, review what was said about the dimensions of nonverbal communication behavior and their bearing on effective communication. Based on this review, list five specific nonverbal communication behaviors you think would aggravate conflict and five nonverbal communication behaviors you believe would be useful in effectively managing conflict.

Be prepared to defend both lists, explaining the reasoning behind your selections.

say something positive about each other and their relationship at the end of counseling sessions. Simply saying, "This has been productive and I feel good about it" may suffice.

Be Positive

Conflict needn't be a negative and unpleasant experience. How conflict turns out simply depends on the attitudes and corresponding behaviors people reveal in the course of conflict. One person leaning back in his or her seat with a sour facial expression will produce a much different transaction than a person leaning forward, with a neutral, or better yet, welcoming expression on his or her face. The following are skills you can use to be positive.[21]

1. *Be immediate.* Immediacy behaviors, as you may recall from Chapter 4, reduce perceptions of distance and increase perceptions of openness and warmth. Immediacy behaviors include smiling, appropriate eye contact, head nodding, and leaning forward.

2. *Be encouraging.* Complement immediacy behaviors with appropriate verbal expression. Encourage the person to speak, "Please . . . go on." When talking try to incorporate positive sentiments with your message. Say such things as "I care about you and our relationship," or "We've invested a lot of love in each other," or "I love you, but I don't like the way you boss me." Box 10-4 reviews ask you to verbal and nonverbal behaviors you can use to manage conflict.

3. *Relieve tension.* Assist each other in relieving tension, should it become too intense. Humor can work well in this regard. Recall a humorous anecdote that involves you and the other person, for example. Remember, though, the

humor must be appropriate to the situation. Sarcasm may increase rather than alleviate tensions during conflict.

Managed properly, conflict can be resolved to everyone's benefit.

Try to think of these five sets of techniques, strategies, and skills as a system for the constructive management of conflict. As is the case with all systems, these skills are interdependent and work best when used together. It won't do much good to follow the advice suggested in one set of skills—for instance, keeping your emotions in check—if you fail to consider the well-being of the other person.

Finally, think about these five sets of techniques, strategies, and skills as a means of framing the conflict. As any artist will tell you, the success of a painting or an illustration depends in part on the manner in which it is framed. An ornate, wooden frame will influence the viewer one way; a plain metal frame will influence the viewer in a totally different way. So it is with conflict and its constructive management. How you and others frame the conflict will affect the probability of your success in resolving it.

Summary

Conflict is not abnormal. It is a central feature of relational life. Conflict need not be destructive. Although conflict can occur as a result of a communication breakdown, it also can occur when there is complete fidelity in a communication transaction. Five common sources of conflict are perceptual bias, interdependence, goals, scarce resources, and outside interference. When conflict does occur, trying to speedily resolve it is not necessarily the best strategy.

Conflict can be constructive. Constructive conflict, which requires willingness to change, is most likely when people are knowledgeable about the sources of conflict, aware of their conflict style, and clear about the differences between distributive and integrative message strategies. Common conflict styles include avoidance, collaboration, competition, compromise, and accommodation. To be constructive, people must actively manage conflict. The effective management of conflict involves the routine use of specific techniques, strategies, and skills.

Techniques for effective conflict management include verbal and nonverbal behaviors that demonstrate people are considerate of each other—for instance, listening actively. Strategies for effective conflict management involve people keeping their emotions in check, avoiding distributive message strategies, judiciously using assertive and argumentative messages, and avoiding the temptation to reciprocate highly critical messages. Skills for the effective management of conflict are equally numerous. These skills have been discussed throughout this book and include verbal and nonverbal immediacy and the use of "I" messages.

Another Look

Articles

Stella Ting-Toomey. "Managing Conflict in Intimate Intercultural Relationships." In *Conflict in Personal Relationships,* edited by Dudley D. Cahn, 47–77. Hillsdale, N.J.: Lawrence Erlbaum, 1994.

What special problems do intercultural couples face in their attempts to constructively manage conflict? Professor Ting-Toomey provides some answers to this question. In the process, she talks about conflict between partners from individualist and collectivist cultures, the importance of saving face across cultures, and conflict styles and strategies.

Shereen G. Bingham. "Sexual Harassment: On the Job, On Campus." In *Gendered Relationships,* edited by Julia T. Wood, 233–52. Mountain View, Calif.: Mayfield, 1996.

Perceptions of sexual harassment differ between men and women. Conflict between the sexes on the topic of sexual harassment is common, even when men and women are close friends. This article makes it clear why disagreement and conflict over what constitutes sexual harassment are common.

Books

Dudley D. Cahn, ed. *Conflict in Personal Relationships.* Hillsdale, N.J.: Lawrence Erlbaum, 1994.

This book of edited readings is excellent in its scope and treatment of relational conflict. Besides the article described above, it features readings on conflict in same-sex relationships, marital conflict, parent–child conflict, and conflict between adults and their aging parents.

Joyce L. Hocker and William W. Wilmot. *Interpersonal Conflict.* 4th ed. Madison, Wis.: Brown and Benchmark, 1995.

This is probably the most widely read and cited book on the relationship between communication and the constructive management of conflict. Hocker is a clinical therapist who uses the book's strategies in her practice. Besides being a university professor, Wilmot is a practicing mediator who has worked extensively with people in conflict management. Their backgrounds make this book more than a scholarly exercise.

Video Rentals

Who's Afraid of Virginia Woolf?   Starring the late Sir Richard Burton and Elizabeth Taylor, this adaptation of Edward Albee's play is a powerful statement about destructive conflict in a soured relationship.

War of the Roses   This is a more entertaining if less insightful treatment of destructive conflict in marital relationships than *Who's Afraid of Virginia Woolf?*. This film, starring Michael Douglas and Kathleen Turner, does an excellent job of showing the escalatory spiral unmanaged conflict can take. It also hints at how different perceptions of the balance of power in a relationship can contribute to the escalation of conflict.

Star Trek: The Unknown Country   Always praised for its meta-message, this final voyage for the original crew looks at intercultural conflict. It shows how competition interferes with communication and how cultural and sociological differences can exacerbate conflict. The film also deals with face and face work and their role in conflict management. Face and face work are terms from collectivist cultures, where it is important to protect the pride (face) of conflicting parties and to practice conflict strategies (face work) that ensure that conflicting parties keep face.

Theory and Research in Practice

1. Research suggests that personal orientations toward conflict depend on gender and culture. In terms of the following list, how do you think men and women differ? How do you think people in individualistic cultures differ from those in collectivist cultures?

   A. Conflict style

   B. Integrative/distributive strategy

   C. Consideration of the other

   Make a list of the differences you've noted and explain in writing why you think each difference occurs.

2. Given the information in this chapter and the preceding one, in which of the following types of families do you think conflict would be most common, most unmanaged, or both? What specifically leads you to this conclusion? Write down your reasons and share them in class.

   A. open family

   B. closed family

   C. random family

   D. enmeshed family

   E. disengaged family

3. Do you think conflict tends to be more frequent in traditional relationships or in independent ones? Why? Once conflict occurs in a traditional or independent relationship, which couple type (described in Chapter 9) do you think is better able to constructively manage the conflict?

4. Rent *Star Trek: The Unknown Country*. Write an analysis of conflict management in the film, paying particular attention to

   A. sources of conflict,

   B. conflict goals,

   C. conflict styles,

   D. message strategies, and

   E. balance of power.

CHAPTER ELEVEN

Interviewing

OBJECTIVES

After reading this chapter you should be able to:

- Conduct an interview to gather information.

- Conduct an effective and legally correct employment interview.

- Effectively present yourself during an interview with a potential employer.

- Construct a résumé and cover letter that effectively present your qualifications to a potential employer.

- Conduct an effective appraisal interview.

- Present yourself effectively when undergoing an appraisal interview.

Imagine the following situation. You are on a panel interviewing an applicant for a position in your firm. After going through the applicant's experience and qualifications, you ask a routine interview question: "What are your greatest strengths and weaknesses?" The potential employee replies: "Well, I can't think of any real strengths. My greatest weakness is that I have a hard time getting to work on time." Guess who isn't going to get the job? This, by the way, is not a fictional account. Although the applicant deserved points for modesty and honesty, the outright admission that being punctual was a problem sealed the applicant's fate.

We all will experience the interview process, most likely from both sides. Chances are you have already been through a number of interviews, as a job applicant, as you sought a college scholarship, or even when you applied for college. You will likely find yourself conducting interviews in the future. As a student you may interview an expert source for a speech, class paper, or the campus newspaper. Once you enter the work force and advance in your career, you are likely to conduct interviews with potential or current employees. If you enter a field such as counseling or medicine, you will undoubtedly conduct many helping interviews. Even finding an apartment or securing a loan for a

interview A communication transaction by an interviewer or interviewers engaging in questioning and discussion with an interviewee for some purpose, such as gathering information, selecting a person for employment, evaluating an employee, or providing therapy.

interviewer The person responsible for guiding and conducting an interview.

interviewee The person who is the subject of an interview.

information-gathering interview Questioning a source for information about one or more topics.

house can involve an interview. Without a doubt, interviewing is a pervasive form of communication.

This chapter deals with this important relational communication tool, the **interview,** a communication transaction by an interviewer or interviewers engaging in questioning and discussion with an interviewee for some purpose, such as gathering information, selecting a person for employment, evaluating an employee, or providing therapy. Interviews initiate the process in which interviewer and interviewee begin to define their relationship. All interviews involve an **interviewer,** the person responsible for guiding and conducting an interview, and an **interviewee,** the person who is the subject of an interview. There are, of course, many types of interviews—from the job selection interview to the television reporter who interviews a president. In this chapter, we look at three important types of interviews you are likely to face in your college career and beyond:

- the information-gathering interview,
- the employment-selection interview, and
- the performance-appraisal interview.

We discuss the roles of both the supervisor and the employee in making the most effective use of the performance-appraisal process. Keep in mind that this chapter only scratches the surface of the interviewing process. Nevertheless, many of the principles we discuss, such as effective preparation and active listening, are vital to all types of interviews.

Interviewing for Information

One of the most common types of interviews is the **information-gathering interview.** Included in this category are interviews with experts, such as a student might use in writing a paper or speech. Other types of information-gathering interviews are those done by survey research firms, by researchers who collect oral history from people who have lived through important experiences, and by journalists.

As a college student you are likely to have several occasions to interview for information—perhaps for an upcoming report, for a group project, or for your school radio station. Far too often students go into an information-gathering interview with little or no background on their topic. In a sense, they expect the expert they interview to write their report or paper for them. Although interviews with experts can offer you useful information and may lead you to other sources, they cannot substitute for doing your own research. Thus, an interview should be conducted only after you've been to the library and done the research necessary to ask intelligent questions.

Finding potential interviewees on most topics is not as difficult as you may think. On the topic of recycling, for example, your community probably has a recycling center. You may be able to arrange an interview with the director of the center. Community leaders, such as members of the city council, also may have information on topics such as recycling, traffic congestion, parking, and growth. At a college or university, most departments have a variety of experts on various topics. Often you can call the relevant department to ask if there is anyone familiar with your specific topic. In other cases, you may simply want to consult a department's course offerings. If someone is teaching a class on ecology, for example, it's a fair bet the person is an expert in that subject.

Another strategy is to contact organizations that are related to your topic and ask if someone is available for you to interview. For example, if you are researching the effects of secondhand tobacco smoke, the American Lung Association is a likely source of potential interviewees.

Sometimes you already know a person who can help you. The authors recall the case of one student who was speaking about a "miracle" weight-loss product. After calling the company's home office and getting the runaround, she contacted her local pharmacist. He informed her that the ingredients in the product were in no way capable of helping a person lose weight and, in fact, they were potentially harmful. A brief interview with the pharmacist gave her information she would have had great difficulty finding on her own.

Once you have decided on an interview, there are some basic guidelines to help you succeed:

Before the Interview

- *Contact the potential interviewee well in advance.* Explain why you want to meet and how much time you think you'll need. Ask for a convenient time and place for a meeting (usually at the interviewee's place of business). If possible, confirm your appointment in writing. Verify where and when you will meet and how much time you have to spend. This will guide you in both formulating questions and determining the number of questions you can reasonably pursue.

- *Do some general reading on your topic.* Read at least a book or two and some recent articles. This will give you a basis for asking your questions and allow you to concentrate on those things you cannot easily find out for yourself.

- *Prepare specific questions in advance.* You should attempt to ask open-ended questions, which will allow the interviewee an opportunity to talk at some length. You should, of course, be prepared to deviate from that list as answers suggest other avenues to follow. But at least you know you won't be wasting time trying to come up with questions on the spot.

During the Interview

- *Show up on time, dressed professionally, and ready to begin.* Introduce yourself and explain how you will use the interview. If you are planning to tape-record the interview, be sure to ask for permission. If an interview is by phone, you have a legal obligation to inform the other party if you are taping the conversation.

- *Begin with general questions.* Using what you've learned about your topic as a guide, begin with general questions and then work to specific ones. Be sure to let the interviewee talk. Don't monopolize the conversation, as this will defeat the purpose of the interview.

- *Ask for leads.* Ask the interviewee if he or she can suggest other sources of information—books, pamphlets, periodicals, or other experts. Often an expert will lead you to sources you never would have thought of yourself. Most fields have their own specialized journals or other publications. If you are lucky, your interviewee may even loan you some relevant materials.

- *Listen effectively.* Use the listening skills discussed in Chapter 6. For an information-gathering interview, comprehensive listening is a must.

- *Take notes.* Either tape-record (with permission) or take complete notes during the interview. If you do not get something down, ask a follow-up question to make sure you get the essential points on paper. If you want to use direct quotes from the interview, make sure they are accurate.

- *Ask for additional information.* When your time is about up, ask the interviewee if there is anything he or she can add to what has been said. Perhaps there is some area that you have completely overlooked.

- *Say thanks.* Thank the interviewee for his or her time and exit graciously.

After the Interview

- *Follow up.* A follow-up thank you letter is common courtesy and may help you get subsequent interviews.

- *Transcribe notes.* Transcribe your tape or your notes while the interview is fresh in your mind. Notes that may have been clear at the moment will quickly fade from memory unless you flesh them out soon after the interview.

- *Follow leads.* Follow up on leads or other interviews suggested by your interviewee.

- *Build credibility.* Interviews not only can provide a rich source of information to you but also can add to your credibility. The fact that you have taken the time to speak directly to an expert shows the lengths to which you will go to gather more than superficial information.

employment interview
Questioning an applicant for a job in an organization.

Employment Interviews

Employment-selection interviews are an important part of everyone's career. Not only will you depend on your interviewing skills to get that all-important

Reporters use the interview as their primary medium of information gathering.

first job after college, statistically you are likely to change jobs several times during your working lifetime. In addition, it is possible that you will someday be in the position to hire someone yourself. Thus, understanding the dynamics of the employment interview is important, not only to prospective interviewees but also to those who conduct the interviews. We begin this section by discussing the interviewer's role.

Interviewer Responsibilities

Preparation   As an employment interviewer, you have some very important responsibilities. Not only are you seeking to find the best available employee for your organization, you are also subject to a number of legal requirements. The discussion below focuses on legal as well as practical aspects of preparing to interview potential employees.

Box 11-1 Critical Thinking

Dealing with Illegal Interview Questions

It was not so many years ago that women applicants for jobs were often asked if they planned to have children. Or, if they were known to have children, questions about child care or how to deal with childhood illnesses sometimes were asked. Questions about religious preferences often surfaced in discussions of whether a person could work Saturdays or Sundays. Only recently were questions related to disability restricted by the passage of the Americans with Disabilities Act. Although all the above questions are now illegal, only a naive person would believe that such questions are no longer asked.

An ethical and pragmatic question, therefore, is how to deal with these illegal questions. Although you may be tempted to become angry and defiant, keep in mind that your objective is to get the job. On the other hand, if a question is a serious viola-

tion of the law, failure to object to it may perpetuate the behavior with other applicants.

What, then, are your options when you are asked illegal interview questions? Without consulting an authoritative source, make a list of questions you think should be off-limits in a job interview. Then visit your campus personnel office and ask to see any available document that tells you the legal limits of the questions that can be asked of you during an employment interview. Compare your self-generated list with the legal document. If you find inconsistencies, bring them up in class and discuss them. Also, if you discover any questions that personally would prove bothersome, talk to your instructor about how you might skillfully answer such questions despite your discomfort.

Although this chapter is too brief to provide a full discussion of the *legal requirements for employers,* it is important that you familiarize yourself with the basic principles. Congress passed the Equal Employment Opportunity (EEO) laws back in the 1960s. Recently, the Americans with Disabilities Act (ADA) was added to the mix. The key to complying with these laws is that you only ask questions of potential employees that are related to *bona fide occupational qualifications* (BFOQs), that is, the requirements essential to performing a particular job. Questions regarding education, work experience, skills, and the like are acceptable. Questions about age, marital status, race, religion, ethnicity, disability, and the like, are not acceptable,[1] although some of them once were. Box 11-1 will help you think about how you would handle being asked illegal questions during a job interview.

In addition to familiarizing yourself with the legal requirements for employment interviews, you should develop a clear set of *criteria for the position* that is being filled. It is often useful to develop a rating scale for the various criteria required for the job. Then, by rating candidates on a numerical system—for example a scale of 1 to 5, with 5 being best—you can ensure you are fairly comparing all the candidates.

When conducting an interview, it's important to try and help the interviewee relax.

Next, you should develop a *preliminary set of questions* to be asked of all prospective employees. Not only will this lead to a more focused interview, it will help protect you against potential charges of discrimination. For example, if you ask different questions of a disabled person than of an able-bodied one, you are inviting an ADA lawsuit.

Finally, before conducting specific interviews, be sure to familiarize yourself with the *applicants' résumés*. That way, you can avoid asking questions that are already answered on paper. In addition, the résumé may raise questions that the applicant can answer. For example, you may want to ask about specific duties at previous jobs or relevant courses of study.

Conducting the Interview   It is important that you conduct an interview in a professional and courteous manner. Remember that for every applicant who is hired, many others will not be accepted. Not only will any signs of discourtesy or unprofessionalism shed a bad light on your organization, they could become the basis of a lawsuit if an applicant believes he or she was discriminated against. Keep in mind that applicants will talk about your organization. Negative experiences in the interview process can come back to haunt you. Furthermore, you never know when a person who was not right for one position might be just the right person for another opening in your organization.

Just like a speech or paper, an interview has an opening, body, and close. Here are some suggestions for each of these phases of the interview:

- *Opening.* You should greet the interviewee in a friendly and professional manner. Shake his or her hand, introduce yourself and anyone else participating in the interview. Make sure the applicant is comfortable. Although it is perfectly appropriate to begin an interview with some small talk, this should be kept to a minimum. Prolonging the casual conversation can create suspense and anxiety on the part of the applicant.[2]

- *Body.* The body of the interview is where you get down to business. It is a good idea to preview for the applicant how the interview will proceed: "First, I'll ask you some questions about your background and experience; second, we'll discuss the position and job expectations; and finally, you'll have an opportunity to ask questions." It is good to begin with open-ended, relatively easy questions, which will help the applicant relax and build rapport. Avoid unstructured, overly general questions, however, such as, "Tell me about yourself."[3]

One of the most interesting findings of research on interviewing is that interviewers often make their decisions within the first four minutes of the interview.[4] While many interviewers tend to begin with an "inverted funnel," asking closed-ended questions first and open-ended questions later in the interview, professors Charles Stewart and William Cash recommend the reverse. They point out that it is best "to begin with a funnel sequence to get the interviewee talking and begin obtaining maximum information immediately."[5]

Interviewers should avoid a number of question types.[6] *Yes/no questions* give the interviewee little opportunity to provide information. *Double-barreled questions* actually combine two questions in one. A *leading question* telegraphs to the interviewer how you want him or her to answer. The *guessing-game question* occurs when the interviewer guesses at the answer and asks the interviewee if that is correct. The *evaluative-response question* reveals the interviewer's feelings about a prospective answer. *Illegal questions,* such as those which violate the EEO or ADA, are obviously taboo. *Yes-response questions* that can only be answered yes are pointless. *Résumé questions* are redundant, since they ask for information that is already provided on the résumé.

More effective are questions that ask about some of the following areas: interest in the organization, general or specific work-related topics, education and training, career paths and goals, previous job performance, salary and benefits, and the career field in general.[7] Questions can also deal with hypothetical or real situations. For example, when the authors interview prospective professors, we often ask them to describe how they would approach a certain class, what texts and assignments they would employ, and how they would grade students.

After you ask questions and obtain the information you need, it is often important to provide the applicant information about the organization, the nature of the job, salary and benefits, and career advancement opportunities. Keep in mind that an interview is a two-way street. In some fields, good applicants have a number of offers. It is important that interviewers are ethical and honest in explaining the benefits of their organization. At the same time, interviewers must ensure that the applicant leaves with a good impression of their organization, whether that person is hired or not.

Finally, be sure to give the applicant a chance to ask questions of you. Not only is this an important information source for the interviewee, it is also another source of information for the interviewer. For example, an employee who is overly concerned about perks and benefits might be less than ideal for your organization. One of the mistakes many interviewers make is to talk too much. The interviewer is there to listen as well as to ask questions.

- *Close.* Sometimes an interviewer has the authority to make an offer on the spot, but this is rare. More likely, there are other applicants to interview. Often there are EEO guidelines that must be met and paperwork that must be processed before an offer can be tendered. The interviewer should honestly explain to the interviewee what will happen next. If there is another level of interview possible, this should be made clear. Finally, a rough indication of the time frame is important. Not only is this fair to the applicant, who may be foregoing another employment possibility while waiting for an offer, it also prevents an applicant from constantly calling to find out what is happening next.

After the Interview   Be sure to make a record of your impressions as soon after the interview as possible. If you have taken notes during the interview, go over them while they are fresh in your mind. Often the organization will have a standardized form for the interviewer to fill out. Otherwise, you may want to draw up your own checklist.

Once a decision is made—to offer employment, to conduct another interview, or to not offer employment—you should communicate this decision in writing to all applicants if feasible. If there are too many applicants to notify those not hired, be prepared for calls of inquiry. It would be wise to let interviewees know that unless they hear further from you, they are no longer in the running.

Assuming you do send letters or otherwise notify those not hired, a polite, noncommittal letter—"We regret to inform you that you were not selected"—is in order. Remember that this letter also reflects on your organization and that those who are not hired may one day be desired by your organization. A good impression at all levels of the interview process is not only common courtesy it is common sense as well.

Interviewee Responsibilities

As an applicant for employment, you will need to give careful attention to every phase of the interview process. The process begins with your search for possible employment and involves developing a résumé and cover letter and preparing for the actual interview. It concludes with a letter of thanks and appropriate follow-up and evaluation of your performance.

Preparation   The first step in preparing for the interview is to determine the career field(s) in which you are qualified for employment. Whereas this is obvious for some majors (accounting, for example), majors in the liberal arts and social sciences often face a wide-open career range. We have seen communication majors employed doing everything from sales to anchoring the evening news. Early in your college career, you should talk to your major advisor about careers in your field. Most campuses have career counselors and placement services. Avail yourself of these services long before you plan to graduate. Knowing what you want to do for a career is one of the essential things you'll need to succeed professionally. Assuming you know your general career area, here are some important steps to follow in preparing for the interview process:

- *Look for leads.* What employment opportunities are there in your field? Obviously placement services, want ads, and professional contacts are a good place to begin. But it is important to pursue unconventional means as well. For example, a survey of Boston area residents who had recently found new jobs found that most of them learned about their jobs from people who were distant associates—college friends, parents of their children's playmates, and the like.[8]

  Depending on your field, trade publications can be an important source of information on job openings. For example, prospective professors know that the *Chronicle of Higher Education* is an indispensable source for job openings in academia. Journalists turn to sources such as *Editor and Publisher.* If you belong to a professional society or student organization related to your field, inquire as to the usual method of posting employment notices.

- *Develop a résumé.* This is a crucial step in pursuing a job. A résumé is your best advertisement. You want to capture in one or two pages the essence of what you have to offer an employer. The basic features of a résumé are the following:

  - Name, address, phone number. If you have a local and a permanent address, be sure to list both.

  - Career objective. Most employers like to see a brief description of what type of employment you are seeking.

  - Education and training. Presumably if you are enrolled in this course, you are pursuing a college degree. Be sure to list your most recent education first and then continue on in reverse chronological order. If you

are not yet a graduate, list your degree and date of graduation (expected). You probably shouldn't list your grade-point average unless it is fairly high.

- Work experience. This information should also be in reverse chronological order, with your last job listed first. By titling this list "work experience," rather than "employment history," you can include non-paid experiences, such as internships. Be sure to list more than the title of the position. Give a brief description of the duties and responsibilities of the job.

- Relevant professional licenses, awards, honors, and the like. For example, in the speech pathology discipline, it is important to have a certificate of clinical competency in either speech pathology or audiology. Without such a license, a person cannot practice professionally or supervise those who are preparing to do so.

- Hobbies and recreational activities are a useful way to indicate that you

Placement agencies and job fairs are helpful for finding out employment opportunities in your field. Prior to a job interview, learn as much as possible about the company and position for which you are applying.

Figure 11-1 Sample Résumés

```
PAT A. JONES
P.O. Box 55
Forest Valley, WA
95860-0549
Phone: 360-555-1234

EDUCATION                           WORKSHOPS AND SEMINARS

Valley State University             Color Therapy Workshop
9/1992 to present                   Valley State University 11/1994
B.A. Degree in Graphic Design,
Minor in Art, expected 6/1997       Portfolio Workshop 12/1992
Coursework completed in             Artists Club, Forest Valley, WA
copy preparation, typography,
photography, packaging,             Basic Line, Halftone and PMT
publication design,                 Techniques 10/1992
and offset lithography.             Fotoprocessing, Inc.

WORK EXPERIENCE                     MEMBERSHIPS

Quality Printing, Inc.              Artists Club
6/1995 to present                   member since 1992
Lithographic stripper, responsible  Treasurer, 1996/1997
for all film assembly and
platemaking, including four         Designers Club, Valley State
color process, in quality oriented  University member since 1992
commercial printing company.        Steering Committee, 1994/1995

Weekly Shopper                      REFERENCES AVAILABLE
7/1993 to 6/1995                    ON REQUEST
Contributing designer and
illustrator,and copy camera
operator for community newspaper.

Scott, Johnson, and Roberts
Advertising, Seattle, WA
6/1993 to 9/1993
Full-time internship position as
graphic designer and production
artist in advertising agency.

Kopy Korner, Inc.
9/1992 to 6/1993
Responsible for all pre-press
operations (paste-up, camera,
stripping, platemaking) and
ran small offset press in
printing shop.
```

are a well-rounded person. Any extracurricular activities you pursued in college help an employer know that you are capable of budgeting your time and meeting your responsibilities.

- References. Many texts advise writing only "references available on request."[9] On the other hand, some employers specifically want a list of references submitted with the résumé. The best advice is to determine

KIM A. SMITH

1234 Cypress Street, Apt. B
San Thomas, CA 92345
310-555-8345

Career Objective

Computer Programmer with emphasis on applications
for World Wide Web

Professional Experience

96   Webmasters, Inc., Youngstown, CA
      Computer Programmer

Responsibilities

Develop computer web sites for clients of local
Internet provider, customized software for
business applications.

Clients/Projects

Shasta Research Center, Shasta, CA
Designed and maintained web sites.

Furniture Mart, Bayville, CA
Customized payroll software for medium sized
chain with 100+ employees.

Middlefield Industries, San Lucas, CA
Designed and maintained web pages,
provided training for employees.

95   Software Solutions,
      San Thomas, CA
      Computer Trainer

Responsibilities

Responsible for training beginning computer users
in use of Windows and Macintosh programs, including
word processing, spreadsheets, and data bases.

Clients

Chamber of Commerce, San Thomas, CA
Trained new employees in use of Windows.

Oakmont Elementary School
Provided training to faculty in use of Macintosh
computers.

Weekly Herald
Provided training to weekly newspaper staff
in Microsoft Word for Windows.

Academic Experience

94   Internship
      Computer City

      Sales and customer service

93   Internship
      University Media Center

      Computer graphics, assisted in design of instructional
      materials for faculty.

Education

95   San Thomas University

      Bachelor of Science, Computer Science
      Minor in Mathematics
      Graduated with Honors
      Coursework included C programming in UNIX environment,
      compilers, databases, human-computer interaction design,
      artificial intelligence, computer graphics.

References Available on Request

what is customary in your field. If you do list references, be sure that you have their permission.

Résumés should be printed, either professionally or on a laser printer, using good quality paper, typically off-white, gray, or beige. There should be a fair amount of white space, and the résumé should be clear and attractive. Sample résumés are shown in Figure 11-1. Keep in mind that potential employers may spend only a few seconds on each résumé.[10] Any grammatical, spelling, or typographical errors are likely to lead to immediate disqualification. A messy or unconventional résumé is likely to make a bad impression.

Avoid any information that violates EEO or ADA guidelines. This means do not include a picture, marital information, age, race, religion, and the like. Some companies, fearing lawsuits, have gatekeepers, such as secretaries, who black out such information.[11] Imagine what it does to your chances to have your résumé mutilated before it ever reaches the eyes of the decision makers.

- *Target your cover letter.* Unlike the résumé, which is general and can be used for numerous applications, your cover letter should be targeted to the specific job you are seeking. Address the letter to the person most responsible for hiring. Don't simply address it to the personnel department. Be sure to put your letter in terms of what you can do for the company based on your preliminary research of the company. It is important that your cover letter address how your training and skills meet the company's employment needs.

  Cover letters should be brief, never over one page, and personalized. Never use a form letter—it is sure to end up in the circular file. Also, as with the résumé, the cover letter should be "letter perfect." Be sure to indicate your desire for an interview. Often it is useful to follow up a letter with a phone call. If you plan to do so, you should so indicate in your letter. Two sample cover letters are shown in Figure 11-2.

- *Do your homework.* As we suggest in Box 11-2, your homework begins well in advance of an invitation to an interview. You should prepare for it, just as you would for a final exam. Do your research on the organization and the position for which you are applying. If it is a major corporation, look at recent annual reports. If you know someone who works in the organization or who has contact with it, ask for as much information as possible. Providing specific information related to the company during the interview not only shows initiative on your part but also shows you are serious about pursuing the job.

- *Rehearse.* If possible, try a "dry run" interview with a friend playing the role of interviewer. Many communication departments offer classes in interviewing or include it as a component of another class. Such classes are an excellent opportunity to practice your interview skills. If you can, videotape or audiotape your interview and review your performance. Video- and audiotapes are useful tools to improve your performance in the real interview.

Being Interviewed   Of course, the moment of truth is bound to come—the actual interview. Assuming you have properly prepared yourself, there is no reason to be overly anxious. It is important to be on time (in fact a few minutes early), properly dressed, well groomed, and in a positive frame of mind for your

Figure 11-2 Sample
Cover Letter (a)

```
P.O. Box 55
Forest Valley, Washington 95860-0549
Phone: 360-555-1234

September 6, 1997

Mr. John Rohan
Design Director
Marketplace and More
1001 First Avenue
Denver, Colorado 80221

Dear Mr. Rohan:

The examples of food packaging systems shown by your firm at
the Design Arts Annual Show intrigued me. The level of your
company's work was well above those of the other entries.  For
years I have admired the unique approach to visual packaging
taken by Marketplace and More.

Susan Swanson who represented your firm at the Arts Show
indicated that you plan to be opening a west coast office
early next year.  As my enclosed résumé indicates, I have the
unique educational and professional experiences that can be
of benefit to your company.

My comprehensive knowledge of the marketing opportunities in
the west coast area can help Marketplace and More gain a
foothold in a highly competitive region.  I have extensive
contacts with a network of buyers and designers which could
be of great assistance to developing a top-notch staff for the
west coast operation.

I will be in Denver from October 1-3 to attend the trade show
at the Civic Center.  Perhaps we can meet briefly during the
show to review my slide portfolio.  I will call to confirm
your availability.

I look forward to meeting with you.

Very truly yours,

Pat A. Jones

Pat A. Jones


Enc: Résumé
```

interview. Depending on the nature of the job, dress should be professionally correct. Usually that means a conservative suit or coat and tie for men and businesslike dress for women. Unusual or flashy jewelry is out. You want to impress your potential employer that you are a serious, businesslike person.

Keep in mind that you will be judged on both your verbal and nonverbal communication. Maintaining eye contact, a friendly smile, and a firm handshake

Figure 1-2 Sample
Cover Letter (b)

1234 Cypress Street, Apt. B
San Thomas, CA 92345
310-555-8345

January 12, 1997

Mr. Paul Benjamin
Personnel Officer
WWW, Inc.
123 Gateway Ave.
San Jose, CA 95008

Dear Mr. Benjamin:

Your presentation at the October World Wide Web symposium in San Francisco
was very stimulating. I have used much of the web page development software
provided by WWW, Inc. in my current work with a local Internet provider. A
recent article in Web Magazine about your company's planned expansion prompts
me to write you.

I would like to join WWW, Inc. as a computer programmer, with a special
emphasis on developing software applications for the World Wide Web. As the
enclosed résumé shows, I have been involved in everything from sales and
customer service at the retail level to developing and maintaining web sites for
a variety of clients. Samples of my work can be found at the following web site:
http://www.webmaster.org.

I will be in the Bay Area next month and would like to arrange an opportunity
to meet with you and discuss my interest in your firm. I will call your office
in a few days to confirm a meeting date.

Sincerely,

Kim A. Smith
Kim A. Smith

Enc: Résumé

all communicate positively. Try to answer questions without undue hesitation or
too many ums and uhs. Avoid slang and distracting fillers, such as "like" and
"you know."

- *Opening.* As we noted earlier, interviewers often make their decision in the
  first four minutes of the interview. Thus, first impressions are crucial. Begin

Box 11-2   Skill Building

A Game Plan for Interview Preparation

Choose a company that you would like to join and which is a leader in the profession you plan on pursuing. Assume that you will be interviewing with the company in the near future. How will you prepare for the interview? For example:

1. What sources do you plan on consulting prior to the interview?

2. Where are these sources located, and how will you gain access to them?

3. What kinds of questions will guide you as you prepare?

4. Do you have a goal for this preparatory process? If so, what is it? If not, why not?

5. Do you plan on contacting anyone within the company prior to the interview? Who and for what purpose?

Answer each of these questions in writing. Also, summarize in writing what you were able to learn about the company once you consulted the sources identified and located in questions 1 and 2. Discuss how this information should help you in preparing for the interview.

---

with a firm handshake, a friendly demeanor, and appropriate ice-breaking conversation. But also convey the impression that you are ready to get down to business. Don't let the interviewer think you are stalling or are not fully prepared to answer the questions.

Be sure to have an extra copy of your résumé available. Presumably the interviewer has seen it, but it is always possible that he or she is not prepared. If asked, you should be able to produce one instantly. If you did not include names of references on your original résumé, be sure to have a printed list of references available. Again, always make sure you have their prior approval.

- *Body.* The bulk of the interview will consist of you answering questions. To be a successful applicant, you need to connect with the employer, support your qualifications, be organized, clarify ideas, contribute to positive delivery, and convey a positive image.[12] Successful applicants give answers that demonstrate they identify with the employer. Unsuccessful applicants, on the other hand, fail to identify with employers' interests. Successful applicants support their claims about themselves with a variety of forms of evidence. Unsuccessful applicants lack evidentiary support for their claims and rely mostly on personal experience for support. Unsuccessful applicants speak for less time than successful applicants, use less active and concrete language, and speak softly and slowly. Successful applicants speak longer, more rapidly, and forcefully. Successful applicants convey a more positive and professional image than unsuccessful applicants, although as

Corporate recruiters give considerable weight to the communication skills a candidate demonstrates during the initial interview.

suggested in Box 11-3, our behavior during interviews is influenced by cultural conditioning. In sum, most of the same communication competencies that we have stressed throughout this book are essential to successful job interviewing.

Be prepared to ask some questions of your own. These should not be self-serving questions but should be an opportunity to further demonstrate how you can serve the organization's best interests. Expect the issues of salary and benefits to be raised and prepare a clear and concise answer. If the interviewer doesn't raise these issues, they are probably best deferred until you have an offer in hand.

- *Close.* It is important to thank the interviewer for the opportunity to interview. Inquire about the next step—will there be further interviews? When can you expect to hear from them? Be sure to indicate how you can be contacted, and offer to provide any additional information desired by the organization. Your departure should be pleasant, professional, and polite.

Box 11-3   Considering Diversity

Differences in Self-Presentation

How we talk about ourselves, including our individual accomplishments, in part reflects our racial heritage. As a result, how we respond in an interview to a question such as "Tell me about your achievements" can be quite different depending on our racial background. Research shows that people of European ancestry in North America are embarrassed by questions such as this one and tend to underestimate their accomplishments and display nonverbal behaviors that show their discomfort. They may shift in their seat, stumble over words, and avoid direct eye contact.

In contrast, African Americans enjoy talking about their accomplishments. African Americans' nonverbal behavior not only corresponds to their comfort in this regard but also emphasizes the magnitude of accomplishments. An African American may raise her or his voice, gesture more, and speak faster.

As you might guess, both races tend to misin-terpret each other's behaviors when talking about their achievements. People of European ancestry perceive African Americans as boastful. African Americans perceive their counterparts' discomfort as insincere.

What problems, if any, do you think these racial differences and perceptions cause in an interview when the parties are Black and White? Do these differences trigger unfair bias in such a scenario? How so?

Talk over this issue with friends from other races for their reaction. Also, talk this over with friends whose ethnic background is Central or Southeast Asian, Pacific Islander, Native American, Central American, and Latino. Ask them whether there are differences between their ethnic group and other groups that are similar to those described between Blacks and Whites in regard to self-presentation in interviews.

SOURCE: Adapted from William B. Gudykunst, Stella Ting-Toomey, Sandra Sudweeks, and Lea P. Stewart, *Building Bridges: Interpersonal Skills for a Changing World* (Boston: Houghton Mifflin, 1995).

After the Interview   Write a follow-up letter as soon as possible. Thank the interviewer and the firm for their hospitality. Be sure to stress important points made in the interview. Again, offer to provide additional information and indicate how you may be contacted. If some information has been requested, provide it in the follow-up letter.

Depending on the time frame, you may also want to make a follow-up telephone call after a few weeks if you have not heard about your status. You don't want to be a pest, but you also want to make sure you are not forgotten.

Performance-Appraisal Interviews

Given the fact you may still be waiting on your first "real job," this topic may seem out of place. The problem is that if you don't learn something about the appraisal interview here, you may never be exposed to information on the topic.

performance-appraisal interview
A databased interview designed to facilitate an accurate assessment of performance—for example, an employer interviewing an employee.

The **performance-appraisal interview** is important, regardless of whether you are the interviewer or the interviewee. Unless conducted appropriately, the performance-appraisal interview may stimulate legal action. If the interviewee is to be dismissed, for example, the interviewer will have to be able to document just cause for the action. The performance-appraisal interview, therefore, has become an important legal process between employers and employees. Performance-appraisal interviews are widely used in American organizations.[13] Unfortunately, some experts believe, "Less than 10% of the nation's companies have systems that are reasonably good."[14]

This section deals with the responsibilities of *both* parties to the interview in the performance-appraisal process. We look at the *mutual* responsibilities of both supervisors and subordinates in the preparation, conduct, and follow-up of performance-appraisal interviews.

Interviewer Responsibilities

The interviewer in a performance-appraisal interview is usually the employee's direct supervisor. In some instances, a panel of interviewers is used. For example, college professors are usually interviewed by a committee of other professors rather than or in addition to an administrator. Regardless of who is conducting the interview, there are several important guidelines to the preparation, conduct, and follow-up.

Preparation   An effective performance appraisal can occur only if the supervisor and the employee have a clear understanding of the *requirements of the job.* Thus, from the outset of employment, the employer and the employee should agree to clearly defined job duties and expectations. Many organizations have detailed job descriptions and performance standards written in a contract or manual. Thus, for example, a fast-food employee should know exactly how the employer wants the food prepared and orders taken, what clean-up duties are required, and so on. A university professor should know what the expectations are for teaching, publication, and committee work. If there are unclear or contradictory job performance expectations, any appraisal is certain to be flawed.

In addition to a clear set of job duties, continuing employees should be engaged in the process of *goal setting* with their supervisor. For example, if productivity is an issue, a numerical quota—so many widgets produced per hour—can be set. In education, student achievement outcomes are becoming increasingly important in assessing how well schoolteachers are doing their jobs. Even a corporate CEO has goals that he or she is expected to reach. If the company does not produce, new leadership is often sought.

Given a clear job description and a set of goals to be met, the immediate supervisor needs to conduct a *regular evaluation* of each employee's job performance. Many companies use only annual or semiannual reviews, but more frequent evaluations are preferable. The longer the time between performance appraisals, the more likely problems will go undetected, and the greater the pressure on the subordinate and the supervisor.

Some type of performance appraisal—whether a standardized scale, a written appraisal, or a self-assessment—needs to be conducted *prior* to an interview. Not only will the results of the assessment guide the interview, it also is typical that the employee will have a chance to read his or her performance assessment before the interview. Thus, there is an opportunity to focus the discussion on those issues of greatest importance. Proper preparation of the performance-appraisal interview is essential to its success.

Conducting the Interview As important as performance-appraisal interviews are for the organization and the employee, "Many supervisors and workers find them stressful, unpleasant, time-consuming and discouraging."[15] There are numerous reasons for these feelings, including the fact that we are not all equally skilled at interviewing. Clearly, employees have reason to fear a negative evaluation of their job performance. Supervisors, even if they feel a need to correct a problem with an employee, also need to maintain a positive working relationship with workers. One supervisor, in reviewing a new employee's previous work record in preparation for the first performance evaluation, was surprised to find nothing but glowing evaluations from a previous supervisor who had often complained about that worker. When asked, the previous supervisor simply replied: "I had to work with Adams every day. What could I do?" Having a previous record of inflated positive evaluations made the next, less positive evaluation more stressful than it would otherwise have been.

As Jack Gibb showed nearly four decades ago from his study of small groups, certain communication behaviors contribute to a defensive whereas others contribute to a supportive climate.[16] According to Gibb, **defensive behavior** "occurs when an individual perceives threat or anticipates threat."[17] **Supportive behavior** is, of course, the opposite: communication that reduces the perception of threat. Communication behaviors that can make people defensive include evaluation, control, strategy, neutrality, superiority, and certainty, many of which are likely to be present in a performance-appraisal interview.

Gibb proposes six behaviors that reduce defensiveness and create a supportive climate. These are the opposites of the defensive climate–producing behaviors. For example, rather than speaking evaluatively, a supervisor can offer a description of the behavior. Instead of saying, "You have a real problem getting to work on time," the supervisor might say, "There were four days last month when you were 10 or more minutes late for work." The first statement immediately puts the employee on the defensive; the second describes a set of facts, which the employee at least can explain or dispute. Rather than the employer seeking control, Gibb recommends that he or she use a problem orientation. Thus, rather than saying, "If you don't start showing up for work on time, we're going to take disciplinary action," the supervisor might ask, "How can we work to ensure that you are able to get to work on time and not leave people waiting for the office to open?" Spontaneity contrasts with strategy. If an employee fears that a supervisor is trying to "build a case" for dismissal, for example, then every performance-appraisal interview is a potential threat. On the other hand, if the supervisor's concerns are clearly spontaneous, motivated by the facts of the cur-

defensive behavior
Defensive communication; threatening messages that create feelings of discomfort and insecurity.

supportive behavior
Supportive communication; nonthreatening messages that create feelings of comfort and security.

rent evaluation, there is less of a threat to the employee's security. An uncaring or neutral supervisor is unlikely to overcome an employee's defensiveness. On the other hand, an empathetic or caring supervisor is far more likely to get the employee to work together with management to solve the problem. For example, if the supervisor says, "I don't really care about you having to get your child to day care; we're paying you to be here from 8 to 5," the employee is going to become defensive. On the other hand, imagine the supervisor says, "I didn't realize day care was the problem for you. I know how that is, when my kids were younger we had a problem getting them to stay at day care without fussing. Maybe we need to look into a more flexible schedule for you." The second response combines empathy with a problem-solving orientation.

Of course a supervisor is a "superior," in one sense, because he or she is the worker's boss. On the other hand, that doesn't mean a supervisor cannot have an attitude of equality with employees. After all, many supervisors have come up through the ranks. It is possible to stress similarities rather than differences and not go on a "power trip" just because you are the boss.

Finally, a supportive climate is much more likely if the supervisor uses language that is provisional rather than certain. Instead of saying, "Lateness is unacceptable, period," the supervisor might say, "It seems to me that lateness creates a real problem for our customers." This is a qualified, less-than-absolute statement. The employee has an opportunity to respond without directly contradicting the boss.

The conduct of the interview should, as far as possible, be such that a supportive rather than defensive climate is fostered. There is no doubt that any performance-appraisal interview in which the employee receives any type of critical comment has the potential to create a defensive reaction. The key to avoiding this reaction is to present the criticism in a constructive and positive way. Jeanne Barone and Jo Switzer offer several suggestions for *constructive criticism*. It should be "focused on work behaviors. It is specific, descriptive, problem solving, limited, and appropriately timed."[18] Consider each of these attributes in turn.

Specific criticism focuses on a detailed description of actual behaviors, not on general attitude or personality traits. For example, consider the general complaint, "You don't seem to care about our customers." That is nonspecific and nondescriptive. The employee is likely to respond, "Of course I care about customers. I've worked like a dog for this company and now you treat me like this." A more specific, behaviorally oriented statement might be: "You tend to ignore customers who are in the store when you answer the phone. On at least three occasions the past week, I observed customers leave the store because you interrupted your conversation with them to take a phone call."

The second statement identifies a problem. Perhaps the store is understaffed during the busiest times, and employees cannot both wait on customers and handle phone calls. Perhaps management has not been clear about who has priority—phone or in-store customers. Maybe a voice-mail or automated answering system would relieve the problem. There are a number of ways this problem could be addressed. Exploring such alternatives, moreover, is far more likely to lead to a solution than berating an employee for answering the phone, which, is presumably, also part of the job.

Criticism should be limited. Barone and Switzer suggest that no more than four areas, and perhaps as few as two, should be targeted for improvement in one performance-appraisal cycle.[19] To find no area at all for improvement suggests to a conscientious employee that maybe the supervisor isn't taking the review process seriously. After all, who of us can claim perfection in anything we do? On the other hand, to list a great many areas of improvement, particularly if some of them seem picky or minor, only invites the fear that this is part of a strategy for potential job termination on the part of the supervisor. Timing is also important. If job reviews are conducted only infrequently, more complaints will pile up. It is always better to deal with a problem as soon as possible, rather than waiting for it to get worse.

Thus, criticism, though essential to the performance-appraisal interview, need not be destructive or hostile, leading to a defensive climate. Put the emphasis on describing actual job behaviors. Focus on the problem, not the employee's personality. Limit criticisms and time them appropriately for maximum effect.

Barone and Switzer also suggest that workers should be part of the process of *setting goals* for them to achieve by the next performance appraisal.[20] The notion that management and workers are a team, and that everyone profits from improving productivity and quality, should promote the setting of common goals. People are more likely to accept decisions if they believe they have been a part of the decision-making process. In the next two chapters we discuss how group decision-making often leads to greater acceptance by those involved in the process. The same principle applies to relational communication in the workplace. To the extent that employees help shape the goals for their job, they are more likely to feel ownership of the resulting targets. If a salesperson agrees that a 10 percent increase in call-backs is a good idea, then the likelihood of achieving that goal is greater than if it is simply imposed from on high.

Finally, Barone and Switzer stress the importance of *effective listening.*[21] In Chapter 6 we discussed the importance of listening in the communication process. An interview is not a one-way conversation. It is just as important for the supervisor to listen to what the employee is saying as it is for the supervisor to present an evaluation. Comprehensive and critical listening skills are particularly important to an effective interview. And in cases involving employees who are having personal problems that impact on their job performance, the supervisor may be engaged in therapeutic listening as well.

Structuring the Interview   In addition to setting general goals for the interview, it is important to structure the interaction. As with all interviews, there is an opening, body, and close to the interaction. You should begin the interview in a pleasant manner. Small talk, perhaps a cup of coffee, and a brief preview of what the interview will cover are all recommended. However, these preliminaries should not be prolonged. After all, both the supervisor and the employee know that it is necessary to get down to business.

The body of the interview should focus first on strengths and then areas that need improvement, keeping in mind the guidelines suggested above—giving constructive criticism, setting goals, and listening to what the employee has to say. Stewart and Cash suggest it is important to summarize the performance appraisal and give employees the opportunity to comment and ask questions before moving on to goal setting.[22] In setting new goals, the supervisor and the employee should review the goals from the prior period and how well they are being met before working together to set new goals. Goals should not be imposed on workers but should be mutually set. Further, Stewart and Cash argue, "Goals should be few, specific, well defined, practical, and measurable."[23]

Finally, closing an interview should not be rushed. End on a positive note, stressing "trust and open communication."[24] Be sure the employee has had an opportunity to ask questions and offer suggestions. Barone and Switzer suggest that the supervisor first summarize the goals that have been agreed to and then end by stating that the interview has been valuable and important.[25] Also keep in mind that job performance appraisals can have important legal consequences. Some organizations will require a signature from employees to verify that they have been properly advised of their job performance. It is best to make sure that both parties understand what has been said. Even if they disagree, at least the parameters of that disagreement should be clear.

After the Interview   Don't leave issues unresolved. If something requires follow-up, be sure that it gets done. If the employee has identified a problem that can be solved, do it. Few things are a bigger morale booster than seeing an organization respond to an employee suggestion. If employee behavioral problems have been identified, make sure that they are being addressed. It is not always necessary to wait for the next formal review to follow up. Frequent, rather than rare, performance appraisals are the best follow-up. If the employee doesn't meet with the supervisor for another year, the whole process loses its significance. Stress and defensiveness are increased with the lack of frequency and familiarity. Even an informal chat now and then can reassure an employee that the supervisor has not forgotten what they discussed in the last performance-appraisal interview.

Interviewee Responsibilities

Although it might seem as if an employee can do little more than react to the supervisor's performance appraisal, actually the employee should try to be an *active* participant in the process. After all, if one hopes to succeed and even advance in the organization, it is essential to know what is expected and how one is doing. The employee should see the performance appraisal interview more as an opportunity than as a threat.

Preparation   To begin with, an employee should try to get as clear a description as possible of the expectations of the job preferably upon hiring. The more

Box 11-4   Self-Assessment

What Are Your Strengths and Weaknesses as an Interviewee?

If you were asked to name and describe your five greatest strengths as an interviewee, what would they be? Write them in order of the strongest to the weakest of the five.

1. _____

2. _____

3. _____

4. _____

5. _____

What are your five greatest weaknesses as an interviewee? List all five and then write out a strategic plan to strengthen each of the weaknesses.

1. _____

2. _____

3. _____

4. _____

5. _____

you know about what is expected, the more likely you will succeed. If an organization uses some sort of evaluation instrument, ask to see a copy of it before you undergo your first performance appraisal. That way, you'll know what your supervisor is looking for.

Second, don't wait until the formal interview process to ask questions or raise concerns. Sometimes it's not a bad idea to ask, "How am I doing?" at least with respect to specific tasks.

Third, prior to the formal interview, prepare a list of things you would like to cover. If there are problems you want to call to the attention of your supervisor, the interview is a good time to do so.[26] Of course many of these issues will be part of your supervisor's agenda as well. But by making a list you can make sure nothing that is important to you is overlooked. Depending on the nature of your job, you may be asked to prepare materials or a portfolio of your work. College professors, for example, are usually asked to provide samples of their classroom materials, articles they have written, and sometimes examples of student work. Whatever the requirements of your job, remember you are an active participant in the appraisal process, not a bystander.

Being Interviewed   Barone and Switzer suggest that those undergoing appraisal interviews will benefit by "reducing their own defensiveness, listening carefully, asking for information, stating disagreement tactfully, and participating actively."[27] Such skills mean that even when confronted with criticism, workers need to respond in a way that is constructive and positive. Box 11-4 will help you identify your strengths and weaknesses as an interviewee. Listen to what is being said, rather than immediately denying or contradicting it. If you disagree with the statements made, try to get to the factual foundation behind the criticism. Perhaps there is a misunderstanding or factual error at the root of the problem. For example, if you have been told not to let the phone ring more than three times, it is unreasonable to receive criticism for interrupting customers to pick up the phone. Maybe you misunderstood the rule or perhaps your employer didn't realize the problem that was being created.

The key to being an effective interviewee is to listen, stick to the facts, and avoid getting angry or defensive, no matter how critical the boss may seem. In the long run, losing your cool can only backfire. If your supervisor appears to be planning an action with which you disagree, be sure to make careful notes immediately after the meeting. Get as many facts as you can to bolster your case. Many organizations have either a union or other mechanism for resolving disputes between supervisors and subordinates. Although such avenues are obviously a last resort, they sometimes need to be pursued in order to ensure fairness. Bad performance evaluations can be expunged from the record if they are arbitrary or unfair. As Stewart and Cash indicate, although there is no legal requirement for performance appraisals, "those that are conducted must be standardized in form and administration, measure actual work performance, and be applied equally to all classes of employees."[28]

After the Interview   Assuming that goals have been set for your job performance as a result of your interview, you need to focus your job efforts after the interview on fulfilling those goals. It is useful to determine what steps you need to take to achieve the goals and to plan out a strategy to do so. In between interviews, you may want to discuss your progress with your supervisor. Sometimes a follow-up note, indicating that you have accomplished some part of the goal, is useful. Continued communication about one's performance is preferable to being surprised at the next interview.

If you have an objection to what has been said in your performance appraisal, there may be an opportunity to put your response in writing. Again, as in the interview itself, it is important to stick to the facts and respond in an unemotional, nonaccusatory way. And you must decide what points are worth disputing. If the disagreement is minor, the ill will created by challenging your supervisor's evaluation may only exacerbate the problem. But if there are serious misstatements about your performance, and these misstatements may have an effect on your course of employment, then a response is in order.

Summary

This chapter has covered three common types of interviews: information gathering, employment selection, and performance appraisal. For an information-gathering interview, you should contact the interviewee well in advance, do general reading on the topic, and prepare specific questions in advance. During the interview, be on time, act professionally, be ready to ask questions, work from general to specific questions, ask the interviewee to suggest other sources of information, use good listening skills, record or take notes on the interview, ask open-ended questions, and thank the interviewee. After the interview, send a follow-up thank you letter, transcribe your tape or notes while the interview is fresh in your mind, and follow up on leads.

The employment interview is the key to your professional future. As an interviewer you need to be fully prepared, including familiarizing yourself with legal requirements, developing criteria for hiring, preparing a set of questions, and familiarizing yourself with the applicants' résumés. The interview is divided into an opening, body, and close. The introduction should put the interviewee at ease and prepare for the questions that follow. The body should begin with general and relatively easy questions, avoiding unproductive types such as yes/no and leading questions. It is best to use a funnel approach, starting with broadly based questions, moving later to more specific ones. Be sure to allow the applicant a chance to ask questions of you. Conclude by letting the applicant know what will come next and when he or she can expect to hear from the company. After the interview, evaluate your impressions of the applicant.

Performance-appraisal interviews are found in most organizations. Interviewers should prepare by conducting a thorough written evaluation of job performance prior to the interview. In conducting the interview, supervisors should attempt to create a supportive, rather than defensive, environment. Behaviors that involve evaluation, control, strategy, neutrality, superiority, and certainty all contribute to a defensive climate. Behaviors that involve description, problem orientation, spontaneity, empathy, equality, and provisionalism help create a supportive climate.

Those undergoing a performance appraisal should begin by obtaining a clear job description, preferably upon hiring. Employees should come to the interview with specific questions and issues that they want to discuss. During the interview, employees should seek to reduce defensiveness, use good listening skills, seek information, disagree tactfully, and participate actively. After the interview, employees should follow up on the goals set. If there is serious disagreement with the performance appraisal, formal grievance channels must sometimes be pursued.

Another Look

Books

Jeanne Tessier Barone and Jo Young Switzer. *Interviewing: Art and Skill.* Boston: Allyn and Bacon, 1995.

This is a comprehensive guide to all types of interviewing, including journalistic, information gathering, employment selection, performance appraisal, employee intervention and discipline, problem solving, and counseling.

Charles J. Stewart and William B. Cash, Jr. *Interviewing: Principles and Practices.* 5th ed. Dubuque, Iowa: Wm. C. Brown, 1988.

This book presents a practical guide for a wide variety of situations, including probing, survey, employment selection, performance appraisal, counseling, persuasion, and health-care interviews.

Video Rentals

All the President's Men   A riveting and Academy Award-winning portrayal of investigative reporters Bob Woodward (Robert Redford) and Carl Bernstein (Dustin Hoffman) and their investigation of the cover-up of the Watergate burglary by President Nixon's White House. The movie illustrates how reporters followed leads and interviewed reluctant sources in an effort to pierce the veil of secrecy that surrounded the Watergate cover-up.

Working Girl   This film is designed as a romantic comedy. Yet, in several scenes, stars Melanie Griffith, Sigourney Weaver, and Harrison Ford are shown in realistic interviewing settings. Organizational sexism also is an interesting subtext in the film.

Broadcast News   Starring Holly Hunter and William Hurt, this film does an excellent job of showing how broadcast journalists manipulate the interviewing setting. The techniques used are routinely practiced by journalists on *60 Minutes* and similar magazine format shows.

Theory and Research in Practice

1. One of the most interesting findings of research on interviewing is that interviewers often make their decisions within the first four minutes of the interview. To test this theory, make an appointment to interview a personnel officer for a local firm. Find out about the interview process in the firm. In particular, inquire about the importance of initial impressions created by an applicant. Write a brief paper or make a short presentation to the class about your findings.

2. Jack Smith is your subordinate. Although you personally like Jack, his performance at work has become increasingly sub-par. He has been late to work on three different occasions, has received a customer complaint from a valued client, and has behaved unpredictably toward co-workers. You want to keep Jack and correct his behavior. You also suspect something in his personal life may be at the bottom of his problems. Call Jack in for a performance-appraisal interview. In advance, prepare the questions you plan to ask and descriptions of behavior you plan on sharing with Jack. Be sure to consult Jack Gibb's advice on creating a supportive climate as you prepare for the interview.

3. Interview a member of your campus or community police who routinely interviews people who are being investigated. Share techniques described in this chapter with the officer and elicit the officer's reaction. Report back to class on what you learned and the degree to which it conformed to the interviewing skills suggested in this chapter.

PART THREE

Dimensions of Small Group Communication

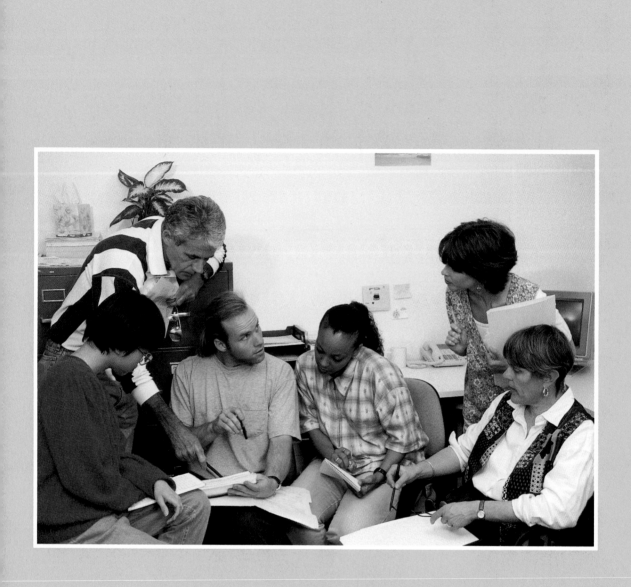

CHAPTER 12

The Nature of Small Group Communication

OBJECTIVES

After reading this chapter you should be able to:

• Identify types of groups.

• Assess the advantages and disadvantages of working in groups.

• Recognize the symptoms and correct the causes of groupthink.

• Explain the importance of group composition to the functioning of groups.

For college students in the 90s, the explosion of the space shuttle *Challenger* was a defining event in their formative years. Because the first teacher in space was on the shuttle, many of today's college students were in elementary school watching the take-off of *Challenger* on that unforgettable day. Organizational communication specialist and former consultant to the National Aeronautics and Space Administration (NASA), Phillip K. Tompkins, describes the scene:

> The date was January 28, 1986, the time 11:38 A.M., and millions of people were watching television. The delays had been frustrating, but in a way they deepened the appetite for the launch. Teachers all over the United States were trying to keep their students' attention focused; one of their own was on center stage. At last they heard the disembodied voice intone the final countdown.[1]

After liftoff, the shuttle launch appeared to be normal. However, unseen by the naked eye was a small puff of black smoke from the right solid-fuel rocket booster—a sign of impending tragedy, one that had been foretold by Roger Boisjoly, an engineer working for Morton Thiokol, the prime contractor for the rocket boosters. According to Tompkins, the night before, Boisjoly had strongly recommended against the launch on the grounds that the O-rings—rubber gaskets that prevent the escape of explosive gases—had never been tested under freezing conditions.[2]

Grade school students, including those of teacher Christa McAuliffe, watched on television and the families of astronauts Greg Jarvis, Ron McNair, Ellison Onizuka, Judy Resnik, Dick Scobee, Mike Smith, and McAuliffe watched in the stands at Cape Canaveral, as 73 seconds into the flight, the *Challenger* exploded in a giant fireball before their eyes.

How could such a tragedy occur? The mechanical explanation was straight-forward. The Presidential Commission on the Space Shuttle *Challenger* Accident, headed by William P. Rogers, a former secretary of state and attorney general, concluded that *"the cause of the Challenger accident was the failure of the pressure seal in the aft field joint of the right Solid Rocket Motor."*[3] But the cause was also a flawed decision-making process. The Rogers Commission pointed out that the people who made the decision to go ahead with the launch were missing some crucial information about the risks of launching any space shuttle when the air temperature outside was less than 53 degrees Fahrenheit.[4]

The flawed decision-making process leading to the *Challenger* tragedy has been the subject of numerous books and articles.[5] The evening before the launch, management personnel and engineers at Morton Thiokol were connected by phone with key decision makers at the Kennedy Space Center in Florida and the Marshall Space Flight Center in Huntsville, Alabama. Engineers Roger Boisjoly and Arnold R. Thompson raised their concern about the safety of launching the shuttle at temperatures below 53 degrees. Boisjoly explained that there had been evidence of gases escaping from the solid rocket boosters on prior shuttle flights. Further, at very low temperatures, the O-rings that sealed the joints of the booster rockets would become too hard to seal properly—like "trying to shove a brick into a crack versus a sponge," said Boisjoly.[6]

However, the Marshall Space Flight Center management seemed to be pressuring Thiokol for launch approval. George Hardy, deputy director of science and engineering at Marshall, is alleged to have said that he was appalled at the engineers' recommendation not to launch.[7] And Lawrence Mulloy, the manager of the Solid Rocket Booster Project at Marshall, is alleged to have said, "My God, Thiokol, when do you want me to launch, next April?"[8]

Thiokol management asked for time to confer. When the teleconference was resumed half an hour later, Thiokol recommended that the launch proceed. Boisjoly testified as to what happened during the off-line caucus:

> After Arnie [Thompson] and I had our last say, Mr. Mason [a senior vice president at Thiokol] said we have to make a management decision. He turned to Bob Lund [vice president of engineering] and asked him to take off his engineering hat and put on his management hat. From that point on, management formulated the points to base their decision on. There was never one comment in favor, as I have said, of launching by any engineer or other non management person in the room, before or after the caucus. I was not even asked to participate in giving any input to the final decision charts.[9]

What happened to exclude the engineers' concerns from Thiokol's ultimate recommendation? According to Boisjoly:

This was a meeting where the determination was to launch, and it was up to us to prove beyond a shadow of a doubt that it was not safe to do so. This is in total reverse to what the position usually is in a preflight conversation or a flight readiness review.[10]

Not only did Thiokol recommend a launch, they also failed to let higher levels know that the engineers were not in agreement with the decision. According to testimony given to the Rogers Commission, one of the managers at the Marshall Space Flight Center even asked if anyone in the loop had a different position or disagreed with the Thiokol recommendation. No one spoke up. Why did the engineers not dissent at this point? Boisjoly summed up the situation: "I had my say, and I never [would] take [away] any management right to take the input of an engineer and then make a decision based upon that input." He added, "I left the room feeling badly defeated, but I felt I really did all I could to stop the launch. I felt personally that management was under a lot of pressure to launch and that they made a very tough decision, but I didn't agree with it."[11]

Although most of us have not been faced with such tragic outcomes from our decision making in groups, each of us confronts the problems of ineffective groups almost daily. How often have you had a class project that left you frustrated after working with a group, or a committee that just seemed to go nowhere, or a group in which you felt totally left out? We have all had these

Despite the concerns of engineers about the effects of freezing temperatures, the shuttle Challenger was launched on an icy January morning. This was a major failure of group decision-making which, unfortunately, resulted in the loss of these astronauts' lives.

experiences. Some people simply prefer to avoid group work at any cost. Yet, numerous studies have demonstrated that most people spend a considerable part of their workday in group meetings. For example, executives are reported to spend an average of 10 hours per week in formal committee meetings, tenured faculty members spend approximately 11 hours per week in meetings, and the average executive spends 700 hours a year in meetings.[12] In business, education, and even volunteer organizations, group work is unavoidable. The question, then, is how to make the most of your experiences in groups. The purpose of this chapter and the next is precisely that—to give you the communicative competence to function effectively as a leader or member of a group.

This chapter is designed to assist you in becoming a more effective leader or member of a group. After defining what we mean by the word *group,* we will look at

- the advantages and disadvantages of using groups,
- the common but avoidable process of groupthink, and
- the multidimensional nature of group composition.

The Basics of Groups

Defining Groups

What exactly constitutes a group? Few would disagree that an officially constituted working committee in business, such as a board of directors, is a group. By the same token, few would consider the collection of people who happen to board the same airplane to be a group. What, then, are the factors that determine what is a group versus a mere collection of individuals? Many different definitions of *group* can be found.[13] Obviously, all men age 21–65 can be considered a group in the demographic sense. A family is another type of group. A group with whom you identify, called a reference group, is another type of group. For our purposes, we are interested in groups small enough to communicate with one another to achieve some goal or goals. Thus, for us, a **group** is three or more individuals who are aware of each other's presence, share a mutually interdependent purpose, engage in communication transactions with one another, and who identify with the norms of the group. Let's discuss each of these parts in turn.

Size   In Chapter 1, we said that as the number of people in a communication system increases, the lines of communication in the system increase geometrically. As Figure 12-1 indicates, the more lines of communication that characterize a system, the more difficult the system is to manage. Groups are no different. The more people in a group, the more difficult it is to manage the group. Although there is no magic number in this regard, such tasks as small group problem solving seem ideally suited to groups of five. A group of five is large

group   Three or more individuals who are aware of each other's presence, share a mutually interdependent purpose, engage in communication transactions with one another, and identify with the norms of the group.

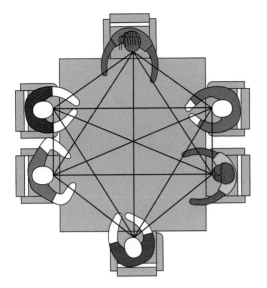

Group of 6 (15 lines of communication)

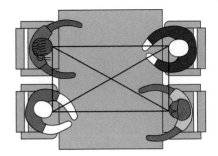

Group of 4 (6 lines of communication)

enough to increase the chances of its membership displaying dissimilar talents and abilities, but also small enough for everyone to participate in the group process.

Interdependent Purpose   What distinguishes a group from a bunch of people who happen to be in the same place at the same time? The difference is that a group shares a purpose that requires mutual effort to achieve. For example, a basketball team is a group, whereas five people standing at a bus stop is not. The basketball team has to work together to achieve their purpose—to score points. Five people at a bus stop, however, can ignore one another entirely and still catch the bus.

Communication   To be a group, individuals must communicate in some way with one another. Although we are principally concerned in this chapter with face-to-face verbal and nonverbal communication, other forms of communication may occur within a group. For example, some groups communicate exclusively via computers. In fact, software now exists that allows group decision making via computers. As long as a transaction is occurring, this criterion of communication is still being met.

Norms   Finally, groups share **norms**, that is, rules of conduct or patterns of behavior that are considered customary. For example, some families may have norms that call for open discussion of problems and concerns. Others may avoid conflicts at all costs. Some work groups operate by the strict parliamentary procedure of *Robert's Rules of Order,* whereas others operate by informal means and

Figure 12-1 Lines of Communication in Groups of Different Sizes.   The lines of communication increase with the size of a group. This may be one reason people are fond of the saying, "Too many cooks spoil the broth."

norms   Rules of conduct or patterns of behavior that are considered customary.

reach decisions by consensus. As a group evolves, the norms become clear to members but are generally unstated unless violated.

Norms can change with time. Philip Tompkins cites the change in norms at NASA over the years from *Apollo* to the space shuttle. As a consultant to Dr. Werner Von Braun at the Marshall Space Flight Center in 1967, Tompkins learned a fundamental norm: "The presumption at NASA had always been that manned space flight should not be undertaken when there were any doubts about the safety of the mission."[14] The astronauts themselves, for example, played a major decision-making role in deciding whether or not to launch during the *Apollo* mission. Yet, two decades later, as Boisjoly pointed out in his testimony, the astronauts were completely out of the decision-making loop.

Types of Groups

Not all groups are the same. At least three different types of groups can be identified based on differences in their purpose. They are formal and informal social groups, therapeutic recovery groups, and task-oriented groups.

Formal and Informal Social Groups   We all belong to a wide variety of social groups. Some are rather informal. The circle of friends we hang around with after work or class may well be a group, in that we are aware of each other's presence, share a common purpose—even if it is just to have a good time—engage in communication transactions, and have standards of behavior to which we all implicitly agree. Yet, such a group is rather informal. If you asked people to name the groups to which they belong, they might overlook such a group entirely, since it has no official status or name and its membership is fluid. Yet, such groups are an important and ever-present part of our lives. In some ways, peer social groups can be every bit as influential on a person's development as schools, parents, and other official institutions.

Formal social groups also exist. Perhaps you belong to a fraternity or sorority. If not, you still belong to some kind of familial group, whether it is the traditional two-parent family, a single-parent, or an extended family of grandparents, aunts, uncles, and the like. Some people have challenged the legal limitations on formally recognized family groupings, arguing for granting legal status to "domestic partners," who share the same household but lack the legal tie of marriage. Some government agencies, for example, the Board of Supervisors of San Francisco, have granted certain rights to such family arrangements.

Clearly, social groups, formal and informal, play a significant part in our lives. They help socialize us to the values that govern our behavior. They reinforce our attitudes and provide norms that we often follow in our daily lives. Some groups promote social good, whereas others, such as gangs, may be destructive. Regardless of the group, however, a recognition of the importance of social groups is essential to our overall understanding of small group communication.

Therapeutic Recovery Groups   Self-help and recovery groups are an ever-present feature of our lives. Table 12-1 lists a few of the groups that you might

Table 12-1   Self-Help Groups

As a society, we have become believers in the power of self-help groups. Here's just a partial listing of organizations that use therapeutic groups to help people deal with problems in their lives:

Alcoholics Anonymous

Alanon (for families of alcoholics)

Compassionate Friends (for those who have children who have died)

Couples in Conflict

Gamblers Anonymous

La Leche League (support for breast-feeding mothers)

Narcotics Anonymous

Overeaters Anonymous

Parents Anonymous (parents and adult survivors of physical or emotional abuse)

PFLAG (Parents and Friends of Lesbians and Gays)

Recovery (for those recovering from mental illness)

Smoke Enders

---

find in your local phone book. Many psychological counselors use therapy groups in their practice. Group reinforcement is critical to the success of people who are recovering from a wide variety of problems—from substance abuse to eating disorders.

The same principles that make social groups important apply to therapeutic groups. The values, attitudes, and behavioral modifications that such groups support can help someone cope with a problem that seems unsolvable alone.

Task-Oriented Groups   When we think of the workplace or school, many of us think of groups formed to accomplish a specific job—solve a problem, help explain a difficult subject, render a decision. These are known as task-oriented groups. Problem solving is a common task assigned to groups. For example, when a business is trying to decide how to revitalize its product line, a group of key employees might be assembled to come up with new ideas. Another common task is education. Many classes use discussion groups to help students understand difficult topics. Even subjects such as mathematics and science often benefit from problem-solving or study groups. The task faced by these groups is mutual enlightenment. Finally, some groups are formed to render a decision. The engineers and managers meeting prior to the *Challenger* launch were such a decision-making group, faced with recommending whether the shuttle launch should be scrubbed due to cold weather.

Another example of a decision-making group is a jury, consisting of (usually) 12 citizens called to render a decision about the guilt or innocence of an accused person or about damages in a civil case. Juries are bound by complicated norms, codified as rules of evidence and law, that must be applied to the specific case in question. You may have already served on a jury. If not, you likely will. Much of what we talk about in this chapter, including the potential disadvantages of using groups, is applicable to the jury system here in the United States.

Advantages and Disadvantages of Groups

Sometimes it seems like it would be easier to just let people solve their problems, make their decisions, and do their jobs alone because groups can be time-consuming and require negotiation and compromise. From our perspective, groups are a valuable form of communication, but they are not a panacea. As one of the authors wrote in a recent issue of *Quality Digest*: "The question is not whether groups can't or won't work. Instead, it is, Why do they so often fall so short of their promise?"[15]

Groups are not always the best way to go about solving a problem or reaching a decision. If the decision on whether or not to launch *Challenger* had been left to the engineers, the crew would be alive today. The problem is how to know in advance who is best able to make a decision. If one knows that there is a genuine expert who is likely to achieve the best decision, it makes little sense to assign the task to a group. On the other hand, if a decision depends on the cooperation of others, a group is generally preferable. So, what are the best situations in which groups should be used? That depends on understanding the assets and liabilities of groups in making decisions.

Assets of Groups

Psychologist Norman R. F. Maier wrote a classic article about group assets and liabilities.[16] Among the advantages of groups that he identified are more information, more approaches to problems, greater acceptance of decisions, and greater comprehension.

1. *More information:*   Groups have a greater sum of knowledge and information than individuals working alone. Where a decision depends on a wide range of information, groups have the advantage. Particularly in an era of complex problems, very few of us, working alone, have all the information we need to reach a good decision. For example, try to list the presidents of the United States in chronological order. How did you do? Most of us get about as far as Jefferson. Now get a group together and tackle the same task. Chances are you will do better than any one of you did on your own. That's because as a group you had more information than any one of you had individually. As you discuss the pos-

sibilities, one person will correct another and perhaps even jog memories of others to recall even more information. One of the key failings of the *Challenger* disaster is that higher levels of decision making were denied information possessed by the engineers at Thiokol.

Quality circle groups meet frequently to insure that people understand each other and their independent roles in a task.

2. *More approaches to problems:*   Groups have more approaches to a problem than an individual working alone. Try this exercise. Take a common household object, say, a paper clip. List all the uses you can think of for it. Now get together in a group and try the same thing. Chances are your group will come up with more uses than any one of you could when working alone. Further, the group interaction will likely suggest new uses none of you thought of on your own. This is the basic principle behind brainstorming. One person will hitchhike on the ideas of others. Thus, when the goal is to think of as many approaches as possible to a problem, groups usually have the edge. The exclusion of all but management approaches to making the launch decision was one factor that doomed *Challenger*.

3. *Greater acceptance of decisions:* By participating in group deliberations, people are more likely to accept the results of the decision. Imagine that your parents announce to you that you will attend College X—no ifs, ands, or buts. Compare this arbitrary decision in which you didn't participate to a decision made jointly by you and your parents. Which result are you most likely to accept? However, some decisions have to be made by those in authority and simply passed down to those affected. For example, American troops waiting offshore Haiti in 1994 were not allowed to decide for themselves whether to attack. In fact, the skillful negotiation of former President Jimmy Carter, Senator Sam Nunn, and General Colin Powell enabled the United States forces to land peacefully. Carter, Nunn, and Powell were able to convince the rulers of Haiti that a peaceful landing would be preferable to the inevitable loss of life on both sides that would follow an invasion.

However, when decisions depend on the support of those affected for their success, the more involved people are in the deliberations, the better the odds of acceptance. This principle is at the foundation of the quality circle movement in much of industry, described in Box 12-1.

4. *Greater comprehension:* People may better understand the results of a decision if they have participated in making it. Not only are people more likely to accept a decision they have helped make, they are also more likely to understand what it means. If people have no role in reaching a decision, the decision makers often have to explain everything from scratch to those affected. Implementing a decision among people who have participated in making it is a far simpler task.

Consider a simple example. An employer wants to improve job efficiency. If all she does is post a new regulation and expect everyone to follow it, the results may be disastrous. Although employees may wish to comply, if they do not understand the procedures or the rationale underlying them, they may not be able to comply. On the other hand, if the employees have participated in the process of change, they are likely to at least understand what is expected, whether they agree with the plan or not.

Liabilities of Groups

On the other hand, Maier also identified a number of liabilities that potentially inhere to groups. Among the most significant are social pressures to conform, premature solutions, dominant individuals, and goal conflict.

1. *Social pressures to conform:* As indicated by Box 12-2, people vary in their susceptibility to conform to pressure. Social pressures may force conformity to decisions, even when such conformity produces disaster. Correct minority opinions may be overlooked. If you doubt the pressure to conform, try this exercise. For a day, violate a norm of behavior in a group (but avoid anything illegal or obscene). For example, sit in a different seat in your class, one that usually is occupied by another student. Or make eye contact with others in an elevator. If you really want to see the effects of conformity, violate dress standards in your

Box 12-1   Considering Diversity

Quality Circles

In the 1960s, "Made in Japan" was generally synonymous with cheap, low-quality merchandise. By the 1990s, "Made in Japan" has come to be a mark of excellence. While there are many factors contributing to the turnabout in Japanese quality of manufacturing, one of them is an American import, the concept of quality circles, developed by W. Edwards Deming. By the 1970s, this innovation had caught the attention of an American corporation, Lockheed, which introduced the concept in 1974. Lockheed claimed to save $3 million through this innovation.

Quality circles are a participative management technique. Typically, a small group of employees who work on similar tasks meet on a regular basis to come up with solutions to task-related problems. Their discussions may be led by a supervisor or by a member of the group. The quality circle's solutions are then presented to the manager in charge of the task, who may accept or reject the proposal.

Not all United States companies have used quality circles with the same success as Lockheed. Do you think quality circles are better suited to corporations in collectivist cultures than corporations in individualistic ones? Or do you think that the effectiveness of quality circles depends on the type of work being attempted, for example, manufacturing as opposed to marketing a product?

Write a one-page opinion piece in which you take a stand on the issues raised by these two questions.

SOURCE: Adapted from Rodney W. Napier and Matti K. Gershenfeld, *Groups: Theory and Experience* (Boston: Houghton Mifflin, 1993), 537–45; J. Dan Rothwell, *In Mixed Company: Small Group Communication,* 2nd ed. (Fort Worth, Tex.: Harcourt Brace, 1995), 215–17.

group. Imagine the reaction of your classmates if you showed up to class in a formal dress or a tuxedo or showed up to work in cutoffs and a baseball cap. We all face social pressures to conform. When those pressures work against a free and open discussion of solutions to problems, bad decisions can follow. Clearly the statement "My God, Thiokol, when do you want me to launch, next April?" pressured those at Morton Thiokol to conform to the Marshall Space Flight Center's desire to proceed with the launch. Later in this chapter we will discuss the extreme results of conformity to social pressure—a phenomenon known as "groupthink," which has led to some disastrous decisions.

2. *Premature solutions:* Once a solution achieves a critical level of voiced support (*valence* is Maier's term), better solutions introduced later have little chance of success. A small minority, if sufficiently vocal, can push a solution over that threshold. Have you ever been in a group where everyone who spoke seemed to feel the same way? You go along, not wanting to offend anyone, thinking you are hopelessly outnumbered. Later you learn that most of the group disagreed, but a vocal minority buffaloed everyone else. That's an example of valence.

3. *Dominant individual:* Maier also argues that one person may emerge as the dominant leader of a group, even if that individual is not the best problem

Box 12-2   Self-Assessment

What Is Your Locus of Control?

One measure of the degree to which you are susceptible to group pressure is locus of control. To assess your personal level of locus of control, choose either true or false for each of the following statements.

T   F   1. It's stupid to oppose the wishes of the group.

T   F   2. People have far less control over things than they think.

T   F   3. You get what you deserve.

T   F   4. Luck is really a consequence of hard work.

T   F   5. I make my own breaks.

T   F   6. Some people are born lucky.

T   F   7. Good fortune is an accident of birth.

T   F   8. I've worked for everything I've received from life.

T   F   9. There are no self-made people.

T   F   10. You might as well accept life on its own terms.

Answering true to statements 1, 2, 6, 7, 9, and 10 indicates a belief that external forces (external locus of control) play a major role in determining what happens to people. People who believe strongly in an external locus of control are more prone to go along with the group than resist it.

In contrast, answering false to 1, 2, 6, 7, 9, and 10 and true to statements 3, 4, 5, and 8 indicates a belief that people are the masters of their own destiny (internal locus of control). People who believe strongly in an internal locus of control tend to resist pressure from the group.

Discuss the degree to which your responses reflect your actual behavior with other members of the class.

SOURCE: Adapted from J. B. Rother, "Generalized Expectancies for Internal Versus External Locus Control of Reinforcement," *Psychological Monographs* 80 (1966): 609.

solver in the group. Sometimes, by virtue of appointed power position, or by strength of personality, a person comes to dominate a group, even when privately the members of the group don't agree with the person. Such dominance can be particularly destructive to the interests of a minority—even a better-informed minority. If group members are afraid of retribution (say, the leader is their boss), the likelihood of failing to challenge the dominant person, regardless of the challenge's merit, is likely to increase.

4. *Goal conflict:*   When individual goals come into conflict with the group's primary goal, bad things happen. Winning arguments can become more important than achieving the best solution. Particularly dangerous are "hidden agendas," private purposes that are at odds with the agreed-on objectives of a group. For example, a group of college professors may meet with the professed group goal of improving faculty productivity in the classroom. Suppose, however, that one faculty member is a technological laggard. He or she may have a private goal, a hidden agenda, to avoid having to learn new technologies. This private

goal might well undermine the group's overall goal of increased productivity, since such a goal often depends on utilizing new technologies to replace the standard 50-minute lecture in class. Groups with conflicting goals may seem to get nowhere and no one can figure out why. The reason is that in reality the group members do not share common goals, as was the case with engineers and managers at Morton Thiokol. The engineers' goal was to make sure their solid rocket booster was safe. Management, on the other hand, wanted to make sure NASA continued to buy its company's product.

Assets or Liabilities of Groups

Finally, Maier identified several factors that can help or hinder a group, depending on the situation. These factors are related to disagreement, conflicting interests, risks, time, and change:

1. *Disagreement:* Disagreement can be good or bad, depending on how it is handled. Learning to separate idea generation from evaluation is essential for positive disagreement. If no one ever disagrees about anything, then unthinking conformity to the first idea voiced results. On the other hand, some people seem to be disagreeable just for the sake of hearing their own voices. Productive disagreement about the problem at hand, not personalities or side issues, is the key to effective group decision making. But agreeing to disagree, put simply, is often easier said than done. It requires a strong norm of toleration of difference within a group.

2. *Conflicting interests:* To achieve agreement on a solution, a group first must agree on the nature of the problem and the goal it seeks to accomplish. Only after the group agrees on the nature of the problem can any solutions be meaningfully discussed. When disagreement focuses not on different solutions to a common problem but on different views of the problem—different objectives for the group—the results can be flawed. "Cooperative problem solving," according to Maier, "can occur only after the mutual interests have been established."[17] The engineers at Thiokol were most interested in ensuring the safety of the mission, whereas management was more interested in satisfying the needs of its major customer to keep the shuttle launches on schedule.

3. *Risks:* Groups tend to be more likely to take risks than individuals. It is a lot easier sometimes to take a risky action when you know there are others taking the risk too. Blame for failure is unlikely to fall on your own shoulders alone. Thus, where risk taking is a desirable goal, groups are well suited to decision making. Investment clubs, in which individuals pool their resources and then make joint investments, are an example of a group that takes risks no one member would be likely to take alone. However, groups may also engage in unnecessarily risky behavior, sometimes known as the "risky shift." The "I'll do it if you do it" syndrome is a common example of the risky-shift phenomenon. Often it produces tragic results. Not long ago "elevator surfing" was the rage at high-rise

dorms at colleges and universities. Groups of risk takers would dare each other to stand on top of elevators in an open elevator shaft. Several people who were doing what everyone else in the group was doing also fell to their death.

4. *Time:*   Groups take more time than individuals to reach decisions. This is simply a function of their size. When five people are involved, assuming each has an opportunity to speak, more time will elapse than when one person just decides. Where time is of the essence (as in an emergency), there is no time for group deliberations. The supervising physician in an emergency room can't poll the other staff before defibrillating a patient's heart. An airline pilot doesn't engage in a lengthy discussion with the rest of the crew when the plane is rapidly descending. Inaction in an emergency is a decision—usually one with disastrous consequences. On the other hand, in situations where time is not limited, groups may produce better decisions. If we are seeking to improve the nation's health-care system, for example, a hasty decision could be disastrous. Time spent on exploring the problem and considering alternative solutions is time well spent.

5. *Change:*   The members of the group who end up changing may be those who originally had the best ideas. If so, the group may produce a bad decision. On the other hand, if the change occurs among those who had the most flawed position prior to the group meeting, the change may be for the better. One of our children was in a math class where group work was used extensively—some tests were even taken as a group. As it happens, she is a good math student and usually gets the right answer. When she was put in a group with other students who were less proficient in math, the group ended up changing her correct answer to the wrong one, which the majority of the group believed was right. Needless to say, they did poorly on the test. The laws of mathematics are not governed by majority rule!

To Maier's list, we add two features of groups that can be either good or bad: shared versus individual responsibility for a decision and anonymity.

6. *Shared versus individual responsibility:*   To some extent, sharing responsibility can be positive. When people feel a stake in a decision, they are more likely to be committed to its success. One of the factors underlying the success of self-help groups, for example, is the shared sense of responsibility members feel for one another. A member of Alcoholics Anonymous or Overeaters Anonymous knows that support is only a phone call away. On the other hand, if shared responsibility is used as an excuse to avoid individual responsibility, it can rapidly lead to a situation in which people take no responsibility for their own actions. The result often is "mob psychology," whereby people do unspeakable things they would never do individually. But when everybody's doing something, individual culpability is obscured.

7. *Anonymity:*   Just as groups can benefit or suffer from shared responsibility, so too can anonymity be a blessing or curse. Juries, for example, benefit from

People are more willing to take risks when members of a group.

the anonymity of their members. Sometimes the facts of a case lead to what the jury knows will be an unpopular decision. Consider the case of the Menendez brothers, accused of murdering their parents. This highly controversial case resulted in a hung jury on first trial. Because they were assured anonymity, jurors were able to vote their individual consciences, despite the potential for considerable public criticism after the trial. On the other hand, anonymity can lead to an abdication of responsibility that makes for risky and dangerous decision making. It becomes easy to blame someone else for group failures, regardless of one's individual role in the process.

Groupthink

Yale professor of psychology Irving R. Janis has developed a theory to explain bad decision making in groups. He finds that groups sometimes are victims of what he calls "groupthink."[18] He defines **groupthink** as "a mode of thinking that

> **groupthink** A mode of thinking that occurs when people are deeply involved in a cohesive group, when desire for unanimity overrides a realistic appraisal of alternatives.

people engage in when they are deeply involved in a cohesive in-group, when the members' strivings for unanimity override their motivation to realistically appraise alternative courses of action."[19] Results of groupthink include the botched invasion of Cuba's Bay of Pigs under President Kennedy, the escalation of the war in Vietnam under President Johnson, the Watergate scandal and cover-up of President Nixon's administration, Jimmy Carter's disastrous attempt to rescue American hostages in Iran,[20] and NASA's decision to launch the space shuttle *Challenger* at temperatures not proven safe.

Symptoms of Groupthink

How do you know if a group is in a state of groupthink? Janis offers eight symptoms: illusion of invulnerability, unquestioned belief in the group's inherent morality, collective rationalizations, stereotyped views of out-group members, direct pressure on dissenters, self-censorship of dissenters, shared illusion of unanimity, and emergence of mindguards.

1. *Illusion of invulnerability:* Sometimes a group feels that it is invulnerable to failure. After 24 successful shuttle launches, for example, NASA's leaders had come to take space travel as routine. They discounted the possibility that the space shuttle *Challenger* would explode simply because temperatures were low at the time of launch. Similarly, when the Democratic Party in 1994 lost control of the House of Representatives for the first time since Eisenhower was president, it was suddenly stunned at its vulnerability to voter dissatisfaction. After 40 years of continuous control by the Democrats, House Republicans were suddenly in control. When a group, even a political party, thinks it cannot fail, that is when it is most likely to fail.

2. *Unquestioned belief in the group's inherent morality:* The view that God is on our side can be a dangerous one. Some of the greatest atrocities in history were committed in the name of a higher authority. Religious wars and ethnic cleansing are the products of unquestioned belief that only one side has morality to support it. Of course, in reality, it is often the case that both sides in a conflict see themselves as uniquely moral. Protestants and Catholics in Northern Ireland, Israelis and Palestinians in the Middle East, and Muslims and Christians in the former Yugoslavia are examples of groups that see themselves as fighting with God on their side.

3. *Collective rationalizations:* We also tend to rationalize the mistakes we make. This is a well-documented fact of human nature. What is true of individuals also is true of groups. When a group of people fail, they rationalize and sometimes try to blame failure on convenient scapegoats. As we indicated in Chapters 2 and 7, we often give unfounded motives and reasons for our own and others' behaviors. These attributions are often biased because we tend to assign situational and external ones to our own shortcomings, but stable and internal ones to others. Presidents are often the victim of such collective ratio-

nalizations. Bill Clinton frequently blamed Republicans for their failure to pass national health-care reform during his first two years in office, despite the fact that the Democrats controlled both houses of Congress and the White House.

Another example of rationalization is explaining away problems as insignificant. Despite evidence that the O-rings in the space shuttle boosters were not sealing properly on previous flights, the decision makers at NASA kept lowering the safety threshold for shuttle launches, engaging in what commission member and Nobel Prize–winning physicist Richard P. Feynman called "a kind of Russian roulette." Feynman noted that when the shuttle had one successful flight in spite of O-ring erosion, O-ring problems were no longer taken so seriously for the next flights. According to Feynman, the prevailing feeling seemed to be that "we can lower our standards a little bit because we got away with it last time."[21]

4. *Stereotyped views of out-group members:* Along with viewing itself as inherently moral, the in-group often negatively stereotypes those outside the group. In November 1994, voters in California passed Proposition 187, which denied most government services to "illegal aliens." Much of the support for this proposition was based on the stereotype that "illegals" were draining taxpayer resources, while contributing little to the state. Yet, some of the supporters of the proposition were themselves dependent on undocumented immigrants for essential work, including a candidate for the United States Senate, who was a strong advocate of the proposition, yet had employed an illegal immigrant to care for his children for several years.

5. *Direct pressure on dissenters:* No one likes a naysayer. History is full of examples of naysayers being pressured to conform or criticized and dismissed as crackpots. They range from Galileo, who said the earth wasn't at the center of the universe, to Camile Paglia, the controversial feminist who has claimed that women who dance nude are not victims of sexual exploitation. Galileo was pressured to conform by the Catholic Church, and Paglia has been roundly criticized by mainstream feminists. Nowhere is pressure on dissenters more prevalent than in governmental decision making. The Republican governor of California, Pete Wilson, made Proposition 187 and the problem of illegal aliens a centerpiece of his reelection campaign. When two prominent Republicans from outside the state of California, former Reagan Cabinet members Jack Kemp and William Bennett, opposed Wilson on Proposition 187, there was an outcry among California Republicans. When someone stands up against the group, if groupthink is present, the dissenter is often shouted down by the group.

6. *Self-censorship of dissenters:* So great are the pressures that greet those who voice opinions contrary to the group, those who might dissent from the majority often remain silent—they engage in self-censorship. Particularly when a high-powered leader is present, those who doubt the wisdom of a group's decision may decide it is not worth the risk of being excluded to express their real views. In the *Challenger* case, once the decision had been made by management, engineers went no further in raising their objections. As Boisjoly put it, once he

had raised his objections and been overruled by management, "There was no point in me doing anything further than I had already attempted to do."[22]

7. *Shared illusion of unanimity:*   Self-censorship leads directly to the false perception that everyone agrees—the illusion of unanimity. Combined with the illusion of invulnerability and the belief in the group's inherent morality, this illusion invites disaster. In the *Challenger* incident, the failure of Morton Thiokol to let higher decision-making levels know of the objections of engineers led to the illusion that there were no objections to the launch, despite the low temperature. The Rogers Commission concluded that

> there was a serious flaw in the decision-making process leading up to the launch. . . . A well-structured and managed system emphasizing safety would have flagged rising doubts about the Solid Rocket Booster joint seal. Had these matters been clearly stated and emphasized in the flight readiness process in terms of reflecting the views of most of the Thiokol engineers and at least some of the Marshall engineers, it seems likely that the launch of 51-L might not have occurred when it did.[23]

Instead of raising doubts, however, lower-level managers hid them, allowing the illusion of unanimity to be maintained at the higher levels of NASA.

8. *Emergence of mindguards:*   Mindguards are like bodyguards. They protect a leader's thinking from dissenting and contradicting opinion. During the height of the Vietnam War, for example, the Joint Chiefs of Staff of the Armed Forces withheld information from President Lyndon Johnson when the information was contrary to Johnson's war policy.

During Watergate, moreover, H. R. Haldeman and John D. Ehrlichman played the role of mindguards for President Richard Nixon. Specifically, they tried to keep from Nixon how badly the Watergate cover-up was unraveling and the magnitude of the threat to Nixon's presidency.

Minimizing Groupthink

With all the dangers of groupthink, how can a group guard against it? First of all, the group needs to know about the phenomenon. If members recognize groupthink starting to take hold, it's time to take some precautions. Professor Janis offers seven suggestions: assign a devil's advocate, avoid revealing leader preferences, have independent groups work simultaneously, discuss group processes with trusted others outside the group, utilize outside experts, consider alternative scenarios for rivals, and have a second-chance meeting.

1. *Assign a devil's advocate:*   It is often helpful to have someone in the group responsible for challenging all ideas, even those that seem to be good ones. The role of devil's advocate was something that had once been part of NASA's tradition. Phillip Tompkins conducted a briefing for the Marshall Space Flight Center

in 1967. He reports that the director of the Marshall Space Flight Center, Werner Von Braun, challenged him at several points during the briefing. Tompkins later "learned that von Braun had been convinced by my arguments early on; this dialectical devil's advocate approach was his way of testing the strength of my evidence and arguments."[24] Had NASA maintained the tradition of the devil's advocate, perhaps the mistakes leading to the loss of *Challenger* could have been avoided.

2. *Leaders should avoid revealing their preferences:*   We've all had the experience of going into a meeting knowing in advance what decision the leader wanted. The leaders of NASA made it clear that they wanted to launch *Challenger* and that they were appalled at the recommendation not to launch. The Rogers Commission concludes that "the Thiokol management reversed its position and recommended the launch of 51-L [*Challenger*], at the urging of Marshall [Space Flight Center] and contrary to the views of its engineers in order to accommodate a major customer."[25] A good leader keeps his or her preferences private until hearing what others have to say. On the eve of D-Day, for example, General Dwight D. Eisenhower is reputed to have solicited opinions from all of those present before announcing his decision to go forward with the Allied forces invasion of France on June 6, 1944. By concealing his preferences, Eisenhower avoided simply being told what the others present thought he wanted to hear.

3. *Have independent groups work simultaneously:*   If time and resources permit, having more than one group work on the same problem is a good way to combat groupthink. The recent COBE (Cosmic Background Explorer) experiment that established proof of the big bang theory of the universe used exactly this method. Because different teams analyzed the data independently, the project leaders could have confidence that their conclusions were not simply the result of wishful thinking.[26]

A similar technique is called the Nominal Group Technique. Individuals work silently in each other's presence but do not interact. Usually, nominal groups are composed of people who have some special expertise relevant to a problem or an issue. Each expert works on the problem, until satisfied with the conclusions he or she reaches. The members then get together to share their ideas with one another and reach a solution to the problem.[27]

4. *Discuss group processes with trusted others and report back to group:* Although in some instances secrecy precludes reporting group deliberations to others (for example, jury members are sworn to secrecy during deliberations), sometimes it is useful to conduct a "reality check" to see if others outside the group think you are on the right track.

5. *Utilize outside experts:*   As implied in Box 12-3, asking an expert is a common method people use in arriving at decisions. Many organizations bring in outside consultants to help them solve their problems. Phillip Tompkins was brought to the Marshall Space Flight Center in 1967 and later, after the *Chal-*

lenger disaster, precisely because of his expertise outside the area of rocket science. Although, by his own admission, he doesn't know which end of a rocket to light, he is a widely respected authority on organizational communication.[28] His analysis of the communication strengths and weaknesses in the space program led to several improvements in communication that helped to make the *Apollo* program one of our nation's crowning achievements. It is a good idea when possible to allow outside experts to provide their input into whatever problem your group is trying to solve.

6. *Consider "alternative scenarios" for rivals:* Putting yourself in the other's shoes is sometimes essential to avoiding groupthink. The hostage crisis with Iran was sparked by President Carter's allowing the deposed shah of Iran to come to the United States for medical treatment. At that time one of us was teaching a class that had several Iranian students. In discussing the situation with them, we were surprised to learn how hated the shah was in his own country. As one student put it, it was as if the U.S. had invited Hitler. Had the Carter administration thought about its hospitality to the shah from the Iranian perspective, perhaps the entire fiasco could have been avoided.

7. *Have a second-chance meeting:* Even if a decision seems sound, it is always a good idea to give yourselves one more chance to change your mind. A second-chance meeting gives members an opportunity to reflect and think about their decisions, discuss it with others, and consider introducing an action vote—ensuring that hasty decisions are not made.

Group Composition

The chances of groupthink occurring also depend on the composition of the group. Some groups are more prone to groupthink than others. Professor of psychology Marvin E. Shaw, for example, has done extensive research on group composition. His research suggests that the likelihood of groupthink reflects three factors specifically: group cohesiveness, group compatibility, and homogeneity/heterogeneity (how similar or dissimilar group members are to each other).[29] He reports a number of findings and suggests several hypotheses with respect to each of these areas.

Cohesiveness

cohesiveness A measure of how attractive a group is to its members. It is the glue that holds a group together.

Cohesiveness is a measure of how attractive a group is to its members. It is the glue that holds a group together. A highly cohesive group is one in which members are highly motivated to belong. You can probably recall groups that you really enjoyed participating in—perhaps a sports team or the cast of a play. On the other hand, we all have belonged to groups that had absolutely no cohesiveness at all. Groups lack cohesiveness when they are imposed on the members, as when an instructor assigns a group project. In comparison to low-cohesiveness

Box 12-3   Skill Building

Decision-Making Methods

The following are common methods people use in arriving at decisions. Write down what you perceive to be the advantages and disadvantages of each method. Pair off with another person and compare your lists of advantages and disadvantages. Then try to reach consensus and produce a combined list that you both agree represents an improvement over your initial lists.

1. Ask an expert to make the decision.

2. Go along with majority rule by vote.

3. Flip a coin.

4. Ask the group leader or boss to decide.

5. Require that any decision be acceptable to at least two-thirds of the group membership.

6. Reach consensus, meaning everyone agrees and is committed to seeing the decision through.

groups, groups with high cohesiveness (1) have more extensive communication among group members; (2) are more positive, friendly, and cooperative; (3) exert higher influence on members; (4) have greater effectiveness in achieving goals; and (5) result in higher member satisfaction.[30]

For the most part, therefore, groups should do what they can to build cohesiveness. However, because cohesive groups exert more influence on their members, if the group is in a groupthink mode, the very cohesiveness of the group can result in worse decision making.

On the whole, however, it is better for a group to be high in cohesiveness than low. Ernest G. Bormann and Nancy C. Bormann suggest several ways to increase a group's cohesiveness:

- Give the group a name with which group members can readily identify.
- Establish group ceremonies and rituals which set the group apart from other groups.
- Stress the importance of teamwork and cooperation.
- Encourage individual group members to recognize each other's contributions.
- Establish group rewards for group achievements.
- Set goals that the group realistically can achieve.
- Treat group members as people, not numbers.[31]

In many ways these suggestions are just common sense—treat others as you would like them to treat you. Make the group a team and share credit and rewards—and blame. These are the steps to increasing your group's cohesiveness and potentially its productivity.

Another way to build cohesiveness is to be in competition with another group, such as a rival team or social organization. The military branches of service in the United States—the Marines, Navy, Air Force, and Army—take great pride in their units. The annual Army–Navy football game, for example, is a way of building cohesiveness for Army cadets and Navy midshipmen.

Compatibility

Compatibility is the degree to which the members of a group meet each others' needs. A group of all leaders or all followers is destined to fail. Just as a basketball team needs five position players, a group needs individuals that can fulfill a wide variety of needs.

Psychologist W. C. Schutz has suggested that groups can potentially fill three basic interpersonal needs: inclusion, control, and affection.[32] The degree to which group members assist each other in satisfying their needs is the key to compatibility. If a group includes both people who have a high need to be controlled by others and people who have a high need to exercise control, then there is compatibility. On the other hand, if everyone in the group needs to exercise control, but no one wants to be controlled, it is a recipe for disaster.

Compatibility has two important benefits: Groups that are compatible are more likely to achieve their goals than incompatible groups, and members of compatible groups are more satisfied.[33]

Homogeneity/Heterogeneity

The final element of group composition is the degree to which group members are homogeneous—that is, similar to one another—or heterogeneous—dissimilar. Marvin Shaw has identified the following effects of heterogeneity for groups: (1) Groups with diverse abilities are more effective than those with similar abilities; (2) styles of communication are affected by the gender composition of the group (which is discussed further in Box 12-4); (3) groups that include both males and females tend to be more effective than single sex groups; (4) mixed groups induce more conformity than groups of one gender; (5) the racial composition of a group can affect a group's feelings and behaviors; and (6) groups with different personality profiles are more effective than those who are homogeneous in this respect.[34]

One of the major differences between the American and Japanese work forces is in terms of their relative homogeneity. Japan is a very homogeneous country. In terms of cultural and ethnic background, people are quite similar to one another. This similarity helps create a harmonious work environment. The United States, on the other hand, is a multicultural, multiethnic nation. We are likely to have very heterogeneous work groups. This diversity can be a very positive factor, but only if conflict is properly managed and not allowed to undermine the cohesiveness of the group.

Box 12-4   Critical Thinking

Gender Differences in Group Communication

In her book *You Just Don't Understand,* linguist Deborah Tannen describes differences between ways men and women communicate. Men, she notes, tend to have a "public speaking," or report-talk, style. They are socialized to use talk in order to get and keep attention. For them, exhibiting knowledge and taking center stage is a way to establish status and independence. Women, on the other hand, are more comfortable with a "private speaking," or rapport-talk style, whose goal is establishing connections and similarities; in other words, their purpose is interdependence rather than independence. Consequently, as Tannen observes, men are generally more comfortable than women speaking out in public settings. It's usually men who ask the questions after a lecture and who call in to radio talk shows.

During a class discussion or a meeting at which men and women are present in approximately equal numbers, make some notes about who speaks and see how the dynamics of the discus-

sion compare to Tannen's description. Do more men talk than women? How many men and how many women make statements in order to exhibit knowledge or expertise? How many of each gender make statements in support of other speakers' points? Who asks questions? Who interrupts? Who is more likely to tell a joke? To share a personal experience?

Tannen's conclusion is not that men's and women's different conversational styles make conversation between them impossible. Rather, she recommends that men and women recognize that since childhood they have been socialized in different conversational styles. She suggests that women learn to push themselves a little harder to enter a group discussion and not wait for a polite pause, until they're sure that no one else wants the floor. She also proposes that men recognize that they and women have internalized different rhythms of conversation and not assume that women find "public speaking" as natural as they do.

SOURCE: Deborah Tannen, *You Just Don't Understand: Women and Men in Conversation* (New York: Morrow, 1990), 74–95.

Summary

A group is three or more people who are aware of each other's presence, have an interdependent purpose, communicate with one another, and operate within norms. Types of groups include formal and informal social groups, therapeutic groups, and task-oriented groups.

Groups are advantageous in that they have more information than individuals, more ways of approaching a problem, greater acceptance, and comprehension of a solution once it is decided. Among the disadvantages of groups are social pressures to conform, a tendency toward premature solutions, the danger of a dominant individual, and the potential for goal conflict. Disagreements, conflicting interests, a greater tendency to take risks, greater use of time, and the results of inducing change may be advantageous or disadvantageous depending on circumstances.

Groupthink occurs when pressures toward uniformity override a realistic appraisal of alternatives in a group. Symptoms of groupthink include illusions of invulnerability, unquestioned belief in the group's morality, collective rationalization, stereotypes of those not in the group, direct pressure on dissenters, self-censorship of dissent, illusions of unanimity, and emergence of mindguards. Ways to avoid groupthink include use of a devil's advocate, leaders who don't reveal their preferences, use of independent groups, discussions with others outside the group, use of outside experts, consideration of alternative scenarios, and second-chance meetings.

The cohesiveness of a group refers to the degree to which members are attracted to and wish to belong to the group. Groups can build cohesiveness by naming their group, building a group tradition, stressing teamwork, recognizing good work, setting clear and attainable goals, giving rewards to the group as a whole, and treating members as people. Compatible groups have a balance between people who need to receive and need to express interpersonal needs such as inclusion, control, and affection. Members of homogeneous groups are highly similar to one another, whereas heterogeneous groups are more diversified. Generally, heterogeneous groups are more effective than homogeneous ones, depending on the exact nature of the task.

Another Look

Articles

Dennis S. Gouran, Randy Y. Hirokawa, and Amy E. Martz. "A Critical Analysis of Factors Related to Decisional Processes Involved in the *Challenger* Disaster." *Central States Speech Journal* 37 (1986): 119–35.

This is an excellent article explaining how the failed launch of *Challenger* can be directly related to the failure of group decision making.

Books

Phillip K. Tompkins. *Organizational Communication Imperatives: Lessons of the Space Program.* Los Angeles: Roxbury, 1993.

This book provides an excellent history of the space program—from its early days under Werner Von Braun to the *Challenger* disaster. Tompkins was a consultant to Von Braun and brings an organizational communication perspective to his history of the space program.

Video Rentals

Twelve Angry Men This film is a classic examination of group interaction in a jury trial. It stars Henry Fonda as the lone juror who questions the rest of the jury's view that the defendant is guilty, and it shows how each juror develops a unique role. This film illustrates how a group, initially bent on a "groupthink" track to a quick conviction, ends up acquitting an innocent man because of the willingness of one juror to challenge the majority view.

The Right Stuff Based on Tom Wolfe's book about the *Project Mercury* astronauts, this film illustrates many of the principles discussed in this chapter. It does an excellent job of showing how groups build cohesiveness and members of groups assist each other in satisfying their respective needs.

Schindler's List This remarkable film shows what is good and bad about groups. On the one hand, it shows the humanity that can arise from membership in a group, but on the other it shows just the opposite, detailing the inhumanity groups also can encourage in their members.

Theory and Research in Practice

1. Individual versus group problem solving: Write down the names of the last 10 presidents of the United States in chronological order. In class, form groups of about 5 students each. Share your lists in the group, and arrive at a common list of the last 10 presidents. The instructor will then reveal the correct answer. Score one point for each correct answer. Compute your individual score, the average of all individual scores in the group, and the group score. Then answer the following questions:

   • Did the group on the average have a better or worse score than the average of your individual scores?

   • Did any one individual in the group begin with a better score than the group score?

   • What happened in the course of the group discussion to cause people to change their minds about the order of the presidents? What factors seemed to be most influential?

2. Individual versus group creativity: The instructor will take a common object and ask you to list as many possible uses for it as you can. After you have made your own list, join a group of about five students to work on a common list of uses. Groups are encouraged to come up with unique uses, those that were not on any member's list. After concluding the discussion, answer the following questions:

   • What was the average number of uses of the object on your list?

   • How many uses did the group have on its final list?

   • How many new uses did the group come up with in addition to those on one or more individual lists?

The additional uses, not on any individual list, represent a bonus of group interaction over individuals working alone.

3. Violate a norm: *Caution: You should do nothing in this exercise that is illegal or violates any of your university or college regulations.* Pick a norm—a customary standard of conduct—and violate it for a day. For example: walk backward; make eye contact with strangers in an elevator; wear unusual clothing; in a library or cafeteria where there are vacant tables, sit next to someone at an occupied table. Write a brief paper in which you describe the norm you violated and people's reactions to you. Did anyone comment on your behavior or ask you what you were doing? Did people react nonverbally (for example, get up and walk away)? What does this exercise tell you about the power of unspoken norms?

CHAPTER THIRTEEN

Small Group Communication in Practice

OBJECTIVES

After reading this chapter you should be able to:

- Recognize the phases of group development.

- Understand the nature of roles and functional behaviors in small groups.

- Identify different leadership styles and practice the style of leadership appropriate to the situation.

- Participate effectively in a task-oriented group.

Anyone who has ever tried to organize a task-oriented group knows that it is easier said than done. Consider the case of a person on our campus who spearheaded the organization of a group dedicated to exploring what he believed were the most pressing issues facing the modern male. He began by seeking formal recognition from the student government. Next, he called for a general meeting of interested people, which was announced in the student newspaper and on printed flyers posted across the campus.

Not only did men show up to the initial meeting, but so did an equal number of women curious about the group's purpose and composition. This mix of people was hardly what the group organizer expected. When this initial meeting turned into a shouting match, moreover, he began to realize how unprepared he was to achieve what he thought was a straightforward and easily realized goal: providing men on campus with a forum to discuss men's issues.

At last report, the group was still in the process of trying to agree on its purpose and functions. The group is now open to women as well as men, and the leaders who replaced the initial organizer hope to elect officers sometime within the next six months. Needless to say, this outcome probably isn't what the group's instigator initially had in mind.

In Chapter 12 we introduced the concept of groups and discussed groupthink, a usually dysfunctional phenomenon that can even plague people who have had considerable experience working in groups. In this chapter we shift our focus to the constructive use of groups and group processes. Major topics include

- the phases common to a group's development,
- the roles and functions group members perform as the group develops,
- the nature of leadership and the responsibilities leadership involves,
- the common forums in which groups report on their deliberations.

Group Development

As our campus organizer learned the hard way, groups take time to develop. Many researchers have examined this process. None has done a better job, though, than communication scholar B. Aubrey Fisher.[1] As a result of observing many groups, he was able to develop a four-phase model of the process through which decision-making groups pass from start to finish. Fisher called these four phases (1) orientation, (2) conflict, (3) emergence, and (4) reinforcement (Figure 13-1).

Phases of Group Development

During Fisher's first phase, *orientation,* members of the group are just becoming acquainted. People are reluctant to disagree. Ideas are expressed vaguely. Basically, this phase involves efforts by group members to reduce their uncertainty about one another and the task at hand.

The second phase, *conflict,* involves the actual argument and disagreement involved in reaching a decision. At this point in the group, attitudes may become polarized and ideas are put to the test. If a group misses this stage, it is likely to fall victim to groupthink. The critical evaluation of ideas is crucial to effective problem solving.

The third phase, *emergence,* is when a consensus may begin to emerge. Although disagreement is not absent, dissent and conflict are in decline. Those opposed to the likely solution tend to seek accommodation. Strong task leadership is helpful to this phase's successful completion.

The final phase, *reinforcement,* occurs when a group has successfully solved its problem, reached a decision, or completed its task. At this point, group members reinforce each other with positive comments. Consensus and commitment to the decision are stressed.

Not all groups progress in order through all four stages. A group may stall at any point and not succeed in completing its task. In addition, researchers, such as Thomas Scheidel and Laura Crowell, have shown that groups move in a cyclical or spiral fashion, which they call "reach-testing."[2] A consensus may appear to have emerged, only to be beaten back by questions from dissenters. A group often thinks it has solved a problem, only to discover a crucial piece of information is missing. Groups are frequently forced to backtrack in order to move forward.

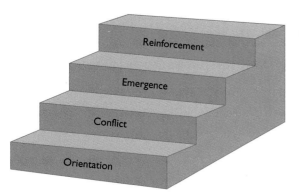

Figure 13-1 Fisher's Model of Group Development

Steps in Group Problem Solving

In contrast to Fisher, other researchers have suggested that groups would be more productive if they followed a predetermined sequence, rather than just letting phases simply happen. Many group discussion agendas are based on the concept of reflective thinking, developed by American philosopher John Dewey. He defined **reflective thinking** as "active, persistent, and careful consideration of any belief or supposed form of knowledge in the light of the grounds that support it and the further conclusions to which it tends."[3] Reflective thinking, according to Dewey, has five steps:

> (1) *suggestions,* in which the mind leaps forward to a possible solution; (2) an intellectualization of the difficulty or perplexity that has been *felt* (directly experienced) into a *problem* to be solved, a question for which the answer must be sought; (3) the use of one suggestion after another as a leading idea or supposition, or *hypothesis,* to initiate and guide observation and other operations in collection of factual material; (4) the mental elaboration of the idea or supposition as an idea or supposition (*reasoning,* in the sense in which reasoning is a part, not the whole, of inference); and (5) testing the hypothesis by overt or imaginative action.[4]

Although originally intended for individual thinkers, Dewey's model has been widely applied to decision-making groups. Among the first to apply this system to group discussion were Russell H. Wagner and Carroll C. Arnold.[5] They apply the principles of reflective thinking to group process using the following steps (Box 13-1 suggests problem topics that a group might address):

Step 1: *Define and limit the problem question.*

One of the big problems most groups face is issue proliferation. Left unchecked people can keep raising so many issues that a group will never be able to discuss, much less solve, them all. It is important at the outset, therefore, that group members consensually agree to a definition of the problem and then limit the problem's scope so that it is manageable.

reflective thinking
A deliberative process that requires group members to evaluate the evidence and reasoning offered as support of a claim.

Defining the problem and limiting its scope, for example, was crucial in the *Apollo 13* space mission, dramatically chronicled in the film *Apollo 13* starring Tom Hanks. Time was precious. The astronauts in the spaceship and the engineers on the ground had to agree what the problem was before they could try to solve it. In this instance, defining the problem incorrectly could have led to the astronauts' death.

Once the problem has been defined and limited, group members can go on to Steps 2 through 6.

Step 2: *Analyze and evaluate the problem.*
    (a) What symptoms suggest a problem really exists?
    (b) What causes produced the problem?
    (c) What forces are already at work to solve the difficulty?

Step 3: *Establish criteria or standards by which solutions will be judged acceptable or unacceptable.*

Step 4: *Examine the consequences of each available solution.*

Step 5: *Select the preferred solution or solutions.*

Step 6: *Put the preferred solution into effect.*

Principles of Group Problem Solving

Small group communication expert John K. Brilhart has suggested some basic principles that groups should follow in structuring their problem solving, regardless of the particular steps they follow.[6] The first principle is to *focus on the problem before thinking and talking about how to solve it.* How good a solution is depends on how well the group understands the problem. Focusing first on the problem forces group members to view it from different perspectives and may reveal new facets of it. If a group jumps too hastily to a conclusion, it is not likely to reach the best solution. For example, a group seeking to improve library service on campus should not begin by deciding that the library should be open every day from 8:00 A.M. until midnight. Maybe that is financially impossible. Perhaps there are better uses of library resources than staying open Friday and Saturday evenings when student use is minimal.

Brilhart's second principle is to *begin with a single, unambiguous problem question.* A group should know at the outset what problem they are trying to solve and what they hope to achieve. Never begin the problem-solving process without first agreeing about your ultimate goal. It is best if the group can agree on a straightforward clearly worded problem question. For example, the group discussing library service might ask, "How can the university library maximize service to students and faculty?"

The third principle of group problem solving is to *map the problem thoroughly.* Group members need to explore the problem, do their homework, and be pre-

Box 13-1   Critical Thinking

What Is the Problem?

The event that alerts us to a problem is normally a symptom rather than the cause of the problem. If we are not careful in this regard, we risk treating the symptom as opposed to attacking the real problem. This tendency to treat the symptom is one of the reasons it is so important for groups to make sure that a problem has been identified and defined correctly before the group moves on. Consider the following topics and the problems they subsume. See if you can identify the cause of the problems you associate with the topic. Structure your discussion according to the first five steps of Wagner and Arnold's system for group problem solving.

- Low voter turnout in national elections
- Teenage pregnancy
- Crack cocaine
- Alcohol abuse
- Water pollution
- AIDS
- Sexual harassment
- Racism
- Illegal immigration
- The federal budget deficit

pared with facts and expert opinion. To simply exchange personal opinions or share ignorance leads to a poor-quality discussion. Group members must consult authoritative sources who can inform them about the nature of the problem. Then they should organize what they have learned from these authoritative sources so that the information can be readily shared.

The fourth principle is to *be sure the group members agree on criteria.* If group members first agree on the principles or standards that will guide their choices, it is often easier than looking at a series of alternatives with no guidelines. For example, recall when you selected your current college or university from the thousands of possibilities. You had to have some standards, or criteria, to guide your decision, for example, cost, closeness to your home, availability of courses in your intended major, and availability of extracurricular activities. In the same way, any group decision needs to be based on specific criteria in order to reach consensus. Not only should the group members agree on criteria, they should also agree on which criteria are most important. A useful way to do this is to rank-order the criteria. For example, doctors have established criteria by which recipients of organ transplants are determined. Factors include age, general health, urgency of the needed transplant, and so forth. Clearly some criteria are more significant than others. If someone will die in a week without a transplant, it makes sense to put that person higher on the list than someone who is at a more desirable age but has many months to live before the transplant need becomes acute.

The fifth principle of group problem solving is to *defer judgment when seeking solutions*. Many times a group will simply jump on the first proposed solution to a problem. This can lead to inferior decision making. Until you know the range of alternatives, it is difficult to determine which of the many possible solutions is best. Sometimes a person will feel intimidated because the first time he or she speaks up with a possible solution, the idea is trashed. Soon, the person will feel defensive and unlikely to make another suggestion. It is far better to get ideas out on the table without evaluation, then go back and evaluate them without consideration of who originated them.

The next principle is one we'll discuss in more detail later in the chapter: *Use constructive argument and other techniques to avoid groupthink*. Sometimes people feel that if they disagree, they will offend other group members. However, it is far better to establish a norm of open and constructive argument. If you have reservations about an idea, you should be able to express them constructively without creating defensiveness or hurt feelings. Thus, the emphasis is on constructive argument. Remember that failure to express disagreement can be disastrous, as it was for the *Challenger* astronauts.

The last principle we'll discuss is to *plan how to implement and follow up on solutions*. All too often groups come up with pie-in-the-sky solutions. A group in one of our classes picked increased teenage smoking as their topic for a problem-solving exercise. Their knowledge of the topic was excellent and they thoroughly discussed the problem. Their solution, however, was highly impractical—ban tobacco products in the United States. (They would continue to allow export—creating a dubious double standard.) Given the nation's experience with prohibition and the difficulty we already have controlling various drugs, to suddenly ban a product used by a significant portion of the population would be impossible to implement. The group gave no thought to how their solution would be implemented or to the negative side effects it might have.

Roles and Functions in a Group

One of the most predictable aspects of group interaction is that group members will evolve a set of differentiated roles. A **role** is a profile of functional behaviors that a member performs for a group. In addition to someone who is capable of performing the role of leader, which we'll discuss shortly, you will find in most groups a person who is very task oriented, seeking to make sure the group gets the job done. There is also usually someone who likes to focus on the social aspects of the group. Perhaps this person likes to bring refreshments or offers his or her apartment or dorm room for meetings. Another group member may be the group clown or tension reliever. Sometimes one member is a computer whiz and ends up being the person who puts together the group's reports. Sometimes roles are dysfunctional—as when a person plays the role of consistent latecomer. The specific behavioral functions that constitute group roles fall into three classifications: task, relationship, and self-centered functions.

role A profile of functional behaviors that a member performs for a group.

Task Functions

Some behaviors help the group accomplish its task—do its job. There are a variety of ways in which group members can advance the task dimension of group process.[7]

- *Initiating and orienting:* Groups need help to get started. For example, once a group is given a task, someone needs to explain to the group members what is expected of them.

- *Information gathering:* Without information, a group discussion is merely an exchange of ignorance. Generally all members of the group should be expected to gather information, although members may choose or be assigned specific topics. As we saw in Chapter 12, the engineers at Morton Thiokol were expected to gather information about the safety of O-rings to support their claims that a launch would be unsafe below 53 degrees Fahrenheit.

Groups need a visual record of their thinking and progress.

- *Information seeking:* During the course of a discussion, members often ask for information from other members. When management at Thiokol asked the engineers to explain the previous instances of O-ring leakage, it was seeking information.

- *Opinion giving:* Groups have to go beyond just the facts—they have to form opinions. When someone makes a statement of judgment or inference, that is opinion giving.

- *Opinion seeking:* Asking for the opinions of others is also part of the process of opinion formation.

- *Clarifying and elaborating:* Because people understand information differently, occasional clarification or elaboration helps to ensure that all group members have a similar understanding of the information that has been presented. For example, one of the Rogers Commission members clarified the maze of technical data by putting a common rubber O-ring from a hardware store in a glass of ice water. The O-ring became hard and lost its resiliency.

- *Evaluating:* Assigning a value judgment is a way for a group to make sure they agree on basic principles. For example, to say that safety should be the number one goal of the space program is to make an evaluation.

- *Summarizing:* Group members occasionally need to summarize what has been said so far in order to keep from plowing the same ground.

- *Coordinating:* Someone in every group needs to ensure that the lines of communication are maintained—whether by coordinating members' busy schedules or by relating various ideas to each other. Often, coordinating takes place as a group nears the completion of its initial meeting.

- *Consensus testing:* At some point in a group discussion, there should be some areas of emerging agreement. "Are we all in agreement that . . . ?" is an important question.

- *Recording:* Keeping the group's minutes, writing down ideas during brainstorming, and jotting down ideas as the group members suggest them are all important recording functions.

- *Suggesting procedure:* Particularly when a group seems to be going nowhere, it is important for someone to suggest a procedure, such as moving to a vote, adjourning until more information is gathered, or breaking into subgroups.

Relationship Functions

Relationship functions are group maintenance functions, because they serve to maintain the group's harmony. Basically, these functions focus on the relationships among group members.

- *Establishing norms:* Some group norms, such as democratic principles, are simply transferred from a larger group or from society at large. However, some-

times groups need to consciously adopt certain norms to deal with specific problems, such as members who are always late or who miss meetings.

- *Gatekeeping:* Who speaks to whom, when, and how long? Gatekeeping helps control the flow of the conversation.

- *Supporting:* Even if someone expresses a view no one else shares, the group should support the importance of hearing everyone's views and thus prevent groupthink.

- *Harmonizing:* When conflict arises, it needs to be resolved and interpersonal harmony rebuilt by trying to find common ground, for example.

- *Tension relieving:* The use of humor to relax a tense situation is often essential to maintaining a good relationship among group members.

- *Dramatizing:* Sometimes telling stories or reliving events can help build group solidarity. In fact, over the long term, groups develop a common history, complete with their own stories.

- *Showing solidarity:* "All for one and one for all" is a useful motto for a cohesive group. Showing solidarity with other group members helps reinforce the ties that bind the group together.

Groups frequently benefit from shared humor.

Self-Centered Functions

Not every behavior performs a positive function in a group. Behaviors that are more self-centered than group-centered can disrupt the group process.

- *Withdrawing:* By withdrawing verbally or nonverbally, a member ceases to be an active part of the group, usually causing hard feelings and resentment. The ultimate withdrawal is the person who simply stops attending a group's meetings.

- *Blocking:* Sometimes there are members who object and try to block anything. In the U.S. Senate, for example, even one senator can hold up important legislation by engaging in a filibuster—at least until he or she can't stay awake or 40 senators vote to close debate. An unwillingness to compromise or an insistence on having one's own way can be destructive to a group. On the other hand, sometimes it is better to block a group than to go along with a dangerous course of action. Imagine if the Thiokol engineers had insisted on forwarding their objections up the chain of command instead of letting management have its way.

- *Status and recognition seeking:* Some members of groups are seeking only their own glorification, and if the group suffers, they couldn't care less. Such grandstanding generally makes for bad feelings for the entire group. A wise person once said, "There is no limit to what you can accomplish if you don't care who gets the credit." It is far more important for a group to accomplish its task than to determine who gets an ego boost.

Box 13-2 describes some specific dysfunctional roles and provides the opportunity to develop strategies for dealing with them.

Leadership and Leaders

One of the key roles in any group is that of the leader. Many of the functions we have discussed are sometimes thought of as "leadership functions." In this section, we discuss leaders, leadership, and various approaches to leading groups.

Defining Leadership

leadership
Influence exerted through communication that helps a group clarify and achieve goals.

leader A person who exercises goal-oriented influence in a group.

There are many ways to look at the concept of leadership. The definitions offered by communication professors John K. Brilhart and Gloria J. Galanes are the best for our purposes. They define **leadership** as "influence exerted through communication that helps a group clarify and achieve goals." A **leader** is "a person who exercises goal-oriented influence in a group" and may either be informally identified by members of the group or designated by appointment or election.[8]

Note that, as these definitions indicate, people become leaders in more than one way. They may exercise leadership functions; the group may self-identify them as leaders; or they may be officially designated leaders. Think of your own

Box 13-2   Skill Building

Dealing with Dysfunctional Group Members

The following list describes five dysfunctional group roles that members sometimes display. Develop a written communication strategy that could be used by group members and leaders for dealing with each role type. Your purpose is to acknowledge the person but to put a stop to the dysfunctional behavior in a way that does not further disrupt the group and allows it to continue working toward its goal. For example, a naysayer could be asked to propose a solution he or she deemed acceptable. The result will be either a constructive contribution to the problem-solving process or, more likely, inability to offer a positive suggestion.

1. *The storyteller:* This person frequently impedes group progress with interesting or entertaining stories that have little to do with the task at hand.

2. *The I'm-so-smart person:* This group member is most interested in impressing the group with how smart he or she is. This person always wants the group to listen to him or her, regardless of the worth of the person's contributions.

3. *The naysayer:* This person says "no" to everything. In his or her mind, no solution to a problem is ever good enough.

4. *The monopolizer:* This person tries to dominate the group verbally and nonverbally, constantly offering advice, opinions, and judgments.

5. *The lobbyist:* This person always wants a solution to accommodate his or her situation, even if it means stepping on the needs of others.

experience. Perhaps you've been asked to lead a group in your fraternity, sorority, temple, or other organization: that would constitute designated leadership. On the other hand, if you were to ask the members of the group who they thought was the leader, they might pick one person who was particularly influential in the group; that person is a leader identified in the course of the group's work. Finally, many people in a group sometimes help it achieve its goals; they could all be thought of as leaders in that they exercise leadership functions, regardless of their particular position in the organization.

Both of the authors have served as leaders. We've been chairs of academic departments, as well as university-wide committees. Despite our designated-leader status, we can point to a number of people in our department or on these committees who were also leaders—particularly influential persons who helped the group to function effectively in achieving its goals.

In sum, all group members have the potential to exercise leadership in the group. The designated leader, should the group have a person in that role, has special responsibilities we will discuss in more detail later in this section.

Leadership Styles

There are many ways to classify leadership styles. One of the most durable classification systems is the tripartite distinction developed by gestalt psychologists

Table 13-1 Leadership Styles and Effects

	AUTHORITARIAN	DEMOCRATIC	LAISSEZ-FAIRE
Leader is clearly identified by role	Yes	Yes	No
How much organization does this kind of leader institute?	Much	Some	None
What are the best kinds of tasks for this leadership style?	Simple	Complex	All kinds
At what rate are decisions made with this style?	Fast	Slow	Slow
What generally tends to be the quality of decision for this leadership style?	Quantity oriented	Quality oriented	Mixed (dependent on input)
How satisfied are work group members with this style?	Low satisfaction	High satisfaction	Mixed satisfaction

SOURCE: Adapted from K. Lewin, R. Lippitt, and R. K. White, "Patterns of Aggressive Behavior in Experimentally Created 'Social Climates,'" *Journal of Social Psychology* 43 (1939), 271–99.

Lewin, Lippitt, and White.[9] They experimentally manipulated adult leadership of groups of boys into three categories: autocratic, democratic, and laissez-faire. Autocratic leaders determine everything for the group—basically functioning as dictators. Laissez-faire leaders, on the other hand, exercise no leadership, leaving everything in the hands of the group. Finally, democratic leaders guide the group, encourage members to participate in decision making, developing policy and means of implementation. Lewin and his colleagues found that democratic leadership produced the best results in terms of the group climate, satisfaction of group members, and quality of product. Table 13-1 compares these three types of leadership. As Box 13-3 explains, some researchers also have found that different ways of leading correspond to differences in gender behaviors.

Situational Leadership

An autocratic style of leadership is called for on a battlefield, but for most problem-solving groups, a democratic style yields better results. There are many variations of democratic style, however, and the best one to use depends on the situation. Business consultants Paul Hersey and Kenneth H. Blanchard have developed a situational model of leadership, which assumes that different leadership styles are appropriate in different situations; the variables are "(1) the amount of guidance and direction (task behavior) a leader gives; (2) the amount of socio-emotional support (relationship behavior) a leader provides; and (3) the readiness ('maturity') level that followers exhibit in performing a specific task, function, or objective."[10] This model leads to a fourfold typology of leadership: telling, selling, consulting, and delegating.

Box 13-3 Considering Diversity

Masculine and Feminine Leadership Styles

In her book *Feminine Leadership, or How to Succeed in Business Without Being One of the Boys*, author Marilyn Loden proposes models of masculine and feminine leadership. In brief, here's how they compare:

	Masculine Style	Feminine Style
Operating Style	Competitive	Cooperative
Organizational Structure	Hierarchy	Team
Basic Objective	Winning	Quality output
Problem-Solving Style	Rational	Combination of rational and intuitive
Key Characteristics	High control, strategic moves, low emotional involvement, analytical approach	Shared control, empathy for employees, collaborative interaction, emphasis on high performance standards

Although no group will be a pure example of either leadership style, the differences in men's and women's communication styles do seem to create differences in the ways they function in groups. In your experience, do men and women lead differently? If you have ever belonged to a same-sex organization (such as Boy Scouts, a sorority, or an athletic team), how did it differ from mixed-sex organizations you have belonged to? In your estimation, what are the strengths and weaknesses of the masculine and feminine leadership styles? What kinds of situations is each style best suited to? Be prepared to explain your answers in specific terms.

SOURCE: Based on Elizabeth J. Natalle, "Gendered Issues in the Workplace" in *Gendered Relationships,* ed. Julia T. Wood (Mountain View, Calif.: Mayfield, 1996), 258–59.

- *Telling:* Low-maturity groups, which are not able or willing to take responsibility, have to be told or directed regarding the task at hand. Little attention is paid to relationship variables. Any recruit who has lived through basic training or boot camp has experienced the "telling" style of leadership of his or her company drill sergeant.

- *Selling:* This style fits groups low to moderate in maturity. These people are willing, but not able, to take responsibility. This style is high on both task and relationship dimensions. It involves persuading or selling people on your ideas, not simply directing them to follow you. This is often the situation faced by a teacher at the beginning of a semester. Students are willing to learn—or they would not have enrolled in the class. But they need to be persuaded or sold on the benefits of sticking it out and working through difficult materials to reap the ultimate benefits of the class.

Figure 13-2
Situational Model of
Leadership

	Task Behavior of Leader	Relationship Behavior of Leader	Maturity of Group
Telling	high	very low	low
Selling	high	high	low to moderate
Consulting	low	high	moderate to high
Delegating	low	low	high

- *Consulting:* This style fits people moderate to high in maturity, who are able to take responsibility but are not willing to follow the leader's direction. This is a style high in relationship behavior, but low on the task dimension. It involves shared decision making between leader and group members. For some classes, students need to participate in their own learning—devising their own projects, feeling that they are a part of the educational process, not merely receptacles for the instructor's wisdom, poured into their heads in 50-minute blocks of lecture.

- *Delegating:* This style is suited to a group of high maturity, which is both willing and able to do the task at hand. The leader in this style has a low task and relationship behavior, since he or she can rely on the group members to take responsibility and do the job. The most mature students frequently can be trusted to do an independent study with minimal supervision by the instructor. In this situation, the instructor uses a delegating style of teaching.

Figure 13-2 compares the four styles of leadership. Fill out Box 13-4 to find out which kind of leader you are.

The best leaders are predictable, yet flexible. In other words, group members know the leader's basic style, but they also know that he or she will change styles if the situation calls for it. The most powerful person in the group is the most flexible one.

Leader Responsibilities

If you are designated leader for your group, you will have certain responsibilities. Based on our experience leading a number of groups, we suggest that as a leader you assume the following responsibilities. Keep in mind that even though you have been designated as the primary spokesperson of your group, that doesn't automatically mean you are a leader in the eyes of group members. Leadership is a perception that results from action.

Box 13-4   Self-Assessment

What Is Your Style of Leadership?

Read each of the following statements. Rate the extent to which you agree or disagree with the statement, using the following scale: 1 = strongly disagree, 2 = disagree, 3 = neither disagree nor agree, 4 = agree, and 5 = strongly agree.

_____ 1. Decisions are best reached when the leader is designated by a higher authority.

_____ 2. Decisions are best reached when the leader emerges from the group itself.

_____ 3. Most people want to participate in making decisions that will affect them.

_____ 4. Most people would rather have decisions made for them.

_____ 5. Everyone's opinions need to be heard when making a decision.

_____ 6. Important people's opinions need to be heard when making a decision.

_____ 7. Usually, group decisions take more time than they are worth.

_____ 8. No decision is better than one in which people haven't had the opportunity to participate.

_____ 9. Leaders must be decisive.

_____ 10. Leaders must be open to others' input.

Scoring: The more you agreed with 1, 4, 6, 7, and 9, the more predisposed you are to an autocratic style of leadership. The more you agree with 2, 3, 5, 8, and 10, the more predisposed you are to a democratic style of leadership. Be sure to consider your score in terms of gender. Research shows that women generally are more democratic in style than men are. Why do you think this may or may not be the case?

First and foremost, leadership involves *competence and character.* Group members must share in the perception that you are competent—knowledgeable about the task you've been given. Group members must also share in the perception that you are a person of high character—someone who can be trusted to do what you say you will do.

Second, leadership requires that you be similar enough to group members that they consider you one of them, but dissimilar enough that they believe you have something to offer they don't. This *balancing act between similarity and dissimilarity* is crucial to your ability to lead. If you are just another one of the guys or gals, group members will give no more weight to your opinion than to anyone else's. If you are perceived as too much of an outsider, however, you'll never get their attention.

As you attempt to lead a group, either you or someone in the group will need to perform a number of specific functions in order to make sure that meetings happen and that something happens at meetings.

• *Determine a meeting time and place.* In classes with group assignments, one of the most common complaints is that the groups cannot find a time to meet. Not only is time important, so is place. If you want to focus on your group task, the local pub is hardly the most conducive place to get the job done.

   If you are assigned to be leader of a group, the first thing to do is to have everybody jot down their schedule, including class, work, and other mandatory activities. Doing this on a grid makes it easy to determine what times are free for everyone in the group. Also, be sure to get everyone's name and address so that you can notify them of any change of plans. It is best to set up your first meeting as soon as possible after the group is formed.

• *Develop an agenda.* It may seem that this is too formal for classroom groups, but you will quickly learn that a group without an agenda is one that will likely flounder. What are the specific items you plan to discuss at your upcoming meeting? Make sure everyone has the agenda in advance so that they are prepared for the discussion. Sometimes there's "homework" to be done before the meeting. For example, suppose you are dealing with the problem of crime on your campus. Rather than just having a "bull session" exchanging your personal experiences with crime, suppose each person in the group is charged with gathering some information prior to the meeting. Then, you might meet with an agenda such as the following:

   1. What is the crime rate on our campus? What specific crimes occur and how often?
      Jim—check with campus security office.
   2. What percentage of crime in our city is committed by college students? What types of crimes are committed against college students?
      Jane—check with city police public information officer.
      Jerry—check local newspaper back files.
   3. What steps have been taken on campus to reduce crime?
      Juan—check back files of campus newspaper.
      Jim—ask campus police.
   4. How do our campus crime rates compare with national statistics?
      Jill—check library sources.
   5. What conclusions can we draw? Is crime "under control" on our campus? Do we need to make changes to reduce crime?
   6. Set agenda for next meeting.

• *Keep the discussion on track.* Although sidetracks and "off topic" discussions can sometimes be productive, more often than not, they are a diversion from the real issues. Particularly disruptive are "isn't it awful" tangents, whereby everyone in the group shares their complaints, about the task, the boss, or whatever. These complaints may have their place, but they are unlikely to help the group get the job done. Most group members are reluctant to criticize their peers as being off the subject, and it is usually the designated leader who has to bring the group back on track. A tactful suggestion that "maybe we're straying from the topic," or a question that refocuses the group on the subject, is usually enough. Even a humorous reminder that the group has wandered can do wonders. After all, most people would rather be someplace else, and if time is wasted on irrelevancies, then the group may have to meet longer or more frequently to finish its task.

• *Ask questions to promote discussion.* There are many types of questions a designated leader (or any member for that matter) can ask. Four of the most important are questions for information, for interpretation, for suggestions, and about procedure. An example of a *question for information* is "What is the average crime rate for colleges our size?" Such a question requires a factually based response. A group member who has done research on this question would be able to provide a specific and factual answer. A *question for interpretation* might be "Do students really feel safe on our campus?" This question is not one that can be answered simply by reading off the statistics. It calls for group members to form conclusions based on the information they've gathered, as well as adding their own subjective interpretation of the information. A question *for suggestions* might be "What can we do to reduce crime on this campus?" This question calls for ideas from group members aimed at solving a problem the group has identified. Finally, a *procedural question* might be asked of the group: "Do we want to brainstorm possible solutions?" This question asks the group if they want to follow a certain procedure. All four types of questions are important if a group is to achieve its goals.

• *Summarize and transition to other points.* At some point it will become apparent that the group is moving in some direction. Although not everyone may agree on every point, the leader can try to summarize those points on which everyone agrees, thus defining which issues need further exploration. For example, the leader might say: "It seems that we all agree that there's a serious crime problem on our campus. Furthermore, it looks like assault and theft are the biggest problems. What we need to figure out is why these problems are getting worse and if there's anything we can do about them. Any ideas?" The function performed here is to move the group off a point that everyone agrees on and on to an issue that needs to be explored.

• *Set the agenda for the next meeting.* Assuming the task has not been completed, the next step is to agree on time and place and agenda items for the next meeting. Particularly important is making sure everyone knows what their individual responsibilities are prior to the next meeting. One of the great advantages of groups is that tasks can be subdivided. But that works only if everyone does what is agreed upon. If you are counting on someone to interview the campus police chief prior to the next meeting and that person "flakes," the whole group is stymied. So the leader needs to be sure those who are assigned crucial tasks are likely to carry them out responsibly.

- *Keep a record of meetings (or see that such a record is kept).* Some groups have a secretary or record keeper. In other groups, that task falls to the designated leader. Particularly in officially constituted groups there may be legal requirements for accurate minutes. Whatever the official requirements, unless some method for keeping accurate records is established a group is likely to spend unnecessary time trying to remember what had already been accomplished.

- *See that the final group decision is accurately reported.* Groups are normally part of some larger organization. For example, the academic department we have chaired reports to a dean. When we are asked to produce a product— for example, a hiring decision—we are expected to make sure the proper paper work is completed. Similarly, many instructors require some type of written report for task groups in their class. Whether the report is written by the leader, by other members of the group, or in sections assigned to subcommittees, the designated leader ultimately needs to make sure the paper work is done.

Member Responsibilities

As noted earlier in this chapter, leadership is a process that can be performed by anyone in the group, not just the designated leader. All the tasks described in the preceding section, therefore, may be performed by others in the group if that is the group's preference. Sometimes, for example, one group member is particularly adept at suggesting procedures to make the group work better. Another may be a good note-taker or report writer. So in a sense, a good group participant should be prepared to exercise any of the leadership functions when called upon to do so or when no one else seems to be getting the job done.

In addition to the leadership tasks described in the preceding section, there are a number of guidelines for effective group participation.

- *Be prepared.* Like the Boy Scout motto says, always be prepared. Do your homework. If you are supposed to do research, conduct an interview, write a section of a report, or bring refreshments, be ready for the meeting.

- *Be there.* One of the most frequent complaints we hear from students in our classes is that people don't show up at meetings. Not only does absenteeism lead to hard feelings and undermine group cohesiveness, it often leaves the group frustrated. Suppose the no-show is the person who has a crucial task assigned for the meeting. The group may just spin its wheels. If you cannot make a meeting, notify the designated leader as soon as possi-

ble. It may make sense to reschedule the whole meeting, rather than have an incomplete group.

- *Focus on ideas, not personalities.* Sometimes group discussions create more heat than light. People become defensive about their ideas and take criticism personally. "How can you say rape isn't a problem on this campus— that's just like a man!" Compare that response to "I can't agree with your conclusion that rape isn't a problem; the statistics I've gathered show that this city is above the national average in rapes per capita." If you keep the focus on facts, you will be less likely to undermine the cohesiveness of the group with personal conflict.

- *Use critical thinking skills to avoid groupthink.* Although this guideline may seem contrary to the preceding recommendation, it is not. We are not suggesting that you should avoid conflict, only that you should not personalize it. But when someone engages in fallacious or illogical thinking, it is important that someone in the group test the idea against the stan-

A panel discussion combines preparation with spontaneity and interaction among members of the group.

dards of reasoning laid out in Chapter 6. Failure to test ideas is a sure path to groupthink.

• *Keep your commitments to the group.* You will undoubtedly be asked to perform various individual tasks for the group—gather some research, set up an interview, write a report. If you don't think you'll be able to do a particular task in the time allotted, by all means say so. If you have developed a cohesive group, chances are someone will offer to help you out or share the task with you. But once you take on a responsibility, do it. It doesn't take long for the group to decide that one of the members is not pulling his or her weight. Just as we often hear complaints from students about difficulty finding meeting times and people not showing up, we also are inevitably confronted by angry group members who tell us some group member isn't doing anything. Although you cannot avoid being in groups with people who are not willing to do their share, you can make sure you are not one of those people. Again, a cohesive group is far more likely to use positive peer pressure to ensure that all members pull their own weight.

Presenting Group Decisions

Once a group has reached a decision, the results of that decision need to be presented in a systematic way. Some groups have the authority to implement their decision directly, but in most cases, groups must report their decision to someone who can then accept, reject, or modify the decision. In classroom situations, groups are normally expected to present their results to their instructor and their classmates. Whatever the specific circumstances your group faces, there at least four ways these decisions can be presented to others: written reports, individual oral reports, panel discussions, and symposiums. In some cases, a group may be expected to present its findings in both written and spoken form.

Written Reports

The Rogers Commission report cited in Chapter 12 is an example of a thorough written report presented by a specially selected commission to the president and the people of the United States. Although it is certainly more extensive than the type of written report expected of classroom groups, it does contain the basic elements of an effective written group report. The basic topics covered in the report are as follows:

Introduction
Events Leading Up to the *Challenger* Mission
The Accident
The Cause of the Accident
The Contributing Cause of the Accident

An Accident Rooted in History
The Silent Safety Program
Pressures on the System
Other Safety Considerations
Recommendations
Appendices

More generally, a written group report should include at least the following:

Introduction
Statement of the Problem
Background of the Problem
Causes of the Problem
Recommendations for Solving the Problem (including steps for implementing solutions)
Appendices (for any background documents)

The writing of a group report can be a difficult task. Obviously, it makes sense to divide tasks among group members, with different sections assigned to those members most familiar with the topic. However, once all the parts have been completed, the assembly of the report is usually best done by one person, who can edit and compile the report so that it reads consistently. The final report should be read by everyone in the group before the group signs off on it. If you read the Rogers Commission report, you will find that each member of the commission signed the report. We require groups in our classes to sign their reports, certifying they agree with the findings of the group and that each member contributed to the final product.

Individual Oral Reports

An oral report often accompanies a written one. The simplest is the individual oral report. The group designates one spokesperson to present the findings of the group to decision makers or (in the case of classroom groups) to the class as a whole.

An oral report is basically a speech. Chapters 14-17 discuss public speaking in greater detail. Briefly, a speech should open with impact, connect with the audience, and focus on the specific task the group tackled. The body of an oral report should include the statement of the problem, background information, causes, and recommendations for solving the problem. A conclusion that summarizes your main points and closes with impact is also expected. As with the written report, it is important to explain how the solution can be implemented.

Writing a group report can be a more difficult task than writing an oral report because everyone in the group needs to agree to what each individual has contributed to the final report.

Panel Discussions

A panel discussion is an extemporaneous group discussion held for the benefit of an audience. In a panel discussion, as in a speech, it is important that the group have a clear outline of the topics to be covered and that members are adequately prepared. On the other hand, the advantage of a panel discussion is that it is a blend of preparation and spontaneity. If members discuss only their specific topics, then it is a symposium (discussed below), not really a discussion. Members should feel free to comment on one another's points, ask questions, and openly discuss points throughout the presentation. However, a panel discussion is more formal than a normal private group discussion.

A panel discussion requires a leader to act as the *moderator* of the presentation. The moderator calls on members and keeps the discussion on track. Members who want to comment on another member's statement should wait to be recognized by the moderator. Most panel discussions also provide an opportunity for audience members to ask questions. Questions-and-answers can occur as the group moves through its outline, or it can be held as a *forum* period at the end of the panel presentation.

The outline for a panel discussion is similar to that for an individual report, with some modifications. The following is an example of a panel discussion outline on the topic of secondhand smoke.

I. Introduction of topic and group members

II. Is secondhand tobacco smoke harmful?

III. What is being done to limit exposure to secondhand smoke?

IV. What is causing these efforts to fall short?

V. Recommendations for new regulations on smoking in public places

Ideally, each member should be able to offer comments on each of these topics, rather than having one member prepared on each topic. A panel discussion should be a true discussion, not a series of individual presentations.

Symposiums

The principal difference between a panel discussion and a symposium is that in the latter each person has a prepared mini-speech on a particular topic. The outline for the panel discussion and the symposium might well be the same, but in the symposium, each member would be responsible for just one topic.

After the presentation, there is usually a forum period, at which time audience members can ask questions and group members may interact. The moderator of a symposium need only introduce each member, ensure that they stay within the time limit, and then lead the question-and-answer period.

Our preference among the four types of group presentations is the panel format. Because it is more spontaneous, it tends to be more interesting. Panel presentations also require everyone in the group to be thoroughly familiar with the group's findings.

Summary

Groups develop in phases, beginning with an orientation phase, moving through a period of conflict, followed by a phase of emergence, and concluding with reinforcement. The reflective thinking sequence has been adapted to group discussion, resulting in a process that moves through phases of definition, analysis, development of criteria, examination of possible solutions, selection of solution, and implementation. In addition to following a sequence of steps, groups are encouraged to focus on problems before trying to come up with possible solutions, begin with a single problem question, map the problem, agree on criteria, defer judgments while seeking solutions, use constructive argument to avoid groupthink, and plan to implement and follow-up solutions.

Group members develop specialized roles and fulfill task, relationship, and occasionally self-centered functions. Leadership is a process whereby influence is exerted that helps a group achieve its goals. A leader is someone who exercises leadership functions, is identified as such by group members, or is designated as the leader. Leadership styles may be autocratic, laissez-faire, or preferably democratic. Situational leadership includes telling, selling, consulting, and delegating. Leadership functions include determining a time and place for meeting, preparing an agenda, keeping the discussion on track, asking questions to promote discussion, providing summary and transition statements, setting the agenda for the next meeting, keeping records, and seeing that the group decision is accurately reported.

All group participants should be prepared for and present at meetings, focus on ideas not personalities, use critical thinking to avoid groupthink, and keep commitments to the group. Group outcomes may be presented in the form of written reports, oral reports, panel discussions, or symposiums.

Another Look

Articles

Stephen C. Schoonover and Murray M. Dalziel. "Developing Leadership for Change." *Management Review,* July 1986, 55–60.

Change in the workplace is inevitable. To be effective, leaders must know how to go about implementing change. This excellent, easy-to-read article offers concrete suggestions on how leaders should expect, foster, plan, direct, and use change for competitive advantage.

Books

Paul Hersey and Kenneth H. Blanchard. *Management of Organizational Behavior: Utilizing Human Resources.* 4th ed. Englewood Cliffs, N.J.: Prentice-Hall, 1982.

The four-part classification of leadership developed by Hersey and Blanchard has become a widely employed model. This book develops these leadership styles in greater depth and is an invaluable resource to leaders.

J. Dan Rothwell. *In Mixed Company: Small Group Com-*

munication. 2nd ed. Fort Worth, Tex.: Harcourt Brace Jovanovich, 1995.

This book is one of the best available about effective participation in groups. We recommend it to students who wish to improve their communication competence in groups, including dealing with the inevitable conflicts that develop in most groups.

Video Rentals

Platoon Tom Berenger and Willem Dafoe exhibit very different styles of leadership in this Oliver Stone film exploring the relationships among men at war. Berenger is autocratic and uses fear to motivate his troops. Dafoe is much more democratic in approach and tries to lead his squad by example.

Prime Suspect Several episodes of this BBC television series are now available on video. Starring Helen Mirren as Chief Inspector Jane Tennison, each episode chronicles the difficulties Tennison faces as a woman leading a predominantly male force of police officers and homicide investigators.

Theory and Research in Practice

1. Make a list of all the groups to which you belong. Include formal and informal groups. Bring the list to class to share. The instructor may divide the class into groups and have each group produce a list of all the types of groups identified by its members.

2. Develop an agenda for a group meeting. Include all the standard elements of an agenda discussed in the chapter. Circulate the agenda among the members of your group and revise the agenda as necessary.

3. Observe a group outside of your class. You could chose a task-oriented group, such as a city council or student government group, or a self-help group, such as Alcoholics Anonymous (if you have the group's permission). Write a brief paper in which you discuss the group in terms of (a) the phases of development you observed; (b) the leadership evident in the group; and (c) the task, social, and self-centered functions performed by the members of the group. Overall, how effective was the group in completing its task or helping its members? Which members played the most positive roles in the group? Were any members detrimental in the roles they played in the group?

PART FOUR
Dimensions of Public Communication

CHAPTER 14

Preparing to Speak

OBJECTIVES

After reading this chapter you should be able to:

- Analyze the basic features of the speech situation as it applies to your speeches.

- Identify the common purposes of public speaking.

- Select an appropriate topic for your first speech.

- Construct a specific purpose for your first speech.

- Invent your first speech, utilizing appropriate sources for information.

- Organize your speech.

Aside from the fact that they are famous in their own right, President Dwight David Eisenhower, *New York Times* columnist William Safire, historian Arthur Schlesinger, Jr., best-selling author and advisor to President Reagan Peggy Noonan, and conservative talk show host Patrick Buchanan share one other distinguishing characteristic: Each of them wrote speeches for other famous people. Eisenhower wrote speeches for General Douglas MacArthur. Safire and Buchanan wrote speeches for President Richard M. Nixon. Schlesinger wrote speeches for President John F. Kennedy, and Noonan wrote the most memorable of speeches delivered by President Ronald Reagan, including his moving eulogy of the *Challenger* astronauts.

Noonan writes at length about her role as a speech writer in the Reagan administration in her book *What I Saw at the Revolution: A Political Life in the Reagan Era*. In the process she writes about the critical role of the presidential speech writer in the history of American politics and comments on how difficult it is to prepare a message that will be delivered by someone else. Noonan also reminds us that "a speech is poetry: cadence, rhythm, imagery, sweep! A speech reminds us that words, like children, have the power to make dance the dullest beanbag of a heart."[1]

This is the first of four chapters that focus exclusively on the art and science of preparing and delivering a public speech. This chapter is designed to show that whether you are preparing a presidential address or an informative speech about buying mutual funds, the process is basically the same.

Often the toughest part of a speaking assignment is deciding where to begin. For example, you may have a general idea about what you would like to speak about but have no clue about where to begin your research. Or you may be like many students, uncertain about whether a topic that you find interesting will be interesting to your audience and appropriate to your classroom.

Let's look at the steps you need to master in order to develop your speeches. These steps will assist you in developing an overall sense of what effective public speaking involves, starting with choosing a topic that suits you, your purpose, and your audience. The steps we will discuss are

- analyzing your audience and speech situation,
- deciding on a purpose,
- choosing a topic that is suitable to both the situation and the purpose chosen,
- inventing your speech, and
- organizing your speech.

Analyzing the Situation

One of your first speech assignments may be to introduce a classmate or yourself, to share a brief story with the class, to prove a controversial point, or to illustrate your pet peeve. Whatever the assignment, you need to understand completely your audience, the situation in which you find yourself, and the expectations that come with the situation.

Audience-Focused Speaking

For starters, you need to know who your audience is. *Audience* is defined as the individuals who share and listen to a public speech. Everything you've read up to this point is important to audience analysis. Giving a speech is every bit as transactional as talking with a friend, resolving a conflict with a parent, and leading a small group. Thus, what you've already learned about communicating competently in these dimensions of communications is applicable to the public speaking dimension as well. Public speaking involves modifying and refining the knowledge and skills you have acquired, rather than learning an entirely new body of knowledge and skills.

Audience analysis, logically enough, begins with a thorough assessment of the accuracy of your current perceptions and attributions about the people to whom you'll be speaking. Will you be speaking to a class of students at a traditional four-year college, a mix of full- and part-time students at a community college, or a group of people who work full-time and are taking the class for professional improvement?

As you check the accuracy of your perceptions and attributions about the audience in general, you also will want to assess the diversity of your audience. Recall that there are three general types of diversity important to your success as a communicator: cultural, group, and individual. Cultural diversity is multidimensional and concerns individualism-collectivism, masculinity-femininity, uncertainty avoidance, and power distance. As we discussed in Chapter 7, the words you choose and the manner in which they are spoken should reflect the cultural make-up of the people with whom you communicate. This is especially true of the speech transaction, where you typically are unable to stop your speech to deal with a cultural misunderstanding between you and audience members.

Group diversity is also an important element of your audience analysis. People in your audience may be members of different religious groups, political parties, generations, social classes, genders, and occupations. The response you receive to your speech will depend heavily on how well you have assessed the extent of group diversity and how you account for it in your speech.

Following your assessment of group diversity, you will need to assess and prepare for the individual diversity present in your audience. Individual diversity, you'll recall, involves people's most significant attitudes, beliefs, and values. Individual diversity, though more difficult to assess among audience members, is not impossible to assess. The messages you receive from people in class are rich in communication cues about individual diversity. Often the messages reveal such things as religious values, political beliefs, and attitudes about people and their lifestyles. However, you may get a more exact picture of your audience if you canvass them in a more systematic way about their attitudes, beliefs, and values. Not only is it appropriate to ask people privately about attitudes, beliefs, and values that will mediate perceptions of you and your speech, it is advisable.

Finally, you'll want to make sure that the purpose of your speech is appropriate for your audience. As we'll explain shortly, not all speeches serve the same purpose. The same is true of audiences: Some audience viewpoints are intractable, regardless of how logical a speech seems. Spending your time trying to change an intractable viewpoint would be a waste of your time and the audience's as well.

Even when an audience is sympathetic to the content of your speech, however, it may not be in a position to help you. Your class, for example, has little power to help you propose federal legislation and see it enacted. On the other hand, your class could be an excellent place to start a campaign for elective office on your campus. The point, then, is that audience-focused speaking requires deciding on a purpose that is appropriate to the audience.

Audience analysis is not a static activity. Good speakers continuously analyze their audiences long after they have concluded their speech. Good speakers know what is true of audiences now may be less so in the future. Every audience is different, even when they are composed of the same people. Recognizing and adapting to this fact will help you become a more audience-responsive speaker.

general purpose
The primary function of a speech, usually to inform, to persuade, or to entertain.

specific purpose
The goal or objective you hope to achieve in speaking to a particular audience.

Selecting an Audience-Focused Purpose

As we have already said, a second key to audience-focused analysis is to think through your purpose in relation to your audience. One of the first decisions a speaker faces is the **general purpose**—the primary function—of the speech. The three most common general purposes are to inform, to persuade, and to entertain. A speaker can seek to *inform* others about things they do not already know or to *persuade* them to believe something or act in certain ways. Persuasive speeches need not seek change; they may seek to reinforce social values, as is usually the case with Fourth of July speeches and sermons. In addition, persuasive speeches may seek to inoculate people against opposing viewpoints. The third kind of speech is one that seeks to *entertain* by sharing an enjoyable experience. Obviously, these three general purposes are not mutually exclusive. A persuasive speech will also inform the audience, and an informative speech should be interesting enough that it persuades the audience to at least listen. Nevertheless, the general purpose you either have been assigned or have chosen will influence the topic you ultimately choose, because some topics will be inappropriate or only marginally appropriate to your purpose. Though controversial topics, for example, lend themselves to a persuasive speech, they are less well suited to an informative speech.

Although you may be assigned a general purpose—to inform, to persuade, or to entertain—for your early speeches, you will not be assigned a specific purpose. The **specific purpose** is the goal or objective you hope to achieve in speaking to a particular audience. What you want to accomplish specifically with your audience rests with you. For example, assume you are asked to introduce yourself to the class. What do you want your classmates to think and feel about you? Do you want them to like, respect, and admire you? Then your specific purpose might be "to have the class develop a favorable opinion of me." Clearly this is a persuasive effort. You are creating attitudes about yourself where none existed before. Thus, even in early speech assignments, you should try to articulate a specific purpose for your speech.

Choosing an Audience-Focused Topic

Once you have clearly identified the response you hope to elicit from your audience, you face one of the hardest tasks for beginning speakers, the selection of your topic. To help you in this process, we offer the following criteria for an appropriate speech topic.

1. *The topic should interest you.* If you don't care about the topic, how can you expect your audience to care?

2. *It should interest your audience or at least be capable of being made interesting.* Knowing as much as possible about your audience will help you know what will interest them.

3. *It should be appropriate for your audience.* Some topics and issues simply are not appropriate for a particular audience. You cannot talk to a group of children about safe sex, but you can talk about it with most audiences of young adults. The children will not necessarily be uninterested, but they may be too psychologically immature for the topic or their parents may object to the topic.

4. *It should be appropriate to the situation.* If your instructor has asked you to speak on your pet peeve, she or he probably is thinking of topics like "dorm food," "roommates," or "people who blow smoke in my face," not the destruction of the rain forests.

5. *It should be appropriate to the time available.* One limitation of a speech is time. Know what is expected and stick to it. Further, consider the time you have available to prepare. If the speech is to be given next week, you won't have time to send for information from your state senator. Pick a topic that you can research in the time available.

6. *It should be manageable.* Don't pick a topic beyond your abilities or resources. One of your greatest assets in speaking is your own **credibility**, or the degree to which your audience trusts and believes in you. Nothing will undermine your credibility faster than speaking on a topic with which you are unfamiliar. Know more about your topic than your audience does.

7. *It should be worthwhile.* Don't waste your audience's time. Pick a topic that will inform, persuade, or entertain by presenting them with ideas or information they haven't already heard.

> **credibility** The degree to which your audience trusts and believes in you.

Given these seven criteria, how can you come up with an appropriate topic? You could make a personal inventory of hobbies, interests, jobs, or experiences you have had that might be interesting to others. Use Box 14-1 to start a list of topics you know well enough to speak about. You could ask friends for suggestions of topics they would like to know more about. Read newspapers, news magazines, and books; reading at least one newspaper a day and one news magazine a week should provide you with an abundance of ideas for topics. Check the Internet; you may well find speech ideas among the subjects discussed on home pages and in chat groups on the Internet. And finally, brainstorm; this is also a good technique for coming up with a list of potential topics.

Inventing Your Speech

It may seem odd to think of a speech as an invention. However, just as it was not enough for Thomas Edison to simply have the idea for the light bulb, it is not enough for you to just have an idea for a speech. You need to invest time and

Your classmates can help you brainstorm for topics.

effort in developing the substance of what you plan to say. **Invention** is the creative process by which the substance of a speech is developed. Among the many sources to which you can turn for materials on your topic are personal experience and knowledge, library resources, interviews, nonprint media, and the Internet.

Using Personal Experience and Knowledge

invention The creative process by which the substance of a speech is developed.

Your own experience and knowledge is frequently the best source to consider as you begin to think about constructing your speech. Speaking about matters with which you have firsthand experience personally connects you to your message. But don't limit your search for information only to what you know firsthand. No matter how intense your experience or extensive your knowledge is, there always is more to learn from additional sources.

Box 14-1   Self-Assessment

What Could You Speak About?

One way to select an appropriate speech topic is to begin with an assessment of your own knowledge and experience. List at least three specific experiences or knowledge areas that you feel fairly confident in speaking about concerning each of the following categories.

Hobbies:

Academics:

Work:

Travel:

Family:

Using Library Resources

The library is the intellectual center of most universities and colleges—the repository of the history of ideas and thought. Although campus libraries vary in size and sophistication, the basic principles of a library search are the same. The first step is familiarization. If you are not already familiar with your library, make it a priority to become familiar immediately. (Tracking down the list of resources in Box 14-2 will help you quickly learn your way around the library.) Then follow these five steps when you do library research.

Select Key Terms   A key term is a word or phrase used in library catalogs and indexes to identify a subject; it is like the combination to a safe. If you have the right combination, you can easily open the door to information on your topic.

Box 14-2   Skill Building

Get to Know Your Library

This directed search is designed to help you familiarize yourself with your college's library as well as develop your skill at library research.

- Find the *New York Times* published on the day of your birth. Make a copy of the front page.
- Find the author, publisher, call number, and copyright date of the following items: a compact disc, a videotape recording, a scholarly journal in communication, and a book.
- Provide the name, issuing agency, and superintendent of documents number for a government document.
- Find out the number of persons living in your home state in the following categories:

  - Caucasians
  - Hispanics/Latinos

  - African Americans
  - men
  - women
  - persons aged 18–21

- Provide the specific location of the following in your library:

  - bound periodicals
  - current periodicals
  - microfilm readers
  - reference materials
  - the card catalog or on-line catalog
  - *Readers' Guide to Periodical Literature*
  - *Dissertation Abstracts*

- Find out the name of one reference librarian and his or her specialty.

The source of key terms in most university library catalogs and indexes is the *Library of Congress Subject Headings (LCSH)*. It also lists topics that are broader and narrower than a particular key term. For example, if you are interested in "green marketing," you might look under the term *recycling*. The *LCSH* indicates that information about the processing of recyclables is found under the term *recycling*, whereas information about reclaiming and reusing larger items is listed under *salvage*. Thus, you would begin your search for sources on "green marketing" with the term *recycling*.

Search the Library Catalog   Although some libraries still use a card catalog to list their book holdings, an increasing number use an online catalog, or a computerized listing of library holdings, which allows you to construct more complex searches. The principles on which the two catalogs are built are the same. They are arranged by subject, author, and title. Because you are just beginning a search on your topic, it is unlikely that you will know specific authors, titles, or call numbers, so the subject heading is the most likely basis for your search.

Computerized databases are an excellent source for information about your topic.

Let's continue to use the example of recycling. Under that term alone, you might find 80 or more publications in the listings by subject. You could look through the list, noting the call numbers of the book titles that seem to relate to your topic. The titles may suggest whether they would be relevant to your topic. Of these, you probably want to select the most recently published books.

If you are using an online catalog, you can use Boolean operators in your search. These are terms such as *and, or,* and *not,* used to narrow or broaden a computerized search of two or more related terms. For example, using the Boolean operator *or* to find books listed under either "recycling" or "landfills" might yield an additional 20 books. The Boolean operator *and* allows you to narrow the search to books that deal with some aspects of recycling. For example, under "recycling and plastics," there might be only two books dealing with both topics. Using the Boolean operator *not,* you can limit your search to books that do not deal with a certain topic. For example, you can find all the books that deal with recycling but not aluminum. Finally, you can also limit your search by specifying the year a book was published.[2]

As you can see, the online catalog can help you to expand, limit, and speed up your search. Some online terminals are connected to printers so that you can print out the results of your search. If you do not have a printed copy of your search of the catalog, however, you should note the author, title, date, and call number of each source that appears promising and then visit the stacks of the books. When you visit the stacks, it is a good idea to do a little browsing as well as finding the specific books you have noted, since it is not unusual to find a book closely related to your topic that you overlooked in your search.

One great advantage of going to books for information first is that the authors have done much of your work for you. Most books have a bibliography or foot-notes that lead to other sources of information about your topic.

Search Relevant Indexes and Abstracts   An index is a listing of sources of information, usually journals and magazines, alphabetically by topic. An abstract is a summary of an article or a report. A good library has hundreds of indexes related to specialized fields. Some indexes both list and abstract articles in journals. On the topic of recycling, for example, a good place to look for information is *Environmental Abstracts.* In addition to abstracting articles from a variety of journals, conferences, and reports, it has a review of the year's key environmental events.

For popular journals, the *Readers' Guide to Periodical Literature* is the old standby. It lists articles in publications like *Newsweek, Time,* and other popular magazines, common to most libraries. Major newspapers, such as the *New York Times, Wall Street Journal,* and the *Christian Science Monitor,* provide printed or computerized indexes that you need to consult before looking through reels of microfilm for newspaper articles on your topic. The computerized database published by InfoTrac includes the *National Newspaper Index,* covering five national newspapers.

Ask a reference librarian what indexes would be suitable for a given topic and where they are located. Make sure you have narrowed down your topic to some-thing specific before going to the librarian. For instance, "I have a speech to give tomorrow on recycling and I need some help" is less helpful than "I'm doing a speech on recycling, and I want to find out how much of our landfill space is being wasted because people don't recycle."

Use CD-ROM Searches   A CD-ROM is a compact disc used for storage and retrieval of data. CD-ROM technology has revolutionized computerized searches. For example, a search of a CD-ROM database on the topic of recy-cling—the *General Science Index (GSI)*—yielded 84 citations under "recycling," 205 under "plastic," and 6 under "recycling and plastic." Two other databases, the *Public Affairs Information Service Index (P.A.I.S.)* and *Government Documents Catalog Service (GDCS),* would undoubtedly provide additional citations.

Consult Reference Books   Frequently you need to find a very specific fact—for example, how much plastic was produced in the United States last year. You could search a dozen articles and never find that number. But a good reference book, such as the *Statistical Abstract of the United States,* puts that kind of information at your fingertips.

Perhaps you need a good quotation to begin or end your speech. Numerous books of quotations are available. A book called *Quotation Location* lists 900 published compilations of quotations.[3]

The World Almanac and Book of Facts provides current information on every topic from abortion to zoology. It also includes a chronology of the preceding year and covers events of the entire world, not just the United States. Another popular annual publication is the *Information Please Almanac.*

Facts on File and *Editorial Research Reports* are useful sources on current events and important public controversies. *Facts on File* provides a weekly digest of world news and has a cumulative index. *Editorial Research Reports* has numerous well-researched reports on topics of public significance. Both of these sources are relatively easy ways to bring yourself up to date on current topics.

Biographies, such as the *Who's Who* series (*Who's Who in America, Who's Who in American Business,* and so on) and the *Dictionary of American Biography,* help you learn about people related to your topic. The *Biography Index* (available online) will help you locate articles and books of a biographical nature.

Although the information in encyclopedias is likely to be general and dated, they can be helpful as an overview of the topic at the beginning of your search. Not only are encyclopedias available in the traditional book form, they are now on CD-ROM. You may also want to consult subject-specific encyclopedias. There are encyclopedias dealing with the social sciences, art, education, science and technology, and organizations. Do not overlook such specialized encyclopedias in conducting your early search for information. The *Encyclopedia of Associations,* for example, provides the address and phone number of relevant groups, such as the Aluminum Recycling Association.

Atlases are valuable in learning about the world. By consulting an up-to-date atlas, which is a must in the changing world, you can learn not only where a country is geographically but also important facts about it. For example, the *World Book Atlas* contains not only maps but also a wealth of information about climates, regions of the earth, natural resources, and population.

Interviews

Interviews can be an excellent source of information. But you should research your topic first; you should not expect the expert to write your speech for you. An interview should be conducted only after you have been to the library and done the research necessary to ask the interviewee intelligent questions. The section "Interviewing for Information" in Chapter 11 provides detailed advice on arranging and conducting an interview.

Nonprint Media

Many universities have extensive collections of nonprint media, including films, videotapes, recordings, photographs, and other nonprint materials that may fit

> ## Box 14-3 Critical Thinking
>
> ### *How Credible Is Internet Information?*
>
> As a speaker, what are your ethical responsibilities in using information you acquire over the Internet? Are you obligated to check the accuracy of the information you read?
>
> Do you see any advantages in using uncensored information you acquire over the Internet? Disadvantages? List the three biggest advantages and disadvantages you see in using Internet information. Share your list with class members and discuss the differences and similarities in your lists.

your topic. Or you may see something on television that is directly relevant to your speech. If you can't tape the program, you may still be able to secure a transcript. The addresses, phone numbers, and prices for ordering transcripts are given at the end of news programs like *20/20* and *60 Minutes*. Some transcripts are also available on the Internet and can be downloaded to your computer directly, saving time and money; Internet addresses are usually provided at the end of a program.

The Internet

One of the most exciting new developments for research is the Internet, a collection of computer networks connecting computers around the world. Although not exactly a superhighway (at least not yet), the Internet does allow the user to travel electronically to almost anywhere in the world. The access to information resources it provides is virtually limitless.

Use of the Internet is increasing rapidly. A survey done by Nielsen Media Research for CommerceNet in 1995 reports that 1 in 6 Americans and Canadians over age 16 have access to the Internet. Nearly 11 percent had used it in the preceding three months, and 18 million people had used the World Wide Web, a collection of thousands of sites called "home pages."[4] Although the survey did not address use by college students specifically, Internet resources are available on many campuses for little or no charge. In the 21st century, there is little doubt that the Internet, or its successor, will be one of the principal resources for speakers in inventing their messages. However, as Box 14-3 points out, speakers need to critically evaluate information they find on the Internet.

Among the most important Internet resources for speakers are e-mail, chat lines, usenet groups, and the World Wide Web.[5] E-mail (electronic mail) is a message sent from one computer, over the network, to one or more other computers. If you know the e-mail address of a source that interests you, contact

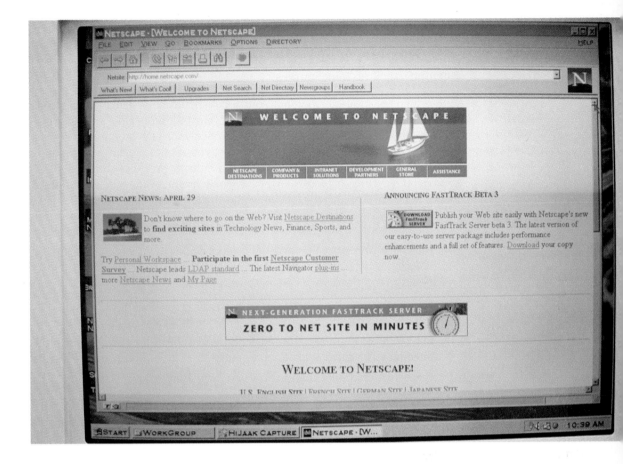

that source directly. You can e-mail most government, education, and commercial institutions.

Chat lines are real-time discussions with other computer users on topics of common interest. Multiple users can participate simultaneously and respond to each other. Although not necessarily reliable as a source of factual information (unless the participants are experts in the field), chat lines can certainly help you get ideas for speech topics. Or you can bounce ideas off other people interested in the same topic.

Usenet groups are electronic "newsletters" to which subscribers can contribute. In the field of speech communication, for example, there are usenet groups for those interested in communication theory and research and those interested in academic debate, to name just two areas.

The most useful aspect of the Internet to speakers, however, is the World Wide Web. Within each home page are connections to other sites, which can link to even more sites. Sites cover everything from sports to literature. For example, you can find the latest scores of your favorite sports or the entire text

The Internet is rapidly becoming one of the best places to search for information you can use in building your speech.

of some books on the web, including atlases, encyclopedias, and government publications. In a sense, the Internet can be thought of as a "virtual library."

Keeping Track of Your Sources

Your search for information about your topic should be systematic. Being systematic in your research not only will make your task more efficient, but it also should help you in organizing your speech once your search is finished. Thus, before beginning in-depth reading on a topic, you should prepare a preliminary bibliography of the sources you have found. You might, for example, find 20 sources on recycling that look like they will be relevant. Using note cards (4 by 6 inches is a good size), list the following information about each source:

- for all sources: author(s), preferably by full name, if an author is listed;
- for books: the exact title and the facts of publication: city, publisher, and date;
- for periodicals: the article title, volume number, date, and pages;
- for government documents: the agency issuing the document, as well as its full title and date;
- for electronic resources: the e-mail address, web site, or path by which the material was located; and
- space for additional information you may learn about as you read the source.

After constructing your preliminary bibliography, look at the most recent and most general sources in it. Beginning with the most recent source can save you a lot of work, because it may review articles and books written earlier, pointing out which are relevant and authoritative and which are not. General articles and books on your topic will give you the broad view of your topic.

As you gather materials, carefully record the facts and quotations you discover. It is important to note not only the substance of what was said but also who said it and where. Documenting such information will build your credibility with your audience and enhance your overall effectiveness as a speaker.

Write important facts, examples, quotations, and statistics on separate note cards. Figure 14-1 is an example of a card with a quotation. The advantage of this technique is that you can organize cards in any way that seems logical when you begin writing your speech.

Another strategy is to selectively photocopy pages from articles or books that seem particularly useful. Then use a highlighter or marker to identify those points you may wish to use in the speech. Cut out the points you plan to quote and paste or tape them to cards. Be sure to note the source and page number on each card.

Finally, if you are doing a computerized search, such as on the Internet, you may be able to directly download information onto a computer. For example, if

Figure 14-1 Sample Note Card for Library Research.

Heading: Number of Smokers Declining

Source: Department of Health and Human Services. (1989).
Smoking tobacco and health: A fact book. (DHHS
Publication No. CDC 87-8397). Washington, DC: U.S.
Government Printing Office, p. 5.

"In 1965, 50.2 percent of American men and 31.9 percent
of women smoked cigarettes; by 1987 this had dropped
to 31.7 and 26.8 percent."

you have access to the World Wide Web, you can find transcripts of CNN programs by going to their web site and following the instructions of your web browser for downloading files.[6]

Organizing Your Speech

There are numerous models people can use to structure their speech. We offer two examples here. The first, *Monroe's motivated sequence,* is a familiar one in communication courses. The second, *Malandro's model of organization,* is less well known but has proven to be highly effective not only in the classroom but also in corporate presentational settings.

Monroe's Motivated Sequence

The **motivated sequence** is a five-step organizational scheme, developed by speech professor Alan Monroe.[7] These five steps overlap somewhat with the introduction, body, and conclusion of a speech. The steps and their counterpart in the traditional three-part organization are the following:

1. *Attention:* Gain your audience's attention (Introduction)
2. *Need:* Show the audience that a need exists that affects them (Body)
3. *Satisfaction:* Present the solution to the need (Body)

Monroe's motivated sequence A five-step organizational scheme, developed by speech professor Alan Monroe, including (1) attention, (2) need, (3) satisfaction, (4) visualization, and (5) action.

4. *Visualization:* Help the audience imagine how their need will be met in the future (Body)

5. *Action:* State what actions must be taken to fulfill the need (Conclusion)

Using the motivated sequence, a speech advocating national health insurance might be organized in the following way:

1. *Attention:* A child dies because her parents couldn't afford to take her to the doctor.

2. *Need:* You could become one of millions of uninsured Americans who face financial ruin if they become seriously ill.

3. *Satisfaction:* National health insurance would guarantee all Americans the right to health care, regardless of their income.

4. *Visualization:* The United States would join nations like Canada, where no one fears seeing a doctor because of the cost.

5. *Action:* Write your senator and representative today, urging the passage of national health insurance.

Obviously, the motivated-sequence pattern is most directly suited to persuasive presentations. However, an informative presentation could use at least some of these steps, since informative speaking typically is the first step in a persuasive campaign. In an informative presentation, it is important to show your audience why they need to learn the information you have presented and, of course, to satisfy that need. Helping an audience visualize how they will use the information is also valuable. And often you will then want them to put what they have learned into action.

Malandro's Model of Organization

According to communication consultant and author Dr. Loretta Malandro, an effective speech should progress through six steps that make up the traditional introduction, body, and conclusion.[8] No step should be skipped, and they should be presented in the order given here:

Introduction

1. Open with impact.
2. Focus on the thesis statement.
3. Connect with the audience.

Body

4. Present the main points.

Conclusion

thesis statement   A statement that expresses the central point of your speech.

5. Summarize the main points.

6. Close with impact.

Let's briefly examine each step and how it relates to the traditional introduction–body–conclusion format of a speech. The first three steps of the Malandro model are elements of the introduction, when the speaker makes a first impression on the audience and either succeeds or fails in engaging their interest.

1. *Open with impact.*   Introduce your presentation dramatically or humorously. Beginning a speech with "Uh, um, well, I guess I'll talk about dorm food today" is a sure turnoff. There are many ways to capture your audience's attention. You can begin with an appropriate joke, a startling statistic, a story, a quotation, a personal experience, a thought-provoking question, or a reference to current affairs, the audience, or the occasion.

2. *Focus on your thesis statement.*   The **thesis statement** expresses the central point of your speech. For example, if you were opposed to a planned tuition hike on your campus, your thesis statement might be "The students of this university should not be forced to pay more for less." If, however, you wanted to inform your audience about the variety of financial assistance available to them, your thesis statement might be "With effort and persistence, you can obtain a student loan or scholarship to help meet your college expenses."

3. *Connect with your audience.*   Answer the questions "What's in this for my audience? Why is it in their personal or professional interest to listen to me? Why should the audience identify with what I'm going to say?" For example, will the proposed tuition hike keep some in your audience from completing their degree? Make the connection to your audience clear in the introduction to the speech.

The introduction is also a good place to build your credibility as a speaker. Let the audience know you understand their concerns and have their best interests at heart. If you have special expertise on the topic, let your audience know now so that they can appreciate what is to come.

4. *Organize the body of your speech.*   The next step in the Malandro model applies to the development of the central idea you want to convey. Usually, the body of the speech is organized around two to four main points, which should be previewed right after the introduction, before treating each point in detail. (We will look further at other elements and organizational patterns in the body of the speech.) The preview may be as simple as saying, "I'm going to present three ways to save money on groceries: clipping coupons, watching for store ads, and buying generic brands." Or it may specifically enumerate the three main points of the speech: "You can save money on your groceries—first, by clipping coupons; second, by watching store ads; and third, by buying generic brands."

5. *Summarize your main points.* The first and most important function of a conclusion is to remind your audience what you told them. Repeat the main points in order and any particularly significant subpoints. Remind the listeners what they have heard.

6. *Close with impact.* The conclusion is your chance to leave a lasting impression. Reinforce your specific purpose and wrap up the presentation. You want your audience to at least think about doing what you've asked them to do. Just as listeners are turned off by a weak introduction, they can be let down by a poor conclusion, such as "Well, I guess that's about it." Here are some ways to finish with a flourish:

- Present a short, memorable *quotation* that will reinforce your specific purpose.
- Use a brief *anecdote* or story that illustrates your point.
- Make a *direct appeal* or "call to action," especially to conclude a persuasive presentation. For example, if you are opposed to a tuition hike, appeal to the audience to contact the board of trustees or sign a petition supporting your position. Perhaps the most famous direct appeal to action was the one President John F. Kennedy made in his inaugural speech: "Ask not what your country can do for you, but what you can do for your country."[9]
- *Return to your opening.* One of the best ways to end a speech is to bring the listeners full circle. If, for example, you began your plea for people to sign organ donor cards with the story of a little girl who needed a liver transplant, at the end of the speech you could describe how her life had been saved because a donor was found for her.

VIDEO FILE

If you have access to the videotape that accompanies this book, view Part V, which includes the speech by Sally Garber, which is outlined here and shown in Segment 1.

Following is a sample speech outline incorporating the six steps of Malandro's model. Notice how the speaker, Sally Garber, introduces her speech with a thought-provoking question and presents some important statistics that show the topic she is addressing is of widespread concern. Her speech has three clear main points, which she previews for her audience. She also cites a number of credible sources (the full bibliographical information about them is given in the reference list at the end of the outline). Finally, she summarizes and closes her speech with impact. We have highlighted a number of these features in the margin of the outline.

Structuring the Body of the Speech

In order to communicate competently with your audience, you need to prepare a speech that is well structured. The main, or most important, points need to stand out and to be worded in a memorable way. The ideas supporting those main points—the subpoints and supporting points—should be clearly stated and presented in an organizational pattern that fits the topic.

main points The key ideas that support the thesis statement of a speech.

Main Points As a result of understanding the **main points,** or key ideas that support the thesis statement, your audience should be informed, persuaded,

Sample Speech Outline
Dieting and Physical Activity
by *Sally Garber*

Specific purpose: To persuade the audience that restrictive dieting is destructive and to empower them to make better lifestyle choices.

Specific purpose is to change both attitudes and behavior.

Introduction

I. **Open with impact:** How many of you took a good look at yourself in the mirror this morning—Did you like what you saw?

   A. Statistics show that a large number of Americans would answer, No.

   B. According to the *University of California Berkeley Wellness Letter,* more than one third of American women and nearly one quarter of men are trying to lose weight at any given time ("A new spin," 1995, p.1).

   C. As a society we are not happy with our looks and are spending billions of dollars a year struggling to achieve ideal bodies.

   D. Yet the percentage of overweight Americans continues to increase.

II. **Focus on thesis statement:** In this struggle to lose weight is where the problem lies.

III. **Connect to audience:** Our methods behind our motives are destructive; dieting is destructive.

Speech begins with a thought-provoking question.

"Focus on thesis, statement" and "Connect with audience" are labeled.

Body

(**Preview:** Today we will take a look at the issue of restrictive dieting. We will explore some recent trends in dieting. We will explore why people turn to dieting, why dieting does not work, and why it is claimed unhealthy and destructive. After discussing the issue, I will then give you some ideas on what you can do to achieve a healthy body.)

Speech is previewed for audience.

I. **Main point:** Every day, Americans struggle with their weight, resulting in desperate attempts to be beautiful.

   A. "The obese now comprise one-third of the American population—58 million Americans, up from just one-quarter 15 years ago—with the trend cutting across race, age and gender. Overall, 58 million Americans are overweight, with adults weighing 8 pounds more on average than they did a decade ago," according to Tufts University, October 1994 ("To diet," 1994, p. 3).

Main points begin with roman numeral I.

Direct quotations are indicated by quotation marks, and the source is cited in parentheses. Your instructor may prefer a different method of citing sources.

B. So what can be done, one might ask? It all depends on who you ask.

   1. Pro-dieters would simply reply, "Go on a diet."

      a. Anyone who has ever struggled with weight loss could tell you that it isn't that easy.

      b. It sure sounds great, though, according to the recent television advertisements—you can have a shake for breakfast, a shake for lunch, and a sensible dinner, and you'll be on your way to a new you!

   2. Anti-dieters would refute this in saying that this way of thinking is where problems arise.

      a. According to *Nutrition Today,* April 1993, "Treatments [for obesity] based on caloric restriction, or dieting, had only temporary effects. . . . [Most] persons treated with restrictive diets will regain lost weight" (Foreyt & Goodrick, 1993, p. 4).

      b. Restrictive diets are ineffective.

C. How do we convince people that dieting is counterproductive to their goal of weight loss?

   1. There is a nondieting approach and it works, but we must first explore why diets fail.

   2. The best way to convince people that it works and that it is ultimately the healthiest way to achieve your goal is to simply give them the facts.

(**Signpost:** So let's explore these facts; why are people turning to diets and why are their weight-loss attempts failing?)

II. **Main point:** Starting about the beginning of this century, Western civilization began to place an extreme emphasis on becoming thin.

A. This resulted in discrimination against the obese, who came to be judged on their appearance rather than their character.

   1. This has led to a situation today in which unloved and unhappy people feel that the only way to be happy is to lose weight.

   2. The tragedy for the overweight occurs when the desperation to be thin is combined with the thought that diets are effective.

B. The continuing popularity of dieting can be explained by the

---

Margin notes:

When a word is added by the speaker to a quotation, it is indicated by [brackets]. Omissions are indicated by ellipses.

Signposts are transitional statements between main points.

emotional cycle in which the obese seem to struggle. [Turn on overhead.]

    1. They begin by feeling fat and unloved.

    2. Wanting to be loved and happy, they feel that they must lose weight in order to gain their desired emotions.

    3. Through many efforts they realize that their goals are unrealistic, leading them to eventually lose self-control, regaining any weight they may have lost.

    4. This leaves them feeling like failures.

    5. Thus, they are further damaged and the cycle continues until something is done. [Turn off overhead.]

    6. These beliefs that they are failures are rooted in the thought that they fail because they lack willpower, which not only is a falsehood but also promotes destructive behavior.

C. At the beginning of a caloric restrictive diet, moods are elevated.

    1. Dieters are feeling good about themselves because they are motivated, their energy increases, and weight is lost.

    2. This is where the misconception that diets work comes into play.

D. Soon after weight is lost the restriction of calories leads to uncontrollable cravings for high-fat foods.

    1. These cravings lead to bingeing and purging, starvation, and other extremely serious eating disorders.

    2. The resulting effect is exactly the opposite of what the dieter intended to achieve.

E. All of these facts have led many to believe that restrictive dieting has more negative than positive effects.

III. **Main point:** Let's explore the alternatives we have to achieve a healthier lifestyle and make better choices. [Overhead]

A. First, we must begin by knowing that successful weight control is a lifelong commitment, not a series of crash diets.

    1. To increase chances of long-term success, it is important to set realistic goals that lead to slow, steady success.

    2. "Gradual changes in diet and physical activity which build on success are expected to lead to more lasting lifestyle changes," states *Nutrition Today*, June 1995 (Blair, 1995, p. 110).

Speaker includes note to herself to turn on the overhead projector.

She also includes note to turn off the projector.

Would a signpost signaling shift to third main point have helped?

B. Second, it is necessary to remember that eating should be a pleasurable experience.

   1. Food should be enjoyed.

   2. "Everyone should use eating as a positive opportunity to relax as they nourish themselves," according to Tufts University, October 1994 ("To Diet," 1994, p. 6).

C. Along with enjoying your meals, wise food choices are equally important.

   1. We have seen that deprivation is not the answer; good healthy choices are.

   2. It is necessary to reduce daily fat intake in order to achieve a healthier body.

   3. Eating less fat will reduce your risk for heart disease, chronic fatigue, and diabetes, as well as other major health problems.

   4. Eating less fat will increase your energy levels, motivating you to get moving and to exercise, which brings me to our last requirement, exercise.

D. In order to achieve a healthy body, you must combine physical activity with a healthy eating plan.

   1. Weight loss will not happen overnight, and it will not happen depriving yourself of your favorite foods; but it cannot happen until you exercise.

   2. Healthy weight loss can occur only when your muscles receive oxygen—you must breathe, you must move.

E. The smallest amount of activity proves beneficial.

   1. Begin by doing work in the yard, or by taking a walk with a friend or pet, or by taking the stairs instead of the elevator.

   2. "Periods as short as 8 to 10 minutes that total 30 minutes by the end of the day are adequate," according to *Nutrition Today*, June 1995 (Blair, 1995, p. 111).

   3. The idea of "no pain, no gain," is dead.

      a. Low-impact exercise, something as simple as walking or riding your bike instead of driving to school is the answer.

      b. But it must coincide with a healthy eating plan that includes choosing lots of fruits, vegetables, and grains, and definitely not deprivation.

   4. There are no more excuses; given these guidelines, it is not impossible to reach your goals.

Conclusion

I. Summarize: It is no secret that those who exercise and eat well regularly have a better chance for survival, they need less medical care, have more energy, and enjoy life to the fullest.

II. Close with impact: Believe it or not, living life to the fullest and achieving a healthy lifestyle can be an enjoyable process.

    A. It's not just about losing weight, it's a matter of choices.

        1. It's about feeling good about yourself.

        2. It's about leading a healthy balanced life.

        3. It's about setting and reaching goals in all areas of your life.

    B. So I leave you with this: enjoy your food, enjoy your exercise, but most importantly, enjoy your life.

Conclusion begins with a summary. But are the main points really summarized here?

References

A new spin on yo-yo diets. (1995, January). *University of California at Berkeley Wellness Letter, 1,* 1–2.

Blair, S. N. (1995). Diet and activity: The synergistic merger. *Nutrition Today, 30,* 108–112.

Foreyt, J. P., & Goodrick, G. K. (1993). Weight management without dieting. *Nutrition Today, 28,* 4–9.

To diet or not? The experts battle it out. (1994, October). *Tufts University Diet and Nutrition Letter, 12,* 3–6.

Speaker lists references at end of speech with full bibliographical citation. Your instructor may prefer a different method of citing sources. Whatever method is used, accurate source citation is important.

or entertained in accordance with your specific purpose. In developing your main points, make sure they are few in number, focused, parallel in structure, simply stated, and balanced in treatment. Let us examine each of those guidelines in turn.

NUMBER Every speech needs to be anchored around two to four main points. (If you have only one, then it is probably the same as your thesis statement, and what you are identifying as subpoints are in fact main points.) More than five main points are too many for an audience to absorb. Three seems to be ideal. The audience (not to mention the speaker) usually can easily grasp three key ideas, especially if they are organized in a memorable fashion. As the number of main points increases, each one tends to become less important, and the chances of the speaker or the audience forgetting one or more of them tend to increase. Obviously, some topics do not fit into three neat pigeonholes, but if you find yourself with six, seven, or eight main points, you may be trying to cover too much in your speech.

FOCUS   The main points should clearly relate to the thesis statement. They should fully develop it, without going beyond the focus of the speech. For example, if the thesis statement of a speech on the structure of the federal government were "The federal government consists of three separate branches that check and balance one another," the three main points would be obvious:

    I. The legislative branch is the Congress.

    II. The executive branch includes the president and the Cabinet.

    III. The judicial branch includes the Supreme Court and the lower courts.

If, for some reason, the speaker decided not to include the judicial branch, the thesis statement would have to account for the omission or risk leaving the audience wondering why such a significant point was left out. If the speech, on the other hand, had a fourth main point, "Corruption in government is a serious problem," the thesis statement would need reformulating or the purpose of the speech would need rethinking.

Each main point should express only one idea. "Corruption exists in Congress, and laws begin in Congress as bills" is a statement of two disparate ideas, which should be expressed in two separate main points:

    I. Laws begin in Congress as bills.

    II. Corruption exists in Congress.

PARALLEL STRUCTURE   Because the main points form the essence of a speech, they should be stated clearly, concisely, and memorably. One of the best ways to make main points memorable is to express them in parallel fashion. To see the effect of parallel construction, compare these two sets of main points:

    I. Congress is corrupt.

    II. There are corrupt members of the executive branch.

    III. Some judges take bribes.

or

    I. Corruption corrodes Congress.

    II. Corruption corrodes the White House.

    III. Corruption corrodes the judiciary.

Obviously, the second set is easier to remember because the main points have a parallel structure. The repetition of the phrase "corruption corrodes" stresses the focus of this speech—that all three branches experience corruption.

SIMPLICITY   Whereas a reader can reread anything that is complex or confusing, an audience listening to a speaker has only a limited opportunity to process information. If you phrase your main points as complex sentences, you may lose your audience. To see how concise and simple language can help make the structure of a speech clear, compare these two sets of main points:

> **subpoint** An idea that supports a main point.

    I. AIDS is transmitted through unprotected sexual relations, including homosexual and heterosexual encounters.

   II. AIDS is transmitted when drug users, often desperate for their next fix, share dirty needles.

  III. AIDS is transmitted by the exchange of blood, such as in a transfusion or between a mother and her unborn child.

or

    I. AIDS is transmitted through unprotected sex.

   II. AIDS is transmitted through sharing of needles.

  III. AIDS is transmitted by blood.

Obviously the second set is easier to understand because the main points are stated as simply and concisely as possible.

BALANCE   Another important characteristic of a good speech is balance among the main points. For example, if one main point takes up two thirds of the speech, audience members may wonder why it is so much more important than the other main points, or they may suspect that the speaker forgot one of the main points. Try to make sure that each main point gets equal treatment.

Subpoints   A **subpoint** is an idea that supports a main point. It is to a main point what a main point is to a thesis statement. Each main point should have at least two and no more than five subpoints. It rarely makes sense to have only one subpoint under a main point. Like main points, subpoints should be parallel in structure, simply stated, and given equal treatment. Here is the outline of the speech on the structure of the federal government, with subpoints added:

  I. The legislative branch makes the laws.   **[main point]**
    A. The House of Representatives is based on population.   **[subpoint]**
    B. The Senate provides each state with equal representation.   **[subpoint]**

  II. The executive branch enforces the laws.
    A. The president is the chief executive officer.
    B. The Cabinet consists of the heads of the executive departments.

  III. The judicial branch interprets the laws.

A. The Supreme Court is the final arbitrator of the law.

B. Lower courts must follow the Supreme Court's rulings.

Supporting Points   Some subpoints require further support and subdivision into **supporting points.** Here is part of the outline of the speech about the federal government, with supporting points added:

[main point]

[subpoint]

[supporting point]

[supporting point]

I. The legislative branch makes the laws.

  A. The House of Representatives is defined in the Constitution.

    1. The qualifications for office are specified in the Constitution.

    2. The powers of the House are specified in the Constitution.

Think carefully before you subdivide supporting points, however. A speech whose structure is too complex probably will lose the audience. What's more, most classroom speeches do not allow enough time to develop most main points beyond the level of supporting points. If a supporting point seems to lend itself to further subdivision, ask yourself first whether it is really a subpoint instead, whether some of the subpoints are really main points, and whether the topic is too broad. If your answer is no to all of these questions, go ahead and subdivide the supporting point, using lowercase letters in your outline to indicate the points of further support:

[main point]

[subpoint]

[supporting point]
[further support]
[further support]
[further support]

I. The legislative branch makes the laws.

  A. The House of Representatives is defined in the Constitution.

    1. The qualifications for office are specified in the Constitution.
      a. At least 25 years of age
      b. Citizen of the U.S. for at least 7 years
      c. Resident of the state represented

Signposts   To highlight and connect the main points of your speech for your audience, use transitional statements, or **signposts.** For example, you might say something as simple as "My second point is . . . " or "Now that you understand the problem, let's examine some possible solutions." Signposts serve as guides along the path of your speech so that your audience will know where you have been, where you are, and where you are going next.

supporting point
An idea that supports a subpoint.

signposts Transitional statements that bridge the main points of a speech.

Organizational Patterns   You can use a number of different patterns to organize the body of your speech, including time, extended narrative, spatial, categorical, and problem–solution. Figure 14-2 gives examples of these patterns, and the following pages describe them further. These are all linear patterns, the organizational structure of preference for mainstream North America culture. As Box 14-4 points out, other cultures may prefer other kinds of patterns, such as waves, spirals, and stars.

Time Pattern
Specific purpose: to inform audience how to change a tire.
I. Remove jack and spare from trunk
II. Use jack to raise car
III. Remove flat tire
IV. Replace with spare tire
V. Lower car

Categorical Pattern
Specific purpose: to inform listeners about types of classes they may take at the university.
I. General education courses
II. Courses in the major
III. Electives

Spatial Pattern
Specific purpose: to inform audience about regions of the U.S.
I. Eastern seaboard
II. Midwest
III. Rocky Mountains
IV. Pacific States

Narrative Pattern
Specific purpose: to entertain the audience with the story of Little Red Riding Hood.
I. Red sets off to deliver goodies to Grandma
II. Red encounters the Wolf and reveals where she is going
III. Red meets Wolf in Grandma's clothing
IV. Wolf is going to eat Red
V. Hunter kills Wolf and rescues Red

Problem-Solution Pattern
I. The problem is explained.
A. The harm of the problem is shown.
B. The qualitative or quantitative significance of the problem is shown.
C. The cause or causes of the problem are identified.
I. The solution to the problem is proposed.
A. The solution is described.
B. The feasibility of the solution is explained.
C. Advantages of the solution are explained.

Figure 14-2
Examples of Organizational Patterns

TIME   Many topics lend themselves to a temporal sequence. A **time pattern** is based on chronology or sequence of events. Topics of a historical nature are likely to follow a time sequence. Suppose you were speaking about the history of the U.S. space program, as did Tom Wolfe in his book *The Right Stuff*. Your speech might be divided into the following main points:

I. The space race begins in the 1950s with the launch of *Sputnik*.

II. The U.S.S.R. puts the first men into space in the 1960s.

III. The U.S. sets the goal to land on the moon by the end of the 1960s.

IV. Neil Armstrong is the first human to land on the moon in July 1969.

time pattern   A pattern of organization based on chronology or a sequence of events.

Speeches about a process, such as "how-to" speeches, are frequently organized by time sequence as well. A speech about learning to ski might be organized around these three main points:

I. Select the right equipment.

II. Invest in lessons.

III. Practice!

EXTENDED NARRATIVE   A second pattern of organization is the **extended narrative,** in which the entire body of the speech is the telling of a story, with a climactic point at the end. This organizational pattern is well suited to speeches whose purpose is to entertain. If, for example, you were to tell the story of your first blind date, you might organize your speech around these main points:

I. I am asked to go out with a blind date.

II. I meet the date.

III. Disaster follows.

A persuasive speech can also be built around an extended narrative of some incident that dramatizes the problem you are addressing. For example, a persuasive speech warning about the risks of drinking too much might be structured as an extended narrative and organized around the following main points:

I. Jim had too much to drink at a fraternity party.

II. His frat brothers dared him to hop a moving freight train.

III. Jim attempted to jump on the moving train.

IV. He lost his balance and fell under the train; both of his legs were severed.

V. Jim lived and has dedicated his life to fighting alcohol abuse.

Notice that a story needs not only a plot line but also characters, including a central character with whom the audience can identify. In this particular story, the speaker would seek to create a sympathetic portrayal of Jim, the protagonist. Each point would be developed in detail, and the audience held in suspense as the story unfolds. The moral of the story should not have to be stated explicitly but should be apparent to the audience by the end. The effectiveness of this kind of speech would be undermined if the thesis were stated at the beginning, as is customary.

extended narrative
A pattern of organization in which the entire body of the speech is the telling of a story.

spatial pattern A pattern of organization based on physical space or geography.

SPACE   A **spatial pattern** of organization is based on physical space or geography. Some topics lend themselves to a spatial or geographic order. For example, if you wanted to discuss weather patterns in the United States, you might divide the topic geographically into east, south, north, and west. If you were trying to explain how a ship is constructed, you might do so in terms of fore, midship, and aft. Or if you were giving a tour of your hometown, your points might look something like these:

Box 14-4   Considering Diversity

Cultural Variations in Organizational Patterns

Not all cultures and groups within a larger culture are comfortable with the kind of linear organizational patterns commonly discussed in public speaking classes. Cheryl Jorgensen-Earp has suggested that women and some ethnic speakers use less linear, more organic patterns. For example, one pattern found in the speeches of many women and African Americans is the "wave." Much like a wave cresting, receding, and then cresting again, a speech following this pattern continually returns to the basic theme, repeating a phrase again and again throughout the speech. Perhaps the most familiar example is Dr. Martin Luther King, Jr.'s, "I Have a Dream" speech, which gets its title from the constant repetition of the phrase. In addition, King uses the theme "Let freedom ring" repeatedly as he brings the speech to its dramatic conclusion.

Other patterns suggested by Jorgenson-Earp include a "spiral" pattern, which repeats points as does the wave, but with each point growing in intensity, as the speech builds to its pinnacle at the conclusion. A third pattern she suggests is the "star" pattern, with all points of the star being of equal importance. Thus, a speaker can present the points in any order in support of the common theme that encircles the star and holds the speech together.

As a speaker, you should carefully consider your audience's cultural background as it affects their organizational preferences as well as your own cultural affinity for certain patterns of organization. Although cultural diversity provides the opportunity to expand the ways in which speeches may be organized, it should not be used as an excuse for a lack of any coherent organizational pattern.

SOURCE: These patterns are cited in Clella Jaffe, *Public Speaking: A Cultural Perspective* (Belmont, Calif.: Wadsworth, 1995), 187–92. They are based on a telephone interview by Jaffe with Jorgensen-Earp, as well as the latter's unpublished works.

I. The east side is mostly residential.

II. The central part of town is the business district.

III. The west side is largely industrial.

CATEGORIES   A **categorical pattern** of organization is based on natural divisions in the subject matter. The federal government, as we have already shown, can be naturally divided into the legislative, executive, and judicial branches. Communication messages can be naturally divided into verbal and nonverbal categories. The essential principle is to divide the topic according to its natural boundaries and avoid creating false categories. Although it may be convenient, for example, to identify people in terms of some specific group, it can also be highly misleading or even offensive. Much social and ethnic prejudice is rooted in the stereotyping of people into arbitrary categories.

PROBLEM–SOLUTION   Some speeches are intended to propose a solution to an ongoing problem. Usually, the purpose of this type of speech is persuasion, and its organizational structure is a **problem–solution pattern** (also known as the

categorical pattern
A pattern of organization based on natural divisions in the subject matter.

problem–solution pattern A pattern of organization that analyzes a problem in terms of (1) harm, (2) significance, and (3) cause, and that proposes a solution, which is (1) described, (2) feasible, and (3) advantageous.

Television meteorologists use spatial patterns of organization to deliver information.

stock issues approach). The problem is analyzed in terms of harm, significance, and cause. The solution is then described, and its feasibility and advantages are explained. A speech about the need for better national health care, for example, would have two main points, each amplified by three subpoints.

[problem]   I.   Millions of Americans do not have access to adequate health care.

[harm]   A. People risk suffering and death without adequate health insurance.

[significance]   B. Over 37 million Americans lack health insurance.

[cause]   C. There is a gap between government-sponsored health care (Medicaid and Medicare) and private insurance.

[solution]   II.   We need a program of national health insurance to fill the gaps.

[description]   A. All businesses will be taxed to provide national health insurance.

[feasibility]   B. Similar programs exist in almost every other industrialized country in the world.

C. No longer will people be denied access to medical care simply   [advantages]
because they cannot pay.

The relationship between harm (subpoint I.A.) and significance (subpoint I.B.) is important. Harm has to do with the adverse consequences of the problem, in this case, potential suffering and death. Significance has to do with the extent of the problem. It would be unfortunate if 100 people in a nation of 250 million were at risk of suffering or death because of an inadequate health care system, but it would not be a significant problem in a nation of that size. If millions of people were at risk, however, then the problem would be significant. Because there can be numerous solutions to a problem, it is also important to stress both the feasibility (subpoint II.B.) and the advantages (subpoint II.C.) of the solution you propose, if you hope to have it adopted.

Summary

To prepare for giving a public speech you need to (1) analyze the situation with which you are faced, (2) decide on both a general and a specific purpose; (3) choose a topic that is suitable to both the situation and the purposes you have chosen, (4) invent the substance of your speech, and (5) organize your speech.

In analyzing the situation, consider both the nature of your assignment and the audience you will face. Look for clues that will help you understand them, such as their cultural, group, and individual diversity. The three most common general purposes, or primary functions, of a speech are to inform, to persuade, or to entertain. Your specific purpose is your goal or objective in speaking to a particular audience.

An appropriate speech topic should (1) interest you, (2) interest your audience, (3) be appropriate to the situation, (4) be appropriate to the time available, (5) be within your abilities and resources, and (6) be worthwhile.

There are many ways to come up with an appropriate topic, including making a personal inventory, talking to friends, reading widely, checking the Internet, and brainstorming. The process of inventing your speech includes looking for sources of information for the substance of your speech. Such sources include your own experience, general sources of information, interviews with experts, computerized searches, and specialized information sources.

You need to develop a clearly organized speech. One pattern is Monroe's five-step, motivated sequence. Another is the pattern developed by Malandro that (1) opens with impact, (2) focuses on the thesis statement, (3) connects with the audience, (4) organizes the speaker's ideas into main points, with subpoints and supporting points, (5) summarizes the main points, and (6) closes with impact. It is useful to preview the main points before discussing them in detail. Common organizational patterns include time, extended narrative, spatial, categorical, and problem–solution. Transitional statements, called signposts, help your audience follow your organizational pattern.

Another Look

Books

C. I. Hovland, W. Mandel, E. H. Campbell, T. Brock, A. S. Luchins, A. E. Cohen, W. J. McGuire, I. L. Janis, R. I. Feierabend, and N. H. Anderson. *The Order of Presentation in Persuasion.* New Haven, Conn.: Yale University Press, 1957.

In what order should a speaker put his or her arguments? If two sides are presented on a topic, which has the advantage—the first or the last one presented? These are questions known in the field as "primacy-recency" effects. It turns out that sometimes the first arguments are more influential—a primacy effect—whereas at other times, the last arguments are more effective—a recency effect. This book represents the classic studies investigating this question.

Peggy Noonan. *What I Saw at the Revolution: A Political Life in the Reagan Era.* New York: Random House, 1990.

Although this entire book is informative and entertaining, Chapter 5 is especially relevant to this textbook. Titled "Speech! Speech! Speech!" it gives an excellent idea about the manner in which professional speech writers go about preparing a speech and the special problems they face. Chapter 5 also does a good job of illustrating just how important public speeches are to presidential politics.

Articles

Ralph L. Rosnow. "Whatever Happened to the Law of Primacy?" *Journal of Communication* 16 (1966): 10–31.

This study reexamines the research on the "primacy-recency" question. Rosnow finds that no general law of primacy exists and that some factors seem to favor primacy and others recency.

Kent E. Menzel and Lori Carrell. "The Relationship Between Preparation and Performance in Public Speaking." *Communication Education* 43 (1994): 17–26.

This study demonstrates that there is a positive relationship between students' preparation for speaking and the quality of their speeches. The quality of the speech is enhanced by total preparation time, time spent preparing visual aids, number of rehearsals, research, and preparation of speech notes, as well as cumulative GPA.

Video Rentals

Speechless This romantic comedy, starring Michael Keaton and Geena Davis, is about two political speech writers who work for opposing candidates. The movie is loosely based on the real-life relationship between James Carville, who managed the Clinton presidential campaign in 1992, and Mary Matalin, who was a high-ranking official in the opposing campaign for then-President George Bush. The movie is not only entertaining but also illuminating regarding the role of the speech writers who craft the words spoken by political candidates.

Theory and Research in Practice

1. Research shows that clear organization will enhance your credibility as a speaker and increase your audience's comprehension of your speech. To practice your organizational skills, see if you can create a logical outline from the scrambled list of points you see here. The outline may be developed as an individual or group exercise, depending on your instructor's instructions.

Place the number of the statement where it best fits in the outline that follows.

1. Use fresh bread, preferably whole-grain.

2. Use a quality jelly or jam, made without artificial additives.

3. Use either plain or chunky peanut butter.

4. You must have the necessary ingredients.

5. Fold the wax paper neatly around the sandwich.

6. Place the sandwich in a paper bag.

7. Use biodegradable wrappers, such as wax paper, rather than plastic wrap.

8. You need to package the sandwich to take to school.

9. Put the two slices together.

10. Spread the first slice with peanut butter.

11. Spread the other slice with jelly or jam.

12. You need to assemble the sandwich.

13. To inform the class how to make a peanut butter and jelly sandwich.

14. First make sure you have the necessary ingredients.

15. Finally, wrap the sandwich.

16. Second, assemble the sandwich.

17. Enjoy your lunch and go to a movie with the money you've saved.

18. You can save money and eat better.

19. Today you will learn how to make the perfect peanut butter and jelly sandwich.

20. Are you tired of spending five dollars for a greasy hamburger and fries?

21. Making a peanut butter and jelly sandwich involves three basic steps: having the ingredients, assembling the sandwich, and packaging the sandwich.

22. After you have the ingredients, you need to make the sandwich.

23. Unless you are eating it immediately, the sandwich must be wrapped to stay fresh.

24. To review, there are three steps:

Specific purpose: _____

Introduction

I. Open with impact: _____

II. Focus: _____

III. Connect with your audience: _____

Body

(Preview:) _____

I. Main point: _____

    A. _____

    B. _____

    C. _____

(Signpost:) _____

II. Main point: _____

    A. _____

    B. _____

    C. _____

(Signpost:) _____

III. Main point: _____

    A. _____

    B. _____

    C. _____

Conclusion

I. Summarize: _____

    A. _____

    B. _____

    C. _____

II. Close with impact: _____

CHAPTER FIFTEEN

Presenting Your Speech

OBJECTIVES

After reading this chapter you should be able to:

- Recognize and manage the common sources of speech anxiety, using techniques such as visualization, relaxation imagery, and constructive self-talk.

- Recognize the strengths and weaknesses of manuscript, memorized, impromptu, and extemporaneous methods for delivering a speech.

- Describe the relationship between delivery and the eight basic components of the nonverbal communication system.

- Display nonverbal communication behaviors characteristic of effective delivery, including control of the speaking environment; proper attire; eye contact and expressive facial cues; vocal variation in pitch, rate, rhythm, and tempo; clear and distinct vocal articulation; and gestures and movements that serve as emblems, illustrators, and regulators.

- Control distracting self-adapting behaviors.

- Use time to enhance your credibility and communicate urgency, drama, humor, and the like during your speech.

- Explain the guidelines for developing a proactive, rather than reactive, delivery.

What an audience thinks during and following a speech depends largely on the content of the message, including the care with which it was invented and organized. But the audience's reaction also depends on how well you deliver the speech, a process on which this chapter focuses. **Delivery,** the nonverbal behaviors by which a speaker conveys his or her message to an audience, should complement the content of the speech. Although effective delivery sometimes can camouflage a poorly prepared speech, it is no substitute for a carefully prepared one.

Delivery is a complex process, one you need to start thinking about well in advance of sharing your speech with an audience. In this chapter we'll look at

delivery The nonverbal behaviors by which a speaker conveys his or her message to an audience.

385

Box 15-1   Self-Assessment

What Is Your Level of Public Speaking Anxiety?

The following is a self-report measure of public speaking anxiety. Respond to each statement honestly and work quickly. Indicate the extent to which you agree or disagree with each statement and score yourself as follows: strongly agree = 1, agree = 2, undecided = 3, disagree = 4, strongly disagree = 5.

____ 1. While preparing for giving a speech I feel tense and nervous.

____ 2. I feel tense when I see the words *speech* and *public speech* on a course outline when studying.

____ 3. My thoughts become confused and jumbled when I am giving a speech.

____ 4. Right after giving a speech I feel that I have had a pleasant experience.

____ 5. I get anxious when I think about a speech coming up.

____ 6. I have no fear of giving a speech.

____ 7. Although I am nervous just before starting a speech, I soon settle down after starting and feel calm and comfortable.

____ 8. I look forward to giving a speech.

____ 9. When the instructor announces a speaking assignment in class I can feel myself getting tense.

____ 10. My hands tremble when I am giving a speech.

____ 11. I feel relaxed while giving a speech.

____ 12. I enjoy preparing for a speech.

____ 13. I am in constant fear of forgetting what I prepared to say.

____ 14. I get anxious if someone asks me something about my topic that I do not know.

____ 15. I face the prospect of giving a speech with confidence.

____ 16. I feel that I am in complete possession of myself while giving a speech.

____ 17. My mind is clear when giving a speech.

____ 18. I do not dread giving a speech.

____ 19. I perspire just before giving a speech.

____ 20. My heart beats very fast just as I start a speech.

____ 21. I experience considerable anxiety while sitting in the room just before my speech starts.

____ 22. Certain parts of my body feel very tense and rigid while giving a speech.

SOURCE: Copyright by the Speech Communication Association, 1970, from James C. McCroskey, "Special Reports: Measures of Communication-Bound Anxiety," *Speech Monographs* 37 (1970): 269–77, by permission.

- the relationship between effective delivery and speech anxiety,
- common methods of delivery,
- the relationship between delivery and audience diversity, and
- the functional role nonverbal communication plays in delivery.

Speech Anxiety

Anxiety is the word we give to feelings of fear and uncertainty usually accompanied by physical symptoms such as butterflies in the stomach, perspiring, and unsteadiness. Not only is anxiety a fact of life for college students, it frequently

Box 15-1   Self-Assessment *(continued)*

What Is Your Level of Public Speaking Anxiety?

_____ 23. Realizing that only a little time remains in a speech makes me very tense and anxious.

_____ 24. While giving a speech I know I can control my feelings of tension and stress.

_____ 25. I breathe faster just before starting a speech.

_____ 26. I feel comfortable and relaxed in the hour or so just before giving a speech.

_____ 27. I do poorer on speeches because I am anxious.

_____ 28. I feel anxious when the teacher announces the date of a speaking assignment.

_____ 29. When I make a mistake while giving a speech, I find it hard to concentrate on the parts that follow.

_____ 30. During an important speech I experience a feeling of helplessness building up inside me.

_____ 31. I have trouble falling asleep the night before a speech.

_____ 32. My heart beats very fast while I present a speech.

_____ 33. I feel anxious while waiting to give my speech.

_____ 34. While giving a speech I get so nervous I forget facts I really know.

To determine your score, first total the numbers you gave yourself for statements 1, 2, 3, 5, 9, 10, 13, 14, 19, 20, 21, 22, 23, 25, 27, 28, 29, 30, 31, 32, 33, and 34. Now subtract this total from 132 and add the difference to your total score on statements 4, 6, 7, 8, 11, 12, 15, 16, 17, 18, 24, and 26. Your score should be no higher than 170 and no lower than 34. If your score is higher than 100, you are moderately to highly fearful of public speaking. A score between 80 and 100 means moderate fear, and anything less than 80 means minimal fear. Your score is only an approximation of your speech anxiety and should be regarded as such. The vast majority of students who have responded to this measure on many campuses in the United States fall in the moderately anxious range. Extremely low and extremely high scores are rare. Whatever score you achieve, you can benefit from the techniques discussed in this chapter.

accompanies public speaking. In fact, as pointed out during a segment of ABC's program *20/20,* speech anxiety is regularly experienced by upwards of 40 percent of all American adults. **Speech anxiety** refers to the feelings of fear and discomfort that people experience before, during, and after speaking in public.

Public speaking anxiety (which you can assess for yourself in Box 15-1) shows itself in two major ways. The first is mental. Before a speech, anxiety is characterized by such mental behaviors as excessive worry, inability to concentrate, and procrastinating. During a speech, it can take the form of feeling helpless, thinking highly negative thoughts, and erroneously believing that the audience wants the speaker to fail. Following a speech, it can express itself in terms of self-criticism, unjustified feelings of embarrassment, and inability to listen.

speech anxiety
Fear of speaking in public, usually accompanied by mental worry and physical signs of excessive arousal such as perspiring, rapid heart beat, and dry mouth.

The second and most easily recognized way that speech anxiety shows itself is physical.[1] Prior to speaking, for example, it typically involves butterflies in the stomach. During a speech, anxiety can take the form of excessive perspiration, trembling hands, and poor eye contact. After a speech, it can leave the speaker feeling physically exhausted, mentally drained, and unable to focus on constructive feedback.

Some degree of anxiety while speaking is normal and even performance enhancing. Moderate feelings of anxiety are accompanied by moderate levels of physiological arousal. Moderate levels of arousal improve thinking and energize performance. Thus, both the moderate feelings of anxiety and the arousal these feelings stimulate are perceived as pleasant by most people. If you interpret a public speaking situation negatively, however, both the feelings of anxiety and levels of arousal you experience are likely to be excessive. Excessive arousal interferes with thinking and performance, as illustrated in Figure 15-1.

The Sources of Speech Anxiety

Not all people have the same reason for being anxious about speaking in public. Still, research over the past three decades has given us a good picture of the most common sources of these anxieties.[2] This picture includes a pessimistic attitude toward speaking, inadequate preparation and practice, negative or insufficient experience, unrealistic goals, inaccurate perception of the audience, and negative self-talk. Let's discuss each of these sources of anxiety in turn.

Pessimistic Attitude Toward Speaking   The first and most immediate source of anxiety is your perception and reaction to the situation you face. Though actual physiological arousal is neither positive nor negative in itself, your perception of it can be either positive or negative. If you perceive and react to a situation positively, the arousal you feel will be perceived as a pleasant rather than an unpleasant sensation. Conversely, if you perceive a situation negatively, you will perceive the arousal you feel as an unpleasant, even worrisome sensation. This perception increases the probability of arousal exceeding the optimal level, as you become more and more anxious, further pushing your physiological arousal level.

Inadequate Preparation and Practice   An obvious reason for viewing the speech transaction as unpleasant is inadequate preparation and practice. Whereas most students would never dream of entering an athletic competition or taking a test crucial to their success in their major without preparation and practice, many seem to think that public speaking is different in this regard. So they put off preparing and practicing their speech until the last moment. Then they wonder why the act of speaking was so traumatic.

Negative or Insufficient Experience   Your prior experiences with any task influence how you approach and complete your present task. If your past experiences with public speaking proved both successful and personally rewarding,

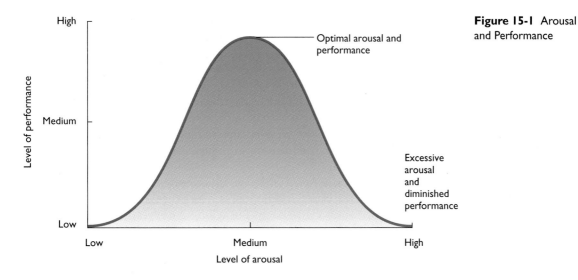

Figure 15-1 Arousal and Performance

chances are you look forward to public speaking. But if your prior experiences with public speaking were unpleasant, chances are you harbor some doubt about your abilities to succeed. Finally, if you have had little or no opportunity to speak in public, you may be mildly or even considerably anxious about speaking in public.

Unrealistic Goals   A common source of anxiety for inexperienced speakers is the goals they set for themselves. Though it is important to set high goals, they also should be realistic. Unrealistic goals can lead to irrational fears about the speaking situation. Research shows that people who set realistic goals for themselves are less anxious and more successful than their counterparts with unrealistic goals. This finding also has been reported in studies of elite athletes, business people, and students enrolled in public speaking courses.[3]

Inaccurate Perception of the Audience   Another source of speech anxiety is the speaker's perception of the audience. Many beginning speakers view the public speaking situation in general, and their audience specifically, as a threat to their mental well-being. They convince themselves that the members of their audience are just waiting for them to commit some social blunder, lose their train of thought, blow a quotation, or mumble through a sentence. Along the same lines, it is not uncommon for beginning speakers to read the nonverbal feedback they receive from their audience as "they're bored to tears" or "they think I'm terrible." These are false conclusions, of course. Audiences, with rare exception, want speakers to succeed and are silently rooting for them to do so.

Negative Self-Talk   Closely aligned with the problem of unrealistic personal goals is the more widespread problem of self-defeating patterns of negative self-

self-talk   Silent communication with oneself, sometimes referred to as intrapersonal communication.

negative self-talk
Self-criticizing, self-pressuring, and catastrophizing statements made to oneself which emphasize doubts about speaking publicly.

talk. **Self-talk** is silent communication with oneself, sometimes referred to as intrapersonal communication. **Negative self-talk** includes self-criticizing, self-pressuring, and catastrophizing statements. Let's look at each of these types of negative self-talk.

Though realistic self-evaluation is important to self-improvement, many of us berate ourselves without sufficient cause. Not just students but people in all walks of life engage in *self-criticism* about their speaking abilities. Many of us do so even though we have never received any training in public speaking and have had few if any opportunities to speak in public. Thus, our lack of skill doesn't justify our self-criticism.

Self-talk can also be *self-pressuring*. We tell ourselves, for example, "I must be the best speaker in the class." It is normal to experience some degree of pressure and arousal when speaking publicly. But telling ourselves that being anything but the best isn't good enough will hurt rather than help our speaking.

Finally, we may *catastrophize,* or blow things out of proportion, when talking to ourselves. For example, a sub-par speech becomes the worst thing that has ever happened to us, something that we will never be able to live down, or a reason to hate ourselves should we receive a low grade.

Controlling Speech Anxiety

In the past 20 years, researchers have learned much about the control of arousal and anxiety. In the process, they have also learned that anyone can benefit from following certain arousal- and anxiety-controlling steps regardless of his or her individual level of anxiety about speaking in public. Let's now look at each of these steps.

Develop an Optimistic Attitude Toward Speaking   To begin with, the slightest shift in your point of view can drastically change the way you see anything, including public speaking. Viewing public speaking as communication rather than performance can make a tremendous difference in the way you look at and respond to the speech transaction. The first step in controlling speech anxiety for many people, then, is to start thinking about public speaking differently. Instead of thinking of it as a public performance during which they will be "on stage," they might be better off viewing it as a slightly different and more formal way of carrying on a conversation with a group of interested friends or perhaps telling them a story.

Don't Put Off Preparing Your Speech   The second step in controlling arousal and anxiety is to commit to preparation well in advance of the actual speech. Although only you know how much time you need to prepare, inexperienced speakers usually need more time than they think they do. So, to avoid excessive anxiety, be sure to allow more time for preparation than you initially think you will need.

VIDEO FILE

If you have the videotape that accompanies this book, please see Segment 1, Part VI, which focuses on overcoming speech anxiety.

Look for Opportunities to Gain Speaking Experience   Of course you have made the first step to gaining public speaking experience by enrolling in this class. Realistically, however, you probably will be able to give only a few speeches during an academic term. To build up your repertoire of public speaking experience, you should seek out other opportunities to speak. Many colleges and universities offer a competitive speech team. Though this might seem intimidating at first, competition is geared to levels of experience, with beginning speakers normally placed at the "novice" level. There may also be other opportunities to speak on your campus or in your community. Some communities have a Toastmasters International club, which provides an opportunity to gain experience in a group devoted to building public speaking confidence.

Set Realistic Goals   Unrealistic goals lead to irrational fears that misguide anxious speakers in the preparation, presentation, and evaluation of their speeches. No one is perfect. To think that *you* always must be perfect simply isn't realistic. By the same token, it is impossible for anyone to be the best at everything. Telling yourself that you must be the best invites unnecessary and anxiety-arousing comparisons with other people. In a public speaking class, you have the opportunity to work on improving your public speaking incrementally. You do not need to be a perfect or ideal speaker with each speech. Rather, as you approach each assignment, focus on one or two areas that you feel are most in need of improvement.

Realize the Audience Wants You to Succeed   Just as anxious speakers set unrealistic goals for themselves, they often fear that their audience will ridicule them and that they will look ridiculous. These fears are as irrational as expecting perfection in yourself as a speaker. In reality, you probably will never find as supportive an audience as in your public speaking class. Remember, every member of the class faces exactly the same challenges you do. If you make a mistake or have problems, their reaction is far more likely to be empathy and support than ridicule.

Practice Constructive Self-Talk   Another step to controlling arousal and anxiety is to engage in **constructive self-talk,** that is, to use positive coping statements instead of negative self-talk. Table 15-1 illustrates positive coping statements that can substitute for negative self-talk and help you manage your arousal and anxiety. Note that positive coping statements (1) accentuate your assets, not your liabilities; (2) encourage you to relax; and (3) emphasize a realistic rather than catastrophic assessment of your situation before, during, and after your speech.

constructive self-talk Positive coping statements we make to ourselves that accentuate our assets, encourage relaxation, and emphasize realistic goals before, during, and after a speech.

Use Visual Imagery to Enhance Performance   Visual imagery is used extensively in competitive sports such as skiing, gymnastics, and figure skating. (One athlete's techniques are described in Box 15-2.) It is a highly effective complement to actual practice. Visually imagining your speech is the opposite of

Table 15-1   Positive Coping Statements for Speeches

BEFORE SPEECH	DURING SPEECH	AFTER SPEECH
TASK STATEMENTS	**TASK STATEMENTS**	**CONTEXT STATEMENTS**
What do I have to do?	Keep using coping statements.	It wasn't as bad as I feared.
Remember to use coping statements.	Speak slowly, it helps.	It was not a big deal.
Speak slowly and I'll be fine.		Each time will get easier.
CONTEXT STATEMENTS	**SELF-EVALUATION**	**SELF-EVALUATION**
It's only my class.	How am I doing?	What did I do well?
It's only one speech.	So far so good.	I used coping statements.
We're all in the same boat.	I've started and it was okay.	I spoke.
I know as much as anyone.	I was anxious, but now I've calmed down.	I spoke slowly.
I can't be any worse than previously, only better.	This is a little easier than I thought.	What do I want to improve next time?
		Remember to speak slowly and rehearse my statements.

rehearsing it. Instead of practicing your speech out loud, you visually imagine yourself confidently and successfully giving it. This technique works best when you are in a relaxed state and familiar with the content of your speech. It involves controlled visualization of all phases of the actual speaking situation, which may require some practice. For example, you might first visualize yourself seated at your desk, relaxed but appropriately aroused as you wait your turn to speak. Next, you might visualize yourself leaving your desk, moving to the front of the room, confidently facing your audience, and introducing your speech. From here on, you would visualize yourself speaking—moving, gesturing, and making eye contact with individual members of your audience right up to your conclusion. Finally, you would see your audience and the teacher enthusiastically responding to your presentation.

Use Relaxation Techniques   Butterflies, a racing heart, trembling hands, and weak knees are the result of the excessive adrenaline that is pumped into your system when you are overly aroused. The best way to prevent these symptoms is to condition your body to relax in situations that are, characteristically, overly arousing. Exercise, relaxation imagery, and muscular relaxation—alone or in combination—are all effective relaxation techniques.

You can help your body relax if you engage in some form of intense exercise one to two hours before you speak. The effects of *physical exercise* on physical

Box 15-2   Critical Thinking

An Athlete's Approach to Anxiety

Champion figure skater Kristi Yamaguchi not only practices physically for a performance; she practices mentally in order to cope with anxiety. Here, she describes her techniques:

> I usually get by myself before I go out for a routine. I walk through the program, visualizing myself completing all the moves. Right before a performance, I start talking to myself: "Okay, get out there, skate like it's an everyday practice."

The techniques Kristi Yamaguchi uses illustrate the importance of practice and mental imaging in dealing with anxiety. Notice that she mentally rehearses her moves right before a performance. She also engages in constructive self-talk when she tells herself that a competition is like an everyday practice. How do you think Yamaguchi's techniques could be successfully used by a public speaker? What can we learn as public speakers from the ways that elite athletes deal with the enormous pressure under which they must perform?

SOURCE: *American Health* © 1992 by Steve McKee.

and mental well-being are well known. Intense exercise assists us in limiting signs of stress and has been linked to improved thinking and performance, regardless of the task.

If exercise is either inconvenient or impractical, another way to induce relaxation before you speak is to use *relaxation imagery.* Imagery is not the same as merely thinking. Imagery involves pictures, whereas thinking is a verbal process. Relaxation imagery involves visualizing pleasant and calming situations such as lying in a hammock or on the beach on a warm summer day. If you linger on such a visual image, your body will become increasingly relaxed and the level of arousal you customarily feel will drop.

Exercise is a great way to manage the stress and anxiety you feel in anticipation of speaking.

Muscular relaxation is a technique using systematic tensing and relaxing of various muscle groups. It usually begins with the muscles in the face and neck, then gradually moves to the middle and lower torso. The idea behind this technique is to teach your body the difference between tension and relaxation. By alternately tensing and relaxing your muscles, you can condition them to relax even under the most stressful circumstances.

There is a good reason for practicing muscular relaxation. When we tense up, the range of movement in our muscles is restricted. In a speaker, you sometimes see tension manifested either in the absence of movement and gestures or in awkward and unnatural movements and gestures.

These techniques work best when used in combination as a habitual routine that you practice as you prepare to speak. Just as elite athletes don't wait to use anxiety-controlling techniques until they are about to compete, so speakers shouldn't put off using them, until the night before they speak. Box 15-3 provides some guidelines for systematically learning to use the various techniques to control anxiety.

Box 15-3   Skill Building

Five Steps to Managing Speech Anxiety

1. Immediately begin to analyze your goals. Ask yourself whether they are realistic, given your experience and commitment to spend time preparing for this class.

2. Begin today to assess the degree to which you routinely engage in negative self-talk. Write down the self-criticizing, self-pressuring, and catastrophizing statements you routinely make to yourself. Describe in writing how these statements affect your level of arousal and anxiety before, during, and following your speeches.

3. Make a list of the positive coping statements you could substitute for the negative ones you

now make. Begin to use these statements as you prepare and practice your speech.

4. Once you're confident that you have thoroughly prepared your speech, find a quiet time when you can practice relaxation imagery and visually rehearse your speech. Do this for 15 minutes every other day, and practice your speech on the other days.

5. Use your positive coping statements as you are about to speak, as you are speaking, and after you speak.

Audience-Focused Delivery

Because speech anxiety can easily interfere with your ability to gesture and sound confident, controlling speech anxiety is a first, important step to effective delivery. Because speaking is a transaction between you and your audience, the next step demands that you give some thought about who your audience will be and which method and style of delivery will be most appropriate to them. Then, and only then, can you begin to concentrate on your use of nonverbal communication behaviors, to enhance your delivery.

VIDEO FILE

If you have the videotape that accompanies this book, see Part V, Segment 2, which concerns delivery.

Choosing an Appropriate Method of Delivery

There is more than one way to deliver a speech. Speeches can be written out word for word and read, delivered from memory, delivered spontaneously, or delivered extemporaneously with the help of notes. As you review your analysis of your audience and your situation, one of your most important choices will be the most appropriate method of speech delivery.

Manuscript Delivery   Writing out the speech and reading it to the audience is called manuscript delivery. This method may be the best choice when the audience requires precise information. When someone is speaking about highly technical matters before a group of engineers, for example, the precision with which the information is delivered may be extremely important. Similarly, people who expect their words to be quoted by others can help to ensure accuracy by having a manuscript of their speech.

Using a manuscript, however, restricts the dynamics of delivery. As we show later in this chapter, eye contact, movement, and gesture are important dimensions of nonverbal communication behavior that may enhance your delivery. Having to read a manuscript limits the ability to move, gesture, and make eye contact. Manuscript speaking also impedes spontaneity between speaker and audience because it limits opportunities to survey and creatively respond to audience feedback. Further, a manuscript demands a lectern, a barrier between speaker and audience. Finally, this method of delivery can sound stilted and artificial—the language of a written message generally is more formal than spoken language.

Memorized Delivery   A speaker using memorized delivery writes out the speech but then commits it to memory so that it can be presented without the use of notes. Most audiences don't expect a memorized speech, unless they are watching a professional speaker, an actor in a play, or a student competing in a speech tournament. In fact, in a typical communication class, an obviously memorized speech probably would strike most students and the instructor as odd. Although memorization allows the speaker to concentrate on eye contact, movement, and gesture, it does so at a price. You may forget parts of your speech. Memorization also requires a much greater investment of time than any other method.

Impromptu Delivery   Impromptu delivery is a spontaneous, unrehearsed method of presenting a speech. Usually, these short speeches are given in response to a request to say a few words, make a toast, or respond to an inquiry. Although an audience is always appreciative of an eloquent impromptu speech, an organized and confidently spoken impromptu message is normally enough to fulfill any audience's expectations.

Extemporaneous Delivery   For most students who are still learning to give a speech, therefore, extemporaneous speaking remains their best choice of delivery method. Extemporaneous delivery combines careful preparation with spontaneous speaking. The speaker generally uses brief notes rather than a manuscript or an outline. Extemporaneous speaking enables you to maintain eye contact, move, gesture, and spontaneously adapt to audience feedback. You may choose not to use a lectern, depending on how extensive your notes are and how comfortable you are moving freely before the audience.

Today's audiences are more likely to expect and appreciate the extemporaneously delivered speech than other methods of presentation. Just as it allows the speaker to remain in contact with the audience, so it allows the audience to remain connected to the speaker. Audiences not only can give feedback to someone speaking extemporaneously but also can assess the degree with which their feedback registers with the speaker.

Extemporaneous speaking is not without its drawbacks. Note cards can be a problem because they can restrict the range of gestures used when you refer to them. Note cards can also be distracting when waved about while you're speak-

Box 15-4   Considering Diversity

Cultural Variations in Audience Response

Both the method and style of delivery should reflect the cultural and group diversity of your audience. For example, consider how three different audiences might respond to the same speech. A North American audience returns eye contact and nods in agreement with the speaker. A British audience also returns eye contact, but their heads remain motionless. And a West African audience avoids making direct eye contact with the speaker altogether. What should a speaker make of the differences in feedback? Before you decide, perhaps it would help to know more: When the British agree with a speaker, they sometimes blink rather than nod their heads. Fur-

ther, the more direct the eye contact of West Africans, the less they respect the person to whom it is directed. Knowing the typical patterns of non-verbal communication behavior in a given culture is essential if you are to accurately interpret their nonverbal communication behaviors.

Another example of differences among diverse audiences concerns the voice. Almost from birth, the norm for the North American culture is "to speak up and let yourself be heard." What is normative here, however, may be loud in Japan or among the upper class in Great Britain. And much as we may want to be heard, we don't want to be perceived as loudmouths.

ing. Finally, you can get carried away with note cards, writing down so many of your thoughts that the note cards become a different kind of manuscript.

Adapting the Style of Delivery to the Situation

How you present your speech depends on the specific situation you face and the kind of delivery your audience is likely to expect. A speech commemorating or honoring a person calls for a formal and dignified delivery. Other speech situations call for an energetic, dynamic delivery. A motivational speaker, for example, usually dispenses with the lectern and moves about the stage, perhaps even into the audience. A lively style is expected and rewarded. Then there are situations that call for a lighthearted, comic style of delivery. For example, "roasts" honoring someone often are punctuated with good-natured joking at the honoree's expense. Unlike a commemorative speech, a delivery at a "roast" should be informal and lively. Moreover, as Box 15-4 illustrates, different cultures and groups have different expectations for the transaction between speaker and audience. The key is to understand what the audience expects in a given situation and match your delivery style to those expectations.

The Nonverbal Elements of Delivery

Delivery involves the nonverbal communication behaviors by which a speaker conveys his or her message to an audience. Delivery is what brings mere words

Figure 15-2 Zone of Interaction in the Traditional Room Setting. Where people are seated in rows and the speaker is stationary, eye contact between speaker and audience is limited to the shaded area.

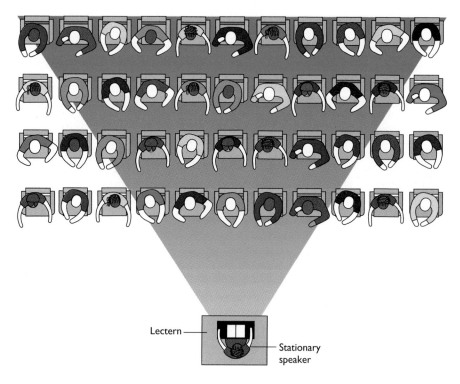

Lectern

Stationary speaker

to life in the public speaking transaction. Recall from Chapter 4 that nonverbal communication is a wordless system of communicating. Remember, too, that nonverbal communication is continuous, uses multiple channels simultaneously, and is spontaneous.

The components of the system of nonverbal communication include the speaking environment, the speaker's appearance, face and eyes, voice, gestures and movement, posture, self-touching behaviors, and time. Because these components are interrelated, a change in one of them can produce changes in others and profoundly affect the delivery of a speech.

The Environment

environment The physical surroundings for a speech and the physical distance separating a speaker from the audience.

Both the surroundings and the distance between speaker and audience have an undeniable impact not only on delivery but also on how the speech is perceived by the audience. The characteristics of the **environment** in which you speak—for example, lighting, temperature, comfort, and aesthetics—will influence both you and your audience physically and psychologically.[4] A bright, aesthetically neutral room, which is neither sterile nor plushly decorated, and in which the temperature is 68 degrees will have a much different overall impact on the

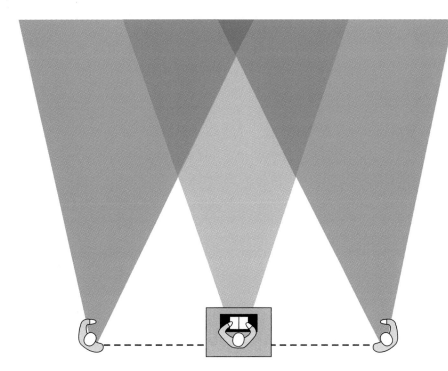

Figure 15-3 Shifting the Zone of Interaction with Movement. Changing positions can increase the perception of inclusiveness as well as add energy to your speech.

speech transaction than a room that is dimly lit, richly furnished, and 85 degrees.

The layout of the room in which you speak will also affect the speech transaction. A room with rows of seats and a lectern at the front is consistent with the needs of a speaker most comfortable with a traditional style of delivery. A room with a circular configuration and a seat for the speaker is consistent with the needs of a speaker whose style is much less formal. Although both styles of delivery can be equally effective, the room layout consistent with the traditional style is more restrictive than its counterpart in two ways. The first way concerns the **zone of interaction,** the area in which the speaker can easily make eye contact with audience members. (See Figure 15-2.) The second concerns the amount of space physically separating the speaker from the audience.

The zone of interaction is limited to the range of the speaker's peripheral vision. The immediate zone of interaction between the speaker and the audience diminishes as a room gets larger. To compensate for this fact, speakers have two choices. Either they can shift the zone of interaction by looking from side to side or they can physically move from one point to another when they deliver their speech. The effect of moving from one point to another is illustrated in Figure 15-3. Obviously, in a very large room the traditional style of delivery limits the speaker to looking from side to side in the attempt to shift the zone of interaction. The consequence is having to ignore part of the audience part of the time.

zone of interaction
The area in which a speaker can easily make eye contact with audience members.

The traditional style of delivery allows less flexibility in manipulating the physical distance separating speakers from their audiences than does a less formal style. Whereas a speaker who moves about the room can reduce or increase distance physically as well as psychologically, a relatively stationary speaker is restricted to psychologically manipulating the distance. Thus, for speakers who prefer a formal style of delivery, eye contact is the primary agent for managing how immediate the audience perceives them to be, a point we discuss shortly.

Appearance

Appearance often has a disproportionately significant effect on audience perceptions of a speaker's message and delivery.[5] Speakers never get a second chance to make a first impression with an audience. The significance of appearance to public speaking can be measured in at least two ways. The first involves audience members' first impressions. The second involves how people perceive themselves as a result of their appearance and the impact this perception has on their self-confidence and delivery.

Audience members use appearance to initially judge a speaker's level of credibility and attractiveness. The consequences of this judgment are far-reaching for speakers. Research reports that speakers perceived as credible and attractive by audience members also are perceived as smart, successful, sociable, and self-confident. As a result, speakers who fall into this category enjoy an audience whose initial impression of them is favorable.

Yet, appearance influences more than an audience's initial impression of a speaker. Appearance also can have a very real effect on a speaker's self-confidence. Research also tells us that speakers who feel they appear attractive report greater self-confidence than those who do not see themselves as attractive.[6]

Although some facets of your appearance and their impact on audience perception are outside your control—for example, body type and height—there is one facet you can easily control: your dress. Simply said, your clothes should be appropriate to the situation. If you are to give a speech to a class, for example, dress a bit more formally than usual. Dressing a bit more formally than your audience is good advice for a majority of speech transactions.

The Face and Eyes

We introduced the concept of nonverbal immediacy in Chapter 4. We said that it concerns perceptions about the degree to which people are perceived as close or distant. The face and eyes are useful in communicating friendliness to an audience, reducing undesirable feelings of distance, and promoting immediacy.

Yet, immediacy is only one of the roles the face and eyes play in enhancing delivery. The face and eyes can also communicate happiness, surprise, fear, anger, disgust, contempt, sadness, and interest.

In the North American culture, eye contact is perceived as a specific message. Speakers who are respectful, trustworthy, friendly, and interested in our well-being make eye contact with us. What's more, the best speakers don't simply make eye contact with the audience but with individual members of the audience as they deliver their speech. This personal eye contact makes it appear to the audience member that he or she is engaged in dialogue with the speaker.

Remember, though, this kind of eye contact is a North American norm, not a universal one. In many cultures, the focus and sustained eye contact North Americans expect would be frowned upon. Such eye contact is viewed by members of many Asian cultures, for example, as rude and even hostile. As both a speaker and an audience member, you should keep such differences in mind.

The Voice

Try reading this familiar nursery rhyme out loud in three different ways. In the first, your goal is to make your audience sad. In the second, your goal is to make your audience happy. And in the third, your goal is to make your audience anxious about the well-being of the characters.

> Mary had a little lamb,
>
> Its fleece was white as snow;
>
> And everywhere that Mary went,
>
> The lamb was sure to go.

Your readings should illustrate that we can use our voices in a number of ways to enhance the delivery of our speeches. Drama, irony, sarcasm, and urgency are but a few of the emotions we can convey vocally.

To gain maximum control of your voice, you need to know two things: the mechanics of the voice and the importance of finding your own voice rather than trying to imitate the voice of someone else.

Vocal Production   To produce vocal sounds, we take in air and expel it through the trachea, across our vocal cords, which are contained in the larynx, and then across our teeth, tongue and lips, as shown in Figure 15-4. Variations in the amount of air expelled, the positioning of the vocal cords, the placement of the teeth and tongue, and the position of the lips will all result in variations in the sounds we produce. Shallow breathing and the rapid expulsion of air across the vocal cords, for example, will produce a much different sound than breathing deeply and then slowly expelling the air. The mechanical operation of the voice, however, is not as important to our purpose as are the mechanical characteristics of the voice. These include volume, pitch, range, rhythm, tempo, and articulation.

Volume is how loudly you project your voice. It is a consequence of both the amount of air you expel when speaking and the force with which you expel it. Some examples of people with "big" voices, capable of speaking with great vol-

Figure 15-4
Physiology of the Voice

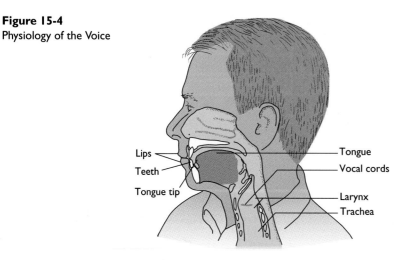

ume, are singer Bette Midler, conservative broadcaster Rush Limbaugh, actor James Earl Jones, and the late congresswoman and distinguished professor Barbara Jordan. Some people, on the other hand, are naturally soft-spoken.

As a public speaker, you need to have enough volume to be heard by your audience. Too soft a voice will simply not be heard. On the other hand, shouting at the top of your lungs can turn off your audience. The key is to speak loudly enough to be heard but not too loudly for the room. Of course, if you have the use of a microphone, you can be heard even if you speak relatively softly. It is also useful to vary your volume during the speech, increasing it to emphasize important points. If the entire speech is delivered at the same volume, nothing will stand out as most important.

Pitch is the highness or lowness of sound. A person who sings bass has a low pitch, whereas a person who sings soprano has a high pitch. The pitch of blues singer B. B. King's voice is low, whereas the pitch of heavy-metal rock star Axl Rose's voice is relatively high. Effective speakers vary their pitch during their speech. They must be careful, however, because an excitable voice can assume a higher-than-normal pitch, and an artificially altered pitch can sound unnatural and may strain the voice.

Range is the extent of the pitch, from low to high, within a person's vocal capacity. Just as a piano, for example, has a tremendous range in pitch, some speakers have a great vocal range. On the other hand, some speakers are like an electric bass guitar, which, no matter how well played, does not have much range. As a speaker, you need to make the fullest use of your normal conversational vocal range. Raising or lowering the pitch of your voice can emphasize a particular word or phrase in your speech. Avoid a monotone delivery, which can lull your audience to sleep.

Rhythm is extremely important to the delivery of your speech. It involves the characteristic pattern of your volume, pitch, and range. Perhaps you have heard someone describe a voice as "singsong," which means that the pitch goes up and down in a predictable and sometimes irritating pattern. Although variation in the rhythm of your voice is certainly to be encouraged, the pattern of variation should not be completely predictable.

Tempo is the rate at which you produce sounds. How quickly or slowly you speak will influence how you are perceived. Tempo tends to vary across and even within cultures. In the Deep South, for example, tempo is relatively slow. In the East, tempo is accelerated. The difference is readily apparent if you compare the tempo of Southern actress Holly Hunter with that of Eastern actress Marisa Tomei.

Speaking too quickly or too slowly can turn off your audience. An excessively rapid pace can be perceived as a sign of nervousness. An excessively slow pace may suggest a speaker is not well prepared. Researchers have found that moderate to fast rates of speaking tend to be associated with the audience being likely to perceive a speaker as competent.[7] Other researchers have noted a ceiling to that effect, however, meaning that too fast a rate of speaking can backfire.[8] In addition, when audiences perceive speech rates as similar to their own, they are more likely to find the speaker socially attractive and to comply with his or her requests.[9] The best advice, therefore, is to moderately vary your tempo. Not only will a variety of tempos accommodate the different preferences of individuals in your audience, it also will enhance the overall effect of your message.

Your tempo is also affected by pauses. Sometimes a brief moment of silence can convey a lot to an audience. Pausing just before delivering the crucial word or phrase helps grab the audience's attention. Pausing after you have made an important point gives it time to sink in. Don't be afraid to use pauses when appropriate. It is better to pause a moment than to fill the air with "ums," "uhs," and "you knows," which are really vocalized pauses.

Articulation refers to the distinctness with which we make individual sounds. We've all experienced the frustration of listening to people whose voice is mushy because they fail to distinctly vocalize sounds. Common causes of articulation problems are running together different sounds or dropping parts of a word: "goin'" instead of "going," "wanna" instead of "want to," or "Whatcha doin'?" in place of "What are you doing?" If you expect an audience to understand what you are saying, you need clear articulation. A good way to test your articulation is to tape-record your speech and listen critically to yourself. If you find consistent articulation problems, you may want to find out if your college or university (probably the drama department) offers a course in voice and articulation. Severe articulation problems, however, are often best treated by a speech pathologist. But for most students giving speeches in class, exercising care, practicing, and slowing down are the keys to being understood by the audience.

Finding Your Own Voice   With these vocal elements in mind, let's now turn to your voice specifically. Are you pleased with the way it sounds and complements your overall delivery? If you are not satisfied with the sound of your own voice, don't try to make it sound like that of some television or radio personality with a great voice. Instead, work on finding your own voice. For example, record your attempts to convey varying emotions in your voice, listen to yourself, and then repeat the process. This kind of exercise will let you hear where your vocal strengths and weaknesses are. Do not be unfairly harsh about how you think you sound. Chances are what you think you hear is quite different from what others hear. If you still think that something about your voice needs to be improved, see the tips in Box 15-5.

Finally, recognize that important as it is, your voice is but a single nonverbal component of your overall delivery. Not all good speakers have tremendous "pipes." For example, Meg Ryan's and Geraldo Rivera's voices may be interesting, but they would hardly be described as rich in timbre.

Gestures and Movement

There is no single standard for gestures and movement relative to delivery. Although Ronald Reagan neither moved nor gestured much when he spoke, he was a consummate public speaker. On the other hand, the Reverend Jesse Jackson, also a public speaker of notable achievement, makes much use of gestures and movement. Thus, before we say more about using gestures and movement as you speak, we want to say this: Your gestures and your movements as you grow as a public speaker should be a refined reflection of what you do naturally.

As is the case with the face and eyes, gestures and movements also can be used to intensify or lessen the emotional impact of verbal messages. Many gestures, for instance, serve as affect displays; that is, they visibly communicate feelings. Placing both hands near the heart at the same time we explain how important a subject is to us is an example. So too are clenched fists, open palms held face up, or lightly slapping the side of the face.

Even though gestures and movement should reflect what you do naturally, they can be purposely used to complement your delivery in several ways.[10] You can use gestures and movement to make your delivery more emblematic, to make it more illustrative, and to regulate the speech transaction.

Emblems The speeches of the best public speakers are usually rich in emblems. An **emblem** is a nonverbal behavior that can be directly translated into words and may replace them.[11] For example, Winston Churchill's "V" was an emblem for victory. Emblems must meet the following criteria:

emblem A meaningful and intentional gesture or movement, or a series of them, that can be translated into words.

1. They must mean something specific to the audience members.
2. They must be used intentionally by the speaker to stimulate meaning.
3. They must be easy to translate into a few words.

Be aware that emblematic gestures are defined by the culture in which they are learned. As a case in point, when Richard Nixon was vice president, he inadvertently incited a protest while deplaning at a South American airport. He greeted

Box 15-5 Skill Building

Tips for Improving Your Voice

L
ike it or not, people will make judgments about you on the basis of the way you sound. George Bush, for example, was criticized for sounding "shrill" near the end of the presidential campaign in 1992. Evidently, the implication was that he was beginning to sound desperate—which is not the way an incumbent president wants to be perceived. On the other hand, Bill Clinton so overused his voice that it became raspy. Near the end of the campaign, Hillary Rodham Clinton was forced to speak for her husband, because he had completely lost his voice.

Although what's most important is to be comfortable with your voice, the following tips may help if you perceive something about your voice that you think needs to be changed.

- *Relaxation:* More than one problem with voice can be solved by monitoring tension in your vocal apparatus. Nasality, shrillness, or screeching, and excessive rate of speech often are a consequence of tension and stress. The relaxation techniques discussed in this chapter can be used to alleviate the impact of tension and stress in your voice.

- *Vocal variation:* Tape-record yourself or have someone tape you when you speak. If you find as a result of monitoring your audiotape that greater vocal variation is needed, pick out someone whose vocal characteristics you admire and repeatedly listen to the person. Then try to model the vocal variation in which the person engages. Repeat this process while using an audiotape recorder.

- *Being heard:* Have a friend monitor your speaking volume. When you speak too softly, tell your friend to raise an index finger within your view. Use this signal to increase the volume of your voice. The goal is to be easily heard, even in the back of the room.

---

the crowd with arms outstretched above his head, the thumb and first finger of each hand joined together in what North Americans take to mean "A-OK." In many South American countries, however, this nonverbal emblem was then synonymous with what we call "giving the finger."

Illustrators   **Illustrators** are nonverbal behaviors that accompany speech and "show" what is being talked about. Although similar to emblems, they are more general and seldom translate into words. The most common way we nonverbally illustrate is with our hands. For example, verbal directions or descriptions beg for the use of the hands. Try giving someone directions or describing an object—say, a spiral staircase—without using your hands.

At the beginning of the semester, we usually ask a student to describe the shapes in Figure 15-5 to other students without showing them or using his or her hands to illustrate the shapes. The listening students are to attempt to reproduce the shapes on paper. Not only do the speaker and the listeners find the task next to impossible, most also consider it frustrating.

illustrators
Nonverbal gestures whose purpose is to "show" what is being talked about.

Natural gestures add to the impact of a speech.

Figure 15-5 Can you instruct a classmate on how to draw an identical set of geometric shapes without using nonverbal expressions or referring back to the figure itself?

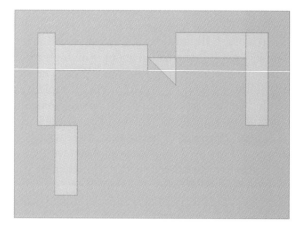

Gestures frequently assist speakers in regulating their transaction with an audience.

Regulators   **Regulators** are gestures that influence the amount and type of feedback received from the audience. If you hold up your hand when asking audience members whether they have ever felt frustrated waiting in line, for example, they are likely to respond by raising their hands as well. If you are stationary throughout a speech, your audience will give you much different feedback than if you were to move and periodically change the zone of interaction. Using gestures and movement to regulate feedback, however, requires planning and rehearsal. An unplanned or inappropriate gesture or specific movement may elicit a response from the audience that you hadn't expected.

   Regulating audience feedback is also important when a speaker answers audience questions. Without regulation, question-and-answer sessions can be dominated by one persistent questioner or disrupted by an angry one.

Posture   This dimension is obviously related to movement, gestures, and overall appearance. Posture is very important to your delivery and the manner in

regulators
Nonverbal gestures whose purpose is to influence the amount and type of feedback received from the audience.

which it is received. People make all kinds of attributions about speakers on the basis of their posture, ranging from how confident a speaker is to how seriously the speaker takes the topic and the situation. At the least, consequently, you will want to guard against an audience making an incorrect attribution about you because you slouched, folded your arms across your chest, stood with one hand on your hip, or kept your hands in your pockets.

Although the norms governing appropriate posture vary across cultures, there are some general steps you can follow to achieve a good posture for delivering your speeches. Remember that the more you slouch and shrink posturally, the less powerful you are likely to be perceived.

- Find your center of balance. Usually this means standing with your feet apart at about shoulder width.
- Pull your shoulders back, sticking your chest out and holding your stomach in.
- Keep your chin up and off your chest.
- Initially let your arms rest at your sides with palms open, which will allow you to gesture easily as you speak.

Touch

Touch, which many experts regard as the most intimate and reinforcing of the nonverbal components, can affect your delivery in at least two ways.[12] The first involves **self-adapting behaviors,** which are distracting touching behaviors that speakers engage in unconsciously.

Frequently, in situations that arouse anxiety, we touch our face, hair, or clothes without realizing it. Just as frequently we touch some convenient object. We may squeeze the arm of a chair, roll our fingers on a tabletop, trace the outside edge of a glass with our fingertip, or mistake the top of a lectern for a conga drum. We do these things unconsciously.

Because public speaking arouses anxiety, it can provoke these self-adaptive forms of touch. Further, they can needlessly detract from your delivery. Tugging at an earlobe, rubbing the outside of your upper arm, or jingling the change in your pocket won't help your delivery. Neither will pounding on the lectern with the palms of your hands or rocking it from side to side.

The second way touch can affect your delivery concerns other people who may be involved in some of your presentations. Corporate trainers, managers, teachers, attorneys, and practitioners of public relations often give informative presentations that involve audience participation. Touch in these scenarios can be as simple, but as important, as shaking a person's hand, or it may involve guiding someone by the hand, patting someone on the back, or even giving a more demonstrative tactile sign of approval. However, speakers need to take care to avoid touch that can be interpreted as inappropriate. For example, there have been several widely reported cases of school teachers accused of inappro-

self-adapting behaviors
Distracting touching behaviors that speakers engage in unconsciously.

priately touching students. Unwelcome touching can, in fact, be grounds for accusations of sexual harassment.

Time

The final nonverbal component to think about relative to delivery is time. Time affects delivery in several ways. If you attempt to cover too much material, for example, time limits may cause you to "hurry" your delivery. Conversely, if you find that you're about to finish your speech in less than the minimum time requirement for an assignment, you may slow down the delivery of your speech.

The audience's perception of your delivery also will be affected by your timing, a term frequently used in reference to actors and comics. Just as their timing of a joke or dramatic monologue can spell the difference between success and failure, so too can your timing. Rushing a punch line or dramatic anecdote, for instance, may negate its intended effect, as may telling a story too slowly.

Because the norms that govern the use of time vary across cultures, you may want to speed up or slow down your delivery, depending on where you are speaking. Whereas a relatively speedy style of delivery may be well received in New York City, it may be received as evidence of your having little time for the audience in parts of the South and Southwest. Conversely, a slow rate of speech, which some mistakenly equate with the speed at which a person thinks, may prove irritating to an audience whose culture is fast paced.

Finally, whether you are on time or late affects your credibility in this culture. People who are on time are efficient and courteous, both attributes that affect perceptions of competence and trustworthiness. People who are routinely late give the impression they are disorganized and not especially considerate of the time needs of an audience.

The Functions of Nonverbal Communication Behaviors in Delivery

The components of nonverbal communication we've been talking about perform a number of important functions in speech delivery.[13] As we've discussed, these components interact to make our speeches more emblematic and illustrative. They also can help us regulate audience feedback and intensify or lessen the emotional impact of what we say during a speech. Other ways that nonverbal communication facilitates the delivery of our messages include complementing, contradicting, and repeating the message; substituting for a verbal cue; increasing the perception of immediacy; exciting the audience; and conveying power.

Complementing the Message

A complementary nonverbal cue serves to reinforce what you verbally share with your audience. A genuine smile on your face as you thank your audience for the opportunity to speak carries more weight than either message standing on its own. There are many ways to complement the delivery of your message nonverbally. Changing the expression on your face, raising the pitch of your voice, or even breaking off eye contact are just a few of them.

Contradicting the Message

Often, people contradict themselves nonverbally while communicating interpersonally. Forcing a smile and saying, "I had a great time," is a classic example. Although the smile sometimes succeeds in covering up the person's real feelings, more often it only serves to contradict the person's words.

Usually, we try to prevent such contradictions between words and nonverbal behaviors. In the case of public speaking, however, we can use contradiction to enhance our delivery, for example, by rolling our eyes, shrugging our shoulders, or by a sarcastic expression. Certainly, Shakespeare knew that contradiction could enhance delivery. He frequently wrote speeches for his characters that invited actors to contradict their verbal statements with nonverbal cues. For example, in Marc Antony's eulogy of Julius Caesar, the line "But Brutus was an honorable man" is usually delivered by an actor in a sarcastic voice that means exactly the opposite. Because it is an attention-getting device, this kind of antithesis in a speech can enhance the impact with which the verbal message is delivered.

Repeating the Message

Repetition is one of the most common ways speakers manipulate their message nonverbally. It's also one of the easiest. Raising three fingers as you say you have three points to make doesn't require the oratorical skill of a Colin Powell.

Repetition differs from complementing in a significant way. Whereas a complementary nonverbal cue reinforces the message, a repetitious one makes it redundant. The classic example is when Star Trek's Mr. Spock makes the Vulcan V sign while saying, "Live long and prosper." Other examples include nodding your head up and down when communicating agreement and shaking your head from side to side when communicating disagreement.

Substituting for a Verbal Cue

Have you ever seen entertainers and politicians raise one or both hands in the attempt to stop an audience's continued applause? They are using a nonverbal cue as a substitute for a verbal one. In many circumstances, such a nonverbal cue is both more appropriate and more effective than a verbal one. An icy stare shot in the direction of someone talking as you speak is likely to be less disruptive, for example, than politely asking the person to be quiet. Shrugging your shoulders, reaching out with open palms, and raising your eyebrows may more clearly communicate your bewilderment than to actually say you're puzzled by something.

Increasing the Perception of Immediacy

As we said in the discussion of the face and eyes, nonverbal behavior can also increase the perception of immediacy, or psychological closeness and approachability, between you and your audience.[14] Generally, the perception of immediacy between people is desirable, because people who are perceived as immediate are also perceived as friendly, stimulating, open to dialogue, and interpersonally warm.

Because public speaking normally takes place in a setting that arbitrarily puts physical distance between speakers and their audiences, speakers usually have to reduce this physical distance psychologically. Distance can be psychologically reduced in at least two ways. The first, which we discussed at length in Chapter 3, is the use of immediate language. The second is to make our delivery more nonverbally immediate. Eye contact is the perfect example. When people are separated by physical distance, eye contact enables them to bridge this distance in a psychological sense. The best public speakers are often the ones who seem to be speaking to us with their eyes as well as their voices. Eye contact is not the only medium, however, through which we can achieve greater immediacy with our audience. It also can be achieved by smiling, by using a conversational rather than condescending tone of voice, and by standing beside the lectern instead of appearing to hide behind it.

Exciting the Audience

One way we gauge the effectiveness of a speech is the degree to which it stimulated us. The best speakers are the ones who make us think, provoke us to laugh, or motivate us to act. Generally, an audience's degree of excitement can be traced to the degree of excitement the audience senses in the speaker.

The level of excitement of public speakers is most noticeable in their nonverbal behavior, including rate and volume of speech and vocal as well as facial expressiveness. Excited speakers speak faster and louder than speakers unaroused by their topic or by the transaction between them and their audience. Excited speakers reveal more of themselves through changes in facial expressions as they speak as well as through changes in the pitch of their voice.

Is excitement all it takes to be a good speaker? Of course not. Too much excitement can be as distracting as too little excitement can be boring. The ideal, then, is to moderate your excitement for your topic or the audience rather than to inappropriately exaggerate it with your delivery.

Conveying Power

When it comes to public speaking, the power of words depends mightily on the manner in which they are delivered. No doubt many speech writers have

Box 15-6   Skill Building

Guidelines for Proactive Delivery

1. **Familiarize yourself with your speaking environment.**
   Familiarity with the environment will influence the quality of your delivery. Know well in advance and plan for such things as seating arrangement, availability and location of lectern, availability and location of overhead screen and projector or easel for displaying poster boards or charts, and lighting.

2. **Dress appropriately.**
   Dressing appropriately is one of the easiest ways to enhance your audience's initial impressions of you. Think about the possible effects of apparel, such as a backwards baseball cap, baggy shorts, or the saying on your favorite T-shirt.

3. **Increase your nonverbal immediacy.**
   Practice using your face and eyes to increase immediacy with your audience. Specifically, practice making eye contact with individual audience members. If possible, videotape your practice session, and review the tape for facial expressions expressing immediacy. On the day of your speech, smile at your audience and establish eye contact before speaking.

4. **Use natural gestures.**
   Review your practice tape to check your gestures. Do they appear natural and complement your delivery, or do they appear forced and constrained? Do your gestures unnecessarily distract from your spoken message?

5. **Work to improve your voice.**
   Review Box 15-5 on tips for improving your voice. Don't be afraid to experiment with your voice. But at the same time, remember to be true to it; don't try to sound like someone else.

6. **Time your speech.**
   Time it more than once and on videotape if you can. Note your timing and the degree to which your rate of speech facilitates the mood you want to communicate. Keep in mind that your practice time will probably be longer than when you actually speak before an audience.

7. **Avoid self-adapting behaviors.**
   During practice, watch out for self-adapting behaviors, such as playing with your hair, tugging on a finger, cracking knuckles, licking your lips, and hiding your hands. Self-adapters such as these will call attention to themselves and undermine perceptions of your power and self-confidence.

8. **Work on posture.**
   Check out your posture and what it conveys about your comfort and level of confidence. Remember, good delivery is next to impossible without good posture.

suffered as the power of the words they so carefully crafted was wiped out by the person delivering them. This shouldn't and needn't be the case. With care and practice, you can use the various dimensions of nonverbal behavior to make the delivery of your speech powerful. Some of the ways you can do this are obvious, and some are more subtle.

Posture is an obvious way to control the power of delivery. Standing tall and self-assured communicates power, especially when combined with movement away from the lectern. You also can enhance the power of your delivery with your eyes and voice, through movement and gestures. In North America, powerful speakers make eye contact, speak in a controlled and confident tone of voice, reduce the distance between themselves and their audience by moving closer to it, and gesture as a natural extension of their spoken message. In contrast, speakers whose delivery lacks power avoid eye contact, fail to speak up, and usually try to tie up their hands by sticking them in pockets, gripping the side of the lectern, or hiding them behind their back.

Taking a Proactive Approach

Knowing something about the nature and functions of nonverbal communication should help you make your speech delivery proactive rather than reactive. To engage in **proactive delivery** means taking the initiative and anticipating and controlling for as many variables as possible, rather then merely reacting to them. Reactive delivery is like the boxer who only counterpunches. This wait-and-see attitude is rarely the mark of a boxing champion, and it can be disastrous for even the most seasoned public speaker. To that end, you'll find some guidelines in Box 15-6 to help you make sure that your nonverbal communication behavior enhances the delivery of your speech.

proactive delivery
Delivery in which a speaker takes the initiative and anticipates and controls as many variables as possible, rather than merely reacting to them.

Summary

Effective speech delivery begins with the recognition and management of speech anxiety. Common sources of speech anxiety include a pessimistic attitude, poor preparation and inadequate practice, negative or insufficient experience, unrealistic goals, and negative self-talk. The effective management of speech anxiety involves an optimistic attitude about speaking, preparation and practice, constructive self-talk, and the routine use of proven techniques such as visual imagery and relaxation.

Effective speech delivery also involves choosing among manuscript, memorized, impromptu, and extemporaneous delivery methods. The method selected depends on the audience and the situation you face.

Effective speech delivery also requires engaging the audience nonverbally. The system of nonverbal communication has eight interdependent components, including the environment, appearance, the face and eyes, the voice, gestures and movement, posture, touch, and time. The environment includes the seating arrangement, the physical layout of the room, and temperature and lighting. Appearance includes dress and what it communicates to the audience. The face and eyes can communicate emotional states such as joy, anger, and sadness. The voice influences audience emotions through volume, pitch, range, rhythm, tempo, and articulation. Gestures and movement—including emblems, illustrators, and regulators—complement verbal behavior and regulate the speech transaction, including audience feedback. Speakers often use touch to compensate for nervousness; slapping the top of the lectern is an example of this kind of self-adapting behavior. Time is important to public speaking in terms of how the audience perceives the speaker and in terms of the timing of the speech. All of these nonverbal communication behaviors independently and collectively function to enhance the delivery of speeches by complementing, contradicting, or repeating a message; substituting for a verbal cue; increasing immediacy; exciting the audience; and conveying power.

Another Look

Articles

John O. Greene, "Speech Preparation Processes and Verbal Fluency." *Human Communication Research* 11 (1984): 61–84.

How important is speech preparation to verbal fluency, or smooth and uninterrupted delivery? This study investigates that question and concludes, not surprisingly, that preparation does help to increase a speaker's fluency.

P. Ekman and W. V. Friesen. "The Repertoire of Nonverbal Behavior: Categories, Origins, Usage, and Coding." *Semiotica* 1 (1969): 49–98.

This seminal article goes beyond the superficial treatment of nonverbal behavior one normally reads in the popular press. It reminds us that nonverbal behavior is both more complex and richer with potential cues than we sometimes think.

Books

Edward T. Hall. *The Silent Language*. Garden City, N.Y.: Anchor Press/Doubleday, 1959.

Edward T. Hall. *The Hidden Dimension*. Garden City, N.Y.: Anchor Press/Doubleday, 1966.

These two books laid the groundwork for much subsequent research on the importance of nonverbal communication, including the differences in unspoken language from culture to culture.

P. Heinberg. *Voice Training for Speaking and Reading Aloud*. New York: Ronald Publishing, 1964.

All too often we underutilize the power of our voice. This brief and practical book is full of exercises and activities that can help you use your voice to its fullest potential.

Video Rentals

A Perfect Candidate This video documentary follows Oliver North's unsuccessful bid for the United States Senate in 1994. It carefully documents the relationship between North and his handlers and clearly establishes the significance they all attached to North's speeches. The video was co-produced by R. J. Cutler, who made the critically acclaimed backstage look at the 1992 Clinton campaign, *The War Room*.

Theory and Research in Practice

1. Although people confuse them, speech anxiety and shyness are quite different. Some performers, such as Jay Leno's predecessor, Johnny Carson, report that they are shy. What do you see as the difference between speech anxiety and shyness?

2. Differences in nonverbal norms, as well as differences in communication styles and patterns, are common across cultures. To investigate this fact, engage in some self-directed research. Choose two or three North American norms for nonverbal behavior—for example, eye contact, gesturing, and time. Interview a student or faculty member from a culture that is not North American about how these communication behaviors differ in his or her culture. Write a brief paper summarizing your findings.

3. Obtain a videotape recording of a public speech. Watch the tape carefully. After doing so, answer the following questions about the delivery:

   - What mode of delivery did the speaker employ?
   - Did the speaker effectively use his or her voice?
   - Did the speaker effectively use his or her face and eyes?
   - Did the speaker effectively use his or her body?
   - How could the speaker have been more effective in delivering the speech?

   If you can obtain a printed copy of the speech, read and compare the experience of reading the speech with seeing and hearing it.

CHAPTER SIXTEEN

Informative Speaking

OBJECTIVES

After reading this chapter you should be able to:

- Explain how to adapt your informative speech to audiences with diverse learning styles.

- Explain the concept of informative speaking in terms of its cognitive, affective, and behavioral components.

- Discuss the relationship between informative speaking and persuasion.

- Use the message attributes novelty, compatibility, comprehensibility, relative advantage, observability, and trialability in your informative speeches.

- Prepare informative speeches that explain, instruct, demonstrate, and/or describe.

- Incorporate presentational aids into your speeches.

Jaime Escalante, whose picture you see in the opening photograph, is not simply a gifted teacher. He is a remarkable person. He immigrated to the United States from Bolivia in 1969, where he had taught mathematics and physics. He spoke not a single word of English. But Escalante had what he called *ganas*—that is, a desire to succeed regardless of the odds against it. As Escalante puts it: "Determination plus hard work plus concentration equals success, which equals *ganas*."[1] Thus, at age 30, he reentered school to work toward his teaching credential, even though it meant subjecting his out-of-shape body to a required course in P.E.

The rest of the story, of course, is probably well known to you. Escalante's life became the subject of the critically acclaimed film *Stand and Deliver*. In the movie, actor Edward James Olmos portrays Escalante, who took East Los Angeles barrio students who could barely do simple math and, in two years of intensive work, prepared them for the Advanced Placement Test in Calculus. His

ganas Desire to succeed.

417

informative speaking
The process by which an audience gains new information from a speaker.

students were so successful that all 18 who attempted the test in 1982 passed, the most of any high school in Southern California. Each year more students passed; by 1987, 87 of his students had passed the exam. Remember, these were students who were not expected to attend college, let alone receive college credit for calculus while still in high school. But as Escalante says, "Students will rise to the level of expectations." When students wanted to quit, Escalante would challenge them by saying, "Do you have the *ganas*? Do you have the desire?"[2]

Although there are many reasons that Escalante was able to overcome odds others would have perceived as insurmountable, we think his success in life as well as in the classroom can be found in that word of his: *ganas.* Not only did Escalante have it when he needed it, but also his life is testimony to the fact that he has instilled it in many of his students. As a result, they too have succeeded.

In a sense, this chapter is about *ganas.* Like Jaime Escalante, the best informative speakers do more than simply pass on information to an audience. With their words and actions, they create a desire in their audience to put the information to constructive use. In the case of Escalante, the desire involved a subject that many students prefer to avoid: mathematics. In yours, it may involve anything from how we treat our environment to the kind of foods we eat.

Informative speaking is the process by which an audience gains new information from a speaker. Put another way, the goal of informative speaking is audience learning. In order for you to be an effective informative speaker, you need to master several skills, which we will look at in this chapter. These skills include

- focusing on your audience and appealing to their various styles of learning;
- understanding the cognitive, affective, and behavioral components of informative speaking;
- recognizing the relationship between informative speaking and persuasion;
- learning to utilize various attributes of messages in informative speaking;
- putting theory into practice in speeches that explain, instruct, demonstrate, or describe; and
- learning to augment your speeches with presentational aids.

Focusing on Your Audience's Learning Styles

Consider the following scenarios. In the first, the president of the United States goes on national TV to explain a foreign-policy situation that could lead to the commitment of our armed forces. In the second, a police officer visits a local elementary school to instruct children about bicycle safety. In the third, an NBA pro at a basketball camp demonstrates to high school students the proper techniques for accurate free-throw shooting. And in the fourth, a NASA spokesperson describes findings from the latest Hubble space telescope transmissions.

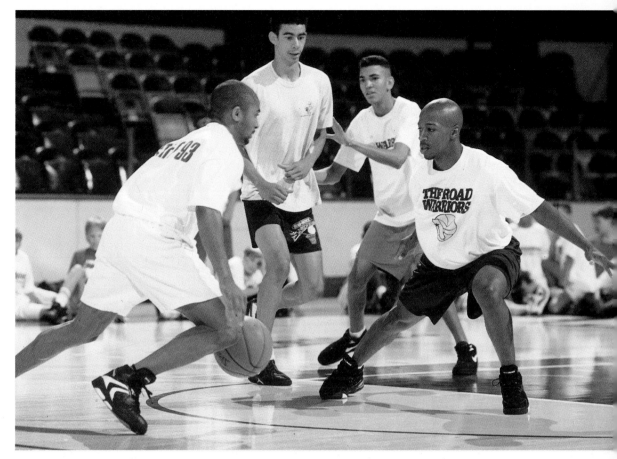

Informative speaking is often informal, as is the case with these basketball instructors.

Each of these scenarios can be viewed as a speaking situation. Further, each involves a speaker publicly *informing* an audience. In each case, the speaker must focus on relating the information to the needs and goals of the audience members. Jaime Escalante had to first reach out to and connect with his students before he could begin to teach them calculus. So too must every informative speaker reach out to and connect with his or her audience before presenting them with information.

Informative Speaking and Styles of Learning

One important consideration in focusing on your audience is recognizing that not everyone has the same style of learning. Not everybody thinks in a linear or "logical" fashion. Some people can simply read a book and absorb the information, whereas others need to hear and see to learn. Still others learn best by doing. Good public speakers recognize these differences and appeal to as many styles as possible. Here is one useful listing of diverse learning styles:[3]

- *Auditory linguistic:* Learning by hearing the spoken word.
- *Visual linguistic:* Learning by seeing the printed word.
- *Auditory numerical:* Learning by hearing numbers.
- *Visual numerical:* Learning by seeing numbers.
- *Audio–visual–kinesthetic combination:* Learning by hearing, seeing, and doing in combination.
- *Individual:* Learning best when by oneself.
- *Group:* Learning best in collaboration with other people.
- *Oral expressive:* Learning by telling others orally.
- *Written expressive:* Learning by writing.

At first, such a long list of diverse learning styles may be intimidating. How can one speech or even a series of speeches adapt to all of these different ways of learning? Of course, a speaker cannot be all things to all people. But teachers confront this variety of learning styles every day. Many teachers use a combination of methods—individual and group work, written and oral assignments, print and visual materials—in an effort to adapt to the variety of learning styles in their classrooms.

Rather than trying to guess which style of learning is most widespread in an audience and focusing on that, it is better to use a combination of methods of learning. That way, you are likely to reach most of your audience members with something that suits their style of learning. In any given audience, there are likely to be individual learners as well as group learners, those who respond best to oral instruction and those who need to read it, and so on. As implied in Box 16-1, there also may be learners whose primary language is different from your own. Utilizing visual aids, discussed later in this chapter, is one excellent way to reinforce visually what you say orally. Distributing a handout after a speech can help visual learners retain what was said. You should provide your audience an opportunity to use as many senses as possible to process your message. If parts of your presentation can be seen, heard, and even touched, you will increase the odds that your message will be understood by the audience.

learning The acquisition of new information.

cognition The purely mental component of learning.

affect The emotional–attitudinal component of learning.

The Components of Learning

Learning is the acquisition of new information. But it is more than just mentally absorbing the knowledge. Learning has three components: cognitive, affective, and behavioral.[4] **Cognition** is the purely mental component of learning. For example, when schoolchildren memorize the Pledge of Allegiance to the flag, they have learned a series of words and phrases. **Affect** is the emotional/attitudinal component of learning, the way you *feel* about having to learn something and your attitude toward the subject matter. The attitude of patriotism and rev-

Box 16-1   Considering Diversity

Overcoming Language Barriers

One advantage Jaime Escalante had in connecting with his students was a shared language. He was able to relate to his students and their parents better than most non-Spanish-speaking teachers. Obviously, there are many situations speakers face where they do not share the culture or even the first language of their audience. However, making an effort to learn at least a few common phrases can assist you in connecting with your audience. For example, Peace Corps volunteers are always instructed in the language of the country in which they will be stationed. Because their purpose is to share information and technology with their hosts, the ability to bridge the language barrier is essential to building trust and conveying a sense of identification.

Given this information, what might you do to facilitate an informative presentation to a group that doesn't share your first language? Is it necessary to be fluent in the language, or are there other ways to connect? If you are speaking through an interpreter, how can you still make a personal connection with your audience?

erence toward the American flag represents the affective component of the Pledge of Allegiance. **Behavior** is the skill component of learning, the ability to do something with the knowledge acquired. Reciting the Pledge of Allegiance is an overt behavior.

Mathematics provides another good example of these three components of learning. Jaime Escalante was not satisfied if his students merely memorized calculus formulas. That would be a purely mental, or cognitive, process. He changed his students' affect, or attitude, toward math. If you have seen the movie based on his life, you know that at first his students didn't believe they could learn calculus. He had to help them have faith in themselves and their ability to achieve in math. Finally, Escalante had to influence his students' behavior. Not only did they need to know the rules of calculus, they also had to perform on the Advanced Placement Test. Thus, their accomplishment was a result of changes in cognition, affect, and behavior. All three components are inextricably linked, as Figure 16-1 shows.

The Informative–Persuasive Continuum

Although academics may be fond of "knowledge for knowledge's sake," most students seek and remember knowledge they find personally and professionally useful. Over the course of a semester or quarter, therefore, part of a teacher's job is to ensure that students understand the usefulness and relevance of the knowledge they acquire. The first step in teaching information to students usually involves some type of informative presentation, most commonly a lecture. In a sense, a good lecture is an effective informative speech. It should provide

behavior The skill component of learning; the ability to do something with the knowledge acquired.

Figure 16-1
Components of
Learning. Learning is the
result of cognition, affect,
and behavior interacting
with each other.

students with information that is stimulating and potentially useful. At the lecture's end, moreover, students should feel that the experience was a positive one and that the information shared is relevant to them. The same is true for any kind of informative speech.

Students often ask how to tell when a speech is merely informative and when it is both informative and persuasive. Some people argue that a speech can be exclusively informative, with no purpose other than passing information along to an audience. Others argue that the distinction between an informative speech and a persuasive speech is blurred.

We are in the second camp. We believe that an informative speech is not worth giving unless it is designed to stay with the audience and influence their lives in some way. What good, for example, is an informative speech about the proper equipment for safe roller blading if it doesn't increase the probability that the audience will seriously consider the information? By the same token, what good is an informative speech on preventive health practices, such as using a condom, if it has no motivational value for an audience?

Instead of looking at the relationship between informative and persuasive speeches as a dichotomy, therefore, think about them in terms of a continuum (shown in Figure 16-2). On one end of the continuum is knowledge, on the other end is behavior. Given the poles of this continuum, behavioral change is seldom the result of a singularly persuasive speech delivered by a singularly credible and charismatic speaker. More typically, persuasion is a process, composed of a series of interdependent messages over time. In the so-called real world, this process—this campaign—begins with someone or some agency providing people with information designed to stimulate them. The information is then used as a base from which to build a more explicitly persuasive campaign to influence people's behavior.

We encourage you to view your informative speeches from the perspective of this continuum. Although a single speech may be predominantly directed toward the informative end of the continuum, it may also contribute to the process of persuading at least some audience members to change at some point in the future. In order to gain experience in the kind of informative speaking you are likely to do in your professional life, select a topic that is reasonably serious and relevant to people's real concerns. Talking about a frivolous topic because you think your goal is simply to provide information is generally a waste of time, both yours and your audience's.

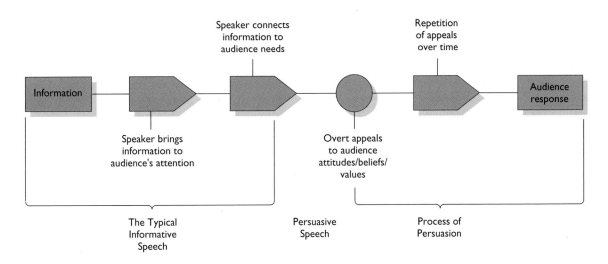

Figure 16-2
Continuum of
Informative to
Persuasive Speaking

Attributes of Effective Informative Speaking

What makes one speaker's presentation so informative and stimulating that you want to learn more about what you initially thought was a boring topic? On the other hand, why does another speaker's presentation leave you cold from the beginning to the end? Is the reason (a) the speaker, (b) the topic, (c) the message, (d) your perceptions, or (e) all of the above? Because the public speaking transaction is an interdependent system, the answer, of course, is "(e) all of the above."

Research over the past two decades suggests that the likelihood of an audience perceiving information as relevant depends significantly on six message attributes: novelty, compatibility, comprehensibility, relative advantage, observability, and trialability.[5] These attributes represent the criteria people use to decide whether a speaker's information is worth the time and effort necessary to pay attention and actively process it.

Novelty

Novelty is the quality of being new and stimulating. Just as plants continuously orient themselves to the sun to activate the process of photosynthesis, people continually orient themselves to new and unique sources of stimulation.

Although novelty alone is not enough to sustain an informative speech, it certainly can make a speech more effective. Research has time and again documented the fact that the perception of novelty heightens selective exposure, selective attention, and selective retention of information. In other words, people are likely to seek out, pay attention to, and remember novel information.

novelty The quality of being new and stimulating.

The most obvious way to get the benefit of novelty in an informative speech is to choose a topic that is novel for your audience. You are much more likely to initially captivate the attention of audience members with the unfamiliar than with the mundane. Novelty, however, shouldn't be confused with obscurity. For example, whereas computer software for accountants probably would be a novel, but obscure, topic for most audiences, the use of the software to save money on taxes might be a novel topic that would interest most people.

Another way to use novelty to your advantage is in the construction of your message. Even though the general rule is to structure your speech so that the audience can predict what comes next, this is not an unbending rule. Sometimes it is to your advantage to violate the expectancies of an audience. Writers, for example, sometimes begin with a story's end and then backtrack. Similarly, a skilled speaker could conceivably start a speech with what normally would be considered its conclusion and build backward.

Finally, novelty in your delivery can work to your advantage when you are speaking informatively. Audiences, for instance, generally are accustomed to speakers who are relatively stationary. Movement may add needed novelty to your presentation, as can the use of vocal variety and well-placed pauses.

Compatibility

Early in this book we said that communication is perceptual and that the process of perception is selective. Basically, people perceive what they choose to perceive. In the effort to reach your audience with an informative speech, you will need to take into account a second message attribute: compatibility. **Compatibility** is the audience's perception that a message is consistent with their attitudes, beliefs, values, and lifestyle. All too often, speakers fail to consider their audience's views when choosing a topic and then constructing their informative speech.

In the past year, for example, we have heard several informative speeches on AIDS and its prevention. We've also had students approach us after class and tell us they were offended or made to feel unjustifiably uncomfortable as a consequence of the information in some of these speeches. These students perceived that these speeches promoted a lifestyle with which they disagreed, and used visual aids they didn't perceive to be in good taste. To a large degree, we were surprised by these reactions to a topic we believe needs to be openly discussed. We don't feel that student speakers should altogether avoid sensitive topics such as this one. However, they do need to consider the question of compatibility so that they can soften or qualify the information and make it appropriate for the audience.

compatibility The perception that a message is consistent with attitudes, beliefs, values, and lifestyle.

Consider, for example, how you might approach an informative speech on the constitutional rights of accused felons for two different audiences. The first audience is composed of law school students. The second is a group of veteran police officers. Both audiences need the information you have at your disposal. Would you give an identical speech to both of them? Probably not. For the police officers, you most likely would have to qualify the information in your speech with such statements as

"I realize some of you take exception with the courts' rulings on the rights of the accused."

"Putting our personal feelings aside, the Constitution is clear . . ."

"Before I begin, I want you to put the shoe on the other foot; assume that you are the accused."

Information that is potentially incompatible with audience members can be made palatable if it is presented in a way that acknowledges the audience's point of view.

Comprehensibility

No matter how simple or complex your topic, your audience should perceive it as something they can understand. **Comprehensibility** is the perception that a message is not too difficult or complex to understand. Research tells us that one of the quickest ways to turn off an audience is to complicate a topic. You don't have to avoid complex topics for your informative speeches; in fact, they are likely to be both novel for your audience and interesting for you to research. The goal is to make complex topics comprehensible and compelling for your audience.

Jaime Escalante's calculus classes in *Stand and Deliver* are models of the presentation of complex information. He broke the lessons into easy-to-digest bits, what he called "step by step." In fact, he would say to his students, "This is easy." It's not so much the complexity of the topic as the complexity of a speaker's explanation that makes a topic difficult for an audience to understand.

An excellent way to reduce the complexity of a speech is through analogies or comparisons. Explain a complex process, for example, by comparing it with a common process based on the same principle. One speech we heard explained nuclear power plants by using an analogy to the steam produced by heating water in a tea kettle.

Visual aids, which are discussed later in this chapter, can also be helpful in reducing complexity. For example, we recall a speech about a complex carbon molecule in which the speaker used a Tinkertoy model to show what the molecule looked like. The speaker also used an analogy, calling the molecule a "soot ball," to help the audience visualize what it would be like.

Relative Advantage

When we introduced the Malandro model of organization in Chapter 14, we talked about the importance of connecting with your audience. Audience members need to know explicitly why it is in their interest to listen to what you have to say.

comprehensibility
The perception that a message is not too difficult or complex to understand.

When we connect with our audience, we are in effect saying, "My topic and message hold some relative advantage for you." **Relative advantage** is the audience's perception that a message will benefit them. It can be anything from a more informed view on some topic to an improved way of behaving. Don't think that just because you have a good idea, people will necessarily see the advantage in adopting it. History is replete with good ideas, the proverbial better mousetraps, that are collecting dust for want of the public's attention. Macintosh users were amused at the hype over Windows 95, pointing out that the same simplicity of use has been available on the Mac for a decade. Yet 90 percent of all personal computers are IBM-compatibles, not Macs. And despite its demise as a format for video recording, Sony's Betamax was technically superior to VHS. The list of great ideas that haven't been adopted is endless. And the key to getting your ideas accepted is to show the audience the relative advantage inherent in adopting them.

All too often, speakers assume that audience members will automatically recognize they have something to gain personally or professionally from a speech. What may be perfectly obvious to the speaker, however, may be just the opposite for the audience. Consider a case with which you already have some experience—college classes. Regardless of their subject matter, most college professors believe that the information they have to share is absolutely essential to every student's intellectual well-being. So secure are they in this belief, in fact, some seldom spend any time convincing students that there are good reasons for their being in the professor's class.

Occasionally, this oversight doesn't much matter—for example, when students are taking a course in their major. Students listen because they know they have to learn what is being taught, regardless of how well it is being taught. This motivation is seldom present, though, when students find themselves in a required course outside their major. "Why do I need a course in art history?" complains the computer science major, while the chemistry major asks, "Why do I need a class in public speaking?" To motivate students in math classes, Jaime Escalante put together a video called *Math: Who Needs It?* starring people like Bill Cosby.

Just as teachers have an obligation to connect their course to the professional aspirations of their students, speakers have the same kind of obligation to their audience. It's not enough that the audience perceives the information as novel or compatible. The audience must also perceive the information—the speech—as something that will benefit them.

relative advantage
The perception that a message is beneficial.

observability The degree to which information can be seen.

Observability

Seeing is believing, or so the saying goes. Information that can be made observable for your audience can work to your advantage. **Observability** is the degree to which information can be seen. For example, in and of themselves, statistics such as gross national product, median income, the consumer price index, and the rate of inflation can ring hollow in the ears of an audience. Yet such information is often the stuff of which informative speeches are made. One way to breathe life into statistics is to augment the speech with creative visual aids. In fact, this kind of augmentation may be what makes your audience nod in understanding instead of staring back at you with blank expressions.

The need for observability is not limited to statistical information. A working model of an internal combustion engine certainly would help a mechanically disinclined audience understand an informative presentation on automotive engineering; a detailed cross section of the human eye would help a group of biology students understand the role of the cornea; and even a visually appealing list of the daily diet of the American teenager might help a group of nursing students relate to an informative speech on nutrition.

Although visual aids may be the most obvious way to give pictorial life to your informative speech, you also can provide word pictures for your audience. For example, in the effort to assist your audience in visualizing information, you can ask them to imagine a situation; you can use examples for which the audience is likely to have a visual referent, such as the Statue of Liberty, a landmark at your school, or a national park; and you can use descriptive adjectives, action words, and visual metaphors. Regardless of how you give visual life to your informative speech, however, the objective is the same: You want your audience to "see" what it is you are talking about.

Trialability

The final message attribute we want to share with you is most relevant to informative presentations that require some demonstration. **Trialability** is the opportunity to experiment with an idea, a product, or a practice without penalty. Simply put, people prefer to "try something on for size" before deciding on its personal or professional worth.

In the business world, for instance, when the PC began to replace the typewriter, and faxes and e-mail began to replace letters, trialability was essential to informative presentations on the uses of these new technologies. One of the lessons learned in the process of computerizing the workplace was that people were quicker to respond favorably to innovations when they had an opportunity to try them out in a nonthreatening environment.

Of course, it is rarely possible to have an entire audience try out something as you speak. Sometimes, the solution is to provide the audience with information on where they can go to try out what you have discussed in your speech. For example, a speech on CPR should include the names and addresses of places that offer hands-on training. On other occasions, you can invite a few audience members to the front of the room and have them try out the process in front of everyone else, showing how it can be done. Then you can urge audience members to try it out on their own. In any case, if some kind of trial experience can be incorporated into a speech, it will enhance the audience's understanding of the subject matter.

At some point in either your educational or professional life, you can expect to have to provide a demonstration for an audience. It may be as simple as explaining your job, or it may be assisting people in the solution of a complex

trialability The opportunity to experiment with an idea, a product, or a practice without penalty.

problem. Whether simple or complex, the best demonstrations are those that involve the people to whom you are speaking. After all, it is much easier to relate to information with which we have hands-on experience than to relate to information that has been conveyed abstractly.

Modes of Informative Speaking

Now that you know some of the principles related to conveying information to an audience, it is time to turn to some practical suggestions for how to give an informative speech. There are four basic ways to inform an audience: explanation, instruction, demonstration, and description. Although we discuss these modes of informing separately, informative speeches may employ more than one of them.

Speeches That Explain

One of the primary functions of an informative speech is to explain some process, object, or concept to an audience. A political science teacher may explain the *process* of democratization of the Eastern European nations. An astronomy teacher may explain the composition of a star, an *object*. A communication teacher may explain how verbal and nonverbal messages differ, a *concept*.

In selecting a topic for a speech that explains something, keep in mind that the topic should be relevant to the audience, something they are capable of understanding, and something you can explain in the time allotted. Even if the theory of relativity is highly relevant to the audience, explaining it in a 5- to 10-minute speech is a tall order.

The message attribute of comprehensibility is important in speeches that explain. Analogies are an effective means of reducing complexity for an audience. Consider the use of analogy in this excerpt from a speech by Jonathan Studebaker, explaining a disease he has:

> I was born with osteogenesis imperfecta, a disease which causes my bones to be fragile. Have you ever accidentally dropped a glass on the floor? What happens? It breaks. Well, my bones kind of break like glass, which is why I tell people, when you carry me, treat me like your best crystal.[6]

This simple analogy of comparing bones to glass helps the audience understand a disease most of us cannot even pronounce. For Jonathan's purpose, which is to introduce himself and explain his disability, that is the extent of the technical information his audience needs to know.

A second attribute that is important in explanatory speeches is observability. Visual aids—such as slides, charts, or overhead transparencies—can make abstract concepts concrete. Because they are observable, the concepts are easier to explain.

Complex topics often need to be explained visually.

During your college career, you undoubtedly will be called on to explain something to an audience, if not in your communication class, then in another setting. Similarly, in the professional world, people are called on to give reports that explain everything from a new product idea to why the last quarter's sales were so low. Using the principles of comprehensibility and observability can help you enhance your explanations.

Speeches That Instruct

Another goal of informative speaking is instruction, or providing new information the audience can put to use. Modern educational theory introduced the notion of observable behavioral objectives to instruction; that is, after receiving instruction, the student should be able to show either by answering questions or by engaging in some activity that he or she has mastered the subject.

The message attributes of novelty and relative advantage are particularly relevant to speeches that provide instruction. Unless the information in your speech presents *new* information to your audience, all you have done is bored them with what they already know. For example, speeches on how to ride a bike or how to pack a suitcase are unlikely to provide anything new to an audience. However, even though information is new, the audience may not find it relevant or of relative advantage. For example, a speech on how to wax skis is irrelevant to nonskiers.

So, the key to speeches that instruct is to provide information that is both new and relevant to your audience. You can use the novelty of your topic to gain interest while pointing out the relative advantage of learning the information to at least the majority of listeners.

Speeches That Demonstrate

Speeches that demonstrate are closely related to those that provide instruction, but they use the message attributes of observability and trialability. In a speech that demonstrates, the speaker shows the audience how to do something. Further, a good demonstration will allow the audience to try out what is being demonstrated, if not during the speech itself, then later on their own. A good example of speeches that demonstrate are the late-night infomercials for a wide variety of products. From "miracle" beauty products to food dehydrators, the products are demonstrated for the audience. The use of the products is clearly observable to the viewers at home and in the studio. Studio audience members are often given a chance to try the product on the spot. Viewers are urged to order the product and try it at home, with a no-risk, money-back guarantee. The combination of observability and trialability has made infomercials highly successful.

Whatever a speaker is demonstrating, he or she needs to provide audience members with enough information to do the activity on their own, or with information on where to obtain further instruction, so that they can try out the activity. For example, although no one can master karate from a single speech, or even a series of speeches, a demonstration of karate moves can spur an audience member to seek out individual instruction in the martial arts. In fact, many martial arts studios make a practice of giving demonstrations in schools and at public events as a way of recruiting new students.

Topics for speeches that demonstrate need to be chosen with care. A complex, difficult task cannot be adequately demonstrated in a few minutes. There can even be the danger of making people think they know how to do something based on a speech when in fact they do not. Few of us could do CPR, for example, based on simply watching a speaker demonstrate the activity. We need the opportunity to try it out (perhaps on a life-size doll) before we can know whether we can do it. On the other hand, another life-saving technique, the Heimlich maneuver, is often the subject of demonstration and can be learned in a reasonably short time.

The key to making your demonstration effective is careful planning. If you have ever watched the show *Home Improvement* you know that Tim (The Tool Man) Taylor rarely has practiced what he is doing. If you plan to demonstrate a process in a speech, you should rehearse it carefully. Also, it is sometimes useful to prepare steps of the process in advance. Watch any chef doing a demonstration on a TV show. The onions are already chopped, the flour is already sifted and measured, and so on. You don't want the audience drifting off as you measure ingredients or sift the flour. Providing a written recipe in a handout or as a visual aid will also save you a lot of time and let the audience focus on watching your demonstration. In short, a demonstration requires extra preparation.

In addition, be sure that the demonstration is an accurate re-creation. If you misinform an audience, you have done more harm than good. Depending on what you are demonstrating, you might even be inviting injury to the audience member or someone else. Make certain, therefore, that you can accurately demonstrate the process in the time allowed.

Failure to properly prepare for a demonstration is the hallmark of Tim Allen's comedy on *Home Improvement*, but it can lead to disaster in an informative speech.

VIDEO FILE

If you have the
videotape that
accompanies this
book, the speech
"Eating Disorders and
Their Warning Signs,"
by Kelli Wells, appears
in Part V, Segment 3.

Finally, make sure the demonstration is visible to the audience. We recall a student who was an expert fisherman and wanted to demonstrate the art of fly tying. Since fishing line is almost invisible and a fishhook is very difficult to see, he used a large-scale fishhook (made from a coat hanger) and colored yarn to tie his fly. Only by enlarging the actual objects was he able to give the audience a meaningful demonstration.

Speeches That Describe

Another function of informative speeches is description. Observability is the key to a descriptive speech. Not only can visual aids be useful but you may also want to provide a word picture of your subject. Consider the following description of a familiar character, Disney's Mickey Mouse, provided by student speaker Jennie Rees:

"They used a circle for his head and oblong circles for his nose and snout. They also drew circles for his ears and drew them in such a way that they appeared to look the same any way Mickey turned his head. They gave him a pearshaped body with pipe-stem legs, and stuffed them in big, oversized shoes, making him look like a little kid wearing his father's shoes."[7]

Can't you almost picture Mickey from that description? Visual language is key to effective description.

Description can be used not only for physical objects but also for scenes or events. Consider the briefings given by General Norman Schwarzkopf during the Persian Gulf War. He used a variety of maps and charts to explain every move. He used terms from football, calling the American troop movements a "Hail Mary pass." Further, rather than merely telling the audience about the success of U.S. smart bombs, he used a video to show the accuracy with which targets were destroyed. In one memorable incident, he pointed to a vehicle passing through the crosshairs of the bomber just before the target was hit. He called the driver "the luckiest man in Iraq."

Putting It All Together

Whether your speech is primarily explanation, instruction, demonstration, or description, it is important that you incorporate as many of the six attributes of effective informative speaking as possible. One attribute that you need to include for every speech, however, is compatibility. If your audience sees the topic as incompatible with their needs, beliefs, attitudes, or values, they will view your speech as a hostile persuasive attempt rather than an informative speech.

What, then, does an effective informative speech look like? For one example, see the sample informative speech "Eating Disorders and Their Warning Signs," in Box 16-2 by Kelli Wells. This speech and the accompanying annotations will help you put together the concepts discussed in this chapter as you plan and prepare your own informative speech.

Box 16-2   Critical Thinking

Sample Informative Speech
Eating Disorders and Their Warning Signs
by Kelli Wells

This speech was prepared and delivered by Kelli Wells, a student in a speech class at California State University, Chico. It is reprinted here with her permission. The text was prepared from a transcript of Kelli's speech. Because extemporaneous speaking frequently leads to unintentional errors, we have edited the speech.

I knew my best friend had a problem. Didn't she know what she was doing to herself? Her weight and food consumption had become an obsession with her. I could see how it was controlling her. But in her mind, it was all she could control. She couldn't eat anything without quickly running to the bathroom. I had to hear daily how fat she was and how her life would be so much better if she was thinner. As she got deeper and deeper into an eating disorder, bulimia nervosa, she was no longer the person I used to know. I know the signs of an eating disorder and I was able to confront her about her problem. She was able to get help and now she's doing much better.

I've seen firsthand how an eating disorder can affect someone. That's why it's important that we all know about them and the warning signs of an eating disorder. You may be able to save a life. Knowing more about eating disorders will enable you to be more aware of what may be going on in the mind of even a friend or a family member.

Tonight, you will be informed of the main types of eating disorders, who are the most likely candidates, and the signs to look for.

The two main types of eating disorders are anorexia and bulimia nervosa. The fear of obesity and the pursuit of thinness represent the driving force in both these mental disorders.

In anorexia nervosa, this fear is expressed through a number of symptoms, including the desire to maintain a very low body weight, body-image disturbance, and avoiding food altogether. There is intense fear of getting fat and an obsession with being thin. These are the two most cognitive features of anorexia.

Anorexic individuals also struggle with body-image disturbance. They have a distorted view in which they perceive their body to be fat, in spite of its thin appearance. They also suffer extreme dissatisfaction with the size or the shape of the body. Food avoidance is another problem. Anorexics will avoid food altogether and obtain only small amounts of diet food, such as salads or fruits.

Young women with bulimia nervosa share many of the same symptoms

Continued on page 434

Notice how Kelli uses a vivid description to capture the audience's attention.

Also, because it is a personal experience, her credibility on the topic is established.

Kelli stresses the relative advantage of learning about eating disorders—you may save a life.

Kelli's preview is clear and direct.

Kelli uses clear language to explain a complex topic in terms everyone can understand.

The difference between the two disorders is clearly explained.

Notice the clear use of signposts in the speech to indicate transitions between points.

By citing statistics on college-age women, Kelli connects with her college-age audience.

Observable symptoms of the disorders are presented. (Would a visual aid have been helpful here?)

Summary is clear and accurate.

Conclusion ties back to introduction. Audience members are urged to use the information in the speech.

as anorexics. Most bulimic women are dissatisfied with their current body weight. Bulimics, however, are not as effective in dieting and usually weigh within the normal range. So they are able to avoid treatment for many years. But actually what they are doing to their bodies is completely destroying their systems. Bulimics binge-eat, which means they eat large amounts of food uncontrollably and then force themselves to purge the calories consumed to avoid weight gain. For many bulimic individuals, the act of eating is associated with the feeling of being out of control. They're able to regain control by purging.

Now that you are informed of the two main types of eating disorders, anorexia and bulimia nervosa, it's important to know who the most likely candidates are for having these disorders.

The most widespread group of people that are affected by these disorders are young women. Our society today believes that the thinner you are, the better your life will be. Young women begin to measure their self-esteem on their dieting success. They believe that eating is the cause and result of many of their problems. So they become trapped in a vicious cycle of rigid behavior focused on food. We're continually confronted in newspapers, magazines, and television, with ads imploring and encouraging us to eat and prepare all kinds of food. At the same time, young women are encouraged and pressured to be thin and maintain perfect figures by fashion designers. This paradox is hard to manage and for most young women results in an eating disorder.

In doing my research, I found statistics for college populations from the book *Eating Disorders: Assessment and Treatment,* by Scholtz and Johnson. In 22 studies done across college campuses, an average of 7.6 percent of college women suffer from some type of eating disorder. As we can see, this is a problem that shouldn't be forgotten.

Now that I have informed you that young women are the most affected by these disorders, it is crucial to know the warning signs. In bulimia nervosa, the warning signs are dehydration, digestive disorders, severe dental problems, and muscle weaknesses. In anorexia, the symptoms are dry skin and hair, cold hands and feet, general weakness, and most importantly extreme weight loss.

In conclusion, let me summarize the three main points I informed you about tonight. First, the two main types of eating disorders are bulimia and anorexia nervosa. Second, young women are the most likely candidates for having these disorders. And thirdly, the symptoms which I shared with you are important to know in helping a friend or even a family member.

My best friend felt what many women feel everywhere, that to be thin equals happiness. Eating disorders are vicious traps that, once you get into, are very hard to get out of. Hopefully now, by knowing more about them, you can help someone you care about.

To what extent does this speech incorporate the principles of novelty, compatibility, complexity, relative advantage, observability, and trialability discussed in this chapter? To what extent would the speech benefit from further use of any of these message attributes? After reading and/or viewing the speech, see if you can construct an outline of the speech, identifying opening, connecting, focus, main points, summary, and close.

Strengthening Your Speech with Presentational Aids

As we have mentioned, observability and comprehensibility are important in informative speaking, and presentational aids are often an ideal way to achieve observability and comprehensivity. **Presentational aids** are visual, audio, and audiovisual devices that augment a speech. They can add an important dimension to it. For example, when you give someone directions to your home, is it clearer to explain it only verbally or to both draw a map and to explain it? Which is the more effective advertising—a radio ad or a full-color television commercial that can be seen as well as heard? Which is more interesting to listen to for a 50-minute class session—an instructor who lectures the entire time or one who uses a variety of visual media to supplement the lecture?

In each case you probably chose the second alternative. Adding visual or even audio information to any presentation is likely to help your audience comprehend, remember, accept, and act on your ideas. A study conducted by the University of Minnesota for 3M found that people who saw a presentation with visual support were more likely to be persuaded, had an improved perception of the speaker, as well as greater comprehension and a higher attention level, and were more likely to agree with the verbal material of the presentation.[8]

Although we introduce presentational aids in the context of informative speaking, they can be used in all types of speeches. Speeches to inform, to persuade, and to entertain can all be enhanced by the use of visual, audio, and audiovisual aids, as long as they are appropriate to the topic and the audience.

Types of Visual Aids

Visual aids are presentational aids that convey their message visually. There are numerous types of visual aids that you may want to consider for your speech, including objects, models, photographic depictions, diagrams and illustrations, and charts, graphs, and maps.

Objects In some cases, you can use the object you are discussing in your speech. A speech about the bagpipe might call for a demonstration on the instrument. A demonstration of karate or judo almost demands that you use people to show how the moves are done.

The key to using people or objects is to make sure they are easily visible to your audience and appropriate to the situation. As our earlier example illustrated,

presentational aids
Visual, audio, and audiovisual devices that augment a speech.

visual aids
Presentational aids that convey their message visually.

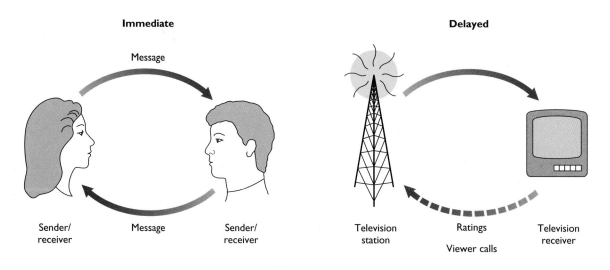

Immediate

Message

Sender/
receiver

Message

Sender/
receiver

Delayed

Television
station

Ratings

Viewer calls

Television
receiver

Figure 16-3 Diagrams such as these can be used to illustrate abstract concepts, such as communication feedback.

the speech demonstrating fly tying could not use actual fishing line because it is almost invisible. So the speaker used a large hook made from a coat hanger and yarn to represent the fishing line. Some inappropriate objects can even create problems. Almost every semester we have students who wish to do speeches on some aspect of firearms. However, firearms are prohibited on our campus (except for those of campus security officers) for obvious reasons. Wine tasting is another popular topic we must veto, because alcohol is also prohibited on our campus. Thus, before you plan a speech using actual objects, be sure to ask your instructor what is appropriate and allowable on your campus.

Models   Often a three-dimensional model of an object can be used when it is impractical to use the actual object. We recall a speech on the common American cockroach. Bringing a live cockroach to class would have been disconcerting, to say the least. However, the student cleverly constructed a large-scale model of a cockroach that she kept hidden in a box until just the right instant, when she revealed the topic of her speech. Not only was the speech informative and entertaining, it also was enhanced by the student's ability to explain her subject vividly with a model.

Photographs   A photograph of your object can be a useful visual aid, as long as it is clearly visible to everyone in the audience. Thus, you must either enlarge the photo to poster size or show it through a slide or overhead projector. A speech on art history, for example, would be greatly enhanced by slides or enlargements of photographs of paintings of various periods and styles.

Diagrams and Illustrations   Sometimes an illustration or a drawing will serve your purpose better than a photograph. Diagrams are a good way to represent the parts of an object. For example, a cutaway drawing of a firearm can be used

Percent Distribution of 1993 State Lottery Proceeds ($9 billion)

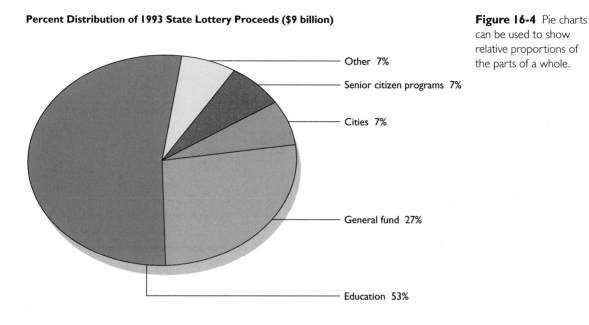

Other 7%

Senior citizen programs 7%

Cities 7%

General fund 27%

Education 53%

Figure 16-4 Pie charts can be used to show relative proportions of the parts of a whole.

to explain its function, and the diagram—unlike a real gun—is neither illegal nor dangerous. Figure 16-3 illustrates a more abstract concept, communication feedback, through use of a diagram.

Charts, Graphs, and Maps   Some speeches call for a particular kind of visual representation of numbers and statistics through charts or graphs. Three types of charts and graphs are especially useful for depicting statistical information: pie charts, line graphs, and bar charts.

A *pie chart* is a circular chart that divides a whole into several parts, each represented by a slice of the circle proportional to its share of the whole. Figure 16-4 shows a typical pie chart representing the distribution of state lottery proceeds. The advantage of pie charts is that they simplify and dramatically illustrate the relative proportions of the parts of a whole.

A *line graph* shows numerical data as a series of points connected by a line. It is well suited to showing changes over time, such as media usage over a 15-year period, as shown in Figure 16-5. By using more than one line (each a different color or pattern), you can show how two or more things compare across the same time period.

A *bar chart* uses vertical bars or horizontal columns to represent various quantities, as shown in Figure 16-6. By grouping two or more bars or by color-coding them, you can compare two or more categories. For example, the first bar chart in Figure 16-6 compares men's and women's participation in the 10 most popular sports. The second chart compares the per capita consumption of various foods in four different years.

Figure 16-5 Line graphs are useful for showing changes over time.

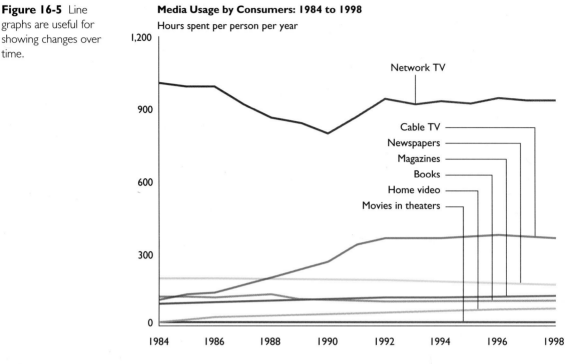

Media Usage by Consumers: 1984 to 1998

Hours spent per person per year

Note: Data for 1993 to 1998 are projected.

An *organizational chart* represents the structure of an organization, using boxes and lines to convey hierarchy and lines of authority, as in Figure 16-7. Such charts are useful in business, industry, and governmental organizations. They can illustrate the organization's structure or show the lines of authority.

A *flow chart* uses boxes and arrows to represent the relationship of steps in a process. Thus, a flow chart, such as Figure 16-8, can show how a process is carried out.

Maps are useful for speeches describing the spatial layout of an area, whether a dangerous intersection in your hometown or the disputed border between hostile nations. Maps can also be used to describe a dynamic process, such as a battle. At the site of the historic battle of Gettysburg, for example, numerous maps display the stages of the battle. One large-scale map uses embedded lights to show the daily progress of the battle.

Visual-Aid Materials

Visual aids can be constructed from a variety of materials. Typical materials for visual aids include poster board, flip charts, overhead transparencies, slides, handouts, and chalkboards. We'll discuss each briefly in turn.

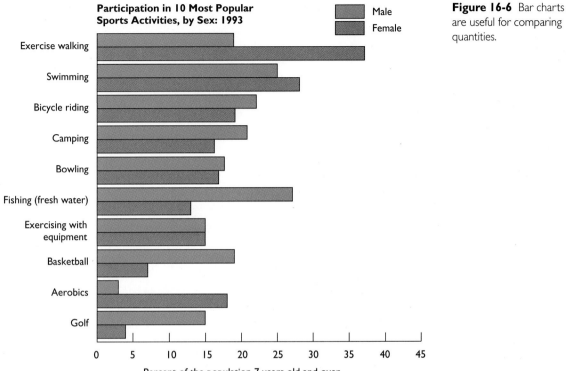

Participation in 10 Most Popular Sports Activities, by Sex: 1993

Percent of the population 7 years old and over

Figure 16-6 Bar charts are useful for comparing quantities.

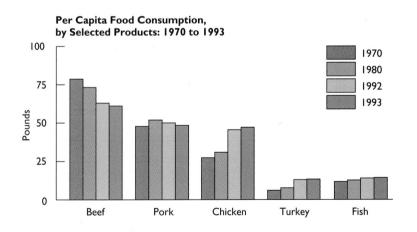

Per Capita Food Consumption, by Selected Products: 1970 to 1993

Poster board is one of the most common materials used for visual aids. One can draw an illustration, a diagram, or a chart on poster board with colored marking pens; enlarged pictures can be pasted on it; and rub-on letters or other

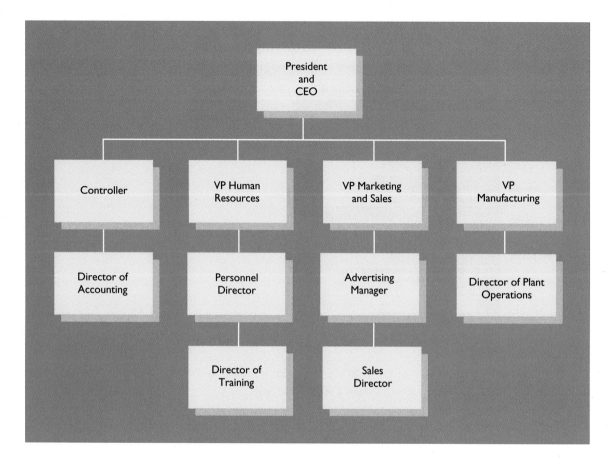

Figure 16-7
Organizational Chart

prepared materials can also be used. Colored poster board may be visually more interesting than white board, as long as it contrasts with the lettering.

Flip charts are a series of drawings, charts, or graphs rendered on large sheets of paper, usually bound at the top and supported on an easel. Speakers use flip charts to present a series of visual aids in a predetermined order. As with poster board, rough out the visual aid in light pencil and then fill it in with permanent marking pens. Be sure that the ink does not bleed through to the next sheet of paper. Put blank sheets between visual aids if you will not be using one right after the other.

An image can be made into an *overhead transparency* by drawing or photocopying it onto a plastic sheet and then projecting it on a screen with an overhead projector. Overhead transparencies are a popular visual aid in business and classroom presentations. They have the advantage of low cost and ease of preparation, and they can be used without dimming the lights. Many classrooms and business conference rooms have overhead projectors, but, you should always check in advance to make sure a projector will be available. It is also wise to check out the equipment in advance, since machines operate differently.

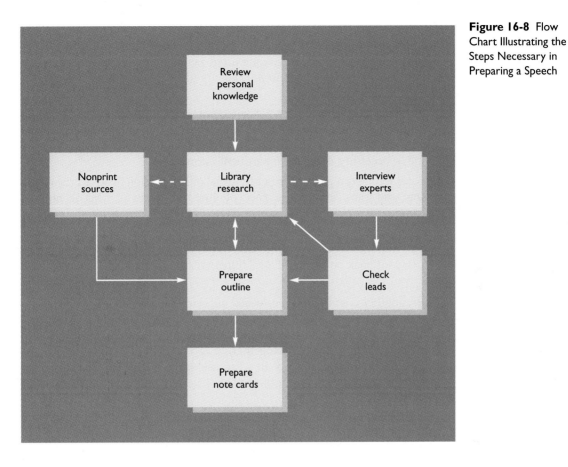

Figure 16-8 Flow Chart Illustrating the Steps Necessary in Preparing a Speech

When making and using overheads, keep the following rules in mind:[9]

- The text must be large enough to be seen when projected on a screen. The smallest image on the screen should be at least 1 inch high for every 30 feet of viewing distance. If something you plan to put on an overhead transparency is too small to be read, unprojected, from 10 feet away, enlarge it with a photocopying machine before you copy it onto a transparency.

- Place the projection screen high enough for those in the back of the room to see clearly, with the bottom at least 48 inches from the floor. Ideally, the screen should be to the right of a right-handed presenter so that he or she can write on the transparency without blocking the light. Also, be sure to consider the audience's line of sight. Don't hesitate to ask if everyone can see, and make the necessary adjustments if some people's view is blocked.

- To maintain eye contact with your audience, don't turn your back on them to point to something on the screen. Instead, use a pointer, such as a pencil, to point to the transparency on the projector.

- Consider using special water-based marking pens to underline or highlight points on overheads as you go along. For example, you could liven up a black-on-clear overhead by using a red pen to underline key words. You can also use colored pens in advance to add color to black-on-clear outlines on charts or graphs.

- Turn off the overhead projector when you are not using it. Don't leave an old overhead up on the screen, and never project an empty screen. On the other hand, leave the overhead on long enough for the audience to read it and, if necessary, copy down pertinent information.

- Consider using a piece of paper to reveal only a portion of an overhead at a time and thus control the pace of your presentation. This technique, known as "revelation," prevents audience members from reading ahead.

- Keep a printed copy of each transparency on the lectern so that you can refer to it instead of having to stare into the glare of the projector's light or turn your back on your audience to read the screen.

Slides, another common type of visual aid, are also a useful way to project a picture or other image onto a screen to ensure that everyone in the group can see. However, slides, unlike overhead transparencies, require a darkened room. So all slides should be presented together.

Organize the slides in advance in a carousel projector. Be sure every slide is properly loaded, as an upside-down or reversed slide can disrupt your presentation.

In addition, you should rehearse with the slides, especially if you must use a colleague to advance them. Although a slide presentation can be effective when done professionally, most beginning speakers should stick to simpler visual aids. Photographs that can be enlarged and placed on poster board, for example, often work just as well as slides and do not require any special equipment.

The primary use of *handouts* is to give the audience something to take with them from the speech, such as a recipe or an address. If you do not plan to directly use the handouts in the speech, pass them out after you are finished speaking. If they are distributed prior to the speech, your audience is likely to be reading them and not listening to what you say. Distributing them during the speech will disrupt the flow of your presentation and take up valuable time.

Chalkboards or erasable marker boards are sometimes useful for putting up brief information, such as a phone number, an address, or a few key words. For anything longer than a few words, use a prepared visual aid, such as an overhead transparency, so that you will not have to turn your back on your audience for more than a moment. Before you read any further, take the visual literacy test in Box 16-3.

Guidelines for Creating Visual Aids

When you begin to create your visual aids, keep four basic principles in mind: simplicity, visibility, layout, and color.[10] Let's consider each of these in turn.

Box 16-3   Self-Assessment

Testing Your Visual Literacy

Without referring to the text, try to answer the following questions.

1. How many ideas should a visual aid attempt to express?
2. How many lines should appear on a visual aid?
3. How many words should appear per line on a visual aid?
4. To be visible from a distance of 30 feet, what is the minimum size type for an effective visual aid?

5. True or false?
    a. Color makes visual aids more memorable.
    b. The more colorful a visual aid is, the more memorable it will be.
    c. Primary colors such as red and blue are preferred to blended colors.
    d. Any use of color is better than no use of color.

To check how well you did, return to the text and the discussion of guidelines for creating visual aids.

Simplicity   It is a common mistake to try to put too much information on any one visual aid. You can't simply take a page from a magazine and copy it onto an overhead transparency or put two or three ideas on one poster. Overcrowding undermines the effectiveness of visual aids. Following are some tips for keeping your visual aids simple.

- Limit yourself to one idea per visual aid.
- Use no more than six or seven words per line.
- Use no more than six or seven lines per visual aid.
- Use short, familiar words and round numbers.
- Keep charts and graphs simple enough to be sketched easily by the audience.

Visibility   Any visual aid is only as good as it is visible to your audience. It will hinder your presentation if audience members have to strain or ask a neighbor what is on the screen. To make your visual aids visible:

- Images should be at least 1 inch high for every 30 feet of viewing distance.
- Transparencies should be readable by the naked eye at 10 feet and use type no smaller than one-quarter inch, which is known as

18 POINT TYPE.

- Nothing should block your audience's view.

Layout An organized, consistent, and uncluttered layout is necessary for an effective visual aid. For the most readable layout:

- Place images near the top of the visual aid to ensure maximum visibility.
- Accentuate key points with bold type, underlining, or color.
- Use horizontal, not vertical, writing for ease of reading.
- Leave a sizable margin, larger on top than bottom and equal on the sides.
- Present information so that it can be read from left to right, top to bottom.

Color Research has shown that the proper use of color helps your audience pay attention to, comprehend, and remember your visuals.

- Primary colors, such as red, blue, and yellow, create the strongest impact.
- Insufficient contrast, such as yellow lettering on a white background, makes things difficult to see.
- Colored backgrounds are visually soothing, as long as the color is not so dark that the message is hard to see.
- Avoid using clashing colors or confusing ones, such as red to show a profit and black to show a loss.

Audio and Audiovisual Aids

Presentations can be enhanced not only with visual aids, but also with sound or sound and pictures in combination. Presentational aids that use sound only, such as a tape recording, are called *audio aids*. A speech on different styles of music, for instance, would be almost impossible without a recording of the music being discussed. A speech about dialects would be enhanced by samples of speech from different regions. A speech on old-time radio shows might include a few snippets from "Superman" or "The Phantom."

The most obvious way to prepare audio aids is with a tape recorder. Because most speech situations don't allow enough time to present a complete song, let alone a symphony, you will want to edit your tape to include only the brief portion of the sounds you need. You can do this with a tape deck or any recording equipment that permits you to dub from tape to tape or from CD to tape.

Audiovisual aids, such as films, videotapes, filmstrips, and slide/tape presentations, combine sound and sight. Films and videotape offer sound and motion, and filmstrips and slide/tape presentations combine still photos with sound.

Videotape has several advantages over film. You do not have to darken the room to show it. Also, you can easily search a videotape for a particular segment. Usually, speakers have their videotapes cued to the points they plan to use. For example, we recall a student who was speaking against the colorization of old black-and-white movies. She brought in two videotape versions of Frank Capra's classic, *It's a Wonderful Life*. In about a minute, she was able to compare a scene originally shot in black and white with the colorized version. Her audience could clearly see for themselves the differences colorization had made in the film. With video, you can also use slow motion or freeze frame to emphasize your point. For example, a speaker explaining gymnastic scoring might want to freeze the tape or use slow motion to call attention to mistakes that call for a deduction in points.

With either film or videotape, the danger is that you will cease to be a speaker and become merely a projectionist or a button pusher. Any use of video or film should be brief (no more than a minute or so for a 10-minute speech) and central to the speech.

Filmstrips or slide/tape presentations basically involve prerecording the speech, which is then presented in coordination with still photos projected on a screen. For most speech classes, this is not an appropriate method, because it replaces your speech with the mediated presentation. However, the slide/tape technology is often useful for sales presentations, as a teaching device, and in situations where a speaker will follow up with a speech. Because the time limits for most speech classes do not allow for this technology, we will not go into it in detail here. Suffice it to say that, with the right equipment, one can prepare an effective slide/tape presentation at a reasonable cost.

Computer-Assisted Presentational Aids

One of the most exciting developments in presentational aids has been the use of computers to create and present visual and audiovisual aids.[11] At a minimum, computers enable you to create charts, graphs, illustrations, and other visual depictions that can be transferred to slides, overheads, or posters. With a color printer, you can create attractive graphics rather easily. Special transparency sheets can be printed on directly by a laser or ink-jet printer.

Because of the wide variety of software and hardware available, we will not specifically discuss any one program or computer. However, among the leading software packages you may have the opportunity to deal with are Adobe™, Persuasion™, or Microsoft® Powerpoint. Whether you use an IBM-compatible PC or a Macintosh, you will find a wide range of programs that can assist you in preparing visual aids for your speeches.

The advantage of using software designed specifically for presentation graphics is that many programs will create appropriate charts or graphs once you enter your information. Also, there are usually prepared templates that you can use in preparing your own graphics. Clip-art images are also typically part of the package, allowing you to pick and choose images that fit your needs. A scanner will allow you to store pictures in your computer for use in graphics. In short, the computer can help you in the creative process of producing graphics to be displayed on the traditional media of visual aids.

Because the screen on a computer is too small to be seen by an audience, you need a way to project your visual aids on a large flat screen, just as you would an overhead transparency or slide. There are thin, transparent display units, called liquid crystal display pads, made for this purpose. The pad is placed on top of

VIDEO FILE

If you have the videotape that accompanies this book, Part IV shows a demonstration of *Power Point*, a popular computer-assisted aid.

Technological innovations in computer software make the creative use of visual aids accessible to even those who can't draw a straight line.

an overhead projector and connected by a cable directly to your computer. At the same time an image is displayed on your computer screen, the pad on the overhead displays the image on a thin panel through which the light from the overhead projector can pass and project the image on the screen for your audience to see. Even animation and sound are possible with the right hardware and software.

Of course, the downside to this technology is that the speaker risks becoming secondary to the equipment. And if you do not know how to correctly operate the computer, or if there is an equipment failure, you risk embarrassment, as Box 16-4 makes clear. Thus, for beginning students, we recommend computers primarily for the creation of more traditional visual aids. However, be aware that the range of computer-assisted presentations is ever increasing and will likely become more common throughout your lifetime.

Summary

To be successful, informative speakers must do as Jaime Escalante did, instill *ganas,* the desire to succeed, into their audiences. Speakers must also adapt their informative speeches to audiences with diverse learning styles. One way to do so is to incorporate multiple methods and channels of learning into their speeches.

Informative speaking is the process by which an audience gains new information from a speaker. Learning is the acquisition of new information and involves

Box 16-4   Skill Building

Murphy's Law and Presentational Aids

Murphy's law is the well-known adage "If anything can go wrong, it will." It applies as much to the use of presentational aids in public speaking as to your car battery on a cold morning. Although you can prepare your visual aids thoroughly, there is no way to be completely prepared for the unexpected. The best defense is to anticipate problems and prepare alternatives. Here are a few of the things that can go wrong (at one time or another, they have all happened to us) and ways to prepare for them.

Problem: The battery in your equipment (tape recorder, microphone, or whatever) is dead.

What to do: Test the equipment the morning of your speech and carry a spare battery.

Problem: There is no overhead projector, even though you reserved one.

What to do: Make sure you call to confirm your reservation on the morning of your speech. Physically check out the projector if possible.

Problem: The overhead projector's light bulb is burned out.

What to do: Most overheads have a spare light bulb. Make sure you know where it is beforehand.

Problem: The slide projector (film projector, VCR, etc.) does not work.

What to do: Again, check it out in advance if possible. If it unexpectedly fails, you will need to verbally describe what is on your slides. We recall one case where a person simply stood in front of a blank screen, pretended to show slides, and described them in elaborate detail as he went along ("As you can clearly see from this slide . . ."). It turned a frustrating situation into a humorous one.

Problem: Your visual aids are out of order or upside-down, or some are missing.

What to do: An ounce of prevention is worth a pound of cure. Check and double-check them before the speech. If you run into this problem, try not to get flustered. Make a joke while you look for the missing visual; if you can't find it, verbally describe the visual or skip that part of the speech.

Problem: There's no chalk for the chalkboard or no dry erase pen for the white board.

What to do: Bring extra chalk or dry erase pens with you.

Problem: It takes a lot longer than you thought to demonstrate a process using your visual aids.

What to do: First, always practice with your visuals so that you know how long it will take. Second, if you are demonstrating a multistep process, prepare various steps along the way in advance.

Remember, nothing can happen to you that hasn't already happened to someone else. Most audiences are sympathetic to speakers who are obviously prepared and yet encounter technical difficulties beyond their control. At the same time, audiences have little sympathy when Murphy's law strikes someone who is just "winging it." And keep in mind, "Murphy was an optimist."

three interrelated components: cognition, the purely mental aspects of learning; affect, the emotional-attitudinal component; and behavior, the skill component. Informative speaking is related to persuasion by virtue of being the first step in the process of influencing people to adopt new ideas, products, and processes.

Informative and persuasive speaking are best viewed as ends of a continuum, rather than totally unrelated types of speaking.

Informative speakers should use the message attributes of novelty, compatibility, comprehensibility, relative advantage, observability, and trialability in their informative speeches. Informative speeches may explain, instruct, demonstrate, and describe. Each of these types of speeches employs one or more of the six attributes of effective informative speaking. Informative speaking is by far the most common type of public speaking and routinely occurs in the classroom, the workplace, and the community.

Presentational aids can make the difference between a successful speech and a failure. People learn more, remember longer, and are more likely to be persuaded by speeches with effective presentational aids. As with all aspects of your speech, be sure to begin by analyzing the situation and the audience in deciding to use presentational aids such as poster board, flip charts, transparencies, slides, handouts, and chalkboards. Other presentational aids include audio, audiovisual, and computer-assisted presentations.

Another Look

Articles

Donald Dean Morley and Kim B. Walker. "The Role of Importance, Novelty, and Plausibility in Producing Belief Change." *Communication Monographs* 54 (1987): 436–42.

The authors tested the role of importance, novelty, and plausibility in causing changes in belief. They found that all three had to be present to result in significant belief change. The results of their test are consistent with our discussion in this chapter.

Walter Kiechel III. "The Big Presentation," *Fortune Magazine,* July 1982, 99.

Making informative presentations doesn't just stop once you have earned your degree. For many of us, in fact, both the number and importance of informative presentations increase as our careers progress. Kiechel's article takes stock of the significant role informative presentations play in the real world of corporate America.

Books

Jay Mathews. *Escalante: The Best Teacher in America.* New York: Henry Holt, 1988.

This is an excellent book about Jaime Escalante. Reading it will give you insight into what makes a truly superb teacher.

C.C. Staley and R. S. Staley III. *Communicating in Business and the Professions: The Inside Word.* Belmont, Calif.: Wadsworth Publishing Company, 1992.

Although this book looks at more than business and professional presentations, it gives you a genuine appreciation of the importance business people place on communication skills. Chapters 4 and 5 specifically address developing and delivering an effective business presentation, paying particular attention to what is unique about business and professional speaking situations.

Video Rentals

Stand and Deliver   This is the award-winning film about Jaime Escalante's life. Actor Edward James Olmos portrays Escalante in a memorable performance. Seeing this film will show you vividly what we can only describe in this chapter, that *ganas* is the key to successful informative speaking.

Dangerous Minds   Michele Pfeiffer stars as a former United States Marine who is put into an "impossible" situation as a new high school teacher. Like *Stand and Deliver,* this movie is based on a true story of an inspiring teacher who overcame impossible odds, and shows the role informative speaking plays in any classroom.

Theory and Research in Practice

1. We have discussed the research that shows people have widely varied learning styles. Develop an outline of a one- to two-minute speech in which you inform an audience about a topic with which you are personally very familiar. Then show how you would adapt that speech to at least three different learning styles: auditory linguistic, visual linguistic, and audio–visual–kinesthetic.

2. On a topic of your choice, explain how you would prepare an informative speech so that it would affect the listeners' cognitive, affective, and behavioral learning. For example, if you were to teach someone to ride a bike, how would you affect all three components of learning?

3. Come up with at least two possible topics each for speeches that explain, instruct, demonstrate, and describe. Do some topics seem to fall naturally into one category? Could other topics be used for more than one type of speech?

CHAPTER 17

Persuasive Speaking

OBJECTIVES

After reading this chapter you should be able to:

• Describe how your assessment of the situation is important to persuasive speaking.

• Describe the four goals persuasive speeches are designed to achieve.

• Define ethos, logos, and pathos.

• Demonstrate how to use Toulmin's model of argument to create a persuasive message.

• Demonstrate how to use first-, second-, and third-order data as evidence in a persuasive speech.

• Explain the rationale for presenting a two-sided persuasive message, and construct such a message.

• Demonstrate how certain types of persuasive appeals are linked to audience members' emotions and primitive beliefs.

The last week in March 1981 was a good time to be a Republican. Ronald Reagan had just been sworn in as president that January, after defeating Democrat Jimmy Carter. It was even better if you happened to hold an important post in the Reagan White House, as did Press Secretary James P. Brady. As a result, Brady was feeling good about himself and his boss, who had just delivered a speech to 3,500 labor leaders.

As usual, a throng of reporters and tourists awaited President Reagan and his entourage as they emerged from the building in which Reagan had just given a speech to the AFL-CIO. As usual, the reporters present immediately began to shout, "Mr. President, Mr. President." And, as usual, Press Secretary Brady stepped ahead of the president to field the questions that the reporters were yelling.

What happened in the next two seconds was horrifying. John Hinckley, Jr., a disturbed young man, fired six shots from a .22 caliber automatic pistol in the direction of President Reagan, hitting the president, Secret Service Agent Tim McCarthy, Washington Patrol Officer Thomas Delahanty, and Brady. Reagan, McCarthy, and Delahanty recovered completely. Brady, wounded in the head, was permanently disabled and would never completely recover his considerable talents as a communicator.

Fast-forward 12 years. Sarah Brady is testifying before Congress about the merits of a handgun-control bill that bears her husband's name. In a short time, the Brady Bill would become law, the culmination for Sarah and Jim Brady of a decade-long campaign to impose a waiting period and background checks for the purchase of guns like the one John Hinckley, Jr., had used. In the course of that campaign, not only did Sarah Brady become the founder of Handgun Control, Inc., a nationwide lobbying group dedicated to changing handgun laws, but she also became a public speaker of unquestionable persuasive skills.[1]

Although you may never find yourself thrust into the national limelight like Sarah Brady, you can still count on preparing and delivering at least a few persuasive speeches over the course of your life. What's more, you can learn a lot about this process from Sarah Brady's example. In this chapter we use her story to illustrate the process of preparing and delivering an effective persuasive speech. The topics covered in this chapter include

- the relationship between persuasive speaking and the rhetorical situation;
- factors to take into account in your attempts to reinforce what audience members believe, to inoculate them against counterpersuasive speeches, to change their attitudes, and to prompt them to act;
- the relationship of persuasive speaking to the concepts of ethos, pathos, and logos;
- how you can use these three concepts to construct an effective persuasive speech; and
- how to respond appropriately to audience questions about your persuasive speech.

Persuading Your Audience

Audience-focused persuasive speaking begins with an assessment of the situation you face as a speaker. You will need a clear understanding of your goals as a speaker, knowledge about your audience, and an assessment of the constraints facing you, including the ethical boundaries you must respect.[2]

The Four Goals of Persuasive Speaking

There are four common, and sometimes interdependent, goals we can achieve through persuasive speaking. The first is to *reinforce* the attitudes, beliefs, and

Speaking persuasively is frequently an unwritten part of a person's job.

values an audience already holds. Keynote speeches at national political conventions, for example, are usually designed to bolster the common core of beliefs, attitudes, and values to which members of a political party subscribe.

The second goal of persuasive speaking is to *inoculate* an audience against counterpersuasion, that is, persuasive messages opposed to your views. Although it is possible to bolster audience members' attitudes, beliefs, and values simply by reinforcing them, it takes more than reinforcement to make them truly resistant to counterpersuasion. Antidrug messages aimed at children, for instance, are most effective when they give sound reasons not to use drugs, rather than telling kids to "just say no." Children can then use these reasons to defend their refusal to use drugs when pressured by their peers to experiment with illegal substances.

The third goal of persuasive speaking is to *change attitudes*. This is a difficult task, especially when the audience disagrees with or is even hostile to your position. For example, a speaker calling for the legalization of marijuana needs to realize that most audiences will not share that point of view. Changing people's attitudes requires incremental change over time. Taking small steps, such as first convincing an audience that marijuana should be legalized for medical purposes, is more likely to achieve success than trying to change people immediately from total opposition to total support.

The fourth goal of persuasive speaking—and the most difficult to achieve—is to prompt an audience to *act*. People are seldom moved to act as a result of a single persuasive speech. A foundation must first be laid that will make the audience likely to act. That takes time and repetition of the message. When people seem to be responding to a single persuasive speech, it usually is the most recent in a long line of messages building momentum for action. Consider the people who respond to an evangelist's call to get out of their seats, move to the stage, and orally proclaim their faith. The fact that they voluntarily committed to being in the audience means they probably were predisposed to act. Thus, the evangelist's persuasive sermon was a catalyst rather than the sole cause of action.

Which of these four goals you will pursue in a given speech depends largely on the audience you are addressing. If they already share your attitudes and values, then a speech of reinforcement is called for. On the other hand, if they are likely to be the subject to counterpersuasion, or if their commitment to your point of view is shaky, then inoculation should be your goal. If you face an audience opposed to your views, you will need to attempt to change their attitudes, usually a time-consuming incremental process. Finally, if your audience has been primed by prior persuasive messages to behave in accordance with your goals, then prompting them to action may be your best approach. Although these four goals are related, any given persuasive speech is likely to focus primarily on one outcome.

Analyzing Audience Diversity

The realization of any of these goals depends on how well the speaker has analyzed the audience. Audience analysis starts with an assessment of the relationship between the audience and the speaker's goal. Not all audiences are capable of acting to help speakers achieve their goals, even if they desire to do so. For example, people who are not U.S. citizens or who are under age 18 cannot vote in elections. The candidate who directs a persuasive campaign to either group is just wasting time and money. To prepare and deliver a persuasive speech intended to induce action, therefore, makes sense only if the audience is capable of acting.

Once you are sure your goal makes sense in relation to your audience, the next step is to analyze audience diversity. Remember, as we discussed in Chapter 7, that there are three levels of audience diversity to consider: cultural, group, and individual. Cultural diversity concerns collective ways of thinking and acting. Group diversity reflects people's social and demographic affiliations, such as the generation to which they belong. Finally, as illustrated in Box 17-1, individual diversity is revealed in people's most deep-seated beliefs, attitudes, and values.

Simply put, the more you know about the diversity of your audience, the better you will be able to predict how it is likely to respond to issues and the people

Box 17-1   Considering Diversity

Adapting Persuasive Messages to Audience Diversity

Using a topic you are considering for a persuasive speech, consider how the following features of audience diversity might affect the construction and delivery of the actual speech. For example, do you think you might have to tone down your claims, use different types of evidence to support your claims, establish your credibility differently, or avoid certain arguments altogether? Record in writing the ways you would have to adapt your speech to accommodate the diversity that follows.

I. Cultural Diversity

    A. Collectivist audience members

    B. Audience members from low-context cultures

    C. Audience members from cultures that feature specific roles based on gender

    D. Audience members from theocratic cultures such as Iran

II. Group Diversity

    A. A racially diverse audience

    B. An audience considerably younger or older than you

    C. A highly religious audience

    D. An audience that doesn't share your political beliefs

III. Individual Diversity

    A. An audience composed of heterosexual, homosexual, and bisexual members

    B. An audience whose members hold a variety of religious beliefs

    C. An audience whose members hold a variety of political beliefs

    D. An audience whose members hold a variety of attitudes about gender roles

---

associated with the issues. A persuasive speech about product safety delivered to the National Association of Manufacturers, for example, would need to be different from one delivered to a group of personal-injury attorneys. In both cases, however, you would have to construct your persuasive message on the basis of what you know about the group.

Ethical Constraints

Finally, audience-focused persuasive speaking is bound by ethical constraints. The realization of your persuasive goal, for example, should not come at the expense of your audience. Selling worthless swampland may help the speaker achieve the goal of making money, but only at the expense of gullible audience members who may lose their savings. The end you hope to achieve must reflect not only your interests but those of your audience as well. Along the same lines, you need to thoroughly think through the persuasive means you plan on using to achieve your goal. Noble ends do not justify ignoble means. As a case in point, we happen to believe that the remaining stands of giant sequoias should be protected from logging. We would be happy to assist someone in preparing and delivering a speech that suggests reasonable means to achieve this end. However, we would not be willing to help someone who, as a part of his or her persuasive message, plans to advocate tree spiking, placing metal spikes in trees to prevent them being cut down. Such activity can lead to serious injury or even the death of loggers.

Sarah Brady's Persuasive Campaign

Sarah Brady's persuasive speeches had one ultimate goal: legislative action. To get there, however, she had to first reinforce the attitudes of those who shared her beliefs and convince them to join her campaign. Brady also had to inoculate sympathetic Republicans in Congress, who knew from the outset that they would receive intense pressure to oppose her efforts. She had to give these members of the House and Senate evidence they could use to counter the arguments of the powerful pro-gun lobby.

Sarah Brady's most significant audience was Ronald Reagan, who initially opposed legislation proposed by Handgun Control, Inc. She knew that if she could win him over to her side, she might convince other opinion leaders in the Republican Party to either support or at least not stand in the way of the legislation. By appealing to the former president on the basis of his own near brush with death and the sacrifice made by her husband, Sarah Brady eventually did win Reagan's support, which considerably expanded the audience of people willing to hear her persuasive message.

One of the things Sarah Brady didn't do was build a persuasive campaign based solely on emotion, which she could have easily done. Although emotional appeal was certainly a part of her campaign, it was balanced with evidence and reasoning. She avoided the temptation to exploit her husband and other victims of gun violence as objects of pity. Instead, she took the ethical high road, going beyond her husband's injury to demonstrate there was considerable evidence to support handgun control. She presented the need for a federally mandated waiting period between the purchase and delivery of handguns. In doing so, Brady stayed within the boundaries of ethical speech.

Roots of Persuasive Speaking

Most contemporary theory and research about persuasive speaking grows out of the observations of the philosopher Aristotle. Not only did he define rhetoric as "the faculty of observing in any given case the available means of persuasion,"[3] he identified three means of persuasion: ethos, logos, and pathos. These three means of persuasion correspond to the three basic elements of any persuasive speech situation: speaker, message, and audience.

Ethos: The Credibility of the Speaker

Aristotle believed that to be persuasive a speaker must be not only competent but also a person of substantial character. He described this combination of competence and character as **ethos,** a personal attribute, which is essential to a speaker's chances of persuading an audience.

Modern communication researchers have substantiated Aristotle's thinking about the importance of ethos. Today's scholars use the term **source credibility,** which is the audience's perception of the speaker's believability.[4] It is a quality conferred by the audience rather than an innate quality. Thus, a speaker might be truly competent in a particular subject matter, but if the audience does not know this, the speaker's expertise cannot increase his or her credibility. Similarly, a speaker may be of good character, but if the audience does not believe it, the speaker will not be given any particular credibility.

Logos: The Message

Aristotle also recognized the power of words (*logos* is Greek for "word") in the process of persuasion. As a result, he spent considerable time theorizing about both the nature of words and the manner in which they were arranged to form a message. **Logos** is the proof a speaker offers to an audience through the words of his or her message. Aristotle believed speakers should use logical proof. Consider two examples. In the first, the speaker claims without any proof that Socrates is a mortal man. In the second, the speaker makes the same point in the form of a syllogism, that is, a conclusion plus the premises supporting it. Specifically, the speaker tells the audience, "All men are mortal. Socrates is a man. Therefore, Socrates is mortal." In this case, the speaker not only has stated a conclusion the audience can either accept or reject but also has communicated proof in support of the conclusion. Aristotle claimed that, in speaking, rhetoricians often use an abbreviated syllogism (called an enthymeme), which follows the rules of formal logic. He believed that speakers could also prove their case through the use of examples and signs. As they did for ethos, modern researchers have found considerable support for Aristotle's theories about logos.

Pathos: Motivating Your Audience

Finally, Aristotle recognized the role of the audience's emotions in the process of persuasion. He reasoned what modern researchers have demonstrated again and again: People are persuaded not simply by cold logic but also by emotional appeals. **Pathos** refers to the emotional states that a speaker can arouse in an audience and use to achieve persuasive goals. These methods are not inherently unethical, but they can be abused by unscrupulous persuaders.

Aristotle cataloged the many emotions a speaker can evoke in the attempt to persuade people. Specific emotions he mentions in his writings about persuasion include anger, fear, kindness, shame, pity, and envy.[5] Although contempo-

ethos A speaker's competence and character.

source credibility The audience's perception of the speaker's believability.

logos The proof a speaker offers through the words of his or her message.

pathos The emotional states that a speaker can arouse in an audience and use to achieve persuasive goals.

rary researchers have studied each of these emotions in relation to persuasion, fear has been of particular interest, a topic we will discuss later in this chapter.

Up to this point, we have been considering theories about persuasive speaking, such as the need for an analysis of the situation the speaker faces—including the speaker's goals, the audience, and the ethical constraints on the speaker—and the need for appeals to be based on ethos, logos, and pathos. Here, we want to shift our focus to the practice of persuasive speaking. We follow Aristotle and contemporary researchers in looking at the three basic means of persuasion: the speaker, the message, and finally the audience.

The Speaker: Persuasion Through Ethos

As we noted earlier, credibility is rooted in audience perceptions of believability. Contemporary communication research shows that this perception is composed of two parts: competence and character.[6] Although both are necessary to sustain the perception of ethos, neither is sufficient in itself to do so. To perceive you as credible, your audience must believe that you are not only competent about your topic but also a person of character who can be trusted.

Credibility is dynamic and changeable. The fact that a speaker is perceived as credible going into a persuasive speech doesn't guarantee the speaker will still be perceived as credible afterward. Similarly, the speaker who begins with little credibility can build credibility in the process of speaking. One of your goals is to build and maintain your credibility as you speak. You want it to be at least as high, and hopefully higher, than it was when you began.

Credibility Before the Speech

Often, speakers' reputations precede their appearance before an audience. In fact, their reputation may be what prompts the audience to attend, especially when the speaker has unique qualifications to speak about the topic. For example, because Sarah Brady was personally touched by the destructive force of a handgun, her audiences had reason to believe she was uniquely qualified to speak about handgun control.

Of course, most of us are not experts and may not even be known to our audience. One way to build your credibility before you speak is to have someone introduce you to the audience. If you do not have an introduction, you will have to establish your credibility by what you say in your speech and how you say it.

Credibility During the Speech

Whatever credibility a speaker has before starting to speak is not sufficient to sustain the perception of believability. Credibility by way of reputation can be negated by the speaker's appearance, message, and delivery. Often, little-known political candidates begin with credibility, which vanishes once the public learns more about them. Ross Perot, for example, once led the public opinion polls in his independent run for the presidency in 1992. But as people learned more about him, and after he temporarily withdrew from the race, his credibility suffered. Although he did garner considerable support in the election, he never regained his original level of credibility with voters.

On the other hand, even speakers with little initial credibility can build their ethos during their speech. Students in an introductory communication course, for example, may have little initial credibility with each other. They don't usually know one another and don't know each other's qualifications to speak on various topics. Practically speaking, then, these students have the chance to begin building their credibility with their first speeches. Their appearance, the care with which they've prepared their message, and their delivery can begin to establish their competence and character with their fellow students and their instructor.

To make certain you are perceived as a credible speaker in a persuasive transaction, though, you'll need to provide your audience with proof of your credibility through the logos of your message. The reasoning and evidence you present in your persuasive speech should support not only the arguments in it but also the audience's perception that you are competent and a person of high character. In addition, if you have special expertise or credentials that are relevant to your topic, you'll want to share the fact with your audience.

Credibility After the Speech

Speakers whose persuasive message has bolstered their credibility with an audience cannot rest on their laurels. Just as initial credibility can suffer from a poor speech, the credibility you have established during your speech can be negated as well. No one knows this better than former President George Bush. Following his acceptance speech at the 1988 Republican convention, in which he proclaimed, "Read my lips: No new taxes," his credibility soared in the eyes of the public. He was, subsequently, elected by a landslide.

During his term of office, however, Bush reneged on his no-new-taxes pledge. Not only did he lose credibility with the public, but his going back on his word became a major issue in the 1992 presidential election. Even though Bush told the public he had been wrong in going along with the congressionally approved tax increase, he was never able to recapture public confidence.

Never lose sight of the fact that perceived credibility is dynamic. Once gained, credibility continues to need nourishment. The following list provides some reminders and tips for maintaining credibility:

- Ask yourself about the degree to which your audience already perceives you as credible. Also ask yourself whether your classroom behavior could have lowered your credibility in the eyes of the other students. For example, coming to class late and interrupting a speaker, not being ready to speak when it was your turn, or delivering speeches that were hastily put together tells other students about your competence and character.

- Dress appropriately for the occasion. Persuasion is serious business and should be approached seriously.

- Incorporate any special expertise or experience you have with your topic into the body of your speech. This information will enhance the audience's perception of your competence.

- Use evidence to support the claims you make. The logos of your speech will help enhance your ethos.

- Engage your audience nonverbally, using the characteristics of effective delivery described in Chapter 15.

- Use inclusive language, discussed in Chapter 3, to make certain all audience members believe they have a stake in the topic of your persuasive speech.

Using Similarity and Dissimilarity

The perception of moderate similarities between communicators and their audiences can augment the persuasive effects of credibility. People tend to be initially suspicious of people they perceive to be dissimilar. Conversely, they tend to be initially trusting of people they perceive as similar.

Like credibility, similarity is a perception and it is composed of several parts. Chief among them are appearance, background, and belief system. We perceive people whose appearance is a reflection of our culture or group to be similar to us. We then use this surface cue to infer similarities in background and belief system.[7]

If you are an 18- to 21-year-old student at a traditional four-year college or university, chances are that you are similar to the audience you will be speaking to in class. If you can couple your similarity with proof that you have more competence on your topic than your audience members do, you will be able to capitalize on your similarity. Should you be unable to demonstrate special competence, however, similarity may undermine your credibility, because the audience is likely to think, "What does that person know that we don't? He [or she] is no different from us."

If you are not similar to your audience, however, don't worry. You can make dissimilarity work to your advantage. For an example, see the sample persuasive speech (Box 17-2) by Ryland G. Hill, Jr., who was older than and in many respects not similar to his classmates. If you are a reentry student, a parent, or a part-time student with a full-time job, you can use your experience to bolster audience perception of your credibility. After all, you have real-world experience that the 18- to 21-year-old undergraduate probably lacks. If you can combine this dissimilar experience with some common ground you share with your audience, you will enhance your credibility and increase your persuasive effect.

VIDEO FILE

If you have the videotape that accompanies this book, view Part V, Segment 4, which shows Ryland G. Hill, Jr.'s persuasive speech, "Fear Is Real Among Freshman Students."

Box 17-2   Critical Thinking

Sample Persuasive Speech

Fear Is Real Among Freshman Students

by Ryland G. Hill, Jr.

After retiring from the Navy, Ryland Hill, Jr. decided to go back to school at age "thirty something." Currently, he's majoring in early childhood education. That's right, the former chief petty officer wants to be an elementary school teacher. Although Ryland is in many respects dissimilar to his classmates, he focused his speech on something he believes he shares with all undergraduates—fear. The following text was prepared from a transcript of his speech. Because extemporaneous speaking frequently leads to unintentional errors, we have edited the speech for you to read.

Eleanor Roosevelt once quoted an unknown author by saying, "You gain strength, courage, and confidence by every experience in which you really stop to look fear in the face. . . . You must do the thing you think you cannot do."

Today, in the 90s, incoming college freshmen often report becoming anxious before entering college. The transition from high school to college brings fears to the surface. Likewise, students who return to college after many years of absence report similar fears.

College freshmen find it difficult to identify exactly where the problem lies. As a reentry student myself, I have experienced the same difficulty and would like to persuade you that it's essential to be aware of the subtle effect that fear has on each and every one of us in each class that we take.

Today we'll look at some reasons why the fear of failure, the fear of the unknown, and self-fulfilling prophecies have paralyzed freshman students from achieving their full potential. And finally we'll discuss three solutions that can eliminate harmful effects that fear can produce.

Freshman students develop fears that create doubt. A common fear is the fear of failure. Some students doubt their ability to succeed at a college level. These students have often received negative feedback throughout their elementary and high school years. They suffer from low self-esteem and are insecure about their new academic experience.

Students in their first year have potential to do well in school, but usually they underachieve and they may be afraid of making mistakes. But in the counseling center at Berkeley's Writer's College, students are told that making mistakes is important. It is a way of learning about our strengths, and what works well for us, and what does not work. It's only when we do not learn from our mistakes and refuse to correct them that we

Continued

Ryland begins his speech with a quotation used by a respected source, Eleanor Roosevelt.

Ryland establishes a connection with the audience despite dissimilarity in age.

Ryland clearly previews the points he will make.

Note the use of authority to support his point about students learning from their mistakes.

Note the signpost. It reminds us of the point just made and prepares us for the next one.

Quotations from authority are used to bolster his point and also his own credibility.

Note still another signpost, summing up and previewing what comes next.

Notice use of analogies to make the point that we don't always fear the future.

Ryland uses a problem–solution format and presents three solutions to the problem of freshman fears.

become failures. People don't reach their full potential because of important challenges in life, as Robert Steinberg wrote in 1986. It is also easier for students to spend a lot of energy and time dodging the system and their work as assigned due to the fear of failure.

Now that we understand why the fear of failure has such a crippling effect on students in their first year, let's examine another reason why fear plays such a pivotal role in the lack of a freshman's success.

Instead of high school counselors making students see that they have the potential to achieve, they make predictions, which students feel are like a prophet predicting their very future. Well-meaning counselors sometimes steer students away from attending college. They advise the students to consider the work force instead. In today's economy, jobs call for more than just a high school diploma. The students receive a "can't do" message, further lowering their self-esteem. Often this leads to a cycle of low grades and achievements, fulfilling the prophecy of failure.

Robert Steinberg's book, *Intelligence Applied,* explains why intelligent people may fail. Steinberg has identified stumbling blocks that get in the way of even the brightest and sharpest freshman students and prevent them from becoming academically successful. "It scarcely matters what talents people have if they are not motivated to use them," he writes.

First-semester students rely on the correctness of their college professors. Students are still immature and rely on others for their external rewards. But a lot of students say that immaturity has nothing to do with their grades here at Chico State University. Steinberg states: "A lack of self-confidence gnaws away at a person's ability to get things done and this becomes a self-fulfilling prophecy." It's all in your mind.

Now that we understand how self-fulfilling prophecies can create fear in freshman students, let's take a brief look at the fear of the unknown and see how it can be a deterrent to our success as first-year students.

Any new experience that one knows little about can be real scary. On holidays and birthdays, for instance, we receive unknown gifts that are new and different, yet we don't fear those types of gifts, do we? Yet maybe it all lies in the way one packages things. An attractive package that we are expecting is the one that we look forward to receiving. College officials here at Chico State University should let freshman students know that there is a beauty and a joy in the gift called a college education.

Now that we can see how fear of the unknown can disguise itself as a problem, let's look at three solutions that can be very helpful in battling fears that we face on our college campuses.

First is to identify some traits that define a successful student. Successful students tend to be risk takers. Just enrolling in college is a risk to some. Yet they do it, and they take the first step toward success. Successful students also learn from their mistakes. Remember, it's not a failure if you're willing to correct your mistake and learn from it. They need to recognize their successes and overcome their failures, as Professor Johnson, 1990, says.

The second solution is that we must look at college life as a challenge. When we view college life as a roller coaster with its ups and its downs, as long as we believe that life is going to return to the top again, we can rise to the challenge and we can persevere.

And lastly, we can envision our future. We must see ourselves as successful people. And even when things become blurry, and even when we're losing our focus, we can maintain the ability to fine-tune our lives and become even more goal-directed.

We must have faith in ourselves and stay persistent, and stay willing to keep trying. When we don't succeed the first time, we can search for solutions until we are successful. It is difficult for many students to appreciate their own success. I'm going to repeat that. It is difficult for many college students to appreciate their own success. Successful students have learned to celebrate their victories, but most importantly, they have learned to overcome their college fears.

To summarize, today we have discussed reasons why fear is real among college freshmen, and we gave practical solutions to overcoming it. Successful freshman students are confident enough to believe in themselves. But most importantly, they expect their classmates to appreciate their abilities.

> Note the clear attempt to sum up what has been said.

As Eleanor Roosevelt reminds us, while thinking about overcoming our college fears, "You gain strength, courage, and confidence by every experience in which you . . . stop to look fear in the face. . . . You must do the thing you think you cannot do. You must do the thing you think you cannot do." Thank you.

> Conclusion ties back to opening by again using the quotation from Eleanor Roosevelt.

What elements of persuasive speaking are present in this speech? How successful was Ryland in establishing his credibility with an audience largely dissimilar to himself? How well do you think Ryland used evidence to support his claim about fear? What specific types of evidence did you notice him using—first-order data, second-order data, or third-order data? Did Ryland make use of pathos? Did he appeal to audience emotions? What specific emotional appeals are you able to identify in the text of this speech? In what ways besides problem–solution might Ryland have organized his presentation?

Also think about Sarah Brady and her audiences. She had access to circles of influence not open to the traditional supporters of handgun-control legislation because of similarity. She was one of the Republican Party's elite, and they saw her as sharing a background and belief system with them.

At the same time, Sarah Brady was not similar to fellow Republicans in at least three respects. First, she and her family had been personally victimized by a man who had no problem purchasing a handgun despite the fact that he had a documented history of mental illness. Second, as a result of what had happened to Jim Brady, she became an expert on the subject of handguns. Finally, as a woman, she was dissimilar in gender to the vast majority of the Republican members of Congress.

To sum up, then, you can use similarity and dissimilarity to increase the audience's perception of your credibility. You simply need to inventory how you resemble and how you differ from your audience and to think through how you can use this knowledge to your advantage. To conduct your inventory, refer to Self-Assessment Box 17-3.

The Message: Persuasion Through Logos

Assuming that you have done your best to establish initial credibility by your appearance and your classroom behavior, it is your message and its delivery that will most influence audience perceptions of your credibility. What you put into your persuasive message and how you structure it are crucial to your success in reinforcing, inoculating, changing attitudes, and prompting people in your audience to act.[8]

Although Ryland Hill's level of credibility prior to his speech was presumably high with his classmates, it was what he did once he began his speech that made him effective. He cited evidence, provided analogies, and quoted respected people like Eleanor Roosevelt to make a persuasive message that his audience could accept. His credibility was therefore enhanced by the content of his message.

To build a successful persuasive message, you need to know at least three steps. First, you need a model of argument you can use as a template for your message. Second, you need to know how to flesh out this model with evidence and reasoning. Finally, you need to know the extent to which you should include both sides of a controversial issue in your message.

The Toulmin Model of Argument

claim A conclusion that persuasive speakers want their audience to reach as a result of their speech.

In Chapter 6, we introduced you to Stephen Toulmin's model of argument, depicted once more in Figure 17.1. Not only can you use this model to critically assess the arguments of others, but you can also use it as a template in constructing the arguments in your own persuasive speech. As you may recall, according to Toulmin, a sound argument involves *at least* a claim, grounds for making the claim, and a warrant that connects grounds and claim.[9] A **claim** is a conclusion

Box 17-3   Self-Assessment

What Do You and Your Audience Have in Common?

Fill out this form before your persuasive speech. In what ways are you similar and in what ways dissimilar to your audience? How can you use your similarities to build your credibility? How can you overcome your dissimilarities or even make them work to your advantage?

	Similar to Audience	Dissimilar to Audience
Background		
Culture		
Demographics		
Age		
Ethnicity		
Religion		
Appearance		
Belief System		
Attitudes about Popular Culture		
Beliefs about Political System		
Values		

that persuasive speakers want their audience to reach as a result of their speech. Speakers may make claims about the facts as they see them, about basic human values, or about public policies, for example.

The assertion of a claim doesn't constitute an argument for its truth, however. An argument requires **grounds,** which is the evidence a speaker offers in support of a claim. This evidence can be based on personal experience, expert testimony, established fact, statistics, or other data. Good persuasive speakers connect the grounds they offer in support of their claim. Such a connection between grounds and claim is called a **warrant.** Although warrants can be implied, we think it is better for the speaker to state them.

grounds Evidence a speaker offers in support of a claim.

warrant The connection between grounds and claim.

backing Support for the warrant.

rebuttal An exception to or a refutation of an argument.

qualifier An indication of the level of probability of the claim.

first-order data Evidence based on personal experience.

second-order data Evidence based on expert testimony.

third-order data Evidence based on facts and statistics.

This is not the complete model, however. Toulmin indicates that three additional parts of an argument *may* be present. First, if the warrant is not obvious to audience members, backing comes into play. **Backing** is support for the warrant. If the audience does not already believe in the warrant, the speaker will need to build additional argument and evidence to support it before attempting to convince the audience of the soundness of the whole argument. Knowing which warrants an audience will accept and which ones will require additional backing is essential to effective persuasion.

Another component is the **rebuttal,** which is an exception to or a refutation of the argument. It is usually preceded by the word "unless," indicating that the claim is true except when conditions stated in the rebuttal are present. As we will discuss shortly, it is important in presenting a two-sided message to let the audience know when a point is an exception to or a refutation of your argument. Finally, unless an argument is 100 percent certain, it will need a **qualifier,** which is an indication of the level of probability of the claim.[10] Qualifiers may be a single word, such as "probably," a brief phrase, such as "very likely," or even a probability expressed as a percentage. Because in human affairs, absolute certainty is rare, acknowledging your degree of certainty helps you avoid appearing to take an extreme or unreasonable position.

As we indicated earlier, arguments are based on different kinds of evidence, such as personal experience, statistics, and expert opinion. Technically, these three types of evidence are called first-, second-, and third-order data.[11]

First-order data is evidence based on personal experience. As we mentioned earlier, the life experience of people can be quite persuasive. Certainly, Sarah Brady's is. In one persuasive message she noted that, in the course of the attempted assassination of President Reagan, her husband became "a statistic in America's handgun war."[12] She also offered first-order data when she said, "Jim Brady knows the importance of a waiting period. He knows the living hell of a gunshot wound."[13]

Second-order data is evidence based on expert testimony. Both sides in the gun-control debate have experts who support their views, including legal experts who interpret the Second Amendment in different ways, depending on their perspective.

Third-order data is evidence based on facts and statistics. Sarah Brady used numerous examples of third-order data in pressing her case. For example, in one message she described specific incidents of gun violence in places like Stockton, California; Louisville, Kentucky; and Colorado. She also cited statistics; such as, "Nearly a quarter of a million Americans die[d] from handguns—four times as many as were killed in the Viet Nam War."[14]

Using the Toulmin model as a template for your own persuasive messages will help you considerably. The model forces you to think about your message critically. It requires you to ask and answer questions that will not only make your message logical but also increase the likelihood that audience members will see it that way as well. Here is a list of the kinds of questions the model encourages you to consider as you construct your persuasive speech:

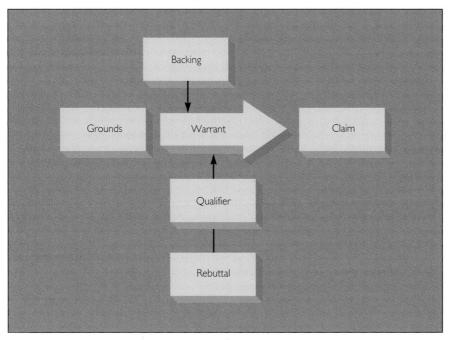

Figure 17-1 The Toulmin Model of Argument

1. What is the nature of the claim or claims I plan on making?

2. What kind of evidence do I need to offer in support of my claim? First-, second-, or third-order data? All three? How will the evidence I offer influence perceptions of my credibility?

3. What can I do to make certain that my audience will make the connection between the claim I make and the evidence I offer as grounds in support of it? Is the warrant really so obvious I don't need to make it explicitly for my audience?

4. Will the warrant need additional support in the form of backing to be acceptable to the audience?

The Importance of Two-Sided Messages

Whereas the research once was equivocal, it now shows that whenever possible, a two-sided persuasive speech is more effective than a one-sided one.[15] A one-sided persuasive speech offers only evidence in support of a claim, but a two-sided persuasive speech makes use of what Toulmin called the qualifier and the rebuttal. With a two-sided message, you need to pay particular attention, therefore, to the inclusion of qualifiers.

Let's say, for example, that you want to persuade your audience to support the claim that the war on drugs is a failure. In a standard one-sided persuasive speech, you would ground the claim with evidence and appeals you believe will prove effective with your audience. In a two-sided speech, you would do all of this and more. After making the claim, giving grounds, and connecting the grounds to the claim with a warrant, you also would include a qualifier in your message and then indicate the rebuttals one might expect to hear to the argument. Of course, acknowledging opposing arguments does not mean you are abandoning your claim. Rather, you would then go on to point out either the weaknesses in the rebuttal or the reasons the rebuttal is not sufficient to set aside your overall claim. Thus, the rebuttal represents the second side of the message. It tells the audience that there are reasonable people who don't support your claim and then gives the audience an example of their evidence. You then refute this example with a further argument or show that in spite of the rebuttal, your overall claim is still strong.

A two-sided message not only is more persuasive than a one-sided message, but it also has at least two other benefits. First, a two-sided message enhances the audience's perceptions of the speaker's credibility. Second, because it gives audience members arguments to rebut those most commonly associated with the opposing view, a two-sided message also makes audience members more resistant to counterpersuasion.

The Audience: Persuasion Through Pathos

To this point, we've been talking about arguments that appeal to reason. Logical argument, however, is neither the only kind of appeal nor always the most effective. Sometimes people's belief systems are so closed that logical appeals have little chance of succeeding. As a result, the speaker may choose to appeal to audience members' emotions or primitive beliefs with messages that people are conditioned to respond to in specific ways. Whereas logical proofs are designed to induce rational thinking on the part of the audience, the appeals described here are designed to provoke audience members to respond without the benefit of such rational thought. These appeals are linked to emotions such as anger, fear, kindness, calmness, confidence, unkindness, friendship, shame, pity, enmity, shamelessness, and envy.[16] To illustrate the way appeals to the emotion operate, we will review one of the best-researched emotional appeals, fear.

Appealing to Emotions: Motivating Through Fear

Common sense tells us that we sometimes do things as a result of fear; for example, we obey the law because we are afraid of the penalties we could suffer should we break it. Yet the research suggests that when it comes to persuasive speaking, fear has its limits. Whether your goal is to encourage the use of shoulder and lap belts while driving, to demonstrate how flossing the teeth can

prevent gum disease, or to convince people everyone needs a gun for self-protection, persuasive messages that arouse moderate levels of fear are much more effective than those using high levels of fear. Moderate fear is an effective motivator especially when the speaker gives audience members a set of clear-cut steps they can take to reduce the fear.[17]

As you can see in Figure 17-2, the relationship between fear and persuasive effects is like the relationship between speech anxiety and performance, explained in Chapter 15. As the level of fear aroused in an audience begins to increase, so do its persuasive effects. Too much fear, however, diminishes persuasive effects because it tends to elicit denial from audience members. In a sense, audience members respond to a speaker's attempt to elicit a high level of fear by saying, "That could never happen to me."

If employed in moderation, however, fear has its uses. Many public service campaigns use moderate levels of fear to encourage positive behaviors such as not smoking, practicing safe sex, and taking advantage of medications that control high blood pressure. The slogan "If not for yourself, then do it for the ones you love" is a good example. Created by the American Heart Association, this

People sometimes draw attention to their cause by relying on emotional appeals, such as shame or unkindness killing of animals, in order to persuade their audience.

Figure 17-2 **The Relationship Between Fear Appeals and Persuasion.** As the level of fear aroused in an audience begins to increase, so do persuasive effects. Too much fear, however, diminishes persuasive effects.

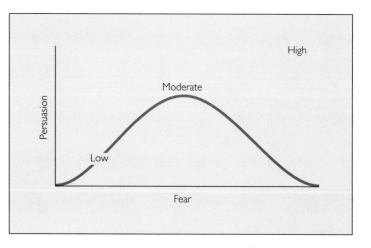

persuasive message tells people with high blood pressure that they need to think about the feelings of the people they would leave behind if they fail to control their high blood pressure. This message involves a mild but effective level of fear. Fear isn't an inherently unethical form of persuasion. Used moderately to achieve an ethical end, it is simply one of many kinds of appeals you can choose.

Appealing to Primitive Beliefs

Emotional appeals frequently are combined with appeals to primitive beliefs. Primitive beliefs are ones instilled since childhood about appropriate ways of behaving in relation to other people. Research shows that the use of appeals that connect with primitive beliefs about reciprocity, liking, authority, social support, scarcity, and commitment is both widespread and effective in persuasive communication.[18]

Reciprocity   A reciprocity-based appeal can work in one of two ways in a persuasive speech. Candidates for political office often promise to give something in return for a person's vote. They may promise to reciprocate by proposing legislation, supporting a specific bill, or voicing a concern of their constituency. The other common way speakers use reciprocity is to call on the audience to reciprocate. During homecoming week, the school president may appeal to alumni for financial support. The appeal is usually couched in terms of "giving something back to the institution that gave you so much." Reciprocity is effective as an appeal because people are conditioned from an early age to return favors, gifts, and services. Reciprocity is a norm; when people receive a promise or are asked to return something received, the conditioned response is to reciprocate in kind.

Liking   Liking is another primitive belief commonly used in persuasive campaigns. Politicians, for instance, enlist film and music stars to speak persuasively on their behalf. The assumption is that if a star is well liked, the feeling may be generalized to the candidate the star endorses. Liking is a staple of advertisers

Advertisers hope that Michael Jordan's popularity generalizes to the products that they pay "Air Highness" to promote.

who employ celebrities as spokespeople for a product. It's not that the celebrity is an expert about the product, but that he or she is well liked by the public. Thus, if Michael Jordan eats Wheaties or Candice Bergen talks up Sprint's long-distance service, the hope is that the public will also like the product being pitched.

Authority Authority-based appeals tap into another primitive belief. Research shows that some people are predisposed to comply with requests from individuals (law-enforcement officers, the clergy) and institutions (the military, the Internal Revenue Service) they perceive as authoritative. Thus, a speaker attempting to encourage a group of Catholics to voice their opposition to abortion might use the words of the pope as an appeal. Similarly, an IRS agent speaking before a group of accountants at a convention might use a written statement from the IRS as part of an appeal.

Social Support An appeal based on social support is nothing more than an appeal based on numbers. There is a tendency among people to think that if enough folks say something is so, then it must be so. In seeking support for the Brady Bill, for example, Sarah Brady wouldn't say "People support gun control." Instead, Brady would say something like, "These public safety measures are supported by the *vast majority of Americans*—including gun owners" (emphasis added).[19] Research shows that when people are confronted with an appeal supported by large numbers, they are much more likely to be persuaded by it. In a sense, they accept social support as a form of grounds for the argument.

Scarcity The appeal to scarcity is based on the law of supply and demand. It is a maxim in economics that when demand exceeds supply, the value of the commodity increases. Thus, an appeal based on scarcity is also one based on relative value. People are conditioned to believe that something that is scarce is valuable enough to merit their attention. Persuasive speeches about the environment frequently use scarcity as the basis of appeal. For instance, the ecological benefits of the rain forests are made even more valuable when the speaker tells the audience that the world's rain forests are disappearing at an alarming rate.

Commitment Commitment is one of the most powerful methods of persuasion. When people make even small commitments as a result of a persuasive message, the principle of psychological consistency comes into play. This principle tells us that we all feel pressure to keep our attitudes, beliefs, and values consistent with our commitments. Thus, if an appeal to commitment leads a person to write a letter, or volunteer to serve, or even sign a petition, it increases the chances of the person's attitudes, beliefs, and values reflecting the commitment. In this case, action may precede a change in attitude, reversing the normal order of persuasive goals.

To reiterate, the appeals you make in your persuasive message should reflect your goal and your audience. Not all audiences will jump on hearing an authority-based appeal. Some people steadfastly refuse to get on a bandwagon, no matter how many other people have already done so. Choosing the right form of appeal or appeals to flesh out your persuasive message, therefore, is part science

and part art. As Box 17-4 indicates, advertising agencies are among the most skilled practitioners of the science and art of persuasion.

The Reverend Billy Graham is one of the century's greatest persuasive speakers.

Persuasive Speaking in Practice

Finally, let us turn to some practical suggestions about preparing and presenting a persuasive speech. We will look at how to adapt your goals to the audience, organize your speech, balance the means of persuasion, and handle the question-and-answer session.

Adapting Your Goals to the Audience

Speeches to reinforce or inoculate an audience presume that its members are either already supportive of your point of view or uninformed about the topic.

These are friendly or neutral audiences, and you can expect your views to receive a fair hearing. You will want to build a strong case, of course, but you need not fear your audience will reject you out of hand.

A speech to change attitudes, by definition, means your audience disagrees with you. This is termed a hostile audience. Although audience members may not be overtly hostile (booing and hissing), they are unlikely to be open to your point of view without a lot of work on your part. A speech to a hostile audience requires you to begin with a common ground on which you and your audience can agree. Only then is it realistic to move them slightly toward your position.

If you were speaking to a group of gun owners about the need for gun control, you would be facing a hostile audience. You might begin by indicating you agree with the Second Amendment and do not seek to infringe on their right to bear arms. Rather, you want to see control of those kinds of weapons that are primarily used by gangs against law-abiding citizens. Perhaps you would simply argue for banning Teflon-coated bullets that can pierce police body armor. In any case, you should not expect a dramatic conversion from this type of audience.

Finally, speeches that seek to prompt people to act presume either that the audience has been prepared by prior messages to take action or that the topic is not inherently controversial. For example, the benefits of flossing one's teeth is not a topic that people are hostile to, though they may not be well informed about it. Such a speech needs to focus on the tangible benefits of action. In the case of an audience already primed by previous messages, your main task is to motivate them to act. People have heard for years about the benefits of wearing seat belts, yet a significant number of people still fail to do so. Rehashing arguments they have already heard is of little use. You need to tell them something new that will get them to finally act. A dramatic story, for example, about how your own life was saved by wearing a seat belt, might be the key ingredient in such a speech.

Organizing Your Persuasive Speech

In Chapter 14 we introduced a number of ways to organize a speech. Two organizational patterns are particularly suited to persuasive efforts. The first is the problem–solution pattern, sometimes called the stock issues approach. This pattern of organization analyzes a problem in terms of harm, significance, and cause and then proposes a solution, which is described as feasible and advantageous. Many persuasive topics are about problems we face individually or as a society. By beginning with a discussion of the problem, the speaker heightens the audience's interest but avoids turning off a hostile audience with a solution they might initially reject. A speech on gun control that begins with a discussion of the growing gang problem is far more likely to receive a hearing from a pro-gun group than a speech that begins by calling for gun control. Even individual problems are susceptible to this pattern of organization. If you examine Ryland Hill, Jr.'s speech which was introduced earlier in this chapter, you'll see that the problem–solution pattern is his basic approach.

Box 17-4   Skill Building

Analyzing Persuasive Messages

Select an advertisement from a newspaper or magazine. In writing, identify the major claim the ad makes, the grounds and backing offered in support of the claim, and any qualifiers mentioned. Next, analyze the ad in terms of the degree to which it effectively uses ethos, logos, and pathos. Finally, analyze the ad in terms of appeals targeted at primitive beliefs such as liking, social support, and authority. What do you conclude about the effectiveness of the ad based on your analysis? Be specific.

The second useful pattern for persuasive speaking is Monroe's motivated sequence, a five-step organizational scheme, including attention, need, satisfaction, visualization, and action. Because the final step is action, this pattern is particularly well suited to speeches calling for your audience to act. As should all good speeches, this type begins by capturing the audience's attention. Like the problem–solution pattern, this pattern focuses on a problem (called a need) before proposing its solution (satisfaction). But this pattern goes further and asks the audience to visualize the satisfaction of the need and then calls on them to act.

Regardless of the organizational pattern you choose, there are two principles of organization you should follow. First, put your best arguments and support either early or late in the speech; do not hide them in the middle. Over the years, research has shown that in some cases people remember best what they hear first, whereas in other cases, what comes last is most memorable. Either way, the middle of the speech is not the place for your best material. Second, with hostile or indifferent audiences, it is particularly important to have some of your best material early in the speech. Otherwise, they will tune you out before you get to the critical points you wish to make.

Balancing the Means of Persuasion

Although it sometimes might seem like we have treated logos, pathos, and ethos as separate means of persuasion, this is not really the case in practice. Your ethos will affect how your audience perceives the logos of your speech. If you have high credibility, the audience is more likely to accept your arguments. Similarly, if you have strong evidence and arguments in your speech, your credibility will grow in the audience members' minds. And unless you touch the audience with pathos, it is unlikely that they will be motivated to act or believe in what they have heard. Although Sarah Brady certainly had credibility and used strong logic in her speeches, were it not for the emotional appeal associated with her husband's gun-inflicted injuries, it is unlikely she would have prevailed in getting the Brady Bill passed. In short, a good persuasive speech relies on all three factors—speaker, message, and audience—for its success.

Answering Audience Questions

Frequently after a speech, particularly a persuasive one, you will be expected to take questions from the audience. You should not be fearful of this situation, as it is an opportunity to gain important feedback from your audience as well as to clarify points that may not have been completely understood. Successfully answering questions, even hostile ones, can add to your credibility as a speaker. The key is to regulate that feedback in a constructive manner. Here are some basic guidelines for handling the question-and-answer period following a speech:[20]

- *Announce at the outset that you will take questions at the end of your speech.* Under no circumstances take questions during the speech, as it will cause you to lose control of the situation. When audience members know they will have the opportunity to ask questions at the end, they will be able to think about them as you speak.

- *Overprepare for your speech.* You need to know more than you cover in the speech if you are to take questions. If you expect a hostile audience, it is a good idea to anticipate their toughest questions and prepare answers in advance.

- *Restate questions if they cannot be heard by all.* If you are speaking with a microphone, someone asking a question from the audience probably cannot be heard. Restating the question not only allows everyone to hear what was asked; it also allows you time to think of an answer. If a question is wordy, hostile, or imprecise, you may be able to rephrase it in a way that neutralizes some of the problems.

- *Answer questions directly with facts to back up your answers.* This requires you to be fully prepared. However, if you don't know the answer, don't be afraid to say so. You can always promise to obtain the facts and get back to the questioner at a later date. It is better to admit you don't know an answer than to be proved wrong because you tried to bluff your way through.

- *Take questions from different audience members.* Don't let yourself get into a debate or an argument with one audience member. Insist that everyone who has a question gets a chance to ask it before you return to a previous questioner. Choose questioners from different parts of the room as well so that everyone feels they will get their chance.

- *Be brief.* Answer questions as succinctly as possible and move on to the next question. Overly long answers bore the audience and frustrate others who want to ask questions.

- *Announce when you are near the end of the Q&A.* When you sense the audience growing restless, the questions have become repetitive, or you are near the end of your allotted time, simply announce that you can take only one or two more questions.

- *At the end of the Q&A, be sure to restate the thesis of your speech and summarize its essential points.* This is your chance to get in the last word and remind the audience of the thesis of your speech. Depending on the situation, you may want to make yourself available for informal discussion after the speech.

These guidelines not only will help you achieve your speech goals, they also will help you to do so in a way that will enhance your credibility by demonstrating your competence for your audience.

Summary

As Sarah Brady's example illustrates, persuasive speaking begins with an assessment of the speech situation, including your persuasive goals, the diversity of your audience, and the constraints you face. Four common goals of a persuasive speech are to reinforce existing beliefs and attitudes, to inoculate against counterpersuasion, to change attitudes, and to prompt the audience to act. The probability of a persuasive speech achieving these goals requires a thorough understanding of the audience's cultural, group, and individual diversity. Finally, speakers should realistically examine the constraints they face, including ethical boundaries.

Aristotle proposed a three-part model of persuasion composed of ethos, logos, and pathos. Ethos, now called source credibility, is essential if a speaker hopes to persuade an audience. Logos, or the words of the speech in the form of logical proof, also has been shown to affect a persuasive speaker's success. Pathos, or the emotions a speaker stirs in the audience, interacts with ethos and logos in the process of persuasion.

Toulmin's template of argument is useful in the construction of a speech designed to provoke a reasoned response from an audience. The template consists of a claim, grounds, and a warrant. The claim is the conclusion the speaker wants the audience to reach. Grounds are evidence a speaker offers in support of a claim. The warrant is the connection between the grounds and the claim. In addition, the speaker may need to provide backing, or further support for the warrant. A rebuttal indicates an exception to or refutation of the claim. And a qualifier indicates the degree of certainty of the claim.

Three types of grounds (evidence) commonly used to support a claim are personal experience, or first-order data; expert testimony, or second-order data; and facts and statistics, known as third-order data.

A two-sided message includes a qualifier and a rebuttal in addition to a claim, grounds, and a warrant. Two-sided persuasive speeches are generally more effective than one-sided speeches. Two-sided messages also confer greater credibility on a speaker and can be used to inoculate an audience against counterpersuasion.

Sometimes, grounds take the form of appeals that are designed to produce conditioned responses from an audience. These appeals are meant to trigger basic emotions such as fear, and they rely on primitive beliefs, such as reciprocity, liking, authority, social support, scarcity, and commitment. Such appeals can be both effective and ethically used by a person constructing a persuasive speech.

Persuasive speaking in practice involves adapting your goals to your audience, organizing your speech for maximum effectiveness, balancing the means of persuasion, and handling audience questions in a way that enhances your credibility as a speaker.

Another Look

Articles

Mike Allen. "Meta-Analysis Comparing the Persuasiveness of One-Sided and Two-Sided Messages." *Western Journal of Communication* 55 (1991): 390–404.

This study reexamines the research on one- and two-sided messages. Its conclusion, that two-sided messages are more successful in inducing attitude change, is a change from earlier research that suggested sometimes one-sided messages were superior. It is a good example of the emerging practice of meta-analysis, which allows researchers to combine the results of several different studies in reaching general conclusions about communication.

William J. McGuire and Demitrios Papageorgis. "Effectiveness of Forewarning in Developing Resistance to Persuasion." *Public Opinion Quarterly* 26 (1962): 24–34.

This is a classic article which develops the theory of inoculation. Just as two-sided messages are preferable to one-sided, persuaders benefit from forewarning an audience to counterarguments they are likely to encounter.

Books

Robert Cialdini. *Influence: Science and Practice.* 2nd ed. New York: HarperCollins, 1988.

Cialdini's six short-cut methods to social influence are developed in this very readable and enlightening book. He explained at length how such principles as reciprocity and liking are used by salespeople and advertisers to influence consumer behavior.

Philip G. Zimbardo, Ebbe B. Ebbesen, and Christina Maslach. *Influencing Attitudes and Changing Behavior.* 2nd ed. Reading, Mass.: Addison-Wesley, 1977.

Although somewhat dated, this book is an entertaining, well-grounded, and fascinating look at social influence—from brainwashing by religious cults to getting people to eat grasshoppers and like it. Zimbardo and his colleagues make social science research on persuasion accessible to readers.

Video Rentals

The War Room Starring the real-life campaign staff of the Clinton campaign, including James Carville and George Stephanopolous, as well as Clinton and his running mate, Al Gore, this film takes you behind the scenes to the "War Room" in Little Rock, Arkansas, where the 1992 campaign of Bill Clinton was headquartered. This documentary provides a fascinating insight into the persuasive techniques used in modern politics.

Theory and Research in Practice

1. Research shows that there are four possible persuasive goals, as discussed in this chapter. Suppose you are giving a speech on the topic of gun control. How would you change your persuasive message to achieve each of the four persuasive goals: reinforcement, inoculation, attitude change, and action? How would these goals differ depending on possible audiences for this topic and the constraints you would face in each situation?

2. Research shows that either too little or too much fear appeal will fail to be persuasive. Consider the following list of topics: (1) preventing AIDS, (2) preventing tooth decay, (3) wearing seat belts. Construct a brief message based on a moderate level of fear appeal for each of these topics. What kinds of messages might induce too much fear and cause audience members to reject your message? At what point do you think arguments based on fear on these topics would become unethical?

3. Research has shown source credibility to be one of the most important tools in the arsenal of any persuasive speaker. Follow up on the list of tips we gave for assessing and enhancing perceptions of your credibility. List the specific factors you believe make you credible about the topic of your persuasive speech. Then describe how you plan on using these specific factors so that they will sustain the perception of credibility as you deliver your speech.

4. Newspaper editorials constitute a persuasive message. To improve your ability in recognizing the types of appeals being used, select a recent column from a nationally syndicated writer such as George Will, William Safire, Molly Ivins, or Ellen Goodman. Highlight what you consider to be appeals the columnist is using. Note whether these appeals are intended to affect your emotions or your primitive beliefs. Finally, label the emotion or belief the appeal is targeted at arousing.

CHAPTER 18

Mass Communication

OBJECTIVES

After reading this chapter you should be able to:

- Describe the nature of mass communication.

- Explain how mass communication differs from face-to-face dimensions of communication.

- List, chronologically, important innovations and events in the history of mass communication.

- Critically discuss the major functions of mass communication.

- Describe and distinguish among various perspectives on the effects of mass communication, including models of direct and indirect effects, uses and gratifications, agenda setting, cultivation and critical theories.

- Describe the behaviors and skills necessary for people to become critical and responsible consumers of mass communication.

- Critically analyze and discuss research focusing on the verifiable effects of sex and violence in mass communication.

In October 1993, MTV's *Beavis & Butt-Head* show was blamed for causing a five-year-old to burn down his mother's mobile home, killing his two-year-old sister. Although dismissing the charge as ridiculous, MTV shifted the show to a later time slot and removed all references to fire. A disclaimer was added that Beavis and Butt-Head were "not role models" and that "some of the things they do would cause a real person to get hurt, expelled, arrested. . . . Don't try this at home."[1]

In November 1995, a cashier at a subway token booth in Brooklyn, New York, was critically burned over 75 percent of his body by two men who sprayed a flammable fluid in the booth's change tray and then ignited it. As the news media were quick to report, this horrible act of violence was remarkably similar to the one depicted in a scene from the action film *Money Train,* starring Wesley Snipes and Woody Harrelson.[2]

Critics of television and film believe that examples such as these are proof of the powerful and often destructive effects of mass communication on society. Critics charge, moreover, that unless the producers of mass communication are held accountable for the content of their creations, matters will get worse.

What do you think? Does mass communication influence society to the degree alleged by its critics? Or do the critics exaggerate the effects of media, such as television and film, on antisocial behavior in order to suit their purposes?

In this chapter we'll look at a variety of perspectives on the relationship between mass communication and human behavior. The chapter is designed to give you some tools for analyzing and responding to mass media. It is also designed to assist you in both processing and responding to the mass communication that you confront daily, which is just as essential to your communication competence as the skills we've discussed thus far in the book. Some of the important topics we discuss are

- the nature of mass communication,
- the historical evolution of mass communication,
- important perspectives on the functions and effects of mass communication, and
- the significance of taking individual responsibility for your behavior as it relates to mass communication.

The Nature of Mass Communication

Mass communication involves one source transmitting a message to a large number of people (an audience). It involves the use of devices to facilitate communication between sources and audiences that are physically separated. Mass communication can be distinguished from face-to-face and mediated dimensions of communication in terms of its audience, its response to feedback, and the degree to which mass communication is subject to regulation.

The Audience

mass communication
One source transmitting a message to a large number of people.

One of the reasons for the proliferation of mediated systems of communication is the degree to which you can pinpoint your audience. Consider the seemingly infinite number of chat rooms available over the Internet. No matter how esoteric your interests, chances are that you can find someone on-line who shares them. What's more, if you enter a chat room only to find no one talking about what most interests you, you can ask if anyone would like to join you in another chat room, where the topic of the day is what interests you specifically.

In contrast traditional mass communication systems, such as network television, target the largest possible audience. Because broadcasters cannot respond immediately to feedback from that audience, they cannot adapt their messages to feedback for some time. Even then, the adaptations are likely to be at only the most general level. If the previous season dramas about emergency-room medicine were successful with the audience, then the new season is likely to offer more of the same. If the ratings slide on talk shows, fewer will be offered next season. In short, the goal of the producers of mass communication's content is to appeal to as many people as possible. This is one of the reasons advertisers are willing to spend millions of dollars annually to buy 30-second spots during widely viewed events such as the Super Bowl and the Olympics. Advertisers

MTV's "Beavis and Butthead" now carries a disclaimer, after a mother blamed the show for the tragic fire her preschool son set, which killed his sister and destroyed the mobile home in which they lived.

assume that the bigger the audience, the better their chances of reaching the audience members they most hope to attract.

Feedback

Another principal difference between mediated systems and the mass communication involves feedback. Mediated systems, such as those offered by AT&T, MCI, and Sprint, have the capability for instantaneous feedback. Telephone communication usually involves a real-time conversation. Chat rooms on the Internet are also real-time mediated communication. However, e-mail involves delayed feedback, since the sender must wait for the recipient's response. Delayed or instantaneous, however, feedback in mediated systems such as these is one on one. The sender of a message knows who is providing the feedback and can take that into account in processing feedback.

In mass communication, feedback is almost always delayed. The most general form of feedback is from ratings for television and radio programs, box-office receipts for movies, circulation figures for print media, and "hits" on Internet sites. Such feedback is not identifiable on an individual basis. Some feedback, of course, can be individual, as when a person calls a television station to protest programming, writes a letter to the editor, or calls to cancel a subscription. Talk radio and television programs even have a form of instantaneous feedback from a few callers. However, the callers are typically not representative of the audience at large and are screened before they are allowed on the air. Thus, there is a difference in terms of both immediacy and representativeness in feedback between mediated and mass communication systems.

Regulation

Another key difference between mediated and mass communication concerns the degree to which the content of the message is regulated. Although this may change, the content of communication over mediated systems such as cellular phones and the Internet is largely unregulated. Although e-mail messages can be monitored, there are few restrictions on the content of the messages people exchange electronically. There has been recent legislation, however, banning the use of the Internet to transmit pornographic messages to children. Such legislation has spurred protests (some Internet sites went "black" for a day).

In the United States, the content of traditional mass media is highly regulated. The Federal Communications Commission (FCC) controls and regulates the licenses of television and radio broadcasters who use the public airwaves to transmit programming and advertising. Although protected by the First Amendment, print media can be subject to regulation for obscenity and pornography. And, of course, libel laws allow individuals to sue those who publish defamatory articles in the print media as well as those who broadcast over the air. Although regulation of traditional mass communication has decreased in recent years, it is still far more regulated than the mediated systems we have described.

History of Mass Communication

The history of mass communication is well beyond the scope of a single chapter. Still, we think it is helpful to know something about the roots of mass communication and its historical evolution. As a result we offer the following overview, which highlights some of the events appearing in the timeline in Figure 18-1.

The Evolution of Print Media

Ancient societies relied primarily on word-of-mouth to communicate. Although writing was invented between about 5000 and 4000 B.C., it wasn't until the Sumerians invented an alphabet of symbols for sounds that written history began to be systematically recorded.

Stone and clay tablets were the earliest media of writing. The Egyptians developed paper from papyrus around 3000 B.C. Later, parchment (tanned sheepskin) and vellum (calfskin) were used. By the second century A.D., paper as we now know it was developed in China. Later imported into Europe, paper became the medium of choice for early books and printing.[3]

At first, books and manuscripts were copied by hand. Thus, when Johann Gutenberg invented the movable-type printing press in 1455, he launched a communication revolution.[4] For the first time in history, it was possible to communicate to large numbers of people—the first "mass communication." He created what Marshall McLuhan later termed "the Gutenberg Galaxy."[5]

The invention of movable type was instrumental to the creation of three major forms of print media we currently enjoy: books, newspapers, and magazines. Today, millions of books are sold each year—ranging from college texts to the latest Stephen King thriller. Currently, for example, over 50 million new book titles and new editions of previously published books appear each year.[6]

Newspapers have been a feature of the American landscape since before the Revolution. Freedom of the press, protected by the First Amendment, is seen by most Americans as an inalienable right. Although newspapers continue to be an important medium of mass communication, they reached their zenith in terms of numbers published and readership around 1910.[7] Newspaper readership has steadily declined ever since, largely as a result of the electronic media. First films, then radio, and now television supplanted newspapers as a source of news and as a medium of advertising. Currently, only about half of the American population reads a daily newspaper.[8]

In contrast to the shrinking number of newspapers available today, the types of magazines have increased. Research in marketing has enabled magazine publishers to identify specific niches of readers, composed of significant numbers of people bound by common interests, such as aviation, gardening, hot rodding, mountain biking, quilting, surfing, and weight lifting. Publishers of special-interest magazines can sell advertising space to the makers of products designed specifically for niche-market readers. Unlike newspapers in the past decade, the number and readership of magazines has risen significantly.[9]

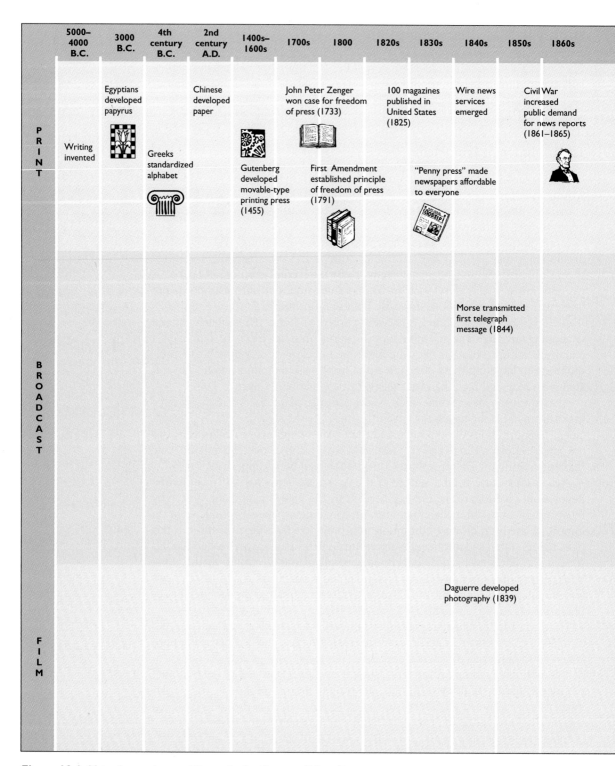

Figure 18-1 Major Innovations and Events in the History of Mass Communication

1870s	1880s	1890s	1900	1920s	1930s	1940s	1950s	1960s	1970s	1980s	1990s	1995

Advent of "yellow Journalism"

First newsmagazines and large-circulation periodicals

Specialty magazines became popular; number of magazine readers increased

5,000 magazines published in United States; height of newspaper circulation

Marconi developed wireless telegraph (1895)

Radio was dominant mass medium; Federal Communications Act was passed to regulate radio airwaves (1934); RCA built prototype TV station (1932)

Cable TV became widely available

The human voice first transmitted by wireless (1906)

1.1% of households had VCRs; over half of U.S. households hooked up to cable

World War I; the military used portable radio transmitters and receivers (1914–1918)

World War II; development of TV was interrupted (1939–1945)

TV is dominant medium (1990s)

First amamteur radio broadcast; first radio station began regular broadcasts

9% of households had TV and watched 4.5 hours a day; video was developed (1952)

6 radios per household; over 10,000 radio stations in United States; 98% of households have TV and watch 7 hours a day; 67% have VCRs; 13% of adults are on-line (1995)

87% of households had TV

Eastman introduced film in rolls (1888); Edison developed motion picture projection system (1889)

40 million Americans attended a movie every week (1914)

Movie attendance dropped to once a week; drive-in movies became popular

People go to a movie once every five weeks; drive-in movies are disappearing

First talking picture, *The Jazz Singer*

Number of nickelodeons rose from 1,000 to 10,000

"Golden age" of movies; people saw an average of 2–3 movies a week

Writing was one of the first steps in the history of mass communication. Shown here is a cuneiform tablet (partially erased) from Sumer, circa 2500 B.C.

Although print media have taken a back seat to electronic media in this century, books, newspapers, and magazines serve functions not fulfilled by electronic mass media. For one, they require readers to be active, rather than passive, information processors. Print media also allow for self-pacing. A reader can decide how quickly or slowly to process the information. Finally, print media allow us to look up a word in the dictionary or consult another author in the attempt to evaluate the credibility of a printed passage.

The Evolution of Electronic Media

The first electronic mass medium of communication was the motion picture film. This medium required several technological breakthroughs to come into existence. Although the basic photographic process was developed in 1839, it was not until the 1880s, when George Eastman developed flexible rolls of celluloid film, that it became possible to create a series of photographs required to create the illusion of motion. American inventor Thomas Edison developed the projection system necessary for motion pictures as we know them. By the end of the 19th century, the technology was in place for the development of motion pictures as a mass medium.[10]

The first movie theaters to cater to mass audiences were known as nickelodeons (because they cost a nickel). Between 1905 and 1910, the number of such theaters grew from 1,000 to 10,000. Nickelodeons were located in industrial cities and catered to immigrants, many of whom spoke no English. Since films were silent, this was not a problem. Unlike print media, which require literacy, movies speak a universal language. However, movie producers sought to expand their appeal to the middle and upper classes and developed "movie palaces" and the "star system." By 1914, 40 million Americans attended movies on a weekly basis.[11] In a little over a decade, movies became even more popular as Warner Brothers and AT&T labs combined efforts to produce the first talkie, *The Jazz Singer,* starring then-popular singer Al Jolson.[12]

Many consider the 1930s and 1940s as the golden age of movies. Not only were such great classics as *Citizen Kane, Gone with the Wind, Casablanca,* and the *Wizard of Oz* produced, but movies became an instrumental agent of patriotism during World War II. At their high point in the 1930s and 40s, movies were seen on an average of two or three times a week by the typical household. Then came television. By the mid 1950s, average movie attendance dropped below once a week per household. By 1989 it was down to barely one fifth of a visit per week per household.[13]

To meet the challenge of TV, movies began to change. Codes limiting what could be shown were relaxed. Greater doses of violence, profanity, and sex became common. Technological innovations, such as wide screens, and Dolby and THX sound systems were tried. But, in many ways, the very medium that threatened the existence of movies has helped bring it new life. Today almost all movies are seen not only in theatrical release but on home video cassettes. The ability to watch a movie on your home TV and even to purchase your own copy has revitalized Hollywood's movie industry. In addition, cable television outlets, such as HBO, have commissioned their own full-length motion pictures. Filmmakers and producers think now in terms of both celluloid and videotape. This change in thinking has enabled the motion picture industry to keep pace.

When most people think of traditional mass media, however, their attention is drawn to *radio* and *television*. Radio and TV have their roots in the telegraph. In 1844 Samuel Morse successfully transmitted the first telegraph message from Baltimore to Washington, D.C. By 1895 Guglielmo Marconi developed a way to send messages via radio, a wireless telegraph. And by 1906 the first human voice was sent by wireless. By World War I, portable radio transmitters and receivers were used by the military.

After World War I, interest grew in home receivers, leading to a demand for regularly scheduled broadcasts. In April 1920, the first amateur radio broadcast began in Pittsburgh. Later that year, KDKA in Pittsburgh became the first radio station to broadcast regularly, beginning with an announcement of the results of the 1920 presidential election. Radio was on the way to becoming a mass medium.[14]

Unlike newspapers, radio stations could not exist free of government regulation. For one thing, if there was no systematic way of assigning broadcast frequencies, stations' signals would overlap. Congress passed the Radio Act of 1927, followed by the Federal Communications Act of 1934. These acts established the principle that the airwaves are the people's and should "serve the public interest, convenience, and necessity."[15]

Owners of radio stations soon discovered that advertisers were willing to pay for the privilege of sponsoring programs. This established the principal means of financing that carried over to television. Between the 1930s and about 1950, radio was the dominant mass medium in America. Programs ranged from big band music to news to sports to comedy to adventure to drama. Some radio dramas, in fact, were able to move an audience to act, as was the case with the Mercury Theater's production of H. G. Wells's novel *War of the Worlds,* in 1938. Many of the early television programs were simply radio programs moved to the small screen. *Batman,* for example, was a radio program before it was adapted for television in the 1960s and later film.

After World War II, television began to preempt radio as well as film as the nation's favorite mass medium. Today, radio is primarily a local phenomenon, with networks limited to news and talk. Like contemporary magazines, today's 10,000 radio stations across the country represent a very segmented medium, targeted at market niches.[16] There are top-40, hard rock, alternative, reggae, oldies, and country music stations. Some stations broadcast in other languages, particularly Spanish in California and the Southwest. And there is a growing market for conservative talk show hosts, such as Rush Limbaugh.

Although we typically think of *television* as a recent innovation, the first experimental broadcast occurred in the 1920s. By 1932 RCA had built a prototype station and by 1936 it began test broadcasts. However, the development of television was interrupted by World War II. After the war, television sets again were manufactured, although they were expensive and primitive by today's standards. From 1948 until 1952, there was a freeze on granting new licenses, as the FCC sorted out the technical requirements. Once television licenses were unfrozen in 1952, the boom in TV began in earnest. In 1950 only 9 percent of households had a TV. By the end of the decade, over 87 percent of households owned a TV. Today, the number of households with television exceeds 98 percent. Not only has the number of TVs increased, the amount of time spent daily

watching television has grown from a household average of 4½ hours in 1950 to over 7 hours today.[17]

Perhaps the two most dramatic examples of television's early influence occurred in 1960 and 1963. In 1960 the two major candidates for president, Richard M. Nixon and John F. Kennedy, faced each other in a series of four television debates. Many attributed Kennedy's razor-thin victory to his superior television image as portrayed in the debates, although the research doesn't consistently support this conclusion.[18] The second event of the 60s was the assassination of John F. Kennedy and his televised funeral. The American people were brought together by the terrible events of November 22, 1963, in a way that few who experienced it would ever forget.

Television became the dominant medium of mass entertainment in the 1950s.

Figure 18-2 Media Usage: 1984 to 1997. You can see in this graph that cable TV has cut into network TV's audience.

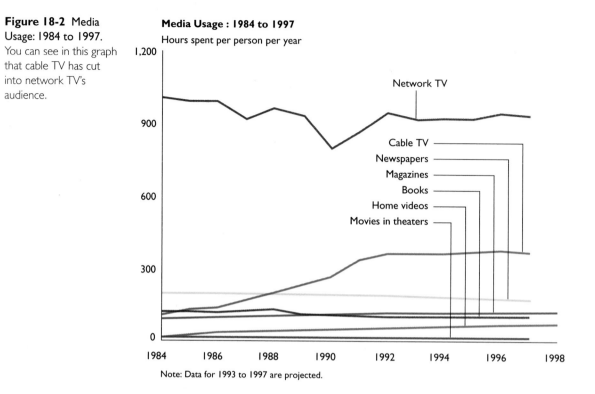

Media Usage : 1984 to 1997

Hours spent per person per year

Note: Data for 1993 to 1997 are projected.

Television has continued to be a powerful and controversial force in American society, as more recent events such as the *Challenger* disaster and the trial of O. J. Simpson have shown. The average high school graduate has spent more time in front of television than in school, and Americans rely more on television for their news than on any other source.[19] As Figure 18-2 shows, television has become the most widely used mass medium of the late 20th century.

Today, new technologies are challenging the dominance of traditional forms of television, such as the three major networks and local affiliates. Cable television and, more recently, Direct Broadcast Satellite systems not only compete with each other for the television audience, but also have become increasingly competitive with the major broadcast networks and their system of local affiliates. New networks such as Fox, moreover, have been successful in attracting the television audience with both innovative programming, such as the *X-Files*, and the former staple of CBS, the National Football League.

The preceding examples are but a small sample of the electronic alternatives to the once-dominate television networks. Hardly a day goes by that we do not learn about yet another innovation that will alter the broadcast landscape. You will want to keep this in mind as we now turn to the functions and effects of traditional mass communication systems.

Functions and Effects of Mass Communication

At one time, researchers focusing on traditional mass media suggested their functions and effects are straightforward. Traditional mass media, they explained, serve to inform people, entertain them, and occasionally alert them to important events, such as elections, natural disasters, and international crises. Contemporary researchers have learned, however, that the influence of mass media is not this simple. They realize that the functions of the traditional media of mass communication not only are complex and subtle but also are not entirely understood. As a result, the number of competing ideas and theories about the functions and effects of mass communication has increased over time. Rather than simply present a chronology of theory and research, therefore, we have organized the following discussion around the specific foci of people who study mass communication functions and effects, including

- how the mass media directly affect specific audience members,
- how audience members use the mass media for the purposes of gratification,
- how the mass media affect us socially and culturally, and
- how the mass media serve to promote the political and economic agendas of the elite and powerful in our society.

Direct Effects

Although scholars now discount what they derisively call the "magic bullet theory," many people continue to think that the mass media powerfully and directly affect the behavior of the people in their audience. This model is represented in Figure 18-3. If you listen to talk radio, for example, you'll frequently hear people complain about the control the mass media exert over the lives of ordinary people. This is hardly a new idea. It's at least 100 years old, going back to those who attributed the Spanish-American War to the pro-war editorials of newspaper magnates William Randolph Hearst and Joseph Pulitzer. Similarly, the later rise of Hitler in Nazi Germany seemed evidence to many people that skillful use of the electronic mass media, particularly radio and film, could be enormously effective in provoking people to act.

It is one thing to hypothesize about powerful and direct mass media effects. It is another to prove media effects with scientific evidence. When the magic bullet model was subjected to scientific scrutiny, it fell into disrepute. In its place came a view that the media had, at most, only minimal effects on their audience.

During the 1940 presidential election, researchers Paul F. Lazarsfeld, Bernard Berelson, and Hazel Gaudet put the question of the effects of mass communication to the test. Their results, published in *The People's Choice,* revolutionized thinking about the power of the media for a generation of scholars.[20] Their intensive interviews with 3,000 Erie County, Pennsylvania, voters led them to conclude that the mass media (radio and print) were far more likely to reinforce

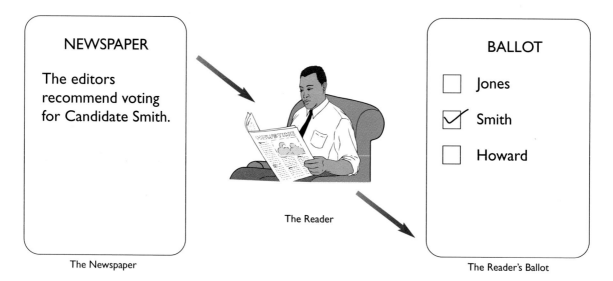

NEWSPAPER

The editors recommend voting for Candidate Smith.

The Reader

The Newspaper

BALLOT

☐ Jones

☑ Smith

☐ Howard

The Reader's Ballot

Figure 18-3 Direct-Effects Model

preexisting political views or activate partisan predispositions than to convert voters. After studying the 1948 election as well, Berelson, Lazarsfeld, and William McPhee summarized their findings, concluding that "media exposure gets out the vote at the same time that it solidifies preferences. It crystallizes and reinforces more than it converts."[21] Media researcher Steven Chaffee wrote in 1975 that "it has been typical in academic circles to assume that communication campaigns can make only minor dents in the political edifice. Citizens' processing of information has been thought to be highly selective, conditioned by partisan predispositions, and subordinate to interpersonal influences."[22] This last condition, interpersonal influence, is related to the theory of the "two-step flow" of public opinion explained next.

If the mass media were not influencing people, what was? Lazarsfeld hypothesized that something stood between the media and the average person. The basic idea of the **two-step flow** of media influence is that "ideas flow *from* radio and print *to* opinion leaders and *from* them *to* less active sections of the population."[23] This model is illustrated in Figure 18-4. **Opinion leaders** are those people who are actively involved in the political process, who pay careful attention to speeches on radio and to newspaper accounts of candidates. According to the two-step flow theory, these people serve as conduits for media influence, directly influencing those who are less concerned about political issues.

To test this theory, Lazarsfeld, along with Elihu Katz, studied ordinary decision making by people in Decatur, Illinois.[24] They looked at decisions about marketing, fashion, motion pictures, and public affairs. The study found that people tend to be more influenced by other people—opinion leaders—than directly by the media.[25]

Who are these opinion leaders? Although they often share the same social status as followers, opinion leaders are likely to be more gregarious, heavier users

two-step flow The theory that ideas flow from the media to opinion leaders and from them to the general population.

opinion leaders People who serve as conduits for media influence, directly influencing those less concerned about political issues.

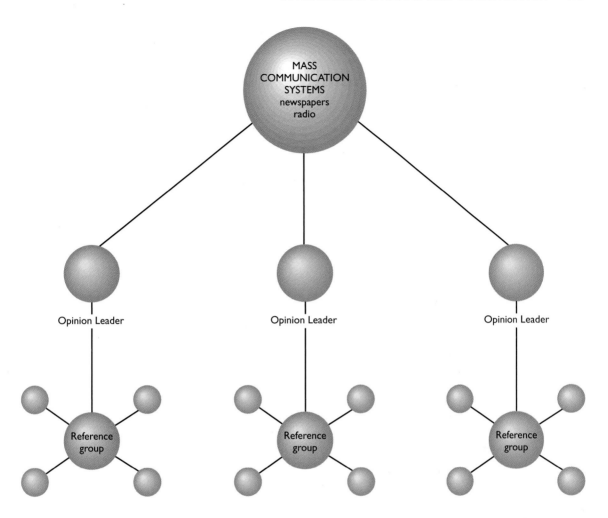

of the media, and more socially active.[26] They also tend to be more sophisticated than the average media consumer and thus less likely to be persuaded by deceptive propaganda. The effect of the media is moderated by opinion leaders who serve as gatekeepers for less informed citizens.

The theory of minimal effects of the mass media was further buttressed by social psychologist Leon Festinger, who found that people tend to reject or distort information that is not consistent with what they already believe.[27] People try to avoid exposing themselves to information that is inconsistent with their beliefs, and if that is not possible, they will perceive that information in a selective way. This selective perception restricts the power of the mass media. Not only do most people rely on interpersonal influence more than on the mass media, but when they do encounter the mass media, they attend to it selectively. People avoid reading, listening to, or watching that which contradicts what they

Figure 18-4 Two-Step Flow of Mass Communication

believe. And when exposed to contrary information, they tend to distort their perception of that information to fit preconceived ideas and to forget that information more quickly than information with which they agree.[28]

One limitation of the minimal-effects perspective is that most of the research supporting it predated television. The presidential campaigns of 1940 and 1948, for example, were conducted largely through radio and print media. Ironically, by the time television had come into prominence, scholarly researchers were not inclined to study it, because the minimal-effects model told them there was not much to study.

During the 1970s some scholars began rethinking the minimal-effects model. A variety of theoretical approaches were developed that suggested that the mass media do have important effects, even if they do not directly convert voters from one side to the other. These theories include uses and gratifications, agenda setting, and the sociocultural effects of media.

Uses and Gratifications

Imagine two different scenarios. In the first, you come home from a hard day's work and turn on the TV hoping to find light entertainment. You channel-surf until you finally settle on a meaningless sitcom, which you half-watch while talking with family members. In the second scenario, you turn on the TV when you come home from work because you are concerned about the latest developments in the Middle East. Someone at work mentioned that there was a hostage situation. You immediately tune in CNN's or MSNBC's breaking coverage of the event. You intently watch the coverage, hoping to learn just what happened and if hostilities are likely to break out. You know it will be topic "A" of conversation tomorrow at work.

These two situations illustrate the basic premise behind the **uses and gratifications** approach to understanding media effects. The audience members' reasons for consuming media messages and the gratifications they seek affect how they process the messages. Thus, communication represents a transaction between the source who provides a message and the audience member who uses it. And one cannot fully understand media effects without first knowing something about why people are attending to the media.

According to Elihu Katz, Jay G. Blumler, and Michael Gurevitch, the uses and gratifications approach makes a number of important assumptions about the role audience members play in determining the impact of mass media. Unlike earlier, direct-effects models, which cast audience members in a passive role, the uses and gratifications approach assumes just the opposite. Audience members are active and make conscious choices about the media they consume. They decide for themselves the functions media will perform in their lives. Mass media, moreover, must compete to attract the participation of potential audience members.[29]

The uses and gratifications approach has been applied to assessing the political impact of the media. In a study of the 1972 presidential election between

uses and gratifications The reasons people have for consuming media messages, and the needs these media satisfy.

Richard Nixon and George McGovern, communication researchers Jack M. McLeod and Lee B. Becker found that television viewers sought five kinds of gratifications and had three reasons for avoiding political content.[30] The five kinds of gratifications were surveillance, vote guidance, anticipated communication, excitement, and reinforcement. *Surveillance* means the desire to keep up on current events, to know what is going on in the world. *Vote guidance* is what happens when people tune in political programs, such as presidential debates, to learn about the candidates to help decide how to vote. *Anticipated communication* is a reason for viewing, for example, when one tunes in an important political event because it is a likely topic of conversation the next day. *Excitement* is often a motive for watching TV events—a fact exploited by politicians who try to hype their events. And it is not unusual for those who already support a candidate to watch programs that *reinforce,* or bolster, a decision already made to support the candidate.

McLeod and Becker found that people avoid political content because of partisanship, relaxation, or alienation. *Partisans* are likely to avoid media expressions of competing groups. For example, Democrats are likely to avoid Republican-sponsored programming and vice versa. When people want to *relax* and have the media provide a diversion from the stress of everyday life, they avoid political content because they feel it is stressful. And, of course, those who are *alienated* from the political system are unlikely to pay much attention to political programming.

The uses and gratifications approach doesn't apply just to overtly political programming. For example, the ground-breaking sitcom of the 1970s, *All in the Family,* was intended to portray Archie Bunker as a narrow-minded bigot. In the program, Archie was pitted against his liberal son-in-law, Michael (who Archie called "Meathead"). Archie expressed every prejudice imaginable—attacking minorities, liberals, gays, and feminists. The producers intended Archie to be so extreme as to be laughable. Yet some viewers took him as expressing correct attitudes, totally missing the satire intended by creator Norman Lear.[31] They used the program to reinforce their own prejudices, rather than the reverse effect intended by the show's creator. The same was found for those who identified not with Archie but his liberal son-in-law. They, too, were reinforced by Michael's exaggerated views.

Agenda Setting

Another important theory that expanded the understanding of media functions and effects is called agenda setting. The basic premise of the **agenda-setting** hypothesis is that although the media might not tell the audience what to think, they can have a significant impact on what audience members think about.[32] For example, how many people in the United States had heard of Bosnia before the outbreak of hostilities there? Would you have ever heard about it without the mass media publicizing it? The mass media's raising an issue to public consciousness is termed the "agenda-setting" effect of the media. Most research on

agenda setting The mass media's ability to determine the issues of public debate by choosing which events to report and which to ignore.

agenda setting is of a correlational nature. That is, researchers measure the amount of air time or print devoted to a given issue and then look for a correlation with public interest in that issue. However, one could also argue that the mass media pay attention to the issues that concern the public. Thus, agenda setting may work in reciprocal ways.

As researchers have explored agenda setting, they have discovered that media are more powerful with some issues than others. For example, on "unobtrusive" issues, that is, issues with which the average person has little familiarity, the media agenda-setting effect seems greatest. On the other hand, with "obtrusive" issues, that is, things that the average person has experienced firsthand, the media agenda-setting effect seems muted.[33]

An important refinement of the agenda-setting hypothesis has to do with a psychological concept called "need for orientation."[34] The greater uncertainty we have about an issue or a situation, the more we will seek out information about it from the media. This is when the effect of media agenda setting is greatest. For example, remember when you were trying to select a college or university to attend? A newspaper or TV story about the latest rankings of universities and colleges probably got your attention. In fact, magazines such as *U.S. News & World Report* and *Money Magazine* publish annual rankings of colleges and universities. Chances are good that prospective college students and their families will pick up these issues of those magazines and that, at least to some extent, they will serve an agenda-setting function. On the other hand, once you are secure in your choice and have begun college, the likelihood that *U.S. News & World Report*'s ranking of your chosen school would cause you to drop out is pretty slim. You no longer have a need for orientation on this issue.

Theories About Mass Communication and Culture

The theories covered so far have been concerned primarily with the relationship between traditional media and individual audience members. Although theories of agenda setting and uses and gratifications have societal implications, they mostly involve each audience member's reaction to media messages. The following approaches paint a broader picture. Rather than looking for functions and effects at the individual level, theories about mass communication and culture look for societal or cultural implications of mass media communication.

The first such approach concerns the role of mass media in the construction of our social reality. The essence of the **social construction of reality** theory is that people create a symbolic reality that is as influential as their physical reality. For example, whether or not there is a high crime rate in your community is a factual question. But regardless of the actual crime rate, if you feel afraid of crime, you will behave as if the crime rate were quite high. The socially constructed reality of a crime-ridden society is a result of communication—mass and interpersonal—and it can have some of the same effects as a real crime wave. People whose fear of crime is unfounded will stay in their homes, arm themselves, and purchase burglar alarms, just as if their fears were based on factual data.

social construction of reality The theory that the symbolic reality people create is as influential as their physical reality.

Researchers discovered that, contrary to its intended effect, the popular 1970s sitcom "All in the Family" reinforced rather than decreased viewer prejudice.

What role do the media play in constructing reality? Consider the preceding example of crime. One study found that "fear [of crime] is out of proportion to the actual danger posed by crime."[35] Scholar Michael J. Robinson has coined the term "video malaise," for the climate of fear, mistrust, and cynicism engendered by negative media coverage.[36] If our socially constructed reality is tinged by the way reality is portrayed in the media, particularly television, then this is a profound effect of the mass media. As you can see, this finding is similar to those of agenda-setting researchers. The difference is that rather than simply determining how a list of issues is prioritized, media are seen as actually affecting public attitudes and behaviors through their false portrayal of the reality in which we live.

Two broad streams of thinking can be identified in terms of the media and culture. The first, growing out of the research of George Gerbner and his associates, is termed *cultivation analysis*. The second, growing out of North American, British, and continental thought, is the use of *critical perspectives*. These two streams of thinking share a common view. Specifically, they assert that the effect of the media in general, and television specifically, is not so much their measurable effects on individuals but their overall impact on the culture of a nation.

Cultivation Analysis   Gerbner and his associates argue, "Television pervades the symbolic environment. **Cultivation analysis** focuses on the consequences of exposure to its recurrent patterns of stories, images, and messages."[37] Unlike traditional-effects studies, cultivation analysis does not attempt to measure the influence of television exposure by comparing "before" and "after" attitudes or behaviors. "Television enters life in infancy," write Gerbner and his associates. "There is no 'before exposure' condition. Television plays a role in the formation of those very 'predispositions' that later intervene (and often resist) other influences and attempts at persuasion."[38]

Three steps are involved in using cultivation analysis. First, the researchers analyze the institutional processes, such as media regulation, that govern the flow of messages through the mass media. Second, they analyze the message system itself. For nearly three decades, Gerbner and his associates have recorded and analyzed the content of samples of U.S. network programming. Finally, researchers examine the answers to questions about social reality as given by audience members based on their levels (heavy, medium, light) of media exposure. If there are measurable differences between people's perceptions of social reality based on differences in media use, and these differences are consistent with the nature of social reality as portrayed in the media, then cultivation is believed to have occurred.

cultivation analysis
The theory that the world view of heavy consumers of mass media is influenced by the predominant perspectives and themes of media programming.

The proponents of cultivation analysis do not argue for a one-directional cause-to-effect relationship, along the lines of the magic bullet model. Rather, they claim that "television neither simply 'creates' nor 'reflects' images, opinions, and beliefs. It is an integral aspect of a dynamic process."[39] In fact, they compare television to "a gravitational process."[40] Traditional-effects researchers were unable to document changes in attitudes or behaviors resulting from media messages. Cultivation analysis argues that absence of change is a result of the *mainstreaming* process, in which outlooks converge, resulting from the consistent images of reality portrayed on television. To learn more about how this process works, respond to the questions in Box 18-1.

Box 18-1   Self-Assessment

What Kind of TV Viewer Are You?

Circle the number that best approximates your agreement or disagreement with each of the following statements. Cultivation analysis suggests that the number you circle will depend on whether you are a light, moderate, or heavy television viewer.

1 = strongly agree   2 = agree   3 = not sure
4 = disagree   5 = strongly disagree

1. Violent crime continues to increase in the United States.
   1   2   3   4   5

2. Violent crimes against middle-class white people have increased for the past three years.
   1   2   3   4   5

3. Drug-related crimes such as the illegal use of marijuana, cocaine, and crack are highest among minority groups.
   1   2   3   4   5

4. The people you see on prime-time TV sitcoms and dramas approximate the median age in the United States.
   1   2   3   4   5

5. Reality shows such as *Cops* and *True Stories of the Highway Patrol* show what the streets of our cities are really like.
   1   2   3   4   5

Add your cumulative score for all five statements.

Heavy TV viewers are much more likely to agree with the preceding statements, all of which are false. High scores on this assessment may suggest your window on the world has been distorted by too much TV. Proponents of cultivation analysis offer this kind of evidence as proof of the power of TV to shape our realities. How did you respond to these statements? Do you think your responses correlated to how much TV you watch? Finally, do you think the producers of TV shows should be obligated to depict such things as the amount of violence in our society accurately? Why or why not? Be prepared to defend your answer in class.

Cultivation analysis has pointed out that there are many differences between the world as portrayed on television and the "real world" of everyday experience. For example, older Americans are greatly underrepresented on television. Heavy TV viewers tend to believe that the numbers of people over age 65 are declining and that people don't live as long as they once did—which is contrary to the facts. Violence is overrepresented on TV. Although the FBI reports that less than 1 percent of Americans are victims of violent crimes in a year, over half of TV characters are involved in violence each week. Not surprising, heavy TV viewers have exaggerated perceptions of the frequency of crime. Gerbner and his associates report that heavy TV viewers are more likely to view society as a "mean world" than are less-frequent viewers. These researchers have also found that heavy viewers have higher ratings on sexism scales and that children are more likely to stereotype gender roles if they are heavy viewers. Finally, heavy TV viewers are more likely to think of themselves as politically moderate than liberal or conservative. All of these cultivation effects are seen as "mainstreaming" audiences into the predominant view of reality that is portrayed on television.[41]

One might suspect that the increased prevalence of cable TV and VCR use would diversify the "reality" presented by television. Gerbner and his associates, however, claim that numerous studies have shown that cable and VCR content is not "fundamentally different from most network-type programs."[42] The same elements that appear on network dramas find their way into cable TV and rental movies. In fact, many cable outlets simply recycle old network programming.

The importance of the research by Gerbner and his associates is that it takes us well beyond limited effects or even agenda setting and uses and gratifications. Functions and effects of television at the societal level are hypothesized. Utilizing social science methods, such as content analysis and survey research, cultivation analysis offers significant insights into the broader societal implications of the mass media and, in particular television.

Critical Perspectives   **Critical perspectives** deal with the fundamental issue of power and its relationship to communication. A number of different approaches to studying media can be classified as critical, including "political economy analysis, cultural studies . . . feminism, semiotics, and discourse analysis."[43] One critical perspective is actually termed **critical theory;** it is a neo-Marxist theory associated with the Frankfurt school of thought in Germany, which combined the theories of Karl Marx with those of Sigmund Freud. Unlike traditional Marxists, who believed that violent revolution was necessary to change society, neo-Marxists believed that through ideological reform society could change without violent upheaval.[44] It is important to realize, however, that one can take a critical *perspective* without embracing *critical theory* or Marxism.

One of the most important critical perspectives is the **cultural studies approach,** as exemplified by the work of researcher Stuart Hall, of the Center for Contemporary Cultural Studies at University of Birmingham in Great Britain. Researchers in the cultural studies tradition are interested in how the dominant ideologies of the ruling class are imposed on popular culture and working-class consciousness. Central to understanding cultural studies is the concept of *hegemony,* which means "dominance" or "control." Cultural studies theorists assert that "mass media are the most important instrument of twentieth-century capitalism for maintaining ideological hegemony because they provide the framework for perceiving reality."[45] In other words, the basic limits on debate within a society are set within a narrow framework that is acceptable to the ruling elite.

Hall goes further than looking at just media content, considering how audiences decode, or interpret, mass media messages for themselves. There are three ways audiences interpret these messages: (1) the audience can accept the media's perspective; (2) it can accept the media's perspective at a general level, but oppose the message in the particular situation; and (3) it can interpret the meaning in terms of a totally different code, which is known as *oppositional decoding.*[46]

critical perspectives
Various perspectives that deal with the fundamental issue of power and its relationship to communication.

critical theory   A critical perspective based on the theories of Karl Marx and Sigmund Freud, which holds that elites use mass media to sustain their privileged positions in society.

cultural studies approach
Perspective that argues mass media are used so that the ruling class can impose its thinking on the working class.

An example of oppositional coding was found by researcher Janice Radway, who studied the content of popular romance novels. Her content analysis revealed that the content of such novels was patriarchal and male dominated. However, after interviewing women who read these novels, she found that they did not support this patriarchal domination. Instead, the readers preferred male characters with a feminine side and female characters who controlled their own lives. According to Baran and Davis, she found that readers of such books actually were engaged in "silent rebellion against male domination."[47]

An extension of the cultural studies perspective is the theory of cultural imperialism. This theory suggests that many Third World and developing nations are fed a diet of cultural images designed to make their people eager consumers of the products they see advertised on TV especially. The power of international corporations to influence world cultures through advertising, as well as the export of television and film, has been studied according to the cultural studies perspective.[48]

One of the most influential figures taking a critical perspective is James Carey, scholar and researcher. Carey distinguishes between two views of communication. Most traditional mass communication research, such as agenda-setting and uses and gratifications, has been based on a "transmission model." Instead, he proposes a "ritual model" of communication. The difference between the two models can be illustrated with the example of newspaper reading:

> If one examines a newspaper under a transmission view of communication, one sees the medium as an instrument for disseminating news and knowledge . . . in larger and larger packages over greater distances. . . .
>   A ritual view of communication will focus on a different range of problems in examining a newspaper. It will, for example, view reading a newspaper less as sending or gaining information and more as attending a mass, a situation in which nothing new is learned but in which a particular view of the world is portrayed and confirmed. News reading, and writing, is a ritual act and moreover a dramatic one.[49]

For Carey, therefore, communication is *not* the transmission of messages through space and time. Rather, it is "a symbolic process whereby reality is produced, maintained, repaired, and transformed."[50]

Michael Real, another communication scholar, has attempted to integrate the cultural studies tradition into a more comprehensive and systematic framework. He identifies three dimensions of society: (1) political-economic institutions, (2) symbolic forms of human consciousness, and (3) communication, either interpersonal or mass, that links the two.[51] For example, in his book *Mass-Mediated Culture,* he examines cases such as Disneyland and the Super Bowl from this perspective.[52] As Robert White explains it, Disneyland is seen by Real as promoting "an ethnocentric U.S. insensitivity to the Third World, an idealization of the United States's past, and a reinforcement of a North American capitalist world view and motivational structure."[53] Although Real acknowledges the use of the media as a means of ideological dominance, he also recognizes that the media are generating countermovements and alienation among some segments of society. In other words, it is also possible for the media to be used as a source of change in society and culture, particularly when there is tension between the political and economic institutions and the symbolic reality present in culture. Thus, a key contribution of cultural studies is that "they tend to see cultural expression as an arena where ordinary people can reinterpret and 'resist' the dominant values and definitions of reality in society and perhaps create their own culture and meanings."[54]

Feminist approaches are another critical perspective on mass communication. Feminists look to the way men and women are employed and portrayed in the media and how gender stereotypes are reinforced in our culture as a result. Of course, even the most extreme gender stereotypes may not be what they seem. Scholar Liesbet Van Zoonen points out in her discussion of the sitcom *Married . . . with Children* that "gender and family stereotypes are taken to extremes . . . and become sources of laughter that expose and undermine dominant gender discourse instead of confirming and strengthening them."[55] Nevertheless, there is considerable evidence that the mass media perpetuate subordinate images of women living in a male-dominated power structure. Box 18-2 investigates some of those images.

You and Mass Media

The preceding discussion should make it clear that the answers one gets about the functions and effects of mass communication depend largely on the questions that are asked and the methods used to answer them. If we ask whether mass media messages directly cause individual audience members to behave in the way the message sender wants, the answer is likely to be no. On the other hand, if we ask whether the public agenda is set on many issues and for many people by what they see and hear in the media, the answer is yes. Depending on the uses that bring audience members to the media, a variety of effects can occur. Some viewers might well vote in accordance with the information they receive from the media, if their purpose in seeking out media messages is vote guidance. Others find reinforcement for their preconceived attitudes by seeking out messages that support their world view. The functions and effects of mass communication are complex and not always obvious.

At a cultural level, research suggests some broad-based societal effects from the mass media. For example, heavy viewers of television have a very different world view than those only lightly exposed to TV. They see a meaner, more dangerous world, with traditional gender roles. Yet, even those lightly exposed to TV cannot discount its effects. After all, the messages of television are so pervasive, they become almost unnoticed. How many of our opinions are based solely on mediated messages? How many of us have ever met a president? Yet the vast majority of us have strong opinions about the current occupant of the White House. How many of us have heard the Beastie Boys or Tori Amos in person? Yet we know whether or not we like their music. And how many of us have person-

Box 18-2   Considering Diversity

Images of Women in the Media

Cultural studies scholars suggest that the media are "culture industries." One of the constant images we see in the mass media is of the "ideal" woman, usually thin, tall, and beautiful. But at least one physician suggests that "the media's image of women could kill them."

Dr. Ann Gerhardt of Sacramento, California, has formed a group called WINS (Women Insisting on Natural Shapes) to promote healthy eating habits and fight the image of thin as the only ideal body shape for women. Her organization has targeted fashion companies and women's magazines it alleges promote an unhealthy image of the ideal woman's body. Members have mailed them letters stating, "I strongly object to your use of excessively thin women as models. . . . You are not only sell-ing a product, you are advocating and promoting an image for women that leads women and girls of all ages to excessive dieting and other practices."

Another object of WINS' wrath is the Barbie doll. "The doll's dimensions, in life-size terms, would be 40-18-32." Yet Lisa McKendall, speaking for Barbie's manufacturer, Mattel Toy Company, claims, "Barbie is an inspirational role model for lit-tle girls. . . . Little girls want to be like her because she shows that little girls can do anything."

To what extent should the media be held accountable for eating disorders? Is the "thin is beautiful" image created by the media or merely a reflection of cultural ideals? What would critical theory suggest as the appropriate response to media images of women?

SOURCE: Jennifer Bojorquez, "The Shape You're In," *Sacramento Bee,* 15 June 1995, Scene 1, 5.

ally witnessed a violent crime? Yet we have opinions about crime, criminals, and punishment based on what we learn from the media.

Critical perspectives take us a step further, suggesting that our mass media play an important role in maintaining the ideology and values of the dominant forces in society. Yet there is the potential for audience members to engage in their own interpretation of media messages, creating their own meanings, which may in fact be in direct opposition to those meanings intended by the origina-tors of the messages.

So, what are the effects of the mass media on individuals and society? The answers are not simple. Certainly we have come a long way from the magic bul-let model of a simple cause-to-effect relationship. At the same time, the assur-ances that media have only minimal effects are not convincing. The mass media do have significant effects on the agenda of public issues, on individuals who seek particular uses and gratifications from the media, and on our culture and society at large. Their effects cannot be ignored.

Become a Critical Consumer of Mass Communication

As a citizen of a democratic society, it is your prerogative to be a critical con-sumer of media content. Ask yourself what messages are being presented, what vision of reality is implied by the media. Apply the same test of critical thinking that you apply to interpersonal and public speaking to the mass media. Remember that research has shown that audiences are not simply passive receivers. You may well create oppositional readings of media messages, just as the readers of romance novels steeped in patriarchy actually use the novels as a way of challenging male dominance.

One of the great changes now taking place is the expansion of media channels. No longer are our choices limited to ABC, CBS, and NBC. Programming on alternative channels, such as Fox, CNN, C-SPAN, and even MTV, provides alternative ways of looking at reality. As the 1992 presidential election demonstrated, political candidates ignore such constituencies at their peril. By going on non-mainstream programs, such as MTV and Arsenio Hall, Bill Clinton was able to reach audiences not normally found watching the big three networks. As a consumer of political communication, you have access to a wide variety of alternatives to the traditional 30-second commercials and evening news sound bites.

Finally, become a conscious consumer of the media. For example, use what you have learned about critical perspectives to assess what ideology is being promoted by television programming. What gender roles are being promoted through the media by programs such as *Baywatch* and *Beverly Hills 90210?* Are you willing to accept those gender roles as valid? What about the level of violence on television? Does that reflect your own sense of reality? What do actual crime statistics reveal? How real is the reality you see on TV? Certainly we all seek and enjoy the escape that comes from mass entertainment—movies, TV, popular books, and the like. But at the same time, we need to critically separate reality from fantasy.

Know the Issues of Concern

Part of separating reality from fantasy involves knowing the degree to which traditional mass media are biased. Thus, we close this chapter with a discussion of three issues of concern often raised about the mass media. Is there a liberal (or conservative) bias in the media? What is the impact of violence on television on society? And finally, what are the limits of freedom of expression and speech in the media? Should some content be censored for the benefit of society at large?

Media Bias   Conservative critics of the media argue that the press has a liberal bias. They point to studies that show the working members of the press are generally more liberal in their attitudes toward issues than the general public to support their view. For example, mass communication researchers S. Robert Lichter and Stanley Rothman surveyed attitudes of "elite" reporters (such as those at the *New York Times, Washington Post,* and the three TV networks) and found them more liberal and overwhelmingly more likely to vote for Democrats for president.[56] On the other hand, scholar Doris Graber points out that the owners of the media tend to more likely reflect conservative Republican values.[57] In fact, as researchers Robert S. Erikson and Kent L. Tedin point out, "Newspapers almost always endorse Republican candidates."[58] They go on to point out

Box 18-3   Critical Thinking

Is Network News Biased?

Do you think network television news is liberal, conservative, or balanced? For one week, watch the nightly news on one of the three major TV networks, ABC, CBS, or NBC. Record the number of news stories that focused on the president, the Republican Party, and the Democratic Party. Rate the content of the story as favorable, unfavorable, or neither. At week's end, tally your results and report back to class. Be sure to include in your report the criteria you established and consistently used in evaluating whether a story was favorable, unfavorable, or neither. Be honest! Try not to let selective perception bias your reporting.

that the public in general sees little overall bias in newspaper coverage and that academic studies of television coverage of presidential campaigns show TV coverage to be fairly balanced. Box 18-3 proposes a way to test the bias of the news for yourself.

If coverage is so balanced, why do so many politicians complain about media bias? Perhaps because coverage is so overwhelmingly negative—*to both sides.* Of course, partisans are more likely to notice negative publicity about their candidate than about the other side. According to political science professor Thomas E. Patterson: "During the [1992] general election, more than 80 percent of network news stories on the Democratic party were negative; 87 percent of all references to the Republican party were unfavorable. Congress was portrayed as a human cesspool: 90 percent of news regarding it was bad. The federal government fared even worse: 93 percent negative."[59] Those findings were not an isolated occurrence. Patterson found that in three of the last four general elections bad news outweighed the good.[60] Thus, if there is a systematic bias in the news media, it may be one of negativity toward all politicians, rather than a selective slant, liberal or conservative.

Of course, those taking a critical perspective would dismiss all of the above findings as missing the point. The whole political system is upheld by the media. By excluding fringe candidates or those who seek to radically change the system, by marginalizing protesters as bizarre and deluded, the media confine the debate to the basic Democratic-Republican dichotomy (with an occasional billionaire thrown in from time to time). Further, critical theorists would note that the media tend to cover the "horse race" aspects of the campaigns (who's ahead in the polls today) rather than the candidates' qualifications, records, or stands on the issues. The predominantly negative coverage of politicians tends to create a cynicism among citizens that makes them apathetic and uninvolved, therefore less likely to challenge the power elite. A critical perspective, therefore, would argue that the way the media frame the political debate reinforces the power of the governing elite and perpetuates the status quo.

Violence and the Media   We have already reviewed Gerbner's findings regarding cultivation analysis. It appears that the media do cultivate a climate that exaggerates the fear of violent crime. But a more pressing question for many critics is "Do the media actually incite the violence they portray?" The examples that began this chapter were all premised on the idea that violence on TV can cause someone to behave violently in real life. Is this empirically true, or is media violence just a convenient excuse for people who were inclined to behave violently in any case?

That TV is a violent medium is unquestionable. But what are the effects of that violence on society? In recent testimony before the House Subcommittee on Telecommunications and Finance, Robert E. McAfee, M.D., president of the American Medical Association, summarized the findings of two decades of research:

> Over the past two decades, a growing body of scientific research has documented the relationship between the mass media and violent behavior. Reports by the U.S. Surgeon General, the National Institutes of Mental Health, the National Academy of Science, the Centers for Disease Control and Prevention, and the Society of Adolescent Medicine, among others, have arrived at a similar conclusion—namely, that programming shown by the mass media contributes significantly to the aggressive behavior and, in particular, to aggression-related attitudes of many children, adolescents, and adults. Analyses of research studies support two conclusions: 1) there is a positive association between televised violence exposure and aggressive behavior across a wide range of ages and measures of aggressive behavior; and 2) exposure to violent programming increases aggressive behavior and is associated with lower levels of prosocial behavior.[61]

McAfee also points out that "it is estimated that by the time children leave elementary school, they have viewed 8,000 killings and more than 100,000 other acts of violence. As they near the end of their teenage years, they have viewed more than 200,000 violent acts in the media, including 40,000 killings."[62]

Former Surgeon General M. Joycelyn Elders, M.D., also testified before the House Subcommittee on Telecommunications and Finances. She cited a 1992 report by the American Psychological Association:

> The accumulated research clearly demonstrates a correlation between viewing violence and aggressive behavior—that is, heavy viewers behave more aggressively than light viewers. Children and adults who watch a large number of aggressive programs also tend to hold attitudes and values that favor the use of aggression to resolve conflict—these correlations are solid. They remain even when many other potential influences on viewing and aggression are controlled, including education level, social class, aggressive attitudes, parental behavior, and sex-role identity.[63]

CALVIN AND HOBBES *Bill Watterson*

Of course, the vast majority of viewers of television violence do *not* go out and commit random acts of violence. But, particularly among heavy viewers of violence who are already prone to aggressive behavior, there is a wealth of evidence that television violence is a contributing factor to actual violent behavior. Add this to cultivation analyses that heavy viewers of television view the world as a meaner, more violent place, and you have the recipe for a serious and undesirable effect of the mass media.

As video recordings and cable TV expand, television violence will only worsen. Violent acts usually edited out of television movies can be seen routinely on cable or video rentals. Particularly among children, the exposure to such violence is a serious social problem that merits parental and perhaps governmental action. However, the nature of the government's response is mitigated by the last issue we discuss, freedom of speech.

Freedom of Speech   The First Amendment to the Constitution guarantees freedom of the press and freedom of speech (as well as the rights to peaceable assembly and to petition). However, television and radio, because of the limited nature of the broadcast spectrum, have been subject to government regulation and restriction since the early part of this century. Broadcast television, in particular, has strong codes prohibiting offensive speech and acts. Yet cable TV and now the Internet are far less subject to regulation. Although legislation has been passed to prohibit the distribution over the Internet to minors of material that is "obscene, lewd, lascivious, filthy, or indecent,"[64] it has been struck down by a federal appeals court. As of this writing, the Supreme Court has not yet ruled on this legislation.

Freedom of speech is a broad cultural value most Americans endorse. However, the question of what limits are appropriate is a vexing one. As Supreme Court Justice Oliver Wendell Holmes declared, freedom of speech does not convey the right to shout "Fire!" in a crowded theatre. We already recognize the right of the government to protect state secrets from publication. Individuals may sue mass media organizations for libel if they believe they are the victims of malicious and false statements. And the broadcast media and motion pictures have codes to regulate what may be shown. Recently, politicians have attacked television for showing violent or sexually offensive programming at times when children are likely to be watching. In fact, some politicians, including President Clinton, have proposed the so-called V-chip to permit parents to lock out offensive programming.

Certainly, freedom of speech also involves tolerance for divergent points of view. Since the abolition of the Fairness Doctrine, it has become more and more difficult for some viewpoints to be heard. For example, talk radio is largely dominated by conservative views. In some communities, no one from the liberal side of the spectrum has access to the airwaves. The question, then, is should the government, in the name of freedom of speech, make an effort to ensure that differing viewpoints are aired? If so, then does freedom of speech belong only to those who control the airwaves and the presses? Is that not, from a critical perspective, yet another institutional impediment to societal change?

Finally, one issue of free speech relates to the effects of allowing sexually degrading depiction of women in the mass media. Scholar Richard Jackson Harris summarizes the research regarding such portrayals of women: "Although there are some negative effects of nonviolent sexual materials, especially on attitudes toward women . . . the research is especially compelling in the case of sexual violence. Sexual violence is arousing to sex offenders, force-oriented men, and sometimes even to 'normal' young men if the woman is portrayed as being aroused by the attack."[65] Harris also notes: "Repeated exposure to sexual violence may lead to desensitization toward violence against women and great acceptance of rape myths."[66]

Does such research justify restricting freedom of speech? This is a controversial issue. Some have argued forcefully for taking action. College professors Andrea Dworkin and Catherine MacKinnon are seeking to restrict materials degrading to women. They argue that pornography is action, rather than speech, and therefore not subject to First Amendment protection. In fact they compare pornography to "saying 'kill' to a trained guard dog."[67] On the other hand, Nadine Strossen, the first woman president of the American Civil Liberties Union, argues that "defending pornography is defending the right of individual people to choose what they want to see or how they want to make a living."[68] Clearly there is no easy answer to this dilemma. Although there appears to be reputable scientific evidence of the harms of pornography, particularly that depicting violence toward women, there is also an important constitutional issue of where to define the limits of free speech. Further, as our discussion of the difficulty of proving direct media effects should make clear, it is far from a scientific certainty that pornography is the cause of violence toward women in any but the most extreme cases. The critical perspective, however, might suggest that we look not so much at the acts of individual violence toward women as a direct effect from mass communication, but rather at the way cultural values are created and maintained that perpetuate a view of women as objects and possessions of men, who can choose to do with them what they wish.

Summary

This chapter began with a review of the principal media of mass communication. Print in the form of books, newspapers, and magazines is the oldest form of mass communication and remains an important medium to this day. The receiver of print communication controls the pace of processing the message and can avoid undesirable communication entirely. Electronic media, such as film, radio, and television, have become increasingly important in our society. Broadcast media, beginning with radio, brought the nation together simultaneously to share common experiences. The advent of television in the 1950s changed radio's role, but radio continues to be an important medium, specializing in various audience segments. Television has been the dominant medium of mass communication for four decades. However, network television's dominance is changing with the development of new technologies, such as cable, video recorders, and computer networks.

Numerous theories have been offered to explain the functions and effects of the mass media. Although the magic bullet theory of powerful direct effects had intuitive appeal, it was not confirmed by research. Instead, early mass media researchers concluded that the media had only minimal effects—primarily reinforcing what people already believed. Opinion leaders were seen as standing between the media and the average citizen, creating a two-step flow of communication. Uses and gratifications researchers concluded that people's reasons for using the media had a significant impact on how messages were processed. Research into agenda setting showed that although the media might not tell the audience what to think, they could have a significant impact on what the audience thought about. Finally, cultural analysis of media effects looked at a broad view of media effects on the social construction of reality. Cultivation analysis suggests that heavy media users are likely to develop a world view more in line with the world of TV—violent, mean, and dangerous—than what the actual facts of the world reflect. Critical perspectives, such as cultural studies and feminist theories are concerned with the role of the mass media in perpetuating the power of elites in our society.

Understanding how media affects audiences and the power that audiences have to modify those effects is important to the critical consumer of media messages. Issues of concern include alleged media bias, media violence, and freedom of speech.

Another Look

Articles

Liesbet Van Zoonen. "Gender, Representation, and the Media." In *Questioning the Media: A Critical Introduction,* 2nd ed., edited by John Downing, Ali Mohammadi, and Annabelle Sreberny Mohammadi, 311–44. Thousand Oaks, Calif.: Sage, 1995.

This thought-provoking article suggests that media historically have reinforced the idea that men and women are quite naturally distinct from each other. More recently, Van Zoonen argues, the media have subtly begun to address the fact that this distinct gender division is a false dichotomy. This is an excellent article for writing a reaction paper.

Books

Marshall McLuhan. *Understanding Media: The Extensions of Man.* New York: McGraw-Hill, 1964.

McLuhan became a widely publicized media guru for his theories about "hot" and "cool" media. His concept that media are extensions of us is an important insight into the effects of television. His vision of a "global village" has become a reality in an era of satellite technology and CNN's 24-hour global reporting.

Mary Matalin and James Carville. *All's Fair: Love, War, and Running for President.* New York: Random House, 1994.

An inside view of the Bush and Clinton campaigns in 1992, this odd couple, romantically involved and yet working opposite sides of the political street, collaborate on revealing what happened behind the scenes in the 1992 presidential campaign. The use and abuse of media by the campaigns (and vice versa) is well chronicled in this entertaining book.

Video Rentals

Broadcast News This 1987 film, written, directed, and produced by James L. Brooks, offers a humorous, but not so unrealistic look behind the scenes at television news. Starring Holly Hunter, William Hurt, and Albert Brooks, who all work in the Washington bureau of a network, the film shows the often absurd antics that are unseen by the average viewer. Holly Hunter plays the producer who has to run the news room. The handsome but shallow anchorman played by Hurt and the bright and unmediagenic reporter played by Brooks are portrayed brilliantly in this excellent comedy, with a ring of truth.

Network Written by Paddy Chayefsky, this 1976 film takes a cynical view of network TV. Howard Beale, played by Peter Finch in his last role before his death, declares that he's "mad as hell and . . . not going to take it anymore." The network's young chief of programming, played by Faye Dunaway, realizes she has a hit on her hands. Soon the network is featuring the "mad prophet of the airwaves," complete with a soothsayer. We don't want to spoil the ending if you have not seen this movie, but suffice it to say that *Network* takes television to new extremes in the quest for ratings.

Theory and Research into Practice

1. Surveys show that Americans spend about seven hours a day exposed to the mass media, three quarters of it television. How much time do you spend with the mass media? For a week, keep a log of all of your exposure to newspapers, magazines, radio, film, and television. How many hours did you average each day with each medium? How do these numbers compare with time spent on other activities: work, school, recreation? How much time is spent simultaneously on other activities and with the media (for example, having the radio on in your car or eating a meal while watching TV)? Turn in your log to your instructor, who may compute averages for the entire class.

2. How much violence is there on TV? Use the following definition of violence: observable acts of physical force against another person, or self-inflicted, or the threat of violence used to compel someone to act against his or her own will. Randomly select five hours of TV programming; watch these programs and count the acts of violence. Do your findings seem consistent with the high amount of violence reported in the research? How hard was it to decide if an act fit the definition? Write a one-page report on your findings.

3. Give up TV for a solid week. Keep track of the other media to which you turned for uses and gratifications. Write about what you learn from this exercise and how these lessons might be used to modify your TV viewing.

Notes

Chapter 1

1. Forum, *National Geographic Magazine,* October 1995.
2. Claude E. Shannon and W. Weaver, *The Mathematical Theory of Communication* (Urbana: University of Illinois Press, 1949).
3. Dominic A. Infante, Andrew S. Rancer, and Deanna F. Womack, *Building Communication Theory,* 2nd ed. (Prospect Heights, Ill.: Waveland Press, 1993).
4. Ludwig Von Bertanlaffy, *General Systems Theory* (New York: Braziller, 1968). Frank E. X. Dance, ed., *Human Communication Theory* (New York: Harper and Row, 1982).
5. Infante, Rancer, and Womack. *Building Communication Theory.*
6. P. Watzlawick, J. Bevin, and D. Jackson, *Pragmatics of Communication: A Study of Interaction Patterns, Pathologies, and Paradoxes* (New York: Norton, 1967).
7. Brian Spitzberg and Michael L. Hecht, "A Component Model of Relational Competence," *Human Communication Research* 10 (1984): 575–99. Sarah Trenholm and Arthur Jensen, *Interpersonal Communication,* 2nd ed. (Belmont, Calif.: Wadsworth, 1992).
8. Dale Leathers, *Successful Nonverbal Communication: Principles and Applications* (New York: Macmillan, 1986). R. Rosenthal, J. A. Hall, R. M. DiMatteo, P. L. Rogers, and D. Archer, *Sensitivity to Nonverbal Communication* (Baltimore, Md.: Johns Hopkins University Press, 1979).
9. E. Langer, *Mindfulness* (Reading, Mass.: Addison-Wesley, 1989).
10. Sarah Trenholm and Arthur Jensen, *Interpersonal Communication,* 3rd ed. (Belmont, Calif.: Wadsworth, 1995).
11. Leathers, *Successful Nonverbal Communication.*
12. Langer, *Mindfulness.*
13. William W. Wilmot, *Dyadic Communication,* 4th ed. (New York: McGraw-Hill).
14. William W. Wilmot. *Dyadic Communication,* 18–19.
15. Bruskin Associates, "What Are Americans Afraid Of?" *The Bruskin Report* 53 (July 1975).
16. Stanley J. Baran and Dennis K. Davis, *Mass Communication Theory* (Belmont, Calif.: Wadsworth, 1995).
17. Shearon A. Lowery and Melvin L. DeFleur, *Milestones in Mass Communication Research: Media Effects,* 2nd ed. (New York: Longman, 1988), Chap. 7.

Chapter 2

1. Howard Goldberg, "Yawning Gulf of Perceptions," *Sacramento Bee,* 3 March 1994, A12.
2. Julian E. Hochberg, *Perception* (Englewood Cliffs, N.J.: Prentice-Hall, 1964).
3. Dominic A. Infante, Andrew S. Rancer, and Deanna F. Womack, *Building Communication Theory,* 2nd ed. (Prospect Heights, Ill.: Waveland Press, 1993). D. O. Sears and J. Freedman, "Selective Exposure to Information: A Critical Review," *Public Opinion Quarterly* 31 (1967): 66–97.
4. Hochberg, *Perception.* See also M. Minsky, ed., *Semantic Information Processing* (Cambridge, Mass.: MIT Press, 1968). A. Paivio, J. C. Yullie, and S. A. Madigan, "Concreteness, Imagery, and Meaningfulness Values for 925 Nouns," *Journal of Experimental Psychology, Monograph Supplement* 76 (1968): 1–25. H. Thomas Hurt, Michael D. Scott, and James C. McCroskey, *Communication in the Classroom* (Reading, Mass.: Addison-Wesley, 1978).
5. Michael Burgoon and E. P. Bettinghaus, "Persuasive Message Strategies," in *Persuasion: New Directions in Theory and Research,* ed. Michael E. Roloff and Gerald R. Miller (Beverly Hills, Calif.: Sage, 1980), 141–69. See also Gerald R. Miller, Michael Burgoon, and Judee K. Burgoon, "The Function of

Human Communication in Changing Attitudes and Gaining Compliance," in *Handbook of Rhetorical Communication Theory,* ed. C. C. Arnold and J. W. Bowers, (Boston, Mass.: Allyn and Bacon, 1989), 400–74.

6. "Happiness," *Sacramento Bee,* 11 February 1995, C1.

7. Charles H. Cooley, *Human Nature and the Social Order* (New York: Scribners, 1902).

8. Julia T. Wood, *Gendered Lives: Communication, Gender, and Culture* (Belmont, Calif.: Wadsworth, 1994).

9. Deborah Tannen, *You Just Don't Understand: Women and Men in Conversation* (New York: William Morrow, 1990).

10. Fritz Heider, *The Psychology of Interpersonal Relations* (New York: Wiley, 1958). Harold Kelley, "The Process of Causal Attribution," *American Psychologist* 28 (1978): 108. Brant R. Burleson, "Attribution Schemes and Causal Inference in Natural Conversations," in *Contemporary Issues in Language and Discourse Processes,* eds. D. G. Ellis and W. A. Donohue (Hillsdale, N.J.: Erlbaum, 1986), 63–86.

11. Alan L. Sillars, "Attributions and Communication in Roommate Conflicts," *Communication Monographs* 47 (1980): 180–200.

12. Loretta A. Malandro, Larry L. Barker, and D. A. Barker, *Nonverbal Communication,* 2nd ed. (New York: Random House, 1989).

13. George Orwell, *Animal Farm* (New York: Penguin Books, 1946).

14. See, for example, Albert Ellis, *Reason and Emotion in Psychotherapy* (New York: Stuart, 1962); A. H. Buss, *Self-Consciousness and Social Anxiety* (San Francisco: W. H. Freeman, 1980); J. A. Daly and J. C. McCroskey, eds., *Avoiding Communication: Shyness, Reticence, and Communication Apprehension* (Beverly Hills, Calif.: Sage, 1980).

15. Alan L. Sillars and Michael D. Scott, "Interpersonal Perception Between Intimates," *Human Communication Research* 10 (1983): 153–76.

16. "'Teen Talk' Mattel Offers Trade-in for Barbie," *Raleigh News and Observer,* 13 October 1992, A3.

17. William K. Rawlins, *Friendship Matters: Communication Dialectics and the Life Course* (New York: Aldine de Gruyter, 1992).

18. Lauren Wispe, "The Distinction Between Sympathy and Empathy: To Call Forth a Concept, a Word Is Needed, "*Journal of Personality and Social Psychology* 50 (1986): 314–21.

19. This is an intentionally simple treatment of the concept. For a detailed look, see V. E. Cronen, B. W. Pearce, and L. M. Harris, "The Coordinated Management of Meaning: A Theory of Communication," in *Human Communication Theory,* ed. Frank E. X. Dance (New York: Harper and Row, 1982), 61–89.

Chapter 3

1. C. K. Ogden and I. A. Richards, *The Meaning of Meaning* (New York: Harcourt Brace Jovanovich, 1923).

2. Benjamin L. Whorf, *Language, Thought, and Reality* (New York: Wiley and Sons, 1956).

3. Tom McArthur, ed., *Oxford Companion to the English Language* (Oxford: Oxford University Press, 1992).

4. McArthur, *Oxford Companion to the English Language.*

5. W. B. Gudykunst and Y. Y. Kim, *Communicating With Strangers* (New York: McGraw-Hill, 1992).

6. Edward T. Hall, *The Hidden Dimension* (Garden City, N.Y.: Doubleday, 1966).

7. Julia T. Wood, "Gender, Relationships, and Communication," in *Gendered Relationships,* ed. Julia T. Wood (Mountain View, Calif.: Mayfield, 1996), 3–20.

8. Julia T. Wood, *Gendered Lives: Communication, Gender, and Culture* (Belmont, Calif.: Wadworth, 1994).

9. Wood, *Gendered Lives.*

10. Cheris Kramarae, "Classified Information: Race, Class, and (Always) Gender," in *Gendered Relationships,* ed. Julia T. Wood (Mountain View, Calif.: Mayfield, 1996), 20–38.

11. Earl Shorris, *Latinos: A Biography of the People* (New York: Norton, 1992), 95–100.

12. H. Giles and J. Wiemann, "Language, Social Comparison, and Power," in *The Handbook of Communication Science,* eds. C. R. Berger and S. H. Chaffee (Newbury Park, Calif.: Sage, 1987), 350–84.

13. J. Wiemann, "Interpersonal Control and Regulation in Conversation," in *Sequence and Pattern in Communicative Behavior,* R. L. Street, Jr., and J. N. Cappella (London: Arnold, 1985), 85–102.

14. Deborah Tannen, *That's Not What I Meant: How Conversational Style Makes or Breaks Relationships* (New York: Ballantine, 1986).

15. "Hate in Cyberspace," *San Francisco Examiner,* 18 December 1994, B2.

16. "Log On Turn Off," *Sacramento Bee,* 18 April 1994, E1.

17. Marilyn Schwartz and the Task Force on Bias-Free Language of the Association of American University Presses, *Guidelines for Bias-Free Writing* (Bloomington: Indiana University Press, 1995), 24.

18. Albert Mehrabian, *Silent Messages* (Belmont, Calif.: Wadsworth, 1971). See also J. Burgoon, D. B. Buller, and W. G. Woodhall, *Nonverbal Communication: The Unspoken Dialogue* (New York: Harper and Row, 1989).

19. Carol Gilligan, *In a Different Voice: Psychological Theory and Women's Development* (Cambridge, Mass.: Harvard University Press, 1982).

20. Steven R. Brydon and Michael D. Scott, *Between One and Many: The Art and Science of Public Speaking* (Mountain View, Calif.: Mayfield, 1994).

Chapter 4

1. Diana Griego Erwin, "Signs Were There; Facts Were Missing," *Sacramento Bee,* 17 December 1995, A2.

2. Erwin, "Signs Were There; Facts Were Missing," A2.

3. J. Burgoon, D. W. Buller, and W. G. Woodhall, *Nonverbal Communication: The Unspoken Dialogue,* 2nd ed. (New York: Harper and Row, 1989). See also M. Knapp and J. A. Hall, *Nonverbal Communication in Human Interaction,* 3rd ed. (Fort Worth, Tex.: Harcourt Brace and Jovanovich, 1992).

4. L. A. Malandro, L. Barker, and D. A. Barker, *Nonverbal Communication,* 2nd ed. (New York: Random House, 1989). See also V. P. Richmond and J. C. McCroskey, *Nonverbal Behavior in Interpersonal Relationships* (Englewood Cliffs, N.J.: Prentice-Hall, 1991).

5. D. Leathers, *Successful Nonverbal Communication: Principles and Practices* (New York: Macmillan, 1986), 90.

6. J. C. Steat, "Size of Nose and Mouth as Components of Facial Beauty," *Dissertation Abstracts International,* (Ph.D. diss., University of Oklahoma, 1977). E. Berscheid and E. Walster, "Beauty and the Best," *Psychology Today* 5 (1972): 42–46.

7. P. Ekman and W. V. Friesen, *Unmasking the Face: A Guide to Recognizing Emotions from Facial Expression* (Englewood Cliffs, N.J.: Prentice-Hall, 1975).

See also P. Ekman, W. V. Friesen, and S. Ancoli, "Facial Signs of Emotional Expression," *Journal of Personality and Social Psychology* 39 (1980): 1125–34.

8. Ekman and Friesen, *Unmasking the Face.* See also Ekman, Friesen, and Ancoli, "Facial Signs of Emotional Expression."

9. Malandro, Barker, and Barker, *Nonverbal Communication.*

10. P. Ekman, *Telling Lies* (New York: Norton, 1985). See also M. B. DePaulo, M. Zuckerman, and R. Rosenthal, "Humans as Lie Detectors," *Journal of Communication* 30 (1980): 129–31; R. E. Kraut, "Verbal and Nonverbal Cues in the Perception of Lying," *Journal of Personality and Social Psychology* 36 (1978): 380–91.

11. K. R. Scherer, H. London, and J. J. Wolf, "The Voice of Confidence: Paralinguistic Cues and Audience Evaluation," *Journal of Research in Personality* 7 (1973): 31–44. J. Thakerar and H. Giles, "They Are—So They Spoke: Non-Content Speech Stereotypes," *Language and Communication* 3 (1981): 255–61.

12. Malandro, Barker, and Barker, *Nonverbal Communication.* See also P. A. Andersen and K. Leibowitz, "The Development and Nature of the Construct Touch Avoidance," *Environmental Psychology and Nonverbal Behavior* 3 (1978): 89–106.

13. Malandro, Barker, and Barker, *Nonverbal Communication.* Andersen and Leibowitz, "The Development and Nature of the Construct Touch Avoidance."

14. R. Sommer, "Man's Proximate Environment," *Journal of Social Issues* 22 (1966): 60. See also R. Sommer, "Sociofugal Space," *American Journal of Sociology* 72 (1967): 655; R. Sommer, *Tight Spaces: Hard Architecture and How to Humanize It* (Englewood Cliffs, N.J.: Prentice-Hall, 1974).

15. R. Sommer, "Sociofugal Space."

16. Michael Ventura, "Trapped in a Time Machine With No Exits," *Sacramento Bee,* 26 February 1995, E1.

17. Leathers, *Successful Nonverbal Communication,* 12. See also Burgoon, Buller, and Woodhall, *Nonverbal Communication;* E. T. Hall, "System for the Notation of Proxemic Behavior," *American Anthropologist* 65 (1963): 1003–26.

18. Stephen Thayer, "Close Encounters," *Psychology Today,* March 1988, 31–36. See also A. Montague, *Touching: The Significance of the Skin* (New York: Harper and Row, 1971).

19. See, for example, J. Fast, *Body Language* (New York: Evans, 1970); S. Young, "Image Makers or Breakers," *Glamour,* October 1987, 32; E. Marshall, *Eye Language: Understanding the Eloquent Eye* (New York: New Trends, 1983).
20. Judee Burgoon, "Nonverbal Communication Research in the 1970s: An Overview," in *Communication Yearbook 4,* ed. D. Nimmo (New Brunswick, N.J.: Transaction Books, 1980), 179–97.
21. Malandro, Barker, and Barker, *Nonverbal Communication.*
22. Ekman, *Telling Lies.*
23. Peter A. Andersen, personal communication, 1995.
24. M. Snyder, "Self-Monitoring and Expressive Behavior," *Journal of Personality and Social Psychology* 30 (1974): 526–37.

Chapter 5

1. Nina Rosenstand, *The Moral of the Story: An Introduction to Questions of Ethics and Human Nature* (Mountain View, Calif.: Mayfield, 1994), 100.
2. Immanuel Kant, *Groundwork of the Metaphysics of Morals,* trans. H. J. Paton (New York: Harper and Row, 1964), 88.
3. Kant, *Groundwork of the Metaphysics of Morals,* 96.
4. John Stuart Mill, *Utilitarianism,* in *Essential Works of John Stuart Mill,* ed. Max Lerner (New York: Bantam Books, 1961), 198–99.
5. William Temple, *Nature, Man and God* (New York: Macmillan, 1934), 405, quoted in Joseph Fletcher, *Situational Ethics: The New Morality* (Philadelphia: Westminster Press, 1966), 27.
6. Aristotle, *Rhetoric,* trans. W. Rhys Roberts (New York: Modern Library, 1954), 22.
7. James A. Jaska and Michael S. Pritchard, *Communication Ethics: Methods of Analysis,* 2nd ed. (Belmont, Calif.: Wadsworth, 1994), 65.
8. W. B. Gudykunst, S. Ting-Toomey, S. Sudweeks, L. P. Stewart, *Building Bridges: Interpersonal Skills for a Changing World* (Boston: Houghton Mifflin, 1995).
9. Karl R. Wallace, "The Substance of Rhetoric: Good Reasons," *Quarterly Journal of Speech* 49 (1963): 248.
10. R. Hart and D. M. Burkes, "Rhetorical Sensitivity and Social Interaction, *Speech Monographs* 39 (1972): 75–91.
11. Jaska and Pritchard, *Communication Ethics.* Several of these speaker and listener responsibilities are also derived from S. Trenholm, *Persuasion and Social Influence* (Englewood Cliffs, N.J.: Prentice-Hall, 1989), 18-20.
12. Stanley Karnow, *Vietnam: A History* (New York: Viking Press, 1983).
13. E. G. Bormann, *Small Group Communication,* 3rd ed. (New York: HarperCollins, 1990).
14. R. L. Johannesen, *Ethics in Human Communication,* 3rd ed. (Prospect Heights, Ill.: Waveland Press, 1990), 62–63.
15. R. L. Johannesen, *Ethics in Human Communication.*

Chapter 6

1. Gavin Edwards, *'Scuse Me While I Kiss This Guy and Other Misheard Lyrics* (New York: Fireside Books, 1995).
2. Ralph G. Nichols and Leonard A. Stevens, *Are You Listening?* (New York: McGraw-Hill, 1957), 1–6. See also Lyman K. Steil, Larry Barker, and Kittie W. Watson, *Effective Listening* (New York: Random House, 1983).
3. Andrew D. Wolvin and Carolyn G. Coakley, *Listening,* 3rd ed. (Dubuque, Iowa: W. C. Brown, 1988).
4. David J. Schneider, Albert H. Hastorf, and Phoebe C. Ellsworth, *Person Perception,* 2nd ed. (Reading, Mass.: Addison-Wesley, 1979). See also H. Thomas Hurt, Michael D. Scott, and James C. McCroskey, *Communication in the Classroom* (Reading, Mass.: Addison-Wesley, 1978), 43–60.
5. Anthony P. Carnevale, Leila J. Gainer, and Ann S. Meltzer, *Workplace Basics: The Skills Employers Want* (Washington, D.C.: American Society for Training and Development and U.S. Department of Labor, 1988), 12.
6. Edward T. Hall and Mildred R. Hall, *Hidden Differences: Doing Business with the Japanese* (Garden City, N.Y.: Anchor/Doubleday, 1987), 7.
7. Russell A. Jones, "Perceiving Other People: Stereotyping Is a Process of Social Cognition," in *Bridges Not Walls,* 6th ed. John Stewart (Belmont, Calif.: Wadsworth, 1994), 158.
8. Wolvin and Coakley, *Listening.*
9. Marilyn Vos Savant, "Ask Marilyn," *Parade Magazine,* 26 February 1995, 6.

10. Lawrence M. Brammer, *The Helping Relationship: Process and Skills,* 2nd ed. (Englewood Cliffs, N.J.: Prentice-Hall, 1979).

11. "Facts and Fantasy," *Newsweek,* 11 July 1994, 6.

12. These techniques are adapted from Richard L. Weaver III, *Understanding Interpersonal Communication,* 7th ed. (New York: Harper/Collins, 1996), 118–37. See also John Stewart and Carole Logan, *Together: Communicating Interpersonally,* 4th ed. (New York: McGraw-Hill, 1993), 189–227.

13. Stephen Toulmin, *The Uses of Argument* (London: Cambridge University Press, 1958). See also Stephen Toulmin, Richard Rieke, and Allan Janik, *An Introduction to Reasoning,* 2nd ed. (New York: Macmillan, 1984).

14. Brooke Noel Moore and Richard Parker, *Critical Thinking,* 3rd ed. (Mountain View, Calif.: Mayfield, 1992).

10. "The Nation," *Chronicle of Higher Education,* 1 September 1994, 5.

11. Rokeach, *Beliefs, Attitudes and Values,* 6–21. See also Milton Rokeach, ed., *Understanding Human Values: Individuals and Societies* (San Francisco: Jossey-Bass, 1968).

12. Roderick P. Hart and Donald M. Burks, "Rhetorical Sensitivity and Social Interaction," *Speech Monographs* 39 (1972): 75–191.

13. Houston and Wood, "Difficult Dialogues, Expanded Horizons," 34–56.

14. Mark Snyder, "The Self-Monitoring of Expressive Behavior," *Journal of Personality and Social Psychology* 30 (1974): 526–37.

15. Benjamin J. Broome, "Building Shared Meaning: Implications for a Relational Approach to Empathy for Teaching Intercultural Communication," *Communication Education* 40 (1991): 235–49.

Chapter 7

1. Edmund Fuller, ed., *2500 Anecdotes for All Occasions* (New York: Avenal Books, 1980), 133.

2. William B. Gudykunst, *Bridging Differences: Effective Intergroup Communication* (Newbury Park, Calif.: Sage, 1991).

3. Geert Hofstede, *Cultures and Organizations: Software of the Mind* (New York: McGraw–Hill, 1991), 44–45.

4. Hofstede, *Cultures and Organizations.*

5. Marsha Houston and Julia T. Wood, "Difficult Dialogues, Expanded Horizons: Communicating Across Race and Class," in *Gendered Relationships,* ed. Julia T. Wood (Mountain View, Calif.: Mayfield, 1996), 39–56.

6. Harry Triandis, "Values, Attitudes, and Interpersonal Behavior," in *Cross-Cultural Perspectives on Learning,* eds. R. Brislin, S. Bochner, and W. Lonner (New York: Wiley, 1975), 42–43, quoted in William Gudykunst and Young Yun Kim, *Communicating with Strangers,* 2nd ed. (New York: McGraw-Hill, 1992), 140–41.

7. Gordon Allport, *The Nature Of Prejudice* (New York: MacMillan, 1954).

8. Julia T. Wood, *Gendered Lives* (Belmont, Calif.: Wadsworth, 1994).

9. Geert Hofstede, *Cultures and Organizations: Software of the Mind* (London: McGraw-Hill), 84.

Chapter 8

1. Alan L. Sillars and Michael D. Scott, "Interpersonal Perception Between Intimates: An Integrative Review," *Human Communication Research* 10 (1983): 153–76.

2. Irwin Altman and Dalmas Taylor, *Social Penetration: The Development of Interpersonal Relationships* (Austin, Tex.: Holt, Rinehart and Winston, 1973).

3. Leslie A. Baxter and Carol Bullis, "Turning Points in Developing Relationships," *Human Communication Research* 12 (1986): 469–93.

4. The first version of this model appeared in Mark L. Knapp, *Social Intercourse: From Greeting to Goodbye* (Boston: Allyn and Bacon, 1978). The most recent version of the model appears in Mark L. Knapp and Anita L. Vangelisti, *Interpersonal Communication and Human Relationships,* 3rd ed. (Boston: Allyn and Bacon, 1996).

5. Steve Duck, *Human Relationships,* 2nd ed. (London: Sage, 1988).

6. Mark L. Knapp and J. Hall, *Nonverbal Communication in Human Interaction,* 3rd ed. (New York: Harcourt Brace Jovanovich, 1992).

7. Ted Huston, ed., *Foundations of Interpersonal Attraction* (New York: Academic Press, 1974). See also Dale G. Leathers, *Successful Nonverbal Communication: Principles and Applications,* 2nd ed. (New York: Macmillan, 1992); Ellen Berscheid, "Physical

Attractiveness," in *Foundations in Experimental and Social Psychology*, Vol. 7, ed. Leonard Berkowitz (New York: Academic Press, 1974), 158–215.

8. Dale G. Leathers, *Successful Nonverbal Communication: Principles and Applications,* 2nd ed. (New York: Macmillan, 1992).

9. Mark L. Knapp and Gerald R. Miller, eds., *Handbook of Interpersonal Communication*, 2nd ed. (Newbury Park, Calif.: Sage, 1994).

10. Duck, *Human Relationships.*

11. Huston, *Foundations of Interpersonal Attraction.*

12. Baxter and Bullis, "Turning Points in Developing Relationships."

13. Erik Erikson, *Childhood and Society* (New York: Norton, 1963).

14. Knapp, *Social Intercourse: From Greeting to Goodbye.*

15. Joyce L. Hockner and William W. Wilmot, *Interpersonal Conflict,* 3rd ed. (Dubuque, Iowa: W. C. Brown, 1991).

16. Daniel J. Canary and Michael J. Cody, *Interpersonal Communication: A Goals Based Approach* (New York: St. Martin's Press, 1993). B. R. Schleker and M. F. Weigold, "Interpersonal Processes Involving Impression Regulation and Management," *Annual Review of Psychology* 43 (1992): 133–68.

17. F. Scott Fitzgerald, *The Great Gatsby* (New York: Charles Scribner and Sons, 1925).

18. Sydney Jourard, *The Transparent Self* (New York: Van Nostrand Reinhold, 1964).

19. Dalmas A. Taylor and Irwin Altman, "Communication in Interpersonal Relationships: Social Penetration Processes," in *Interpersonal Processes: New Directions in Communication Research,* eds. M. E. Roloff and G. R. Miller (Newbury Park, Calif.: Sage, 1987).

20. Lawrence R. Wheeless, "Self-Disclosure and Interpersonal Solidarity: Measurement, Validation, and Relationships," *Human Communication Research* 3 (1976): 47–61.

21. Wheeless, "Self-Disclosure and Interpersonal Solidarity."

22. Joseph Luft, *On Human Interaction* (Palo Alto, Calif.: National Press, 1969).

23. Geert Hofstede, *Cultures and Organizations: Software of the Mind* (London: McGraw-Hill).

24. Julia T. Wood, ed., *Gendered Relationships* (Mountain View, Calif.: Mayfield, 1996).

25. V. E. Cronen, W. B. Pearce, and L. M. Harris, "The Coordinated Management of Meaning: A Theory of Communication," in *Human Communication Theory: Comparative Essays,* ed. Frank E. X. Dance (New York: Harper & Row, 1982). See also Donald P. Cushman, "The Rules Perspective as a Theoretical Basis for the Study of Human Communication," *Communication Quarterly* 25 (1977): 30–45.

26. Judee Burgoon

27. William K. Rawlins, *Friendship Matters: Communication, Dialectics, and the Life Course* (New York: Aldine de Gruyter, 1992).

28. Rawlins, *Friendship Matters.*

29. Laurie P. Arliss, *Contemporary Family Communication: Messages and Meanings* (New York: St. Martin's Press, 1993), 34.

30. Rawlins, *Friendship Matters,* 9–24.

31. Rawlins, 9–24.

32. Joseph N. Capella, "The Management of Conversations," in *Handbook of Interpersonal Communication,* 2nd ed., ed. Mark L. Knapp and Gerald R. Miller (Newbury Park, Calif.: Sage, 1994), 393–438.

33. Kathleen K. Reardon, *Interpersonal Communication: Where Minds Meet* (Belmont, Calif.: Wadsworth, 1987). Margaret McLaughlin, *Conversation: How Talk Is Organized* (Beverly Hills, Calif.: Sage, 1984).

34. Reardon, *Interpersonal Communication,* 107–8. See also H. Grice, "Logic and Conversation," in *Syntax and Semantics,* Vol. 3, eds. P. Cole and J. Morgan (New York: Academic Press, 1975), 45–46.

35. Frank Millar and Edna F. Rogers, "A Relational Approach," in *Explorations in Interpersonal Communication* (Beverly Hills, Calif.: Sage, 1976) 87–103.

36. Millar and Rogers, "A Relational Approach," 87–103.

37. Kathleen K. Reardon, *Interpersonal Communication,* 116–119.

Chapter 9

1. Gregory Nava, writer and director, *My Family/Mi Familia,* American Zoetrope, Turner Home Entertainment, New Line Productions, Inc., 1995.

2. See, for example, Laurie P. Arliss, *Contemporary Family Communication: Messages and Meanings* (New York: St. Martin's Press, 1993).

3. The system types were adapted from Kathleen M. Galvin and Bernard J. Brommel, *Family Communi-*

cation: Cohesion and Change, 4th ed. (New York: HarperCollins, 1996), 29–30, 171–74. See also David Kantor and William Lehr, *Inside the Family* (San Francisco, Calif.: Jossey-Bass, 1976).

4. Erving Goffman, *The Presentation of Self in Everyday Life* (Garden City, N.J.: Doubleday, 1959).

5. Galvin and Brommel, *Family Communication*, 153.

6. Janet Yerby, Nancy Buerkel-Rothfuss, and Arthur P. Bochner, *Understanding Family Communication*, 2nd ed. (Scottsdale, Ariz.: Gorsuch Scarisbrick, 1995), 256.

7. Yerby, Buerkel-Rothfuss, and Bochner, *Understanding Family Communication*, 60–61.

8. Yerby, Buerkel-Rothfuss, and Bochner, *Understanding Family Communication*, 61–62.

9. Yerby, Buerkel-Rothfuss, and Bochner, *Understanding Family Communication*, 61.

10. Yerby, Buerkel-Rothfuss, and Bochner, *Understanding Family Communication*, 62–63.

11. Yerby, Buerkel-Rothfuss, and Bochner, *Understanding Family Communication*, 63.

12. Yerby, Buerkel-Rothfuss, and Bochner, *Understanding Family Communication*, 64.

13. Basil Bernstein, *Class Codes and Control* (London: Routledge and Kegan Paul, 1971).

14. Patricia Noller and Mary Anne Fitzpatrick, *Communication in Family Relationships* (Englewood Cliffs, N.J.: Prentice-Hall, 1993). See also J. G. Miller, *Living Systems* (New York: McGraw-Hill, 1978).

15. Walter R. Fisher, *Human Communication as Narration* (Columbia: University of South Carolina Press, 1987). See also J. Bruner, *Acts of Meaning* (Cambridge, Mass.: Harvard University Press, 1990).

16. Yerby, Buerkel-Rothfuss, and Bochner, *Understanding Family Communication*, 210–11.

17. N. Denzin, *Interpretive Interactionism* (Newbury Park, Calif.: Sage, 1989).

18. This list is adapted from Yerby, Buerkel-Rothfuss, and Bochner, *Understanding Family Communication*, 230–33.

19. Mary Anne Fitzpatrick, *Between Husbands and Wives* (Newbury Park, Calif.: Sage, 1988). Although this discussion of spousal roles is largely based on marital relationships, Fitzpatrick's typology also has application for unmarried couples living together, including gay and lesbian couples.

20. Laurie P. Arliss, *Contemporary Family Communication*, 1993. This book does a particularly good job of examining how different types of parents cope with their roles.

21. Although these particular dialectics reflect William Rawlins's book *Friendship Matters: Communication, Dialectics, and the Life Course* (New York: Aldine de Gruyter, 1992), the discussion also reflects the research of Leslie A. Baxter. See also Leslie A. Baxter, "A Dialectical Perspective on Communication Strategies in Relationship Development," in *A Handbook of Personal Relationships*, ed. S. W. Duck (New York: Wiley, 1988), 257–73.

22. Joseph Campbell with Bill Moyers, *The Power of Myth* (New York: Doubleday, 1988).

23. William Rawlins and Melissa Holl, "Adolescents' Interaction with Parents and Friends: Dialectics of Temporal Perspective and Evaluation," *Journal of Social and Personal Relationships* 5 (1988): 27–46.

24. Linda K. Acitelli, "When Spouses Talk to Each Other About Their Relationship," *Journal of Social and Personal Relationships* 5 (1988): 185–200.

25. David Olson and Hamilton McCubbin, *Families: What Makes Them Work* (Newbury Park, Calif.: Sage, 1983).

26. S. A. Anderson, "Changes in Parental Adjustment and Communication During the Leaving Home Transition," *Journal of Personal and Social Relationships* 7 (1990): 47–68.

27. Noller and Fitzpatrick, *Communication in Family Relationships*, 280–81.

28. Noller and Fitzpatrick, *Communication in Family Relationships*, 290–91.

Chapter 10

1. Joyce L. Hocker and William W. Wilmot, *Interpersonal Conflict*, 4th ed. (Madison, Wis.: Brown and Benchmark, 1995), 20.

2. Hocker and Wilmot, *Interpersonal Conflict*, 5.

3. Hocker and Wilmot, *Interpersonal Conflict*, 29.

4. Hocker and Wilmot, *Interpersonal Conflict*, 29.

5. Hocker and Wilmot, *Interpersonal Conflict*, 30.

6. Hocker and Wilmot, *Interpersonal Conflict*, 30.

7. Hocker and Wilmot, *Interpersonal Conflict*, 20.

8. R. A. Baron, "Reducing Organizational Conflict: An Incompatible Response Approach," *Journal of Applied Psychology* 69 (1984): 272–79.

9. A.L. Sillars, G. R. Pike, T. S. Jones, and K. Redmon, "Communication and Conflict in Marriage." In

Communication Yearbook 7, ed. R. Bostrom (Beverly Hills, Calif.: Sage, 1983), 414–22.

10. Dudley D. Cahn, ed., *Conflict in Personal Relationships* (Hillsdale, N.J.: Lawrence Erlbaum, 1994).

11. Linda I. Putnam and Michael E. Roloff, eds., *Communication and Negotiation* (Newbury Park, Calif.: Sage, 1992).

12. Hocker and Wilmot, *Interpersonal Conflict,* 37.

13. Hocker and Wilmot, *Interpersonal Conflict,* 37.

14. Alan L. Sillars and J. Weisberg, "Conflict as a Social Skill," in *Interpersonal Processes: New Directions in Communication Research,* ed. Michael J. Roloff and Gerald R. Miller (Newbury Park, Calif.: Sage, 1987), 140–71.

15. E. Jones and C. Gallois, "Spouses' Impressions of Rules for Communication in Public and Private Marital Conflicts," *Journal of Marriage and the Family* 51 (1989): 957–67.

16. C. H. Coombs, "The Structure of Conflict," *The American Psychologist* 42 (1987): 355–63. Jones and Gallois, "Spouses' Impressions of Rules for Communication in Public and Private Marital Conflicts," 957–67.

17. Dominic A. Infante, *Arguing Constructively* (Prospect Hills, Ill.: Waveland Press, 1988). See also Dominic A. Infante, T. Chandler Sabourin, J. E. Rudd, and E. A. Shannon, "Verbal Aggression in Violent and Nonviolent Marital Disputes," *Communication Quarterly,* 38 (1990): 361–71.

18. Infante et al., "Verbal Aggression in Violent and Nonviolent Marital Disputes."

19. Infante et al., "Verbal Aggression in Violent and Nonviolent Marital Disputes."

20. J. M. Gottman, "The Roles of Conflict Engagement, Escalation, and Avoidance in Marital Interaction: A Longitudinal View of Five Types of Couples," *Journal of Consulting and Clinical Psychology* 61 (1993): 6–15.

21. Jack R. Gibb, "Defensive Communication," *Journal of Communication* 11 (1961): 141–48. J. K. Alberts, "The Use of Humor in Managing Couples' Conflict Interactions," in *Intimates in Conflict: A Communication Perspective,* ed. D. D. Cahn (Hillsdale, N.J.: Lawrence Erlbaum, 1990).

Chapter 11

1. Charles J. Stewart and William B. Cash, Jr., *Interviewing: Principles and Practices,* 5th ed. (Dubuque, Iowa: Wm. C. Brown, 1988), 132.

2. John W. Cogger, "Are You a Skilled Interviewer?" *Personnel Journal* 61 (1982): 842–43.

3. Stewart and Cash, *Interviewing,* 137.

4. Stewart and Cash, *Interviewing,* 138.

5. Stewart and Cash, *Interviewing,* 138.

6. Stewart and Cash, *Interviewing,* 139–40.

7. Stewart and Cash, *Interviewing,* 140–41.

8. Mark S. Granovetter, "The Strength of Weak Ties," *American Journal of Sociology* 78 (1973): 1360–80.

9. See, for example: Stewart and Cash, *Interviewing,* 147; Ronald B. Adler, *Communicating at Work: Principles and Practices for Business and the Professions* (New York: Random House, 1989), 153.

10. Stewart and Cash, *Interviewing,* 146.

11. Stewart and Cash, *Interviewing,* 147.

12. Lois J. Einhorn, "An Inner View of the Job Interview: An Investigation of Successful Communicative Behaviors," *Communication Education* 30 (1981): 217–18.

13. Jeanne Tessier Barone and Jo Young Switzer, *Interviewing: Art and Skill* (Boston: Allyn and Bacon, 1995), 274.

14. Brian S. Moskal, "Employee Ratings: Objective or Objectionable?" *Industry Week,* 8 February 1982, 47.

15. Barone and Switzer, *Interviewing,* 274.

16. Jack R. Gibb, "Defensive Communication," *Journal of Communication* 11 (1961): 141–48.

17. Gibb, "Defensive Communication," 141.

18. Barone and Switzer, *Interviewing,* 292.

19. Barone and Switzer, *Interviewing,* 292.

20. Barone and Switzer, *Interviewing,* 293.

21. Barone and Switzer, *Interviewing,* 293.

22. Stewart and Cash, *Interviewing,* 185.

23. Stewart and Cash, *Interviewing,* 185.

24. Stewart and Cash, *Interviewing,* 186.

25. Barone and Switzer, *Interviewing,* 294.

26. Barone and Switzer, *Interviewing,* 294–95.

27. Barone and Switzer, *Interviewing,* 297.

28. Stewart and Cash, *Interviewing,* 180.

Chapter 12

1. Phillip K. Tompkins, *Organizational Communication Imperatives: Lessons of the Space Program* (Los Angeles: Roxbury, 1993), 1.

2. Tompkins, *Organizational Communication Imperatives,* 2.

3. William P. Rogers, *Report of the Presidential Commission on the Space Shuttle Challenger Accident* (Washington, D.C.: U.S. Government Printing Office, 1986), 72.

4. Rogers, *Report of the Presidential Commission*, 82.

5. In addition to Tompkins's book and the Rogers Commission report, see Randy Y. Hirokawa, Dennis S. Gouran, and Amy E. Martz, "Understanding the Sources of Faulty Group Decision-Making: A Lesson from the *Challenger* Disaster," *Small Group Behavior* 19 (1988): 411–33; Dennis S. Gouran, Randy Y. Hirokawa, and Amy E. Martz, "A Critical Analysis of Factors Related to Decisional Processes Involved in the *Challenger* Disaster," *Central States Speech Journal* 37 (1986): 119–35; James A. Jaska and Michael S. Pritchard, Chapter 8, "Ethics in Organizations: The *Challenger* Explosion," *Communication Ethics: Methods of Analysis* (Belmont, Calif.: Wadsworth, 1988); and M. McConnell, *Challenger: A Major Malfunction* (Garden City, N.Y.: Doubleday, 1987).

6. Rogers, *Report of Presidential Commission*, 89.

7. Rogers, *Report of Presidential Commission*, 94.

8. Rogers, *Report of Presidential Commission*, 96.

9. Rogers, *Report of Presidential Commission*, 93.

10. Rogers, *Report of Presidential Commission*, 93.

11. Rogers, *Report of Presidential Commission*, 93.

12. Stewart L. Tubbs, *A Systems Approach to Small Group Interaction*, 2nd ed. (Reading, Mass.: Addison-Wesley, 1984), 5–6.

13. For a review of a number of possible definitions of *group*, see Marvin E. Shaw, *Group Dynamics: The Psychology of Small Group Behavior*, 3rd ed. (New York: McGraw-Hill, 1981), 4–8.

14. Tompkins, *Organizational Communication Imperatives*, 11.

15. Michael D. Scott, "Why Small Groups Don't Work," *Quality Digest* 11 (June 1991): 47.

16. Norman R. F. Maier, "Assets and Liabilities in Group Problem Solving: The Need for an Integrative Function," *American Psychological Review* (1967) 74, 239–49.

17. Maier, "Assets and Liabilities in Group Problem Solving," 243.

18. Irving R. Janis, *Groupthink*, 2nd ed. (Boston: Houghton-Mifflin, 1983).

19. Janis, *Groupthink*, 9

20. Michael W. Mansfield, "Political Communication in Decision-Making Groups," in *New Directions in Political Communication: A Resource Book*, eds. David L. Swanson and Dan D. Nimmo (Newbury Park, Calif.: Sage, 1990), 255–304.

21. William P. Rogers, *Report of the Presidential Commission on the Space Shuttle Challenger Accident* (Washington, D.C.: U.S. Government Printing Office, 1986).

22. Rogers, *Report of Presidential Commission*, 93.

23. Rogers, *Report of Presidential Commission*, 104.

24. Tompkins, *Organizational Communication Imperatives*, 87.

25. Rogers, *Report of Presidential Commission*, 104.

26. For an excellent discussion of the COBE project, see George Smoot and Roger Lewis, *Wrinkles in Time* (New York: Morrow, 1993).

27. Andre L. Delbecq, Andrew H. Van de Ven, and David H. Gustafson, *Group Techniques for Program Planning: A Guide to Nominal Group and Delphi Processes* (Glenview, Ill.: Scott Foresman, 1975).

28. Tompkins, *Organizational Communication Imperatives*, 99.

29. Marvin E. Shaw, "Group Composition and Group Cohesiveness," in *Small Group Communication: A Reader*, 5th ed., eds. Robert S. Cathcart and Larry A. Samovar (Dubuque, Iowa: Wm. C. Brown, 1988), 42–49.

30. Shaw, "Group Composition and Group Cohesiveness," 43–44.

31. Ernest G. Bormann and Nancy C. Bormann, *Effective Small Group Communication*, 4th ed. (Edina, Minn.: Burgess, 1988), 74–76.

32. W. C. Schutz, *FIRO: A Three-Dimensional Theory of Interpersonal Behavior* (New York: Rinehart, 1958).

33. Shaw, "Group Composition and Group Cohesiveness," 44–45.

34. Shaw, "Group Composition and Group Cohesiveness," 45–47.

Chapter 13

1. B. Aubrey Fisher, "Decision Emergence: Phases in Group Decision-Making," *Speech Monographs* 37 (1970): 53–66.

2. Thomas M. Schiedel and Laura Crowell, "Idea Development in Small Group Discussions," *Quarterly Journal of Speech* 50 (1964): 140–45.

3. John Dewey, *How We Think* (Boston: D. C. Heath, 1933), 9. Italics omitted.

4. Dewey, *How We Think*, 107.

5. Russell H. Wagner and Carroll C. Arnold, *Handbook of Group Discussion*, 2nd ed. (Boston: Houghton Mifflin, 1965), 70–72.

6. John K. Brilhart, *Effective Group Discussion*, 5th ed. (Dubuque, Iowa: Wm. C. Brown, 1986), 203–305. John K. Brilhart and Gloria J. Galanes, *Effective Group Discussion*, 6th ed. (Dubuque, Iowa: Wm. C. Brown, 1989), 174–77.

7. Brilhart and Galanes, *Effective Group Discussion*, 189.

8. Brilhart and Galanes, *Effective Group Discussion*, 189.

9. K. Lewin, R. Lippitt, and R. K. White, "Patterns of Aggressive Behavior in Experimentally Created 'Social Climates,'" *Journal of Social Psychology* 43 (1939): 271–99.

10. Paul Hersey and Kenneth H. Blanchard, *Management of Organizational Behavior: Utilizing Human Resources*, 4th ed. (Englewood Cliffs, N.J.: Prentice-Hall, 1982).

Chapter 14

1. Peggy Noonan, *What I Saw at the Revolution: A Political Life in the Reagan Era* (New York: Random House, 1990), 68.

2. Based on Meriam Library, *How to Use the On-Line Catalog* (Chico: California State University, 1991).

3. Patricia McColl Bee and Walter Schneider, *Quotation Location* (Ottawa: Canadian Library Association, 1990).

4. "Cyberspace Survey Finds That 1 of 6 Uses Internet," *Sacramento Bee*, 31 October 1995, E1.

5. David Wallechinsky, "Be at Home on the Internet," *Parade Magazine*, 19 November 1995, 6, 9.

6. http://www.cnn.com/

7. Alan Monroe, *Principles and Types of Speech* (New York: Scott, Foresman, 1935). See also the most recent edition: Bruce E. Gronbeck, Raymie E. McKerrow, Douglas Ehninger, and Alan H. Monroe, *Principles and Types of Speech Communication*, 12th ed. (New York: HarperCollins, 1994).

8. The eight-part formula (assuming three main points) was developed by Dr. Loretta Malandro and is taught in her program "Speak With Impact," offered by Malandro Communication Inc., Scottsdale, Arizona.

9. John F. Kennedy, "Inaugural Address," in *American Rhetoric from Roosevelt to Reagan*, 2nd ed., edited by Halford Ross (Prospect Heights, Ill.: Waveland Press, 1987), 158.

Chapter 15

1. William J. Fremouw and M. G. Harmatz, "A Helper Model for Behavioral Treatment of Speech Anxiety," *Journal of Consulting and Clinical Psychology* 43 (1975): 652–60.

2. J. A. Daly and J. C. McCroskey, eds., *Avoiding Communication: Shyness, Reticence and Communication Apprehension* (Beverly Hills, Calif.: Sage, 1984).

3. Albert Ellis and Robert A. Harper, *A New Guide to Rational Living* (Hollywood, Calif.: Wilshire Book Company, 1975).

4. R. Sommer, "Man's Proximate Environment," *Journal of Social Issues* 22 (1966): 60.

5. Ellen Berscheid and Elaine Walster, "Beauty and the Best," *Psychology Today*, February 1972, 42–46.

6. Loretta Malandro, Larry Barker, and D. A. Barker, *Nonverbal Communication*, 2nd ed. (New York: Random House, 1989).

7. George B. Ray, "Vocally Cued Personality Prototypes: An Implicit Personality Theory Approach," *Communication Monographs* 53 (1986): 366–76.

8. Richard L. Street and Robert M. Brady, "Evaluative Responses to Communicators as a Function of Evaluative Domain, Listener Speech Rate, and Communication Context," *Communication Monographs* 49 (1982): 290–308.

9. David B. Buller and R. Kelly Aune, "The Effects of Speech Rate Similarity on Compliance: An Application of Communication Accommodation Theory," *Western Journal of Speech Communication* 56 (1992): 37–53.

10. Judee Burgoon, "Nonverbal Communication Research in the 1970s: An Overview," in *Communication Yearbook* 4, ed. D. Nimmo (New Brunswick, N.J.: Transaction Books, 1980), 79–97.

11. Joseph A. Devito, *The Communication Handbook: A Dictionary* (New York: Harper and Row, 1986), 105.

12. Stephen Thayer, "Close Encounters," *Psychology Today*, March 1988, 31–36. See also A. Montague, *Touching: The Significance of the Skin* (New York: Harper and Row, 1971).

13. Judee Burgoon, David Buller, and W. G. Woodhall, *Nonverbal Communication: The Unspoken Dialogue*

(New York: Harper and Row, 1989). E. T. Hall, "System for the Notation of Proxemic Behavior," *American Anthropologist* 65 (1963).

14. Malandro, Barker, and Barker, *Nonverbal Communication.*

Chapter 16

1. Jay Mathews, *Escalante: The Best Teacher in America* (New York: Henry Holt, 1988), 191.

2. *Stand and Deliver,* director Tom Menendez, with Edward James Olmos, Lou Diamond Phillips, Rosana DeSoto, and Andy Garcia (An American Playhouse Theatrical Film, A Menendez/Musca & Olmos Production, Warner Bros., 1988).

3. P. Friedman and R. Alley, "Learning/Teaching Styles: Applying the Principles," *Theory into Practice* 23 (1984): 77–81. Based on R. Dunn and K. Dunn, *Teaching Students Through Their Individual Learning Styles: A Practical Approach* (Reston, Va.: Reston Publishing, 1978).

4. Michael D. Scott and L. R. Wheeless, "Instructional Communication Theory and Research: An Overview," in *Communication Yearbook 1,* ed. Brent D. Ruben (New Brunswick, N.J.: Transaction Books, 1977), 495–511.

5. Michael D. Scott and Scott Elliot, "Innovation in the Classroom: Toward a Reconceptualization of Instructional Communication" (paper presented at the annual meeting of the International Communication Association, Dallas, Texas, 1983).

6. Jonathan Studebaker, "Who Am I?" (speech given at California State University, Chico, 1992).

7. Jennie Rees, "Mickey: A Changing Image" (speech given at California State University, Chico, 1992).

8. Donald R. Vogel, Gary W. Dickson, and John A. Lehman, "Persuasion and the Role of Visual Presentation Support: The UM/3M Study," commissioned by Visual Systems Division of 3M, 1986, cited in John J. Makay, *Public Speaking: Theory into Practice* (Fort Worth, Tex.: Harcourt Brace Jovanovich, 1992), 172–73.

9. Minnesota Western, *Visual Presentation Systems* (Oakland, Calif.: Minnesota Western, 1988–89), 170–81.

10. Minnesota Western, *Visual Presentation Systems,* 180–81.

11. Margaret Y. Rabb, ed., *The Presentation Design Book: Projecting a Good Image with Your Desktop Computer* (Chapel Hill, N.C.: Ventana Press, 1990).

Chapter 17

1. Sarah Brady, "And the Case Against Them [firearms]," *Time Magazine,* 29 January 1990, 23.

2. For a discussion of the factors present in the speech situation, see Lloyd Bitzer, "The Rhetorical Situation," *Philosophy and Rhetoric* 1 (1968): 1–14.

3. Aristotle, *Rhetoric,* trans. W. Rhys Roberts (New York: Modern Library, 1954), 25.

4. Sarah Trenholm, *Persuasion and Social Influence* (Englewood Cliffs, N.J.: Prentice-Hall, 1989).

5. Aristotle, *Rhetoric.*

6. James C. McCroskey, *An Introduction to Rhetorical Communication,* 5th ed. (Englewood Cliffs, N.J.: Prentice-Hall, 1986).

7. D. J. O'Keefe, *Persuasion: Theory and Research* (Newbury Park, Calif.: Sage, 1990).

8. O'Keefe, *Persuasion: Theory and Research.* See also John C. Reinard, "The Empirical Study of the Persuasive Effects of Evidence: The Status After Fifty Years of Research," *Human Communication Research* 15 (1988): 3–59.

9. Stephen Toulmin, Richard Rieke, and Allan Janik, *An Introduction to Reasoning,* 2nd ed. (New York: Macmillan, 1984).

10. Toulmin originally termed this the *qualifier,* but added the term *modality* in his later works. We prefer the simpler term, *qualifier,* which is what we will use in this book.

11. James C. McCroskey, *An Introduction to Rhetorical Communication.*

12. Brady, "And the Case Against Them," 23.

13. Brady, "And the Case Against Them," 23.

14. Brady, "And the Case Against Them," 23.

15. Mike Allen, "Meta-Analysis Comparing the Persuasiveness of One-Sided and Two-Sided Messages," *Western Journal of Communication* 55 (1991): 390–404.

16. Aristotle, *Rhetoric.*

17. Irving Janis, "Effects of Fear-Arousal on Attitude Change: Recent Developments in Theory and Experimental Research," in *Advances in Experimen-*

tal and Social Psychology, vol. 3, ed. L. Berkowitz (New York: Academic Press, 1967), 166–224.

18. Robert Cialdini, *Influence: Science and Practice,* 2nd ed. (New York: HarperCollins, 1988).

19. Brady, "And the Case Against Them," 23.

20. Some of these guidelines are based on a pamphlet by Robert Haakensan, *How to Handle the Q&A* (Philadelphia: Smith Kline & French Laboratories, Department of Public Relations, n.d.).

Chapter 18

1. Mark Caro, "Taking It Out On TV; Does What You See Influence How You Act?" *Chicago Tribune,* 26 October 1993, Kidnews, 3.

2. Joe Baltake, "Escaping into Reality," *Sacramento Bee,* 5 December 1995, C-1.

3. Melvin L. DeFleur and Everett E. Dennis, *Understanding Mass Communication,* 4th ed. (Boston: Houghton Mifflin, 1991), 43, 47.

4. DeFleur and Dennis, *Understanding Mass Communication,* 48–49.

5. Marshall McLuhan, *The Guttenberg Galaxy* (Toronto: University of Toronto Press, 1962).

6. U.S. Bureau of the Census, *Statistical Abstract of the United States: 1994,* 114th ed. (Washington, D.C.: 1994), 574.

7. DeFleur and Dennis, *Understanding Mass Communication,* 85.

8. DeFleur and Dennis, *Understanding Mass Communication,* 102.

9. DeFleur and Dennis, *Understanding Mass Communication,* 132.

10. DeFleur and Dennis, *Understanding Mass Communication,* 140–43.

11. DeFleur and Dennis, *Understanding Mass Communication,* 144–45.

12. DeFleur and Dennis, *Understanding Mass Communication,* 145.

13. DeFleur and Dennis, *Understanding Mass Communication,* 148.

14. DeFleur and Dennis, *Understanding Mass Communication,* 181–91.

15. Doris A. Graber, *Mass Media and American Politics* (Washington, D.C.: Congressional Quarterly, 1993), 51.

16. DeFleur and Dennis, *Understanding Mass Communication,* 197.

17. DeFleur and Dennis, *Understanding Mass Communication,* 207–10.

18. See Sidney Kraus, ed., *The Great Debates: Kennedy vs. Nixon, 1960* (Bloomington: Indiana University Press, 1962 [reissued 1977]).

19. Graber, *Mass Media and American Politics,* 2.

20. Paul F. Lazarsfeld, Bernard Berelson, and Hazel Gaudet, *The People's Choice* (New York: Columbia University Press, 1948).

21. Bernard Berelson, Paul F. Lazarsfeld, and William N. McPhee, *Voting: A Study of Opinion Formation in a Presidential Campaign* (Chicago: University of Chicago Press, 1954), 248.

22. Steven H. Chaffee, *Political Communication: Issues and Strategies for Research* (Beverly Hills, Calif.: Sage, 1975), 19.

23. Lazarsfeld, Berelson, and Gaudet, *The People's Choice,* 151 (emphasis added)

24. Elihu Katz and Paul F. Lazarsfeld, *Personal Influence: The Part Played by People in the Flow of Mass Communication* (Glencoe, Ill.: The Free Press of Glencoe, 1955).

25. Shearon A. Lowery and Melvin L. DeFleur, *Milestones in Mass Communications Research: Media Effects,* 2nd ed. (New York: Longman, 1988), chap. 7.

26. Stanley J. Baran and Dennis K. Davis, *Mass Communication Theory* (Belmont, Calif.: Wadsworth, 1995), 119.

27. Leon Festinger, *A Theory of Cognitive Dissonance* (Stanford, Calif.: Stanford University Press, 1957).

28. Joseph T. Klapper, *The Effects of Mass Communication* (New York: Free Press, 1960), 19.

29. Elihu Katz, Jay G. Blumler, and Michael Gurevitch, "Utilization of Mass Communication by the Individual," in *The Uses of Mass Communications: Current Perspectives on Gratifications Research* eds. Jay G. Blumber and Elihu Katz (Beverly Hills, Calif.: Sage, 1974), 21–22.

30. Jack M. McLeod and Lee B. Becker, "Testing the Validity of Gratifications Measures Through Political Effects Analysis," in Blumler and Katz, eds., *The Uses of Mass Communications,* 137–64.

31. Baran and Davis, *Mass Communication Theory,* 221.

32. Sidney Kraus and Dennis Davis, *The Effects of Mass Communication on Political Behavior* (University Park: Pennsylvania State University Press, 1976), 213.

33. Maxwell McCombs, "New Influence on Our Pictures of the World," in *Media Effects: Advances in Theory and Research*, ed. Jennings Bryant and Dolf Zillmann (Hillsdale, N.J.: Lawrence Erlbaum, 1994), 7–8.

34. McCombs, "New Influence on Our Pictures of the World," 8.

35. Margaret T. Gordon and Linda Heath, "The News Business, Crime, and Fear," in *Agenda Setting: Readings on Media, Public Opinion, and Policymaking*, ed. David T. Protess and Maxwell McCombs (Hillsdale, N.J.: Lawrence Erlbaum, 1991), 72.

36. Michael J. Robinson, "American Political Legitimacy in an Era of Electronic Journalism: Reflections on the Evening News," in *Television as a Social Force: New Approaches to TV Criticism*, ed. Richard Adler (New York: Praeger, 1975), 97–139.

37. George Gerbner, Larry Gross, Michael Morgan, and Nancy Signorielli, "Growing Up with Television: The Cultivation Perspective," in *Media Effects: Advances in Theory and Research*, eds. Jennings Bryant and Dolf Zillmann (Hillsdale, N.J.: Lawrence Erlbaum, 1994), 37.

38. Gerbner, Gross, Morgan, and Signorielli, "Growing Up with Television," 37.

39. Gerbner, Gross, Morgan, and Signorielli, "Growing Up with Television," 23.

40. Gerbner, Gross, Morgan, and Signorielli, "Growing Up with Television," 24.

41. Gerbner, Gross, Morgan, and Signorielli, "Growing Up with Television," 29–31.

42. Gerbner, Gross, Morgan, and Signorielli, "Growing Up with Television," 19.

43. John Downing, Ali Mohammadi, and Annabelle Sreberny-Mohammadi, eds., *Questioning the Media: A Critical Introduction*, 2nd ed. (Thousand Oaks, Calif.: Sage, 1995), xxi.

44. Baran and Davis, *Mass Communication Theory*, 314–41.

45. Robert A. White, "Mass Communication and Culture: Transition to a New Paradigm," *Journal of Communication* 33 (Summer 1983): 291 (emphasis omitted).

46. White, "Mass Communication and Culture," 292.

47. Janice Radway, *Reading the Romance: Women, Patriarchy, and Popular Culture* (Chapel Hill: University of North Carolina Press, 1984) and Janice Radway, "Identifying Ideological Seams: Mass Culture, Analytical Method, and Political Practice," *Communica-

tion* 9 (1986): 93–123 as described in Baran and Davis, *Mass Communication Theory*, 323.

48. White, "Mass Communication and Culture," 292.

49. James W. Carey, *Communication as Culture: Essays on Media and Society* (Boston: Unwin Hyman, 1989), 20.

50. Carey, *Communication as Culture*, 23.

51. White, "Mass Communication and Culture," 294.

52. Michael R. Real, *Mass-Mediated Culture* (Englewood Cliffs, N.J.: Prentice-Hall, 1977).

53. Micheal R. Real, *Mass-Mediated Culture*, as descibed in White, "Mass Communication and Culture," 295.

54. Downing, Mohammadi, and Sreberny-Mohammadi, *Questioning the Media: A Critical Introduction*, xxiv.

55. Liesbet Van Zoonen, "Gender, Representation, and the Media," in Downing et al., *Questioning the Media*, 322.

56. S. Robert Lichter and Stanley Rothman, "Media and Business Elites," *Public Opinion*, October/November 1981, excerpted in L. Brent Bozell III and Brent H. Baker, eds., *And That's the Way It Isn't: A Reference Guide to Media Bias* (Alexandria, Va.: Media Research Center, 1990), 20–26.

57. Graber, *Mass Media and American Politics*, 105.

58. Robert S. Erikson and Kent L. Tedin, *American Public Opinion*, 5th ed. (Boston: Allyn and Bacon, 1995), 243.

59. Thomas E. Patterson, *Out of Order* (New York: Alfred A. Knopf, 1993), 18.

60. Patterson, *Out of Order*, 21.

61. "Statement of the American Medical Association to the Subcommittee on Telecommunications and Finance, House Committee on Energy and Commerce, Presented by Robert McAfee, M.D., Re: Violence and the Media," in *Violence in Video Games: Hearing Before the Subcommittee on Telecommunications and Finance of the Committee on Energy and Commerce, House of Representatives, One Hundred Third Congress, Second Session*, June 30, 1994, Serial No. 103-124 (Washington: U.S. Government Printing Office, 1994), 20–21.

62. "Statement of Robert McAfee," 21.

63. "Statement of M. Joycelyn Elders, M.D., Surgeon General, U.S. Public Health Service," in *Violence on Television, Hearing Before the Subcommittee on Telecommunications and Finance of the Committee on Energy and Commerce, House of Representatives, One Hundred Third Congress, First Session*, September

15, 1993, Serial No. 103–79 (Washington: U.S. Government Printing Office, 1994), 373.

64. "Dealing with Cyberporn," *Sacramento Bee,* 28 March 1995, B-6.

65. Richard Jackson Harris, "The Impact of Sexually Explicit Media," in *Media Effects: Advances in Theory and Research,* ed. Jennings Bryant and Dolf Zillman (Hillsdale, N.J.: Lawrence Erlbaum, 1994), 266.

66. Harris, "The Impact of Sexually Explicit Media," 267.

67. David Barton, "The Debate Over Porn," *Sacramento Bee,* 10 March 1995, Scene, 3.

68. Barton, "The Debate Over Porn," Scene, 1.

Credits

Illustrations and Photographs

Chapter 1   pg. 2, © Richard Pasley/Stock Boston; pp. 4 and 5, Fig. 1-1 and Fig. 1-2, Claude E. Shannon and Warren Weaver, *The Mathematical Theory of Communication,* Copyright © 1949 by the Board of Trustees of the University of Illinois. Used with permission of the University of Illinois Press; pg. 7, Everett Collection; pg. 9, © 1996 M.C. Escher/Cordon Art-Baarn-Holland. All rights reserved.; pg. 15 (top left), © Bob Daemmrich/The Image Works; pg. 15 (top right), © John Eastcott/Yva Momatiuk/Stock Boston; pg. 15 (bottom), © Ron Sherman/Stock Boston

Chapter 2   pg. 22, © David Young-Wolff/PhotoEdit; pg. 24, © Pola Lopez; pg. 28, © Larry Prosor/Sports Illustrated; pg. 31, Everett Collection; pg. 35, © Frank Siteman/Stock Boston

Chapter 3   pg. 44, © Karen Borchers; pg. 47, © Chris Brown/SABA; pg. 49, © Joel Gordon; pg. 55, © Rose Carrillo/PhotoEdit; pg. 59, © Bob Daemmrich/Stock Boston

Chapter 4   pg. 70, © Addison Geary/Stock Boston; pg. 75 (left), Everett Collection; pg. 75 (right), © Chris Brown/SABA; pg. 81, © Jonathan Nourok/PhotoEdit; pg. 82, © Charles Gupton/Stock Boston; pg. 84, Salvador Dali, *The Persistence of Memory*. 1931. Oil on canvas, 9 1/2 x 13" (24.1 x 33 cm). The Museum of Modern Art, New York. Given anonymously. Photograph © 1996 The Museum of Modern Art, New York

Chapter 5   pg. 96, © Charles Kennard/Stock Boston; pg. 99, © AP/Wide World Photos; pg. 105, © Reuters/Mike Theiler/Archive Photos; pg. 109, © UPI/Corbis-Bettmann; pg. 112, © Roberto Soncin Gerometta/Photo 20-20

Chapter 6   pg. 116, © Bob Daemmrich/The Image Works; pg. 123, © 1996 Phiz Mezey; pg. 131, © Tony Freeman/PhotoEdit; pg. 135, © Steve Skjold/PhotoEdit; pg. 142, Fig. 6-4, From An Introduction to Reasoning, Second Edition, by Stephen Toulmin, Richard Rieke, and Allan Janik. Copyright © 1984. Adapted by permission of Prentice-Hall, Inc., Upper Saddle River, NJ.; pg. 144, © Bob Daemmrich/The Image Works

Chapter 7   pg. 150, © Bob Daemmrich/Stock Boston; pg. 169, © Karen Thomas/Stock Boston; pg. 173, © Steve Vidler/Leo de Wys, Inc.; pg. 174, © Alan Oddie/PhotoEdit

Chapter 8   pg. 180, © Bill Horsman/Stock Boston; pg. 183, © Michael Newman/PhotoEdit; pp. 184–186, Fig. 8-1, Fig. 8-2, Fig. 8-3, and Fig. 8-4, I. A. Altman and D. A. Taylor, *Social Penetration: The Development of Interpersonal Relationships* (Holt, Rinehart, and Winston, 1973). Reprinted by permission of the authors.; pg. 189, © Joan Liftin/Actuality, Inc.; pg. 197, © Tony Freeman/PhotoEdit; pp. 199 and 201, Fig. 8-6 and Fig. 8-7, J. Luft, *Group Processes: An Introduction to Group Dynamics,* 3rd ed. © 1984, 1970, 1963 by Joseph Luft. Reprinted by permission of Mayfield Publishing Co.; pg. 205, © David Simson/Stock Boston

Chapter 9   pg. 212, © David Young-Wolff/PhotoEdit; pg. 214, Everett Collection; pg. 218, © Bill Bachmann/Leo de Wys, Inc.; pg. 219, © Tony Freeman/PhotoEdit; pp. 220 and 221, Fig. 9-1 and 9-2, Adapted from Kathleen M. Galvin and Bernard J. Brommel, *Family Communication: Cohesion and Change,* 4th ed. (New York: HarperCollins, 1996) 97–99.; pg. 225, Everett Collection; pg. 231, © Martin Cleaver/AP/Wide World Photos; pg. 238, © R. Sidney/The Image Works

Chapter 10 pg. 242, © Bob Daemmrich/Stock Boston; pg. 245, © Michelle Bridwell/PhotoEdit; pg. 247, Fig. 10-1, Adapted from Joyce L. Hocker and William W. Wilmot, *Interpersonal Conflict,* 4th ed. (Madison, Wis.: Brown and Benchmark, 1995) 33.; pg. 253, Courtesy Drill Team/Fear of a Day-Job Music; pg. 259, © Rob Crandall/Stock Boston; pg. 263, © Tom McCarthy/PhotoEdit

Chapter 11 pg. 266, © Rhoda Sidney/Stock Boston; pg. 271, © Joe Marquette/AP/Wide World Photos; pg. 273, © Bob Daemmrich/Stock Boston; pg. 277, © Bob Daemmrich/Stock Boston; pg. 284, © Robert Brenner/PhotoEdit

Chapter 12 pg. 296, © Myrleen Ferguson/PhotoEdit; pg. 299, Courtesy NASA; pg. 305, © Charles Harbutt/Actuality, Inc.; pg. 311, © Jeff Greenberg/PhotoEdit

Chapter 13 pg. 322, © Addison Geary/Stock Boston; pg. 325, Fig. 13-1, Based on B. Aubrey Fisher, "Decision Emergence: Phases in Group Decision-Making," *Speech Monographs* 37 (1970) 53–56.; pg. 329, © Mark Richards/PhotoEdit; pg. 331, © Jim Pickerell/Stock Boston; pg. 336, Fig. 13-2, Based on Paul Hersey and Kenneth Blanchard, *Management of Organizational Behavior: Utilizing Human Resources,* 4th ed. (Englewood Cliffs, NJ.: Prentice-Hall, 1982); pg. 341, © Joel Gordon; pg. 344, Gary Conner/PhotoEdit

Chapter 14 pg. 351, © Alán Gallegos/AG Photographs; pg. 356, © Cindy Charles/PhotoEdit; pg. 359, © David Young-Wolff/PhotoEdit; pg. 363, © Bonnie Kamin; pg. 380, © David Young-Wolff/PhotoEdit

Chapter 15 pg. 384, © Michael Newman/PhotoEdit; pg. 393, © Reuters/Corbis-Bettmann; pg. 394, © Ben Davidson/Photo 20-20; pg. 406, © Najlah Feanny/SABA; pg. 407, © Martin Simon/SABA

Chapter 16 pg. 416, © David Butow/SABA; pg. 419, © Sam Forencich; pg. 429, © Beringer/Dratch/The Image Works; pg. 431, Everett Collection; pg. 437, Fig. 16-4, Source: U.S. Bureau of the Census, *Statistical Abstract of the United States: 1995,* 115th Edition (Washington, D.C.: 1995) 298.; pg. 438, Fig. 16-5, Source: U.S. Bureau of the Census, *Statistical Abstract of the United States: 1995* 115 edition (Washington, D.C.: 1995) 568.; pg. 439, Source: U.S. Bureau of the Census, *Statistical Abstract of the United States: 1995* 115th edition (Washington, D.C.: 1995) 250, 106.; pg. 446, © 1994 David J. Sams/Stock Boston

Chapter 17 pg. 450, © John Duricka/AP/Wide World Photos; pg. 453, © Steve Ferry/P & F Communications; pg. 467, Fig. 17-1, Adapted from An Introduction to Reasoning, Second Edition, by Stephen Toulmin, Richard Rieke, and Allan Janik. Copyright © 1984. Adapted by permission of Prentice-Hall, Inc.; Upper Saddle River, NJ.); pg. 469, © Robert Brenner/PhotoEdit; pg. 471, Everett Collection; pg. 473, © David Burns/AP/Wide World Photos

Chapter 18 pg. 480, ABC/Everett Collection; pg. 483, Everett Collection; pg. 488, © Lee Boltin Picture Library; pg. 491, © AP/Wide World Photos; pg. 499, Everett Collection

Text Credits

Page 71, Diana Griego Erwin, news columnist, *The Sacramento Bee.* Excerpted with permission.

Please see the Notes (pages 513–526) and boxes and tables within the chapters for additional text credits.

Index